FIFTH EDITION

Accounting for Canadian Colleges

TED PALMER
Business Education Council of Niagara

DONNA P. GRACE

VIC D'AMICO
NECTAR Foundation

PEARSON
Addison
Wesley

Toronto

To our families, students and colleagues.

Library and Archives Canada Cataloguing in Publication

Palmer, Ted, 1945–
    Accounting for Canadian colleges / Ted Palmer, Donna P. Grace, Vic D'Amico.–5th ed.

Includes index.
ISBN-13: 978-0-321-41553-0
ISBN-10: 0-321-41553-1

    1. Accounting-Textbooks. I. Grace, Donna P. II. D'Amico, Victor L., 1936– III. Title.

HF5635.P33 2008   657'.042   C2006-905531-9

ISBN-13: 978-0-321-41553-0
ISBN-10: 0-321-41553-1

Editor-in-Chief: Gary Bennett
Executive Editor: Samantha Scully
Marketing Manager: Cas Shields
Developmental Editor: Rema Celio
Production Editor: Laura Neves
Copy Editor: Marg Bukta
Proofreader: Shirley Corriveau
Production Coordinator: Avinash Chandra
Composition: Bill Renaud
Permissions Research: Sandy Cooke
Art Director: Julia Hall
Cover Design: Geoff Agnew
Interior Design: Chris Tsintziras
Cover Image: istock and Getty Images/Reza Estakhrian

8 9 10   14 13 12

Printed and bound in Canada.

PEARSON
Addison
Wesley

Contents

PREFACE

WHY STUDY ACCOUNTING?

Many students ask: "Why should I study accounting when I am not going to become an accountant?"

The subject accounting is often called the language of business. The purpose of accounting is to provide accurate information that you can use to make an informed decision in a situation where financial information is required. An understanding of basic accounting principles, practices, and terminology will be helpful in both your personal life and business career. Whether you are employed in the service sector, for example, tourism, or in a merchandising business, such as a retail store, a basic knowledge of accounting can help you be successful in your chosen career. Should you decide to open your own business, it will be essential.

The expectations and demands of the business world are continually changing and employers are seeking employees who understand accounting procedures, exhibit thinking skills, are computer literate, and show well-developed personal characteristics.

This textbook, *Accounting for Canadian Colleges*, Fifth Edition, has been designed to meet these requirements, and is part of a complete first-year introductory accounting curriculum package for students who are not planning to specialize in accounting. Included are:

- A Textbook
- A set of Student Working Papers
- An Instructor's Manual that includes all the answers

ORGANIZATION OF THE TEXT

Accounting for Canadian Colleges, Fifth Edition, contains thirteen chapters that are divided into thirty-one units. Each unit presents learning objectives, the theory to be covered, review questions, and practical exercises.

The text introduces basic Generally Accepted Accounting Principles, where relevant, when presenting accounting procedures and practices to students. The theory is presented in such a way as to encourage clear understanding of the principles and purposes of accounting. Decision making based on the examination of financial data is encouraged throughout the text. *Accounting for Canadian Colleges*, Fifth Edition, uses a systems approach to illustrate the accounting procedures followed in the processing of data and in the control of company assets. Descriptions of accounting systems from companies such as Henley Sporting Goods and Malibu Gym are presented to further illustrate and reinforce accounting systems and procedures.

Relevant activities in various formats are a major method of reinforcing the accounting principles and procedures presented. In addition to questions and exercises at the end of each unit, summary application problems of varying degrees of difficulty and case studies are included at the end of each chapter. Major activities, called Integrative Activities, are interspersed throughout the text to reinforce student learning.

NEW TO THIS EDITION

Based upon suggestions from teachers and students using the fourth edition, some topics have been given less or more focus, others have been updated, and new material has been added. In Chapter 5, the straight-line method of amortization has been given increased attention. Chapter 7 has been significantly revised to include a full examination of the perpetual inventory system. Chapter 12 contains the most recent payroll tables and the web address where changes to the tables can be accessed. All chapters contain a new section titled Internet Resources, which provides links to useful and current information appropriate for the text. Many chapters have additional application and challenge problems of varying difficulties. Three Integrative Activities in Chapters 6, 11, and 12 deal with the accounting topics covered in these chapters. These activities are ideal for pre-test review. New cases have been added to many of the chapters, the most significant being the new Ethics Cases.

Ethics issues in business are constantly reported in the media. Consider the following examples:

- Martha Stewart was sentenced to five months in prison, five months of home confinement, and two years' probation for conspiracy, obstruction of justice, and lying about a stock sale. Stewart also had to pay a $30 000 fine. She was not indicted on the original charge of insider trading.
- H. Radler, former publisher of the Chicago Sun-Times, pleaded guilty to charges of making improper payments. He was accused of diverting funds from the company into his and other managers' pockets. This could result in a combination of fines and a prison term.
- The president of a government agency was accused of extravagant misuse of government funds, including unreasonable travel claims and entertainment expenses. This resulted in his forced resignation from his position.

These situations indicate a need for greater focus on business ethics.

Business ethics is the study of decision making in a business context according to moral judgments and concepts. It involves the rules, principles, duties, and obligations that should guide people in conducting any type of business. These moral obligations apply to everyone, including company presidents, financial officers, accountants, managers, and office and plant workers.

This textbook examines ethics from the points of view of business executives, internal and external accountants, all those who work in business, and society in general. The Ethics Cases illustrate breach of trust, insider trading, fraud, misappropriation of company or government funds, and undue personal influence.

INTEGRATIVE ACTIVITIES

Three major activities are provided to reinforce students' knowledge of the accounting process. The activities can require both group and individual work in order to encourage the development of organizational skills, leadership qualities, and social interaction.

GOODS AND SERVICES TAX AND HARMONIZED SALES TAX

Goods and Services Tax is used in the majority of provinces in Canada. Harmonized Sales Tax is used in the Atlantic provinces at the time of publication. You are strongly recommended to research subsequent changes by accessing the Canada Revenue Agency Web site at www.cra-arc.gc.ca. In certain examples and exercises, the PST and/or GST have been deliberately omitted in order to focus attention on specific accounting concepts.

ACKNOWLEDGMENTS

We sincerely appreciate the materials, encouragement, and ideas provided to us in the preparation of *Accounting for Canadian Colleges*, Fifth Edition. Source documents, illustrations, and descriptions of accounting systems were provided by the Canadian Institute of Chartered Accountants; Janet Allen at KPMG; and Pat Holmes, CGA. Special thanks are extended to our colleagues at The Business Education Council of Niagara and Sheridan College Institute of Technology and Advanced Learning, Louise Edwards for her assistance, and Maurice J. Pothier for his useful suggestions.

We would like to acknowledge the staff of Pearson Education Canada and in particular Samantha Scully, Executive Editor, and Rema Celio, Associate Editor.

On a personal note, Ted appreciates the encouragement of his wife Sherry Campbell and the clan, Ryan Palmer, Kyle and Rachael Campbell; and as always MOM. Vic appreciates the support of Cecilia and the rest of the family and the assistance received from Chris Chapman, Sandi Bender, and the staff at Pearson Education Canada.

Ted Palmer
Donna P. Grace
Vic D'Amico

REVIEWERS AND CONSULTANTS

Alice Beddoe, *Fanshawe College*
Grace Credico, *Lethbridge Community College*
Ken Hartford, *St. Clair College*
Deb Kindopp, *Red Deer College*
Douglas A. Leatherdale, *Georgian College*
Wayne Schweitzer, *Selkirk College*

The Balance Sheet

UNIT 1   Financial Position

Learning Objectives

After reading this unit, discussing the applicable review questions, and completing the applications exercises, you will be able to do the following:

1. **DETERMINE** the financial position of a business.

2. **CLASSIFY** items as assets, liabilities, or owner's equity.

3. **CALCULATE** owner's equity.

4. **PREPARE** a balance sheet.

5. **USE** correct recording procedures.

Ⓕ INANCIAL POSITION OF AN INDIVIDUAL

Sadoun Janabi is a loan officer in a community branch of United Credit Union. As part of his duties, he authorizes loans to individuals and to businesses wishing to borrow money.

Recently, a young person named Louise Wong visited Sadoun to apply for a loan. Louise is a graduate of her local college's retail management program and has been working in a fashionable ladies' boutique for the past few years.

Louise has the entrepreneurial spirit — that is, she would like to own and run her own business. Although she is quite young, Louise feels that her college training, combined with the practical experience she has gained over the past five years, will enable her to start her own successful small boutique.

Louise needs $10 000 to start the business and is applying to Sadoun's bank for a loan. In deciding whether to grant a loan, Sadoun examines the financial position of the applicant. This is what she does. First, she lists the items owned by the applicant:

Items Owned by Louise Wong:	
Cash	$ 3 000
Government Bonds	6 000
Clothing	4 000
Furniture	9 000
Computer	4 000
Automobile	18 000
	$44 000

A creditor is a person or business that has extended credit or loaned money.

Next, Sadoun lists what Louise owes to creditors. **Creditors** are people or businesses that extended credit when items were purchased or who loaned money used to purchase possessions. These creditors must be paid before an individual has complete title to his/her possessions.

Debts Owed to Creditors by Louise Wong:	
Credit Card Debt	$ 1 500
Student Loan	7 500
	$9 000

Now Sadoun determines the financial position of the applicant.

Calculation of Financial Position

Louise's financial position is determined by making the following calculation:

Total Value of Items Owned	−	Total Owed to Creditors	=	Personal Net Worth
$44 000		$9 000		$35 000

By calculating the cost of the items owned by an individual and subtracting the debts owed, it is possible to determine a person's net worth at any given time. The net worth represents the difference between the total owned and the debts owed. Thus, Sadoun has determined that Louise Wong's net worth is $35 000.

Accounting Terminology

The subject **accounting** is often called the *language of business*. An understanding of accounting terminology will help you in both your personal life and your business career. Starting with the items owned by Louise, let's translate her financial position into the language of accounting.

The "language of business." The purpose of accounting is to provide accounting information for decision making.

Assets

In accounting, items of value owned by a business or a person are called **assets**. The total of Louise's assets is $44 000.

Assets are items of value owned by a business or a person.

Liabilities

Debts or amounts owed to others by a business or a person are called **liabilities**. Louise's liabilities total $9000.

Liabilities are the debts of a business or a person.

Personal Equity

Personal equity is a term that represents a person's net worth. Louise's personal equity or net worth is $35 000. Because of the substantial difference between Louise's assets and liabilities, the bank gave her the loan. Louise's very positive net worth indicated to the bank that Louise has a secure financial position and should be able to repay the loan.

Personal equity is a person's net worth, the difference between items owned and debts owed.

Accounting Equation

The **financial position** of a person or a business can be stated in the form of an equation called the **accounting equation**:

$$\text{Assets} = \text{Liabilities} + \text{Owner's Equity}$$

In Louise's case, the accounting equation is:

$$\$44\ 000 = \$9\ 000 + \$35\ 000$$

or $\$44\ 000 = \$44\ 000$

This accounting equation is the basis for much of the accounting theory you will learn.

Listing of the assets, liabilities, and equity of a person or business.

Assets = Liabilities + Owner's Equity

Balance Sheet

Louise's financial position is illustrated in Figure 1-1 in the form of a balance sheet. This is a financial statement that lists assets, liabilities, and personal equity (net worth) at a specific date.

FIGURE 1-1
Personal balance sheet

Louise Wong
Personal Balance Sheet
August 31, 2004

Assets		Liabilities	
Cash	$ 3 000	Credit Card Debt	$ 1 500
Government Bonds	6 000	Student Loan	7 500
Clothing	4 000	Total Liabilities	9 000
Furniture	9 000		
Computer	4 000		
Automobile	18 000	**Personal Equity**	
		Louise Wong, Net Worth	35 000
		Total Liabilities	
Total Assets	$44 000	and Personal Equity	$44 000

FINANCIAL POSITION OF A BUSINESS

The financial position of a business is determined in the same way as that described for Louise Wong. In the next few pages, we will examine the financial position and the balance sheet for a small business called Malibu Gym. Malibu Gym will be used in this text to demonstrate a variety of accounting procedures. This business will be followed from its formation through its first year of operation, thereby presenting an opportunity to examine both accounting and non-accounting procedures, problems, and decision making faced by all business proprietors.

Background Information

An entrepreneur is a person who organizes and operates a business.

Troy Montana opened Malibu Gym in Niagara Falls, Ontario. Many factors were involved in Troy's decision to become an **entrepreneur** and open his own business.

Troy's background and continued interest in athletics, combined with his formal education, provided the expertise necessary to operate this type of business. His athletic background included playing professional sports. Troy capitalized on his interest in athletics by completing a degree in physical education and returned to college to obtain a post-graduate diploma in business. A career as an accountant, combined with a hobby as a bodybuilder, provided him with additional experience that he could use in fulfilling his ambition to open a successful business in the field of fitness.

Troy felt that his unique background and interests, together with a capacity for hard work and a desire to succeed, qualified him to become a successful entrepreneur in the area of physical fitness. This idea was particularly appealing, given the increase in popularity of leisure and fitness-related activities. Troy decided to investigate the potential in the Niagara Region for opening a fitness centre for men and women. Through his former hobby of bodybuilding, he had become familiar with Malibu Gym, which had started in California and had spread across the United States and Europe but which had only begun to enter the Canadian market. Troy felt that the use of the Malibu name and promotional material would assist him in building a clientele for his gym, so he applied to become a licensee. A licensee pays a monthly fee to Malibu Gym International for the use of the Malibu name in a particular region of the country, but operates the business as his or her own. Because of Troy's background, he was approved as the licensee for the Niagara Region.

As with any business, starting this business required the owner to take risks in the hope of being successful. Troy collected all his available cash and applied for a loan and mortgage from the bank to start his business. He decided he would work part-time at the fitness centre, and continue in his present position as an accountant. Malibu Gym, Niagara, officially opened on September 1.

Purpose of Accounting

The purpose of accounting is to provide financial information for decision making.

Organized method of performing accounting tasks.

The primary **purpose of accounting** is to provide financial information for decision making. In addition, accurate information is required for many purposes, including calculating income tax for Canada Revenue Agency. To fill this need, Troy had to develop an **accounting system** for Malibu. An accounting system is an organized method of performing accounting tasks. Every accounting system must:

• Record the day-to-day activities of the business.

- Summarize and report information in financial statements for analysis and decision making.

Introducing Generally Accepted Accounting Principles

It is very important to the users of accounting information, whether they are owners, creditors, bankers, or investors, that the information presented to them be prepared according to a common set of rules. Only in this way can users compare the data of various businesses to make decisions. **Generally Accepted Accounting Principles (GAAP)** and their underlying assumptions provide a set of consistent rules used by all accountants to prepare financial statements such as the balance sheet. In Canada, the Canadian Institute of Chartered Accountants (CICA) publishes the *CICA Handbook* containing these principles. Where appropriate throughout this text, a simplified version of GAAP and concepts will be discussed to assist you in understanding the significance of the accounting procedures that you are undertaking.

Generally Accepted Accounting Principles (GAAP) are standard rules and guidelines.

Business Entity Assumption

In this chapter, the study of accounting will begin with a look at the balance sheet, which is one of the financial statements for Malibu Gym. It should be pointed out at this time that to prepare accurate financial statements the financial data for the business must be kept *separate* from Troy's personal financial data. Each business should be considered as a separate unit or *entity* for the purpose of keeping accounting records. This is known as the **business entity assumption**.

Each business should be considered as a separate unit or entity for the purpose of keeping accounting records.

COMPANY BALANCE SHEET

The financial position of Malibu Gym on opening day is shown in Figure 1-2 in a **balance sheet**. Just as with the personal balance sheet shown for Louise Wong, a company balance sheet is a formal report or statement showing the financial position of a business at a certain date. It lists assets, liabilities, and owner's equity. **Owner's equity** is an accounting term for the owner's claim against the assets of the company.

A balance sheet is a financial statement that lists the assets, liabilities, and owner's equity at a specific date.

Owner's equity is the owner's claim against the assets of the company.

FIGURE 1-2

Company balance sheet

Malibu Gym			
Balance Sheet			
September 1, 2007			
Assets		**Liabilities**	
Cash	$ 5 000	Accounts Payable	$ 4 000
Accounts Receivable	6 000	Bank Loan	65 000
Office Supplies	500	Mortgage Payable	80 000
Land	35 000	Total Liabilities	149 000
Building	110 000		
Training Equipment	94 500	**Owner's Equity**	
		T. Montana, Capital	102 000
		Total Liabilities	
Total Assets	$251 000	and Owner's Equity	$251 000

The company's financial position can also be described in terms of the accounting equation:

Assets	=	Liabilities	+	Owner's Equity
$251 000	=	$149 000	+	$102 000
$251 000	=	$251 000		

In this equation, the two sides balance. The left side ($251 000) equals the right side ($251 000).

Notice that the balance sheet also balances. The total of the left side equals the total of the right side. This is why it is called a *balance sheet*.

Accounting Terms

Notice also that accounting terminology is used for all items on the balance sheet. The amount owed by customers for memberships, $6000, is called *Accounts Receivable*. The amount owed as debts to creditors, $4000, is *Accounts Payable*. The loan (mortgage) owed on the building, $80 000, is *Mortgage Payable*.

Balance Sheet Preparation

The opening balance sheet for Malibu Gym will be used as an example to discuss the correct format and procedures followed to prepare a balance sheet. This is known as a formal report since it is prepared according to a specific set of rules, outlined in the following steps.

Step 1: Prepare Statement Heading

The three-line heading is centred at the top of the page and is designed to provide information in this sequence:

Line 1: Who? — Malibu Gym — business name
Line 2: What? — Balance Sheet — statement name
Line 3: When? — September 1, 2007 — date of statement

Step 2: List Assets

The assets are listed on the left side of the page. Before the assets are totalled, the liabilities must be listed and totalled. Then, if required, the necessary number of blank lines must be inserted before the owner's equity section and before the assets total so that the final totals on both sides of the statement will be on the same line.

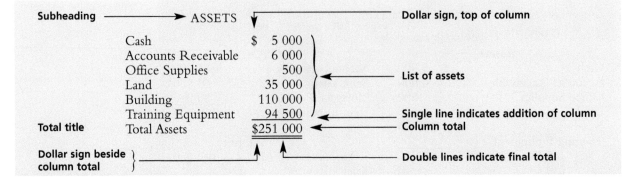

Step 3: List Liabilities

The liabilities are listed and totalled on the right side of the page:

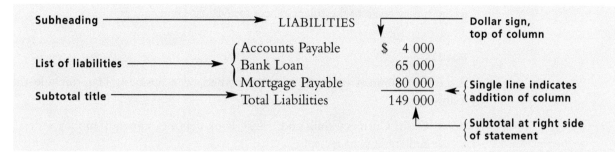

Step 4: Show Owner's Equity

The owner's equity section, showing the owner's investment, is on the right side of the page after the liabilities section. As explained previously, the final totals of each side must be on the same line. This allows for an attractive presentation of the information and emphasizes the fact that the left side of the balance sheet equals the right side, that is, $A = L + OE$.

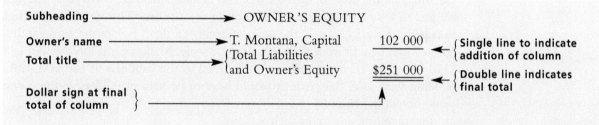

Facts to Remember

The total assets and the total liabilities and owner's equity are written on the same line:

The appearance of the balance sheet is very important since the statement may be viewed by a variety of people inside and outside the business. Statements such as this create an impression regarding the business and should be prepared as attractively and accurately as possible. In addition to the specifications for balance sheet preparation given in the examples, the following requirements should be considered:

(1) No abbreviations should be used in the statement.
(2) The statement should contain no corrections.
(3) For the balance sheet, dollar signs should be placed as follows:

- Beside the first figure in each column.
- Beside the *final* total on both sides of the statement.

Additional Accounting Terminology

Earlier in the chapter, you started to build your accounting vocabulary by learning what assets, liabilities, and equity were. Here is additional information regarding these terms as they relate to the balance sheet for Malibu Gym.

Assets

Assets are resources or items of value owned by a business. They include the following:

- **Cash:** Currency (bills and coins), bank deposits, cheques, money orders, and credit card receipts.
- **Accounts Receivable:** The total amount due from **debtors** (customers). Debtors are persons or businesses that owe a business money as a result of purchasing goods or services on credit. The amount is normally due within 30 days.
- **Office Supplies:** Items purchased for use within the business office.

Persons or businesses that owe a business money as a result of purchasing goods or services on credit.

Liabilities

Liabilities are the debts of the business. The creditors who are owed these amounts are said to have a claim against the assets of the business. This claim by the creditors is the right to be paid the amount owing to them before the owner of the business can benefit from their sale. For example, Malibu Gym lists a building at $110 000 as an asset. A mortgage is included in the liabilities at $80 000. If the building were sold, the creditor would have to be paid in full before the owner could obtain the balance.

Liabilities include items such as:

- **Accounts Payable:** The total amount owed to the creditors for the purchase of goods or services of the business. These amounts are normally due in 30 days.
- **Bank Loan:** The amount of loans owing to the bank. These loans vary in length of time (1–5 years). Some bank loans are "demand" loans and are due whenever payment is demanded by the bank.
- **Mortgage Payable:** The amount borrowed from financial institutions usually to purchase buildings or land. The lender has the right to obtain control of the property in the event that the borrower fails to repay the debt. Since this liability is normally large in amount, the time to repay is longer than other liabilities (for example, 25 years).

Equities

Equities are claims against the assets of a company.

The assets are listed on the left side of the balance sheet. On the right side are the claims against the assets. These claims are called **equities**.

The liabilities section lists the claims of the creditors. The *owner's equity* section lists the owner's claim. The owner's claim is what the company is "worth to the owner," or the net worth. It is listed on the balance sheet using the word **Capital** beside the owner's name (see *T. Montana, Capital* — page 5). The owner's equity is the difference between the assets and the liabilities (OE = A − L).

Order of Items on the Balance Sheet

The assets and liabilities on the balance sheet are listed in a particular order.

Assets

Assets are listed in order of their **liquidity**. This is the order in which they would likely be converted to cash. Using the balance sheet for Malibu Gym as an example, the order would be Cash, Accounts Receivable, and Office Supplies, since this is the order in which these items could be converted to cash. After assets such as Cash, Accounts Receivable, and Office Supplies comes a different type of asset — assets that *last a long time* and are used for a long period of time to operate the business. Examples include Land, Building, and Training Equipment. They are listed in order of useful life to the business with the longest lasting listed first:

Liquidity order is the order in which assets can be converted into cash.

ORDER OF ASSETS		REASONS
Cash	$ 5 000	Most liquid asset.
Accounts Receivable	6 000	Received within 30 days.
Office Supplies	500	Easily converted to cash.
Land	35 000	Assets listed in order of length of
Building	110 000	useful life in the business. Longest life
Training Equipment	94 500	listed first and shortest life last.

Liabilities

Liabilities are listed according to their payment due date, from most recent to longest term. This is known as the **maturity date rule**.

The maturity date rule specifies that liabilities are listed according to the date they are due to be paid.

ORDER OF LIABILITIES		REASONS
Accounts Payable	$ 4 000	Payable within 30 days.
Bank Loan	65 000	Payable usually within 1–5 years.
Mortgage Payable	80 000	Payable usually within 25 years.

Valuation of Items on the Balance Sheet

All the items on the balance sheet have a dollar value. There are accounting rules governing the methods used to assign dollar values. One of them is the cost principle.

Cost Principle

Assets are valued according to the **cost principle**. When assets are obtained, they are recorded at their actual cost to the business. This figure is never changed even though the owner might think that the value of the assets has increased.

The cost principle requires assets to be recorded at their actual cost to the business.

Users of the Balance Sheet

For a variety of reasons, a number of people and organizations could be interested in the financial position of a business. The following chart provides a brief introduction to users of a balance sheet and lists reasons for their interest. When you consider the number of users of this financial information and the importance of the decisions they are making, it is easy to see why it is essential to employ the most objective, accurate data available in preparing the balance sheet.

USERS	REASONS FOR INTEREST
Owner	Indicates his or her claim on the assets. Comparing balance sheets at different points in time will show whether or not the financial position is improving.
Creditors	Companies considering extending credit or loaning money are interested in liquid assets available to meet payments as well as claims on assets.
Investors	Investors investigate the financial position of a business as one of the factors they consider in deciding whether or not to invest in the business. They want to protect their investment and are interested in much the same information as are creditors.
Government	Government departments need information for policy decision making, statistical reports, and taxation.

COMMON RECORDING PRACTICES

There are several common recording practices followed by most accountants. They are described and illustrated below:

(1) When ruled accounting paper is used, dollar signs and decimals are not required.
(2) A single line indicates addition or subtraction.
(3) Double lines indicate final totals.

ASSETS				
				← Ruled accounting paper
Cash		500	00	
Accounts Receivable	1	200	75	
Equipment	5	000	00	{ A single line indicates
Total Assets	6	700	75	{ addition or subtraction
				← Double lines indicate final totals

(4) When ruled accounting forms are not used, dollar signs and decimals are used.
(5) Dollar signs are placed before the first figure in a column and beside final column totals when accounting forms are not used.

ASSETS

Cash	$ 500.00
Accounts Receivable	1 200.75
Equipment	5 000.00
Total Assets	$6 700.75

(6) Abbreviations are not used on financial statements unless the official name of the company contains an abbreviation. For example, Lumonics Inc. *does* contain a short form (Inc.) in its official name and should be written as *Lumonics Inc.* Goldcorp Investments Limited should not be written in short form since the company uses *Limited*, not Ltd., as part of its official name.

(7) Accounting records must be neat and legible. They are used by many people and are kept for a long period of time. They are either printed, keyed, or written in ink. Care must be taken to write numbers and words clearly and legibly.

1. What is meant by "financial position"?

2. Define "asset" and give an example of an asset.

3. (a) Define "liability" and give an example.
   (b) Define "owner's equity."

4. What is the accounting equation?

5. What is the balance sheet?

6. Why did Troy Montana decide to go into business for himself? What risks did he take?

7. How is the owner's equity calculated?

8. In what order are assets listed on the balance sheet?

9. In what order are liabilities listed on the balance sheet?

10. What does a single ruled line on a financial statement indicate? What do double lines mean?

11. What is meant by "Generally Accepted Accounting Principles"?

12. What is the business entity assumption?

13. What is the cost principle?

1. Complete the following equations in your study guide or notebook:

A	=	L	+	OE
$ 75 000		$25 000		$50 000
?		72 000		35 000
96 000		49 000		?
65 000		?		33 000
87 000		43 000		?

2. Classify the following items as assets, liabilities, or owner's equity:

Cash
Accounts Payable
Equipment
Land
Mortgage
Building
Owner's Investment in the Business
Accounts Receivable

3. The balance sheet items for the College Clothing Company are listed in random order below.
   (a) Prepare lists of the assets, the liabilities, and the owner's equity.
   (b) Complete the accounting equation for the College Clothing Company in your study guide or notebook, following the format shown below.
      Assets $_____ = Liabilities $_____ + Owner's Equity $_____

Cash	$16 500
Building	78 000
Land	45 000
Bank Loan	20 500
Mortgage	38 600
Equipment	30 000
K. Campbell, Capital	110 400

4. The balance sheet items for the Means Company at April 30, 2007 are listed in random order below.
   (a) Prepare lists of the assets, the liabilities, and the owner's equity.
   (b) Complete the accounting equation for the Means Company in your study guide or notebook, following the format shown below:
      Assets $_____ = Liabilities $_____ + Owner's Equity $_____

Building	$70 000
Cash	12 600
Land	25 000
Bank Loan	9 500
Mortgage	38 000
Equipment	15 000
T. Means, Capital	78 100
Accounts Receivable	7 500
Accounts Payable	4 500

5. Using the format in Figure 1-1 (page 3) and Figure 1-2 (page 5), prepare a balance sheet for Means Company (refer to exercise 4 above).

6. The balance sheet items for West Coast Tourist Trips are listed below. Prepare a balance sheet dated April 15, 2007, listing assets and liabilities in correct order.

Cash	$ 4 200
Accounts Receivable	?
Office Equipment	7 200
Bank Loan	4 100
Accounts Payable	2 700
Building	58 000
L. Dupont, Capital	53 500
Land	25 000
Mortgage Payable	37 000
Supplies	1 600

7. Chili Pepper is a restaurant owned by Michael Kurri. The restaurant's assets and liabilities on May 31, 2008, are as follows:

Cash	$ 19 000
Food Supplies	3 000
Restaurant Supplies	7 500
Furniture and Fixtures	58 000
Land and Building	190 000
Payable to Suppliers	12 000
Mortgage Payable	85 000
Bank Loan	27 000

(a) Calculate Kurri's equity.
(b) Prepare a balance sheet.

8. The assets and liabilities of Mike Jackson, a lawyer, are as follows on July 31, 2008:

Cash	$12 800
Due from Clients	35 000
Office Supplies	2 800
Office Equipment	30 000
Bank Loan	12 500
Owed to Creditors	10 000

(a) Classify each item as an asset or a liability.
(b) Calculate Jackson's equity.
(c) Prepare a balance sheet.

UNIT 2 Business Transactions

Learning Objectives

After reading this unit, discussing the applicable review questions, and completing the applications exercises, you will be able to do the following:

1. **RECORD** transactions affecting assets, liabilities, and owner's equity on a transaction sheet.

2. **PROVE** the arithmetical accuracy of a transaction sheet.

3. **PREPARE** a balance sheet from a completed transaction sheet.

INTRODUCING TRANSACTIONS

The balance sheet for Malibu Gym was prepared on September 1, 2007. Events will occur in the business after this date that will change the value of the balance sheet items. For example, customers will pay the remainder owing on their memberships, equipment will be purchased for the business, and payments will be made to creditors. All these events are examples of transactions.

A business transaction is an exchange of things of value.

A *transaction* is an event occurring during the operation of a business that results in a financial change. A **business transaction** always includes an exchange of things of value:

Transaction

Something of value ⟷ Something of value
is given   is received

The balance sheet provides a detailed picture of the financial position on a certain date. This same information is presented in summary form by the accounting equation:

Assets = Liabilities + Owner's Equity

To assist in the examination of transactions and their effect on the balance sheet, a *transaction analysis sheet* will be used. This places the balance sheet items in equation form to more easily examine the effect of transactions on these items as well as on the equation. Transaction analysis sheets are not used in business, but the technique of analysis developed by their use will be helpful throughout your career.

A number of common transactions will be analyzed and recorded for Malibu Gym. This example will begin with the information found on the September 1, 2007 balance sheet; it will conclude with the preparation of a new balance sheet at the end of this accounting period. The **accounting period** is the length of time between the preparation of financial reports. This time varies from monthly to annually, depending on many factors such as business size and current need for the data contained in the reports.

The accounting period is the period of time covered by financial statements.

USING A TRANSACTION ANALYSIS SHEET

The first step in preparing a transaction analysis sheet is to restate the balance sheet in balance sheet equation form on the transaction analysis sheet. Figure 1-3 below shows the September 1 balance sheet for Malibu Gym.

FIGURE 1-3

September 1 balance sheet

Malibu Gym Balance Sheet September 1, 2007			
Assets		**Liabilities**	
Cash	$ 5 000	Accounts Payable	$ 4 000
Accounts Receivable	6 000	Bank Loan	65 000
Office Supplies	500	Mortgage Payable	80 000
Land	35 000	Total Liabilities	149 000
Building	110 000		
Training Equipment	94 500	**Owner's Equity**	
		T. Montana, Capital	102 000
		Total Liabilities	
Total Assets	$251 000	and Owner's Equity	$251 000

Figure 1-5 on page 17 is a transaction analysis sheet containing the opening balance information. Notice that the left side contains the assets and the right side the liabilities plus owner's equity.

The following transactions will cause changes in items on the balance sheet:

Sep.   2   *Purchased new training equipment for $3500 cash.*
      5   *Bought office supplies for $115, on credit from Central Supply Co.*
    10   *Received $4000 cash from customers (various accounts receivable) who owed money.*

These transactions must now be analyzed to determine the changes in value caused to the items on the balance sheet. The changes will then be recorded on the transaction analysis sheet.

Transaction Analysis

Transaction 1: Asset Purchased for Cash

Sep.   2   *Purchased new training equipment for $3500 cash.*

The following questions are asked to assist in analyzing a transaction:

(a) Which items change in value as a result of the transaction?
(b) How much do the items change?
(c) Do the items increase or decrease in value?
(d) After the change is recorded, is the equation still in balance?

In the first transaction, *Training Equipment* and *Cash* will change. Training Equipment will *increase* since the company now owns more equipment. Cash will *decrease* by $3500 since the company has spent money. Notice how these changes are shown on the transaction analysis sheet in Figure 1-6 on page 17. After the transaction is recorded, the total assets ($251 000) still equal the liabilities plus owner's equity ($251 000).

Transaction 2: Asset Purchased on Credit

Sep.   5   Bought office supplies for $115, on credit from Central Supply Co.

Which items on the balance sheet change? Do they increase or decrease? If you said the asset, *Office Supplies, increases* by $115 and the liability, *Accounts Payable*, also *increases* by $115, you were correct. Look at how this transaction is recorded on the transaction analysis sheet in Figure 1-7 on page 17. Is the equation still in balance? If you add up the asset balances after the second transaction, you will get a total of $251 115. The liabilities and owner's equity now total $251 115. The equation is still in balance.

Transaction 3: Cash Received from Customers

Sep.   10   Received $4000 cash from customers (various accounts receivable) who owed money.

Which items change? Do they increase or decrease? Look at Figure 1-8 on page 18 to see how this transaction is recorded. Is the equation still in balance?

Additional Transactions

Look at the next four transactions. For each of them, ask yourself which items change. Do they increase or decrease?

Sep.   15   Sold some unused equipment for $400 cash.
*   18   Paid $375 cash to Central Supply Co. in payment of an account payable that had become due.*
*   21   Owner invested an additional $2500 cash in the business.*
*   25   Purchased equipment from Niagara Sport Ltd. at a cost of $3000. Of the total price, $2000 was paid in cash and $1000 will be paid in 30 days.*

Now look at Figure 1-9, on page 18 and follow the recording of each of these transactions. Note that the final transaction involves changes in three items.

ⓅREPARING A NEW BALANCE SHEET

The completed transaction analysis sheet now contains the changes caused by the September transactions. The equation is still in balance; that is, the total of the left side equals the total of the right side. The new balances are used when the new balance sheet is prepared on September 30, 2007. Figure 1-4 below shows the September 30 balance sheet.

FIGURE 1-4

September 30 balance sheet

Malibu Gym			
Balance Sheet			
September 30, 2007			
Assets		**Liabilities**	
Cash	$ 6 025	Accounts Payable	$ 4 740
Accounts Receivable	2 000	Bank Loan	65 000
Office Supplies	615	Mortgage Payable	80 000
Land	35 000	Total Liabilities	149 740
Building	110 000		
Training Equipment	100 600	**Owner's Equity**	
		T. Montana, Capital	104 500
		Total Liabilities	
Total Assets	$254 240	and Owner's Equity	$254 240

FIGURE 1-5

Transaction analysis sheet — opening balances

	ASSETS						=	LIABILITIES			+	OWNER'S EQUITY
	Cash	Accts. Rec.	Off. Supps.	Land	Bldg.	Train. Equip.		Accts. Pay.	Bank Loan	Mtge. Pay.		T. Montana, Capital
Bal.	$5 000 +	$6 000 +	$500 +	$35 000 +	$110 000 +	$94 500	=	$4 000 +	$65 000 +	$80 000	+	$102 000

FIGURE 1-6

Transaction analysis sheet — Sep. 2 transaction

	ASSETS						=	LIABILITIES			+	OWNER'S EQUITY
	Cash	Accts. Rec.	Off. Supps.	Land	Bldg.	Train. Equip.		Accts. Pay.	Bank Loan	Mtge. Pay.		T. Montana, Capital
Bal.	$5 000 +	$6 000 +	$500 +	$35 000 +	$110 000 +	$94 500	=	$4 000 +	$65 000 +	$80 000	+	$102 000
Sep. 2	-3 500					+3 500						
New Bal.	1 500 +	6 000 +	500 +	35 000 +	110 000 +	98 000	=	4 000 +	65 000 +	80 000	+	102 000

FIGURE 1-7

Transaction analysis sheet — Sep. 5 transaction

	ASSETS						=	LIABILITIES			+	OWNER'S EQUITY
	Cash	Accts. Rec.	Off. Supps.	Land	Bldg.	Train. Equip.		Accts. Pay.	Bank Loan	Mtge. Pay.		T. Montana, Capital
Bal.	$5 000 +	$6 000 +	$500 +	$35 000 +	$110 000 +	$94 500	=	$4 000 +	$65 000 +	$80 000	+	$102 000
Sep. 2	-3 500					+3 500						
New Bal.	1 500 +	6 000 +	500 +	35 000 +	110 000 +	98 000	=	4 000 +	65 000 +	80 000	+	102 000
Sep. 5			+115					+115				
New Bal.	1 500 +	6 000 +	615 +	35 000 +	110 000 +	98 000	=	4 115 +	65 000 +	80 000	+	102 000

FIGURE 1-8

Transaction analysis sheet — Sep. 2–10 transactions

	Cash	Accts. Rec.	Off. Supps.	Land	Bldg.	Train. Equip.	=	Accts. Pay.	Bank Loan	Mtge. Pay.	T. Montana, Capital
						ASSETS	=	LIABILITIES			OWNER'S EQUITY
Bal.	$5 000	+ $6 000	+ $500	+ $35 000	+ $110 000	+ $94 500	=	$4 000	+ $65 000	+ $80 000	+ $102 000
Sep. 2	−3 500					+ 3 500					
New Bal.	1 500	+ 6 000	+ 500	+ 35 000	+ 110 000	+ 98 000	=	4 000	+ 65 000	+ 80 000	+ 102 000
Sep. 5			+ 115					+ 115			
New Bal.	1 500	+ 6 000	+ 615	+ 35 000	+ 110 000	+ 98 000	=	4 115	+ 65 000	+ 80 000	+ 102 000
Sep. 10	+ 4 000	− 4 000									
New Bal.	5 500	+ 2 000	+ 615	+ 35 000	+ 110 000	+ 98 000	=	4 115	+ 65 000	+ 80 000	+ 102 000

FIGURE 1-9

Transaction analysis sheet — Sep. 2–25 transactions

	Cash	Accts. Rec.	Off. Supps.	Land	Bldg.	Train. Equip.	=	Accts. Pay.	Bank Loan	Mtge. Pay.	T. Montana, Capital
						ASSETS	=	LIABILITIES			OWNER'S EQUITY
Bal.	$5 000	+ $6 000	+ $500	+ $35 000	+ $110 000	+ $94 500	=	$4 000	+ $65 000	+ $80 000	+ $102 000
Sep. 2	−3 500					+ 3 500					
New Bal.	1 500	+ 6 000	+ 500	+ 35 000	+ 110 000	+ 98 000	=	4 000	+ 65 000	+ 80 000	+ 102 000
Sep. 5			+ 115					+ 115			
New Bal.	1 500	+ 6 000	+ 615	+ 35 000	+ 110 000	+ 98 000	=	4 115	+ 65 000	+ 80 000	+ 102 000
Sep. 10	+ 4 000	− 4 000									
New Bal.	5 500	+ 2 000	+ 615	+ 35 000	+ 110 000	+ 98 000	=	4 115	+ 65 000	+ 80 000	+ 102 000
Sep. 15	+ 400					− 400					
New Bal.	5 900	+ 2 000	+ 615	+ 35 000	+ 110 000	+ 97 600	=	4 115	+ 65 000	+ 80 000	+ 102 000
Sep. 18	− 375							− 375			
New Bal.	5 525	+ 2 000	+ 615	+ 35 000	+ 110 000	+ 97 600	=	3 740	+ 65 000	+ 80 000	+ 102 000
Sep. 21	+ 2 500										+ 2 500
New Bal.	8 025	+ 2 000	+ 615	+ 35 000	+ 110 000	+ 97 600	=	3 740	+ 65 000	+ 80 000	+ 104 500
Sep. 25	− 2 000					+ 3 000		+ 1 000			
New Bal.	$6 025	+ $2 000	+ $615	+ $35 000	+ $110 000	+ $100 600	=	$4 740	+ $65 000	+ $80 000	+ $104 500
						$254 240	=	$149 740			+ $104 500
						$254 240	=	$254 240			

Ⓐ CCOUNTING TERMS

Accounting	The "language of business." The purpose of accounting is to provide accounting information for decision making. (p. 3)
Accounting Equation	Assets = Liabilities + Owner's Equity. (p. 3)
Accounting Period	The period of time covered by financial statements. (p. 14)
Accounting System	An organized method of performing accounting tasks. (p. 4)
Accounts Payable	Amount owed to suppliers of the business for the purchase of goods or services on credit. (p. 8)
Accounts Receivable	Total amount due from customers for goods and services purchased on credit. (p. 8)
Assets	Resources or items of value owned by a business or person. (p. 3)
Balance Sheet	Financial statement that lists assets, liabilities, and owner's equity at a specific date. (p. 5)
Business Entity Assumption	Each business should be considered as a separate unit or entity for the purpose of keeping accounting records. (p. 5)
Business Transaction	An exchange of things of value. (p. 14)
Capital	Owner's net worth found in the Owner's Equity section of the balance sheet. (p. 8)
Cost Principle	Assets are recorded at the actual cost to the business. (p. 9)
Creditor	A person or business that has extended credit or loaned money. (p. 2)
Debtor	A person or business that owes a business money as a result of purchasing goods or services on credit. (p. 8)
Entrepreneur	A person who organizes and operates a business. (p. 4)
Equities	Claims against the assets. Found on the right side of the balance sheet. (p. 8)
Financial Position	Listing of the assets, liabilities, and equity of a person or business. (p. 3)
Generally Accepted Accounting Principles	Consistent accounting rules published by the Canadian Institute of Chartered Accountants needed to prepare financial statements. (p. 5)
Liabilities	Debts or amounts owed to others by a business or a person. (p. 3)
Liquidity	The order in which assets would likely be converted into cash. (p. 9)
Maturity Date Rule	Liabilities are listed on the balance sheet according to payment due date from most recent to longest term. (p. 9)
Owner's Equity	A person's net worth. The owner's claim against the assets of the business. (p. 5)
Personal Equity	The difference between personal assets and personal liabilities. (p. 3)
Purpose of Accounting	To provide financial information for decision making. (p. 4)

1. Define the term "transaction."

2. What four questions are asked when analyzing a business transaction?

3. Define the term "accounting period."

UNIT 2

REVIEW QUESTIONS

1. For each of the items listed below, give an example of a business transaction that will have the desired effect on the accounting equation:

(a) Increase an asset and increase owner's equity
(b) Increase a liability and decrease a liability
(c) Decrease an asset and decrease a liability
(d) Increase an asset and increase a liability
(e) Increase an asset and decrease an asset

2. The June 30 balance sheet for Y. Bissonette Secretarial Service is shown below.

Yolanda Bissonette Secretarial Service
Balance Sheet
June 30, 2008

Assets		Liabilities	
Cash	$ 4 500	Accounts Payable	$ 3 000
Accounts Receivable	5 000	Mortgage Payable	45 000
Office Supplies	6 000	Total Liabilities	48 000
Building	95 000	**Owner's Equity**	
		Y. Bissonette, Capital	62 500
		Total Liabilities	
Total Assets	$110 500	and Owner's Equity	$110 500

The following transactions occurred in July:

Jul. 4 Paid $900 cash on some accounts payable.

15 Received $1600 cash from an account receivable.

20 Purchased office supplies for $1000 on credit (payment is due in 30 days).

29 The owner, Y. Bissonette, invested an additional $4000 in the business.

(a) Place the June 30 balances on a transaction sheet.
(b) Record the transactions on the transaction sheet. Follow the format of the transaction sheet in Figure 1-9. Be sure that the total assets equal the total liabilities and owner's equity after each transaction.
(c) In your study guide or notebook, complete the equation on July 31 following this format:
Assets $_____ = Liabilities $_____ + Owner's Equity $_____
(d) Prepare a new balance sheet on July 31.

3. Mail-O-Matic Printing produces a variety of advertising materials such as brochures and flyers and distributes them door-to-door for retail stores. The February 1 balance sheet for Mail-O-Matic Printing and several transactions that occurred during February are given below.

Feb. 1 Purchased printing supplies for $1050 from Office Products, on credit.

10 Some of the printing supplies bought on February 1 were damaged when received. Returned damaged supplies that cost $150 to Office Products for credit.

15 Paid $2300 to Clear Chemicals Ltd., a supplier, to reduce balance owing.

21 Purchased a new $15 000 copier from Conway Manufacturers. A down payment of $4000 cash was made, and the balance of $11 000 is to be paid later.

28 Made a $3500 payment on the bank loan.

Mail-O-Matic Printing Balance Sheet February 1, 2007			
Assets		**Liabilities**	
Cash	$ 24 000	Accounts Payable	$ 16 500
Accounts Receivable	23 000	Bank Loan	20 000
Printing Supplies	18 900	Total Liabilities	36 500
Equipment	97 000	**Owner's Equity**	
		R. Francis, Capital	126 400
		Total Liabilities	
Total Assets	$162 900	and Owner's Equity	$162 900

(a) Complete a transaction sheet for Mail-O-Matic.
(b) Prepare a new balance sheet on February 28.

4. The following is the balance sheet for Corbett Auto Repair as of November 1:

Corbett Auto Repair Balance Sheet November 1, 2007			
Assets		**Liabilities**	
Cash	$ 6 500	Accounts Payable	$ 4 700
Accounts Receivable	15 300	Bank Loan	1 500
Equipment	64 000	Total Liabilities	6 200
		Owner's Equity	
		K. Corbett, Capital	79 600
		Total Liabilities	
Total Assets	$85 800	and Owner's Equity	$85 800

The following transactions took place during November:

Nov.   3 Received $2950 cash from M. Lynch, a customer.

4 Purchased a new $9500 air compressor from K.D. Manufacturers, on credit.

5 Borrowed $10 000 cash from bank.

8 Paid $950 to General Auto Parts, a supplier, to pay off some of the balance owing to them.

15 Made a $600 cash payment on the bank loan.

20 The owner, K. Corbett, invested a further $2500 in the business.

(a) Prepare a transaction sheet for Corbett Auto Repair and record the transactions.
(b) After the last transaction has been recorded, prepare the accounting equation to prove the accuracy of your work.

CHAPTER 1

**PROBLEMS:
CHALLENGES**

1. The completed transaction sheet for Quick Cleaners, Figure 1-10, is on page 23. For (a) to (f), describe the transactions that must have occurred in the business to produce the changes shown on the transaction sheet.

   Example:

   (a) Cash increased by $500 as a result of the collection of $500 from a customer (an account receivable).

2. At first glance, the following balance sheet for Red Deer Company may appear to be correct, but it has several major and minor errors.

   (a) List the errors.
   (b) Prepare a correct balance sheet.

Red Deer Company Balance Sheet December 31, 2008				
Assets			**Liabilities**	
Cash	$ 3 500		Bank Loan	$ 54 400
Truck	20 600		Accounts Payable	13 600
Building	162 500			
Less Mortgage	76 000			
Land	42 300		Red Deer Company,	
Equipment	25 100		Capital	110 000
	$178 000			$178 000

3. There are several mistakes in the set-up and content of this balance sheet. Can you locate them?

M. Mancini & Company Balance Sheet August 31, 2009			
Assets		**Liabilities**	
Cash	2 000	Accounts Receivable	3 000
Accounts Payable	2 000	Equipment	6 000
Supplies	1 000	Bank Loan	30 000
Building	90 000	Total Liabilities	39 000
		Owner's Equity	
		M. Mancini, Capital	68 000
		Total Liabilities	
Total Assets	95 000	and Owner's Equity	106 000

FIGURE 1-10

Transaction analysis sheet for Quick Cleaners

	ASSETS					=	LIABILITIES		+	OWNER'S EQUITY
	Cash	Accts. Rec.	Clean. Equip.	Bldg.	Land		Accts. Pay.	Mtge. Pay.		Z. Sharif, Capital
Bal.	$5 000	+ $2 000	+ $7 500	+ $42 000	+ $18 000	=	$750	+ $38 000	+	$45 750
(a)	+500	−500								
New Bal.	5 500	+ 1 500	+ 7 500	+ 42 000	+ 18 000	=	750	+ 38 000	+	45 750
(b)	−700		+1 500				+800			
New Bal.	4 800	+ 1 500	+ 9 000	+ 42 000	+ 18 000	=	1 550	+ 38 000	+	45 750
(c)	+2 000									+2 000
New Bal.	6 800	+ 1 500	+ 9 000	+ 42 000	+ 18 000	=	1 550	+ 38 000	+	47 750
(d)	−800						−800			
New Bal.	6 000	+ 1 500	+ 9 000	+ 42 000	+ 18 000	=	750	+ 38 000	+	47 750
(e)	+300	+700	−1 000							
New Bal.	6 300	+ 2 200	+ 8 000	+ 42 000	+ 18 000	=	750	+ 38 000	+	47 750
(f)	−3 000							−3 000		
New Bal.	3 300	+ 2 200	+ 8 000	+ 42 000	+ 18 000	=	750	+ 35 000	+	47 750

4. Following is a list of items Mari Ross presented to her accountant to have a balance sheet prepared for her business, Ross Dance Studio. Mari has included all items she felt were important.

Cash in Business Bank Account	$ 3 800
Personal Bank Account	2 500
Accounts Receivable	1 500
Accounts Payable	500
Personal Car Loan	15 000
House and Lot	245 000
Dance Studio Building (Cost)	300 000
Dance Studio Building (Current Market Price)	350 000
Land	120 000
Personal Car	28 000
Mortgage on Dance Studio	200 000
Mortgage on House	132 000
Studio Equipment	10 000
Bank Loan on Studio Equipment	6 000
Personal Property	10 000

(a) Prepare a balance sheet for Ross Dance Studio on December 31, 20—.

(b) Explain why some of the items listed above were not included in the balance sheet you just prepared. Refer to the GAAP that influenced your decision.

(c) Which GAAP was applied to determine the value of the dance studio building on the balance sheet?

(d) Using the data and concepts from (a), (b), and (c), prepare a personal balance sheet.

ETHICS CASE

Ethics issues in business are constantly reported in the media. For example:
- Martha Stewart was sentenced to five months in prison, five months of home confinement, and two years' probation for conspiracy, obstruction of justice, and lying about a stock sale. Stewart must also pay a $30 000 fine. She was not indicted on the original charge of insider trading.
- H. Radler, former publisher of the *Chicago-Sun Times*, pleaded guilty to charges of making improper payments. He was accused of diverting funds from the company into his and other managers' pockets. This could result in a combination of fines and prison term.
- The president of a government agency was accused of extravagant misuse of government funds, including unreasonable travel claims and entertainment expenses. This resulted in his forced resignation from his position.

These situations indicate a need for business and society to focus on business ethics.

Business ethics is the study of decision making in a business context according to moral judgements and concepts. It involves the rules, principles, duties, and obligations that should guide people in conducting any type of business. These moral obligations apply to everyone, including company presidents, financial officers, accountants, managers, and office and plant workers.

This textbook examines ethics from the points of view of business executives, internal and external accountants, all those who work in business, and society in general. The business ethics case studies illustrate breach of trust, insider trading, fraud, misappropriation of company or government funds, and undue personal influence.

CASE 1

Use of Business Funds for Personal Reasons

You are the accountant for Superior Personnel. This firm specializes in supplying temporary office employees to firms in need of short-term assistance during peak work periods. It has ten branch offices.

Fatima Alharad, the president of the company, has just purchased a car for her daughter and instructs you to list the car as an asset of the company. You are to make the monthly car payments from the business bank account. When you ask why she would like the transaction handled in this manner, she informs you that she is the president of the company and can use the business funds however she wishes.

(a) Is Fatima correct in her assumption? Which accounting concept should you use to support your answer?
(b) From an ethical point of view, whose interests are being affected if the business pays for the car?

CASE 2
Evaluation of Assets

Jamie Burnstein owns a small delivery service. He asks you, his accountant, to prepare a balance sheet for him to present to the bank for evaluation to obtain a bank loan. A friend of his who works in the real estate business has indicated that Jamie's building would probably be worth $250 000 if offered for sale. The current records of the business show the building has a value of $190 000 which is what Jamie paid five years ago when he moved to this location. Jamie feels the higher amount should be used on the balance sheet since it better reflects the current value of his business to the bank manager.

(a) Should you follow Jamie's instructions when preparing the balance sheet? Include any GAAP and accounting concepts that you have considered in your answer.
(b) Would the bank be interested in the current market price of the building? Why?

CASE 3
Owner's Claim on Assets

Lin Chang, the owner of a retail store, has come to you for advice. She shows you her latest balance sheet. The assets total $200 000, the liabilities are $130 000, and the owner's equity is $70 000. Included in the assets are old equipment and merchandise at a value of $120 000. Realistically, these assets are now worth $40 000.

Lin is considering selling all the assets. She feels she could get about $120 000 if all the assets were sold. She would then take her investment (equity of $70 000) and close down the business. The remaining $50 000 from the sale of the assets would be available to the creditors as their claim against the assets.

What advice would you give Lin concerning her proposal?

CHAPTER 1

INTERNET RESOURCES

Explore these Web sites for information on professional accounting associations.

1. **Canadian Institute of Chartered Accountants   www.cica.ca**

   This site includes news on issues relevant to chartered accountants, information on becoming a CA and career development, research and guidelines, and a list of services and products. Extensive material, including frequently asked questions, is available on privacy issues. The Standards section includes the *CICA handbook.*

2. **Certified General Accountants Association of Canada www.cga-online.org**

   This site provides information about CGAs, including educational standards, professional guidelines, international issues, and available services. Comprehensive detail is included on the CGA Program of Professional Studies.

3. **Canadian Society of Management Accountants**
    www.cma-canada.org

    This site includes news of issues related to management accountants, a comprehensive career site, business publications, courses, and conferences. Members can access Canada's internationally recognized business publications, as well as an online library.

4. **Institute of Chartered Accountants of Ontario   www.icao.on.ca**

    This provincial organization offers news via a media room, career connections, and information on training and certification programs. The extensive professional development resources include a handy list of acronyms and links to related sites. The section on serving the public provides information on a variety of topics, from locating a CA to free CA tax clinics. Each Canadian province and territory has a similar site with a regional focus.

Balance Sheet Accounts

UNIT 3 Recording Transactions in T-Accounts

Learning Objectives

After reading this unit, discussing the applicable review questions, and completing the applications exercises, you will be able to do the following:

1. **RECORD** the opening balances on a balance sheet in a T-account ledger.

2. **ANALYZE** transactions to determine which accounts are changed and whether the changes are recorded as debits or credits.

3. **RECORD** transactions in T-accounts.

4. **CALCULATE** the balances in accounts.

5. **PREPARE** a trial balance to verify the mathematical accuracy of the ledger.

6. **PREPARE** a balance sheet from the trial balance.

INTRODUCING T-ACCOUNTS

Transaction analysis sheets were used in Chapter 1 to demonstrate the process of analysis necessary to record changes in the balance sheet items caused by business transactions. In actual practice, the use of a transaction analysis sheet is impractical due to the large number of financial events occurring each day in a business. A more efficient method of collecting, recording, and summarizing these events is to keep a separate record of the changes for each item. This record is called an **account**. To introduce the concepts and practices involved in recording data in accounts, a simplified form of this record, called a **T-account**, will be used in this chapter.

An account is a form in which changes caused by transactions are recorded.

For every item on the balance sheet, an account is prepared. As transactions occur, the changes that happen as a result of these transactions are recorded in accounts. Following is an example of a T-account. It is shaped like a "T" and has two sides just like a balance sheet prepared in account format:

A T-shaped account.

Account Title	
Left Side	Right Side
Debit	Credit

Debit is the accounting term used for the *left side* of the account. **Credit** is the accounting term used for the *right side* of the account. Following is an account used to record transactions involving cash. It has a debit (left) side and a credit (right) side. One side is used to record increases in cash, that is, money received, and the other side is used to record decreases in cash, that is, money paid out.

Debit refers to the left side of an account.

Credit refers to the right side of an account.

Cash	
Debit	Credit

T-accounts are not needed in business but are often used by accountants for their rough work when analyzing transactions. They are used at this time to introduce a number of basic accounting procedures and concepts.

On the next few pages, we will examine the use of accounts by recording transactions for Malibu Gym. As a first step, look again at the September 30 balance sheet for Malibu Gym shown in Figure 2-1.

Recording Balances in Accounts

There is a separate **balance sheet account** for each asset, for each liability, and for the owner's equity. For Malibu Gym, ten accounts are required because there are six assets, three liabilities, and one equity account. These ten accounts are shown a little further ahead in Figure 2-2 on page 31 The beginning amounts on the balance sheet are called *balances*. For each item on the balance sheet, the balance is recorded in a T-account. The Cash account is shown on page 31 after the beginning balance has been recorded. Since Cash appears on the left side of the balance sheet, the beginning balance is recorded on the left side of the Cash account. This rule applies to all **asset accounts**.

There is a separate account for each asset and liability and for the owner's equity.

Asset accounts are found in the asset section of the balance sheet.

Asset balances are recorded on the left side of asset accounts.

FIGURE 2-1

Sep. 30 balance sheet

Malibu Gym Balance Sheet September 30, 2007			
Assets		**Liabilities**	
Cash	$ 6 025	Accounts Payable	$ 4 740
Accounts Receivable	2 000	Bank Loan	65 000
Office Supplies	615	Mortgage Payable	80 000
Land	35 000	Total Liabilities	149 740
Building	110 000		
Training Equipment	100 600	**Owner's Equity**	
		T. Montana Capital	104 500
		Total Liabilities	
Total Assets	$254 240	and Owner's Equity	$254 240

Since assets are located on the left side of the balance sheet, the beginning balance of an asset is recorded on the debit (left) side of its account.

Cash	
Sept. 30 6 025	

Since liabilities are located on the right side of the balance sheet, the opening balance of a liability account is placed on the credit (right) side of the **liability account**. For the same reason, the opening balance for the **owner's equity account** is placed on the credit side of its account. This rule applies to all liability and owner's equity accounts.

Since liabilities and owner's equity are located on the right side of the balance sheet, their opening balances are recorded on the credit or right side of their accounts.

A liability account is found in the liability section of the balance sheet.

An owner's equity account is found in the owner's equity section of the balance sheet.

Liability and owner's equity balances are recorded on the right side of liability accounts.

INTRODUCING LEDGERS

A ledger is a group of accounts.

A **ledger** is the place where the accounts are found. It may be in the form of a book containing pages for each account in a manual accounting system, or stored on disk or tape for computerized accounting systems. The accounts in the ledger are designed to collect the data concerning changes in value of each item on the balance sheet on an individual basis.

Opening the Ledger

The balance sheet shown on page 31 can be visualized as a large "T" with the assets on the left and the liabilities and owner's equity on the right. This will help you remember that asset accounts normally have debit balances (balances shown on the left side of the T-account), while liabilities and owner's equity accounts have credit balances (balances shown on the right side of the T-account).

Enter the balances as shown on the balance sheet in the accounts found in the ledger.

To **open the ledger**, these steps should be followed:

- Place the account name in the middle of each account.
- Record the date and balance from the balance sheet in the account on the appropriate side.

The ledger for Malibu Gym is shown in Figure 2-2 on page 31. A separate account has been opened for each item on the balance sheet.

Left Side		Right Side	
Assets		**Liabilities**	
Cash	$ 6 025	Accounts Payable	$ 4 740
Accounts Receivable	2 000	Bank Loan	65 000
Office Supplies	615	Mortgage Payable	80 000
Land	35 000	Total Liabilities	149 740
Building	110 000		
Training Equipment	100 600	**Owner's Equity**	
		T. Montana, Capital	104 500
		Total Liabilities	
Total Assets	$254 240	and Owner's Equity	$254 240

Now let's analyze Figure 2-2. Since assets are found on the left side of the balance sheet, the value of each asset account has been recorded on the left (debit) side of the account. Since liabilities are found on the right side of the balance sheet, the value of each liability account has been recorded on the right (credit) side of the account. Since owner's equity is found on the right side of the balance sheet, the value of the owner's equity account has been recorded on the right (credit) side of the account.

Debits:

$6 025 + $2 000 + $615 + $35 000 + $110 000 + $100 600 = $254 240

Credits:

$4 740 + $65 000 + $80 000 + $104 500 = $254 240

Total of debit balances must equal total of credit balances. Note that if the debit balances are added together, they equal the total of the credit balances.

This is known as having the ledger in balance. This relationship must continue as transactions are recorded, in keeping with the important principle of double-entry accounting.

FIGURE 2-2
Ledger for Malibu Gym showing balances in each account

Cash		Accounts Payable	
Sep. 30 6 025			Sep. 30 4 740

Accounts Receivable		Bank Loan	
Sep. 30 2 000			Sep. 30 65 000

Office Supplies		Mortgage Payable	
Sep. 30 615			Sep. 30 80 000

Land		T. Montana, Capital	
Sep. 30 35 000			Sep. 30 104 500

Building	
Sep. 30 110 000	

Training Equipment	
Sep. 30 100 600	

Double-Entry Accounting

One of the most important principles of accounting is the **double-entry principle**. For each transaction, a debit amount equal to a credit amount must be recorded in the accounts. Thus, all transactions are recorded in one or more accounts as a debit and in one or more accounts as a credit. The total of the debit amounts must always equal the total of the credit amounts for each transaction.

Double-entry accounting requires a debit amount equal to the credit amount for each transaction.

RECORDING TRANSACTIONS IN ACCOUNTS

Determining which accounts are debited and credited in order to record transactions.

These steps are followed in **analyzing transactions** and recording them in accounts:

- **Step 1:** Determine *which* accounts change in value as a result of the transaction. Note that two or more accounts will change in value as a result of each transaction.
- **Step 2:** Identify the *type of account* that has changed. Is the account that has changed an asset, a liability, or an owner's equity account?
- **Step 3:** Decide whether the change is an *increase* or a *decrease* in the account.
- **Step 4:** Decide whether the change is recorded as a *debit* or a *credit* in the account. Note that the ledger must remain in balance.

The following transactions for Malibu Gym occurred during October 2007. These transactions will be analyzed and entered in the ledger to illustrate how the four steps described previously are followed. As you read the examples, note that each transaction has a debit amount that is equal to the credit amount. Note also that the debit portion of the entry is always shown before the credit portion.

Transaction Analysis

Transaction 1

Oct.   2   Received $500 cash from members as payments on memberships.

Assets increase on the debit side.

The two accounts that are affected are Cash and Accounts Receivable. The Cash account is increased with a debit for the following reasons:

- Cash is an asset.
- The asset Cash is increasing (money has been received).
- Assets are found on the left side of the balance sheet and increase on their debit (left) side.

The $500 increase is recorded in the Cash account as illustrated below:

	Cash
Sep. 30 6 025	
Oct. 2 500	

Assets decrease on the credit side.

The asset, Accounts Receivable, is also affected. The balance for this asset decreases because customers have paid some of the amount owed by them. An account *decreases* on the side *opposite* to its opening balance. The decrease in Accounts Receivable is recorded as a credit, as shown below:

Accounts Receivable	
Sep. 30 2 000	Oct. 2 500

Here is a summary of how this transaction was recorded:

ACCOUNT AFFECTED	TYPE OF ACCOUNT	INCREASE/DECREASE	DEBIT/CREDIT	
Cash	Asset	Increase	Debit	$500
Accounts Receivable	Asset	Decrease	Credit	500

Notice that in recording the transaction, there is a debit of $500 and a credit of $500. A general rule for recording transactions can now be stated:

Accounts increase on the same side as they appear on the balance sheet and they decrease on the opposite side.

Following are four specific statements based on this general rule:

(1) If assets increase, the amount is recorded on the debit side.
(2) If assets decrease, the amount is recorded on the credit side.
(3) If liabilities or owner's equity increases, the amount is recorded on the credit side.
(4) If liabilities or owner's equity decreases, the amount is recorded on the debit side.

Transaction 2

Oct.   5   *Purchased office supplies for $60 from a creditor, Central Supply Co., with 30 days to pay.*

Which accounts are changed by this transaction? What type of accounts are they? Do they increase or decrease, and are they debited or credited to record the changes? The answers to these questions will help you to understand how this transaction is recorded.

The asset account Office Supplies increases because the company now has more supplies. Assets are found on the left side of the balance sheet; therefore, the increase in supplies is recorded on the debit (left) side of the Office Supplies account.

The company now owes more money to an account payable. Therefore, the liability account Accounts Payable increases. Since liabilities are found on the right side of the balance sheet, the liability Accounts Payable increases on the credit (right) side. The transaction is shown recorded in the accounts below:

Liabilities increase on the credit side.

Office Supplies		Accounts Payable	
Sep. 30 615		Sep. 30 4 740	
Oct. 5 60		Oct. 5 60	

Here is a summary of how this transaction was recorded:

ACCOUNT AFFECTED	TYPE OF ACCOUNT	INCREASE/DECREASE	DEBIT/CREDIT	
Office Supplies	Asset	Increase	Debit	$60
Accounts Payable	Liability	Increase	Credit	60

An asset increased by $60 and was debited. A liability increased by $60 and was credited. There was a debit of $60 and an equal credit of $60.

Transaction 3

Oct.   5   *Paid $705 now due to Equipment Unlimited for goods previously purchased but not paid for.*

Can you determine which account is debited? Which account is credited? The asset Cash decreases because money was paid out. Assets decrease on the credit side; therefore Cash is credited.

The liability Accounts Payable also decreases because less money is now owed
to the creditor. Liabilities decrease on the debit side; therefore, Accounts Payable
is debited. This transaction is shown in the accounts below.

Accounts Payable				Cash			
Oct. 5	705	Sep. 30	4 740	Sep. 30	6 025	Oct. 5	705
		Oct. 5	60	Oct. 2	500		

Here is a summary of how this transaction was recorded:

ACCOUNT AFFECTED	TYPE OF ACCOUNT	INCREASE/DECREASE	DEBIT/CREDIT	
Accounts Payable	Liability	Decrease	Debit	$705
Cash	Asset	Decrease	Credit	705

An asset decreased by $705 and was credited. A liability decreased by $705 and
was debited. Therefore, the ledger remains in balance. The total of the debits will
still equal the total of the credits.

Transaction 4

*Oct.   7   Purchased three new exercycles for $545 each (total of $1635). Cash down pay-
ment of $535 made. Remaining amount ($1100) to be paid at a later date.*

This transaction involves changes in three accounts. They are the assets Cash and
Training Equipment and the liability Accounts Payable. Can you determine the
debits and credits?

Training Equipment increases by $1635. Cash decreases by $535. Accounts
Payable increases by the amount still owing, $1100. This is how the transactions
are recorded in the accounts:

Training Equipment			Cash					Accounts Payable			
Sep. 30	100 600		Sep. 30	6 025	Oct. 5	705	Oct. 5	705	Sep. 30	4 680
Oct. 7	1 635		Oct. 3	500	7	535			Oct. 5	60
									7	1 100

Here is a summary of how this transaction was recorded:

ACCOUNT AFFECTED	TYPE OF ACCOUNT	INCREASE/DECREASE	DEBIT/CREDIT	
Training Equipment	Asset	Increase	Debit	$1 635
Cash	Asset	Decrease	Credit	535
Accounts Payable	Liability	Increase	Credit	1 100

Remember that assets are recorded at cost price whether or not they are fully paid
for at the time of purchase. The asset increase of $1635 (debit) is balanced by an
asset decrease of $535 (credit) and a liability increase of $1100 (credit). Therefore,
the ledger remains balanced. The total debits are equal to the total credits.

Transaction 5

Oct.   7   Owner invested an additional $7500 in the business.

This transaction causes the company's cash to increase. It also causes the
owner's equity to increase because the business is now worth more. The two
accounts that change, Cash and T. Montana, Capital, are shown on the following
page.

	Cash					T. Montana, Capital	
Sep. 30	6 025	Oct. 5	705			Sep. 30	104 500
Oct. 2	500	7	535			Oct. 7	7 500
7	7 500						

Here is a summary of how this transaction was recorded:

ACCOUNT AFFECTED	TYPE OF ACCOUNT	INCREASE/DECREASE	DEBIT/CREDIT	
Cash	Asset	Increase	Debit	$7 500
T. Montana, Capital	Owner's Equity	Increase	Credit	7 500

Note that the proprietor's investment of additional cash increases the owner's equity. The company's Cash account increases by $7500 (debit), and this is balanced by the owner's equity account increase of $7500 (credit). Therefore, the ledger remains in balance.

CALCULATING NEW BALANCES IN THE ACCOUNTS

The accounts in the ledger of Malibu Gym now contain the opening balances from the September 30, 2007, balance sheet plus entries to record changes in value of these accounts up to October 7, 2007. To determine the new balance in the accounts, the following calculations are made for each account:

(1) Add up the debit side of the account.
(2) Add up the credit side of the account.
(3) Subtract the smaller amount from the larger and place the answer on the side of the account with the larger balance. This is the new account balance. Two examples are provided below:

> The difference between the two sides of an account is called the account balance.

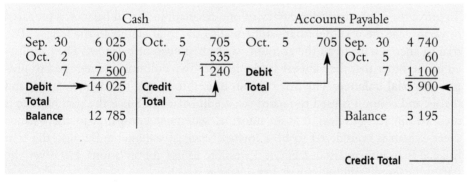

> The account balance is placed on the side of the account with the larger total.

Note that the final balance in the Cash account was placed on the debit side and the Accounts Payable balance was placed on the credit side. The balances are always placed on the side of the account that has the larger total. For assets, this is usually the debit side; for liabilities and owner's equity, this is usually the credit side. The ledger for Malibu Gym would appear as shown in Figure 2-3 after the October 7 balances have been calculated for all the accounts.

FIGURE 2-3

Ledger for Malibu Gym
with balances calculated in
each account

Cash					Accounts Payable			
Sep. 30	6 025	Oct. 5	705		Oct. 5	705	Sep. 30	4 740
Oct. 2	500	7	535				Oct. 5	60
7	7 500		1 240				7	1 100
	14 025							5 900
Balance	12 785						Balance	5 195

Accounts Receivable					Bank Loan			
Sep. 30	2 000	Oct. 2	500				Sep. 30	65 000
Balance	1 500						Balance	65 000

Office Supplies				Mortgage Payable		
Sep. 30	615				Sep. 30	80 000
Oct. 5	60				Balance	80 000
Balance	675					

Land				T. Montana, Capital		
Sep. 30	35 000				Sep. 30	104 500
Balance	35 000				Oct. 7	7 500
					Balance	112 000

Building		
Sep. 30	110 000	
Balance	110 000	

Training Equipment		
Sep. 30	100 600	
Oct. 7	1 635	
Balance	102 235	

PREPARING A TRIAL BALANCE

To prove the mathematical accuracy of our calculations, a trial balance is prepared to verify that the total debits are still equal to the total credits in the ledger. The trial balance is a list of all the accounts with their current balances. They are listed in the order that they appear in the ledger. Two columns are required to prepare the **trial balance**. The first column is used to record the debit balances and the second column is used to record the credit balances. Since the trial balance is used within the business, it is an informal statement compared to the balance sheet, which is considered to be a formal financial statement. Because the trial balance is an informal statement, it is possible to use abbreviations. However, the statement should still be prepared as neatly as possible.

A trial balance is a list of the ledger account balances. The total of the debit balances should equal the total of the credit balances.

The trial balance for Malibu Gym, dated October 7, 2007, is shown in Figure 2-4. The format for the trial balance is as follows:

Heading

Line 1: Who? — Malibu Gym
Line 2: What? — Trial Balance
Line 3: When? — October 7, 2007

FIGURE 2-4
Trial balance for Malibu Gym

Body Accounts listed in ledger order	Column 1 Debit balances	Column 2 Credit balances

**Malibu Gym
Trial Balance
October 7, 2007**

ACCOUNT	DEBIT	CREDIT
Cash	$ 12 785	
Accounts Receivable	1 500	
Office Supplies	675	
Land	35 000	
Building	110 000	
Training Equipment	102 235	
Accounts Payable		$ 5 195
Bank Loan		65 000
Mortgage Payable		80 000
T. Montana, Capital		112 000
Totals	$262 195	$ 262 195

Limitations of the Trial Balance

The trial balance simply indicates the mathematical accuracy of the ledger. It shows that the total debits equal the total credits. It verifies that a debit amount was recorded for each credit amount; that is, that the principle of double-entry accounting was followed. However, the trial balance does not indicate if the wrong accounts were used in recording a transaction.

If, for example, the first transaction given in this unit was recorded incorrectly by reversing the debit and credit, the error would not be discovered on a trial balance. In that first transaction, $500 cash was received from members who owed Malibu Gym payments on their memberships. The transaction was analyzed correctly as:

Cash	Debit	$500
Accounts Receivable	Credit	500

If this was mistakenly recorded as:

Accounts Receivable	Debit	$500
Cash	Credit	500

the error would not be discovered on a trial balance.

Examine the two accounts involved as they are shown below. The Oct. 2 entry for $500 is incorrectly recorded as a credit in the Cash account. It is also incorrectly recorded as a debit in Accounts Receivable:

Cash				Accounts Receivable		
Sep. 30	6 025	Oct. 2	500*	Sep. 30	2 000	
Oct. 7	7 500	5	705	Oct. 2	500*	
	13 525	7	535	Balance	2 500	
			1 740			
Balance	11 785					

*Incorrect entry

The $11 785 balance of the Cash account is $1000 too low. The $2500 balance of the Accounts Receivable account is $1000 too high. However, the trial balance will balance mathematically because the errors offset each other. The totals on the trial balance are the same but two accounts are incorrect. Here is a summary:

REFERENCE	CORRECT BALANCE	INCORRECT BALANCE	DIFFERENCE
Cash account	$ 12 785	$ 11 785	−$1 000
Accounts Receivable account	1 500	2 500	+ 1 000
Trial balance	$262 195	$262 195	No change

Note that when the amount is placed on the opposite side in the account, the error is double the original amount. Remembering this will help in locating errors, as will be discussed in Chapter 4. It is sufficient to remember at this time that the trial balance only indicates that there have been equal debit and credit entries made for each transaction and that no errors have been made in calculating the account balances. Limitations of the trial balance and error location will be covered more fully in Chapter 4.

Preparing a New Balance Sheet

To provide a formal statement of financial position on October 7, 2007, a new balance sheet, as prepared from the information contained in the trial balance, is shown in Figure 2-5:

FIGURE 2-5

October 7 balance sheet

<table>
<tr><td colspan="4" align="center">Malibu Gym
Balance Sheet
October 7, 2007</td></tr>
<tr><td colspan="2" align="center">Assets</td><td colspan="2" align="center">Liabilities</td></tr>
<tr><td>Cash</td><td>$ 12 785</td><td>Accounts Payable</td><td>$ 5 195</td></tr>
<tr><td>Accounts Receivable</td><td>1 500</td><td>Bank Loan</td><td>65 000</td></tr>
<tr><td>Office Supplies</td><td>675</td><td>Mortgage Payable</td><td>80 000</td></tr>
<tr><td>Land</td><td>35 000</td><td>Total Liabilities</td><td>150 195</td></tr>
<tr><td>Building</td><td>110 000</td><td></td><td></td></tr>
<tr><td>Training Equipment</td><td>102 235</td><td colspan="2" align="center">Owner's Equity</td></tr>
<tr><td></td><td></td><td>T. Montana, Capital</td><td>112 000</td></tr>
<tr><td></td><td></td><td>Total Liabilities</td><td></td></tr>
<tr><td>Total Assets</td><td>$262 195</td><td>and Owner's Equity</td><td>$262 195</td></tr>
</table>

SUMMARY OF DEBIT AND CREDIT THEORY

- Double-entry accounting requires that, in recording transactions, the total of the debit amounts must always equal the total of the credit amounts.
- Assets are located on the left side of the balance sheet. Asset accounts increase on the debit (left) side and decrease on the credit (right) side.
- Liabilities and owner's equity are located on the right side of the balance sheet. Liability and owner's equity accounts increase on the credit (right) side and decrease on the debit (left) side. These concepts, known as the rules of debit and credit, are summarized in the following chart:

Assets		=	Liabilities		+	Owner's Equity	
Debit	Credit		Debit	Credit		Debit	Credit
Increase	Decrease		Decrease	Increase		Decrease	Increase

- A trial balance proves the mathematical accuracy of the ledger. It does not indicate that transactions were all correctly recorded as debits and credits.

SUMMARY OF ACCOUNTING PROCEDURES

Figure 2-6 summarizes, in chart form, the important accounting procedures and concepts that have been covered in this chapter.

FIGURE 2-6

Summary of accounting procedures discussed in this chapter

Balance Sheet
Left Side = Right Side
Assets = Liabilities + Owner's Equity

Ledger
Beginning balances from the balance sheet recorded in the T-accounts.
Left Side = Right Side
Debits = Credits

Transactions
Transactions recorded in T-accounts using the principle of double-entry accounting. An equal debit and credit amount recorded for every transaction.
Left Side = Right Side
Debits = Credits

Determine T-Account Balances
Calculate the total of both sides of each account. Subtract the smaller total from the larger to determine the account balance.

Trial Balance
Debit balances equal credit balances.
Debits = Credits

New Balance Sheet
Left Side = Right Side
Assets = Liabilities + Owner's Equity

ACCOUNTING TERMS

Account	A form in which changes caused by business transactions are recorded. (p. 29)
Account Balance	The difference between the debit and credit sides of an account. (p. 35)
Analyzing Transactions	Determining which accounts are debited and credited in order to record transactions. (p. 32)
Asset Accounts	Accounts found in the asset section of the balance sheet. (p. 29)
Balance Sheet Accounts	A separate account is required for each asset, liability, and owner's equity on the balance sheet. (p. 29)
Credit	Right side of an account. (p. 29)
Debit	Left side of an account. (p. 29)
Double-Entry Accounting	All transactions are recorded in one or more accounts as a debit and one or more accounts as a credit. The total debit amount must equal the total credit amount. (p. 31)
Ledger	A group of accounts. It may be found in various forms such as a book containing pages for each account or stored on tape or disk for computerized accounting systems. (p. 30)
Liability Account	Account found in the liability section of the balance sheet. (p. 30)
Open the Ledger	Enter the balances as shown on the balance sheet in the accounts found in the ledger. (p. 30)
Owner's Equity Account	Account found in the owner's equity section of the balance sheet. (p. 30)
T-Account	A T-shaped account. (p. 29)
Trial Balance	A list of ledger account balances. The total of the debit balances should equal the total of the credit balances. This proves the mathematical accuracy of the ledger. (p. 36)

1. What is the meaning of each of the following?
   (a) Account   (c) Credit
   (b) Debit   (d) Ledger

2. On which side of the account is the balance of an asset normally recorded? Why?

3. On which side of the account is the balance of a liability normally recorded? Why?

4. On which side of the account is the balance of the owner's equity normally recorded? Why?

5. On which side of the account would the opening balance for each of the following accounts normally be recorded?
   (a) Cash   (f) Bank Loan
   (b) Inventory   (g) Land
   (c) Mortgage Payable   (h) Building
   (d) Accounts Payable   (i) Delivery Truck
   (e) Computer Equipment   (j) Owner, Capital

6. List the increase and decrease side for each of the following:
   (a) Asset account
   (b) Liability account
   (c) Owner's Capital account

7. Explain the principle of double-entry accounting.

8. How many accounts are there in a ledger?

9. What are the three steps followed in determining the balance for an account?

10. (a) What is a trial balance?
    (b) What does a trial balance indicate?

---

1. The June 1 balance sheet for the Victoria Restaurant is shown below.

   (a) Open accounts in a ledger for each of the assets and liabilities and for the owner's equity. You will need seven T-accounts.
   (b) Record the June 1 balances in the accounts.

   Victoria Restaurant
   Balance Sheet
   June 1, 2008

Assets		Liabilities	
Cash	$ 6 400	Accounts Payable	$ 17 000
Supplies	12 000	Mortgage Payable	85 000
Building	200 000	Total Liabilities	102 000
Equipment	50 000		
		Owner's Equity	
		R. Savard, Capital	166 400
		Total Liabilities	
Total Assets	$268 400	and Owner's Equity	$268 400

2. Window World has contracts to wash the windows of large office buildings. Using the information from their balance sheet, set up accounts and record the opening balances.

Window World Balance Sheet August 1, 2007			
Assets		**Liabilities**	
Cash	$ 12 500	Accounts Payable	$ 18 700
Cleaning Supplies	24 400	Bank Loan	22 500
Equipment	35 000	Total Liabilities	41 200
Truck	42 500		
		Owner's Equity	
		J. Schmidt, Capital	73 200
		Total Liabilities	
Total Assets	$114 400	and Owner's Equity	$114 400

3. Calculate the balance for each of the following accounts using the procedure shown on page 36.

Cash	
1 800	250
400	635
2 100	

Accounts Receivable	
2 000	1 300
4 200	350
1 800	165

Accounts Payable	
300	615
	450
	75

4. Dennis Air Service provides aviator training and leases or rents aircraft. The transactions below occurred during the first week of May. Analyze each transaction using the format indicated in the example. List the debit part of the entry before the credit part.

Example:

TRANSACTION	ACCOUNT AFFECTED	TYPE OF ACCOUNT	INCREASE/ DECREASE	DEBIT/CREDIT
May 1	Bank Loan	Liability	Decrease	Debit $600
	Cash	Asset	Decrease	Credit 600

May 1 Made the regular monthly payment of $600 on the bank loan.

2 Purchased a new air pump from Cadence Industries for $1700, payment to be made later.

4 Secured a further bank loan of $29 000 to pay for future purchases of aircraft.

5 Purchased a new aircraft for $57 000 from Airways Manufacturing by paying a $25 000 down payment with the $32 000 balance to be paid later.

7 Received $3500 cash from L. Rosewood, a customer.

5. (a) The Victoria Restaurant had the following transactions to record during the first week of June. Analyze each transaction using the format indicated in this chapter. List the debit portion of the entry before the credit portion. The June 1 transaction is done for you as an example.

Jun.   1   Purchased a new oven from Restaurant Supplies for $1780 on credit.

2   Made the regular monthly payment of $1080 on the mortgage.

3   Paid $1800 to reduce the balance owing to Wholesale Foods Limited.

5   Purchased a new table and four chairs from Owen Furniture for a $1750 cash down payment and $450 due in 30 days.

6   Owner, R. Savard, invested an additional $6000 cash in the business.

Example:

TRANSACTION	ACCOUNT AFFECTED	TYPE OF ACCOUNT	INCREASE/ DECREASE	DEBIT/CREDIT
Jun. 1	Equipment	Asset	Increase	Debit $1780
	Accounts Payable	Liability	Increase	Credit 1780

(b) Now record the June 1–6 transactions in the ledger accounts prepared for exercise 1.

(c) Calculate the new balance for each of the accounts.

(d) Prepare a trial balance.

6. In the ledger you opened for Window World in exercise 2:

(a) Record the following transactions.

(b) Prepare a trial balance on August 15, 2007.

Aug.   4   Bought soap, towels, and other cleaning supplies for $550 cash.

7   Bought a new hoist for the scaffolds. The hoist cost $4500. A down payment of $1800 was made today, with the remainder to be paid at a later date.

10   Cash of $4100 was paid to the bank to reduce the bank loan.

15   Mr. Schmidt invested $4200 of his personal savings in Window World.

7. Utopia Salon and Spa has been in operation for a number of years. The March 1 balance sheet for the business is shown on the next page.

(a) Prepare T-accounts for Utopia Salon and Spa using the accounts and balances given in the March 1 balance sheet.

Utopia Salon and Spa
Balance Sheet
March 1, 2007

Assets		Liabilities	
Cash	$ 4 800	Accounts Payable	$ 800
Accounts Receivable	3 600	Bank Loan	2 700
Supplies	2 400	Mortgage Payable	88 000
Land	30 000	Total Liabilities	91 500
Building	90 000		
Equipment	40 000	**Owner's Equity**	
		C. Williams, Capital	79 300
		Total Liabilities	
Total Assets	$170 800	and Owner's Equity	$170 800

(b) Record the March transactions listed below in the accounts.

(c) Calculate the account balances and prepare a trial balance on March 7, 2007.

Mar. 2 Purchased shampoo, hair spray, etc., from Beauty Products, $300 on credit.

3 Received $75 credit from Beauty Products for supplies purchased yesterday. Order incorrectly filled.

4 Received $2500 cash from customers who paid their accounts.

4 Made the regular $1100 payment on the mortgage.

5 Bought four hair dryers for $12 000 from Beauty Products. The business made a $4000 cash deposit on the dryers and the balance was to be paid later.

6 Obtained a bank loan of $10 000, part of which will be used to pay for the hair dryers.

7 Paid Beauty Products $8225, payment in full of the amount owing to them.

8. Shirley Bowman, CGA, operates a single proprietorship offering a wide range of accounting services to her clients. The balance sheet for this firm on March 31 is shown below.

(a) Open a T-account ledger for Shirley Bowman Accounting Services using the accounts and balances provided in the March 31 balance sheet.

(b) Record the April transactions listed in the ledger.

Shirley Bowman Accounting Services
Balance Sheet
March 31, 2007

Assets		Liabilities	
Cash	$ 4 200	Accounts Payable	$ 3 750
Accounts Receivable	6 500	Taxes Payable	830
Office Supplies	2 700	Bank Loan	6 300
Land	25 500	Mortgage Payable	44 000
Building	75 000	Total Liabilities	54 880
Office Equipment	27 100		
		Owner's Equity	
		S. Bowman, Capital	86 120
		Total Liabilities	
Total Assets	$141 000	and Owner's Equity	$141 000

(c) Calculate the account balances and prepare a trial balance on April 9, 2007.

Apr. 1 Received cheques from clients totalling $1500 in the mail today in payment of amounts previously billed.

1 Made regular monthly payment of $420 on the bank loan.

2 Purchased a new computer system for the office from Computer Accounts Co. for $3250. A down payment of $1200 was made today, and the balance will be due in 30 days.

3 The owner, S. Bowman, invested an additional $4700 in the business.

4 Paid $750 to various creditors to reduce balances owing to them.

5 Purchased additional supplies for the copier for $600 cash.

6 Returned supplies that cost $75 for a cash refund since they were unsuitable.

9 The owner had recently purchased a laser printer for personal use. Since the firm required a similar piece of equipment, the owner decided to place this printer in the business on a permanent basis instead of buying another one for the business after incurring the expense of the computer system. The printer cost S. Bowman $350. (Note: This transaction represents an additional investment by the owner in the business.)

CHAPTER 2

PROBLEMS: CHALLENGES

1. The following accounts contain a series of transactions for Video Jockeys Unlimited. For each of the entries labelled (a) to (e), indicate how accounts have changed and describe the transaction that must have occurred to cause the entry. Use a chart similar to the one below where transaction (a) has been done for you.

Example:

TRANSACTION	ACCOUNT AFFECTED	TYPE OF ACCOUNT	INCREASE/ DECREASE	DEBIT/CREDIT
(a)	Accounts Payable	Liability	Decrease	Debit $150
	Cash	Asset	Decrease	Credit 150

Paid an account payable.

Cash				Truck	
Balance	1 500	(a)	150	Balance	7 500
(b)	425	(d)	100		
		(e)	250		

Accounts Receivable				Accounts Payable			
Balance	1 000	(b)	425	(a)	150	Balance	500
				(e)	250	(c)	650
						(d)	300

Tapes			Bank Loan	
Balance	2 000		Balance	2 500
(d)	400			

Equipment			O. Sharif, Capital	
Balance	5 500		Balance	14 500
(c)	650			

2. The T-accounts below contain a number of transactions for Action Auction Sales. For each of the entries labelled (a) to (f), indicate how the accounts have changed and the transaction that must have taken place to generate the entry. The chart below, with transaction (a) done as an example, will assist you in describing the transactions correctly.

Example:

TRANSACTION	ACCOUNT AFFECTED	TYPE OF ACCOUNT	INCREASE/ DECREASE	DEBIT/CREDIT
(a)	Cash	Asset	Increase	Debit $12 000
	D. Lord, Capital	Owner's Equity	Increase	Credit 12 000

Since the Cash and Capital accounts both increased, the owner must have invested cash in the business.

Cash				Accounts Payable			
(a)	12 000	(b)	750	(d)	1 750	(c)	2 000
(f)	6 500	(c)	1 000			(e)	5 000
		(d)	1 750				

Supplies			Bank Loan	
(b)	750		(f)	6 500

Furniture			D. Lord, Capital	
(c)	3 000		(a)	12 000

Equipment	
(e)	5 000

3. Dr. W. Lucey has the following account balances on September 30, 2008. The balances have been listed in no particular order: Cash $35 000; Accounts Payable/Suppliers $4000; Equipment $130 000; Accounts Receivable/Patients $6000; Bank Loan $7000; Accounts Receivable/Provincial Health Plan $14 000; Dr. W. Lucey, Capital $176 000; Medical Supplies $2000.

(a) Open a T-account ledger in the correct order from the balances listed above.
(b) Record the following October transactions in the ledger.
(c) Prepare a trial balance.
(d) Prepare a balance sheet on October 15, 2008.

Oct. 2 Dr. Lucey invested an additional $68 000 cash in the business to assist in financing a new office.

      3 C. Patten, a patient, paid $150 (an amount owed).

      4 Bought surgical bandages and other medical supplies from Medical Suppliers, $259 on credit.

      5 Returned supplies costing $43 to Medical Suppliers because they were not the type ordered.

      6 Paid $315 to Pharmaceutical Products, a creditor, to reduce the amount owing to it.

      7 Made the regular $425 payment on the bank loan.

      8 Received a cheque from the Provincial Health Plan for $15 500.

      9 Dr. Lucey located a satisfactory office building for his practice. The property cost $292 000, with the land worth $150 000 and the building worth the remainder ($142 000). A mortgage was secured from Canada Bank for $200 000, and the balance was paid in cash.

     10 Purchased a new computer and printer from Ace Computers for $3500 cash.

     12 Purchased the software necessary for the computer from the same supplier for $2500, on credit.

     15 Sold an old printer for $50 cash.

4. The ledger accounts of The Pastry Shoppe contain the following balances on July 31 of this year. Prepare a trial balance with the accounts arranged as shown on page 37. Fill in the missing amount for Capital.

Accounts Payable	$ 6 000
Accounts Receivable	2 500
Baking Equipment	22 500
Baking Supplies	3 500
Bank Loan	11 500
Building	105 000
Capital	?
Cash	7 000
Delivery Trucks	57 000
Land	35 000
Mortgage Payable	95 000

5. Avadasian Realty has been in business for several years. Here in random order are the balances in the accounts on October 1: Cash ?; Accounts Payable $20 000; Land $200 000; Bank Loan $25 000; Accounts Receivable $7000; Building $300 000; Mortgage $200 000; Equipment $10 000; S. Avadasian, Capital $283 000; Supplies $5000.

(a) Calculate the October 1 balance in the Cash account.
(b) Open a T-account ledger in correct order and record the October 1 balances.
(c) Record the October transactions in the ledger.
(d) Prepare a trial balance and a balance sheet on October 15, 20—.

Oct.   1   Received $1000 due from a client.

       2   Purchased office supplies for $2000 cash.

       4   Obtained an additional bank loan for $18 000 to purchase a company car.

       5   Purchased a new telephone system for the office for $5000. A down payment of $1000 was required, with the balance due on receipt of the invoice.

       6   Made the regular $2500 monthly mortgage payment.

       9   An office chair purchased on credit last month was returned to the supplier since it was defective. The chair originally cost $300.

      10   Sold an unused portion of the land beside the office for $80 000 cash. This amount was equal to the original cost of the land.

      11   Purchased a car from Cullen Motors for $30 000 cash.

      12   Avadasian purchased postage stamps that cost $100 for the business using his own funds.

      14   Paid $900 to a creditor.

CASE 1
Transaction Recording Errors

CHAPTER 2

CASE
STUDIES

Four errors were made by the accountant for Sunrise Services when recording transactions during the month of October. They are described below. Which of the errors would be found by preparing a trial balance? Explain your answer for each error.

(a) A $300 payment was received from a client and recorded in the ledger by a debit to Accounts Receivable and a credit to Cash.
(b) A payment was made by Sunrise Services on an account payable in the amount of $100. It was recorded by debiting Accounts Payable for $10 and crediting Cash $10.
(c) Equipment was purchased for $500 on credit. It was recorded by debiting Equipment $500 and debiting Accounts Payable $500.
(d) The owner invested an additional $1000 cash in the company. The transaction was recorded by debiting Cash $1000 and crediting Capital $100.

CASE 2
Unbalanced Trial Balance

When Grimwood Printers prepared a trial balance on May 31, it did not balance. As a result of checking through the recording of transactions, an error was discovered; namely, $250 received from a customer was recorded by a debit to Cash of $5 and a credit to Accounts Receivable of $250. The total of the credit side of the trial balance was $52 225. Answer the following questions regarding the preceding trial balance information. Explain each of your answers fully.

(a) Was the Accounts Receivable account too high, too low, or correct?
(b) Was the Cash account too high, too low, or correct?
(c) Was the trial balance credit total of $52 225 too high, too low, or correct?
(d) What was the amount of the debit total on the unbalanced trial balance?
(e) Was this debit total too high, too low, or correct?

CASE 3
Double-Entry Accounting

A student has learned the double-entry method of accounting. The student states that it is based on the idea that items owned equal claims against items owned. Further, because of this relationship, debits must always equal credits if the accounting equation, $A = L + OE$, is to remain in balance. The student then states this false conclusion: "In recording a transaction, an asset must change and either a liability or the owner's equity must also change."

Using your knowledge of double-entry accounting, explain the fallacy in the student's thinking.

CASE 4
Interpreting Accounting Data

County Fuels is a small business selling home fuel. It has 400 customers who purchase an average of $900 of products each year. A friend of yours has just inherited the business and comes to you for advice.

Items Owned by the Business

Cash in bank	$ 5 000
Accounts receivable	6 000
Two delivery trucks	40 000 each
Storage tanks	30 000
Inventory	50 000
Yard equipment	45 000
Office supplies	2 000
Office equipment	15 000
Other assets	5 000

Company Debts

Accounts payable	25 000
Salaries owing	8 000
Taxes owing	5 000
Bank loan	30 000

Other information

All values are recorded according to the cost principle. The two trucks are over five years old. None of the assets is less than two years old except the cash, accounts receivable, and inventory. The company employs four full-time and two part-time employees. The previous owner worked full time in the business.

Your friend asks you to help determine the following:

(a) What is the business worth?

(b) Should your friend keep the business or sell it?

(c) A competitor, Exodus Fuels, has offered your friend $50 000 for the entire business. Would you recommend selling at this price? Why?

ETHICS CASE
Business Ethics Apply to Everyone

It is well documented how a number of executives at corporations such as Enron, Bre-Ex, Tyco, and Worldcom abused their positions of trust for personal gain. Significant losses were sustained by customers, shareholders and company workers due to the unethical actions of the executives. However, it is not only executives and managers who should act in an ethical manner. Business ethics apply to consumers as well. Consider the following.

(a) Matthew was planning to attend a family reunion and decided it would be nice to videotape the event. He went to a local retailer and purchased the most expensive piece of equipment available. Matthew had no intention of keeping the expensive product. He knew that the retailer had a guaranteed 30-day return policy. After using the camera for 20 days, he returned it to the store and received a full refund.

    i. What costs did Matthew's actions cause the retailer to absorb?

    ii. Do you feel that Matthew was unethical in this situation? Why?

    iii. Should the retailer change its policy?

(b) Melody went shopping at a supermarket and left the store with her purchases in a large shopping cart. She took the cart home, unloaded her groceries and then abandoned the cart in a nearby park. The cost of the cart is $300. Melody feels the supermarket is "rich" and can afford to lose the cart.

    i. Cite examples of similar consumer behaviour.

    ii. How do you feel about Melody's actions?

    iii. What effect does the $300 loss have on the supermarket's finances?

(c) Ashley and her friends feel it is "cool" to go to the mall and to shoplift items such as cosmetics, clothes, school supplies, and novelties.

    i. What effect does this shoplifting have on business in general?

    ii. What actions do retailers take to curb shoplifting? Do you think that such actions infringe on individual rights?

CHAPTER 2

INTERNET
RESOURCES

These Web sites provide accounting career information and resources.

1. Accounting.com   **www.accounting.com**

   You can post your résumé and search for jobs at this site. Accounting resources are also listed.

2. *CA Magazine*   **www.camagazine.com**

   CA Magazine provides current job postings, news, and trends in accounting. It is worthwhile to do a search for "careers."

3. Job Search Canada   **www.jobsearch.ca**

   Find information on many jobs including accounting at this site. Current job openings and descriptions are provided.

4. Careers in Accounting   **www.careers-in-accounting.com**

   This site provides an overview of many accounting opportunities including job information, salaries, skills required, links, and resources.

5. SkillNet Canada   **www.skillnet.ca/index.htm**

   The SkillNet site provides job postings for a variety of careers including accounting and accounting career information.

The Income Statement

UNIT 4   Preparing the Income Statement

Learning Objectives

After reading this unit, discussing the applicable review questions, and completing the applications exercises, you will be able to do the following:

1. **CLASSIFY** items as revenue or expenses.

2. **PREPARE** an income statement.

3. **EXPLAIN** the accrual basis of accounting for revenue and expenses.

4. **PREPARE** an income statement and report form of balance sheet from a trial balance.

REVIEWING THE PURPOSE OF ACCOUNTING

In Chapter 1, you were told that the purpose of accounting is to provide information that is used to make decisions. This involves two types of accounting activity:

- Recording daily transactions
- Preparing reports that summarize daily transactions

In Chapters 1 and 2, you learned how daily business transactions were recorded and how a statement called a balance sheet was prepared. The balance sheet presented the assets, liabilities, and owner's equity at a specific date. In this chapter, you will expand your knowledge of business transactions and learn how and why a second financial statement, called an *income statement*, is prepared.

PROFIT AND LOSS

People go into business for themselves for a variety of reasons. Troy Montana, the owner of Malibu Gym, Niagara, started his business:

- To use his personal talents and abilities to the fullest
- To achieve a pride of ownership of his own business
- To gain the satisfaction of building a successful business
- To earn a profit on his investment of money and labour

Once Malibu Gym was established, it grew and became successful as a result of the owner's hard work and business knowledge. One of the major criteria of success for a business is its profitability. A business cannot survive for very long unless it earns a profit.

Defining Profit and Loss

Profit is the increase in owner's equity that results from successful operation of a business. In this chapter, we will determine how to calculate whether a business is profitable. When a business is not successful, a **loss** occurs and owner's equity decreases.

A **business** sells *goods* such as cameras, automobiles, clothes, and furniture or it sells *services* such as television repairs, transportation, and hair styling. The money or the promise of money received from the sale of goods or services is called **revenue**.

To sell goods and services, money is spent to operate the business. Money is spent on salaries, advertising, deliveries, and many other things required to run a business. These items are called **expenses**. Take the case of a television set that has a selling price of $500. The seller has to spend $400 to sell the TV. When the TV is sold, does the seller make a profit or is there a loss? There is a profit of $100.

As the television example illustrates, when the revenue is greater than the expenses there is *profit*. **Net income** is the preferred accounting term for profit. Net income occurs when the revenue is greater than the expenses:

$$\text{Revenue} - \text{Expenses} = \text{Profit or Net Income}$$

However, if the expenses are greater than the revenue, there is a loss or **net loss**:

$$\text{Revenue} - \text{Expenses} = \text{Loss or Net Loss}$$

Profit is the increase in owner's equity resulting from the successful operation of a business.

Loss is a decrease in owner's equity that results from unsuccessful operation of a business.

A business sells goods or services.

Revenue is amounts received or promised to the business from the sale of goods or services during the routine operation of the business.

Expenses are the costs of items or services used up in the routine operation of the business.

Net income is the difference between revenue and expenses when revenue is greater than expenses.

Net loss is the difference between revenue and expenses when expenses are greater than revenue.

The following equation mathematically illustrates how the net income or net loss on the sale of the television set is determined:

Revenue	–	Expenses	=	Net Income or Net Loss
(Selling Price)		(All Expenses)		
$500	–	$400	=	$100 Net Income
500	–	550	=	(50) Net Loss

Notice that the $50 loss is shown in brackets. The use of brackets to indicate a loss is a commonly accepted procedure in accounting.

THE INCOME STATEMENT

In Chapter 1, we prepared a **financial statement** called a balance sheet to show the financial position of Malibu Gym at a certain date. The second major financial statement that every business prepares is an **income statement**. It summarizes the items of revenue and expense and determines the net income or loss for a stated period of time. This period of time is called an **accounting period**. The accounting period may be a week, a month, a quarter, a year, or any other regular period of time. The **time-period assumption** requires the definition and consistent use of the same period of time for the accounting period. This allows the owners and other users of the financial statements to compare data for similar periods of time. For example, the owner can determine if the business is as profitable this year as in previous years if one year is used as the accounting period.

A synonym for accounting period is **fiscal period**. Businesses prepare statements on a yearly basis for tax purposes. The statements prepared for this purpose are said to be prepared for the fiscal year. This fiscal year may or may not coincide with a calendar year. For example, a company's fiscal year may extend from July 1: Year 1 to June 30: Year 2, while the calendar year starts January 1: Year 1 and ends December 31: Year 1.

> The two main financial statements are an income statement and balance sheet.
>
> An income statement is a financial statement that presents the revenue, expenses, and net income/loss for a specific period of time.
>
> The accounting period is the period of time covered by the financial statements.
>
> The time-period assumption is the definition and consistent use of the same period of time for the accounting period.
>
> Fiscal period is a synonym for accounting period.

Income Statement Preparation

An income statement prepared for Malibu Gym for the month of October 2007 will be used to discuss the correct format and procedures followed to prepare a formal financial statement. This income statement is shown in Figure 3-1 below.

FIGURE 3-1

October income statement

Malibu Gym Income Statement For the Month Ended October 31, 2007		
Revenue		
Members' Fees	$16 500	
Tanning Bed Rental	2 650	
Towel Rental	450	$19 600
Expenses		
Salaries Expense	5 850	
Advertising Expense	3 450	
Telephone Expense	290	
Maintenance Expense	1 720	
Licence Expense★	1 100	
Interest Expense	500	
Laundry Expense	380	13 290
Net Income		$ 6 310

★Licence Expense is the amount that is paid to the parent company for the exclusive rights to the Malibu Gym name in the Niagara Region.

The four steps followed in preparing an income statement are described below.

Step 1: Prepare Statement Heading

The three-line heading is centred at the top of the page and is designed to provide information in this sequence:

Line 1: Who? — Malibu Gym
Line 2: What? — Income Statement
Line 3: When? — For the month ended October 31, 2007

Note: The income statement provides data for a given time period (week, month, year), while the balance sheet provides data on a specific date. The income statement loses its usefulness if the accounting period is not specified. Thus, if Line 3 were omitted from our example, we would have no way of knowing whether the net income $6310 was for a week, a month, or a year. The owner would have a very different reaction when reading the statement if the income shown was for a week versus a year.

Step 2: Prepare Revenue Section

The revenue received from the business operations is listed under the subheading Revenue. The largest revenue item is usually listed first. The revenue is totalled, and the total is placed in the right column:

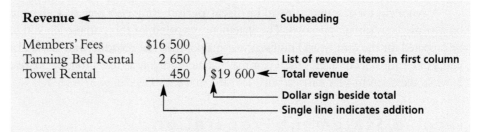

Step 3: Prepare Expenses Section

The expense items are listed in the order in which they appear in the ledger:

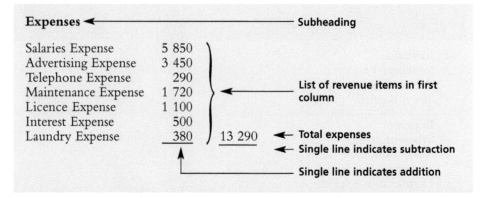

Step 4: Determine Net Income or Net Loss

The difference between total revenue and total expenses is the *net income* or the *net loss*. There is a net income (profit) when the total revenue is greater than total expenses. There is a net loss when the expenses are greater than the revenue.

In Figure 3-1 there is a net income of $6310. This is determined by subtracting the expenses from the revenue ($19 600 − $13 290 = $6310). Notice in Figure 3-1 that there is a dollar sign beside the net income and the net income is ruled with a double line. Double lines are ruled below the net income or net loss. They indicate the final total.

Facts to Remember

For the income statement, dollar signs should be placed as follows:

- Beside the first figure in each column
- Beside the net income or net loss figure at the bottom of the statement

ACCURACY OF THE INCOME STATEMENT

It is important when determining the net income for an accounting period to include only revenue earned during that period and only expenses incurred to produce that revenue. The net income or loss calculated will then accurately reflect only the business activities that took place during that period of time. This matching of the revenue for a specific accounting period with the related expenses for the same period is called the **matching principle**. In this text, two simple rules will assist you in recording the appropriate revenue and expenses for an accounting period.

> The matching principle requires that costs recorded for expenses be matched with revenue generated during the same time period.

Rules for Recording Revenue and Expenses

1. Revenue Is Recorded as It Is Earned.

According to the **revenue recognition principle** revenue is recorded when the service is performed or goods are shipped to a customer even if cash has not been received. For demonstration purposes regarding this point, we will consider the accounting methods in a legal firm.

> Revenue is recorded when the service is performed or the goods are shipped to a customer, even if cash has not been recorded.

During the first week in September, lawyer Simone Beaudry performed a variety of services for a number of clients. Some of the clients paid cash for services totalling $1500. The remainder of the clients were billed $4700 for the services. The total revenue recorded for September was $6200 even though only $1500 cash was received:

Services Performed and Paid For in Cash	+	Services Performed on Credit	=	Total Revenue
$1 500		$4 700		$6 200

What is the effect of earning this revenue on the accounting equation of Simone Beaudry's law firm?

	A	=	L	+	OE
Cash:	+ $1 500	=	No Change	+	$6 200
A/R:	+ 4 700				

When revenue is earned, it produces an increase in owner's equity.

> Revenue increases owner's equity.

2. Expenses Are Recorded When the Cost Is Incurred.

Expenses are the costs incurred to generate the revenue. Expenses are recorded when the cost is incurred whether paid in cash or on credit. In normal practice, the receipt of a bill for the expense item provides evidence that the expense was incurred and should be recorded. A separate account is kept in the ledger for each of the expenses, as explained further in the next unit. The transactions are recorded in the expense accounts whether they are cash transactions or credit transactions. Remember, expenses are recorded as they are incurred. When expenses are incurred, they produce a decrease in owner's equity.

Expenses decrease owner's equity.

Accrual Basis of Accounting

A business that records revenue when earned and expenses when incurred is using the **accrual basis of accounting**. This method produces an accurate picture of profitability for an accounting period because it matches revenue earned with the expenses necessary to produce the revenue during the accounting period. The accrual basis of accounting will be used throughout this book.

Accrual accounting is a commonly used method where revenue is recorded when earned and expenses when incurred.

ⒻURTHER STUDY OF OWNER'S EQUITY

Introducing the Owner's Drawings Account

At the beginning of the chapter, it was indicated that one of the reasons people start their own business is to earn a profit and increase the value of the owner's equity. The owner of the business may make a regular practice of withdrawing money or other assets for personal use. This withdrawal of assets decreases the value of the owner's equity. This event is similar to an expense transaction since owner's equity is reduced. However, as you know, expenses are only recognized if the cost was incurred to produce revenue. Therefore, the withdrawal of assets by the owner is not an expense. This transaction is recorded in an account called Drawings. Since the withdrawal of assets affects the owner's investment, the owner's Drawings account is an equity account. This account appears in the equity section of the ledger and decreases owner's equity on the balance sheet. The Drawings account normally has a debit balance since withdrawals by the owner decrease owner's equity.

The owner's Drawings account records the withdrawal of assets from the business by the owner.

The **owner's Drawings account** is debited whenever assets are withdrawn by the owner for personal use. Examples of this are:

- Withdrawing cash
- Removing merchandise for personal use
- Taking equipment from the business for personal use
- Using company funds for personal expenses of the owner or the owner's family

S. Beaudry, Drawings	
Debit	Credit
Withdrawals are recorded as debits because they *decrease* Capital.	

On October 15, for example, S. Beaudry, the owner, withdrew $1500 cash from the business for personal use. The effect of this withdrawal is illustrated by these T-accounts:

S. Beaudry, Drawings		Cash	
Oct. 15 1 500			Oct. 15 1 500

Owner's Salary

A salary may be paid by a business to the person who owns that business. However, for income tax purposes, the business may not record the payment in an expense account such as the Salaries account. Therefore, payment of wages or salaries to the owner must be recorded in the owner's Drawings account.

Drawings Account in the General Ledger

The study of the General Ledger can now be summarized. You have learned that a *ledger* is a group of accounts. In the General Ledger, there is one account for each asset, for each liability, and for the owner's equity. As transactions occur, the changes caused by the transactions are recorded in these accounts. There is also an account required in the General Ledger for each revenue account, each expense account, and the Drawings account.

At the end of the accounting or fiscal period, a trial balance is prepared. The assets, liabilities, and owner's equity accounts (including the Drawings account) are used to prepare the balance sheet. The revenue and expense accounts are used to prepare the income statement. A complete summary of some typical General Ledger accounts, the account classifications, and the financial statements prepared from these accounts is shown in Figure 3-2 on page 58.

Equity Accounts on the Balance Sheet

The owner's Capital and Drawings accounts.

The owner's Capital account and the owner's Drawings account appear in the owner's equity section of the balance sheet. The Capital account is a record of the owner's investment in the business. It is the owner's claim against the assets. The Capital account increases if there is a net income earned or if the owner increases the assets of the business by further investment in the business. The Capital account decreases if there is a net loss or if the owner withdraws assets from the business for personal use. The owner's Drawings account is used to record the withdrawals. The results of increases or decreases in the Capital account are shown in the equity section of the balance sheet.

Figures 3-3, 3-4, and 3-5, on page 59, show the owner's equity section of three balance sheets. On the October balance sheet shown in Figure 3-3, the business had a net income of $4500; the owner, S. Beaudry, withdrew $1500 for personal use; and the Capital account increased, by $3000, to $23 000. Notice how three money columns are used to record this information.

FIGURE 3-2

Ledger containing asset, liability, owner's equity, revenue, and expense accounts

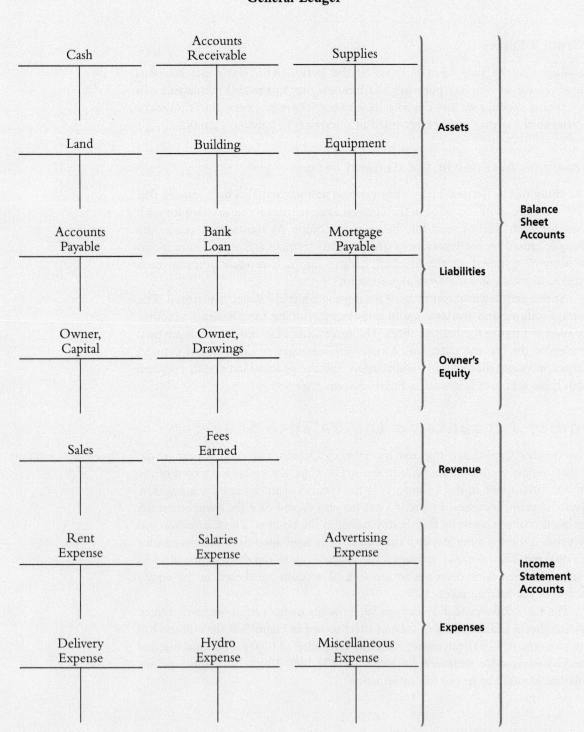

FIGURE 3-3

Capital increases when withdrawals are less than net income.

Owner's Equity			
S. Beaudry, Capital October 1		$20 000	
Add: Net Income for October	$4 500		
Less: S. Beaudry, Drawings	1 500		
Increase in Capital		3 000	
S. Beaudry, Capital October 31			$23 000

In the November balance sheet shown in Figure 3-4, the Capital account increased because the owner withdrew only $2000 while the net income was $3800. The result was an increase in Capital of $1800. Again, three money columns are used to show the changes in Capital.

FIGURE 3-4

Capital decreases when withdrawals are greater than net income.

Owner's Equity			
S. Beaudry, Capital November 1		$23 000	
Add: Net Income for November	$3 800		
Less: S. Beaudry, Drawings	2 000		
Increase in Capital		1 800	
S. Beaudry, Capital November 30			$24 800

In the December balance sheet shown in Figure 3-5, the Capital account decreases because of a net loss of $1200 and drawings of $800. The total decrease in Capital is $2000. Therefore, Capital decreases from $24 800 to $22 800.

FIGURE 3-5

Capital decreases when there is a loss or the owner has withdrawn assets.

Owner's Equity			
S. Beaudry, Capital December 1		$24 800	
Less: Net Loss for December	$1 200		
Less: S. Beaudry, Drawings	800		
Decrease in Capital		2 000	
S. Beaudry, Capital December 31			$22 800

ℝEPORT FORM OF THE BALANCE SHEET

The concept to be introduced now in this chapter is a new form for writing a balance sheet. Up to this point, the **account form** of balance sheet has been used. The account form of balance sheet was essential to establishing the concept:

Left Side = Right Side

From this concept, the accounting equation was established:

Assets = Liabilities + Owner's Equity

The accounting equation is an inflexible rule and the basis of the double-entry accounting system.

The balance sheet does not usually appear in the account format, however. Another form of balance sheet is the **report form** (see Figure 3-6 on page 60). In the report form, the assets, liabilities, and owner's equity are listed vertically. The report form is easier to prepare since there is no need to move lines of figures to have the final balances appear opposite each other. In addition, it presents information in a format that is useful for statement analysis.

The account form of the balance sheet lists the assets on the left side and the liabilities and owner's equity on the right side.

The report form of the balance sheet lists the assets, liabilities, and owner's equity vertically.

In Figure 3-6, of course, the first step involved in deriving the accounting equation, Left Side = Right Side, no longer applies because the balance sheet is written *vertically*, and there is no left side and right side. Remember that the accounting equation still applies:

$$\underset{\$256\ 050}{\text{Assets}} = \underset{\$149\ 740}{\text{Liabilities}} + \underset{\$106\ 310}{\text{Owner's Equity}}$$

Facts to Remember

A slight modification of the rule given in Chapter 1 for the placement of dollar signs on the balance sheet is now required. For the report form of the balance sheet, dollar signs should be placed as follows:

- Beside the first figure in each column in both sections of the statement
- Beside the final total in both sections of the statement

FIGURE 3-6

Report form of balance sheet

Malibu Gym Balance Sheet October 31, 2007			
Assets			
Cash		$ 8 335	
Accounts Receivable		1 500	
Office Supplies		615	
Land		35 000	
Building		110 000	
Training Equipment		100 600	
Total Assets			$256 050
Liabilities and Owner's Equity			
Liabilities			
Accounts Payable		$ 4 740	
Bank Loan		65 000	
Mortgage Payable		80 000	
Total Liabilities			$149 740
Owner's Equity			
Montana, Capital October 1		102 000	
Add: Net Income for October	$6 310		
Less: Montana, Drawings	2 000		
Increase in Capital		4 310	
Montana, Capital October 31			106 310
Total Liabilities and Owner's Equity			$256 050

ⓟREPARING FINANCIAL STATEMENTS FROM THE TRIAL BALANCE

Figures 3-7, 3-8, and 3-9 illustrate how the financial statements are prepared from the trial balance, in this order:

Trial Balance → Income Statement → Balance Sheet

First, Figure 3-7 shows all of the accounts on the trial balance.

Remember that the trial balance is a list of the accounts and balances from the General Ledger in ledger order. The accounts are arranged in the General Ledger so that the balance sheet accounts precede the income statement accounts. However, since you must calculate the net income/loss for the accounting period to complete the equity section of the balance sheet, the income statement is prepared before the balance sheet.

Malibu Gym Trial Balance November 30, 2007		
Balance Sheet Accounts		
Cash	$ 7 650	
Accounts Receivable	2 200	
Office Supplies	695	
Land	35 000	
Building	110 000	
Training Equipment	102 735	
Accounts Payable		$ 5 150
Bank Loan		63 000
Mortgage Payable		80 000
Montana, Capital		106 310
Montana, Drawings	2 400	
Income Statement Accounts		
Members' Fees		14 600
Tanning Bed Rental		725
Towel Rental		465
Salaries Expense	3 850	
Advertising Expense	2 880	
Telephone Expense	190	
Maintenance Expense	650	
Licence Expense	1 100	
Interest Expense	500	
Laundry Expense	400	
	$270 250	$270 250

FIGURE 3-7
Trial balance containing all ledger accounts

Figure 3-8 is the income statement that is prepared using the revenue and expense accounts.

Malibu Gym Income Statement For the Month Ended November 30, 2007		
Revenue		
Members' Fees	$14 600	
Tanning Bed Rental	725	
Towel Rental	465	$15 790
Expenses		
Salaries Expense	$ 3 850	
Advertising Expense	2 880	
Telephone Expense	190	
Maintenance Expense	650	
Licence Expense	1 100	
Interest Expense	500	
Laundry Expense	400	9 570
Net Income		$ 6 220

FIGURE 3-8
Income statement

Remember that even though Drawings has a debit balance, it is not an expense account and is not included on the income statement. Drawings will be used along with the net income ($6220) in the equity section of the balance sheet.

Figure 3-9 is the balance sheet. It contains assets, liabilities, and owner's equity accounts. It is prepared in the report form.

FIGURE 3-9

Report form of balance sheet

Malibu Gym
Balance Sheet
November 30, 2007

Assets

Cash	$ 7 650	
Accounts Receivable	2 200	
Office Supplies	695	
Land	35 000	
Building	110 000	
Training Equipment	102 735	
Total Assets		$258 280

Liabilities and Owner's Equity

Liabilities

Accounts Payable	$ 5 150	
Bank Loan	63 000	
Mortgage Payable	80 000	
Total Liabilities		$148 150

Owner's Equity

Montana, Capital November 1		106 310	
Add: Net Income for November	$6 220		
Less: Montana, Drawings	2 400		
Increase in Capital		3 820	
Montana, Capital November 30			110 130
Total Liabilities and Owner's Equity			$258 280

UNIT 4

REVIEW QUESTIONS

1. Name two financial statements.

2. Write definitions for each of the following:

   (a) Revenue   (c) Net income
   (b) Expense   (d) Net loss

3. What is the purpose of the income statement?

4. What are the three parts of the heading of an income statement?

5. What are the two main sections of the body of the income statement?

6. How is the net income determined?

7. When is there a net loss?

8. Write definitions for:

   (a) Income statement
   (b) Accounting period
   (c) Balance sheet

9. List the four steps followed in preparing an income statement.

10. What is the time-period assumption?

11. Explain the matching principle.

12. Explain the accrual basis of accounting.

13. (a) Give an example of a transaction that is recorded in the owner's Drawings account.
    (b) On which financial statement does the owner's Drawings account appear?

14. In which account is a payment of a salary to the owner recorded?

15. Which financial statement is prepared first? Why?

16. What is the difference between the account form and the report form of the balance sheet?

UNIT 4

PROBLEMS: APPLICATIONS

1. Classify the following accounts as an asset, a liability, owner's equity, a revenue, or an expense; (a) has been done for you as an example.

   (a) Bank Loan   (f) Interest Expense
   (b) Cash   (g) Commissions Earned
   (c) Accounts Payable   (h) Salaries Expense
   (d) Building   (i) Accounts Receivable
   (e) Fees Earned   (j) Owner, Capital

   Example:
   (a) Bank loan — Liability

2. Calculate the net income or net loss for each of the following; then identify the accounting period.

   (a) Revenue for May $110 000
       Expenses for May   85 000
   (b) Revenue for 6 months   349 000
       Expenses for 6 months   382 000
   (c) Revenue for the year   583 000
       Expenses for the year   375 000
   (d) Revenue for July 1 – September 30   295 000
       Expenses for July 1 – September 30   240 000
   (e) Revenue for October   73 950
       Expenses for October   81 300

3. Prepare an income statement for Dr. Mark Tompkins for the year ended December 31, 2008, by using the following accounts from the ledger: Income from Fees $225 000; Investment Income $17 800; Automobile Expense $4200; Supplies Expense $4600; Rent Expense $24 000; Salaries Expense $53 000; Donations Expense $4500; Utilities Expense $12 300; Insurance Expense $6500; Miscellaneous Expense $5000.

4. Prepare an income statement for Truro Cleaners for the month ended June 30, 2008, by using the ledger accounts given here in random order: Salaries Expense $4000; Advertising Expense $2100; Telephone Expense $925; Delivery Expense $2000; Cleaning Revenue $14 500; Office Expense $3000; Repairs Revenue $2300; Rent Expense $5000.

5. (a) From the trial balance for Citywide Movers, classify each account as an asset, a liability, an owner's equity, a revenue, or an expense, and indicate whether it appears on the balance sheet or on the income statement.

Example:
Cash — an asset that appears on the balance sheet.

(b) Using the appropriate accounts, prepare an income statement for Citywide Movers for the year ended August 31, 2008.

Citywide Movers Trial Balance August 31, 2008		
Account Title	Debit	Credit
Cash	$ 37 000	
Accounts Receivable	41 000	
Land and Buildings	165 000	
Moving Vans	113 700	
Accounts Payable		$ 19 100
Bank Loan		31 000
R. Martin, Capital		232 000
Storage Fees Revenue		35 200
Moving Service Revenue		179 200
Salaries Expense	95 300	
Moving Vans Expense	34 000	
Utilities Expense	10 500	
	$496 500	$496 500

6. Complete the following chart by indicating the increase or decrease in Capital and showing the amount of the Capital.

BEGINNING CAPITAL	NET INCOME	NET LOSS	DRAWINGS	INC. OR DEC. IN CAPITAL	ENDING CAPITAL
(a) $ 9 000	$1 000	—	$ 500	?	?
(b) 25 000	3 000	—	1 500	?	?
(c) 21 000	—	$3 500	1 800	?	?
(d) 12 000	4 200	—	2 100	?	?

7. Prepare the owner's equity section of the balance sheet for each of the following three months for Dr. R. Wong.

(a) Capital balance July 1 $47 000
    Net loss for July   4 000
    Drawings for July   7 100
(b) Capital balance August 1   ?
    Net income for August   3 000
    Drawings for August   5 000
(c) Capital balance September 1   ?
    Net income for September   5 700
    Drawings for September   4 200

8. Perfect Cruises had the following assets and liabilities at the beginning and the end of fiscal year April 30, 2008:

	Assets	Liabilities
May 1, 2007	$ 81 000	$62 000
April 30, 2008	110 000	74 000

Calculate the net income (or net loss) for the year using the following unrelated scenarios:

(a) The owner made an additional investment of $18 000 but made no withdrawals during the year.

(b) The owner withdrew $25 000 during the year but made no additional investments.

(c) The owner withdrew $2500 per month and made an additional investment of $48 000.

9. (a) Prepare the income statement for Fortune Industries from the trial balance given for the month ended September 30, 2007.

(b) Prepare a report form balance sheet for Fortune Industries on September 30, 2007.

Fortune Industries Trial Balance September 30, 2007		
Cash	$ 4 500	
Accounts Receivable	9 100	
Office Supplies	2 000	
Office Equipment	10 300	
Furniture	18 750	
Accounts Payable		$ 2 475
Bank Loan		8 500
J. McLean, Capital		29 450
J. McLean, Drawings	2 500	
Fees Earned		14 300
Salaries Expense	5 000	
Office Expense	1 850	
General Expense	725	
	$54 725	$54 725

**Revenue and
Expense Accounts**

Learning Objectives

After reading this unit, discussing the applicable review questions, and completing the applications exercises, you will be able to do the following:

1. ANALYZE transactions involving asset, liability, equity, revenue, and expense accounts.

2. RECORD the transactions in ledger accounts.

3. PREPARE financial statements from a trial balance.

To have the information necessary to prepare an income statement, accounts must be kept for the revenue and expense data for the accounting period. As you learned in Unit 4, the General Ledger must contain all the accounts required to prepare both financial statements: the balance sheet and the income statement. It will contain asset, liability, and owner's equity accounts for the balance sheet. It will also contain revenue and expense accounts for the income statement. The General Ledger will include these in the order shown:

General Ledger

TYPE OF ACCOUNT	USE
Asset	
Liability	Preparation of balance sheet
Owner's Equity	
Revenue	Preparation of income statement
Expense	

INCOME STATEMENT ACCOUNTS

Revenue and expense accounts are found in the General Ledger.

There are two main sections in the body of the income statement, the *revenue* section and the *expense* section. For each item of revenue, there is an account in the General Ledger. For each item of expense, there is an account in the General Ledger.

Revenue Accounts

Revenue is the proceeds arising from the sale of goods or services to customers. Revenue is generated in different ways in various types of businesses. A fitness centre obtains revenue from members' fees; a real estate firm earns commissions from selling houses; professionals such as lawyers, accountants, and dentists earn fees from their clients for their services; a company selling a product earns sales revenue.

A separate revenue account is set up for each distinct type of revenue earned by a company. Therefore, the type of revenue earned determines the type and number of revenue accounts necessary to accurately collect and summarize the revenue data.

Expense Accounts

Expenses are the costs incurred to generate the revenue. A separate expense account is set up for each major type of expense. Therefore, the number and type of expense accounts will be determined within each individual business according to its requirements. The major criteria used to decide whether a separate expense account is needed are: (1) frequency of usage, and (2) dollar value of expenditure. For each expense item that occurs frequently, a separate account is set up in the General Ledger. A separate account is also set up for any items that involve large amounts of money. Small expenditures that occur infrequently are normally collected in one or more non-specific accounts, such as Miscellaneous Expense or General Expense.

Rules of Debit and Credit for Revenue and Expense Accounts

In Chapter 2, the procedure for entering transactions in the balance sheet accounts was explained as summarized in Figure 3-10.

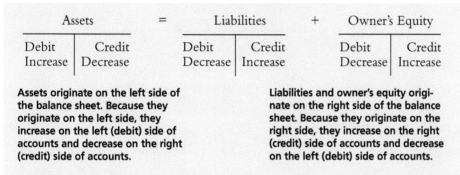

FIGURE 3-10

Theory summary for recording debits and credits in balance sheet accounts

The procedure for recording transactions that affect revenue and expense accounts will now be demonstrated.

Before a transaction can be recorded in the accounts, it is necessary to determine whether the account will be debited or credited. As was shown earlier, net income and revenue increase owner's equity. Owner's equity is increased on the credit side. Therefore, when revenue occurs, it is recorded on the credit side of the revenue account.

Revenue is recorded on the credit side.

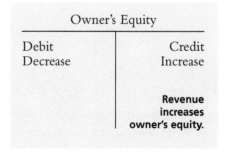

Expenses decrease
owner's equity.

Expenses are recorded on
the debit side.

A net loss and expenses decrease owner's equity. Owner's equity is decreased on the debit side. Therefore, when expenses occur, they are recorded on the debit side of the expense accounts.

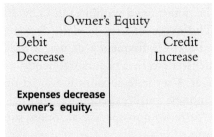

Debits and credits in revenue and expense accounts are determined by the effect of each transaction on owner's equity. *Revenue increases equity and is recorded as a credit. Expenses decrease equity and are recorded as debits.* These points are illustrated in Figure 3-11 and Figure 3-12 below.

FIGURE 3-11

Determining debits and credits in revenue and expense accounts

FIGURE 3-12

Theory summary for recording debits and credits in income statement accounts

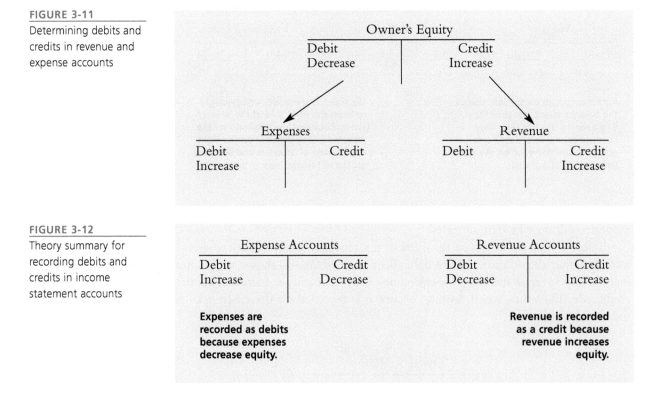

Reason for Revenue and Expense Accounts

If revenue increases equity, expenses decrease equity, and net income is eventually added to the owner's equity on the balance sheet, why are revenue and expense accounts necessary? Why not enter transactions directly into the equity account?

The answer is that one of the main purposes of accounting is to provide information to management about the operations of the business. Separate accounts for items of revenue and expense show at a glance which accounts are bringing in the company's revenue and which expenses are increasing too rapidly. Individual accounts for revenue and expenses provide managers with detailed information that helps them to make decisions about the business they are running and to control expenses, increase revenue, and operate the business effectively.

Transaction Analysis

As you have already learned, at least two accounts are involved in every business transaction. There is an equal debit amount recorded for every credit amount. In this chapter, you will see that the same principles of double-entry accounting apply when recording transactions involving revenue and expense accounts. For every debit amount, an equal credit amount is recorded. The transactions in this chapter will involve five types of accounts: asset, liability, equity, revenue, and expense.

Following are six transactions for lawyer R. Munro. Examine carefully how each transaction is analyzed and the position of the debit and the credit in the T-accounts.

Transaction 1: Asset and Revenue Transaction

Aug.   1   *Received $375 cash from client for drawing up new will.*

The accounts affected are Cash and Fees Earned. Cash is an asset that increases. Therefore, the account should be debited. By completing the performance of a service, the firm earned revenue in the form of fees. Since revenue increases owner's equity, the revenue account Fees Earned would be credited.

Cash	Fees Earned
Aug. 1 375	Aug. 1 375

ACCOUNT AFFECTED	TYPE OF ACCOUNT	INCREASE/DECREASE	DEBIT/CREDIT
Cash	Asset	Increase	Debit $375
Fees Earned	Revenue	Increase	Credit 375

Transaction 2: Asset and Revenue Transaction

Aug.   2   *Billed client fee of $2 100 for legal services required to close purchase of new home.*

The accounts affected are Accounts Receivable and Fees Earned. Accounts Receivable is an asset that increases. Therefore, the account is debited. By performing a service, the firm earned revenue. Revenue should be recorded when the service is completed whether the bill is paid or not. Since revenue increases owner's equity, it is credited on Aug. 2.

Accounts Receivable	Fees Earned
Aug. 2 2 100	Aug. 1 375
	2 2 100

ACCOUNT AFFECTED	TYPE OF ACCOUNT	INCREASE/DECREASE	DEBIT/CREDIT
Accounts Receivable	Asset	Increase	Debit $2 100
Fees Earned	Revenue	Increase	Credit 2 100

Transaction 3: Asset and Asset Transaction

Aug.   3   Received $900 from client as partial payment of $2100 billed on Aug. 2.

The accounts affected are Cash and Accounts Receivable. This transaction does *not* involve revenue because the revenue was previously recorded in Fees Earned on Aug. 2. The asset Cash increases and is debited. The asset Accounts Receivable decreases and is credited.

Cash			Accounts Receivable		
Aug. 1	375		Aug. 2 2 100	Aug. 3	900
3	900				

ACCOUNT AFFECTED	TYPE OF ACCOUNT	INCREASE/DECREASE	DEBIT/CREDIT	
Cash	Asset	Increase	Debit	$900
Accounts Receivable	Asset	Decrease	Credit	900

Transaction 4: Expense and Asset Transaction

Aug.   4   Paid $95 to Bell Canada for telephone bill received today.

The accounts affected are Telephone Expense and Cash. The cost of the telephone is incurred to produce revenue and should be recognized as an expense when the bill is received. The expense decreases owner's equity and should be debited. Cash is an asset that decreases and should be credited.

Telephone Expense			Cash		
Aug. 4	95		Aug. 1	375	Aug. 4 95
			3	900	

ACCOUNT AFFECTED	TYPE OF ACCOUNT	INCREASE/DECREASE	DEBIT/CREDIT	
Telephone Expense	Expense	Increase	Debit	$95
Cash	Asset	Decrease	Credit	95

Transaction 5: Expense and Liability Transaction

Aug.   5   Received a bill from the Hamilton Spectator for $230 for advertising the new location of the practice. The terms of payment allow 30 days to pay. The bill will be paid later.

The accounts affected are Advertising Expense and Accounts Payable. The cost of advertising was incurred to produce revenue and is an expense. It should be recorded upon receipt of the bill whether or not the bill is paid. Since an expense decreases owner's equity, it should be debited. Accounts Payable is credited since it is a liability that increases.

Advertising Expense		Accounts Payable	
Aug. 5	230	Aug. 5	230

ACCOUNT AFFECTED	TYPE OF ACCOUNT	INCREASE/DECREASE	DEBIT/CREDIT	
Advertising Expense	Expense	Increase	Debit	$230
Accounts Payable	Liability	Increase	Credit	230

Transaction 6: Liability and Asset Transaction

Aug.   6   *Paid $160 to Hamilton Spectator as partial payment of its bill for $230 received on*
              Aug. 5.

The accounts affected are Accounts Payable and Cash. Notice that even though a bill is paid, an expense does not result. The expense was recorded when the bill was received on Aug. 5. This is a simple payment of an account payable. Accounts Payable is a liability that decreases and is debited. Cash is an asset that decreases and is credited.

Accounts Payable				Cash				
Aug. 6	160	Aug. 5	230	Aug. 1	375	Aug. 4	95
				3	900	6	160

ACCOUNT AFFECTED	TYPE OF ACCOUNT	INCREASE/DECREASE	DEBIT/CREDIT	
Accounts Payable	Liability	Decrease	Debit	$160
Cash	Asset	Decrease	Credit	160

The six transactions described above were analyzed and recorded in a systematic fashion. The answers to the following four questions helped to correctly record the transactions:

- Which accounts were affected?
- Were the accounts asset, liability, owner's equity, revenue, or expense accounts?
- Did the accounts increase or decrease?
- Were the accounts debited or credited?

SUMMARY OF DEBIT AND CREDIT THEORY

Accurate recording of transactions is based on the rules of debit and credit. The basis for recording transactions in balance sheet and income statement accounts is shown below.

Balance Sheet Accounts

The debits and credits for balance sheet accounts are determined by the accounting equation:

Assets		=	Liabilities		+	Owner's Equity	
Debit	Credit	Debit		Credit	Debit		Credit
Increase	Decrease	Decrease		Increase	Decrease		Increase

The following rules are based on the equation:
  (1) Assets are on the left side of the equation.
  (2) Asset accounts increase on the left, or debit, side.
  (3) Asset accounts decrease on the right, or credit, side.
  (4) Liabilities and owner's equity are on the right side of the accounting
        equation.
  (5) Liabilities and owner's equity accounts increase on the right, or credit, side.
  (6) Liabilities and owner's equity accounts decrease on the left, or debit, side.

Income Statement Accounts

The income statement accounts (revenue and expenses) have debits and credits determined by their effect on equity:

Owner's Equity	
Debit	Credit
Decrease	Increase
Expenses	Revenue

The following rules are based on the equity account:
  (1) Equity increases on the right, or credit, side.
  (2) Revenue increases equity.
  (3) Revenue is recorded on the credit side of revenue accounts.
  (4) Equity decreases on the left, or debit, side.
  (5) Expenses decrease equity.
  (6) Expenses are recorded on the debit side of expense accounts.

ⒶCCOUNTING TERMS

Account Form of Balance Sheet	The account form of the balance sheet lists the assets on the left side and the liabilities and owner's equity on the right side. (p. 59)
Accounting Period	The period of time covered by the financial statements. (p. 53)
Accrual Basis of Accounting	A commonly used method of accounting where revenue is recorded when earned and expenses are recorded when incurred. (p. 56)
Balance Sheet Accounts	Asset, liability, and owner's equity accounts found in the General Ledger. (p. 59)
Business	The purpose of a business is to sell goods and/or services. (p.52)
Equity Accounts	The owner's Capital and Drawings accounts. (p. 57)
Expenses	Costs of items or services used up in the routine operation of the business. (p. 52)
Financial Statement	Income statement and balance sheet. (p. 53)
Fiscal Period	A synonym for accounting period. (p. 53)
Income Statement	A financial statement that summarizes the items of revenue and expense and determines the net income or loss for a stated period of time. (p. 53)
Income Statement Accounts	Revenue and expense accounts found in the General Ledger. (p. 53)
Loss	The decrease in owner's equity that results from unsuccessful operation of a business. (p. 52)
Matching Principle	Matching the revenue earned during a specific accounting period with the related expenses for the same period of time to obtain an accurate net income. (p. 55)
Net Income	Occurs when revenue is greater than expenses for the accounting period. (p. 52)
Net Loss	Occurs when expenses are greater than revenues for the accounting period. (p. 52)
Owner's Drawings Account	Used to record the withdrawal of assets by the owner for personal use. This withdrawal decreases the value of owner's equity. (p. 56)

Profit	The increase in owner's equity that results from successful operation of a business. (p. 52)
Report Form of Balance Sheet	Lists the assets, liabilities, and owner's equity vertically. (p. 59)
Revenue	Amounts earned by a business from the sale of goods or services during the routine operation of the business. (p. 52)
Revenue Recognition Principle	Revenue is recorded when the service is performed or the goods are shipped to a customer, even if cash has not been received. (p. 55)
Time-Period Assumption	Requires the definition and consistent use of the same period of time for the accounting period. (p. 53)

1. (a) Does revenue increase or decrease owner's equity?
   (b) Do expenses increase or decrease owner's equity?

2. (a) What is the increase side for revenue accounts? Why?
   (b) What is the increase side for expense accounts? Why?

UNIT 5

REVIEW QUESTIONS

1. Following are some of the accounts found in the General Ledger of Clarenville Nursery School: Cash; Accounts Receivable; Playground Equipment; Accounts Payable; S. Andrews, Drawings; Fees Earned; Advertising Expense; Automobile Expense; Salaries Expense. Referring to these accounts, analyze the transactions shown below for this business. Use the format demonstrated in this chapter to assist you. List the debit portion of the entry before the credit portion. Transaction (a) has been done for you as an example.

   (a) Received $325 cash for a client's weekly nursery school fees.
   (b) Paid $35 cash for gas used in transporting children to school.
   (c) Received a bill from the *Standard* for $165 for advertising.
   (d) Purchased a new swing set for the playground from School Supply for $2150 on credit.
   (e) Paid the weekly salary of $3000 to the staff.
   (f) The owner, S. Andrews, withdrew $750 for personal use.
   (g) Paid the $165 bill received previously from the *Standard*.

   Example:

UNIT 5

PROBLEMS: APPLICATIONS

TRANSACTION	ACCOUNT AFFECTED	TYPE OF ACCOUNT	INCREASE/ DECREASE	DEBIT/CREDIT
(a)	Cash	Asset	Increase	Debit $325
	Fees Earned	Revenue	Increase	Credit 325

2. Record the following transactions in the General Ledger of T. Bauer Ltd. containing five T-accounts. The accounts are: Cash; Accounts Receivable/ K. Ross; Accounts Receivable/B. Hodge; Accounts Receivable/B. Ianizzi; Sales Revenue.

   May 1 Sold goods for cash, $18 000.

        3 Sold goods on account to K. Ross $9300.

 4   Sold goods on account to B. Hodge $19 000.

 5   Sold goods to B. Ianizzi, $11 200; terms half cash, balance on account.

 8   B. Hodge returned goods that cost $315 sold May 4. The goods were not what was ordered.

 9   Received $7000 from K. Ross.

3. Record the following transactions in a General Ledger with these eight accounts: Cash; Equipment; Accounts Payable/Acme Ltd.; R. Cheng, Capital; R. Cheng, Drawings; Salaries; Advertising Expense; Rent Expense.

Oct.   1   R. Cheng invested $25 000 cash in a business.

 2   Paid $510 cash to the *Naperville News* for advertising.

 3   Bought equipment for $8000 on account from Acme Ltd.

 6   Paid rent, $2100.

 7   Paid Wilco Printers $370 cash for advertising circulars.

 8   Paid salaries, $1900 cash.

 8   Paid $4500 cash to Acme Ltd. on account.

 10   R. Cheng withdrew $1200 cash for personal use.

4. Bert's Service Centre repairs automobiles on a cash or credit basis. Accounts in the General Ledger include: Cash; Accounts Receivable; Tools; Accounts Payable; B. Tham, Capital, $10 000; B. Tham, Drawings; Repair Service Revenue; Advertising Expense; Rent Expense; Telephone Expense. Transactions that occurred during November are given below.

(a) Record the transactions in a T-account ledger.
(b) Prepare a trial balance.

Nov.   1   Paid the monthly rent of $4000 to Lakeland Ltd.

 3   Repaired the car of a client, Kim Jones, and billed her $615.

 4   Purchased a new set of tools for $1575 on credit from Tool Supply.

 7   Received a bill for $475 from the *Aurora Times* for advertising.

 10   Paid Tool Supply $1000 for amounts owing to them.

 12   Paid the telephone bill received today, $115.

 15   The owner, B. Tham, withdrew $1050 for his own use.

 16   Received $295 cash from a customer for a tune-up and oil change done today.

 19   Received $118 cash from a customer who was sent a bill last month.

5. Record the following transactions in a General Ledger for Mabry Driving School with these accounts: Cash; Accounts Receivable/L. Starr; Furniture; Automobiles; Accounts Payable/Grant's Esso; H. Mabry, Capital; Revenue from Lessons; Salaries Expense; Advertising Expense; Automobile Expense; Utilities Expense.

Feb. 1 H. Mabry invested $60 000 cash.

2 Purchased furniture for $4200 cash.

4 Purchased two cars from Roberts Motors for $58 000 cash.

5 Received $1100 cash from customers taking driving lessons.

7 Paid $920 cash for instructor's salary for the first week.

9 Paid $57 cash to the telephone company.

10 Received $650 cash from customers taking driving lessons.

11 Issued a bill of $150 to L. Starr, a customer who is taking lessons but will pay at a later date.

11 Received a bill for $97 from Grant's Esso for gas used by cars.

12 Paid $180 cash for hydro and electricity.

13 Sent a $290 cheque to the *Taber Times* for advertising space.

14 Received $150 cash from L. Starr in payment of bill sent previously.

(a) Balance the accounts and prepare a trial balance.
(b) Prepare an income statement for the two weeks ended February 14.

6. Eight transactions were recorded in the following T-account ledgers. Describe each transaction; include the dollar amount in your answer.

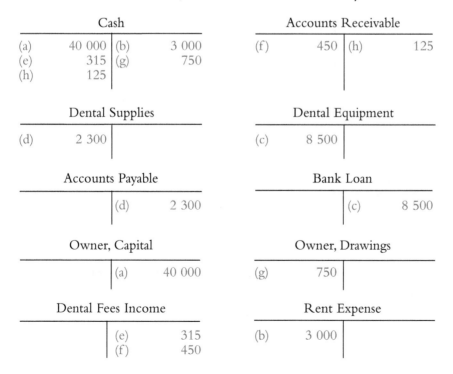

	Cash		
(a)	40 000	(b)	3 000
(e)	315	(g)	750
(h)	125		

	Accounts Receivable		
(f)	450	(h)	125

	Dental Supplies		
(d)	2 300		

	Dental Equipment		
(c)	8 500		

	Accounts Payable		
		(d)	2 300

	Bank Loan		
		(c)	8 500

	Owner, Capital		
		(a)	40 000

	Owner, Drawings		
(g)	750		

	Dental Fees Income		
		(e)	315
		(f)	450

	Rent Expense		
(b)	3 000		

1. The Bluebirds are a minor league professional baseball team owned by S. Greening. A partial list of the accounts used by the team is as follows: Cash $10 000; Equipment; Accounts Payable; Bank Loan, $10 000; S. Greening, Capital; S. Greening, Drawings; Gate Receipts; Parking Revenue; Concession Revenue; Advertising Expense; Players' Salaries Expense; Interest Expense; Rent Expense; Transportation Expense. Set up the T-account General Ledger for the Bluebirds Baseball Club Inc., and record the cash balance and the following transactions.

Apr.   1   S. Greening, the owner, invested an additional $50 000 in the team.

        1   Received a bill from the *Herald* for advertising. The bill for $750 is due in 30 days.

        2   Purchased a new speaker system for the field from Electronics Inc. Paid $750 cash and the remaining $2500 is to be paid in 30 days.

        5   Paid the players' salaries for the week, $29 400.

        7   The game today produced gate receipts $4500, parking revenue $490, and concession revenue $1575.

        9   Signed a new player to a standard player's contract calling for a payment of $925 per week for the remainder of the season. The player will join the club for tomorrow's game.

       10   Made the regular monthly payment on the bank loan. The payment consisted of $1500, of which $300 was interest and $1200 was used to reduce the amount of the loan.

       12   Today's game generated gate receipts $4100, parking revenue $425, and concession revenue $1300.

       14   Paid rent on the stadium for the last two games. The rent was calculated on the basis of 10 percent of gate receipts.

       15   The owner, S. Greening, withdrew $735 to make the monthly payment to GMAC on his personal car loan.

       15   Received a bill today from Grier's Transit for the bus used on the last road trips, $3100. Sent a cheque in full payment.

2. On April 1, Mike Weir's Golfing School had the following accounts, some with balances and some without: Cash $3000; Accounts Receivable/P. Moores $150; Accounts Receivable/L. Troop; Equipment $4700; Accounts Payable/Jack's Repair Shop $750; M. Butler, Capital $7100; Fees Income; Advertising Expense; Rent Expense; Equipment Repairs Expense; Utilities Expense.

   (a) Set up the General Ledger for Mike Weir's Golfing School on April 1 and record the following transactions.
   (b) On April 14, balance the accounts and prepare a trial balance, an income statement for the two weeks, and a balance sheet.

Apr.   2   Received $760 cash from customers for golfing lessons.

        2   Issued a bill for $115 to L. Troop for lessons that will be paid for later.

3 Paid $2500 cash to Remo Management for the monthly rent.

4 Received $85 cash from P. Moores.

5 Received a $175 bill from Jack's Repair Shop for repairing equipment.

8 Received $2000 cash from customers for lessons.

8 Issued another $45 bill to L. Troop for lessons.

9 Received $65 cash from P. Moores who paid the balance of money owed by him.

10 Received a $575 bill for a piece of equipment bought from Jack's Repair Shop. The amount is to be paid at a later date.

12 Paid $155 cash for electricity and water.

14 Paid $650 cash to Jack's Repair Shop to reduce balance owing for work done.

14 Paid $355 cash to the *Chronicle* for advertising.

3. On September 1, the Peace River Women's Hockey Team, owned by R. Brady, had the following accounts, some with balances and some without: Cash $12 000; Accounts Receivable/Stokes Dept. Stores; Equipment $4000; Bus $29 000; Accounts Payable/Klaman Motors $5300; R. Brady, Capital $39 700; Ticket Sales; Income from Concessions; Players' Salaries Expense; Bus Maintenance Expense; Arena Rental Expense; Advertising Expense.

(a) Set up the General Ledger for the hockey team, on September 1, and record the transactions given below for the month of September.

(b) On September 30, balance the accounts and prepare a trial balance, an income statement for the month, and a balance sheet.

Sep.   2 Received $92 000 cash from sales of season's tickets.

4 Purchased equipment for $5000 cash.

8 Received a $438 bill from Klaman Motors for repairs to the team bus.

9 Issued a bill of $3200 to Wal-Mart which bought a block of 200 tickets for the team's opening home game. (The store will use the tickets for promotional purposes.)

10 Paid $3100 rental fee for use of the arena for the last two weeks of practice.

14 Issued cheques for $18 000 to pay the players' salaries for the past two weeks.

16 Paid $350 cash to KCV TV for advertising the first home game on September 26.

17 Paid $515 to the *Daily Reporter* for advertising.

20 The week's sale of tickets for the opening game brought in $4300.

24 Paid $130 cash for gas for the bus on the first away-from-home game.

26 Received a further $8700 cash for ticket sales on the opening game.

28 Paid $3100 cash to the arena for rental for the last two weeks.

29 Issued cheques for $18 000 to pay the players' salaries for the rest of the month.

30 Received $19 500 cash from concession stands.

4. The T-accounts shown below and on the following page contain a series of transactions for Hoskins Realty. For each of the labelled entries, indicate how the accounts have changed and the transaction that must have occurred to generate the entry. The following chart, with transaction (a) done as an example, will assist you in completing the question.

TRANSACTION	ACCOUNT AFFECTED	TYPE OF ACCOUNT	INCREASE/ DECREASE	DEBIT/CREDIT
(a)	Cash	Asset	Increase	Debit $ 500
	Accounts Receivable	Asset	Decrease	Credit 500

Cash increased and Accounts Receivable decreased. Therefore an account receivable was collected.

General Ledger

Cash			
Balance	2 500	(b)	850
(a)	500	(d)	1 900
(f)	4 700	(g)	1 800
(i)	2 000	(h)	115
		(j)	245

L. Hoskins, Drawings	
(b) 850	

Accounts Receivable			
Balance	3 500	(a)	500
(c)	1 500		

Commissions Earned			
		(c)	1 500
		(f)	4 700

Office Furniture	
Balance 8 000	

Office Salaries Expense	
(d) 1 900	

Office Equipment	
Balance 12 000	

Advertising Expense	
(e) 500	

General Ledger (continued)

Accounts Payable				Rent Expense		
	Balance	1 700		(g)	1 800	
	(e)	500				

Bank Loan				Telephone Expense		
	Balance	9 000		(h)	115	

L. Hoskins, Capital				Utilities Expense		
	Balance	15 300		(j)	245	
	(i)	2 000				

CHAPTER **3**

CASE
STUDIES

CASE 1
Income Statement Analysis

You are the loan manager for a bank. A customer, Lethbridge Enterprises, has applied for a loan to expand its business. In support of the loan application, the company has supplied an income statement for the last six months that shows a net income of $52 000.

The following factors were not considered in the preparation of the income statement.

- Salaries of $7000 are owed to workers for last month but have not been paid or recorded as an expense.
- Interest of $4000 is owed to another bank.

(a) What effect does the omission of the two items have on the net income?
(b) What is the correct net income?
(c) What Generally Accepted Accounting Principle has not been followed?

CASE 2
Income Statement Errors

(a) There are several errors in the following income statement. Prepare a list of the errors.
(b) What is the correct net income or net loss?

D. Dobbs and Associates Income Statement June 30, 2008		
Revenue		
Sales		$50 000
Investment Income		2 000
Cash		7 000
		59 000
Expenses		
Advertising	$ 2 000	
Salaries	40 000	
Accounts Payable	5 000	
Rent	8 000	
General	1 000	56 000
Net Income		$ 3 000

CASE 3
Recording Transactions

National Products is a very large manufacturer of household products. It has several factories producing items that are sold by 45 branch offices located throughout the country. As an incentive for the branch managers, a bonus is offered if yearly budgeted net income figures are exceeded.

You are the accountant for a branch office of National Products. The manager of the branch is Charles Waite. You are aware that Charles has obtained a new position and plans to leave National Products early in January. Late in December he instructs you to omit from your records several large expenses including insurance, overtime pay for December, and fuel and hydro expenses. He tells you to pay these expenses as usual in December but to delay recording the items until some time in the new year.

(a) What will be the effect of not recording the expenses in December?
(b) What would you do? What are your alternatives? What are the consequences of each alternative?
(c) What GAAP is involved in this case?

CASE 4
Interpreting Accounting Data

One of the purposes of accounting is to provide information for decision making. Having knowledge of accounting is important for more than accountants. Others who benefit from having a background in accounting are bankers, investors, credit managers, business managers, owners, and government employees such as taxation workers. They all use their knowledge of accounting to analyze data used in making business decisions.

Here is an example of accounting information that is used by management to make decisions.

The *condensed* income statements for four years for Van Dyk Enterprises are shown following.

Van Dyk Enterprises Condensed Income Statement For the years 2—7, 2—6, 2—5, 2—4 (in thousands of dollars)				
	2—7	**2—6**	**2—5**	**2—4**
Net Sales	$251	$240	$225	201
Cost of Goods Sold	175	155	130	100
Gross Profit	76	85	95	101
Expenses	70	65	63	61
Net Income	16	20	32	40

A condensed financial statement highlights certain information. Single totals are provided for key items such as sales and expenses. The information is presented in a visual format that indicates trends requiring further investigation.

(a) What is happening (the trend) in sales?
(b) What is happening to gross profit over the four years?
(c) What is the trend in net income?
(d) What is happening to expenses?
(e) What significant information is provided by an analysis of this information?
(f) How might management use this information to make decisions?

ETHICS CASE
Industrial Pollution

Enviro Growth is a producer of agricultural products such as chemical fertilizers. It is located just outside a small, picturesque town. One of the attractions of the area is the Ontabar River that meanders through and around the town.

Local citizens are concerned about the industrial waste that Enviro Growth releases into the river. They are also worried about the quantity of water the company withdraws daily from the river for use in its production processes. They feel that the quality of the river water and the fish population are being harmed by the company's practices.

Jamie Lever is the environmental manager for Enviro Growth. She is working on recommendations concerning the local issues of pollution and water usage. The company is currently operating within the environmental rules and regulations for the region and Jamie feels no laws are being broken. The level of pollutants and the amount of water used in the factory could be reduced with the introduction of very expensive new equipment and processes.

Company officials have not planned for the purchase, installation, and training required if changes are made. Profits for this year and several years in the future will be greatly reduced if the new technology is implemented. Shareholders will be greatly displeased and share prices will decrease. Layoffs may be required if the company is to survive. Local citizens may lose their jobs.

1. Should the company introduce the new technology and processes? Give reasons for your answer.
2. Should the company decide to not introduce the new technology and processes? Give reasons for your answer.
3. List suggestions for solving this dilemma.

CHAPTER 3

*INTERNET
RESOURCES*

Explore these Web sites for information on personal skills desirable in business.

1. Canada: Training and Careers   **www.jobsetc.ca/toolbox/checklists/
employability.jsp?lang=e**

   On this site is an interactive tool that allows you to assess your skills in a variety of areas including communication, managing information, thinking and problem solving, teamwork, and personal management. The instrument is based on Employability Skills 2000+ from The Conference Board of Canada.

2. Model Business Skills Assessments   **http://honolulu.hawaii.edu/
intranet/committees/FacDevCom/guidebk/teachtip/BSrate.htm**

   This site contains a self-assessment instrument for employability skills, communication and interactive skills, other business core skills, supervisory and leadership skills, information and computer technology skills, and general business skills. A hardcopy document is available that includes both the assessment tools and extended definitions and resources.

3. Career, Business Lesson Plans   **www.moneyinstructor.com**

   This site presents a series of informative lesson plans on developing personal skills in business. Materials relate to resume writing, interviewing, career planning, and communicating. Although useful for instructors, this site offers helpful information for those interested in upgrading or polishing their skills.

4. Business Skills Sites   **www.helpself.com/directory/business.htm**

   This site provides links for various resources including print materials and courses on developing skills in leadership, innovation, presenting, and communication. Examples of links include Outward Bound Professional, Master New Media, and The Writing Solution.

The Journal and the Ledger

The Journal

Learning Objectives

After reading this unit, discussing the applicable review questions, and completing the applications exercises, you will be able to do the following:

1. **EXPLAIN** the purpose of a journal.

2. **RECORD** transactions in a General Journal.

3. **EXPLAIN** the use of a compound entry.

Imagine a business, such as Canadian Tire, that has a very large number of accounts. Now imagine that a $1025 error was made in recording one of the transactions in the ledger accounts. The debit of $1025 was placed in the wrong account. How would the $1025 error be traced? The accountant would have to go through all the accounts until the incorrect entry was located. The debit and credit parts of the transaction would be in widely separated parts of the ledger, and it could take a long time to locate the error. This type of difficulty is eliminated by the use of a *journal*.

INTRODUCING THE JOURNAL

A journal is a record of transactions recorded in chronological order (date order).

The general journal is the main journal of a business.

A journal is where transactions are first recorded.

FIGURE 4-1

Transactions are first recorded in a journal.

The **journal** records all parts of a transaction in one place. The date, debit, credit, and an explanation for each transaction are recorded together. Transactions can be conveniently located because they are recorded *chronologically,* that is, in the order in which they take place. The main journal of a business is often called the **General Journal**. Other types of journals will be discussed in later chapters.

A journal is sometimes called a **book of original entry** because it is where transactions are first recorded (see Figure 4-1). Transactions may be written in a journal manually or they may be prepared using a computer.

Business Transactions ⟶ Journal

Journal Entries

Each transaction recorded in a journal is called a **journal entry**.

Journalizing is the recording of transactions in a journal.

Each transaction recorded in a journal is called a **journal entry**. The process of recording transactions in a journal is called **journalizing**. Each journal entry has four parts as shown in Figure 4-2:

- Date of the transaction
- Account debited and amount
- Account credited (indented) and amount
- Explanation giving details of the transaction

Sample Transactions

Figure 4-2 illustrates how the following four transactions appear when they are recorded in the General Journal:

Jun. 1 *Provided services for $1600 cash.*
      3 *Paid $400 for advertising.*
      5 *Paid secretary's salary, $950.*
      6 *Purchased a new office computer for $4500. A cash down payment was made today of $1500 and the remaining $3000 will be paid to The Computer Store in 30 days.*

In the previous chapters you learned to analyze transactions and record them directly in T-accounts. Many businesses, however, first record entries in a journal when the transaction occurs. They later transfer the information to the ledger account. This second step is explained in Unit 7.

In T-account form the first transaction would be recorded as follows:

Cash		Service Revenue	
Jun. 1 1 600			Jun. 1 1 600

In Figure 4-2, the same transaction is shown in the journal. Notice that in the journal Cash is debited $1600 and Service Revenue is credited $1600 just as in the accounts.

FIGURE 4-2

Transactions recorded in a
General Journal

GENERAL JOURNAL			P.R.	DEBIT	CREDIT
DATE		PARTICULARS			
2008 Jun.	1	Cash		1 600	
		Service Revenue			1 600
		Provided services to R. Heino for Cash, Sales Slip 1.			
	3	Advertising Expense		400	
		Cash			400
		Paid cash for newspaper ad, Cheque 1.			
	5	Salaries Expense		950	
		Cash			950
		Paid secretary's weekly salary, Cheque 2.			
	6	Office Equipment		4 500	
		Cash			1 500
		Accounts Payable/The Computer Store			3 000
		Purchased a computer, Cheque 3 — 30 day account.			

Notice that in the General Journal illustrated in Figure 4-2, debits and credits are determined according to the same rules you learned in previous chapters. Note also that there is a consistent procedure for recording debits and credits in the General Journal. An entry such as the transaction on June 6, which shows more than one debit or credit, is called a **compound entry**. All entries must have equal debit and credit amounts.

A compound entry is an entry that has more than one debit or more than one credit.

Journal Recording Procedures

There are four steps in recording transactions in a journal. All of them are shown in Figure 4-2.

Step 1: Record the Date

In a journal, the first entry on each page must show the year, the month, and the day. Only the day of the month needs to be recorded for other entries on the page unless the month changes before a page is completed. In that event, the new month is shown in the date column.

The year, month, and day are shown on each journal page.

Step 2: Record the Debit

The name of the account debited is written next to the date. It should be written exactly as it appears in the ledger. For example, if cash is received, the appropriate account title would be Cash, not Cash Received. The dollar amount of the debit is written in the debit column.

The debit is shown first.

Step 3: Record the Credit

The credit is recorded on the next line. It is indented about the same as a paragraph indent to distinguish it visually from the debit. The dollar amount is written in the credit column.

The credit is indented.

Step 4: Record the Explanation

On the next line, starting at the margin, an explanation of the transaction is written. The invoice or cheque number is included.

Advantages of the Journal

Although transactions may be recorded directly into the ledger accounts, many businesses prefer to record transactions in a journal first for the following reasons:

- The complete transaction is recorded in one place.
- The use of a journal reduces errors. When entries are recorded directly into ledger accounts, it is easy to make a mistake by recording two debits and no credits or by recording only the debit or only the credit. Such errors are less likely to occur in a journal, but if they do, they are easy to spot. A quick check of each page in a journal will reveal any entry that does not show a debit and an equal credit.

A journal presents a history of all the company's transactions.

- A journal represents a chronological history of all the business transactions recorded by date.
- A journal makes it possible to determine the daily, weekly, or monthly volume of business and to identify busy periods more easily.
- A convenient picture of each day's business is provided.

Double-Entry Accounting

You have already learned that when recording a transaction the debit amount(s) must always equal the credit amount(s). This principle applies even if more than two accounts are used in recording the transaction. You will continue to apply the principle of double-entry accounting as you learn to use a journal. Look again at the journal entries in Figure 4-2. Notice that for every entry, the debit (left side) equals the credit (right side).

UNIT 6

REVIEW QUESTIONS

1. What is a journal?

2. Why is a journal sometimes called a book of original entry?

3. What is a journal entry?

4. What is journalizing?

5. What is a compound entry?

6. Name the four parts of a journal entry.

7. Which part of a journal entry is indented?

8. (a) Describe four advantages of using a journal.
   (b) In what order do entries appear in a journal?

9. Explain the principle of double-entry accounting.

1. Journalize the following transactions for the Odeon Theatre, using these accounts: Cash; R. Buddin, Capital; Ticket Sales; Refreshment Sales; Salaries Expense; Film Rental Expense; Hydro Expense; Advertising Expense.

Apr.   1   R. Buddin invested $130 000 cash.

       5   Ticket sales for the week, $25 000.

       5   Refreshment sales for the week, $9200.

       7   Paid for film rental, $13 500.

       8   Paid salaries, $3300.

      12   Paid the *Citizen* for newspaper advertising, $1200.

      14   Paid the hydro bill, $1900.

2. Journalize the following transactions for Bowman Child Care Centre, using these accounts: Cash; Equipment; Accounts Payable/Sears; M. Bowman, Drawings; M. Bowman, Capital; Child Care Fees; Salary Expense; Advertising Expense; Utilities Expense; Food Expense.

Jul.   1   M. Bowman invested $36 000 cash.

       4   Purchased new equipment for the centre; $1200 was paid immediately and the remaining $3200 was charged to the centre's account with Sears.

       5   Food items for the children's lunches this week were purchased for $625.

       6   Paid $150 for classified advertising in the *Gazette*.

       7   Paid salaries for the week, $2500.

       7   M. Bowman withdrew $825.

       7   Collected fees from parents for the week, $5600.

3. Journalize the following transactions for the Lynch Driving School, using these accounts: Cash; Accounts Receivable/L. Starr; Office Supplies, Office Furniture; Automobiles; Accounts Payable/Grant's Esso; J. Lynch, Capital; Revenue from Lessons; Salaries Expense; Advertising Expense; Automobile Expense; Utilities Expense.

May   1   J. Lynch invested $85 000 cash.

       2   Paid $900 for office supplies.

       2   Paid $3800 for office furniture.

       4   Purchased two cars from Forest Motors. Paid $27 000 each.

       5   Received $1500 from customers taking driving lessons.

       7   Paid $2800 for instructors' salaries for the week.

       9   Paid $110 to the telephone company.

      10   Received $1800 from customers taking driving lessons.

      11   Issued a bill for $425 to L. Starr, a customer who is taking lessons but will pay at a later date.

11   Received a bill from Grant's Esso for gas, $510.

12   Paid $795 for hydro and electricity.

13   Sent a $350 cheque to the *Daily Star* for advertising space.

14   Received $425 from L. Starr, to pay off amount owing for lessons.

4. Journalize the following transactions in the General Journal of Singh Accountants. Select appropriate accounts for each transaction. Note: This firm keeps a separate account for each account receivable and each account payable.

Nov.   1   S. Singh invested $37 000 cash in the business.

2   Provided services for $800 to B. Silva, for cash.

3   Provided services to W. Anderson, $515 on credit.

4   Provided services to R. Mehta, $1100 on credit.

5   Received $285 from W. Anderson as part payment of amount owing.

8   Received $1100 cash from R. Mehta in full payment of amount owing.

8   The owner, S. Singh, paid the office rent for the month, $2400.

9   Purchased a new computer from Office Systems for $3300. Paid a 10-percent down payment today and the remainder within 30 days.

10   Received the hydro bill for $725, to be paid in 10 days.

UNIT 7   Posting to the General Ledger

Learning Objectives

After reading this unit, discussing the applicable review questions, and completing the applications exercises, you will be able to do the following:

1. **USE** a chart of accounts.

2. **POST** journal entries to General Ledger accounts.

3. **PREPARE** the opening entry.

4. **PREPARE** trial balances in three forms:
   • Formal trial balance
   • Informal listing of debits and credits
   • Calculator tape listings

5. **LOCATE** errors.

6. **DEFINE** posting, journal, chart of accounts.

The General Journal is a systematic record of all transactions. It shows the accounts debited and credited for every transaction in the order in which the transactions occur. However, the General Journal does not provide the balance for each account. The General Journal does not tell the accountant how much cash is on hand, and it also does not record the balance of each of the items that will appear on the financial statements. This type of information is found in the accounts in the General Ledger. The information in the General Journal (as well as the other journals to be discussed later in the book) is transferred to the General Ledger by a process called **posting**. The flow of accounting information is shown in Figure 4-3.

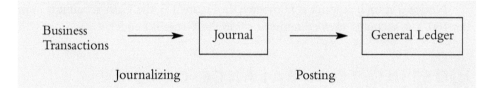

FIGURE 4-3

Posting is the transfer of information from a journal to the accounts in the ledger.

INTRODUCING THE BALANCE-COLUMN FORM OF LEDGER ACCOUNT

The T-account was introduced in Chapter 2 as a simple form of recording transactions in ledger accounts. It is an ideal form for learning the rules of debit and credit, but the T-account is not very practical for use in business. The balance in the account is not available for reference after each transaction. The most widely used form of account is the **balance-column account**, which is sometimes called a three-column account.

A form of account that shows a continuous balance after each transaction.

In Figure 4-4 a number of transactions are recorded in a Cash T-account. Exactly the same transactions appear in Figure 4-5 in the form of a balance-column account. Why is it called a balance-column form of account?

FIGURE 4-4

Transactions recorded in a Cash T-account

	Cash		
Oct. 1	2 000	Oct. 3	150
3	75	6	200
5	100		350
	2 175		
Balance	1 825		

FIGURE 4-5

Transactions shown in Figure 4-4 recorded in a balance-column ledger account

GENERAL LEDGER						
ACCOUNT Cash						NO. 100
DATE	PARTICULARS	P.R.	DEBIT	CREDIT	DR. CR.	BALANCE
2008						
Oct. 1		J1	2 000		DR.	2 000
3		J1	75		DR.	2 075
3		J1		150	DR.	1 925
5		J2	100		DR.	2 025
6		J3		200	DR.	1 825

The DR./CR. column
indicates whether the
account balance is a debit
or a credit.

Compare the information in the T-account in Figure 4-4 with the same information shown in the balance-column form of account in Figure 4-5. Notice that in the balance-column form of account a running balance is provided on each line. The accountant can see at a glance how much cash the company has at the close of each transaction. The DR./CR. (debit/credit) column indicates that the balance in the example is a debit balance; that is, the debits are greater than the credits. Although entries in the account on October 3 and 6 are credits, the DR./CR. column on these dates indicates that there is still a debit balance. The DR./CR. column of the account also indicates the column of the trial balance in which the account will appear. Since the $1825 balance in the Cash account in Figure 4-5 is a DR. (debit), the Cash account balance will be listed in the debit column of the trial balance.

Notice that each account is numbered. In Figure 4-5, the Cash account is number 100. The accounts are filed numerically in the General Ledger.

℗OSTING TO A BALANCE-COLUMN FORM OF LEDGER ACCOUNT

Figure 4-6 shows how a $1300 General Journal entry is posted to the Cash account in the balance-column form of ledger account.

FIGURE 4-6

Steps for posting the journal to the General Ledger

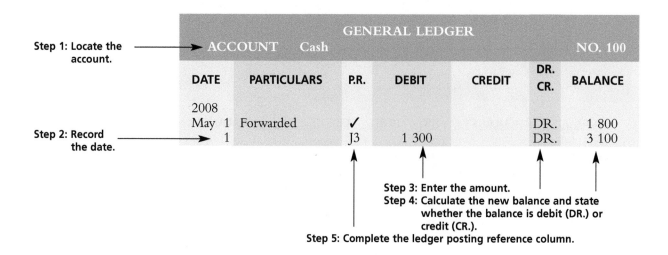

Step 6: Complete the journal posting reference column.

Step 1: Locate the account.

Step 2: Record the date.

Step 3: Enter the amount.
Step 4: Calculate the new balance and state whether the balance is debit (DR.) or credit (CR.).
Step 5: Complete the ledger posting reference column.

Steps in Posting

To avoid mechanical errors in the posting procedure, follow these steps, which are illustrated in Figure 4-6.

Step 1: Locate the Account

Look at the name of the account to be posted to and locate that account in the General Ledger. On May 1 in Figure 4-6, that account is Cash.

Step 2: Record the Date

The transaction date is recorded in the account. The month and year need not be repeated if they are already recorded on that page of the account.

Step 3: Enter the Amount

The amount of $1300 is recorded in the debit column of the account.

Step 4: Calculate the New Balance

Since the previous balance was $1800 (debit) and another debit of $1300 is being entered in the account, the new balance is $3100 (debit). The two amounts are added ($1800 + $1300) because they are on the same side of the account, the debit side. Record the new balance of $3100 and indicate that it is a debit balance by writing DR. in the DR./CR. column.

Step 5: Complete the Ledger Posting Reference Column

Enter the General Journal page number from which the amount was posted (J3) in the posting reference (P.R.) column of the ledger account. The page number is preceded by the letter J to indicate that the amount came from the General Journal. The (✓) in the posting reference column indicates the forwarded balance came from a previous ledger page rather than the journal.

Step 6: Complete the Journal Posting Reference Column

Copy the account number (100) from the ledger account into the posting reference column of the General Journal. This number indicates that the amount in the General Journal has been posted to the General Ledger in account 100.

Figure 4-7 shows the General Journal and the Service Revenue account after the credit has been posted to the Service Revenue account. The six steps in posting have all been repeated. What does the number 400 in the journal posting reference column represent? What does J3 in the account posting reference column indicate?

FIGURE 4-7
Posting to the Service
Revenue account

GENERAL JOURNAL				PAGE 3
DATE	**PARTICULARS**	**P.R.**	**DEBIT**	**CREDIT**
2008 May 1	Cash	100	1 300	
	Service Revenue	400		1 300
	Provided services to A. Trieu, for cash, Invoice 1.			

GENERAL LEDGER						
ACCOUNT Service Revenue						NO. 400
DATE	**PARTICULARS**	**P.R.**	**DEBIT**	**CREDIT**	**DR. CR.**	**BALANCE**
2008 May 1		J3		1 300	CR.	1 300

Posting References

Numbers in the posting reference columns serve an important purpose. They are cross references that link particular journal entries to corresponding postings in the ledger accounts.

Indicates where more information regarding the entry can be located.

A journal page number in the ledger account **posting reference column** indicates where more information about the transaction can be found. For instance, the information explaining the transaction with A. Trieu (Figure 4-6) can be located by referring to page 3 of the General Journal.

The ledger account number in a journal posting reference column indicates that the amount has been posted. It tells the accounting clerk where he or she left off in posting to the General Ledger.

Periodically, all companies have their records audited by an outside accountant. An *audit* is a systematic check of accounting records and procedures. The cross reference provided by posting reference numbers helps the auditor to check the accuracy of the journalizing and posting of transactions. The posting reference numbers allow the transactions to be traced from a journal to the General Ledger and also from the General Ledger to a journal.

Figure 4-8 represents page 12 of a General Journal used by Jacobs Painting Contractors. Figure 4-9 is a portion of the company's ledger to which the transactions have been posted. Trace the transactions from the General Journal to the General Ledger. The posting reference column will help you.

OPENING THE BOOKS

Figures 4-8 and 4-9 illustrated how routine transactions are recorded in the General Journal and then are posted to the General Ledger. The special procedures followed when a business first begins operations will now be examined.

GENERAL JOURNAL			PAGE 12	
DATE	PARTICULARS	P.R.	DEBIT	CREDIT
2008				
Mar. 1	Cash	100	1 300	
	Service Revenue	400		1 300
	Provided services to S. Mills.			
3	Advertising Expense	500	275	
	Cash	100		275
	Paid *Hamilton Spectator* for a newspaper advertisement.			
5	Salaries Expense	502	425	
	Cash	100		425
	Paid secretary's salary.			
6	Cash	100	900	
	Service Revenue	400		900
	Painted house for L. Hoskins.			

FIGURE 4-8

Page 12 of the General Journal for Jacobs Painting Contractors

GENERAL LEDGER

ACCOUNT   Cash   NO. 100

DATE	PARTICULARS	P.R.	DEBIT	CREDIT	DR. CR.	BALANCE
2008						
Mar. 1	Forwarded	✓			DR.	5 100
1		J12	1 300		DR.	6 400
3		J12		275	DR.	6 125
5		J12		425	DR.	5 700
6		J12	900		DR.	6 600

FIGURE 4-9

Portion of the General Ledger for Jacobs Painting Contractors affected by the transactions in Figure 4-8

ACCOUNT   Service Revenue   NO. 400

DATE	PARTICULARS	P.R.	DEBIT	CREDIT	DR. CR.	BALANCE
2008						
Mar. 1		J12		1 300	CR.	1 300
6		J12		900	CR.	2 200

ACCOUNT   Advertising Expense   NO. 500

DATE	PARTICULARS	P.R.	DEBIT	CREDIT	DR. CR.	BALANCE
2008						
Mar. 3		J12	275		DR.	275

ACCOUNT   Salaries Expense   NO. 502

DATE	PARTICULARS	P.R.	DEBIT	CREDIT	DR. CR.	BALANCE
2008						
Mar. 5		J12	425		DR.	425

The Opening Entry

A special entry, called an **opening entry**, is prepared when a business first begins operations. Following are the procedures M. Jacobs used when starting a painting business.

On January 2, 2008, M. Jacobs borrowed money from a bank and started a painting business. He invested $7500 cash, a small truck worth $14 500, and equipment worth $1900. The assets of the new business are:

Cash	$ 7 500
Equipment	1 900
Truck	14 500
Total	$23 900

The business has one liability:

Bank Loan	$10 000

Jacobs' equity is calculated by applying the equation:

$$A = L + OE$$
$$\$23\ 900 = \$10\ 000 + \$13\ 900$$

Jacobs' equity is $13 900.

To open the books of the business, the General Journal is set up, and the business' assets, liability, and owner's equity are recorded. The first entry, as illustrated in Figure 4-10, is called the opening entry.

Opening entry in the General Journal for Jacobs Painting Contractors

GENERAL JOURNAL				PAGE 1
DATE	PARTICULARS	P.R.	DEBIT	CREDIT
2008 Jan. 2	Cash		7 500	
	Equipment		1 900	
	Truck		14 500	
	Bank Loan			10 000
	M. Jacobs, Capital			13 900
	Started a painting business with the above assets, liability, and owner's equity.			

Notice that the opening entry shows three debits and two credits, with the three debit amounts ($23 900) equal to the two credit amounts ($23 900). You learned in Unit 6 that an entry that shows more than one debit or credit is called a compound entry. Remember, however, that all entries must have equal debit and credit amounts. After the opening entry is journalized, the daily entries of the business can be recorded.

Opening Ledger Accounts

Next, the General Ledger is prepared by opening accounts required to post the opening entry (Figure 4-10). As business transactions occur, they are journalized. As new accounts are required, they are opened in the ledger. Follow these procedures when opening a new balance-column account:

(1) Write the name of the account to the right of the word "account."
(2) Write the account number at the far right on the top line.
(3) Write the date in the date column.

(4) Write "Opening Balance" on the first line in the column identified by the heading "particulars." This will help distinguish the opening entry from the changes that will occur in the account as business transactions take place.

(5) Write J1 for General Journal page 1 in the posting reference column.

(6) Record the amount in the correct debit or credit column.

(7) Enter the balance in the balance column.

(8) Depending on the balance, write DR. or CR. in the DR./CR. column.

(9) Enter the ledger account number in the posting reference column of the General Journal.

(10) Insert the account in numerical sequence in the ledger.

Figure 4-11 shows the posting of the opening entry to the General Ledger accounts. For each item in the opening entry, an account has been prepared. Notice that "Opening Balance" has been written in the particulars column and that the six steps in posting have been followed.

FIGURE 4-11

General Ledger after posting the opening entry

GENERAL LEDGER

ACCOUNT   Cash   NO. 100

DATE	PARTICULARS	P.R.	DEBIT	CREDIT	DR. CR.	BALANCE
2008 Jan. 2	Opening Balance	J1	7 500		DR.	7 500

ACCOUNT   Equipment   NO. 141

DATE	PARTICULARS	P.R.	DEBIT	CREDIT	DR. CR.	BALANCE
2008 Jan. 2	Opening Balance	J1	1 900		DR.	1 900

ACCOUNT   Truck   NO. 142

DATE	PARTICULARS	P.R.	DEBIT	CREDIT	DR. CR.	BALANCE
2008 Jan. 2	Opening Balance	J1	14 500		DR.	14 500

ACCOUNT   Bank Loan   NO. 221

DATE	PARTICULARS	P.R.	DEBIT	CREDIT	DR. CR.	BALANCE
2008 Jan. 2	Opening Balance	J1		10 000	CR.	10 000

ACCOUNT   M. Jacobs, Capital   NO. 300

DATE	PARTICULARS	P.R.	DEBIT	CREDIT	DR. CR.	BALANCE
2008 Jan. 2	Opening Balance	J1		13 900	CR.	13 900

CHART OF ACCOUNTS

Each account in the General Ledger has an account title and an account number. Accounts are placed in the General Ledger in numerical sequence so that they may be located quickly. A list of the account names and numbers — called a **chart of accounts** — is used by accounting employees. The chart of accounts is an aid in deciding which accounts to use when transactions are journalized and in locating accounts when posting to the General Ledger.

The accounts in the General Ledger are numbered in the same order as they appear on the balance sheet and income statement. Notice that in the chart of accounts for Jacobs Painting Contractors (Figure 4-12) a series of numbers is assigned to each type of account:

100–199	Asset accounts	400–499	Revenue accounts
200–299	Liability accounts	500–599	Expense accounts
300–399	Owner's equity accounts		

In large companies with a large number of accounts, a four-digit series of numbers may be required to cover all the accounts. For example, asset accounts might be numbered 1000–1999, and liability accounts might be numbered 2000–2999. In computer accounting, the account number becomes a numeric code and is used in place of the account title when journalizing transactions. Only the number is entered on the keyboard. The account name then automatically appears on the screen.

FIGURE 4-12

Chart of accounts for Jacobs Painting Contractors

Jacobs Painting Contractors
Chart of Accounts

Assets

100	Cash
110	Accounts Receivable/F. Zammit
111	Accounts Receivable/B. Kennedy
131	Painting Supplies
141	Equipment
142	Truck

Liabilities

200	Accounts Payable/International Paints
201	Accounts Payable/Hardware Supply Store
221	Bank Loan
231	Mortgage Payable

Owner's Equity

300	M. Jacobs, Capital
301	M. Jacobs, Drawings

Revenue

400	Service Revenue

Expenses

500	Advertising Expense
501	Rent Expense
502	Salaries Expense

FORWARDING PROCEDURE

The active accounts of a business will have many transactions recorded on the pages of the General Ledger. When an account page is filled, a new page is opened according to the following procedure:

(1) Head up a new page using the same account name and number (Figures 4-13 and 4-14).

(2) Write "Forwarded" on the last line of the old page in the particulars column (Figure 4-13).

ACCOUNT	Accounts Receivable/F. Zammit					NO. 110
DATE	PARTICULARS	P.R.	DEBIT	CREDIT	DR. CR.	BALANCE
2008						
Mar. 3	Opening Balance	J1	1 200		DR.	1 200
3		J1	500		DR.	1 700
4		J1		1 000	DR.	700
5		J2	100		DR.	800
5		J2		300	DR.	500
6		J3	400		DR.	900
7		J3	1 600		DR.	2 500
7	Forwarded	J3		2 175	DR.	325

FIGURE 4-13
Ledger page that has been filled and forwarded

(3) On the first line of the new page, write the date (year, month, day), "Forwarded" in the particulars column, and the balance in the balance column. Indicate the type of balance. Place a check mark in the posting reference column as shown in Figure 4-14.

ACCOUNT	Accounts Receivable/F. Zammit					NO. 110
DATE	PARTICULARS	P.R.	DEBIT	CREDIT	DR. CR.	BALANCE
2008						
Mar. 7	Forwarded	✓			DR.	325

FIGURE 4-14
New ledger page

Note that aside from the "Opening Balance" and "Forwarded" notations, the particulars column is seldom used. If further information is required about a transaction, use the posting reference numbers to trace the entry back to the General Journal where more detailed information can be found.

REVIEWING THE TRIAL BALANCE

At regular intervals, usually monthly, a trial balance is prepared. A trial balance is proof of the mathematical accuracy of the General Ledger. As you learned in Chapter 2, a trial balance is a list of the debit account balances and the credit account balances. The total of the debit balances should equal the total of the credit balances. The formal trial balance for Jacobs Painting Contractors is illustrated in Figure 4-15.

A trial balance is proof of the mathematical accuracy of the General Ledger.

FIGURE 4-15

Formal trial balance

ACCOUNT TITLE	ACC. NO.	DEBIT	CREDIT
Jacobs Painting Contractors			
Trial Balance			
March 31, 2008			
Cash	100	$ 2 170	
Accounts Receivable/F. Zammit	110	150	
Accounts Receivable/ B. Kennedy	111	385	
Equipment	141	3 250	
Truck	142	14 500	
Accounts Pay./International Paints	200		$ 695
Accounts Pay./Hardware Supply Store	201		420
Bank Loan	221		10 000
M. Jacobs, Capital	300		9 340
		$20 455	$20 455

Forms of the Trial Balance

The trial balance may take several forms:

- Formal trial balance (Figure 4-15)
- List of the debit and credit account balances in which the debits total equals the credits total (Figure 4-16)
- Machine tape listing the account balances in which the debits minus the credits equal zero (Figure 4-17)

FIGURE 4-16

List form of trial balance — total debits equal total credits

Jacobs Painting Contractors
Trial Balance
March 31, 2008

DEBIT	CREDIT
$ 2 170	$ 695
150	420
385	10 000
3 250	9 340
14 500	
$20 455	$20 455

FIGURE 4-17

Machine tape form of trial balance — debits minus credits equal zero

Jacobs Painting Contractors
Trial Balance
March 31, 2008

0

2 170 +
150 +
385 +
3 250 +
14 500 +
695 –
420 –
10 000 –
9 340 –
0

DEALING WITH ERRORS

Avoiding Posting Errors

By following the six steps in posting given previously, the following types of errors can be avoided:

- Not posting an entire transaction
- Not posting either the debit or credit part of a transaction
- Posting to the correct side but to the wrong account
- Posting to the wrong side of an account
- Calculating the balance incorrectly
- Transposing figures (posting 96 instead of 69)

Locating Trial Balance Errors

The trial balance is a test or trial to prove that the General Ledger is mathematically in balance. If the totals of the debit and credit columns of the trial balance are not the same, the error must be located before the financial statements are prepared.

Locating errors can be very discouraging and time consuming. The suggestions that follow represent procedures for identifying the type of error that has occurred and methods for tracking it down.

(1) Add the columns over again to check for arithmetic errors.
(2) Determine the difference between the debit and credit totals.
(3) If the difference is 1, 10, 100, etc., there may be an addition or subtraction error.
(4) Check to see if an account in the General Ledger with the same balance as the difference (Step 2) has been omitted from the trial balance.
(5) Divide the difference (Step 2) by 2. Look for that amount on the wrong side of the trial balance.
(6) If the difference is divisible evenly by 9, the error may be due to a transposition of numbers (for example 97 written as 79).
(7) Check to see if the amount of the difference has been omitted when it was posted from a journal to the General Ledger.
(8) If the error still escapes you:
  (a) Check each balance in each column in the ledger.
  (b) Check the posting reference column of each journal to locate unposted items.
  (c) Recheck each posting.
(9) If you still have not found the error — relax! Go on with something else, then return later with a clear frame of mind and try again.

Example of a Transposition Error

Following is a list of debits and credits from a trial balance. The totals do not balance because an error has been made. The debit total is $2075 and the credit total is $2165.

DEBIT	CREDIT
$ 150	
400	
560	
200	
765	
	$ 495
	1 670
$2 075	$2 165

To find the error, the following is done:

(1) Re-add the columns to ascertain if an addition error has been made.
(2) Determine the difference. The difference between the debit total ($2075) and the credit total ($2165) is $90.
(3) Is the difference divisible by 9, evenly? Since the difference is divisible by 9 evenly (90 ÷ 9 = 10), the error may be a **transposition error**. That is, numbers may be reversed.
(4) Check each number for a reversal. A check of each ledger account balance indicates that an account balance of $560 was incorrectly written. It should be $650. The 5 and the 6 have been transposed.

A transposition error occurs when numbers are reversed, such as writing 63 rather than 36.

The correct trial balance follows.

DEBIT	CREDIT
$ 150	
400	
650	
200	
765	
	$ 495
	1 670
$2 165	$2 165

Correcting Errors

The accepted method of correcting errors is to rule out the mistake and to rewrite the correction:

~~1143~~ 1134

Some businesses insist that all corrections be initialled:

~~871~~ 817 M.P.

Correcting Journal Entries

Suppose the following entry had been made in the journal and posted to the ledger accounts:

Aug. 2	Supplies	30	
	Cash		30
	Cheque 141, purchase of supplies.		

The amount of the entry should have been $300. One method of correcting this error is to cancel the entry and re-enter the transaction. This is done as illustrated below.

Cancel the entry:

Aug. 3	Cash	30	
	Supplies		30
	To cancel the Aug. 2 entry for Cheque 141, incorrect amount.		

Re-enter the transaction:

Aug. 3	Supplies	300	
	Cash		300
	Cheque 141, purchase of supplies.		

Checking for Accuracy

When using a printing calculator to check calculations, follow these procedures (see Figure 4-18):

(1) Clear the calculator.
(2) Enter the data.
(3) Label the tape.
(4) If the totals being checked do not balance, audit the tape by checking the numbers on the tape against the source. This step will locate errors made in entering numbers on the machine keyboard.
(5) Staple the labelled tape to the material being checked.

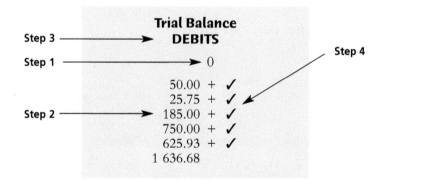

FIGURE 4-18

Checking a trial balance using a printing calculator

Checking Accounts

The balance of an account may be checked on a printing calculator by entering each debit with the plus (+) key and each credit with the minus (−) key. Take the total after the last entry. Figure 4-19 illustrates this procedure.

Another method of checking accounts is to use the subtotal or equals key to check the balance column after each entry (Figure 4-20). This technique specifically identifies the line on which an error may occur.

FIGURE 4-19

Checking accounts by calculator

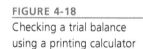

Cash Account

0	
2 190.00	+
25.00	+
395.00	−
620.00	+
895.60	−
8.70	+
699.20	=
2 786.10	

FIGURE 4-20
Subtotal method

Cash Account

2 190.00	+
25.00	=
2 215.00	
2 215.00	−
395.00	=
1 820.00	
1 820.00	−
620.00	=
1 200.00	
1 200.00	+
895.60	=
2 095.60	
2 095.60	−
8.70	=
2 086.90	
2 086.90	+
699.20	=
2 786.10	

ACCOUNT   Cash   **NO. 100**

DATE	PARTICULARS	P.R.	DEBIT	CREDIT	DR. CR.	BALANCE
2007						
Dec. 1	Forwarded	✓			DR.	2 190.00
2		J16	25.00		DR.	2 215.00
3		J16		395.00	DR.	1 820.00
5		J16		620.00	DR.	1 200.00
5		J17	895.60		DR.	2 095.60
5		J17		8.70	DR.	2 086.90
5		J18	699.20		DR.	2 786.10

INTRODUCING THE ACCOUNTING CYCLE

The accounting cycle is the set of accounting procedures performed in each accounting period.

You have seen that business transactions are first recorded in a journal and are then posted to the ledger. If the ledger is in balance, the financial statements (the income statement and the balance sheet) are then prepared. These steps are completed in sequence in each accounting period and together are called the **accounting cycle** (see Figure 4-21).

FIGURE 4-21
Accounting cycle

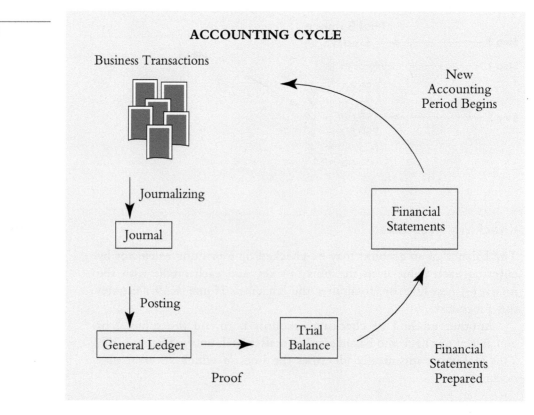

ACCOUNTING CYCLE

1. What is posting?

2. What are the six steps followed in posting?

3. What is written in the posting reference column of a journal and a ledger?

4. What is an opening entry?

5. What is a chart of accounts?

6. What is the accounting cycle?

7. An account with a $735 debit balance is incorrectly placed on the trial balance as a $735 credit.

   (a) State how much the difference will be between the trial balance debit and credit totals.
   (b) How is such an error identified?
   (c) What is a transposition error? Give an example.

8. (a) The difference in the totals of a trial balance is $100. What type of error has probably been made?
   (b) If the difference is $270, what type of error may have been made?

1. (a) The following Cash account has incomplete DR./CR. and balance columns. Prepare a copy of the account, completing the DR./CR. column and the balance column on each line of the account.
   (b) Assume that the account page for Cash is filled. Apply the forwarding procedure and forward the balance to a new account page for Cash.

ACCOUNT	Cash					NO. 100
DATE	PARTICULARS	P.R.	DEBIT	CREDIT	DR. CR.	BALANCE
2007						
Feb. 1	Forwarded	✓			DR.	5 261.00
2		J16	400.00		DR.	5 861.00
2		J16		175.00	DR.	5 686.00
3		J16	162.50			
3		J16	843.75			
4		J17		61.30		
5		J17	119.34			
5		J17		4 825.59		

2. On April 1, R. Campbell, an architect, opened a business. A chart of accounts for the business is given below.

   (a) Journalize the April transactions using accounts from the chart of accounts. Use General Journal page 1.
   (b) Open ledger accounts using account titles and numbers from the chart of accounts.
   (c) Post the General Journal entries.
   (d) Prepare a trial balance.

100	Cash
110	Accounts Receivable/Kendrik Contractors
141	Office Equipment
142	Automobile
200	Accounts Payable/Downtown Motors
300	R. Campbell, Capital
400	Fees Earned
505	General Expense
507	Rent Expense
508	Salaries Expense
510	Telephone Expense

Apr. 1 R. Campbell invested $45 000 cash in an architectural consulting business.

2 Bought office equipment, $4500 cash.

3 Bought an automobile for business from Ajax Ford Ltd. on credit. The cost price of the car was $31 300.

4 Received $820 for services provided to a customer.

5 Sent a bill for $4000 to Kendrik Contractors for services provided.

5 Paid the April rent, $2500.

5 Paid office salaries, $1900.

5 Paid $450 for the installation of a second telephone line.

3. An accounting clerk has prepared three mini trial balances that do not balance. Calculate the difference in the debit and credit totals and indicate the probable type of error made by the clerk in each case.

(a)

DEBIT	CREDIT
$ 3 000	
1 000	
700	
420	
	$ 2 950
	2 170
$5 120	$5 020

(b)

DEBIT	CREDIT
$200	
300	
50	
	$ 75
	25
	300
	200
$550	$600

(c)

DEBIT	CREDIT
$ 3 000	
1 000	
700	
240	
	$ 2 950
	2 170
$4 940	$5 120

4. The Supplies account shown on the following page contains a number of errors.

(a) List the errors.
(b) Prepare a corrected Supplies account.

ACCOUNT Supplies						NO. 122
DATE	PARTICULARS	P.R.	DEBIT	CREDIT	DR. CR.	BALANCE
2009 Aug. 1	Forwarded	✓			DR.	2 300
2		J3		300	CR.	2 000
3		J3	400		DR.	2 400
4		J3	250		DR.	2 650
5		J3	150		DR.	2 500

5. Ahmad Nauman opened an insurance agency on July 1 with the following assets and liabilities: Cash $2500; Equipment $5500; Building $105 000; Land $25 000; Bank Loan $8000; Mortgage $85 000; A. Nauman, Capital $45 000. Record the opening entry for the business in a General Journal.

6. Myassa Khittan opened a secretarial service business on February 1, 2007 with the following assets and liabilities: Cash $2800; Equipment $4300; Bank Loan $4200.

   (a) Prepare an opening entry in a General Journal. (Remember that your entry must balance.)
   (b) The following events occurred in February. Journalize the items in the books of the company. Revenue should be recorded in the Fees from Clients account.

   Feb.   1   Paid the first month's rent on the office, $1200 cash.

           1   Completed keying a report for a client, J. Jamison, and mailed the bill for $325.

           2   Received a bill from the *Express* for advertising, $155.

           3   Purchased office supplies from Gladstone Stationery, $240 on credit.

           4   Received $280 from a client for work completed today.

           5   Mailed a cheque drawn on the company bank account, $930 to pay Ms. Khittan's apartment rent.

           8   J. Jamison paid the bill issued February 1 in full.

           9   Returned a $65 box of envelopes purchased February 3 to Gladstone Stationery because they were the incorrect size. Gladstone agreed to give a credit for the amount. (The firm now owes Gladstone $65 less as a result of this transaction.)

          10   Paid the *Express* bill of February 2.

          11   Paid Gladstone in full.

UNIT 8   Source Documents

Learning Objectives

After reading this unit, discussing the applicable review questions, and completing the applications exercises, you will be able to do the following:

1. **IDENTIFY** and **RECORD** source documents.

2. **EXPLAIN** why source documents are prepared for every transaction.

As business transactions occur, information about them is recorded on some form of business document. For example, when a cash sale is made, a sales slip is prepared. A copy is given to the customer and a copy is kept by the seller. The accountant for the seller uses the sales slip as the source of information that a sale has been made. The accountant for the buyer uses the copy of the same document as a source of information that a purchase has been made. This is where the term **source document** comes from. The most commonly used source documents will be described in this chapter.

> A source document is any business form that is the original source of information.

Source documents are proof that a business transaction did in fact occur. A document is a concrete object. The source document is generally prepared with at least two copies. The two parties to a transaction, generally the seller and the buyer, each receive an exact copy. An important principle of accounting is:

A source document must be prepared for every business transaction.

CASH SALES SLIPS

> Source document for a cash sale.

Figure 4-22 is a **cash sales slip** used by many retail stores. Three copies of the cash sales slip are prepared when a cash sale is made. These are distributed as follows:

- Copy 1: Given to the customer.
- Copy 2: Used by the accounting department of the seller to record the transaction.
- Copy 3: Kept in a numerical file that serves as a record of all cash sales. Every sales slip must be accounted for in this file.

This entry is made by the seller's accountant from Copy 2:

Mar. 17	Cash	49.99	
	Sales		49.99
	Sales Slip 43785.		

It should be noted that in actual practice, groups of sales slips would be combined and an entry similar to the preceding one would be made to record the total of the group of slips.

FIGURE 4-22
Cash sales slip — a source
document used by retail
stores

160 SPRUCE STREET   OTTAWA, ON K1R 6P2   TEL (613) 236-0716

CASH SALE
VENTE AU COMPTANT

International Paints (Canada) Limited
Marine, Industrial, Railway, Aircraft & Household Finishes

DATE March 17   2007

**NAME
NOM**   Campbell Sports

**ADDRESS
ADRESSE**   2579 Base Line Rd., Ottawa, ON K2H 7B3

CODE NUMBER NUMÉRO DU CODE	ORDERED COMM	UNIT SIZE FORMAT	DESCRIPTION	UNIT PRIX L'UNITÉ	AMOUNT MONTANT	
CM 230000	1	1 L	Exterior Paint		49	99
CASH ✓	CHX.	REF.	CHEQUE	PROV. TAX TAXE PROV.		
SALESPERSON VENDEUR/EUSE B.L.				TOTAL	49	99

43785   **CUSTOMER'S COPY
COPIE DU CLIENT**

The buyer uses Copy 1 as the source of information to record this entry:

Mar. 17	Building Repairs Expense	49.99	
	Cash		49.99
	Purchased paint for cash.		

The diagram in Figure 4–23 on page 108 illustrates how both the buyer and the seller use copies of the same source document to record a transaction.

FIGURE 4-23
Both the seller and the buyer use the same source document to record a transaction.

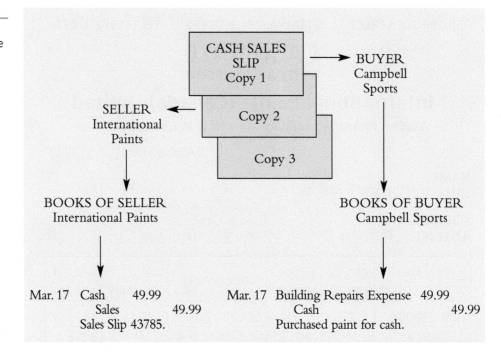

SALES INVOICES

Source document for a sale on credit.

Figure 4-24 is an example of another source document called a **sales invoice**. It is the bill of sale or simply the bill completed by the seller and given to the buyer as a record of a credit sale. A *credit sale* is one in which the customer agrees to pay at a later date. Other terms used to describe a credit sale are *charge sale* or *on account sale*.

The selling company makes several copies of the sales invoice and distributes them as follows:

- Copies 1 and 2: Sent to the customer.
- Copy 3: Used by the accounting department of the seller as the source of information to record the transaction.
- Copy 4: Kept by the sales department as a record of the sale.
- Copies 5 and 6: Given to the shipping department of the seller. Copy 5 is used to pack and label the shipment. Copy 6 is placed inside the shipment as a packing slip. The packing slip tells the customer what should be in the shipment.

This entry is made by the accounting department of the seller from Copy 3:

Apr.	1	Accounts Receivable/Campbell Sports	210	
		Sales		210
		Invoice 5870, letterhead paper and		
		envelopes.		

FIGURE 4-24
Sales invoice with details
of a charge sale

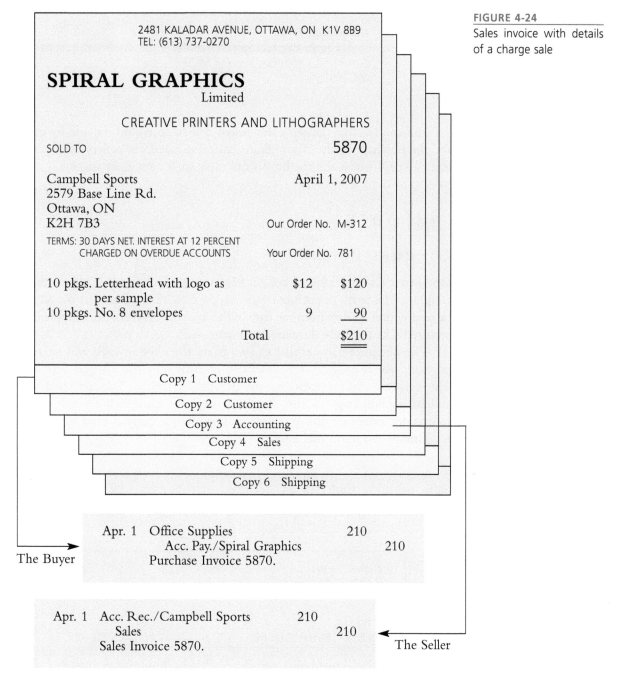

PURCHASE INVOICES

Look again at Figure 4-24. What is the name of the seller? The buyer? To the seller, Spiral Graphics, this is a *sales invoice* and Copy 3 of this sales invoice is used to prepare the entry shown at the bottom of page 102. To the buyer, Campbell Sports Ltd., this is a **purchase invoice**. Copies 1 and 2 are records of what Campbell has purchased and indicate how much is owed to the seller.

Source document for a purchase on credit.

When must Campbell Sports pay the $210? What happens if the invoice is not paid on time? The buyer, Campbell Sports, would make this journal entry to record the purchase invoice:

Apr.	1	Office Supplies	210	
		Accounts Payable/Spiral Graphics		210
		Purchased stationery, Invoice 5870		
		net 30 days.		

You can see that the same document is used to record the sale by the seller and the purchase by the customer. As has been stated, the sellers call their document a sales invoice and the buyers call their copy a purchase invoice.

CHEQUES

Cheques Paid

On April 1, Campbell Sports bought $210 worth of office supplies from the Spiral Graphics. The terms of payment were net 30 days. This means that the $210 must be paid within 30 days from the date of the invoice. On April 30, Campbell Sports prepared Cheque 1624 illustrated in Figure 4-25.

The cheque form consists of two parts, the cheque itself and an attached portion, which provides the details to explain why the cheque was written. The original cheque form is sent to Spiral Graphics. The attached portion and/or a photocopy of the cheque is kept by Campbell Sports and is the source document for this transaction. The cheque copy is used by Campbell's accountant to record this entry:

Apr.	30	Accounts Payable/Spiral Graphics	210	
		Cash		210
		Issued Cheque 1624 to pay Invoice 5870.		

FIGURE 4-25

Cheque issued by
Campbell Sports

```
Campbell Sports                                    No. 1624
2579 Base Line Rd.
Ottawa, Ontario  K2H 7B3              April 30, 2007

PAY TO THE
ORDER OF   Spiral Graphics --------------------- $210.00

Two hundred ten---------------------- 00/100 DOLLARS

  CANADA BANK
  2573 Bond St.
  Ottawa, Ontario  K2B 7C3        B. Watson
                                  Campbell Sports

⑂18⁊2 003 2⁊1 428 6
(Detach and retain this statement)
   THE ATTACHED CHEQUE IS IN PAYMENT OF ITEMS LISTED BELOW

DATE      ITEM      AMOUNT      DISCOUNT    NET AMOUNT

April 30  Inv. 5870  $210.00                $210.00

              Copy to Accounting
```

Cheques Received

Cheque 1624 is mailed to Spiral Graphics. When it is received by Spiral Graphics, the cheque is separated from the record portion (bottom half). The cheque is endorsed with a restrictive endorsement ("deposit only to the account of Spiral Graphics") and immediately deposited in the Spiral Graphics' bank account.

An *endorsement* is the signature placed on the back of a cheque by the person or company depositing the cheque. A *restrictive endorsement* is used to control what will happen to the funds from the cheque. The record portion of the cheque is used to prepare the following entry:

May	2	Cash	210	
		Accounts Receivable/Campbell Sports		210
		Received Cheque 1624 for Invoice 5870.		

List of Cheques Received

Companies that receive a large number of cheques each day prepare a list of the cheques. The cheques are then deposited in the bank. The list is used by the accountant to prepare the journal entries to record the money received and to lower the amounts owing on the customer accounts.

FURTHER FACTS ABOUT SOURCE DOCUMENTS

Prenumbered Source Documents

Source documents are prenumbered, and every document must be accounted for. The numbering of documents is a control procedure designed to prevent errors and losses due to theft or the use of false documents. Source documents are kept on file and must be made available to persons who have the authority to check a company's records. These include:

- Owners and managers of the business
- Outside accountants hired to check the records
- Federal income tax personnel
- Provincial sales tax and Ministry of Labour personnel
- Officials of the courts

Source documents are an important part of a company's accounting system. Every business should take care to produce neat, legible documents that are numbered and filed in a well-organized manner.

Source Documents as Evidence for Transactions

Source documents provide evidence that a transaction has actually occurred. If a check is made on a company's accounting records, the company must be able to prove that the transactions did happen. Source documents such as cash sales slips, sales invoices, and purchase invoices provide the necessary proof.

Further checks on the accuracy of a company's records can be made by comparing the source document copies of both the buyer and the seller. The information on the documents should be the same.

The Principle of Objectivity

The dollar values used in transactions should be determined in a very objective way. The source documents provide objective, verifiable evidence to support the value placed on transactions.

A company could overstate the value of its assets by recording them at a high value. This would make the company appear to be more valuable than it really is. To avoid such situations, accountants follow the **principle of objectivity**. The priciple of objectivity requires evidence to support the value used to record transactions.

Dollar values used in recording transactions should be verified by objective evidence such as source documents.

Summary

Remember that, as has already been stated, it is an important principle of accounting that:

> A source document must be prepared for every business transaction.

The following chart summarizes the source documents used in this chapter:

Source Document	Business Transaction
Cash sales slip	Cash sale to a customer
Sales invoice	Sale on account to a customer
Purchase invoice	Purchase on account
Cheque paid	Payment made to a creditor (account payable)
Cheque received	Payment received from a customer (account receivable)

Ⓐ CCOUNTING TERMS

Accounting Cycle	The set of accounting procedures performed in each accounting period. (p. 102)
Balance-Column Form of Account	A form of account that shows a continuous balance after each transaction. (p. 89)
Book of Original Entry	The journal is referred to as the book of original entry. Transactions are recorded in a journal as they occur. (p. 84)
Cash Sales Slip	A source document for a cash sale. (p. 106)
Chart of Accounts	A list of the names and account numbers of all the accounts in the General Ledger. (p. 96)
Compound Entry	An entry that has more than one debit or more than one credit. (p. 85)
General Journal	The main journal of a business. (p. 84)
Journal	A record of transactions recorded in chronological (date) order. (p. 84)
Journal Entry	Each transaction recorded in a journal. (p. 84)
Journalizing	Process of recording transactions in a journal. (p. 84)
Opening Entry	Records the assets, liabilities, and owner's equity when a business first begins operation. (p. 94)
Posting	Transfer of information from a journal to the ledger. (p. 89)
Posting Reference Column	Indicates where more information regarding the entry can be located. (p. 92)
Principle of Objectivity	Dollar values used in recording transactions should be verified by objective evidence such as source documents. (p. 112)
Purchase Invoice	Source document for a purchase on credit. (p. 109)
Sales Invoice	Source document for a sale on credit. (p. 108)

Source Document	A business form that is the original source of information for a transaction. (p. 106)
Transposition Error	Where numbers are reversed, such as writing 63 rather than 36. (p. 100)

UNIT 8

REVIEW QUESTIONS

1. (a) What is a source document?
   (b) Give four examples of source documents.
   (c) Why are source documents prenumbered?
   (d) Name a source document for each of the following:
      (i) Cash sale
      (ii) Sale on account
      (iii) Purchase on account
      (iv) Payment by cheque

2. Explain the concept of objectivity.

UNIT 8

PROBLEMS: APPLICATIONS

1. For the Birchwood Manufacturing Company invoice shown below, answer the following:

   (a) Who is the seller?
   (b) Who is the buyer?
   (c) What is the invoice number? Invoice date? Invoice total?

BIRCHWOOD MANUFACTURING COMPANY
WOODEN THREAD SPOOLS AND WOOD TURNINGS
MANDEVILLE, BERTHIER COUNTY, QUEBEC J0K 1L0

VIA   C.P. EXPRESS

SHIP TO WABASSO LTD.   **INV. NO.** 17429

ADDRESS 2069 LINCOLN ST.
WELLAND, ONTARIO
L3B 4R8

INVOICE DATE	SHIPPING DATE	CUST. ORDER NO.	OUR ORDER NO.	CUST. PROV. SLS. TAX LIC. NO.
Aug. 7, 2007	Aug. 8, 2007	6821	20529	0231

SOLD TO SAME AS SHIP TO

PACKAGES	DESCRIPTION	QUANTITY PER PKG.	QUANTITY TOTAL	PRICE	TOTAL
1	4 cm WOOD SPOOLS	200	200	$0.16	$32
1	2.5 cm WOOD SPOOLS	100	100	0.11	11
	TOTAL				$43

TERMS: NET 30 DAYS F.O.B. OUR MILL.
1 1/2% MONTHLY SERVICE CHARGE ON PAST DUE ACCOUNT.   **INVOICE — SALES**

CHAPTER 4

PROBLEMS: CHALLENGES

1. (a) Using the trial balance on the following page, open the accounts in the ledger for Mike's TV Repairs.

   (b) At the end of each week, Mike Murphy does his accounting from the source documents that he received or issued for that week. Record the source documents for the week ending September 15 in the General Journal. Assign page 39 to the General Journal. The source documents are shown on pages 114 to 117.

		Mike's TV Repairs		
		Trial Balance		
		September 15, 2007		

ACCOUNT TITLE	ACC. NO.	DEBIT	CREDIT
Cash	100	$ 6 800.00	
Accts. Rec./H. Williams	110	647.43	
Accts. Rec./River Road Motor Hotel	111	198.76	
Accts. Rec./E. Schmidt	112	325.50	
Equipment	141	12 900.00	
Truck	142	28 000.00	
Accts. Pay./Electronics Suppliers	200		$ 2 047.50
Accts. Pay./Roger's Service Stn.	201		1 276.89
Bank Loan	221		7 200.00
M. Murphy, Capital	300		38 347.30
Sales Revenue	400		0
Hydro Expense	504	0	
Truck Expense	506	0	
Equipment Repairs Expense	507	0	
		$48 871.69	$48 871.69

Sales Invoices:

INVOICE
Winnipeg Electronics
1750 Elgin Street, Winnipeg, Manitoba   R3E 1C3

DATE: Sept. 15, 2007
INV. NO: 1501
TERMS: Net 30 days

SOLD TO:

H. Williams
141 Dynes Road
Winnipeg, Manitoba   R2J 0Z8

RE: C.R.A. Colour TV

	Labour	$160.00
	Parts	89.85
		$249.85

AMOUNT OF THIS INVOICE: $249.85

INVOICE
Winnipeg Electronics
1750 Elgin Street, Winnipeg, Manitoba   R3E 1C3

DATE: Sept. 15, 2007
INV. NO: 1502
TERMS: Net 30 days

SOLD TO:

River Road Motor Hotel
1460 River Road
Winnipeg, Manitoba   R2M 3Z8

RE: TVs in rooms 117, 119, and 212

	Labour	$356.00
	Parts	137.50
		$493.50

AMOUNT OF THIS INVOICE: $493.50

Purchase Invoices:

ELECTRONICS SUPPLIERS

147 Industrial Blvd., Winnipeg, Manitoba R2W 0J7

Montreal
Toronto
Winnipeg
Vancouver

Tel. 475-6643   Terms: Net 15 days

SOLD TO	SHIP TO
Winnipeg Electronics 1750 Elgin Street Winnipeg, Manitoba R3E 1C3	SAME

Prov. Sales Tax No.	Date Invoiced	Invoice No.
435 70913	09/13/2007	7463

Quantity	Description	Unit Price	Amount
1	Equipment	$453.90	$453.90

Pay this amount <u>$453.90</u>

INVOICE
Gaucher Auto Repair
1553 Park Drive, Winnipeg, Manitoba   R3P 0H2

Date: Sept. 13, 2007   Terms: Net 15 days   Inv. No. B-151

Part No.	Part Name	Total		
X340	Oil filter	$ 19.99	Make:	GMC Truck
	4 L oil	21.50	Licence:	A-4597
316-092	Tire	189.00	Name:	Winnipeg Electronics
			Address:	1750 Elgin Street
				Winnipeg, Manitoba
				R3E 1C3

WORK COMPLETED	AMOUNT
Oil Change	$ 41.49
Tire	<u>$189.00</u>
PAY THIS AMOUNT	<u>$230.49</u>

Cheques Issued:

Winnipeg Electronics	No. 216
1750 Elgin Street	
Winnipeg, Manitoba R3E 1C3	Sept. 15 2007

PAY TO THE
ORDER OF   Electronics Suppliers ----------------------------- $2,047.50

Two thousand and forty-seven-------------------------- 50/**100 DOLLARS**

CIBC
3017 Lelland Road
Winnipeg, Manitoba R2K 0J7   *M. Murphy*

Winnipeg Electronics

⑊⑊⑊⑊⑊⑊ 28629 008 416 285 9

- -

(Detach and retain this statement)

THE ATTACHED CHEQUE IS IN PAYMENT OF ITEMS LISTED BELOW

DATE	ITEM	AMOUNT	DISCOUNT	NET AMOUNT
Aug. 29	Inv. 7393	$2,047.50		$2,047.50

Winnipeg Electronics	No. 217
1750 Elgin Street	
Winnipeg, Manitoba R3E 1C3	Sept. 15 2007

PAY TO THE
ORDER OF   Winnipeg Hydro ------------------------------------ $369.75

Three hundred and sixty-nine ------------------------- 75/**100 DOLLARS**

CIBC
3017 Lelland Road
Winnipeg, Manitoba R2K 0J7   *M. Murphy*

Winnipeg Electronics

28629 008 416 285 9

- -

(Detach and retain this statement)

THE ATTACHED CHEQUE IS IN PAYMENT OF ITEMS LISTED BELOW

DATE	ITEM	AMOUNT	DISCOUNT	NET AMOUNT
Sept. 15	Inv. B-741	$369.75		$369.75

Cash Receipts:

Daily Cash Receipts September 15, 2007		
CUSTOMER	**INVOICE**	**AMOUNT**
E. Schmidt	1370	$ 225.50
River Road Motor Hotel	1269	398.76
Cash sales		2 475.98
		$3 100.24

(c) In the General Journal, record the September 16 source documents listed below.

(d) Post the General Journal to the ledger and prepare a trial balance.

Sep. 16   Sales invoices issued to:
E. Schmidt, No. 1503, $477;
River Road Motor Hotel, No. 1504, $573.60.

Purchase invoice received from:
Electronics Suppliers, No. 7533, $550.80 for servicing the equipment.

Cheques issued to:
Roger's Service Station, No. 218, $740.50 on account;
Electronics Suppliers, No. 219, $625 on account.

Cash received:
H. Williams, $325.40;
River Road Motor Hotel, $450.50;
Cash sales, $1956.79.

2. Following is the May 1 balance sheet for the Mountain Top Inn owned by Giselle Savard.

Mountain Top Inn Balance Sheet May 1, 2008			
Assets		**Liabilities**	
Cash	$ 14 000	Accounts Payable/	
Supplies	1 700	Acme Supply	$ 5 000
Office Equipment	6 800	Bank Loan	20 500
Furniture	63 000	Mortgage Payable	80 000
Automobile	28 000	Total Liabilities	105 500
Building	157 000		
		Owner's Equity	
		G. Savard, Capital	165 000
		Total Liabilities and	
Total Assets	$270 500	Owner's Equity	$270 500

The chart of accounts contains the accounts shown on the balance sheet plus the following:

301	G. Savard, Drawings	502	Salaries Expense
400	Room Rentals	503	Telephone Expense
500	Advertising Expense	505	Utilities Expense
501	General Expense	506	Automobile Expense

(a) Journalize the opening entry.

(b) Journalize the May transactions using account titles found in the balance sheet and in the chart of accounts.

(c) Open the ledger accounts. Assign account numbers using the numbering system shown on p. 96.

(d) Post the opening entry and the May General Journal entries.

(e) Prepare a trial balance.

(f) Prepare the May financial statements.

May 1 Paid $110 for automobile expenses.

2 G. Savard withdrew $240 cash for personal use.

3 Paid $2000 to Acme Supply to reduce the amount owing.

4 Paid $275 for the previous month's telephone charges.

5 Received $3750 for room rentals for the week.

8 Purchased cleaning supplies from Acme Supply, $160, but did not pay for them.

10 Paid $280 for repairs to Savard's personal car.

11 Bought a computer for the office, paid $3000.

12 Received $2100 for room rentals for the week.

12 Paid $42 cash for postage stamps (General Expense).

12 Paid the hydro bill, $290, and the water bill, $175.

15 Paid $245 for the printing of an advertising brochure.

15 Paid $150 for a small advertisement in the local newspaper.

16 Paid $300 to G. Savard, the owner, for her own use.

16 Paid salaries for the first half of the month, $2200.

18 The bank sent a memorandum (letter) informing G. Savard that $350 had been taken out of the business bank account to pay for interest on the bank loan. (Open a new account numbered 507 for Interest Expense.)

19 Received $3250 for room rentals for the week.

22 Received a $450 bill from Acme Supply for new linen and towels.

23 Received an $85 bill from Poirier Motors for gasoline and oil used in the business car. (A new account will have to be opened for Poirier Motors.)

25 Paid $500 to Acme Supply, on account.

26   Received $2525 for room rentals for the week.

31   Paid salaries for the rest of the month, $2850.

31   Sold an old typewriter for $50. The typewriter was included in the Office Equipment account at $200. (You will need to set up a new expense account called Loss on Sale of Equipment.)

31   Paid the telephone charges for the rest of the month, $325.

31   Paid the hydro bill, $405, and the water bill, $295.

31   G. Savard withdrew $360 cash for personal use.

3. Sam Gelicor began a business called Storm Hair Style on May 1, 2008. Several transactions were completed during the month. Sam's knowledge of accounting is very limited, but he knows how to record journal entries and prepare a trial balance. Presented below are the journal entries and the trial balance for the May activities.

May 1	Cash	59 000	
	S. Gelicor, Capital		59 000
2	Rent Expense	2 500	
	Cash		2 500
3	Insurance Expense	550	
	Cash		550
4	Salon Furniture	3 000	
	Salon Equipment	15 000	
	Bank Loan		18 000
4	Salon Supplies	1 700	
	Accounts Payable		1 700
5	Advertising Expense	1 200	
	Cash		1 200
6	Sam officially opened his business		
7	Cash	150	
	Service Revenue		150
8	Accounts Receivable	275	
	Service Revenue		275
9–15	Cash	1 200	
	Accounts Receivable	2 700	
	Service Revenue		3 900
15	Salaries Expense	1 400	
	Cash		1 400
16	Accounts Payable	1 700	
	Cash		1 700
16	Cash	225	
	Service Revenue		225
17	Salon Supplies	1 100	
	Accounts Payable		1 100

19	Cash	275	
	Accounts Receivable		275
19	Accounts Receivable	180	
	Service Revenue		180
20	Advertising Expense	1 500	
	Cash		1 500
23	Cash	1 700	
	Accounts Receivable		1 700
24–31	Cash	2 100	
	Accounts Receivable	3 200	
	Service Revenue		5 300
27	Cash	180	
	Accounts Receivable		180
29	S. Gelicor, Drawings	1 300	
	Cash		1 300
30	Bank Loan	5 000	
	Cash		5 000
31	Salaries Expense	1 600	
	Cash		1 600

Note: Each journal entry would normally include an explanation; these were omitted to conserve space.

Trial Balance Storm Hair Style May 31, 2008		
Cash	$50 280	
Accounts Receivable	4 200	
Salon Supplies		$ 2 800
Salon Furniture	3 000	
Salon Equipment	15 000	
Accounts Payable		1 100
Bank Loan		1 700
S. Gelicor, Capital		59 000
S. Gelicor, Drawings		1 300
Service Revenue		10 030
Rent Expense	2 500	
Insurance Expense	550	
Advertising Expense		2 700
Salaries Expense	2 800	
	$78 330	$78 630

Sam remembers that a trial balance should balance and realizes that the one she prepared must have at least one error.

(a) To help Sam find the mistakes, open a ledger and post the entries to the accounts. Use the following accounts:

100	Cash	300	S. Gelicor, Capital
110	Accounts Receivable	301	S. Gelicor, Drawings
121	Salon Supplies	400	Service Revenue
131	Salon Furniture	500	Rent Expense
141	Salon Equipment	501	Insurance Expense
200	Accounts Payable	502	Advertising Expense
220	Bank Loan	503	Salaries Expense

(b) Prepare a correct trial balance.

4. Robert Chin operates a real estate agency that earns money from three sources:

- Commissions earned on sales of property
- Management fees
- Investment income

The management fees are a result of renting and maintaining homes and condominiums for owners who are not living in them but who lease them to others. For a fee, Chin manages such properties for the owners. The company has invested past net incomes (profits) in shares and bonds. Interest and dividends received on these investments are recorded in the Investment Income account.

(a) Record the April 2008 transactions on page 28 of a General Journal. Use the accounts from the chart of accounts on the next page.

Apr. 1 Received $3400 as a commission for handling the sale of a house.

  1 Paid $2100 for the month's rent for the office.

  3 Received a bill from Bert's Auto for $475 for gas, oil, and repairs to the company automobile. The bill is not to be paid until Apr. 15.

  5 Received a bill for $210 for the printing of letterhead, envelopes, and sales contract forms from The Print Shop. This bill is to be paid on Apr. 15.

  6 Paid $190 cash for a new filing cabinet for the office.

  8 Sold an old filing cabinet to a friend for $20. This cabinet was recorded in the Furniture and Equipment account at the original cost of $175.

  8 Received $8000 commission for a sale of property.

  8 Paid office salaries, $1400.

  11 Paid $290 for newspaper advertising.

  12 Received a $450 fee for renting a home owned by a client.

  13 R. Chin, the owner, withdrew $1200 for personal use.

  14 Received commissions totalling $15 500 from the sale of properties.

14   Paid $275 for telephone bill.

15   Paid Bert's Auto $475 for the invoice received on Apr. 3.

15   Paid The Print Shop $210 for the invoice received on Apr. 5.

15   Paid $150 for the hydro bill.

15   Donated $40 to a charitable organization.

15   Received $90 in dividends from investments owned.

15   Purchased $2800 worth of Government of Canada bonds.

15   Paid office salaries, $1400.

15   Paid $5000 in commissions to R. Chin Agency's salespeople.

100	Cash	401	Management Fees Earned
131	Office Supplies	402	Investment Income
141	Furniture and Equipment	500	Advertising Expense
142	Automobile	501	Automobile Expense
170	Investments	502	Commissions Expense
200	Accounts Payable/	503	Rent Expense
	Bert's Auto Centre	504	Salaries Expense
201	Accounts Payable/	505	Telephone Expense
	The Print Shop Stationery	506	Utilities Expense
300	R. Chin, Capital	507	Miscellaneous Expense
301	R. Chin, Drawings	508	Loss on Sale of Furniture
400	Commissions Income		and Equipment

(b) Open a ledger using the chart of accounts.

(c) Record the April 1 balances that follow in the ledger accounts. (Record the date, and balance, and put a check mark (✔) in the posting reference column.)

Cash	$ 9 500
Office Supplies	1 700
Furniture and Equipment	5 900
Automobile	24 100
Investments	20 000
R. Chin, Capital	61 200

(d) Post the April 1–15 General Journal entries.

(e) Prepare a trial balance.

(f) Prepare an income statement.

(g) R. Chin asks you, his accountant, to devise a statement that would show him the change in his equity for this accounting period. Prepare the statement.

CASE 1
Source Documents

Joan Means is the owner of Barrhaven Enterprises. While glancing through the company's General Ledger, Joan notices a December 12 credit of $398 in the Sales account. Suspecting that the $398 amount should be $39.80, Joan decides to check the original source document to determine the correct amount.

(a) How can Joan trace the entry back to the original source document to check the amount?
(b) What type of source document(s) could have been prepared for the December 12 transaction?
(c) What is the quickest way to locate the source document?

CASE 2
Accrual Method of Accounting

The following data were collected for Fast Cleaners for the month of August.

(a) Payments received on previous accounts receivable, $2400.
(b) Cash received for cleaning services performed this month, $6000.
(c) Cleaning services performed for credit customers this month, $3500.
(d) Payments made on previous accounts payable, $3000.
(e) Expenses of this month paid in cash, $4000.
(f) Expenses incurred this month that remain unpaid at month end, $3200.

Fast Cleaners follows the accrual system of accounting for revenue and expense. State the amount of revenue, expense, and net income for the month of August.

CASE 3
Transposition Errors

You have learned that a transposition of figures is the reversing of the numbers of an amount. For example, $75 written as $57 is a transposition error. A transposition error may be indicated if the difference in a trial balance is exactly divisible by 9. If the difference in the two totals of a trial balance is $81, the difference may have been caused by transposition, since 81 is divisible evenly by 9.

Once a transposition error is suspected, it may be located by the following rule: The number of times the amount of the difference is divisible by 9 is the difference between the two digits transposed.

Suppose the difference is 81. The difference is divisible by 9 (81 divided by 9 is 9). Therefore, the difference between the two numbers transposed is 9. The only two numbers with a difference of 9 are 0 and 9. Therefore, the amounts transposed must have been 90 written as 9, or 9 written as 90. By looking for 9 or 90 on the trial balance, you will locate the error.

Suppose the error is 63. Since 63 divided by 9 is 7, the difference between the transposed number is 7. Therefore, the numbers transposed must be 7 and 0, or 2 and 9, or 8 and 1.

As the accountant for Joanne's Dressmaking Service, you examine four trial balances that have differences as follows:

(i)   Difference of 72
(ii) Difference of 27
(iii) Difference of 36
(iv) Difference of 54

For each of these trial balance differences state:

(a) The amount the difference is divisible by 9.
(b) The combination of numbers that might be transposed.

CASE 4
General Journal Errors

There are several errors in the following General Journal.
(a)   Prepare a list of the errors.
(b)   Prepare a corrected General Journal.

GENERAL JOURNAL					PAGE 3
DATE		PARTICULARS	P.R.	DEBIT	CREDIT
20--					
Oct. 1		Cash		900	
		Sales			900
		Sold services to R. Heino, for cash, Sales Slip 1.			
	3	Supplies		100	
		Cash			100
	3	Advertising Expense			400
		Cash		400	
		Paid cash for a newspaper ad, Cheque 1.			
Oct .		Accounts Receivable		700	
		Sales			700
		Sales invoice 871			
		5 Salaries Expense		900	
		Cash		900	
		Paid secretary's weekly salary, Cheque 2.			

ETHICS CASE
Vendor Relationships

Canada Advanced Communications Ltd. is a very large telecommunications company located in Toronto. Its sales are over $2 billion a year. Anne-Marie Swenson is responsible for purchasing major technology components. In January, one of her senior managers came to her with this situation:

A long-time, reliable supplier, ATM Tech, would like to pick our brains on our technology needs so they can map out the future plans for their products. They are offering an all expense paid trip to California for a representative we send. The Senior Manager involved is asking if it is ethical for us to take them up on this offer.

Swenson responded, "Although we have no problem engaging in discussions on the technology, it should be at our own expense, since ATM Tech is one of our suppliers and it could be deemed that this is a perk provided to us in exchange for future business. You should request that the session be held in Toronto so that there would be no travel involved for our participation, or that we should pay the employee's way to California (out of his budget), so that Canada Advanced Communications is "squeaky-clean."

Swenson mentions that Canada Advanced Communications holds a similar conference each year where customers are invited to see the latest and greatest technology being built in their labs, and meetings are held with them to see how Canada Advanced Communications' solutions might fit into their future networks. Canada Advanced Communications hosts the meals during the conference, but does not pay for the customers' travel to attend.

(a) Should Canada Advanced Communications accept the trip to California?

(b) What are the implications of accepting the offer?

Explore these Web sites for information on accounting software programs.

CHAPTER 4

INTERNET RESOURCES

1. **Small Business Canada**
   http://sbinfocanada.about.com/cs/software/tp/accountsoft.htm

   Information is provided on software programs for use in small business accounting tasks. Included are reports and tools for effectively using financial data. Five accounting packages are described: Simply Accounting, MYOB Plus, Intuit Quickbooks, Peachtree Computer Accounting Software, and AccountEdge.

2. **Business.com   www.business.com/directory/accounting/software**

   This site describes accounting software related to specific accounting topics such as accounts payable and receivable, auditing, bank reconciliation, payroll.

3. **Tax and Accounting Sites   www.taxsites.com/software2.html**

   News and reviews are provided on accounting software for small business. Topics include Web-based products, project accounting, accounting research, and property management.

4. **Journal of Accounting**
   www.aicpa.org/pubs/jofa/sep2003/johnston.htm

   This article by R.P. Johnston delineates a strategy for finding the right accounting software program. Outlined are the steps to take in locating a package that meets specific business needs within a budget.

The Work Sheet and Classified Financial Statements

The Work Sheet

Learning Objectives

After reading this unit, discussing the applicable review questions, and completing the applications exercises, you will be able to do the following:

1. **EXPLAIN** the function of a work sheet.

2. **PREPARE** a work sheet when given a trial balance.

3. **PREPARE** an income statement and a balance sheet from a work sheet.

Figure 5-1, on the next page, illustrates the steps in the accounting cycle as they have been described up to this point. The end of the fiscal period is a particularly important time for accountants because they do a great deal of work at that time. They must prove the mathematical accuracy of the ledger by preparing a trial balance; then they prepare the income statement and the balance sheet. As an aid in avoiding errors and to help organize their work, accountants use a device called a work sheet.

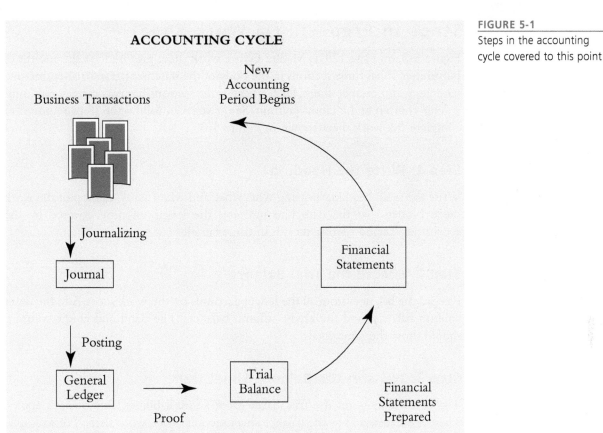

ACCOUNTING CYCLE

FIGURE 5-1

Steps in the accounting cycle covered to this point

INTRODUCING THE WORK SHEET

A **work sheet** is a device that organizes accounting data required for the preparation of financial statements. It is one of the few forms that may be completed in pencil since it is not part of permanent accounting records. It is designed to discover and to eliminate errors before they become part of permanent records. The work sheet represents a rough draft of the work completed at the end of the accounting cycle and is sometimes called the accountant's working papers. It is not a formal statement provided for management, for the owners, or for persons interested in the financial position of the business.

Figure 5-2, below, illustrates the basic principles of the six-column work sheet. All the account balances are taken from the ledger and written on the work sheet in the trial balance section. The account balances are then transferred to either the income statement section or the balance sheet section of the work sheet.

A work sheet is a device that organizes accounting data required for the preparation of financial statements.

FIGURE 5-2

Basic principles of the six-column work sheet

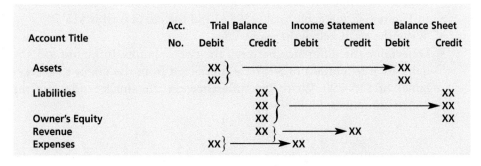

Account Title	Acc. No.	Trial Balance Debit	Trial Balance Credit	Income Statement Debit	Income Statement Credit	Balance Sheet Debit	Balance Sheet Credit
Assets		XX XX				XX XX	
Liabilities			XX XX				XX XX
Owner's Equity			XX				XX
Revenue			XX		XX		
Expenses		XX		XX			

Steps in Preparing a Work Sheet

Figure 5-3, on page 129, is Malibu Gym's work sheet prepared for the month of November. It has three sections in the body of the statement: trial balance, income statement, and balance sheet. Each of the three sections has two money columns: a debit column and a credit column. See if you can follow the steps required to complete the work sheet shown in Figure 5-3.

Step 1: Write the Heading

Write the main heading showing who, what, and when across the top of the work sheet. Notice that the date line indicates the length of time covered by the accounting period — one month in this example.

Step 2: Record the Trial Balance

Record the balances from all the ledger accounts on the work sheet. Add the debit column balances and the credit column balances. The debit and credit columns should show the same totals.

Step 3: Transfer the Balance Sheet Items

The first accounts on the trial balance are assets, liabilities, and owner's equity. These are transferred to the balance sheet section of the work sheet. For example, the Cash debit of $7650 is extended to the debit column of the balance sheet section since Cash is an asset. Extend the remaining assets, the liabilities, and equity accounts to the appropriate debit or credit column of the balance sheet section.

Step 4: Transfer the Income Statement Items

The revenue and expense accounts on the trial balance are now transferred. The Members' Fees account is a revenue account with a credit balance of $14 600. This amount is transferred to the credit column of the income statement section. The remaining revenue and expense accounts are transferred to the income statement section. The expense accounts have debit balances and are transferred to the debit column.

Step 5: Complete the Income Statement Section

The net income or net loss is now determined by doing the following:

- Rule a single line and add the income statement debit and credit columns.
- In Figure 5-3, the debit total is $9570 and the credit total is $15 790.
- Write the totals below the single line.
- Determine the difference between the two columns. In Figure 5-3, the debit total (expenses) of $9570 is subtracted from the credit total (revenue) of $15 790. Write the difference on the smaller side (see the $6220 amount in Figure 5-3).

FIGURE 5-3
Steps in preparing a work sheet

Malibu Gym
Work Sheet
For the month ended November 30, 2008

Step	ACCOUNT TITLE	ACC. NO.	TRIAL BALANCE DEBIT	TRIAL BALANCE CREDIT	INCOME STATEMENT DEBIT	INCOME STATEMENT CREDIT	BALANCE SHEET DEBIT	BALANCE SHEET CREDIT
Step 1: Write the heading								
Step 2: Record the trial balance	Cash	100	7 650				7 650	
	Accounts Receivable	101	2 200				2 200	
	Office Supplies	110	695				695	
Step 3: Transfer the balance sheet items	Land	120	35 000				35 000	
	Building	121	110 000				110 000	
	Training Equipment	122	102 735				102 735	
	Accounts Payable	200		5 150				5 150
	Bank Loan	221		63 000				63 000
	Mortgage Payable	231		80 000				80 000
	T. Montana, Capital	300		106 310				106 310
Step 4: Transfer the income statement items	T. Montana, Drawings	301	2 400				2 400	
	Members' Fees	400		14 600		14 600		
	Tanning Bed Rental	401		725		725		
	Towel Rental	402		465		465		
Step 5: Complete the income statement section	Salaries Expense	500	3 850		3 850			
	Advertising Expense	501	2 880		2 880			
	Telephone Expense	502	190		190			
	Maintenance Expense	503	650		650			
	Licence Expense	504	1 100		1 100			
	Interest Expense	505	500		500			
	Laundry Expense	506	400		400			
			270 250	270 250	9 570	15 790	260 680	254 460
Step 6: Complete the balance sheet section	Net Income				6 220			6 220
Step 7: Rule the work sheet					15 790	15 790	260 680	260 680

In Figure 5-3, is there a net income or a net loss? If the credit column exceeds the debit column, a net income has been made during the accounting period. The amount of this net income is entered below the total of the debit column, so that when these two amounts are added, the two columns are equal. "Net Income" is written in the account titles section opposite the amount of the net income. If the debit column exceeds the credit column, a net loss has occurred. The difference between the two columns is written in the credit column opposite the words "Net Loss."

Step 6: Complete the Balance Sheet Section

Net income increases owner's equity.

Net loss decreases owner's equity.

Rule a single line and total the columns in the balance sheet section. Enter the *net income* amount below the total of the *credit* column of the balance sheet section. The *net income* represents the increase in the owner's equity for the period. If there has been a net loss, enter the amount of the *loss* below the *debit* column total. If the amount of the net income or net loss added to the appropriate column total makes the two final column totals equal in the balance sheet section, the work sheet is mathematically correct.

Step 7: Rule the Work Sheet

Rule double lines below the final column totals to indicate completion and proof that the work is mathematically correct.

Recording a Net Loss on a Work Sheet

Figure 5-4, below, illustrates a work sheet that has a net loss. (Only part of the work sheet is shown.) Following is a description of how a loss is handled:

- Obtain the amount of the loss by subtracting the smaller total, revenue ($84 000), from the larger, expenses ($97 000). The difference, or net loss ($13 000), is written under the credit (revenue) total.
- Write "Net Loss" in the account title section on the same line as the loss ($13 000).
- Enter the loss in the balance sheet section column.
- Rule double lines.

FIGURE 5-4

Recording a net loss on a work sheet

		Brulé Services Work Sheet For the Month Ended July 31, 2008					
		TRIAL BALANCE		**INCOME STATEMENT**		**BALANCE SHEET**	
ACCOUNT TITLE	**ACC. NO.**	**DEBIT**	**CREDIT**	**DEBIT**	**CREDIT**	**DEBIT**	**CREDIT**
Cash	100	5 000				5 000	
Accounts Receivable	101	7 200				7 200	
Owner, Capital	300		184 000				184 000
Maintenance Expense	510	2 000		2 000			
		246 000	246 000	97 000	84 000	171 000	184 000
Net Loss					13 000	13 000	
				97 000	97 000	184 000	184 000

USING THE WORK SHEET

When the work sheet is complete, it contains, in an organized, systematic, and convenient form, all the information that the accountant needs to prepare formal financial statements.

Preparing the Income Statement

The information from the income statement section of the work sheet is used to prepare the formal income statement. When the credit column of this section shows a greater total than the debit column, the amount of the difference is the *net income*. When the debit column exceeds the credit column, the difference is called *net loss*. When the formal income statement is complete, the conclusion (net income or net loss) should be the same as the matching conclusion on the work sheet.

The *income statement* shows the operating results for a business over a period of time. Figure 5-5, below, is the income statement of Malibu Gym for the month of November. Notice that the heading clearly shows the period of time covered by the statement.

The information for the body of the income statement is taken from the income statement section of the work sheet. The *revenue* information is found in the credit column of that section. The *expense* data are found in the debit column. The net income of $6220 appears on both the work sheet (Figure 5-3) and the income statement (Figure 5-5).

FIGURE 5-5

Income Statement

Malibu Gym Income Statement For the Month Ended November 30, 2008		
Revenue		
Members' Fees	$14 600	
Tanning Bed Rental	725	
Towel Rental	465	$15 790
Expenses		
Salaries Expense	3 850	
Advertising Expense	2 880	
Telephone Expense	190	
Maintenance Expense	650	
Licence Expense	1 100	
Interest Expense	500	
Laundry Expense	400	9 570
Net Income		$ 6 220

Preparing the Balance Sheet

A *balance sheet* presents the financial position of a business at a specific date. Figure 5-6 is the balance sheet of Malibu Gym prepared on November 30. It shows the assets, liabilities, and owner's equity at that specific date.

Just as the information for the income statement originated in the work sheet, so does the information for the balance sheet. Notice that in Figure 5-6 all the data used on the balance sheet came from the balance sheet section of the work sheet. Notice also that the net income of $6220 increases the Capital in the owner's equity section of the balance sheet. The balance sheet in Figure 5-6 has been prepared in the report form.

FIGURE 5-6
Balance Sheet

Malibu Gym
Balance Sheet
November 30, 2008

Assets
Cash	$ 7 650	
Accounts Receivable	2 200	
Office Supplies	695	
Land	35 000	
Building	110 000	
Training Equipment	102 735	
Total Assets		$258 280

Liabilities and Owner's Equity

Liabilities
Accounts Payable	$ 5 150	
Bank Loan	63 000	
Mortgage Payable	80 000	
Total Liabilities		$148 150

Owner's Equity
T. Montana, Capital November 1		106 310	
Add: Net Income for November	$6 220		
Less: T. Montana, Drawings	2 400		
Increase in Capital		3 820	
T. Montana, Capital November 30			110 130
Total Liabilities and Owner's Equity			$258 280

UNIT 9

REVIEW QUESTIONS

1. What is a work sheet?

2. What three items of information are included in the work sheet heading?

3. What fiscal period (accounting period) is covered by the November work sheet for Malibu Gym, Figure 5-3?

4. What are the three major sections in the body of a work sheet?

5. Which accounts from the trial balance are extended to the balance sheet section of the work sheet?

6. Which accounts from the trial balance are extended to the income statement section of the work sheet?

7. When the debit column total of the income statement section of the work sheet is greater than the credit column total, what is the difference called?

8. When the credit column total of the income statement section is greater than the debit column total, what is the difference called?

9. When is a work sheet considered to be mathematically correct?

10. Why is the net income from the income statement section of the work sheet transferred to the credit column of the balance sheet section of the work sheet?

11. What is the difference between the report form and the account form of the balance sheet?

12. Prepare a diagram illustrating the steps in the accounting cycle.

---

1. Following is a list of account titles. Prepare a form like the one in the example and indicate on which statement section and in which column of the work sheet each account would appear. The first one, Cash, is done for you.

UNIT 9

PROBLEMS: APPLICATIONS

ACCOUNT TITLE	INCOME STATEMENT		BALANCE SHEET	
	DEBIT	CREDIT	DEBIT	CREDIT
Cash			✓	
Supplies				
Rent Expense				
M. Sharif, Capital				
Office Equipment				
Accounts Payable				
Advertising Expense				
Light, Heat, Water Expenses				
Bank Loan				
Sales Revenue				
Accounts Receivable				
Investment Income				
Land				
M. Sharif, Drawings				
Loss on Sale of Equipment				

2. Prepare a work sheet for the month of July from the following trial balance:

J. Reid Trial Balance July 31, 2009			
ACCOUNT TITLE	ACC. NO.	DEBIT	CREDIT
Cash		$13 000	
Accounts Receivable		14 300	
Equipment		23 900	
Accounts Payable			$12 500
J. Reid, Capital			33 000
Sales Revenue			20 750
Salaries Expense		13 250	
General Expense		800	
Advertising Expense		1 000	
		$66 250	$66 250

3. Prepare a work sheet for the month of May from the following trial balance:

ACCOUNT TITLE	ACC. NO.	DEBIT	CREDIT
J. Williams			
Trial Balance			
May 31, 2009			
Cash		$15 100	
Accounts Receivable		8 000	
Equipment		36 500	
Accounts Payable			$13 700
J. Williams, Capital			36 175
Sales Revenue			18 250
Salaries Expense		5 900	
General Expense		1 125	
Advertising Expense		1 500	
		$68 125	$68 125

4. Prepare a work sheet for the month of March from the trial balance that follows:

ACCOUNT TITLE	ACC. NO.	DEBIT	CREDIT
L. Rabak			
Trial Balance			
March 31, 2008			
Cash		$ 8 600	
Accounts Receivable		3 100	
Supplies		1 150	
Equipment		18 000	
Delivery Truck		78 000	
Accounts Payable			$ 2 250
Loan Payable			17 000
L. Rabak, Capital			69 500
L. Rabak, Drawings		13 000	
Sales Revenue			51 200
Salaries Expense		8 300	
Rent Expense		4 200	
Miscellaneous Expense		1 800	
Office Expense		2 550	
Telephone Expense		1 250	
		$139 950	$139 950

5. Prepare a work sheet for the month of June from the trial balance that follows:

ACCOUNT TITLE	ACC. NO.	DEBIT	CREDIT
M. Ali Enterprises			
Trial Balance			
June 30, 2007			
Cash		$ 10 200	
Accounts Receivable		4 350	
Supplies		1 160	
Building		105 000	
Equipment		31 700	
Accounts Payable			$ 2 500
Bank Loan			21 000
Mortgage Payable			57 000
M. Ali, Capital			76 795
M. Ali, Drawings		3 900	
Sales Revenue			16 870
Salaries Expense		9 900	
Miscellaneous Expense		2 500	
Office Expense		3 420	
Telephone Expense		435	
Advertising Expense		1 600	
		$174 165	$174 165

UNIT 10 Classified Financial Statements

Learning Objectives

After reading this unit, discussing the applicable review questions, and completing the applications exercises, you will be able to do the following:

1. **PREPARE** a classified balance sheet.

2. **DEFINE** current and capital assets and current and long-term liabilities.

3. **PREPARE** supporting schedules for financial statements.

The purpose of financial statements is to provide financial information about a company to owners, management, creditors, and government. By classifying items on the statements into special categories, it is possible to provide more information and to provide it in a way that is more easily interpreted.

CLASSIFIED BALANCE SHEET

Items on the balance sheet are placed in categories to provide additional information to statement users.

In Figure 5-7, balance sheet information from the previous unit is presented in **classified balance sheet** format to answer the following questions:

- Which debts must be paid within a year?
- Is there sufficient cash (or assets) on hand to pay debts?
- Which debts must be paid in future years?

Look at Figure 5-7 and answer the preceding questions.

FIGURE 5-7

Balance Sheet

Malibu Gym Balance Sheet November 30, 2008		
Assets		
Current Assets		
Cash	$ 7 650	
Accounts Receivable	2 200	
Office Supplies	695	
Total Current Assets		$ 10 545
Capital Assets		
Land	35 000	
Building	110 000	
Training Equipment	102 735	
Total Capital Assets		247 735
Total Assets		$258 280
Liabilities and Owner's Equity		
Current Liabilities		
Accounts Payable		$ 5 150
Long-Term Liabilities		
Bank Loan	$ 63 000	
Mortgage Payable	80 000	
Total Long-Term Liabilities		143 000
Total Liabilities		148 150
Owner's Equity		
T. Montana, Capital November 1	106 310	
Add: Net Income for November	$6 220	
Less: T. Montana, Drawings	2 400	
Increase in Capital	3 820	
T. Montana, Capital November 30		110 130
Total Liabilities and Owner's Equity		$258 280

Assets and Liabilities

The balance sheet of Malibu Gym illustrated in Figure 5-7 includes the standard classifications usually found on balance sheets. The assets are divided into two main groups: *current* and *capital*. The liabilities are divided into two groups: *current* and *long-term*.

Current Assets

Assets that are converted into cash in the ordinary course of business, usually within one year, are called **current assets**. The list that follows provides some examples and the order in which current assets usually appear. They are listed in *order of liquidity*, that is, the order in which these assets may be converted into cash.

> Current assets are assets that are/could be converted to cash within one year.
>
> Current assets are listed in order of liquidity.
>
> Liquidity order is the order in which assets may be converted into cash.

CURRENT ASSETS
Cash
Short-Term Investments
Accounts Receivable
Merchandise Inventory
Prepaid Expenses

Short-term investments, such as Canadian government treasury bills, money market funds or term deposits, are easily converted into cash. For that reason, they are placed immediately after Cash in the current assets section of the classified balance sheet. Accounts Receivable, debts that most customers pay within 30 days, come next.

Merchandise Inventory is an asset account used to record the value of merchandise on hand for sale to customers. When the merchandise is sold, cash will be eventually received for it. For that reason, Merchandise Inventory is listed after Accounts Receivable.

> The Merchandise Inventory account records the value of merchandise on hand for sale to customers.

Prepaid Expenses are items such as Prepaid Rent and Prepaid Insurance. They represent the value of insurance policies owned by the company and rental leases for which payment has been made in advance. Although they are not generally converted into cash in the normal operations of the business, they could be if necessary. For example, many insurance policies have a cash value equal to the value of the unused portion. A company in need of cash could "cash-in" an insurance policy. Prepaid Expenses are listed after Cash, Short-term Investments, Accounts Receivable, and Merchandise Inventory on the balance sheet.

> Prepaid expenses are expense payments made in advance.

Capital Assets

Capital assets are assets such as land, buildings, equipment, and trucks that are used in operating the business to generate revenue and that have a long life. The capital assets that have the longest life are generally listed first.

> Capital assets are assets that have a long life and contribute to the business for more than one year. These may be tangible or intangible in nature.
>
> Capital assets may be tangible or intangible in nature.

CAPITAL ASSETS
Land
Building
Equipment
Delivery Trucks

The above are tangible capital assets. Intangible capital assets do not possess a physical substance. Examples are trademarks, patents and copyrights. These assets are also held to produce revenue. Capital assets are recorded using the price at which they were purchased (cost principle). This is a standard principle used by all accountants.

Current Liabilities

Current liabilities are liabilities due to be paid within a year.

The term **current liabilities** generally refers to liabilities that must be paid within a year or less. If possible, current liabilities are listed in the order that they are to be paid.

CURRENT LIABILITIES

Salaries Owing
Accounts Payable
Taxes Payable
Loans Payable

Long-Term Liabilities

Long-term liabilities are liabilities that are not due to be paid for at least a year.

Long-term liabilities are liabilities that are not due to be paid for at least a year. A loan payable in two years and a mortgage payable in 25 years are examples of long-term liabilities.

Owner's Equity Section of the Balance Sheet

The owner's equity in a business increases when the business operates profitably. Owner's equity decreases when there has been a net loss or when the owner withdraws assets from the business.

The owner's equity section of the balance sheet in Figure 5-7 is an example of equity increasing as a result of Malibu Gym earning a net income that is greater than the owner's withdrawals from the business. Figure 5-8, below, shows how the equity section of a balance sheet is set up to record a net loss.

It is possible for a business to earn a net income yet still have a decrease in owner's equity. This happens when the withdrawals by the owner are greater than the net income. Figure 5-9 illustrates the set-up of the equity section when withdrawals are greater than net income.

FIGURE 5-8

Net loss

OWNER'S EQUITY			
T. Montana, Capital November 1		$106 310	
Less: Net Loss for November	$1 200		
Less: T. Montana, Drawings	1 800		
Decrease in Capital		3 000	
T. Montana, Capital November 30			$103 310

FIGURE 5-9

Withdrawals greater than net income

OWNER'S EQUITY			
T. Montana, Capital November 1		$106 310	
Add: Net Income for November	$1 000		
Less: T. Montana, Drawings	1 800		
Decrease in Capital		800	
T. Montana, Capital November 30			$105 510

SUPPORTING STATEMENTS AND SCHEDULES

In addition to the basic income statement and balance sheet, a number of additional statements or schedules may be used to provide financial information.

Statement of Owner's Equity

The **statement of owner's equity** is an example of a *supporting statement*. This statement provides the owner of the business with the data regarding the change in value of owner's equity for an accounting period. It is prepared separately from the balance sheet. The owner's equity balance at the end of the period is shown on the balance sheet instead of the full calculation. Figure 5-10 illustrates a statement of owner's equity.

The statement of owner's equity describes the changes in owner's equity for the accounting period.

Malibu Gym		
Statement of Owner's Equity		
For the Month Ended November 30, 2008		
T. Montana, Capital November 1		$106 310
Add: Net Income for November	$6 220	
Less: T. Montana, Drawings	2 400	
Increase in Capital		3 820
T. Montana, Capital November 30		$110 130

FIGURE 5-10
Statement of Owner's Equity

The balance sheet for Malibu Gym in Figure 5-7 could have been presented with the separate statement of owner's equity shown in Figure 5-10. In such a case, the final balance of the Montana, Capital account, $110 130, would be shown on the balance sheet in place of the complete equity calculation. This is illustrated in the balance sheet in Figure 5-11 on the following page.

Schedule of Accounts Receivable

Supporting schedules are used to provide details about an item on a main statement. An example of a supporting schedule is the **schedule of accounts receivable**, shown in Figure 5-12 on page 140. It provides a list of the individual accounts receivable and the amounts owed. This provides the details regarding the Accounts Receivable total on the balance sheet. In Figure 5-11, the Accounts Receivable total on the balance sheet is $2200. Further information about the amount owed by each customer is found on the schedule in Figure 5-12. Notice that the total of the schedule, $2200, is the same as the Accounts Receivable total on the balance sheet (Figure 5-11).

A supporting schedule provides details about an item on a main statement.

A schedule of accounts receivable provides list of individual accounts receivable and amounts owed to provide details regarding the accounts receivable total on the balance sheet.

Supporting schedules and statements may be prepared whenever the accountant feels they would provide additional useful information for the readers of the financial statements.

FIGURE 5-11
Balance Sheet

Malibu Gym
Balance Sheet
November 30, 2008

Assets

Current Assets

Cash	$ 7 650	
Accounts Receivable	2 200	
Office Supplies	695	
Total Current Assets		$ 10 545

Capital Assets

Land	35 000	
Building	110 000	
Training Equipment	102 735	
Total Capital Assets		247 735
Total Assets		$258 280

Liabilities and Owner's Equity

Current Liabilities

Accounts Payable		$ 5 150

Long-Term Liabilities

Bank Loan	$ 63 000	
Mortgage Payable	80 000	
Total Long-Term Liabilities		143 000
Total Liabilities		$148 150

Owner's Equity

T. Montana, Capital November 30		110 130
Total Liabilities and Owner's Equity		$258 280

FIGURE 5-12
Schedule of Accounts
Receivable   .

Malibu Gym
Schedule of Accounts Receivable
November 30, 2008

B. Adams	$ 250
C. Bartoshewski	150
L. Grace	200
W. Lane	100
D. McIssac	200
K. Owen	100
R. Poirier	200
G. Singh	250
B. Taylor	150
H. Vanede	300
K. Wier	100
A. Wong	200
Total Accounts Receivable	$2 200

ACCOUNTING TERMS

Capital Assets	Assets that have a long life and contribute to the business for more than one year. These may be tangible or intangible in nature. (p. 137)
Classified Balance Sheet	Items on the balance sheet are placed in categories to provide additional information to statement users. (p. 136)
Current Assets	Assets that are/could be converted to cash within one year. (p. 137)
Current Liabilities	Liabilities due to be paid within one year. (p. 138)
Long-Term Liabilities	Liabilities not due to be paid for at least a year. (p. 138)
Schedule of Accounts Receivable	A list of individual accounts receivable and amounts owed to provide details regarding the accounts receivable total on the balance sheet. (p. 139)
Statement of Owner's Equity	Provides information regarding the change in value of the owner's equity for an accounting period. (p. 139)
Supporting Schedule	Provides details about an item on a main statement. (p. 139)
Work Sheet	A device that organizes accounting data required for the preparation of financial statements. (p. 127)

UNIT 10

REVIEW QUESTIONS

1. What is a classified financial statement?

2. Explain the following terms:

   (a) Current asset
   (b) Capital asset
   (c) Liquidity order
   (d) Current liability
   (e) Long-term liability

3. Explain the cost principle as it is applied to capital assets on the balance sheet.

4. What effect does a withdrawal of assets from the business by the owner have on owner's equity?

5. (a) What effect does a net loss have on the owner's equity?
   (b) What effect does a net income have on the owner's equity?

UNIT 10

PROBLEMS: APPLICATIONS

1. Classify each of the following as a current asset, capital asset, current liability, or long-term liability:

   (a) Accounts Receivable
   (b) Land
   (c) Bank Loan (6 months)
   (d) Office Supplies
   (e) Delivery Truck
   (f) Prepaid Rent
   (g) Automobile
   (h) Mortgage Payable
   (i) Taxes Owing
   (j) Government Bonds
   (k) Accounts Payable
   (l) Patent

2. The completed work sheet for the month of April for J. Ling, a lawyer, is shown below. Prepare the income statement and classified balance sheet.

ACCOUNT TITLE	ACC. NO.	TRIAL BALANCE DEBIT	TRIAL BALANCE CREDIT	INCOME STATEMENT DEBIT	INCOME STATEMENT CREDIT	BALANCE SHEET DEBIT	BALANCE SHEET CREDIT

J. Ling
Work Sheet
For the Month Ended April 30, 2009

ACCOUNT TITLE	ACC. NO.	TRIAL BALANCE DEBIT	CREDIT	INCOME STATEMENT DEBIT	CREDIT	BALANCE SHEET DEBIT	CREDIT
Cash		4 000				4 000	
Accounts Receivable		1 200				1 200	
Office Equipment		6 000				6 000	
Automobile		35 000				35 000	
Willson Supply Ltd.			400				400
J. Ling, Capital			39 900				39 900
Fees Income			11 200		11 200		
Automobile Expense		100		100			
Rent Expense		2 800		2 800			
Salaries Expense		1 900		1 900			
General Expense		500		500			
		51 500	51 500	5 300	11 200	46 200	40 300
Net Income				5 900			5 900
				11 200	11 200	46 200	46 200

3. Trial balance figures for July and August for a business owned by D. Howes are shown on page 143.

(a) Prepare a work sheet, an income statement, a statement of owner's equity, and a balance sheet for July.

(b) Prepare a work sheet and financial statements for August (including a statement of owner's equity).

4. (a) Using the trial balance at the bottom of page 143, prepare a work sheet for the three months ended September 30, 2008, for the Rolling Hills Golf Club.

(b) Prepare an income statement, a statement of owner's equity, and a classified balance sheet.

	JULY		AUGUST	
Cash	$5 000		$4 000	
Accounts Receivable	7 000		6 000	
Prepaid Insurance	800		600	
Land	30 000		30 000	
Building	90 000		90 000	
Furniture	5 000		5 000	
Accounts Payable		$4 000		$ 3 000
Taxes Owing		2 000		2 000
Bank Loan (2-year)		15 000		14 000
Mortgage Payable		40 000		38 000
D. Howes, Capital		75 000		76 800
D. Howes, Drawings	4 500		6 500	
Sales Revenue		22 000		26 100
Salaries Expense	12 000		14 000	
Delivery Expense	1 200		900	
Utilities Expense	700		700	
Advertising Expense	1 100		1 400	
Miscellaneous Expense	300		200	
Insurance Expense	400		600	
	$158 000	$158 000	$159 900	$159 900

Rolling Hills Golf Club Trial Balance September 30, 2008			
ACCOUNT TITLE	**ACC. NO.**	**DEBIT**	**CREDIT**
Cash		$ 4 000	
Supplies		7 500	
Land		200 000	
Equipment		47 000	
Accounts Payable			$ 2 000
Bank Loan			92 000
G. Liley, Capital			110 000
G. Liley, Drawings		6 000	
Membership Fees			123 400
Salaries Expense		50 000	
Maintenance Expense		3 900	
Utilities Expense		7 000	
Office Expense		2 000	
		$327 400	$327 400

1. Below is the December 31 trial balance for the Rolling Hills Golf Club.
   (a) Prepare a work sheet for the three months ended December 31, 2008.
   (b) Prepare an income statement.
   (c) Why do you think the operating results for this three-month period are different from the three-month period in exercise 4 on page 142?

ACCOUNT TITLE	ACC. NO.	DEBIT	CREDIT
Rolling Hills Golf Club			
Trial Balance			
December 31, 2008			
Cash		$ 2 700	
Supplies		3 400	
Land		200 000	
Equipment		59 000	
Accounts Payable			$ 750
Bank Loan			90 000
G. Liley, Capital			164 500
G. Liley, Drawings		6 000	
Membership Fees			38 200
Salaries Expense		12 000	
Maintenance Expense		6 000	
Insurance Expense		1 850	
Utilities Expense		2 000	
Office Expense		500	
		$293 450	$293 450

2. A work sheet for the Cheung Law Firm is presented on page 145. Certain amounts are missing or misplaced. Determine the amounts that should be entered into these spaces.

3. Trial balance figures for February for a business owned by T. Hood are shown on page 145.
   (a) Prepare a work sheet, an income statement, a statement of owner's equity, and a balance sheet for February.

Cheung Law Firm Work Sheet For the Year Ended December 31, 2009						
ACCOUNT	TRIAL BALANCE		INCOME STATEMENT		BALANCE SHEET	
TITLE	DEBIT	CREDIT	DEBIT	CREDIT	DEBIT	CREDIT
Cash					7 500	
Fees Receivable					5 000	
Office Supplies	1 400					
Office Furniture	7 000					
Office Equipment					11 000	
Land	40 000					
Building					145 000	
Accounts Payable						2 300
Taxes Owing		3 500				
Bank Loan		11 500				
Mortgage Payable						110 000
C. Cheung, Capital		87 000				
C. Cheung, Drawings					18 000	
Fees Income				78 900		
Salaries Expense	42 000					
Advertising Expense			7 200			
Telephone Expense	2 800					
Utilities Expense	1 300					
Insurance Expense		3 600				
Miscellaneous Expense		1 400				
		293 200		78 900		214 300
Net						

T. Hood Trial Balance February 28, 20--			
ACCOUNT TITLE	ACC. NO.	DEBIT	CREDIT
Cash		$ 3 000	
Accounts Receivable		7 000	
Prepaid Insurance		800	
Land		30 000	
Building		90 000	
Furniture		5 000	
Accounts Payable			$ 4 000
Taxes Owing			1 000
Bank Loan (2 year)			15 000
Mortgage Payable			40 000
T. Hood, Capital			72 100
T. Hood, Drawings		1 000	
Sales			20 000
Salaries Expense		12 000	
Delivery Expense		1 200	
Utilities Expense		700	
Advertising Expense		900	
Miscellaneous Expense		300	
Insurance Expense		200	
		$152 100	$152 100

CHAPTER 5

CASE STUDIES

CASE 1
Comparative Balance Sheets

The July 31 and November 30 balance sheets for Arnold's Sports Club (owned by T. Altman) are shown below and on the following page. Compare the two balance sheets and answer these questions. Give reasons for all of your answers.

(a) Has the financial position of the business improved, weakened, or stayed approximately the same during the first few months of operation?
(b) What additional information would you want to see to determine whether or not Altman has been successful in this venture up to now?
(c) Does the current balance sheet indicate any potential problems for Altman?
(d) Why has the value of the mortgage stayed approximately the same even though Altman has made regular monthly payments?

	Arnold's Sports Club Balance Sheet July 31, 20--	
Assets		
Current Assets		
Cash	$ 5 000	
Accounts Receivable	6 000	
Office Supplies	500	
Total Current Assets		$ 11 500
Capital Assets		
Land	25 000	
Building	110 000	
Training Equipment	94 500	
Total Capital Assets		229 500
Total Assets		$241 000
Liabilities and Owner's Equity		
Current Liabilities		
Accounts Payable		$ 4 000
Long-Term Liabilities		
Bank Loan	$ 65 000	
Mortgage Payable	80 000	
Total Long-Term Liabilities		145 000
Total Liabilities		149 000
Owner's Equity		
T. Altman, Capital July 1		92 000
Total Liabilities and Owner's Equity		$241 000

CASE 1 CONTINUED

Arnold's Sports Club
Balance Sheet
November 30, 20--

Assets

Current Assets

Cash	$ 7 800	
Accounts Receivable	7 510	
Office Supplies	695	
Total Current Assets		$ 16 005

Capital Assets

Land	25 000	
Building	110 000	
Training Equipment	94 325	
Total Capital Assets		229 325
Total Assets		$245 330

Liabilities and Owner's Equity

Current Liabilities

Accounts Payable		$ 9 380

Long-Term Liabilities

Bank Loan	$ 63 000	
Mortgage Payable	80 000	
Total Long-Term Liabilities		143 000
Total Liabilities		152 380

Owner's Equity

T. Altman, Capital November 1		92 000	
Add: Net Income for November	$2 450		
Less: T. Altman, Drawings	1 500		
Increase in Capital		950	
T. Altman, Capital November 30			92 950
Total Liabilities and Owner's Equity			$245 330

CASE 2

Financial Condition

Following are the current assets and current liabilities of a business:

Current Assets		Current Liabilities	
Cash	$2 500	Accounts Payable	$5 000
Accounts Receivable	4 000	Taxes Payable	1 700
Supplies	1 500	Salaries Payable	4 000
	$8 000		$10 700

(a) How would you describe the financial condition of this business?
(b) What advice might you give management of the business?
(c) The owner of this business applied to you for a short-term loan, explaining that the business makes a profit of $2000 per month and therefore would have enough cash to pay loan payments. In your opinion, would this business be a good risk for a short-term loan?

CASE 3

Income Tax

B. Joanisse owns the Hillside Distributing Company. The company is organized as a sole proprietorship; that is, it is owned by one person, B. Joanisse. Hillside Distributing is very successful and Joanisse receives a monthly salary of $4000 for managing the business. For the last fiscal year, the company's operating results were:

Revenue	−	Expenses	=	Net Income
$370 000	−	$340 000	=	$30 000

Included in the expense total is $48 000 paid to Joanisse as a salary for managing the business. Joanisse feels justified in paying personal income tax only on this income or salary of $48 000.

Read the following income tax and accounting principles and then answer the questions.

1. A sole proprietorship does not pay income tax on its net income. However, the net income is considered to be the income of the owner.
2. For tax purposes, a proprietorship must record salary payments to its owner in the owner's Drawings account.

(a) Applying the preceding principles correctly, complete this equation:

Revenue	−	Expenses	=	Net Income
$370 000	−	?	=	?

(b) For personal income tax purposes, what is Joanisse's income for the year?
(c) In the company ledger, what is the year-end balance in the Drawings account? Assume there were no withdrawals other than those mentioned.

CASE 4
Financial Position

The Cascade Inn incurs a relatively large amount of debt at the beginning of each tourist season. Supplies to operate the Inn are bought in large quantities. Repairs are made to television sets and to the plumbing. Painting and landscaping are done to spruce up the property. These expenses are paid off as money is received throughout the tourist season. Arrangements are made with creditors so that payments may be spread out over the summer.

(a) How would you assess the financial position of the business after examining the statements shown below and on the next page? Give reasons for your comments.

(b) If you operated a television repair business, would you do $2000 worth of repair work for the Cascade on credit? What other information might you require to make this decision.

The Cascade Inn Income Statement For the month ended June 30, 20--		
Revenue		
Room Rentals	$250 000	
Restaurant Income	6 000	$256 000
Expenses		
Salaries Expense	$100 000	
Advertising Expense	10 000	
Telephone Expense	2 000	
Laundry Expense	36 000	
Maintenance Expense	60 000	
Interest Expense	20 000	228 000
Net Income		$ 28 000

The Cascade Inn
Balance Sheet
June 30, 20--

Assets

Current Assets

Cash	$ 38 000	
Supplies	17 000	
Total Current Assets		$ 55 000

Capital Assets

Land	250 000	
Building	750 000	
Room Furniture	225 000	
Office Equipment	25 000	
Total Fixed Assets		1 250 000
Total Assets		$1 305 000

Liabilities and Owner's Equity

Current Liabilities

Accounts Payable		$ 50 000

Long-Term Liabilities

Bank Loan	$ 70 000	
Mortgage Payable	280 000	
Total Long-Term Liabilities		350 000
Total Liabilities		400 000

Owner's Equity

B. Galotta, Capital June 1		879 000	
Add: Net Income for June	28 000		
Less: B. Galotta, Drawings	2 000		
Increase in Capital		26 000	
B. Galotta, Capital June 30			905 000
Total Liabilities and Owner's Equity			$1 305 000

ETHICS CASE
Cash Payments

M. Strenach is the owner and president of Canadian Imagery Ltd., a company in the multimedia industry. The revenue of the business is about $16 million a year. In the past several years, Strenach has spent the following:

- Swimming pool built at his home: $40 000
- Renovations to his cottage: $7500
- Landscaping around his home: $4000
- Plumbing and air conditioning installed in his home: $6000.

Although each of these expenditures was of a personal nature, Strenach requested that invoices for the charges be sent to his company, Canadian Imagery. All of the expenditures were recorded in the books of the company in various expense accounts. Payments were made from company funds. Examples of the accounting procedures used follow:

	GENERAL JOURNAL		PAGE	
DATE	**PARTICULARS**	**P.R.**	**DEBIT**	**CREDIT**
Jun. 30	Building Repairs Expense		40 000	
	Cash			40 000
	Cheque 7849 to Kerr Kontractors.			
30	Landscaping Expense		4 000	
	Cash			4 000
	Cheque 7850 to Green Valley Landscaping.			

(a) From an accounting theory point of view, what is wrong with recording the transactions as expenses of the business?
(b) What is the effect on the company's net income and income tax?
(c) Comment on this case from an ethical point of view.

CHAPTER 5

INTERNET RESOURCES

Explore these Web sites for information on accounting software programs.

1. **Canada Business   www.canadabusiness.gc.ca**

    This site provides business information unique to each province. You can obtain information on planning and starting a business, information guides, government rules and regulations, and information on e-business, including a brochure "The Internet—a Tool for Business."

2. **Globe Investor   www.globeinvestor.com**

    This site provides the latest financial information about Canadian companies. Do a site search for "financial reports" and you will find financial information on the top 1000 Canadian businesses, including links to their current financial reports.

3. **Pro2Net   www.pro2net.com**

    The Ethics and Compliance section of this site provides the latest news involving business and accounting ethics, issues, and cases. Included are news articles and general accounting news and information.

4. **PRARS—Annual Reports   www.prars.com**

    This American site provides and ships free annual reports on hundreds of companies. Reports may be viewed online.

5. **Practical Money Skills   www.practicalmoneyskills.ca**

    This site provides information and resources for teachers, consumers and students on topics such as loans and credit, banking and credit, consumer knowledge and decision making, and debt loads.

Completing the Accounting Cycle for a Service Business

UNIT 11 Adjusting the Books

Learning Objectives

After reading this unit, discussing the applicable review questions, and completing the applications exercises, you will be able to do the following:

1. **EXPLAIN** why adjustments are necessary.

2. **PREPARE** adjusting entries for prepaid expenses.

3. **RECORD** amortization for the accounting period.

The basic accounting cycle was introduced in the first five chapters of this text. In this chapter, the accounting procedures performed at the end of the accounting cycle will be introduced. These procedures include adjustments, financial statements, and closing the books.

One of the main purposes of accounting is to provide information for decision making. The information is presented in the form of financial statements. If decisions are to be made based on data in the financial statements, it is essential that the statements be as accurate as possible.

INTRODUCING ADJUSTMENTS

Revenue from one period and expenses from the same period are matched together to determine net income or net loss.

It is not enough that the debits equal the credits and that the statements are mathematically correct. They must also be accurate.

Many transactions are begun in one accounting period but have an effect for several accounting periods. It is essential that all revenue and expenses be recorded. In addition, the matching principle discussed in Chapter 3 requires that the revenue of a particular accounting period be matched with the expenses of the same accounting period to produce an accurate picture of profitability. All asset, liability, and equity account balances must be correct. The purpose of **adjusting the books** is to ensure that the account balances and the financial statements are accurate.

The purpose of adjusting the books is to ensure that the accounts and financial statements are accurate.

The balance sheet must show, as accurately as possible, the value of all the assets, liabilities, and equity accounts at the end of the accounting period. The income statement must accurately present the revenue and expenses for the accounting period it covers.

Accounting period could be 1 month, 3 months, or 1 year.

Adjusting the Books

Suppose that employees work overtime or earn bonuses that have not been recorded by the end of the accounting period. What will be wrong with the financial statements? Both the income statement and the balance sheet will be incorrect.

The expenses will be too low because the Salaries Expense does not include the overtime. This failure to accurately match the expense of this accounting period with the revenue earned will result in the income statement's understating expenses and showing a net income that is overstated.

The liabilities will be incorrect because the debt owing to the workers, called Salaries Payable, will not be shown on the balance sheet. This will result in the total liabilities of the company being understated.

It is necessary to adjust the books to ensure that all accounts have correct balances. In this chapter, some of the accounts of a business called Management Consultant Services will be examined, and the adjustments to the accounts which are required before the financial statements are prepared will be described. L. Jennings is the owner of Management Consultant Services. This business provides business management advice to other companies and is located in a rented office.

PREPAID EXPENSES

In Chapter 3, expenses were defined as the cost of items used up in operating a business. Payments made in advance for items such as rent, insurance, and supplies are called **prepaid expenses**. Often, the payments are made in advance for more than one accounting period. Prepaid expenses are items of value. They are assets.

Prepaid expenses are expense payments made in advance.

Prepaid expenses are current assets.

Prepaid expenses are considered to be assets — items of value owned — until they are used up or no longer have value. For example, office supplies are assets as long as they are owned by a business and are unused. Once they have been used, they no longer have value and therefore are no longer assets. They have changed to expenses.

When a prepaid expense such as office insurance is purchased, it is recorded as an asset. When it is used, the value of the asset has decreased by the amount used and the asset account should be decreased. Since a portion of the asset has changed to an expense, the amount used should be recorded in the appropriate expense account. This change from prepaid asset to expense may occur on a regular basis; however, the actual recording of the change is normally made at the time financial statements are prepared. At the end of the accounting period, journal entries are made to record the conversion of prepaid assets to expenses to correct the account balances for the balance sheet and to record the appropriate expense for the period on the income statement. These entries are called **adjusting entries**. The adjusting entries involve a change in both an income statement account (revenue or expense) and a balance sheet account (asset or liability).

Journal entries made at the end of the accounting period to ensure the balances in the ledger accounts are accurate before the financial statements are prepared.

Prepaid Rent

The rental lease of L. Jennings' business, Management Consultant Services, requires that rent of $2500 a month be paid in advance for three months. Therefore, on September 1, a cheque for $7500 is issued in payment of the September, October, and November rents. Because the rent is being paid in advance for three months, Rent Expense is not debited. Instead, an account called **Prepaid Rent** is debited.

Rent paid in advance.

At the end of September, Management Consultant Services prepares financial statements covering one month. Should Prepaid Rent be shown as a current asset with a value of $7500? The answer is no. After one month, one-third of the asset Prepaid Rent has been used. The business has used up one-third, or $2500, of the value of the prepaid rent. The value of the prepaid rent must be reduced by $2500 if the asset Prepaid Rent is to be correct. It is now worth $5000, not $7500.

Furthermore, since $2500 of the rent has been used, an expense of $2500 must be recorded. The following entry, called an *adjusting entry*, is made:

Sep. 30	Rent Expense	2 500	
	Prepaid Rent		2 500
	To record one month's Rent Expense and to decrease the asset Prepaid Rent.		

This adjusting entry has two effects:

- It records the Rent Expense for September.
- It decreases the asset Prepaid Rent by $2500.

The entry in T-account form is:

Prepaid Rent				Rent Expense		
Sep. 1	7 500	Sep. 30	2 500	Sep. 30	2 500	
Balance	5 000					
	$5 000				$2 500	

Balance Sheet   **Income Statement**

When the financial statements for the month ended September 30 are prepared, Rent Expense of $2500 will be shown on the income statement. Prepaid Rent of $5000 will appear on the balance sheet. If this adjusting entry were not made, the expenses would be too low and, as a result, the net income would be too high. Also, the assets would be too high.

Supplies

The Supplies account is another prepaid expense. At the beginning of September, supplies worth $1400 are purchased by Management Consultant Services. These supplies will last for several accounting periods.

Each working day in September, small amounts of the supplies are used up. The Supplies account is not decreased because it would be time-consuming and inconvenient to record a decrease in the Supplies account every time supplies were used. Thus, the Supplies account is deliberately allowed to become incorrect. However, at the end of September, when financial statements are prepared, the Supplies account must be adjusted. This is how it is done.

First, a count of all supplies left on September 30 is made. The value of the unused supplies is $1100. Then, the amount of supplies used is determined by this calculation:

Supplies purchased	$1 400
Less: Supplies left	1 100
Supplies used	$ 300

Supplies Expense is the value of supplies used.

The value of supplies used is the Supplies Expense. The asset Supplies should be decreased by the amount used. The following adjusting entry is made:

Sep. 30	Supplies Expense	300	
	Supplies		300
	To adjust the Supplies account and to		
	record the Supplies Expense for the month.		

The effect of this adjusting entry is shown in these T-accounts:

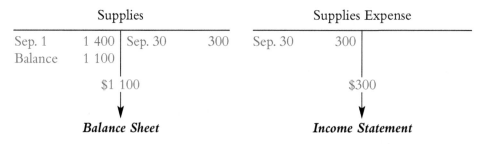

When the September 30 financial statements are prepared, the asset Supplies, with a value of $1100, appears on the balance sheet. The Supplies Expense of $300 appears on the income statement.

Insurance premiums paid in advance.

Prepaid Insurance

On September 1, a comprehensive insurance policy covering fire, theft, and accidental damage to all office furniture and equipment is purchased. The cost of the insurance for one year is $2400.

At the end of September, one month's insurance has been used and must be recorded as an expense. The cost of one month's insurance is 1/12 of $2400, or $200. This adjusting entry is made:

Sep. 30	Insurance Expense	200	
	Prepaid Insurance		200
	To record one month's Insurance Expense		
	and to decrease the asset Prepaid Insurance.		

The effect of this adjusting entry is shown in these T-accounts:

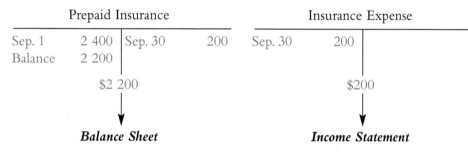

On the September financial statements, Prepaid Insurance of $2200 appears in the asset section of the balance sheet. Insurance Expense of $200 appears on the income statement.

INTRODUCING AMORTIZATION

Management Consultant Services purchased office equipment for $12 000 on September 1, 2008. This purchase is recorded by decreasing Cash and increasing the capital asset account Equipment.

The equipment will be used to help operate the business. Computer equipment, fax machines, and telephones are only some of the equipment used by companies. Such equipment is necessary for the operation of most businesses.

Early in this text, you learned a simple definition of an expense: money spent on things used to operate a business over the years. Since the equipment is used up in operating the business, it does in some way contribute to the expenses of the business. For example, Management Consultant Services may estimate that the equipment purchased will probably last for five years. After that time, it will be worthless. The $12 000 spent on the equipment will have been used up.

However, the equipment does not suddenly become worthless — it loses value each year. The cost of the equipment should be assigned or allocated as an expense to each year's operation. Each year, part of the equipment cost should become an expense.

This allocation of the cost of the capital asset as an expense during the accounting period when the asset is used to produce revenue is consistent with the matching principle. There is a cost of using capital assets during an accounting period to produce the revenue for that accounting period. This cost should therefore be shown as an expense on the income statement for that period.

An expense is the cost of items used to produce the revenue for a business.

Recording Amortization

The assignment of costs, or division of the initial cost over the life of the asset, is called **amortization**. By dividing the initial cost ($12 000) over the life (five years)

Amortization is the allocation of the cost of an asset to the accounting periods in which it is used.

of the equipment, the amortization figure would be $2400 each year or $200 each month, ($2400 × 1/12). This assumes that the equipment is worthless after five years and has no residual value.

The allocation of the cost of assets is recorded in an expense account called **Amortization Expense**. The amortization or using up of capital assets is an expense of operating a business.

The entry to record the amortization of the equipment at the end of the first month is:

Amortization is an expense on the income statement that represents the cost of a capital asset allocated to that accounting period.

Sep. 30	Amortization Expense — Equipment	200	
	Accumulated Amortization — Equip.		200
	To record amortization for the month.		

After this entry has been posted, three accounts relating to the equipment and its amortization are affected:

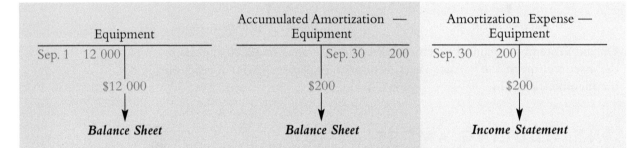

The Amortization Expense — Equipment account appears on the income statement in the expense section. Both Equipment and Accumulated Amortization — Equipment appear on the balance sheet. They are in the capital assets section. **Accumulated Amortization** is a deduction from Equipment as shown in the partial balance sheet in Figure 6-1.

Accumulated amortization appears on the balance sheet.

FIGURE 6-1

Accumulated Amortization appears in the capital assets section of the balance sheet

| Management Consultant Services |
| Partial Balance Sheet |
| September 30, 2008 |

Capital Assets		
Equipment	$12 000	
Less: Accumulated Amortization	200	$11 800

Amortization is a method of spreading the cost of a capital asset over the life of the asset. It is a process of converting the cost of capital assets into expenses over the time the asset will make a contribution to the business. There is a separate Amortization Expense account and a separate Accumulated Amortization account for each group of capital assets such as Buildings, Equipment, Delivery Trucks, and Machinery. Once an asset has been amortized 100 percent, no further amortization is allowed. Suppose an asset costs $10 000 and, over the years, 20 percent is deducted each year. When the Accumulated Amortization account reaches $10 000, no further amortization is available.

You might ask why it is necessary to use an Accumulated Amortization account. Why not simply credit Equipment to show the decrease in its value? The use of the Accumulated Amortization account as well as the asset account Equipment provides two types of information. One is the *original cost* of the equipment. This is found in the asset account Equipment. The other is the *total amount of amortization* recorded over the years. Accounts such as Accumulated Amortization are set up to record subtractions from related accounts. These valuation, or contra, accounts reduce the value of assets on a balance sheet.

Valuation, or Contra, Accounts

The Accumulated Amortization account is sometimes called a **valuation account** because it is used to arrive at the net value of an asset. It is also known as a *contra-asset account* because it has a credit balance rather than the normal debit balance found in most asset accounts. It has a credit balance because it is subtracted from the value of an asset to show the correct net balance sheet value or **net book value**.

> A valuation account is an account used to arrive at the net value of an asset.

> Net book value is the cost of an asset minus the accumulated amortization.

When an asset is purchased, it is recorded at its cost price. Each year, amortization builds up in the Accumulated Amortization account. The net book value of the asset is the cost minus the accumulated amortization. This value is the value according to the books of the company. It is not the actual value, which is the amount received if the asset is sold.

Look again at Figure 6-1. In the capital asset section of the balance sheet, Equipment is shown at its cost price of $12 000. The accumulated amortization to date of $200 is subtracted to arrive at a net book value of $11 800. However, amortization is not valuation. The fact that in Figure 6-1 a current figure of $11 800 is shown for the equipment does *not* mean that the equipment is worth $11 800. It does *not* mean that the equipment can be sold for $11 800. The figures simply mean:

- The equipment cost $12 000.
- Amortization of $200 has been recorded.
- Of the original cost, $11 800 remains to be amortized.

The term "net book value" is used to describe the $11 800 unamortized cost.

Contra accounts provide information to the reader of the financial report. It is clear that the equipment cost was $12 000, that the amortization charged to date is $200, and that additional amortization charges are available in the future. The net book value of Equipment shown on the balance sheet is $11 800. The $11 800 represents the unamortized value of this capital asset at the end of the accounting period.

> Contra accounts reduce the value of assets on the balance sheet.

> Accumulated amortization is a contra-asset account on the balance sheet that shows the total amount of amortization recorded to date over the life of the capital asset.

METHODS OF CALCULATING AMORTIZATION

There are several methods for calculating amortization. The two methods that will be discussed in this chapter are:

- Straight-line method
- Declining-balance method, fixed percentage

Straight-Line Method

The most commonly used method of calculating amortization in business is the **straight-line method**. As shown in Figure 6-1, the equipment's amortization was $200 per month or $2400 per year.

> The straight-line method of amortization allocates the same amount of amortization to each accounting period.

Calculation:

$$\frac{\text{Cost}}{\text{Number of years of use}} = \frac{12\ 000}{5} = \$2400/\text{year}$$

After five years, a total of $12 000 amortization will have been recorded (5 × 2400 = 12 000). Each year, the same amount of amortization, or $2400, is recorded. The table in Figure 6-2 summarizes the calculation of amortization by the straight-line method. The rate is established by using the following calculations:

$$\frac{100\%}{\text{Number of years of use}} = \frac{100\%}{5} = 20\%\ \text{per year}$$

FIGURE 6-2

Amortization by the
straight-line method

Amortization Schedule — Equipment Straight-Line Method			
Year	Calculation	Amortization Expense	Accumulated Amortization
1	20% × $12 000	$ 2 400	$ 2 400
2	20 × 12 000	2 400	4 800
3	20 × 12 000	2 400	7 200
4	20 × 12 000	2 400	9 600
5	20 × 12 000	2 400	12 000
		$12 000	

The adjusting entry for the straight-line method of amortization shows the same amount each year:

Year 1	Amortization Expense — Equipment	2 400	
	Accumulated Amortization — Equip.		2 400
	To record first year's amortization.		
Year 2	Amortization Expense — Equipment	2 400	
	Accumulated Amortization — Equip.		2 400
	To record second year's amortization.		

Scrap or Residual Value

In actual fact, a capital asset may still have some value at the end of the amortization period. The amortization calculation can reflect this to get a more accurate amount recorded as an expense each year than the calculation shown above. If the calculation does not include this residual amount, the asset is shown as having no value at the end of the five-year period. This is true in many cases. The business has to make the decision on whether to include scrap value or not. The decision is based on the calculation that gives the most accurate value for the asset.

To calculate amortization including scrap value, the equation is:

$$\frac{\text{Cost} - \text{Scrap Value}}{\text{Number of Years of Use}} = \text{Annual Amortization}$$

$$\frac{\$12\ 000 - \$2000}{5} = \$2000\ \text{per year}$$

This calculation results in the asset having a book value (Cost − Amortization) of $2000 at the end of five years.

Declining-Balance Method, Fixed Percentage

The straight-line method of amortization allocates an equal amount of amortization to each accounting period. It can be argued that this is not accurate because amortization is greatest in the first few years of an asset's life. For example, an automobile's amortization is greatest in its first year.

A greater amount of amortization is allocated to the first years when the **declining-balance method** is used. Suppose that equipment, worth $12 000, is amortized using the declining-balance method. Each year, a fixed percentage, for example, 20 percent of the declining balance, is charged. The table in Figure 6-3, below, shows the calculation of amortization using the declining-balance method.

The declining-balance method of amortization allocates a greater amount of amortization to the first years of an asset's life.

FIGURE 6-3

Amortization by the declining-balance method

Amortization Schedule — Equipment Declining-Balance Method			
Year	Unamortized cost	Amount of amortization 20%	Declining balance, end of year
1	$12 000.00	$2 400.00	$9 600.00
2	9 600.00	1 920.00	7 680.00
3	7 680.00	1 536.00	6 144.00
4	6 144.00	1 228.80	4 915.20
5	4 915.20	983.04	3 932.16

Notice that each year, as the asset grows older, the amortization is smaller. The cost of the capital asset is never completely written off as long as the asset is being used. However, each year's amortization is progressively smaller.

Journal Entries for the Declining-Balance Method

The adjusting entry used for the declining-balance method of amortization must show a different amount each year:

Year 1	Amortization Expense — Equip.	2 400	
	Accumulated Amortization — Equip.		2 400
	To record the first year's amortization.		
Year 2	Amortization Expense — Equip.	1 920	
	Accumulated Amortization — Equip.		1 920
	To record the second year's amortization.		

The book value (Cost – Amortization) after five years is $3932.16.

Amortization and Income Taxes

For income tax purposes in Canada, the declining-balance method must be used by business. This method is called **capital cost allowance** under the *Income Tax Act*.

The maximum percentage of amortization (capital cost allowance), as well as the method used, is controlled by the government. Assets are grouped into classes and a maximum percentage of amortization allowed for income tax purposes is set for each class. Complete information can be found on the Canada Revenue Agency Web site, www.cra-arc.gc.ca.

For income tax purposes, amortization is called capital cost allowance.

The term used for amortization under the Income Tax Act. The declining-balance method using specified percentages must be used in the calculation.

Land is not amortizable.

It is important to note that land is not amortizable. For income tax purposes, a business may not claim amortization expense (capital cost allowance) on land. Land has an unlimited life — it does not wear out or deteriorate. Unlike a building or equipment, it does not eventually have to be replaced. Because land is so permanent, it is not an asset for which amortization is recorded.

UNIT 11

REVIEW QUESTIONS

1. (a) What is meant by the term "adjusting the books"?
   (b) Why are adjustments necessary?
   (c) List three parties that would be interested in studying accurate financial statements for a company.

2. (a) What type of accounts are prepaid expenses?
   (b) On which financial statement do they appear?

3. (a) Why is the account Supplies allowed to become incorrect?
   (b) Why is it not credited each time supplies are used?
   (c) On which financial statement does the account Supplies appear? On which statement is Supplies Expense found?

4. (a) What type of account is Prepaid Insurance?
   (b) What type of account is Insurance Expense?

5. Define "amortization."

6. Which assets amortize?

7. On which financial statement do Amortization Expense and Accumulated Amortization appear?

8. "Amortization is not valuation." What does this mean?

9. Two methods of calculating amortization are the straight-line method and the declining-balance method. Explain each of them.

10. What is capital cost allowance?

11. For income tax purposes, which method of amortization must be used?

12. What is a contra, or valuation, account? Give an example.

UNIT 11

PROBLEMS: APPLICATIONS

1. Set up T-accounts for Cash, Prepaid Rent, and Rent Expense.

   (a) In the T-accounts, record the following entry: May 1, cheque No. 467 for $6000 was issued to Triangle Realtors as advance payment for four months' rent.
   (b) On May 31, record an adjustment for one month's rent expense.
   (c) Indicate what type of accounts Prepaid Rent and Rent Expense are, and indicate the financial statement on which each appears.

2. The asset account Supplies had a balance of $635 at the beginning of the accounting period. At the end of the accounting period, an inventory shows supplies worth $125 on hand.

   (a) What was the value of supplies used during the accounting period?
   (b) What is the Supplies Expense for the accounting period?

(c) What should the balance in the asset account Supplies be at the end of the accounting period?

(d) Prepare the adjusting entry to record the supplies used.

(e) What is the amount of the Supplies Expense that will appear on the income statement?

(f) What is the value of the asset Supplies that will appear on the balance sheet?

3. On March 1, a one-year insurance policy was purchased for $2160 cash. Prepare the March 31 adjusting entry to record one month's insurance expense.

4. Prepare adjusting entries for the month of January for the following:

   (a) Balance of Supplies account on January 1: $700. Supplies on hand on January 31: $350.

   (b) Rent was paid for three months on January 1, $3900.

   (c) A 12-month insurance policy was purchased on January 15, for $1200.

5. Three accounts related to the capital asset account Automobile (which was bought one year ago for $36 000) follow:

Automobile	Accumulated Amortization — Automobile	Amortization Expense — Automobile
Jan. 1 36 000		

   (a) On December 31, prepare the General Journal adjusting entry to amortize the automobile for one year at the rate of 30 percent.

   (b) Post the entry to T-accounts.

   (c) Give the accounts and balances that appear in the balance sheet and the income statement.

6. It has been estimated that equipment bought for $36 000 will have a useful life of six years, at which time it will be thrown away.

   (a) Using the straight-line method of amortization, what will be the amount of amortization each year?

   (b) Complete your own copy of the following chart for a period of six years.

Year	Value at beginning of year	Amortization for the year	Accumulated amortization	Net book value at end of year
1	$36 000	$6 000	$6 000	$30 000
2				
3				
4				
5				
6				

   (c) How would the equipment appear in the capital asset section of the balance sheet at the end of year five? year six?

7. (a) Make your own copy of the chart shown below and complete it for the amortization of machinery, purchased for $60 000, with a life of five years and a scrap value of $10 000.

   (b) Show the journal entries required to record the amortization expenses in the first four years.

Year	Value at beginning of year	Amortization for the year	Accumulated amortization	Net book value at end of year
1	$60 000	$	$	$
2				
3				
4				

8. Expert Plumbing prepares monthly financial statements. Capital assets owned by the company include Equipment valued at $24 000 and Delivery Truck worth $32 000. Estimated scrap value after three years of life is $5000 for the truck. Prepare adjusting entries to record one month's amortization, using the straight-line method. The equipment has an expected life of six years and has no scrap value.

 **Work Sheets, Adjustments, Financial Statements**

Learning Objectives

After reading this unit, discussing the applicable review questions, and completing the applications exercises, you will be able to do the following:

1. **PREPARE** adjustments on a work sheet for prepaid expenses and amortization of capital assets.

2. **COMPLETE** an eight-column work sheet.

3. **COMPLETE** a ten-column work sheet.

4. **PREPARE** financial statements from a work sheet.

So far in this chapter you have learned:

- That adjustments are necessary if financial statements are to be correct
- How to adjust prepaid expenses such as Supplies, Rent, and Insurance
- How to adjust capital assets by recording Amortization Expense

Adjustments are first prepared on the work sheet.

In this unit, you will learn how the adjustments are prepared on the work sheet and how the financial statements are prepared.

EIGHT-COLUMN WORK SHEET

The trial balance for Management Consultant Services is shown in Figure 6-4, on page 165, on an eight-column work sheet. In Chapter 5, you learned how a six-column work sheet is used to help organize the financial statements. The trial balance is written on a work sheet. The accounts on the trial balance are then transferred to either the income statement section or the balance sheet section of the work sheet. The revenue and expense items are transferred to the income statement section. The

FIGURE 6-4
Eight-column work sheet

Management Consultant Services
Work Sheet
For the Year Ended December 31, 2007

ACCOUNT TITLE	ACC. NO.	TRIAL BALANCE DEBIT	TRIAL BALANCE CREDIT	ADJUSTMENTS DEBIT	ADJUSTMENTS CREDIT	INCOME STATEMENT DEBIT	INCOME STATEMENT CREDIT	BALANCE SHEET DEBIT	BALANCE SHEET CREDIT	
1 Cash	100	13 000								1
2 Accounts Receivable	110	7 000								2
3 Supplies	131	1 000								3
4 Prepaid Insurance	132	900								4
5 Prepaid Rent	133	5 100								5
6 Equipment	141	12 000								6
7 Acc. Amort. — Equip.	142		2 400							7
8 Accounts Payable	200		1 000							8
9 Bank Loan	221		3 000							9
10 L. Jennings, Capital	300		10 400							10
11 L. Jennings, Drawings	301	15 000								11
12 Fees Earned	400		144 000							12
13 Salaries Expense	500	89 500								13
14 Utilities Expense	501	1 300								14
15 Rent Expense	502	15 300								15
16 Miscellaneous Expense	503	700								16
17		160 800	160 800							17

difference in the totals of the income statement section is the net income or the net loss for the accounting period. The difference in the totals of the balance sheet section is also the net income or the net loss. This difference must, of course, be the same as that obtained in the income statement section.

The eight-column work sheet serves the same purpose. It is prepared in the same way as a six-column work sheet, but an *adjustments* section is added. It is also used by the accountant to rough out or plan the necessary adjustments so that the financial statements will be correct. There are four sections on an eight-column work sheet, as shown in Figure 6-4:

- Trial balance section
- Section to plan the adjustments
- Income statement section
- Balance sheet section

In the next few pages, the work sheet will be completed for Management Consultant Services. The period of time covered by this work sheet will be one full year, January 1 to December 31, 2007. The first step in preparing the work sheet is to gather the information required to complete the adjustments. This information includes the following:

- A count made of all supplies on hand shows $400 worth left on December 31.
- On January 1, a three-year insurance policy was purchased. One year of the policy is now expired.
- The balance in the Prepaid Rent account represents a payment on October 1 for the October, November, and December rents.
- The equipment amortizes 20 percent a year. The declining-balance method is used.

Using this information, the adjustments are prepared on the work sheet.

PREPARING ADJUSTMENTS

In this example, four accounts need to be adjusted. They are:

- Supplies
- Prepaid Insurance
- Prepaid Rent
- Equipment

Supplies

The asset account Supplies has a $1000 balance. However, the inventory taken at the end of the accounting period indicates only $400 worth of supplies are left. This means that $600 worth of supplies has been used and should be recorded as an expense.

Supplies purchased	$1 000
Supplies left	400
Supplies Expense	$ 600

It is necessary to record the Supplies Expense of $600 and to decrease the asset Supplies by $600. This is done by debiting Supplies Expense and crediting Supplies. Figure 6-5, on page 167, shows how this adjustment is prepared on the work sheet.

FIGURE 6-5
The adjustment for Supplies is shown on lines 3 and 18 of the work sheet.

Management Consultant Services
Work Sheet
For the Year Ended December 31, 2007

	ACC. NO.	TRIAL BALANCE		ADJUSTMENTS		INCOME STATEMENT		BALANCE SHEET		
ACCOUNT TITLE		DEBIT	CREDIT	DEBIT	CREDIT	DEBIT	CREDIT	DEBIT	CREDIT	
1 Cash	100	13 000								1
2 Accounts Receivable	110	7 000								2
3 Supplies	131	1 000			(a) 600					3
4 Prepaid Insurance	132	900								4
5 Prepaid Rent	133	5 100								5
6 Equipment	141	12 000								6
7 Acc. Amort. — Equip.	142		2 400							7
8 Accounts Payable	200		1 000							8
9 Bank Loan	221		3 000							9
10 L. Jennings, Capital	300		10 400							10
11 L. Jennings, Drawings	301	15 000								11
12 Fees Earned	400		144 000							12
13 Salaries Expense	500	89 500								13
14 Utilities Expense	501	1 300								14
15 Rent Expense	502	15 300								15
16 Miscellaneous Expense	503	700								16
17		160 800	160 800							17
18 Supplies Expense	504			(a) 600						18

In preparing the adjustment, it is necessary to add the account Supplies Expense to the bottom of the trial balance because the account Supplies Expense does not appear on the trial balance. The new account Supplies Expense is debited $600 in the adjustments debit column. The asset Supplies is reduced by entering a credit of $600 in the adjustments credit column on the same line as Supplies. The effect of this adjustment, in T-account form, is:

Supplies				Supplies Expense	
Dec. 31	1 000	Dec. 31	600	Dec. 31	600
Balance	400				

This adjustment decreases the asset Supplies by $600 to the correct balance of $400. It also records the amount of supplies used ($600) in the Supplies Expense account.

Prepaid Insurance

In January, a $900, three-year insurance policy was purchased. At the end of the current year, two years of insurance remain. One-third of the policy has expired or been used up, and it is necessary to reduce Prepaid Insurance by $300 (1/3 × 900 = 300) and record an expense of $300. This is done by adding the account Insurance Expense to the work sheet. A debit of $300 is written beside Insurance Expense in the adjustments debit column. The asset Prepaid Insurance is reduced by entering a credit of $300 in the adjustments credit column opposite Prepaid Insurance. The work sheet in Figure 6-6, on page 169, illustrates how Prepaid Insurance is adjusted.

The effect of this adjustment is to lower the asset Prepaid Insurance to $600 and to record the Insurance Expense for one year of $300.

Prepaid Rent

On October 1, rent of $5100 was prepaid for October, November, and December. On December 31, the rent for those three months is no longer prepaid. It has been used up and an expense must be recorded.

Since there is already a Rent Expense account on the trial balance, all that is required to adjust Prepaid Rent is to decrease the asset by a credit of $5100. The rent expense for the three months is recorded by debiting Rent Expense $5100. Because the rent is no longer prepaid, the effect of the credit to Prepaid Rent is to reduce this asset to zero. Figure 6-7, on page 170, illustrates the rent adjustment.

Equipment

Capital assets such as Equipment amortize each year. Equipment may be amortized at a rate of up to 20 percent a year. For income tax purposes, the declining-balance method must be used. The year's depreciation on Equipment using a 20 percent rate on the declining balance is $1920.

To record the amortization, a debit is entered in the Amortization Expense — Equipment account and a credit is entered in the Accumulated Amortization — Equipment account. It is necessary to add Amortization Expense — Equipment to the work sheet. This account is debited $1920 in the adjustments debit column. The Accumulated Amortization — Equipment account is credited $1920 in the adjustments credit column. Figure 6-8, on page 171, illustrates this adjustment.

FIGURE 6-6
The adjustment for Prepaid Insurance is shown on lines 4 and 19.

Management Consultant Services
Work Sheet
For the Year Ended December 31, 2007

ACCOUNT TITLE	ACC. NO.	TRIAL BALANCE DEBIT	TRIAL BALANCE CREDIT	ADJUSTMENTS DEBIT	ADJUSTMENTS CREDIT	INCOME STATEMENT DEBIT	INCOME STATEMENT CREDIT	BALANCE SHEET DEBIT	BALANCE SHEET CREDIT	
1 Cash	100	13 000								1
2 Accounts Receivable	110	7 000								2
3 Supplies	131	1 000			(a) 600					3
4 Prepaid Insurance	132	900			(b) 300					4
5 Prepaid Rent	133	5 100								5
6 Equipment	141	12 000								6
7 Acc. Amort. — Equip.	142		2 400							7
8 Accounts Payable	200		1 000							8
9 Bank Loan	221		3 000							9
10 L. Jennings, Capital	300		10 400							10
11 L. Jennings, Drawings	301	15 000								11
12 Fees Earned	400		144 000							12
13 Salaries Expense	500	89 500								13
14 Utilities Expense	501	1 300								14
15 Rent Expense	502	15 300								15
16 Miscellaneous Expense	503	700								16
17		160 800	160 800							17
18 Supplies Expense	504			(a) 600						18
19 Insurance Expense	505			(b) 300						19

FIGURE 6-7
The adjustment for Prepaid Rent is shown on lines 5 and 15.

Management Consultant Services
Work Sheet
For the Year Ended December 31, 2007

	ACC. NO.	TRIAL BALANCE DEBIT	TRIAL BALANCE CREDIT	ADJUSTMENTS DEBIT	ADJUSTMENTS CREDIT	INCOME STATEMENT DEBIT	INCOME STATEMENT CREDIT	BALANCE SHEET DEBIT	BALANCE SHEET CREDIT	
ACCOUNT TITLE										
1 Cash	100	13 000								1
2 Accounts Receivable	110	7 000								2
3 Supplies	131	1 000			(a) 600					3
4 Prepaid Insurance	132	900			(b) 300					4
5 Prepaid Rent	133	5 100			(c) 5 100					5
6 Equipment	141	12 000								6
7 Acc. Amort. — Equip.	142		2 400							7
8 Accounts Payable	200		1 000							8
9 Bank Loan	221		3 000							9
10 L. Jennings, Capital	300		10 400							10
11 L. Jennings, Drawings	301	15 000								11
12 Fees Earned	400		144 000							12
13 Salaries Expense	500	89 500								13
14 Utilities Expense	501	1 300								14
15 Rent Expense	502	15 300		(c) 5 100						15
16 Miscellaneous Expense	503	700								16
17		160 800	160 800							17
18 Supplies Expense	504			(a) 600						18
19 Insurance Expense	505			(b) 300						19

FIGURE 6-8

Completed work sheet

Business Management Services
Work Sheet
For the Year Ended December 31, 2007

ACCOUNT TITLE	ACC. NO.	TRIAL BALANCE DEBIT	TRIAL BALANCE CREDIT	ADJUSTMENTS DEBIT	ADJUSTMENTS CREDIT	INCOME STATEMENT DEBIT	INCOME STATEMENT CREDIT	BALANCE SHEET DEBIT	BALANCE SHEET CREDIT	
1 Cash	100	13 000						13 000		1
2 Accounts Receivable	110	7 000						7 000		2
3 Supplies	131	1 000			(a) 600			400		3
4 Prepaid Insurance	132	900			(b) 300			600		4
5 Prepaid Rent	133	5 100			(c) 5 100					5
6 Equipment	141	12 000						12 000		6
7 Acc. Amort. — Equip.	142		2 400		(d) 1 920				4 320	7
8 Accounts Payable	200		1 000						1 000	8
9 Bank Loan	221		3 000						3 000	9
10 L. Jennings, Capital	300		10 400						10 400	10
11 L. Jennings, Drawings	301	15 000						15 000		11
12 Fees Earned	400		144 000				144 000			12
13 Salaries Expense	500	89 500				89 500				13
14 Utilities Expense	501	1 300				1 300				14
15 Rent Expense	502	15 300		(c) 5 100		20 400				15
16 Miscellaneous Expense	503	700				700				16
17		160 800	160 800							17
18 Supplies Expense	504			(a) 600		600				18
19 Insurance Expense	505			(b) 300		300				19
20 Amort. Expense — Equip.	506			(d) 1 920		1 920				20
21				7 920	7 920	114 720	144 000	48 000	18 720	21
22 Net Income						29 280			29 280	22
23						144 000	144 000	48 000	48 000	23

Coding the Adjustments

Four adjustments have now been made on the work sheet and placed in the adjustments section; each adjustment has been *coded*. For example, the supplies adjustment has an (a) beside the debit and an (a) beside the credit. The other adjustments were labelled (b), (c), and (d), respectively. These labels ensure that there is a debit for every credit and provide a reference for checking the adjustments.

The mathematical accuracy of the adjustments section of the work sheet is proved by adding the two columns. The debit column total should equal the credit column total. If this is the case, the columns are double-ruled.

COMPLETING THE WORK SHEET

After the adjustments have been completed and the adjustments columns totalled, the items on the trial balance are transferred to either the income statement or balance sheet sections of the work sheet. The income and expenses are transferred to the income statement section. The asset, liability, and equity accounts are transferred to the balance sheet section.

For example, Figure 6-8 shows that Cash, $13 000, is transferred to the balance sheet debit column (line 1). Accounts Receivable, $7000, is also transferred to the balance sheet debit column (line 2). However, there is a complication on line 3 of the work sheet. The asset Supplies has a debit of $1000 and a credit of $600 in the adjustments section. The difference between a debit of $1000 and a credit of $600 is $400. Because Supplies is an asset account, the $400 balance is transferred to the balance sheet debit column.

Prepaid Insurance is handled in the same way as Supplies. The difference between the $900 debit and the $300 credit is $600. This amount ($600) is transferred to the balance sheet debit column (line 4). On line 5, the difference in the Prepaid Rent account is zero (5100 debit − 5100 credit = 0). Therefore, there is no balance shown in the balance sheet section for Prepaid Rent. There is no change in the Equipment account. Thus $12 000 is transferred to the balance sheet debit column (line 6). On line 7, there are two credits for Accumulated Amortization — Equipment. These are added and the balance, $4320, is transferred to the balance sheet credit column. Accounts Payable, Bank Loan, and L. Jennings, Capital are all transferred to the balance sheet credit column, and L. Jennings, Drawings is transferred to the balance sheet debit column.

Fees Earned, on line 12, is the revenue of Management Consultant Services and is transferred to the income statement credit column.

Salaries Expense, Utilities Expense, and Miscellaneous Expense did not require adjustment and are transferred to the income statement debit column. Rent Expense on line 15 has two debits. These are added and the total of $20 400 appears in the income statement debit column. At the bottom of the work sheet are found the remaining expenses, including Supplies Expense, Insurance Expense, and Amortization Expense — Equipment, which required adjustments. These expenses are transferred to the income statement debit column.

Determining the Net Income or Net Loss

After all the amounts have been transferred to either the balance sheet or income statement sections, it is quite simple to determine the net income or net loss. First, add the income statement debit and credit columns and then find the difference between them. This difference is the net income or the net loss. There is net income if the credit column total is greater than the debit column total. Conversely, there is net loss if the debit column has a greater total than the credit column. Looking at Figure 6-9, it can be seen that the credit column total of the income statement section is greater and thus shows a net income ($29 280).

Next, add the balance sheet debit and credit columns and determine the difference between them. The difference is the net income or net loss. There is net income if the debit column total is greater than the credit column total, and net loss if the credit column total is the greater of the two. Notice that the debit column total in Figure 6-8 is greater and the difference is the same as the difference in the income statement columns — both differences are $29 280. This should come as no surprise because both differences are measuring the same thing — net income.

Balancing the Work Sheet

After the net income (or net loss) has been determined, the amount (in this example $29 280) is added to the lesser column total of both the income statement and the balance sheet sections of the work sheet. The net income figure is added to both the debit side of the income statement section and the credit side of the balance sheet. A net loss would be added to the credit side of the income statement section and to the debit side of the balance sheet section. The columns are then double-ruled as shown in Figure 6-8.

Steps in Preparing the Eight-Column Work Sheet

To summarize, these are the steps followed when preparing an **eight-column work sheet**:

> A sheet that contains columns for trial balance, adjustments, income statement, and balance sheet. It is used to rough out the adjustments and organize the financial statements.

(1) Write the heading on the work sheet.
(2) Write the trial balance on the work sheet.
(3) Gather the data needed to prepare the adjustments.
(4) Prepare the adjustments and total, balance, and rule the adjustment columns.
(5) Transfer all items to either the income statement or balance sheet columns.
(6) Total the income statement and balance sheet columns and determine the net income or net loss.
(7) Balance and rule the work sheet.

TEN-COLUMN WORK SHEET

Many businesses use a **ten-column work sheet** instead of the eight-column work sheet. The extra two columns are used to prepare an **adjusted trial balance**. This trial balance is prepared on the work sheet after the adjustments have been completed. It is prepared to ensure that the ledger accounts are still in balance; that is, to ensure that the debit balances equal the credit balances. If the ledger is still in balance, then the accountant proceeds to complete the work sheet. The work sheet for Management Consultant Services is shown in Figure 6-9, on page 174 using the ten-column format. Notice that the adjusted trial balance section comes after the adjustments section and before the financial statement sections.

> Similar to an eight-column work sheet, but also contains adjusted trial balance columns to ensure the accounts remain balanced after adjustments are calculated.

> Verifies that the ledger is mathematically correct after the adjusting entries are posted.

FIGURE 6-9
Ten-column work sheet

Management Consultant Services
Work Sheet
For the Year Ended December 31, 2007

ACCOUNT TITLE	ACC. NO.	TRIAL BALANCE DEBIT	TRIAL BALANCE CREDIT	ADJUSTMENTS DEBIT	ADJUSTMENTS CREDIT	ADJUSTED TRIAL BALANCE DEBIT	ADJUSTED TRIAL BALANCE CREDIT	INCOME STATEMENT DEBIT	INCOME STATEMENT CREDIT	BALANCE SHEET DEBIT	BALANCE SHEET CREDIT	
1 Cash	100	13 000				13 000				13 000		1
2 Accounts Receivable	110	7 000				7 000				7 000		2
3 Supplies	131	1 000			(a) 600	400				400		3
4 Prepaid Insurance	132	900			(b) 300	600				600		4
5 Prepaid Rent	133	5 100			(c) 5 100							5
6 Equipment	141	12 000				12 000				12 000		6
7 Acc.Amort. — Equip.	142		2 400		(d) 1 920		4 320				4 320	7
8 Accounts Payable	200		1 000				1 000				1 000	8
9 Bank Loan	221		3 000				3 000				3 000	9
10 L. Jennings, Capital	300		10 400				10 400				10 400	10
11 L. Jennings, Drawings	301	15 000				15 000				15 000		11
12 Fees Earned	400		144 000				144 000		144 000			12
13 Salaries Expense	500	89 500				89 500		89 500				13
14 Utilities Expense	501	1 300				1 300		1 300				14
15 Rent Expense	502	15 300		(c) 5 100		20 400		20 400				15
16 Miscellaneous Expense	503	700				700		700				16
17		160 800	160 800									17
18 Supplies Expense	504			(a) 600		600		600				18
19 Insurance Expense	505			(b) 300		300		300				19
20 Amort. Exp. — Equip.	506			(d) 1 920		1 920		1 920				20
21				7 920	7 920	162 720	162 720	114 720	144 000	48 000	18 720	21
22 Net Income								29 280			29 280	22
23								144 000	144 000	48 000	48 000	23

Steps in Preparing the Ten-Column Work Sheet

These steps are followed when completing a ten-column work sheet:

(1) Write the heading on the work sheet.
(2) Write the trial balance on the work sheet.
(3) Gather the data needed to prepare the adjustments.
(4) Prepare the adjustments and total, balance, and rule the adjustment columns.
(5) Transfer all items to the adjusted trial balance columns and recalculate the balances where necessary. Total, balance, and rule the adjusted trial balance columns.
(6) Transfer all items from the adjusted balance to either the income statement or the balance sheet columns.
(7) Total the income statement and balance sheet columns and determine the net income or net loss.
(8) Balance and rule the work sheet.

℗REPARING THE FINANCIAL STATEMENTS

When the work sheet has been completed, the formal financial statements are prepared. All the information necessary for the preparation of the income statement is found on the work sheet in the income statement columns. Similarly, all the necessary data for the balance sheet is found on the work sheet in the balance sheet columns.

Figures 6-10 (below) and 6-11 (page 176) illustrate the financial statements prepared from the completed work sheet. Note the following about the two statements:

• The new expenses resulting from the adjustments are included on the income statement. These are Supplies Expense, Insurance Expense, and Amortization Expense — Equipment.
• The Accumulated Amortization is shown as a subtraction from Equipment in the capital asset section of the balance sheet.

Management Consultant Services
Income Statement
For the Year Ended December 31, 2007

Revenue		
Fees Earned		$144 000
Expenses		
Salaries Expense	$89 500	
Utilities Expense	1 300	
Rent Expense	20 400	
Miscellaneous Expense	700	
Supplies Expense	600	
Insurance Expense	300	
Amortization Expense — Equipment	1 920	114 720
Net Income		$ 29 280

FIGURE 6-10

Income statement prepared from the work sheet

FIGURE 6-11

Balance sheet prepared
from the work sheet

Management Consultant Services
Balance Sheet
December 31, 2007

Assets

Current Assets

Cash	$13 000	
Accounts Receivable	7 000	
Supplies	400	
Prepaid Insurance	600	
Total Current Assets		$21 000

Capital Assets

Equipment	12 000	
Less: Accumulated Amortization	4 320	
Total Capital Assets		7 680
Total Assets		$28 680

Liabilities and Owner's Equity

Current Liabilities

Accounts Payable	$ 1 000	
Bank Loan	3 000	
Total Current Liabilities		$ 4 000

Owner's Equity

L. Jennings, Capital January 1		10 400	
Add: Net Income for the Year	$29 280		
Less: L. Jennings, Drawings	15 000		
Increase in Capital		14 280	
L. Jennings, Capital December 31			24 680
Total Liabilities and Owner's Equity			$28 680

Net Book Value of Assets

The concept of *net book value* is an important one in accounting. In Unit 11, you learned that the net book value is the amount remaining after the accumulated amortization has been subtracted from the cost price of a capital asset.

The net book value of Equipment owned by Management Consultant Services is $7680. This is the net value of the asset. It is determined by subtracting the Accumulated Amortization from the cost of the asset. The net book value should not be confused with the market value or cost of the asset. It is simply the remaining value of the asset that has not yet been converted to expense (i.e., the unamortized value).

UNIT 12

REVIEW QUESTIONS

1. (a) What are the two new columns added to an eight-column work sheet?
   (b) For what purpose are the two new columns used?

2. How is the net income or net loss determined on the work sheet?

3. When there is a net loss, which column of the income statement section of the work sheet is greater? Which column of the balance sheet section is greater when there is a net loss?

4. When there is a net income, to which columns on the work sheet is the amount of the net income added?

5. List the seven steps in preparing an eight-column work sheet.

6. How is the net book value of an asset determined? Give an example.

---

1. The trial balance for M. Porter Sales follows. Prepare an eight-column work sheet for the year ended December 31, 2008, using the additional information given.

UNIT 12

**PROBLEMS:
APPLICATIONS**

Additional Information:

• Supplies on hand at December 31 are valued at $900.

• The declining-balance method of amortization is used, and Equipment amortizes at the rate of 20 percent per year.

ACCOUNT TITLE	ACC. NO.	DEBIT	CREDIT
M. Porter Sales Trial Balance December 31, 2008			
Cash	100	$ 12 000	
Accounts Receivable	110	4 000	
Supplies	131	1 700	
Equipment	141	18 000	
Accumulated Amortization — Equip.	142		$ 6 480
Accounts Payable	200		2 000
M. Porter, Capital	300		33 600
M. Porter, Drawings	301	19 080	
Sales Revenue	400		66 000
Salaries Expense	500	44 000	
Rent Expense	501	4 000	
Telephone Expense	502	1 400	
Miscellaneous Expense	503	900	
Office Expense	504	3 000	
		$108 080	$108 080

2. The trial balance for Music Man Video DJ is shown at the top of page 178. Prepare an eight-column work sheet for the year ended December 31, 2007, using the additional information given.

Additional Information:

• Supplies on hand at December 31 are valued at $150.

• The straight-line method of amortization is used, and Equipment has an estimated life of five years and no scrap value.

3. Prepare an eight-column work sheet for Erdman and Associates using the trial balance shown at the bottom of page 178 and additional information below. The accounting period is one year.

Additional Information:

• Supplies on hand on December 31 are valued at $450.

• The three-year insurance policy was purchased on January 1 for $2700.

• The declining-balance method of amortization is used to record amortization for Office Equipment (20 percent per year) and Automobile (30 percent per year).

Music Man Video DJ
Trial Balance
December 31, 2007

ACCOUNT TITLE	ACC. NO.	DEBIT	CREDIT
Cash	100	$ 5 000	
Accounts Receivable	102	4 000	
Supplies	131	700	
Equipment	141	20 000	
Accumulated Amortization — Equip.	142		$ 8 000
Accounts Payable	200		3 500
B. Schneider, Capital	300		15 300
B. Schneider, Drawings	301	8 000	
Sales Revenue	400		61 200
Salaries Expense	500	42 000	
Rent Expense	501	4 000	
Telephone Expense	502	400	
Miscellaneous Expense	503	900	
Office Expense	504	3 000	
		$88 000	$88 000

Erdman and Associates
Trial Balance
December 31, 2007

ACCOUNT TITLE	ACC. NO.	DEBIT	CREDIT
Cash	100	$ 6 500	
Accounts Receivable	102	17 000	
Supplies	131	2 000	
Prepaid Insurance	132	2 700	
Office Equipment	141	11 000	
Acc. Amortization — Office Equip.	142		$ 3 760
Automobile	143	12 000	
Acc. Amortization — Automobile	144		5 760
Accounts Payable	200		1 500
M. Erdman, Capital	300		28 280
M. Erdman, Drawings	301	18 000	
Fees Income	400		122 000
Salaries Expense	500	80 000	
Rent Expense	501	7 200	
Automobile Expense	502	800	
Utilities Expense	503	1 100	
Office Expense	504	3 000	
		$161 300	$161 300

4. Prepare a ten-column work sheet for Lakeshore Travel, for July, using the trial balance on page 180 and additional information below.

Additional Information:

- Lakeshore Travel prepares a work sheet each month.
- Supplies on hand at the end of July cost $900.
- The straight-line method of amortization is used to record amortization for Office Equipment (five years' life) and Automobile (three years' life and a scrap value of $5000).

ACCOUNT TITLE	ACC. NO.	DEBIT	CREDIT
Cash	100	$ 12 000	
Accounts Receivable	102	22 000	
Supplies	131	4 000	
Office Equipment	141	15 000	
Acc. Amortization — Office Equip.	142		$ 6 000
Automobile	143	29 000	
Acc. Amortization — Automobile	144		8 000
Accounts Payable	200		2 000
Bank Loan	220		3 000
L Dupont, Capital	300		31 500
L Dupont, Drawings	301	15 000	
Sales Revenue	400		120 800
Advertising Expense	500	3 500	
Salaries Expense	501	57 000	
Rent Expense	502	9 800	
Office Expense	503	4 000	
		$171 300	$171 300

Lakeshore Travel
Trial Balance
July 31, 2009

5. Prepare a ten-column work sheet for S. Campbell, Psychotherapists using the trial balance at the top of page 180 and additional information given below. The accounting period is one year.

Additional Information:

- Supplies on hand at December 31 are valued at $650.
- A three-year insurance policy was purchased on April 1 for $6600.
- The declining-balance method of amortization is used to record amortization for Office Equipment (20 percent per year) and Automobile (30 percent per year).

6. Rita Lynch opened a beauty salon on March 1, 2008. Presented at the bottom of page 180 is a list of selected accounts, with their normal debit and credit balances, from the December 31, 2008, trial balance and adjusted trial balance. Prepare the adjusting entries that would explain the differences between the two trial balances.

S. Campbell, Psychotherapists
Trial Balance
December 31, 2009

ACCOUNT TITLE	ACC. NO.	DEBIT	CREDIT
Cash	100	$ 15 500	
Accounts Receivable	110	17 000	
Supplies	131	2 000	
Prepaid Insurance	132	6 600	
Office Equipment	141	16 000	
Acc. Amortization — Office Equipment	142		$ 3 200
Automobile	143	42 000	
Acc. Amortization — Automobile	144		12 600
Accounts Payable	200		11 500
S. Campbell, Capital	300		78 680
S. Campbell, Drawings	301	24 000	
Fees Income	400		142 720
Salaries Expense	500	90 000	
Rent Expense	501	24 200	
Automobile Expense	502	5 800	
Utilities Expense	503	2 600	
Office Expense	504	3 000	
		$248 700	$248 700

Rita Lynch Balances

	TRIAL BALANCE	ADJUSTED TRIAL BALANCE
Cash	$ 8 150	$ 8 150
Accounts Receivable	0	300
Prepaid Rent	9 600	1 600
Prepaid Insurance	3 000	500
Salon Supplies	1 720	750
Salon Furniture	21 000	21 000
Accumulated Amortization —		
Salon Furniture	0	1 750
Accounts Payable	0	515
Interest Payable	0	150
Salaries Payable	0	1 400
Bank Loan	35 000	35 000
R. Lynch, Capital	77 500	77 500
R. Lynch, Drawings	5 600	5 600
Service Revenue	68 500	68 800
Salaries Expense	14 000	15 400
Rent Expense	0	8 000
Insurance Expense	0	2 500
Salon Supplies Expense	9 830	10 800
Amortization Expense —		
Salon Furniture	0	1 750
Interest Expense	1 885	2 035
Utilities Expense	5 150	5 665

UNIT 13   Adjusting and Closing Entries

Learning Objectives

After reading this unit, discussing the applicable review questions, and completing the applications exercises, you will be able to do the following:

1. **PREPARE** adjusting entries from a work sheet.

2. **EXPLAIN** how closing entries update the Capital account and prepare revenue and expense accounts for entries of the next accounting period.

3. **CLOSE** revenue, expense, Drawings, and income summary accounts.

4. **EXPLAIN** why asset, liability, and Capital accounts are not closed.

The books of a company consist of the various journals and ledgers. The work sheet is not part of a company's permanent records. The work sheet is used by the accountant as an aid in organizing data used to prepare the financial statements.

In the example used in this chapter, the assets Supplies, Prepaid Insurance, Prepaid Rent, and Accumulated Amortization — Equipment were adjusted. Changes were made to some expenses, and three expenses were added: Insurance Expense, Supplies Expense, and Amortization Expense — Equipment. All these adjustments were made on the work sheet. The accounts themselves in the General Ledger have not as yet been changed. The ledger accounts are incorrect and must be changed to reflect the adjustments made on the work sheet. The purpose of *adjusting entries* is to record the adjustments in the ledger accounts.

The ledger accounts must be updated to be in agreement with the adjusting entries on the work sheet.

Adjusting entries are necessary to record the adjustments in the ledger accounts.

ADJUSTING ENTRIES

The recording of adjusting entries is quite simple because the adjustments have already been made on the work sheet. It is only necessary to record the adjustments in journal form and to post them to the General Ledger.

When the adjustments were made on the work sheet, they were coded (a), (b), (c), and (d). The debit and credit for the Supplies adjustment were coded (a). By referring to the work sheet and finding the (a) adjustment (Figure 6-8 on page 171), this entry is journalized:

Dec. 31 Supplies Expense	600	
Supplies		600
To record supplies used.		

Similar entries are recorded in the General Journal for each of the adjustments. These are shown in Figure 6-12 at the top of page 182.

FIGURE 6-12

General Journal entries to record the adjustments

DATE	PARTICULARS	P.R.	DEBIT	CREDIT
2007				
Dec. 31	Supplies Expense		600	
	Supplies			600
	To record supplies used.			
31	Insurance Expense		300	
	Prepaid Insurance			300
	To record the Insurance Expense			
	for the year.			
31	Rent Expense		5 100	
	Prepaid Rent			5 100
	To record Rent Expense for three			
	months.			
31	Amortization Expense — Equip.		1 920	
	Acc. Amortization — Equipment			1 920
	To record one year's amortization,			
	declining-balance method.			

Posting the Adjusting Entries

After the adjusting entries have been journalized, they are posted to the General Ledger. Some of the General Ledger accounts of Management Consultant Services are shown in Figure 6-13 below. These T-accounts contain the end-of-the-accounting-period balances found on the trial balance before adjustments have been made.

In the accounts shown in Figure 6-13, several expense accounts have no balance. If the adjustments were not journalized and posted, Supplies Expense, Insurance Expense, and Amortization Expense — Equipment would all have nil balances at the end of the accounting period. That would be wrong since supplies were used, insurance did expire, and amortization is an expense. As well, the balance of $15 300 in the Rent Expense account would be incorrect since it would not include the $5100 rent for the last three months.

FIGURE 6-13

Partial General Ledger in T-account form before end-of-year adjustments have been posted

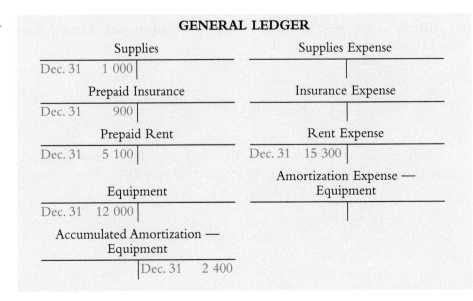

GENERAL LEDGER

The following T-accounts illustrate the effect of this entry on the two accounts:

```
                    Income Summary
   Dec. 31   37 100 | Dec. 31    90 000
        31   52 900 | Balance    52 900
                 ┌──┘
                 │                      ┌──
               D. Hubert, Capital       │
                    | Balance   33 000  │
                    | Dec. 31   52 900 ←┘
```

This entry increases the balance of the owner's Capital account by $52 900, the amount of the net income for the accounting period.

Step 4: Closing the Drawings Account

During the accounting period, withdrawals of cash and other assets by the owner are recorded in the owner's Drawings account. Since withdrawals by the owner affect the owner's investment, the Drawings account is closed with the following entry:

Dec. 31 D. Hubert, Capital   26 000
            D. Hubert, Drawings   26 000
            To close the Drawings account.

The following T-accounts illustrate the effects of this entry:

```
                 D. Hubert, Drawings
   Balance  26 000 | Dec. 31   26 000
                   │       │
                   │       │
          ┌────────┘       │
          ↓  D. Hubert, Capital
   Dec. 31   26 000 | Balance   33 000
                    | Dec. 31   52 900
                    | Balance   59 900
```

This entry reduces the owner's Capital account by $26 000, the amount that has been withdrawn from the business by the owner. Since the owner has withdrawn assets from the business, the owner's equity is decreased. The effect of this entry is to decrease the Capital account.

After these last two entries have been posted, the Income Summary account has been closed (reduced to zero), the Drawings account has been closed, and the Capital account has been updated so that it agrees with the balance for Capital shown on the balance sheet.

Summary

In summary, there are four steps involved in closing the books:

    (1) Close the revenue accounts into the Income Summary account.
    (2) Close the expense accounts into the Income Summary account.
    (3) Close the Income Summary account into the Capital account.
    (4) Close the Drawings account into the Capital account.

See if you can follow the four steps in Figure 6-16 on the next page.

FIGURE 6-16

Closing the books

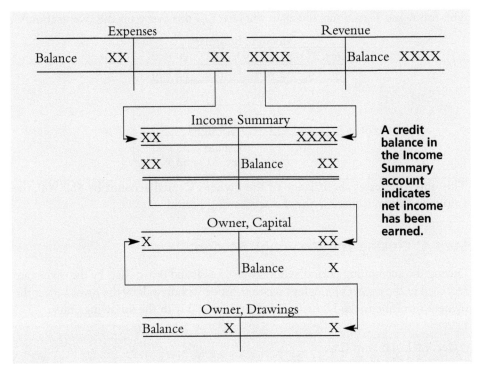

Closing the Books from the Work Sheet

The completed work sheet for Management Consultant Services is found in Figure 6-8 on page 171. The revenue and expense accounts are found in the income statement columns of the work sheet. If you examined the General Ledger *before* closing the books, you would see that L. Jennings' Capital account has a balance of $10 400. The balance sheet shown for Management Consultant Services in Figure 6-11 on page 176 shows the actual Capital balance on December 31 to be $24 680. Why does the ledger balance not agree with the balance sheet? How will the closing entries bring them into agreement? As we journalize and post the closing entries, remember the purposes served by these entries.

Reviewing the Purpose of Closing Entries

Two main purposes are served by closing entries:

(1) Revenue and expense accounts are prepared for the next accounting period.
(2) The Capital account is updated.

Closing Revenue Accounts

On the work sheet (Figure 6-8), the revenue account Fees Earned has a credit balance of $144 000. To reduce it to zero, the Fees Earned is debited $144 000. This closing entry is journalized:

Dec. 31 Fees Earned	144 000	
Income Summary		144 000
To close the revenue account.		

Closing Expense Accounts

There are seven expenses in the debit column of the income statement section of the work sheet. Each is credited to reduce it to zero. This entry is journalized:

Dec. 31 Income Summary	114 720	
Salaries Expense		89 500
Utilities Expense		1 300
Rent Expense		20 400
Miscellaneous Expense		700
Supplies Expense		600
Insurance Expense		300
Amortization Expense — Equip.		1 920
To close the expense accounts.		

Updating the Equity Account

Two entries are required to update the owner's equity account. The first is to transfer the net income or net loss to the Capital account from the Income Summary. The net income of $29 280 earned during the year increases the owner's Capital account. In very simple terms, the net income belongs to the owner. For this reason, the net income is credited to the owner's Capital account. This increases the owner's Capital. If there was a net loss, Capital would be decreased. This entry is journalized:

Dec. 31 Income Summary	29 280	
L. Jennings, Capital		29 280
To transfer net income to the owner's		
Capital account.		

A second entry involving owner's equity is needed to close the Drawings account into the Capital account. This entry is journalized:

Dec. 31 L. Jennings, Capital	15 000	
L. Jennings, Drawings		15 000
To close the Drawings account into the		
Capital account.		

The closing entries just described are all recorded in the General Journal. The sources of information are the income statement columns of the work sheet except for the Drawings account, which is found in the balance sheet columns of the work sheet.

After the closing entries have been journalized, they are posted to the General Ledger. Selected accounts from the General Ledger are shown on the following three pages in Figure 6-17. This ledger contains the adjusting entries and the closing entries that have been posted from the General Journal. All the revenue and expense accounts have a zero balance. They are double-ruled and are now ready to receive data for the new accounting period. Notice that the Drawings account and the Income Summary account are also closed. The asset, liability, and owner's Capital accounts are *not* closed. Their balances continue into the next accounting period.

Asset, liability, and owner's Capital accounts are not closed at the end of an accounting period.

Partial General Ledger for Management Consultant Services after adjusting and closing entries have been posted

GENERAL LEDGER

ACCOUNT   Cash   NO. 100

DATE	PARTICULARS	P.R.	DEBIT	CREDIT	DR. CR.	BALANCE
2007 Dec. 31	Forwarded	✓			DR.	13 000

ACCOUNT   Supplies   NO. 131

DATE	PARTICULARS	P.R.	DEBIT	CREDIT	DR. CR.	BALANCE
2007 Dec. 31	Forwarded	✓			DR.	1 000
31	Adjusting Entry	J34		600	DR.	400

ACCOUNT   Prepaid Insurance   NO. 132

DATE	PARTICULARS	P.R.	DEBIT	CREDIT	DR. CR.	BALANCE
2007 Dec. 31	Forwarded	✓			DR.	900
31	Adjusting Entry	J34		300	DR.	600

ACCOUNT   Equipment   NO. 141

DATE	PARTICULARS	P.R.	DEBIT	CREDIT	DR. CR.	BALANCE
2007 Dec. 31	Forwarded	✓			DR.	12 000

ACCOUNT   Accumulated Amort. — Equipment   NO. 142

DATE	PARTICULARS	P.R.	DEBIT	CREDIT	DR. CR.	BALANCE
2007 Dec. 311	Forwarded	✓			CR.	2 400
31	Adjusting Entry	J34		1 920	CR.	4 320

ACCOUNT   Accounts Payable   NO. 200

DATE	PARTICULARS	P.R.	DEBIT	CREDIT	DR. CR.	BALANCE
2007 Dec. 31	Forwarded	✓			CR.	1 000

ACCOUNT   L. Jennings, Capital   NO. 300

DATE	PARTICULARS	P.R.	DEBIT	CREDIT	DR. CR.	BALANCE
2007						
Dec. 31	Forwarded	✓			CR.	10 400
31	Net Income for Year	J35		29 280	CR.	39 680
31	Drawings	J35	15 000		CR.	24 680

ACCOUNT   L. Jennings, Drawings   NO. 301

DATE	PARTICULARS	P.R.	DEBIT	CREDIT	DR. CR.	BALANCE
2007						
Dec. 31	Forwarded	✓			DR.	15 000
31	Closing Entry	J35		15 000		0

ACCOUNT   Income Summary   NO. 302

DATE	PARTICULARS	P.R.	DEBIT	CREDIT	DR. CR.	BALANCE
2007						
Dec. 31	To Close Fees Earned	J35		144 000	CR.	144 000
31	To Close Expenses	J35	114 720		CR.	29 280
31	To Close Inc. Summary	J35	29 280			0

ACCOUNT   Supplies Expense   NO. 504

DATE	PARTICULARS	P.R.	DEBIT	CREDIT	DR. CR.	BALANCE
2007						
Dec. 31	Adjusting Entry	J34	600		DR.	600
31	Closing Entry	J35		600		0

ACCOUNT   Insurance Expense   NO. 505

DATE	PARTICULARS	P.R.	DEBIT	CREDIT	DR. CR.	BALANCE
2007						
Dec. 31	Adjusting Entry	J34	300		DR.	300
31	Closing Entry	J35		300		0

ACCOUNT	Amortization Expense — Equipment				NO. 506	
DATE	PARTICULARS	P.R.	DEBIT	CREDIT	DR. CR.	BALANCE
2007 Dec. 31	Adjusting Entry	J34	1920		DR.	1 920
31	Closing Entry	J35		1 920		0

Post-Closing Trial Balance

The post-closing trial balance is prepared after the closing entries have been posted to the General Ledger.

The post-closing trial balance contains only asset, liability, and Capital accounts.

After the adjusting and closing entries have been posted to the General Ledger, a **post-closing trial balance** is prepared (Figure 6-18). The purpose of this trial balance is to prove the mathematical accuracy of the General Ledger. If the debit total equals the credit total, the ledger is assumed to be *in balance*. It is ready for the next accounting period. The post-closing trial balance is quite a bit shorter than other General Ledger trial balances. This is because it contains only asset, liability, and Capital accounts with balances. The revenue, expense, and Drawings accounts have been reduced to zero and do not appear on this final trial balance.

FIGURE 6-18

Post-closing trial balance prepared after the closing of the books

Management Consultant Services Post-Closing Trial Balance December 31, 2007			
ACCOUNT TITLE	ACC. NO.	DEBIT	CREDIT
Cash	100	$13 000	
Accounts Receivable	102	7 000	
Supplies	131	400	
Prepaid Insurance	132	600	
Equipment	141	12 000	
Accumulated Amortization — Equip.	142		$ 4 320
Accounts Payable	200		1 000
Bank Loan	221		3 000
L. Jennings, Capital	300		24 680
		$33 000	$33 000

Effect of a Net Loss

How is the closing process affected when a business has a net loss? Revenue and expense accounts are closed as already described in this chapter. However, because there is a loss, the owner's Capital account will decrease. Look at this example:

Expenses	Revenue	Owner, Capital
Dec. 31 63 000	Dec. 31 51 700	Dec. 1 110 900

As you can see, the expenses are greater than the revenue. The first two entries are shown as follows:

Dec. 31 Revenue	51 700	
Income Summary		51 700
To close the revenue accounts.		
31 Income Summary	63 000	
Expenses		63 000
To close the expense accounts.		

After these entries have been posted, the Income Summary account has a debit balance of $2800 — this is a net loss. What effect will this loss have on the owner's Capital account?

Expenses				Revenue			
Dec. 31	63 000	Dec. 31	63 000	Dec. 31	51 700	Dec. 31	51 700

Income Summary				Owner, Capital			
Dec. 31	63 000	Dec. 31	51 700			Dec. 1	110 900
Balance	11 300						

The entry to close the Income Summary account and to transfer the loss to the Capital account is shown below:

Dec. 31 Owner, Capital	11 300	
Income Summary		11 300
To close the Income Summary		
account and to transfer the		
loss to the Capital account.		

The owner's Capital account has now been updated. The Capital balance has been decreased by the net loss suffered during the accounting period.

Income Summary				Owner, Capital			
Dec. 31	63 000	Dec. 31	51 700	Dec. 31	11 300	Dec. 1	110 900
		31	11 300			Balance	99 600

At the beginning of the accounting period, Capital was $110 900. At the end of the period, Capital has decreased to $99 600 because of the net loss.

Additions to the Accounting Cycle

Figure 6-19 illustrates the accounting cycle with the addition of the adjusting and closing entries and the post-closing trial balance.

FIGURE 6-19

The accounting cycle is a continuous process

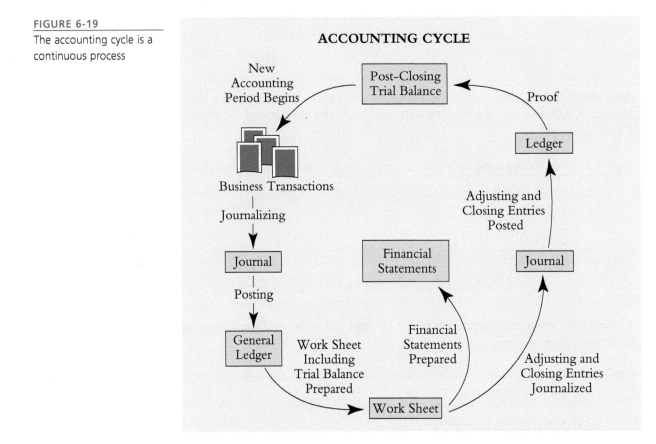

ACCOUNTING TERMS

Accumulated Amortization A contra-asset account on the balance sheet that shows the total amount of amortization recorded to date over the life of the capital asset. (p. 158)

Adjusted Trial Balance Verifies that the General Ledger is mathematically correct after the adjusting entries are posted. (p. 173)

Adjusting Entries General Journal entries made at the end of the accounting period to ensure the balances in the General Ledger accounts are accurate before the financial statements are prepared. (p. 155)

Adjusting the Books General Journal entries made at the end of an accounting period to ensure that the account balances and the financial statements are accurate. (p. 154)

Amortization The allocation of the cost of a capital asset to the accounting periods in which it is used. (p. 157)

Amortization Expense	An expense on the income statement that represents the cost of a capital asset allocated to that accounting period. (p. 158)
Capital Cost Allowance	The term used for amortization under the *Income Tax Act*. The declining-balance method using specified percentages must be used in the calculation. (p. 161)
Closing the Books	The process of preparing the revenue and expense accounts for the next accounting period by reducing them to zero and updating the owner's capital account. (p. 184)
Contra Accounts	Reduce the value of assets on the balance sheet. (p. 159)
Declining-Balance Method of Amortization	A method of calculating amortization in which the amortization allowance is a constant percentage of the book value of the asset. (p. 161)
Eight-Column Work Sheet	A sheet that contains columns for trial balance, adjustments, income statement, and balance sheet. It is used to rough out the adjustments and organize the financial statements. (p. 173)
Income Summary Account	A temporary account used during the process of closing the books to collect the revenue and expenses of the period and transfer the net income or loss to the owner's Capital account. (p. 184)
Net Book Value	Historical (original) cost of an asset minus the accumulated amortization. (p. 159)
Post-Closing Trial Balance	Verifies that the General Ledger is mathematically correct after the closing entries have been posted. It contains only asset, liability, and Capital accounts. (p. 192)
Prepaid Expenses	Expense payments that are made in advance. They are current assets. (p. 154)
Prepaid Insurance	Insurance premiums paid in advance. (p. 156)
Prepaid Rent	Rent paid in advance. (p. 155)
Straight-Line Method of Amortization	A method of calculating amortization that allocates the same amount of amortization to each accounting period. A salvage, or scrap, value may be taken into account in this calculation. (p. 159)
Ten-Column Work Sheet	Similar to an eight-column work sheet but also contains adjusted trial balance columns to ensure the accounts remain balanced after adjustments are calculated. (p. 173)
Valuation Account	An account used to arrive at the net value of an asset. (p. 159)
Work Sheet Code	As adjustments are made on the work sheet, they are coded by letter. (p. 181)

UNIT 13

REVIEW QUESTIONS

1. Why is it necessary to record adjusting entries in the journal?

2. What two purposes are served by closing the books?

3. What type of accounts are closed?

4. (a) Which accounts are permanent?

   (b) Which accounts are temporary?

5. Is a revenue account debited or credited to close the revenue account?

6. To close an expense, is a debit or a credit necessary in the expense account?

7. Into which account are revenue and expenses closed?

8. Into which account are the Income Summary account and the Drawings account closed? Why?

9. What is the purpose of the post-closing trial balance?

10. Which accounts appear on the post-closing trial balance?

PROBLEMS: APPLICATIONS

1. Refer to the work sheet completed in Unit 12, Problems: Applications exercise 1 on page 177 for M. Porter Sales and record the adjusting entries in a General Journal.

2. Refer to the work sheet in Unit 12, Problems: Applications exercise 3 on page 177 and 178 for Erdman and Associates and record the adjusting entries in a General Journal.

3. Use the T-account ledger below to:

   (a) Prepare Aug. 31 closing entries in a journal and post them to the T-accounts in the ledger.
   (b) Calculate the final balance on Aug. 31 in the B. Purdy, Capital account.

B. Purdy, Capital 300		Auto Expense 501	
	Aug. 31 60 000	Aug. 31 1 000	
B. Purdy, Drawings 301		**General Expense 502**	
Aug. 31 5 000		Aug. 31 3 000	
Income Summary 302		**Rent Expense 503**	
		Aug. 31 5 000	
Sales Revenue 400		**Salaries Expense 504**	
	Aug. 31 53 000	Aug. 31 27 000	
Advertising Expense 500			
Aug. 31 2 000			

4. The completed six-column work sheet for J. Fioravanti is shown on the following page.

   (a) Open a General Ledger using the accounts and balances on the trial balance and account 302, Income Summary.
   (b) Prepare closing entries in a General Journal.
   (c) Post the closing entries to the General Ledger.
   (d) Prepare a post-closing trial balance.

		TRIAL BALANCE		INCOME STATEMENT		BALANCE SHEET	
ACCOUNT TITLE	**ACC. NO.**	**DEBIT**	**CREDIT**	**DEBIT**	**CREDIT**	**DEBIT**	**CREDIT**
Cash	100	2 000				2 000	
Accounts Receivable	101	4 300				4 300	
Equipment	110	16 200				16 200	
Accounts Payable	200		2 500				2 500
J. Fioravanti, Capital	300		10 000				10 000
Sales Revenue	400		13 000		13 000		
Salaries Expense	500	1 200		1 200			
General Expense	501	800		800			
Advertising Expense	502	1 000		1 000			
		25 500	25 500	3 000	13 000	22 500	12 500
Net Income				10 000			10 000
				13 000	13 000	22 500	22 500

J. Fioravanti
Work Sheet
For the Month Ended May 31, 2008

---

1. Refer to Unit 12, Problems: Applications exercise 1, M. Porter Sales on page 177.

   (a) Prepare the closing entries in a General Journal.
   (b) What should the balance in the Income Summary account be after closing the revenue and expense accounts?
   (c) What will the new balance be in Porter Capital after the closing entries have been posted?

2. The trial balance for Music Man Video DJ is shown below.

   (a) Open a General Ledger using the accounts and balances on the trial balance and account 302, Income Summary.
   (b) Journalize the adjusting and closing entries for the month of December.
   (c) Post the closing entries.
   (d) Prepare a post-closing trial balance.
   Refer to Chapter 6, Unit 12, exercise 10.

CHAPTER 6

PROBLEMS:
CHALLENGES

Music Man Video DJ
Trial Balance
December 31, 2008

ACCOUNT TITLE	ACC. NO.	DEBIT	CREDIT
Cash	100	$ 5 000	
Accounts Receivable	102	4 000	
Supplies	131	700	
Equipment	141	20 000	
Accumulated Amortization — Equip.	142		$ 8 000
Accounts Payable	200		3 500
B. Schneider, Capital	300		15 300
B. Schneider, Drawings	301	8 000	
Sales Revenue	400		61 200
Salaries Expense	500	42 000	
Rent Expense	501	4 000	
Telephone Expense	502	400	
Miscellaneous Expense	503	900	
Office Expense	504	3 000	
		$88 000	$88 000

3. The trial balance for Lakeshore Travel is shown below.

(a) Open a General Ledger using the accounts and balances on the trial balance and account 302, Income Summary.
(b) Journalize the adjusting and closing entries for the month of July.
(c) Post the closing entries.
(d) Prepare a post-closing trial balance.

ACCOUNT TITLE	ACC. NO.	DEBIT	CREDIT
Lakeshore Travel			
Trial Balance			
July 31, 2009			
Cash	100	$ 12 000	
Accounts Receivable	102	22 000	
Supplies	131	4 000	
Office Equipment	141	15 000	
Acc. Amortization — Office Equip.	142		$ 6 000
Automobile	143	29 000	
Acc. Amortization — Automobile	144		8 000
Accounts Payable	200		2 000
Bank Loan	220		3 000
L. Dupont, Capital	300		31 500
L. Dupont, Drawings	301	15 000	
Sales Revenue	400		120 800
Advertising Expense	500	3 500	
Salaries Expense	501	57 000	
Rent Expense	502	9 800	
Office Expense	503	4 000	
		$171 300	$171 300

4. Listed below are the month-end closing entries for The Dental Clinic, which were prepared by an inexperienced accountant. Upon review of these entries you discover a number of errors.

		Debit	Credit
Sep. 30	Dental Fees Earned	9 800	
	Salaries Payable	1 650	
	Utilities Expense	950	
	Amortization Expense	1 300	
	Owner, Drawings	2 500	
	Income Summary		16 200
Sep. 30	Income Summary	8 705	
	Salaries Expense		3 300
	Rent Expense		1 800
	Accounts Payable		2 275
	Insurance Expense		550
	Dental Supplies Expense		780
Sep. 30	Owner, Capital	7 495	
	Income Summary		7 495

Prepare the correct closing entries for The Dental Clinic.

5. Answer these questions involving end of fiscal period adjustments for the Sun Lei Travel Services.

(a) The Supplies account has a balance of $1700. At the end of the accounting period, an inventory count shows supplies costing $400 on hand.
   (i)   What is the value of the supplies used during the fiscal period?
   (ii) What is the supplies expense?
   (iii) What should the balance be in the Supplies account after the adjusting entry is made and posted at the end of the fiscal period?
   (iv) What is the amount of supplies expense that will appear on the income statement?
   (v)   What is the value of the asset, Supplies, that will appear on the balance sheet?

(b) Equipment was purchased for $50 000 and is amortized at the rate of 20 percent a year using the straight-line method.
   (i)   What is the yearly amount of amortization?
   (ii) At the end of the second year, what is the balance in the Accumulated Amortization — Equipment account?
   (iii) At the end of the second year, what is the amount in the Amortization Expense — Equipment account?
   (iv) At the end of the second year, what is the net book value of the equipment account shown on the balance sheet?
   (v)   At the end of the fifth year, what is the net book value of the Equipment account shown on the balance sheet?

(c) Equipment was purchased for $50 000 and is amortized at the rate of 20 percent a year using the declining-balance method.
   (i)   At the end of the first year, what is the amount of amortization?
   (ii) At the end of the second year, what is the balance in the Accumulated Amortization — Equipment account?
   (iii) What is amount of the second year's amortization expense?
   (iv) At the end of the second year, what is the amount in the Amortization Expense — Equipment account?
   (v)   At the end of the fifth year, what is the net book value of the Equipment account shown on the balance sheet?
   (vi) At the end of the fifth year, what is the balance in the Accumulated Amortization — Equipment account?

(d) On October 1, an insurance policy on the equipment was purchased for one year for $2400.
   (i)   What is the amount in the Prepaid Insurance account on Oct. 1 when the purchase of the insurance policy is recorded?
   (ii) What is the amount of the expired insurance on December 31?
   (iii) What is the amount of the insurance expense after the adjustments are made on December 31?
   (iv) On December 31, what amount will appear on the balance sheet for prepaid insurance?
   (v)   On December 31, what amount will appear on the income statement for insurance expense?

1

THE ACCOUNTING CYLE

Red Deer Cineplex

INTRODUCTION

This activity includes all the steps in the accounting cycle covered to this point in *Accounting for Canadian Colleges.* It is a comprehensive review of Chapters 1 to 6. There are four parts to the project — Parts A, B, C, and optional part D.

Part A: The first task is to complete the work sheet and financial statements for the month of March and then prepare and post adjusting and closing entries and prepare a post-closing trial balance. You are given the March 31 trial balance from which to work.

Part B: In this part you will journalize the April transactions, post to the General Ledger accounts, and prepare a trial balance.

Part C: Your next job is to complete the work sheet, financial statements, adjusting and closing entries, and post-closing trial balance for April.

Optional — Financial Analysis

Part D: The next task is to examine the financial results for the theatre for two months and to make recommendations to the owners.

Part A

The Red Deer Cineplex is a franchise and rents its premises from the Red Deer Town Centre. The business has been open for a month, and management wishes to find out if the business has made a profit or a loss. Using the additional information and the trial balance provided, do the following:

1. Complete an eight-column work sheet.
2. Prepare the monthly financial statements.
3. Set up a General Ledger with the appropriate accounts and balances.
4. Journalize and post the adjusting and closing entries.
5. Prepare a post-closing trial balance.

Additional Information:

- The straight-line amortization method is used by Red Deer Cineplex. The equipment amortizes 20 percent per year. (Note: Calculate the amortization to the nearest dollar value.)
- Rent was prepaid for three months on March 1.
- Insurance was prepaid for one year effective March 1.
- Supplies on hand March 31 were valued at $310.

Red Deer Cineplex
Trial Balance
March 31, 2008

ACCOUNT TITLE	ACC. NO.	DEBIT	CREDIT
Cash	100	$ 6 953	
Prepaid Rent	115	9 000	
Prepaid Insurance	116	2 800	
Supplies	117	1 580	
Equipment	120	94 030	
Accounts Payable	200		$ 2 210
Bank Loan	201		10 203
M. Edwards, Capital	300		96 312
M. Edwards, Drawings	301	2 900	
Ticket Sales	400		26 500
Confectionery Income	401		4 505
Salaries Expense	500	6 700	
Advertising Expense	501	3 563	
Film Rental Expense	502	5 563	
Cleaning Expense	503	850	
Telephone Expense	504	135	
Rent Expense	505	2 293	
Film Transportation Expense	506	248	
Heating Expense	507	1 650	
Electricity and Water Expense	508	1 115	
General Expense	509	350	
		$139 730	$139 730

Additional Accounts:

Accumulated Amortization — Equipment	121
Income Summary	302
Amortization Expense — Equipment	510
Rent Expense	511
Insurance Expense	512
Supplies Expense	513

Part B

The following source documents came across the desk of the accountant during the month of April. Do the following:

1. Journalize the source documents and post to the General Ledger.
2. Prepare a trial balance.

Apr. 7 Cash register tapes from the box office for the week show total sales of $3100. The money was deposited in the bank account.

Weekly sales report for the confectionery shows a net income of $260. The money was deposited in the bank account.

Purchase invoices received from:

Electronics Canada Ltd., $256 for final adjustments to the projector;

The Red Deer Advocate, $750 for newspaper advertisements.

Cheques issued to:

City Hydro, No. 375, $480 for electricity and water;

Bell Canada, No. 376, $60.

Apr.   14   Cash register tapes from the box office for the week show total sales of $6150.

Weekly sales report for the confectionery shows a net income of $515.

Purchase invoices received from:

International Film Distributors, $1289 for rental of the film shown from Apr. 1 to 7;

Commercial Cleaners Ltd., $580 for cleaning the premises in the first half of the month.

Cheques issued to:

Craig Stationers, No. 377, $112 for supplies;

International Film Distributors, No. 378, $890 on account;

M. Edwards, the owner, No. 379, $515 for drawings;

Employees, No. 380 to 390, for a total of $2890 for salaries from Apr. 1.

Apr.   21   Cash register tapes from the box office for the week show total sales of $7950.

Weekly sales report for the confectionery shows a net income of $630.

Purchase invoices received from:

Air Canada, $235 for transportation of film;

Red Deer Radio and TV, $371 for spot advertising;

Stinson Fuels, $675 for heating oil.

Cheques issued to:

Electronics Canada Ltd., No. 391, $256 on account;

The Red Deer Advocate, No. 392, $750 on account;

Best Office Supply, No. 393, $385 for supplies.

Apr.   28   Cash register tapes from the box office for the week show total sales of $8225.

Weekly sales report for the confectionery shows a net income of $785.

Purchase invoices received from:

International Film Distributors, $2658 for rental of film from Apr. 8 to 28;

Commercial Cleaners Ltd., $610 for cleaning of premises.

Cheques issued to:

Commercial Cleaners Ltd., No. 394, $580 on account;

M. Edwards, the owner, No. 395, $545 for personal drawings;

Employees, No. 396 to No. 406, for a total of $3110 for salaries from Apr. 15.

Part C

Using the additional information given, complete the following procedures for the end of April:

1. Prepare an eight-column work sheet.

2. Prepare the financial statements.
3. Journalize and post the adjusting and closing entries.
4. Prepare a post-closing trial balance.

Additional Information:

• Supplies on hand, April 30, were valued at $418.

Part D — Optional — Financial Analysis

1. On behalf of the owner, M. Edwards, prepare a short written report for use in answering the following questions:

   (a) Is the business profitable at this time?
   (b) Is the profitability increasing or decreasing?
   (c) If the business were to apply for a $20 000 bank loan to purchase further equipment, would it be approved? Focus your response on the firm's ability to repay the loan and the bank's chance of recovering its money if the firm cannot meet its loan payments.
   (d) Has the value of the business increased or decreased over the first two months of operation?
   (e) Should the present method of operating the confectionery be changed? C. Jacobs has submitted a proposal to M. Edwards to take over operation of the confectionery in the theatre and to pay Red Deer Cineplex 25 percent of sales. At present, the salary for the booth operator is $390 per week and the cost of the merchandise sold represents approximately 50 percent of the sales revenue (Example: Sales $300 × 0.50 = $150 = Cost of Merchandise Sold). Based on this information and the confectionery income for the first two months, Edwards would like an opinion on whether it would be more profitable to run the booth or to lease it to Jacobs.

CASE 1
Overstating Net Income

At the end of the year, the accountant for Smith Painting Contractors prepares financial statements but neglects to prepare the adjustment for the Supplies account. The balance in the Supplies account at the end of the year is $2500. An actual count shows that the value of supplies on hand at the end of the year is $700.

The net income for the year as calculated by the accountant is $42 000 and the total assets are $110 000. However, these figures are incorrect because Supplies has not been adjusted.

(a) By how much is the net income overstated?
(b) By how much are the assets overstated?
(c) What are the correct figures for the net income and the total assets?

CASE 2
Recording Amortization

C. Lisney is the owner of a furniture restoration and refinishing business. The business has a delivery van with a net book value of $41 000 and equipment with a net book value of $24 000. Amortization has not been recorded on these capital assets.

(a) What effect does the omission of amortization have on the operating results of the business?
(b) How is income tax affected?
(c) Why might amortization have been deliberately not recorded?
(d) What method of amortization should have been used?
(e) What GAAP is involved?

CASE 3
Interpreting Accounting Data

County Fuels is a small business selling home fuel. It has 400 customers who purchase an average of $900 of products each year.

A friend of yours has just inherited the business and comes to you for advice.

Items Owned by the Business	
Cash in bank	$ 5 000
Accounts receivable	6 000
Two delivery trucks	40 000 each
Storage tanks	30 000
Inventory	50,000
Yard equipment	45 000
Office supplies	2 000
Office equipment	15 000
Other assets	5 000
Company Debts	
Accounts payable	25 000
Salaries owing	8 000
Taxes owing	5 000
Bank loan	30 000

Other information

All values are recorded according to the cost principle. The two trucks are over five years old. None of the assets is less than two years old except the cash, accounts receivable, and inventory. The company employs four full-time and two part-time employees. The previous owner worked full-time in the business. Your friend asks you to help determine the following:

(a) What is the business worth?
(b) Should your friend keep the business or sell it?
(c) A competitor, Exodus Fuels, has offered your friend $50 000 for the entire business. Would you recommend selling at this price? Why?

ETHICS CASE
Social Costs of Business Decisions

Metalco is a very large producer of several types of metals. It mines, refines, and ships metal products to customers located in many different countries. The following chart presents a summary of operating results for the last five years and projected results for the next two years.

Operating Results (in millions of dollars)							
			Last Five Years			Projection Next Two Years	
	Yr. 1	Yr. 2	Yr. 3	Yr. 4	Yr. 5	Yr.6	Yr. 7
Sales	500	490	480	470	460	400	390
Costs and Expenses	380	390	390	400	400	410	410
Net Income	120	100	90	70	60	(10)*	(20)*

*Amounts in brackets represent a net loss.

This chart illustrates a decrease of $40 million in sales from Year 1 to Year 5. Costs and expenses have increased slightly. Net income has decreased dramatically from $120 million to $60 million.

Management of Metalco is aware of the causes of the unfavourable trends. World prices and the demand for its products have decreased and competition has increased. In the next two years, sales and net income are projected to decrease even more substantially.

This forecast is based on increased competition from foreign producers located in countries with very low labour costs compared to Canada's.

Metalco is faced with a very difficult problem. The major company expense is wages. The company does not need the services of about 2000 of its workers because of new automated equipment and because production is decreasing. In the last five years, these unneeded people have been kept on staff because the company felt a loyalty towards its workers. If they had been laid off, their families would have suffered severe economic hardships. However, had they been laid off, the company's net income would have averaged about $98 million a year.

Metalco must decide what to do in the next two years. If it does not lay off unneeded workers, the company will suffer losses. If unneeded workers are laid off, the company will be able to decrease total expenses by about $60 million over the two years projected.

1. What will be the estimated net income for the next two years if unneeded workers are let go?
2. What are the social costs to the community if workers are let go?
3. What are the economic costs to the community if workers are let go?
4. What obligation does Metalco have to the shareholders who have invested their savings in Metalco shares?
5. What do you feel is the correct decision and action to make in the interest of:
   (a) the community?
   (b) the shareholders?
   (c) the company's future?
6. If you were a member of Metalco's management team, what decision would you make? Why?

INTERNET RESOURCES

1. **NetMBA   www.netmba.com**

   Go to this site and select Accounting. You will find a detailed explanation of each step of the accounting cycle along with accounting definitions. The site contains information on a number of subjects including economics, finance, marketing, statistics and management.

2. **Ontario Ministry of Education www.edu.gov.on.ca/eng/career/employab.html**

   This site provides information on careers, skills required by employers, and a personal skills quiz as well as links to other skills sites.

3. **Canada Business http://canadabusiness.gc.ca/gol/cbec/site.nsf/en/index.html**

   This federal government site provides all you need to know about operating a business in Canada and specifically in each province. Included is information on starting a business, taxation, employee regulations, marketing, planning, finance and accounting, and importing and exporting. Links to similar sites for each province are listed.

4. **Starting a Business http://canadabusiness.gc.ca/gol/cbec/site.nsf/en/bg00328.html**

   This section of the Canada Business site provides information on starting a business such as planning, information guides, and start-up guides for specific types of businesses.

The Merchandising Company

UNIT 14   Merchandising Accounts

Learning Objectives

After reading this unit, discussing the applicable review questions, and completing the applications exercises, you will be able to do the following:

1. **NAME** and **DEFINE** the function of the three major types of companies.

2. **PREPARE** a schedule of cost of goods sold.

3. **PREPARE** an income statement for a merchandising business.

4. **RECORD** transactions for a merchandising business including the following accounts: Sales, Sales Returns and Allowances, Sales Discounts, Purchases, Purchases Returns and Allowances, Purchases Discounts, Transportation-in, and Delivery Expense.

TYPES OF BUSINESS OPERATIONS

There are three basic types of business operation—service, merchandising, and manufacturing companies. They are shown in Figure 7-10.

Service Companies

Up to this point, accounting procedures have been illustrated mainly by reference to businesses such as a fitness centre, motel, cinema, contractor, doctor, etc. All of these businesses offer services to their customers. They do not sell products such as mouthwash or tires; they sell services and are called **service companies**.

A service company sells services.

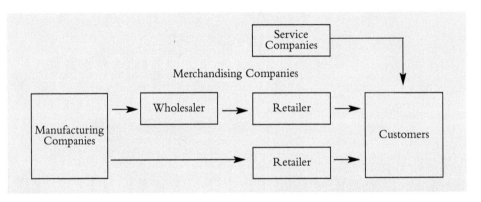

Merchandising Companies

A merchandising company sells a product.

Many businesses sell products, not services, and are known as **merchandising companies**. Both wholesalers and retailers are included in this group. Retailers usually buy merchandise from wholesalers or manufacturers and sell it to their customers at a price that covers their costs and provides a net income.

Manufacturing Companies

A manufacturing company makes a product.

A firm that converts raw materials into saleable products is called a **manufacturing company**. Usually, a manufacturer sells products to merchandising companies such as retailers and wholesalers.

Campbell Sports: A Merchandising Company

The accounting procedures of a merchandising company are a little different from those of a service company. The difference can be illustrated by examining Campbell Sports, a retail store located in Niagara Falls.

Campbell Sports buys bicycles, hockey equipment, baseball equipment, and hundreds of other sporting goods from manufacturers such as Spalding, CCM, Nike, Slazenger, and a variety of wholesalers. The goods bought from these manufacturers and sold to Campbell's customers are called **merchandise**. The total dollar value of goods on hand for resale is found in an account called *Merchandise Inventory*.

Goods bought for resale are called merchandise.

DETERMINING THE NET INCOME FOR A MERCHANDISING COMPANY

In Chapter 3, you learned that expenses are the cost of goods or services used in the operation of a business. To calculate the net income for a service business, expenses are subtracted from the revenue. This calculation is illustrated by the equation:

$$\text{Revenue} - \text{Expenses} = \text{Net Income}$$

A merchandising company must buy and pay for the merchandise it sells as well as pay the expenses of operating the business. The following two equations illustrate how net income is calculated for a merchandising company:

Revenue	–	Cost of Goods Sold	=	Gross Profit
Gross Profit	–	Expenses	=	Net Income

Net income occurs when revenue from sales exceeds both the cost of goods sold and the operating expenses.

The preparation of the income statement for a merchandising enterprise is a little more complicated than for a service business. Figure 7-2, below, shows an income statement for a merchandising company. Notice that there are three sections in the body of the statement — revenue, cost of goods sold, and operating expenses. Can you locate the following equations on the income statement, Figure 7-2?

Revenue	–	Cost of Goods Sold	=	Gross Profit
$164 000		$104 000		$60 000

Gross Profit	–	Expenses	=	Net Income
$60 000		$30 600		$29 400

One of the major expenses for a merchandising company is the cost of the goods that it buys for resale. Since the cost of goods sold is a major expense, it receives special attention on the income statement or in a separate schedule.

Campbell Sports		
Income Statement		
For the Month Ended May 31, 2008		
Revenue		
Sales		$164 000
Cost of Goods Sold		
Cost of Goods Sold (per schedule)		104 000
Gross Profit		60 000
Operating Expenses		
Advertising Expense	$12 400	
Delivery Expense	700	
Office Expense	1 400	
Miscellaneous Expense	500	
Rent Expense	3 600	
Salaries Expense	10 400	
Utilities Expense	1 600	
Total Expenses		30 600
Net Income		$29 400

FIGURE 7-2

Income statement for Campbell Sports

The value of Cost of Goods Sold is determined in two ways dependent upon the inventory system the merchandising firm has implemented.

INVENTORY SYSTEMS

There are two inventory accounting systems that are used by businesses. How do they compare?

Perpetual Inventory System

The perpetual inventory method is a continuous record of all merchandise on hand.

This system provides a current value for inventory since it records changes as items are purchased and sold. Its features include:

- This system is best suited to merchandising firms that offer a large number of items for sale, such as Sears, Canadian Tire, Wal-Mart, etc.
- It is the more common system due to the increased use of scanners in merchandising stores.
- The business must be able to afford a scanner system.
- This method provides up-to-date information regarding the number of items in inventory sold, the price sold for; when the item is sold at the time it is scanned.
- A year-end physical count of inventory is still required to see if the count of actual inventory matches the amount indicated by the perpetual records.
- Any difference can be used to identify necessary corrective action. Where a shortfall amount is increasing, has it been stolen, lost, or destroyed?
- Any difference in the amount is reconciled through a journal entry so that the value of the ending inventory is corrected in the ledger to begin the next accounting period.
- Record keeping is more involved than for the periodic system.

Where the business has a large volume of items for resale and can afford a scanner, this method is probably the better inventory system since it provides more accurate, faster information.

Periodic Inventory System

The actual amount of inventory on hand is determined by physical count when financial statements are prepared.

This system does not provide a current value for inventory since it is based on a physical count that is done periodically. In most cases this is done yearly.

- This method is best suited to merchandising businesses such as small variety stores that cannot afford a scanner; however, it can be used for any merchandising business.
- The value of inventory is determined at the end of the period by counting the items and multiplying by their respective prices.
- The system requires less record keeping than the perpetual method.

Remember: Both systems arrive at the same value for ending inventory at the end of the fiscal year! Why? Both methods require a count of the inventory to determine what items are actually in stock at the end of the period times. To arrive at a value multiply the number of items by the price of each item.

This chapter will discuss in detail the concepts and journal entries required to calculate the value of inventory and the cost of goods sold for the fiscal period.

The accuracy of these values is extremely important to the business since they are used to calculate the net income or net loss for the period.

PERIODIC INVENTORY SYSTEM

Let's start by discussing the periodic system of accounting for inventory. As mentioned above this method is still used by many small businesses in Canada.

Schedule of Cost of Goods Sold

A **schedule** is a supporting statement providing details of an item or items on a main statement.

In the income statement format used by Campbell Sports in Figure 7-2, a single total, $104 000, appears in the **cost of goods sold** section. This total includes all the costs involved in purchasing the merchandise to be sold. It is arrived at by the completion of the *schedule of cost of goods sold* as illustrated in Figure 7-3. The use of this schedule simplifies the presentation of the income statement. This schedule is used in the periodic inventory system to show how the cost of goods sold is calculated.

A schedule is a supporting statement providing details of an item on a main statement.

The total of all costs involved in purchasing the merchandise to be sold.

Campbell Sports
Schedule of Cost of Goods Sold
For the Month Ended May 31, 2008

Merchandise Inventory, May 1	$ 72 000	
Add: Purchases	60 000	
Total Cost of Merchandise	132 000	
Less: Merchandise Inventory, May 31	28 000	
Cost of Goods Sold		$104 000

FIGURE 7-3

Schedule of cost of goods sold for Campbell Sports

Preparing a Schedule of Cost of Goods Sold

The steps followed in preparing a schedule of cost of goods sold can be illustrated as follows:

Beginning Merchandise Inventory + Purchases of Merchandise = Cost of Merchandise Available for Sale − Ending Merchandise Inventory = Cost of Goods Sold

However, there are several other items that affect the cost of goods sold. These include:

- Purchases returns and allowances
- Purchases discounts
- Transportation-in

How do each of these items affect the total cost of merchandise? Figure 7-4, the expanded schedule of cost of goods sold, contains each of these additional items.

Purchases Returns and Allowances

If goods that have been purchased and recorded in the Purchases account are *returned,* the cost of purchases decreases. The *Purchases Returns and Allowances account* is used to record such returns. On the schedule of cost of goods sold (Figure 7-4), the amount shown for the Purchases Returns and Allowances account is a subtraction.

An account used to record the return of merchandise previously purchased for resale.

Purchases Discounts

When a cash discount off the invoice price is received, the discount is recorded in
the Purchases Discounts account. The cost of the merchandise decreases because of
the discount received. Therefore, on the schedule, Figure 7-4, the amount shown for
the Purchases Discounts account is subtracted from the Purchases account.

FIGURE 7-4

Expanded schedule of cost
of goods sold including net
purchases calculation and
transportation cost

Campbell Sports Schedule of Cost of Goods Sold For the Month Ended June 30, 2008			
Merchandise Inventory, June 1			$ 28 000
Add: Purchases		$42 400	
Less: Purchases Returns			
and Allowances	$8 000		
Purchases Discounts	400	8 400	
Net Purchase Cost		34 000	
Add: Transportation-in		2 000	
Total Cost of Merchandise Purchased			36 000
Cost of Merchandise Available for Sale			64 000
Less: Merchandise Inventory, June 30			22 000
Cost of Goods Sold			$42 000

Net Purchase Cost

The Purchases account figure less the Purchases Returns and Allowances account
figure and the Purchases Discounts account figure equals net purchase cost. The
calculation is shown below:

Calculation of Net Purchases		
Purchases		$42 400
Less: Purchases Returns and Allowances	$8 000	
Purchases Discounts	400	8 400
Net Purchase Cost		$34 000

Transportation on Purchases

The cost of merchandise purchased for resale is increased by the cost of trans-
porting the merchandise to the retailer's place of business. **Transportation-in**,
Transportation on Purchases, or *Freight-in* is the account used to record this cost.
Figure 7-4 shows how the transportation cost is added to the net purchases total.
The $2000 transportation cost is added to $34 000 (net purchase cost) to arrive
at a total of $36 000, called *total cost of merchandise purchased*.

The Merchandise Inventory account balance appears in the current assets section of the balance sheet as shown in Figure 7-5:

Campbell Sports		
Partial Balance Sheet		
June 30, 2008		
Assets		
Current Assets		
Cash	$ 8 000	
Accounts Receivable	54 000	
Merchandise Inventory (at cost)	22 000	
Office Supplies	2 000	
Total Current Assets		$86 000

FIGURE 7-5
The Merchandise Inventory account balance is shown in the current assets section of the balance sheet.

Chart of Accounts for a Merchandising Business

As you have learned, the income statement for a merchandising company contains a new expense section — the cost of goods sold section. For each item in this section, there is an account in the General Ledger. Figure 7-6 lists the accounts usually found in the General Ledger of a merchandising company.

Merchandising Company Chart of Accounts		
SECTION	**NO.**	**TITLE**
(1) Assets	101	Cash
	110	Accounts Receivable
	120	Merchandise Inventory
	125	Office Supplies
	126	Store Supplies
	150	Building
	151	Equipment
	160	Land
(2) Liabilities	200	Accounts Payable
	205	PST Payable
	206	GST Payable
	207	GST Refundable
	210	Bank Loan
	250	Mortgage Payable
(3) Owner's Equity	300	Owner, Capital
	301	Owner, Drawings
	302	Income Summary
(4) Revenue	400	Sales
	401	Sales Returns and Allowances
	402	Sales Discounts
(5) Cost of Goods Sold	500	Purchases
	501	Purchases Returns and Allowances
	502	Purchases Discounts
	503	Transportation-in
	550	Cost of Goods Sold
(6) Expenses	600	Advertising Expense
	601	Delivery Expense
	602	Miscellaneous Expense
	603	Office Expense
	604	Salaries Expense
	605	Utilities Expense

FIGURE 7-6
Chart of accounts for a merchandising company

Notice that there are six sections in the General Ledger of a merchandising company: assets, liabilities, owner's equity, revenue, cost of goods sold, and expenses. The General Ledger of a service business has only five sections. It does not have a cost of goods sold section. Most of, but not all, the new merchandising accounts are found in the new section — the cost of goods sold. The new merchandising accounts are shown in Figure 7-6 and include:

NEW MERCHANDISING ACCOUNTS

120	Merchandise Inventory	500	Purchases
205	PST Payable	501	Purchases Returns and Allowances
206	GST Payable	502	Purchases Discounts
207	GST Refundable	503	Transportation-in
400	Sales	550	Cost of Goods Sold
401	Sales Returns and Allowances	601	Delivery Expense
402	Sales Discounts		

Debit and Credit Rules for Merchandising Accounts

In this chapter, you will learn additional debit and credit rules for the accounts of a merchandising company. The rules are based on the equation:

$$\text{Assets} = \text{Liabilities} + \text{Owner's Equity}$$

You will remember that income statement accounts are related to the owner's equity account. The two basic principles determine the debit and credit rules for the new accounts:

- Revenue increases owner's equity.
- Expenses decrease owner's equity.

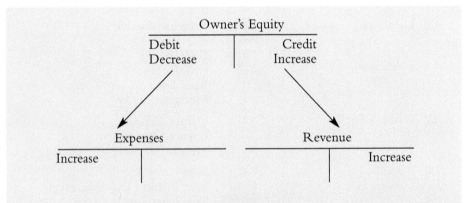

- Expenses decrease owner's equity and are recorded as debits. Expense accounts increase on the debit side and decrease on the credit side.
- Revenue increases owner's equity and is recorded as a credit. Revenue accounts increase on the credit side and decrease on the debit side.

Income Statement Accounts

The income statement in Figure 7-2 on page 209 demonstrates the three sections of the statement for a merchandising enterprise and the calculations necessary to determine net income. This section of the unit will discuss the new accounts necessary to record the sale and purchase of merchandise for a merchandising company.

Revenue Section of the Income Statement

For a business to record a net income (have a net profit), the revenue from sales must exceed the cost of goods sold and the operating expenses (rent, advertising, light, heat, salaries, etc.). Figure 7-7 is the revenue section for Campbell Sports for June:

Campbell Sports Partial Income Statement For the Month Ended June 30, 2008		
Revenue		
Sales		$62 000
Less: Sales Returns and Allowances	$1 500	
Sales Discounts	500	2 000
Net Sales		$60 000

FIGURE 7-7

Revenue section of the income statement

Recording Revenue Account Transactions

Sample transactions involving Campbell Sports' revenue accounts follow.

Sales

Sales means the amount of cash sales and credit sales made by the business during the accounting period. When merchandise is sold to a customer, it is recorded in the **Sales account**.

An account used to record the cash and credit sales of merchandise by the business.

Transaction 1: Cash Sale

Jun.   1   *Cash register total for the day, $4250.*

Cash sales are entered into the cash register or computerized point-of-sale terminal at the time of the sale. At the end of the day, a total is obtained and is recorded by journal entry:

Jun. 1	Cash	4 250	
	Sales		4 250
	To record cash sales for Jun. 1.		

Transaction 2: Credit Sale

Jun.   2   G. Giles purchased a pair of used skates and three hockey sticks, $150 on account.

This transaction is recorded as follows:

Jun. 2	Accounts Receivable/G. Giles	150	
	Sales		150
	Sold merchandise on account.		

The first two transactions are shown in the T-accounts below:

Cash		Accounts Receivable/G. Giles		Sales	
Jun. 1 4 250		Jun. 2 150		Jun. 1 4 250	
				2 150	

Sales Returns and Allowances

There is always a chance that the buyer of merchandise may not be satisfied with the goods received. The goods may be the wrong size or colour; they may be defective; or they may be unsatisfactory for other reasons. Either the goods are returned to the seller for a full refund, or the seller gives the customer an allowance on the selling price. Normally, a customer is given a cash refund if the merchandise was paid for, and a credit to his or her account if the merchandise was purchased on account and the bill is unpaid.

The Sales Returns and Allowances account is used by the seller to record merchandise returned by a customer.

The **Sales Returns and Allowances** account is used to record a return of merchandise by the customer. Since this, in effect, cancels all or a portion of a previous sale, this transaction reduces sales revenue. The Sales Returns and Allowances account is often called a *contra-revenue account* because its debit balance is the *opposite* of the credit balance of the revenue account, Sales. The Sales account could be debited to record these transactions, but most retailers use a Sales Returns and Allowances account to have separate information in this important area. It is important since increasing sales returns and allowances result in decreaseing revenue for the period. Continued increases in returns may indicate a number of problems, such as poor handling of merchandise, shipping problems, or problems with the quality of the merchandise.

Transaction 3: Sales Return on a Credit Sale

Jun.   3   G. Giles returned one defective hockey stick, priced at $15, from merchandise purchased on Jun. 2.

This transaction represents a sales return from a credit customer. Therefore, the customer's account balance must be reduced (credit) and the amount recorded as a sales return and allowance. The Sales Returns and Allowances account is debited to record a reduction in revenue (contra revenue) as a result of a return:

Jun. 3	Sales Returns and Allowances	15	
	Accounts Receivable/G. Giles		15
	Goods returned by G. Giles.		

This transaction is shown in the following T-accounts:

Sales Returns and Allowances		Accounts Receivable/G. Giles		
Jun. 3	15	Jun. 2	150	Jun. 3	15

Transaction 4: Sales Return on a Cash Sale

Jun.   4   *Customer returned merchandise worth $25 with the cash sales slip for a refund. The goods were bought for cash on Jun. 1.*

Since the customer originally paid for the merchandise, a cash refund is given. The journal entry would be as follows:

Jun. 4	Sales Returns and Allowances	25	
	Cash		25
	Goods returned for cash refund.		

This transaction is shown in the T-accounts below:

Sales Returns and Allowances		Cash		
Jun. 3	15	Jun. 1	4 250	Jun. 4	25
4	25			

A sales return represents a decrease in revenue and is recorded as a debit. Since revenue accounts like Sales increase on the credit side, they decrease on the debit side. The amount of the Sales Returns and Allowances account is subtracted from the Sales account figure in the revenue section on the income statement (see Figure 7-7).

Credit Invoices

All business transactions must be supported by an original source document. The source document that is completed when goods sold on account are returned is the **credit invoice**, as shown in Figure 7-8. The credit invoice is prepared by the seller, in this case Campbell Sports, and sent to the customer, G. Giles. A copy is kept by the seller and used as the basis for the entry reducing the customer's account and for recording the sales return in the Sales Returns and Allowances account. A credit invoice provides the details about a reduction in a customer's account, the amount, the reason, and the original invoice number.

> A credit invoice is a source document issued by the seller to indicate the amount of credit allowed to a customer for returned or defective goods purchased on account.

The credit invoice and its copy are used by both the seller and the buyer to prepare an entry to record the return. The seller records a sales return, and the buyer records a purchase return. Other terms used for credit invoice are *credit memorandum* and *credit note*.

Sales Discounts

The second item that results in a reduction in sales is a cash discount given to customers for prompt payment. A discount given to a customer for early payment is called a **sales discount**. Such discounts are indicated in the terms of sale agreed upon between the seller and the customer.

> A cash discount offered to encourage early payment of customer account balances.

FIGURE 7-8

Credit invoice recording goods returned by G. Giles

CAMPBELL SPORTS

3000 Base Line Road
Niagara Falls, ON L2J 1H2
Tel: 613-684-1287   Fax: 613-684-5381

CREDIT INVOICE

Sold To	No. 149
G. Giles	Date June 3, 2008
32 Cleary Ave.	
Ottawa, ON K2A 4A1	

Quantity	Description	Unit Price	Amount
1	Re: Our Invoice 896 — defective hockey stick	$15	$15
	CREDIT		

An agreement between the buyer and seller of an item regarding the method of payment.

Terms of Sale

The invoice sent by the supplier to the buyer contains the agreed-upon terms for payment of the items purchased. If payment is to be made immediately, the terms are *cash* or *cash on receipt of invoice*. If the buyer is allowed a period of time for payment, the terms are said to be *on account,* or *on credit,* and the sale is called a credit sale. Some firms offer the same terms to all customers. Other firms offer a variety of terms to customers. Here is a list of some commonly used terms of sale:

- **C.O.D.:** Payment must be made when the goods are delivered (cash on delivery).
- **Receipt of invoice:** Payment is to be made when the invoice is received.
- **Net 30:** The full amount of the invoice is due 30 days from the invoice date.
- **EOM:** Payment is due at the end of the month.
- **10th following:** Payment is due on the tenth day of the following month.
- **2/10, n/30:** The buyer may deduct a 2 percent discount from the invoice amount if payment is made within 10 days from the date of the invoice. The full amount (net) is due in 30 days if the buyer does not pay within 10 days.
- **1/10, n/30 EOM:** A 1 percent discount may be taken if payment is made within 10 days. The full amount must be paid within 30 days after the end of the month.

It is common practice for firms to negotiate the terms of sale with their customers. Favourable terms, for example net 60 days, may be offered to a valued customer. Less favourable terms may be offered to customers who buy small amounts of goods or services or who have a very poor record of paying amounts owed. You have just learned that sellers offer discounts to customers to encourage early payment of account balances. Transactions 5 and 6 are examples of a sale to a customer involving a discount for early payment of the invoice.

Transaction 5: Credit Sale Offering Sales Discount

Jun.   5   *Sold merchandise to W.P. Mulvihill, Invoice 907, terms 3/10, n/30, $620 on account.*

To encourage early payment, terms of 3/10, n/30 were offered to Mulvihill. On Jun. 5, Campbell's accounts appeared as follows, in T-account form:

Accounts Receivable/ W.P. Mulvihill	Sales
Jun. 5 620	Jun. 5 620

Transaction 6: Recording the Sales Discount

Jun.   15   Received cheque for $601.40 from W.P. Mulvihill in payment of Invoice 907.

Mulvihill decided that it was worth paying within 10 days because it meant a saving of $18.60 (0.03 × 620 = 18.60). Therefore, on June 15, exactly 10 days from the date of the invoice (June 5), payment of $601.40 was made to Campbell. Campbell received the cheque, and it was recorded in their accounts as follows, in T-account form:

Cash	Sales Discounts	Acc. Rec./W.P. Mulvihill
Jun. 15 601.40	Jun. 15 18.60	Jun. 5 620.00 | Jun. 15 620.00

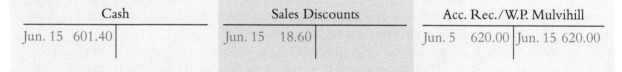

Note that the Sales Discounts account is debited. The debit represents a decrease in revenue; therefore, Sales Discounts is a contra-revenue account like Sales Returns and Allowances. The company has lost or given away $18.60 to encourage early payment. Note also that Mulvihill's account is credited for the full amount owing, $620, even though only $601.40 was received from Mulvihill. The $601.40 cancels the full amount owing of $620.

Sales discounts decrease owner's equity and are recorded as debits.

In General Journal form these entries would appear as follows:

Jun. 5	Accounts Receivable/W.P. Mulvihill	620.00	
	Sales		620.00
	Invoice 907, terms 3/10, n/30.		
15	Cash	601.40	
	Sales Discounts	18.60	
	Accounts Receivable/W.P. Mulvihill		620.00
	Cash received for Invoice 907.		

After these two entries are posted, there is a zero balance in the Mulvihill Accounts Receivable account.

Sales discounts reduce the total revenue that will be received from sales. Since a reduction in revenue decreases Capital, discounts given to customers are recorded as debits in the Sales Discounts account. The amount in the Sales Discounts account is subtracted from the Sales account figure on the income statement, as shown in Figure 7-9.

Campbell Sports
Partial Income Statement
For the Month Ended June 30, 2008

Revenue		
Sales		$62 000
Less: Sales Returns and Allowances	$1 500	
Sales Discounts	500	2 000
Net Sales		$60 000

FIGURE 7-9

The total of sales discounts and sales returns and allowances is subtracted from sales.

For the month of June, Campbell's total sales were $62 000. However, since some customers returned merchandise (sales returns of $1500), the amount of sales for the month must be decreased by $1500. Also, since sales discounts of $500 were given to customers for early payment, sales must be decreased by $500.

On the income statement, Figure 7-9, the total of sales returns and allowances and sales discounts, $2000 ($1500 + $500), is subtracted from sales in the revenue section. The result, $60 000, is called **net sales**.

Net sales = Sales – Sales Returns and Allowances – Sales Discount.

Relationship Between Sales Discounts and Sales Returns

When merchandise is returned to a supplier as unsuitable, a credit invoice (also called a credit memorandum) is issued to the customer. The discount period for that original sales invoice is calculated from the date of the credit invoice. Following is an example illustrating this type of situation.

On June 5, Campbell Sports sold $500 worth of sports equipment to the Parks and Recreation Commission with terms of 2/10, n/30. When the goods were received by Parks and Recreation, it was discovered that part of the order was different merchandise from what was ordered, so it was returned. A credit invoice for $100 was issued by Campbell on June 10. Can you determine by which date the original invoice must be paid to take advantage of the discount?

The discount period begins from the date of the credit invoice, which is June 10. If the invoice is paid 10 days from June 10, the discount may be taken by the customer.

Disallowance of Sales Discounts

If a payment is received from a customer after the discount period, but with the discount subtracted, it is necessary to inform the customer that the discount is disallowed. The amount of the discount is still owed by the customer and remains as a balance on the customer's account.

Recording Cost of Goods Sold Account Transactions

In the next part of this unit, the rules of debit and credit for the cost of goods sold accounts will be described. Some sample transactions for Campbell Sports follow.

Purchases

The cost of merchandise purchased for resale is recorded in the Purchases account.

The **Purchases account** is used to record the cost of merchandise bought for resale. The cost of goods purchased is one of the major costs of operating a merchandising business. Because costs (like expenses) decrease net income and ultimately decrease owner's equity, the Purchases account is debited when merchandise for resale is purchased.

Transaction 7: Cash Purchase of Merchandise

Jun.   8   *Purchased sports equipment from CCM, $500 cash.*

For this transaction, Campbell Sports issues a cheque in payment. The two accounts involved are Cash and Purchases. Cash, an asset, decreases and is credited. Purchases, a cost account, is debited because it reduces owner's equity. In General Journal format, the entry is:

Jun. 8	Purchases	500	
	Cash		500
	Purchased sports equipment for cash from CCM.		

This transaction is shown in the T-accounts below:

Purchases		Cash	
Jun. 8 500			Jun. 8 500

Transaction 8: Credit Purchase of Merchandise

Jun.   9   Purchased tennis equipment from Spalding Ltd., net 30, $200 on account.

The two accounts involved are Purchases and Accounts Payable/Spalding Ltd. Spalding Ltd. is a liability account; it increases and is credited. Purchases is a cost account and it is debited because it reduces owner's equity. Following is the journal entry to record the transaction:

Jun. 9	Purchases	200	
	Accounts Payable/Spalding Ltd.		200
	Purchased tennis equipment, terms of payment net 30 days.		

This transaction is shown in the T-accounts below:

Purchases		Accounts Payable/Spalding Ltd.	
Jun. 8 500			Jun. 9 200
9 200			

Recognition of Costs

As indicated earlier in this text, costs and expenses are recorded when incurred, not when paid. Therefore, both cash and credit purchases are recorded in the Purchases account to obtain the correct balance for purchases for the accounting period. **Net purchases** is the purchases minus both purchases returns and allowances and purchases discounts.

Net purchases = Purchases – Purchases Returns and Allowances – Purchases Discounts.

Purchases Returns and Allowances

If the merchandise purchased from suppliers is unsuitable for resale, it is returned. The accounting entries and procedures for purchases returns are similar to sales returns. When the purchaser returns merchandise, a cash refund is given for items previously paid for, and a credit is given for unpaid invoice items. A **Purchases Returns and Allowances account**, often called a *contra-cost account* because it reduces the cost of a purchase, is used to record the returns on the books of the purchaser.

The Purchases Returns and Allowances account is used by the buyer to record the return of goods.

Transaction 9: Goods Returned for Cash Refund

Jun.   10   Returned to CCM merchandise worth $100, purchased for cash on Jun. 8. Received refund cheque for $100 from CCM.

To record this transaction, Cash, an asset, is increased with a debit of $100. Purchases Returns and Allowances, because it is a contra-cost account, is credited $100. This transaction results in an increase in equity, and therefore the Purchases Returns and Allowances account is credited. The journal entry is as follows:

Jun. 10 Cash	100	
Purchases Returns and Allowances		100
To record cash refund received from CCM.		

T-accounts for this transaction are shown below:

Cash		Purchases Returns and Allowances	
Jun. 10 100			Jun. 10 100

Transaction 10: Goods Returned for Credit

Jun.   11   *Returned to Spalding Ltd. defective tennis equipment purchased for $200, on account, on June 9. Received Credit Invoice 981 for $200 from Spalding Ltd.*

The Accounts Payable account Spalding Ltd. decreases and is debited. The Purchases Returns and Allowances account is credited because it decreases Purchases. Following are the journal entry and the T-accounts:

Jun. 11 Accounts Payable/Spalding Ltd.	200	
Purchases Returns and Allowances		200
To record Credit Invoice 981 for the return of defective merchandise.		

Accounts Payable/ Spalding Ltd.		Purchases Returns and Allowances	
Jun. 11 200	Jun. 9 200		Jun. 10 100
			11 200

Credit Invoice

The source document that is completed when goods are returned is the credit invoice. The credit invoice is prepared by the seller and sent to the customer. The seller keeps a copy and uses it to enter the amount by which the customer's account is reduced. As well, the seller uses the credit invoice to record the return of merchandise in the Sales Returns and Allowances account. The purchaser, on the other hand, uses the credit invoice to record the purchase return in its books.

Purchases Discounts

Just as Campbell offers discounts to its customers for early payment of bills, it receives discounts for the same reason from its creditors. When Campbell receives such a discount, it is called a **purchases discount**. The next two transactions illustrate how purchases discounts are recorded.

The cash discount received off the purchase price in return for early payment of the invoice.

Transaction 11: Credit Purchase with Purchases Discount Available

Jun.   12   *Received Purchase Invoice 4918 for $500 from Spalding Ltd., terms 2/15, n/30.*

Campbell checked the invoice for accuracy and, since the merchandise was received in good condition, the invoice was approved for payment. Campbell's accounts recording the invoice appeared as follows, in T-account form:

Purchases		Accounts Payable/ Spalding Ltd.	
Jun. 12 500			Jun. 12 500

Transaction 12: Recording the Purchases Discount

Jun.   27   Sent cheque for $490 to Spalding Ltd. in payment of Invoice 4918.

When Invoice 4918 was received, it was placed in a date file in a folder dated June 25. Then, on June 25, when the cheque for $490 was prepared and sent to Spalding Ltd., it was recorded in Campbell's accounts as follows, in T-account form:

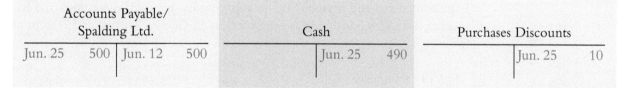

Accounts Payable/ Spalding Ltd.		Cash		Purchases Discounts	
Jun. 25 500	Jun. 12 500	Jun. 25 490			Jun. 25 10

In General Journal form, these two entries would be made as follows:

Jun. 12	Purchases		500	
	Accounts Payable/Spalding Ltd.			500
	Invoice 4918, terms 2/15, n/30.			
25	Accounts Payable/Spalding Ltd.		500	
	Cash			490
	Purchases Discounts			10
	Paid Invoice 4918, less 2 percent discount.			

Purchases discounts reduce the total cost of goods purchased and are recorded as credits in the Purchases Discounts account. Purchases Discounts, like Purchases Returns and Allowances, is often called a contra-cost account because it reduces the cost of a purchase.

> Purchases discounts increase owner's equity and are recorded as credits.

The Purchases Discounts account appears in the schedule of cost of goods sold, where it is subtracted from the cost of purchases. This is illustrated in the schedule of cost of goods sold in Figure 7-10.

Campbell Sports
Schedule of Cost of Goods Sold
For the Month Ended June 30, 2008

Merchandise Inventory, June 1			$28 000
Add: Purchases		$42 400	
Less: Purchases Returns and Allowances	$8 000		
Purchases Discounts	400	8 400	
Net Purchase Cost		34 000	
Add: Transportation-in		2 000	
Total Cost of Merchandise Purchased			36 000
Cost of Merchandise Available for Sale			64 000
Less: Merchandise Inventory, June 30			22 000
Cost of Goods Sold			$42 000

FIGURE 7-10

Expanded schedule of cost of goods sold, including net purchases calculation and transportation cost

Transportation on Purchases

The cost of merchandise purchased for resale is increased by the cost of transporting the merchandise to the retailer's place of business. Transportation-in or *Transportation on Purchases* is the account used to record this cost. Figure 7-10 shows how transportation adds to the final cost of goods purchased during the accounting period.

Transaction 13: Transportation-in

Jun.   14   Received $55 invoice from CN Express, net 30, for transportation of merchandise purchased.

The invoice received from CN Express is to cover the cost of transporting merchandise from a manufacturer to Campbell's store. Since this transaction adds to the costs of operating the business, owner's equity is reduced and therefore the Transportation-in account is debited. The liability account Accounts Payable/CN Express increases and is credited. The company has incurred more costs and has another debt. The transaction is shown below in General Journal and T-account form:

Jun. 14 Transportation-in	55	
Accounts Payable/CN Express		55
Invoice from CN for the transportation of merchandise purchased.		

Transportation-in		Accounts Payable/CN Express	
Jun. 14 55			Jun. 14 55

Delivery Expense

An account used to record the cost of delivering merchandise to customers.

The cost of delivering merchandise to customers is recorded in the **Delivery Expense account**. This account appears in the expenses section of the income statement as shown in Figure 7-11, on the next page.

Transaction 14: Delivery Expense

Jun.   18   Paid $75 to a local cartage firm for delivering merchandise sold to customers.

The expense of delivering goods to customers is recorded in the Delivery Expense account. Delivery Expense reduces owner's equity and is debited. The asset Cash decreases and is credited. This transaction is shown below in General Journal and T-account form:

Jun. 18 Delivery Expense	75	
Cash		75
Cash payment for the delivery of goods to customers.		

Delivery Expense		Cash	
Jun. 18 75			Jun. 18 75

FIGURE 7-11

Income statement for a
merchandising company

Campbell Sports
Income Statement
For the Month Ended June 30, 2008

Revenue			
Sales		$62 000	
Less: Sales Returns and Allowances	$1 500		
Sales Discounts	500	2 000	
Net Sales			$60 000
Cost of Goods Sold			
Cost of Goods Sold (per schedule)			42 000
Gross Profit			18 000
Operating Expenses			
Delivery Expense		2 400	
Office Expense		800	
Miscellaneous Expense		600	
Rent Expense		2 400	
Salaries Expense		2 600	
Utilities Expense		400	
Total Expenses			9 200
Net Income			$8 800

The 14 sample transactions described in this unit involved the new accounts used by merchandising. Look at Figure 7-10, the schedule of cost of goods sold, and Figure 7-11, the income statement. Can you locate the new accounts? What effect do they have on the statements?

Debit and Credit Summary

Several new income statement accounts have been introduced in this chapter. Figure 7-12, on page 226, summarizes the recording of debits and credits in these new accounts.

Transactions involving five of the new accounts normally cause a decrease in owner's equity. These accounts are Delivery Expense, Purchases, Transportation-in, Sales Returns and Allowances, and Sales Discounts. These five accounts usually have a debit balance.

In previous chapters, you learned that transactions involving the Sales account increase the owner's equity and are recorded as credits. Transactions for two other accounts—Purchases Returns and Allowances and Purchases Discounts—also increase the owner's equity and are recorded as credits.

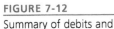

FIGURE 7-12
Summary of debits and credits for the new accounts introduced in this chapter

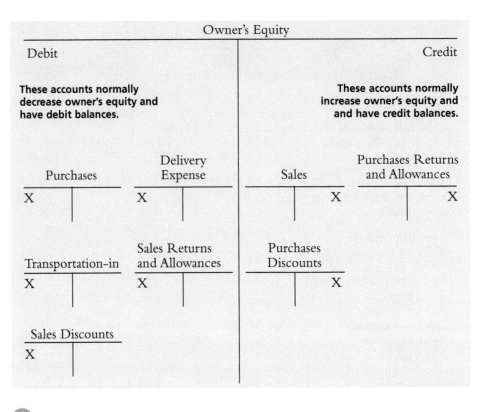

PERPETUAL INVENTORY SYSTEM

The perpetual inventory system keeps a running balance of the value of inventory during the accounting period. This inventory method also calculates the value of Cost of Goods Sold in a different manner from the periodic system that you just learned. It is determined by recording items purchased directly into the Inventory account at cost price and items sold at retail price directly into both the Inventory and Cost of Goods Sold accounts. The result is that the business has a running balance of the value of Inventory and Cost of Goods Sold.

How does it work? As you remember, we indicated earlier in the chapter that this method does require an increased number of entries, but you will discover the accounts and entries you learned in the Periodic System will be very helpful in learning this one.

Recording Increases to Inventory Value

In this example, assume that Inventory has a value of $90 000 at the beginning of the month of July. What journal entries will be required to record purchases and the related accounts that are used to record net purchases. How will this change the value of inventory?

The periodic system that you learned earlier determined the total cost of merchandise purchased in the following manner:

$$Purchases - Purchases\ Returns - Purchases\ Discounts$$
$$= Net\ Purchase\ Cost + Transportation\text{-}in$$
$$= Total\ Cost\ of\ Merchandise\ Purchased$$

In the perpetual system all of the journal entries related to purchases are made directly to Merchandise Inventory to ensure the inventory value at cost price is current.

Jul.   2   Campbell Sports purchased merchandise for $5000 cash.

Jul. 2	Merchandise Inventory	5 000	
	Cash		5 000
	Purchases for cash		

Jul.   5   Campbell Sports purchased merchandise for $7500 on account, terms of 2/10, net 30.

Jul. 5	Merchandise Inventory	7 500	
	Accounts Payable		7 500
	Purchase on account terms 2/10, net 30.		

Jul.   13   Campbell Sports paid the account payable in time to deduct the purchase discount.

Jul. 13	Account Payable	7 500	
	Cash		7 350
	Merchandise Inventory		150
	Payment on account less discount.		

Why does this increase the value of Merchandise Inventory? Remember, purchases are entered directly into the Merchandise Inventory account at the purchase price. The additional items purchased increase the value of the inventory by the cost of the purchase. Discounts on purchases reduce the value of the inventory.

Jul.   14   The store returned a $500 item to the company that they purchased merchandise for cash from on July 2.

How would you record this entry to keep inventory value correct? Right! The value of inventory should be reduced since we returned an item.

Jul. 14	Cash	500	
	Merchandise Inventory		500
	Returned an item for a cash refund.		

Jul.   16   Campbell Sports paid a $100 transportation charge on the purchase made on July 14.

How does this change the value of Merchandise Inventory? This time, the value increases as a result of the transportation-in cost.

Jul. 16	Merchandise Inventory	100	
	Cash		100
	To record the transportation charge on July 14 purchase.		

How is this different from the entry for transportation costs in the periodic system? All purchase-related items are recorded directly into the Inventory account so there is no need to make a separate calculation to determine the total cost of merchandise purchased.

Recording Decreases in Inventory Value

The perpetual inventory system requires **two entries** to the Merchandise Inventory account to decrease the value of inventory.

Recording Sales

In the periodic system, net sales was calculated as follows:

Sales − Sales Returns − Sales Discounts = Net Sales

Cost of Goods Sold was calculated as:

Beginning Inventory + Total of Merchandise Purchased − Ending Inventory
= Cost of Goods Sold

In the perpetual system, net sales are still recorded at the retail price, but the cost price of the same sales-related accounts must be recorded as a decrease in Merchandise Inventory and an increase in Cost of Goods Sold. It requires **two entries** to record these changes.

Let's see how this works!

Jul.   3   Campbell Sports sold $550 worth of merchandise for cash.

Remember: Sales are recorded the same as in the periodic system, which you have already learned.

Jul. 3	Cash	550	
	Sales		550
	To record cash sales.		

Now we need to record the decrease in inventory and the increase in cost of goods sold for the same sale.

Jul. 3	Cost of Goods Sold	350	
	Merchandise Inventory		350
	To record cost of goods sold.		

Why the difference in amount between the $550 recorded in Sales and the $350 recorded in the second entry? Of course, the first entry is recorded at retail price and the second is recorded at cost price. The same principle applies to a sale on account.

Jul. 4	Accounts Receivable	1 000	
	Sales		1 000
	To record sale on account.		
Jul. 4	Cost of Goods Sold	650	
	Merchandise Inventory		650
	To record cost of goods sold.		

How would you record Sales Returns and Sales Discounts?

On July 4, the customer returned an item from the July 3 sale for a $100 refund. The result is an increase in inventory since the item is placed back in inventory, and a decrease in cost of goods sold since it is no longer a cost.

Jul. 4	Sales Returns	100	
	Cash		100
	To record a sales return for cash.		
Jul. 4	Merchandise Inventory	65	
	Cost of Goods Sold		65
	To adjust inventory and cost of goods sold.		

Sales Discount? Red Deer High School paid their bill for $2000 less a 1 percent discount.

Jul. 5	Sales Discount	200	
	Cash	1 800	
	Accounts Receivable		2 000
	To record sales discount.		

You will notice this entry has no effect on inventory or the cost of goods sold since it is simply a payment on account.

The final result is an updated Merchandise Inventory account and Cost of Goods Sold account anytime during the accounting period.

UNIT 14

REVIEW QUESTIONS

1. A business may be classified according to what it does. A company that sells services to customers is called a service business. Name two other types of businesses and describe what they do.

2. Prepare a list of firms in your area. The list should include the names of five companies in each of the three classifications identified in question 1.

3. In a periodic inventory system:
   (a) Which account is debited when merchandise is purchased?
   (b) In which account does the value of the merchandise on hand appear?

4. How would the answers to 3 (1a) and (b) be different in a perpetual inventory system?

5. Name the statement (balance sheet, income statement, or schedule of cost of goods sold) and section of the statement in which each of the following items appears. The first item is done for you as an example.

   Example:

ITEM	STATEMENT	SECTION
(a) Cash	balance sheet	current asset

   (b) Accounts Receivable
   (c) Sales
   (d) Office Supplies
   (e) Purchases
   (f) Sales Returns and Allowances
   (g) Salaries Expense
   (h) Purchases Returns and Allowances
   (i) Delivery Expense
   (j) Transportation-in
   (k) Building
   (l) Beginning Inventory
   (m) Ending Inventory
   (n) Sales Discounts
   (o) Purchases Discounts

6. Indicate whether each of the following increases or decreases the cost of the merchandise:

   (a) Transportation-in
   (b) Purchases returns and allowances
   (c) Purchases discounts

7. Explain the difference between a periodic inventory system and a perpetual inventory system.

8. In a periodic inventory system:
   (a) Which account is debited when a customer returns merchandise bought

on credit because the merchandise is unsatisfactory? Which account is credited?

(b) Which account is debited when a cash refund is given to a customer for returned merchandise? Which account is credited?

8. Does the balance in the Sales Returns and Allowances account increase or decrease revenue?

9. How would the answers to 8 (a) and (b) change in a perpetual inventory system?

10. What source document is prepared when goods are returned for credit?

11. (a) Do sales discounts increase or decrease revenue?
    (b) Are sales discounts recorded as debits or credits? Why?

12. We sold merchandise worth $1000 to R. Heidebrecht. The terms of sale were 3/10, n/30. We received a cheque for $970 from Heidebrecht within 10 days. When recording the $970 cheque, is Heidebrecht's account credited for $1000 or $970?

12. Why do businesses offer cash discounts when the final effect is a reduction in net revenue?

13. A cash discount is recorded in the books of the buyer and seller. What account would be used to record the discount in the ledger of (a) the buyer, and (b) the seller?

14. What effect does a return have on the discount period offered by a business?

15. What is the difference between the Purchases account and the Office Supplies account?

16. What is the difference between the Purchases account and the Merchandise Inventory account in a periodic inventory system?

17. What account is debited for each of the following items purchased by Johnson's Hardware in a perpetual inventory system?

    (a) 1 desk and chair for the office
    (b) 10 ladders
    (c) 1 box of continuous computer paper
    (d) 2000 bags for the checkout counter
    (e) 150 lengths of rope for clothes lines

18. What is the difference between the Delivery Expense account and the Transportation-in account?

19. Name the increase side (debit or credit) for each of the following accounts and give a reason for your answer:

    (a) Purchases
    (b) Delivery Expense
    (c) Transportation-in
    (d) Purchases Returns and Allowances
    (e) Sales Returns and Allowances
    (f) Purchases Discounts
    (g) Sales
    (h) Sales Discounts

1. In January, St. John General Store had net sales of $8500 and cost of goods sold of $4700.

  (a) What is the gross profit?

  (b) If expenses totalled $2800, what is the net income or net loss?

2. In February, St. John General Store' net sales were $6200 and the cost of goods sold was $4100. Expenses totalled $1840.

  (a) What is the gross profit for the month?

  (b) What is the net income or the net loss for the month?

3. St. John General Store's March figures were net sales $3500, cost of goods sold $1900, total expenses $1750.

  (a) What is the gross profit?

  (b) What is the net income or net loss?

4. Complete the following equations by supplying the missing term in each one:

  (a) Net Sales − Cost of Goods Sold = ?

  (b) ? − Sales Returns and Allowances − Sales Discounts = Net Sales

  (c) Net Income + Operating Expenses = ?

  (d) Cost of Goods Sold + Ending Inventory = ?

  (e) Beginning Inventory + ? − Purchases Returns and Allowances − Purchases Discounts + Transportation-in = Cost of Goods Purchased

5. The cost accounts of Batasar Variety follow. Prepare a schedule of cost of goods sold for each of the following months.

  (a) February 1: Inventory $3000; Purchases $4500; February 28 Inventory $3500.

  (b) March 1: Inventory $3500; Purchases $2900; Purchases Returns and Allowances $300; Purchases Discounts $100; Transportation on Purchases $190; March 31 Inventory $3100.

6. Batasar Variety uses a periodic inventory system.

  (a) How would the March 31 inventory value of $3100 be determined if this was the end of the fiscal year and financial statements were being prepared?

  (b) How would the April 1 inventory total be determined?

7. What would be the answers to 6 (a) and (b) if Batasar Variety used a perpetual inventory system?

8. Prepare the revenue section of the income statement for Batasar Variety on March 31 from the following information:

  • Sales Discounts $210

  • Sales $31 000

  • Sales Returns and Allowances $490

9. (a) The documents on page 232 were issued by Campbell Sports. Campbell uses a periodic inventory system.

    (i) What kind of source documents are they?

    (ii) Prepare journal entries to record them.

  (b) Record the transactions listed on page 233 in a journal for Campbell

CAMPBELL SPORTS
3000 Base Line Road
Niagara Falls, Ontario   L2J 1H2

INVOICE   Order No.

Sold To   **Ship To**

A.N. Myer Secondary School   Same
6338 O'Neil Street
Niagara Falls, ON   L2J 1H2

Date Jan. 4, 2008   Invoice No. 26   Terms Net 30 days   Cash   Charge

Quantity	Description	Unit Price	Amount
30	Hockey Sticks	$30	$900

CAMPBELL SPORTS
3000 Base Line Road
Niagara Falls, Ontario   L2J 1H2

CREDIT INVOICE

Sold To   **No. 118**

A.N. Myer Secondary School   Date Jan. 10, 2008
6338 O'Neil Street
Niagara Falls, ON   L2J 1H2

Quantity Amount	Description	Unit Price
5	Re: Our Invoice 26 — hockey sticks received in damaged condition	$30 $150

CREDIT

Sports. Use the accounts Cash, Accounts Receivable, Sales, and Sales Returns and Allowances.

Feb. 1 Cash register summary:
Cash received from sales, $1850.

2 Sales invoices:
No. 301, Niagara Hockey Association, $1950;
No. 302, Stamford Collegiate, $850;
No. 303, S. Edgerton, $85.

3 Cash refund slip:
No. 29, for $87, refund for the return of a pair of children's skates.

8 Cash register summary:
Cash received from sales, $2120.

9 Credit invoices:
No. 89, for $350, hockey jackets returned by Niagara Hockey Association — wrong size.

10 Sales invoices:
No. 304, Vineland Tennis Club, $875;
No. 305, H. Burger, $63.

15 Cash receipts:
Cheques received from Niagara Hockey Association ($1600) and S. Edgerton ($85).

10. Prepare the journal entry for 9 (a) (ii) if Campbell uses a perpetual inventory system where the cost price is 50 percent of the sales price.

11. (a) On what date is the amount to be paid for each of the following invoices? Discounts are not to be taken. In your notebook, use a third column headed "Payment Date" to record your answers.

Invoice Date	Terms
August 5	EOM
August 6	n/30
August 8	n/60
August 14	15 EOM
August 17	2/10, n/30
August 19	C.O.D.
August 20	Receipt of invoice
August 25	1/10, n/30

(b) Determine the amount of the discount, the last day for obtaining the discount, and the amount to be paid for each of the following. All invoices are paid on the last day of the discount period. Record your answer in columns headed:

• Discount Date
• Amount to Be Paid
• Amount of Discount

Amount of Invoice	Terms	Invoice Date
$ 180	2/10, n/30	August 1
1 500	1/15, n/30	August 2
420	3/10, n/60	August 5
150	2/10, n/30	August 12
295	1/10, n/60	August 25

12. (a) Set up the following T-accounts for Water's Men's Wear:

   101 Cash

   112 Accounts Receivable/C. Baker

   113 Accounts Receivable/A. Jonsson

   114 Accounts Receivable/T. Mathews

   401 Sales

   402 Sales Returns and Allowances

   403 Sales Discounts

   (b) Journalize and post the following source documents, using the General Journal model used in Chapter 4.

   Oct. 10   Sales invoices issued to:
             A. Jonsson, No. 1035 for $3250, terms 2/10, n/30;
             C. Baker, No. 1036 for $709, terms 2/10, n/30;
             T. Mathews, No. 1037 for $1750, terms 2/10, n/30.

        14   Credit invoice issued to A. Jonsson, $650 for goods returned. Goods were sold to Jonsson on Oct. 10. It was agreed to change the discount period to date from Oct. 14.

        17   Cheque received from C. Baker, $694.82 for Invoice 1036.

        20   Cheque received from T. Mathews, $1715 for Invoice 1037.

        24   Cheque received from A. Jonsson, $2548 for Invoice 1035 less credit invoice $650, and less discount.

   (c) Calculate the net sales for the two-week accounting period.

13. Which of the following transactions should be recorded in the Purchases account for Lepp Hardware?

   (a) Purchase of advertising in the *St. Catharines Standard*
   (b) Purchase of a new salesperson's car from Nemeth Motors
   (c) Purchase of 12 snowblowers from John Deere for a special pre-winter sale
   (d) Purchase of a new liability insurance policy
   (e) Payment of three months' advance rent on the building

14. The following source documents have been received by Campbell Sports, which uses a periodic inventory system.

   (a) Identify the source documents.
   (b) Prepare a General Journal entry to record each source document.

BROOMBALL MANUFACTURING
331 Marion Street
Oshawa, Ontario   L1J 3A8

SOLD TO	SHIPPED TO	WI-60505
Campbell Sports 3000 Base Line Road Niagara Falls, Ontario L2J 1H2	Same	PLEASE QUOTE THIS NUMBER WHEN REFERRING TO OR PAYING THIS INVOICE

SHIP VIA	PPD.	COLL.	CUSTOMER'S ORDER NO.	TERMS	SALESPERSON	DATE MO.	DAY	YEAR
Pick-up			1214	Net 30 days	Phone	12	10	2008

NO.	DESCRIPTION	QUANTITY	UNIT	AMOUNT
25	Pairs of Broomball shoes	25	$80	$2000

PLEASE PAY THIS AMOUNT $2000

WILSON OFFICE SUPPLIERS
6350 Main Street
Niagara Falls, Ontario   L2J 2N3

Campbell Sports 3000 Base Line Road Niagara Falls, Ontario L2J 1H2	SHIP TO Same	INVOICE NUMBER T110982

DATE	SHIP VIA	ORDER NUMBER	TERMS
Dec. 22, 2008	--	1215	n/30

QUANTITY ORDERED	SHIPPED	PRODUCT NO. DESCRIPTION	UNIT PRICE	AMOUNT
1	1	IBM Intelli Station M Personal Computer	$4350	$4350

THIS IS YOUR INVOICE
NO OTHER WILL BE SENT

SPORTING EQUIPMENT

347 Tachereau Blvd.
Montréal, Québec   H2C 3B3

SOLD TO Campbell Sports
3000 Base Line Road
Niagara Falls, Ontario L2J 1H2

SHIPPED TO   Same

INVOICE
NUMBER

TR89-6153

Cust. Order No.	Our Order No.	Date Received	Date Shipped	Shipped Via	Invoice Date
1190	16150	Dec. 13, 2008	Jan. 4, 2009	Our Truck	Jan. 10, 2009

	Terms	F.O.B.	Salesperson
	Net 30 days		

Qty.	Description	Price	Total
50	Dolphin Clear Goggles	$15.50	$775.00

PRICES SUBJECT TO
CHANGE WITHOUT NOTICE

ORIGINAL INVOICE

OVERLAND TRANSPORT   MONTREAL
OTTAWA
TORONTO

HEAD OFFICE:
1473 Blake Road
Montréal, Québec   H3J 1E4

Shipper:

Broomball Manufacturing
331 Marion Street
Oshawa, Ontario L1J 3A8

Consignee:

Campbell Sports
3000 Base Line Road
Niagara Falls, Ontario L2J 1H2

TERMS Net 30 days   DATE Dec. 12, 2008   INV. NO. CK 4376

Quantity	Containers	Mass	Rate	Amount
3	Boxes	20 kg	$3.75/kg	$75.00

Pay this amount $75.00

CITY DELIVERY
576 Portage Rd.
Niagara Falls, Ontario   L2J 1N8

Charge

Campbell Sports
3000 Base Line Road
Niagara Falls, Ontario   L2J 1H2

Deliver to

Niagara Broomball League
1476 Braeside Street
Niagara Falls, Ontario   L2J 2M4

INV. NO. T-7437   **TERMS** Net 30 days   **DATE** Dec. 20, 2008

Description

5 Boxes

Amount

$55.65

CREDIT INVOICE

SPORTING EQUIPMENT
347 Tachereau Blvd.
Montréal, Québec   H2C 3B3

SOLD TO Campbell Sports
3000 Base Line Road
Niagara Falls, Ontario   L2J 1H2

January 12, 2009

CREDIT NUMBER 1195

WE CREDIT YOUR ACCOUNT AS SPECIFIED BELOW

Re: Invoice TR89-6153, dated January 10, 2009

6 damaged Dolphin Goggles @ $15.50 $93.00

TOTAL CREDIT DUE $93.00

15. Journalize the following transactions for Campbell Sports, which uses a perpetual inventory system.

    Mar. 1 Purchase invoices:
    Cooper Bros., $825.60 for hockey sticks;
    CN Express, $112.50 for transportation charges on purchases.

    2 Cheque copies:
    No. 94, to Dinardo Delivery, $275 for delivery charges on sales to schools;
    No. 95, to Stamford Collegiate, $143 for return of unordered sporting goods. The cost price of the items is $75.

    10 Cheque copies:
    No. 96, to Spalding Bros., $425 on account;
    No. 97, to Tanyss Imports for tennis shoes, $627.50.

    15 Purchase invoices:
    Hofstra Ltd., $1873 for skis;
    Smith Transport, $92.75 transportation charges on purchases;
    Dinardo Delivery, $210.20 for delivery of goods to customers.

    16 Credit note:
    Cooper Bros., $116 for goods returned to them because they were received in a damaged condition. The cost price of the items is $50.

16. Following are the March sales figures for Campbell Sports: Sales $29 300; Sales Returns and Allowances $1400; Sales Discounts $290.

    (a) What is the net sales total for March?
    (b) Determine the cost of goods sold for March for Campbell Sports from the following:
    Beginning Inventory $35 000; March Purchases $17 600; Purchases Returns and Allowances $1300; Transportation-in $875; Ending Inventory $37 000.
    (c) Determine the March gross profit for Campbell Sports using the answers from parts (a) and (b) of this exercise.

17. (a) Prepare a schedule of cost of goods sold for Campbell Sports for May from the following figures:
    Beginning Inventory $37 900; Purchases $18 800; Purchases Returns and Allowances $800; Purchases Discounts $210; Transportation-in $975; Ending Inventory $35 900.
    (b) Prepare an income statement for Campbell Sports for May using the cost of goods sold from part (a) and the following figures:
    Sales $40 750; Sales Returns and Allowances $1950; Sales Discounts $180; Salaries $6800; Rent $1850; Delivery Expense $900; Other Expenses $2100.

17. Pilates and Such had the following transactions occur during June of this year:

Jun. 2 Purchased $3500 merchandise from Sportsplus; terms 2/10, n/30.

      3 Sold $270 merchandise to B. Comeau; terms EOM.

      4 Paid $375 freight charges on the June 2 purchases.

      4 Sold merchandise for $84 cash.

      6 Returned $250 merchandise to Sportsplus; received a credit memo.

      8 Sold $480 merchandise to M. Tompkins; terms 2/10, n/30.

      9 Sold merchandise for $187 cash.

     10 Paid Sportsplus for the June 2 purchase less the discount and the return.

     12 Purchased store supplies $115.

     14 Purchased $2800 merchandise from Relax Mats; terms 2/10, n/30.

     16 Paid $295 freight charges on the June 14 purchase.

     18 Received payment from M. Tompkins for the June 8 transaction less the discount.

     19 Sold merchandise for $450 cash.

     22 Owner invested $5500 additional cash in the business.

     24 Sold $1275 merchandise to R. Ouellette; terms 2/10, n/30.

     25 Paid $92 delivery charges for the merchandise sold on June 24.

     26 Received $115 merchandise returned by R. Ouellette; issued a credit memo.

     27 Sold $215 merchandise to S. Butler; terms 2/10, n/30.

     28 Sold merchandise for $129 cash.

     30 Received payment from B. Comeau for the June 2 transaction.

     31 Owner withdrew $1500 for personal living expenses.

Record the above transactions in the general journal. (Ignore PST and GST for the above journal entries.) Pilates and Such uses a perpetual inventory system. The cost price of items sold is 50 percent of the sales price.

Sales and Goods and Services Tax

Learning Objectives

After reading this unit, discussing the applicable review questions, and completing the applications exercises, you will be able to do the following:

1. **CALCULATE** Goods and Services Tax on sales.

2. **CALCULATE** sales tax on retail sales.

3. **JOURNALIZE** transactions involving Provincial Sales Tax and federal Goods and Services Tax.

INTRODUCING SALES TAX

In Canada, both the federal and most provincial governments impose sales taxes. The companies that sell taxable items become, by law, agents for the government for the collection of sales tax. A customer pays sales tax to a company and the company sends the money to the government. Manufacturers, wholesalers, and most retailers are required to register with the federal government to collect the national Goods and Services Tax (GST). Retailers are also required to register with their provincial governments to receive a Provincial Sales Tax licence. In most provinces, retailers collect both Provincial Sales Tax and federal Goods and Services Tax. New Brunswick, Nova Scotia, and Newfoundland harmonized their provincial sales taxes with the GST to create the Harmonized Sales Tax (HST).

The Federal Goods and Services Tax

A tax charged on the sale of most goods and services in Canada.

The federal **Goods and Services Tax** (GST) is a simple concept that becomes more complex in actual practice. For the purposes of this text, only the basic GST principles and introductory accounting procedures will be discussed.

The Goods and Services Tax is a 6 percent tax charged on most sales of service and merchandise made within Canada. Manufacturers, wholesalers, and retailers of both merchandise and services must add the tax to the selling price of each item sold.

Goods or Services Selling Price	$100.00
6% GST	6.00
Total Cost	$106.00

A number of items such as basic groceries, prescription drugs, health and dental services, daycare services, residential rents, and education services are exempt, or free, from GST.

The GST is collected by businesses that are registered with Canada Revenue to collect the tax, and the tax is then forwarded to the federal government. To register for GST or HST (see page 248 for a description of HST), you are required to fill out a Request for Business Number (BN) form, shown in Figure 7-13 on pages 242–243. This form can be found on the Canada Revenue Web site www.cra-arc.gc.ca.

How Does the GST Work?

A product can be bought and sold by several businesses before you, the consumer, actually purchase the item. For example, a mountain bike is purchased by a wholesaler from the manufacturer. The wholesaler sells the bike to a retailer who in turn sells the bike to you. Each of these businesses must add the 6 percent GST to the selling price. However, the federal government receives only 6 percent of the *final* sales price. How is that possible? It's possible because the business sends the federal government only the difference between GST collected and GST paid. A business collects the 6 percent GST on the sales price of all goods and services sold. Before remitting, or sending, the tax collected to the federal government, the business deducts all GST paid to other businesses when purchasing goods and services. This deduction is called an **input tax credit**. The input tax credit ensures that the federal government is not receiving more than 6 percent GST on the final sales price of the goods or service that you purchase. Let's follow the mountain bike through each step and see how the GST system actually works.

A credit for GST paid on business purchases.

Mountain Bike				
	SALES PRICE	GST COLLECTED	GST INPUT TAX CREDIT	AMOUNT REMITTED
Materials sold to Manufacturer	$100	$ 6	$ 0	$ 6
Mountain bike sold to Wholesaler	$400	$24	($6)	$18
Mountain bike sold to Retailer	$500	$30	($24)	$ 6
Mountain bike sold to Customer	$700	$42	($30)	$12
Total GST remitted to Federal Government				$42

In the example shown above, the retailer sold the mountain bike for $700 plus $42 Goods and Services Tax. The retailer, however, sent only $12 ($42 GST minus $30 input tax credit) to the federal government. This represented the amount of GST collected from the customer minus the amount paid on the purchase of the bike from the wholesaler. The federal government received in total 6 percent, or $42, in GST from all the businesses involved in getting the product to the final consumer. In this chapter, we will discuss the basic accounting procedures used by retailers to record the federal Goods and Services Tax as well as Provincial Sales Tax.

FIGURE 7-13

Request for a Business
Number (BN)

Canada Customs and Revenue Agency	Agence des douanes et du revenu du Canada	BN	FOR OFFICE USE ONLY

REQUEST FOR A BUSINESS NUMBER (BN)

Complete this form to apply for a Business Number (BN). If you are a sole proprietor with more than one business, your BN will apply to all your businesses. **All businesses have to complete parts A and F.** For more information, see our pamphlet called *The Business Number and Your Canada Revenue Agency Accounts (RC2)*. If you have questions, including where to send this form, call us at 1-800-959-5525.
Note: If your business is in the province of Quebec and you wish to register for GST/HST, do not use this form. Contact Revenu Québec. However, if you wish to register for any of the other three accounts listed below, complete the appropriate parts indicated in the following instructions.
- To open a GST/HST account, complete parts A, B, and F
- To open a payroll deductions account, complete parts A, C, and F.
- To open an import/export account, complete parts A, D and F.
- To open a corporate income tax account, complete parts A, E and F.

Part A – General Information

A1   **Identification of business** (For a corporation, enter the name and address of the head office.)

Name	Operating, trading, or partnership name (if different from the name on the left). If you have more than one business, or if your business operates under more than one name, enter the name(s) here. If you need more space, include the information on a separate piece of paper.

Business address (This must be a physical address, not a post office box.)	Postal or zip code

Mailing address (if different from business address)	Postal or zip code

Contact person – Complete this area to identify an employee of your business as your contact person in all matters pertaining to your BN accounts. To identify a person for specific accounts, complete the "Contact Person" lines in Area B1, C1, D1, or E1. To authorize a representative who is not an employee of your business, complete Form RC59, *Business Consent Form*. See our pamphlet for more information.

First name	Last name	Title	Telephone number ( )	Fax number ( )

A2   **Client ownership type**   Language of correspondence ☐ English   ☐ French

☐ **Individual**   If so, are you a sole proprietor?   Yes ☐   No ☐   Are you an employer of a domestic?   Yes ☐   No ☐

☐ **Partnership**

☐ **Other**   Are you incorporated?   Yes ☐   No ☐   (All corporations have to provide a copy of the certificate of incorporation or amalgamation.)

Complete this part to provide information for the individual owner, partner(s), corporate director(s), or officer(s) of the business. If you need more space, include the information on a separate piece of paper. The Social Insurance Number is mandatory for individuals (sole proprietors) applying to register for a GST/HST account (*Social Insurance Number Disclosure Regulations, Excise Tax Act*).

First name	Last name		Work telephone number ( )	Work fax number ( )
Title		Social insurance number	Home telephone number ( )	Home fax number ( )
First name	Last name		Work telephone number ( )	Work fax number ( )
Title		Social insurance number	Home telephone number ( )	Home fax number ( )

A3   **Type of operation**   Check the box below that best describes your type of operation.

☐ Charity	☐ Union	☐ Association	☐ Financial institution	☐ University/school	☐ Municipal government
☐ Society	☐ Hospital	☐ Non-profit	☐ Religious body	☐ Trust	☐ None of the above

A4   **Major commercial activity**

Clearly describe your major business activity. Give as much detail as possible in the space provided.

Specify up to three main products that you mine, manufacture, or sell, or services you provide or contract. Also, estimate the percentage of revenue that each product or service represents.   % % %

RC1 E (05)   (Ce formulaire existe en français.)   Canada

| A5 | **GST/HST information** – For more information, see our pamphlet called *The Business Number and Your Canada Revenue Agency Accounts (RC2)*. |

Do you provide or plan to provide goods or services in Canada or to export outside Canada?
If *no*, you generally cannot register for GST/HST. However, certain businesses may be able to register. See our pamphlet for details.   Yes ☐   No ☐

Are your annual **worldwide** GST/HST taxable sales, including those of any associates, more than $30,000 ($50,000 if you are a public service body)?
If *yes*, you have to register for GST/HST.
Note: Special rules apply to charities and public institutions. See our pamphlet for details.   Yes ☐   No ☐

Do you solicit orders in Canada for prescribed goods to be sent by mail or courier to an address in Canada? Prescribed goods include printed materials such as books, newspapers, periodicals, magazines, and an audio recording that relates to those publications and that accompanies them when they are sent to Canada.   Yes ☐   No ☐

Do you operate a taxi or limousine service?   Yes ☐   No ☐
Are you a non-resident who charges admissions directly to audiences at activities or events in Canada?   Yes ☐   No ☐
If you answer *yes* to either of these questions, you **have** to register for GST/HST, regardless of your revenue.

Do you wish to register voluntarily? By registering voluntarily, you must begin to charge GST/HST and file returns even if your worldwide GST/HST taxable sales are $30,000 or less ($50,000 or less if you are a public service body). See our pamphlet for more information.   Yes ☐   No ☐

Part B - GST/HST account information -
Complete B1 to B4 if you need a BN GST/HST account (except for businesses in the province of Quebec.) See our pamphlet for details.
Do you want us to send you GST/HST information?   Yes ☐   No ☐

| B1 | GST/HST account identification – Check the box if the information is the same as in Part A1. ☐ |

Mailing address for GST/HST purposes
c/o
Account name (enter the name under which you carry on business.)
Address
Postal or zip code

Contact person – Complete this area to identify an employee of your business as your contact person in all matters pertaining to your GST/HST account. To authorize a representative who is not an employee of your business, complete Form RC59, *Business Consent Form.* See our pamphlet for more information.
First name   Last name   Language of correspondence ☐ English ☐ French
Title   Telephone number ( )   Fax number ( )

| B2 | Filing information |

Enter your fiscal year-end. Month ___ Day ___
If you do not provide us with a date, we will enter December 31. If you want to select a fiscal year-end that is not December 31, see our pamphlet for more information.
Enter the effective date of registration for GST/HST purposes. Year ___ Month ___ Day ___
See our pamphlet for information about when you need to register for GST/HST.

| B3 | Reporting period |

Unless you are a charity or a financial institution, we will assign you a reporting period based on your total estimated annual GST/HST taxable sales in Canada (including those of your associates). In the column on the left below, check the box that corresponds to your estimated sales. In certain cases, you may be able to change this assigned reporting period. To do so, check the box in the column on the right below that corresponds to your choice. For more information, see our pamphlet.

Total estimated annual GST/HST taxable sales in Canada (including those of your associates)	Reporting period assigned to you, unless you choose to change it (see next column)	Options
More than $6,000,000 ☐	Monthly	No options available
More than $500,000 up to $6,000,000 ☐	Quarterly	☐ Monthly
$500,000 or less ☐	Annual	☐ Monthly or ☐ Quarterly
Charities ☐	Annual	☐ Monthly or ☐ Quarterly
Financial institutions ☐	Annual	☐ Monthly or ☐ Quarterly

| B4 | Type of Operation |

04 ☐ Listed financial institution   08 ☐ Non-resident   09 ☐ Taxi or limousine operator   99 ☐ None of these types

| B5 | Voluntary direct deposit routing information - The account holder identified below requests and authorizes the Minister of National Revenue to directly deposit into the account identified below, amounts payable to the account holder under Part IX of the *Excise Tax Act.* |

Complete the information area below or attach a blank cheque and write "VOID" across the front. This method provides a faster, more convenient, and dependable way of receiving refunds. The CRA will deposit your GST/HST refund into your bank account.

Branch No.   Inst. No.   Account number

Name(s) of account holder(s):

Source: Copyright © Canada Customs and Revenue. Reproduced with permission of the Minister of Public Works and Government Services Canada, 2005.

Provincial Sales Tax

All provinces, except Alberta, impose a sales tax on retail sales. The tax is charged on the price of goods sold to consumers. In most provinces, the tax is charged only on tangible commodities, although a few services (such as telephone service) are taxed. Such items as food, drugs, children's clothes, school supplies, and farm equipment are exempt from sales tax in many provinces. Provincial Sales Tax (PST) is charged in addition to GST collected by the federal government. It can be calculated on the base price only or on the base price plus GST (see below).

Each province determines the rate of PST to be charged. These rates change from time to time. At the time of writing, these rates were in effect:

Alberta	0%	
British Columbia	7%	
Manitoba	7%	
New Brunswick	8%	Included in
Newfoundland and Labrador	8%	Harmonized Sales
Nova Scotia	8%	Tax (HST)
Ontario	8%	
Prince Edward Island	10%	
Quebec	7.5%	
Saskatchewan	6%	

A retailer who sells taxable items is required by law to collect the PST. Each retailer in Ontario is issued a retail sales tax vendor's permit by the provincial government, and similar licences or permits are issued by the other provinces.

Calculating GST and PST

When you purchased your mountain bike in the previous example, you saw that the selling price was $700 plus $42 GST. In all provinces, except Alberta, the final amount you will have to pay for the bike will also include PST. How much would you finally pay in a province where the PST is 8 percent?

Calculation of GST and PST

Mountain Bike Selling Price (base price)	$700.00
Goods and Services Tax (0.06 × $700)	42.00
	$742.00
Provincial Sales Tax (0.08 × $700)	56.00
Final Price to Customer	$798.00

This method of calculating sales tax eliminates the problem of paying tax on tax since both GST and PST are calculated as a percentage of the base price.

Each province can decide which method will be used to calculate PST. At the time of writing, British Columbia, Saskatchewan, Manitoba, and Ontario calculate PST on base price only, while New Brunswick, Newfoundland, and Nova Scotia pay HST, which includes PST on the base price alone.

GST and PST Payable Accounts

As a retailer, Campbell Sports is responsible for collecting both the GST and PST from customers. The accounting system must include the accounts necessary to record both GST collected from customers and GST paid to suppliers (input tax credits) to calculate the correct amount to remit to the federal government. Remember, Campbell will remit GST collected minus GST paid. In addition, an account is required to record the PST collected to remit the tax to the provincial government. This sounds complicated, but the ledger requires only three new accounts: PST Payable, GST Payable, and GST Refundable. Why are two GST accounts necessary? You must have information on both GST collected and GST paid by your firm.

| GST Collected | – | GST Paid | = | Net GST Owed |
| GST Payable | – | GST Refundable | = | GST Due to Federal Government |

How would Campbell Sports record the sale of the mountain bike in the previous example? The selling price was $700, the GST at 6 percent was $42, and the PST was $56 calculated on the base price. The customer paid a total of $798 cash for the bike. Campbell would record the following journal entry:

Jan. 18	Cash	798	
	Sales		700
	GST Payable		42
	PST Payable		56
	Cash sale of bike.		

PST Payable

The amount of sales tax collected is owed to the provincial government. The sales tax collected during the month is credited in the **PST Payable** (or Sales Tax Payable) account. This account is a liability. It increases when taxable goods are sold and taxes are collected. It decreases when the seller of taxable goods sends the tax to the provincial government.

The PST Payable account is a liability account.

An account used to record the sales tax collected for a period of time that is payable to the provincial government.

PST Payable		
	Jan. 3	73.43
	4	35.62
	6	55.62
	9	41.74
	10	31.50
	31	43.65
		1 243.62

PST Payable	
Debit	Credit
Decrease	Increase
Debit the account when sales tax is remitted to the government.	Credit the account when taxable goods are sold and taxes are collected.

At the end of the month, the amount of tax collected is calculated. In January, Campbell collected $1243.62 in PST and must remit this amount to the Provincial Treasurer. (Note: In some provinces, the remittance is made to the Minister of Finance. You should check the title for your province.) When the cheque is issued, the following journal entry is made:

Feb. 15	PST Payable	1 243.62	
	Cash		1 243.62
	Cheque 299 to Provincial		
	Treasurer for January sales		
	tax collections.		

Recording Sales Tax Commission

Several provinces pay commission to companies in return for the collection of sales tax. For example, in New Brunswick, a company receives 2 percent commission on the first $250 of tax it collects and 1 percent on amounts over $250.

> An amount of money earned by the retailer for collecting the sales tax on behalf of the province.

The commission earned by a company is usually recorded in an account entitled Miscellaneous Revenue or **Sales Tax Commission**.

The entry, in General Journal form, to record a payment to the government and the commission earned is:

Jun. 15	PST Payable	300	
	Cash		291
	Sales Tax Commission		9
	To remit May sales tax and to record		
	commission earned.		

GST Payable

The amount of Goods and Services Tax collected is also a liability. It is owed to the federal government. The amount of GST collected during the month is credited to the **GST Payable** account.

> An account used to record GST collected.

Is this the amount of tax that is sent to the federal government? No. The retailer remits GST collected *minus* GST paid. How does Campbell record GST paid (input tax credit) on goods or services purchased for the business?

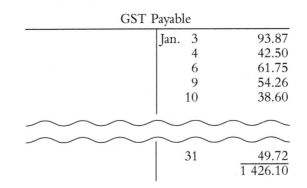

	GST Payable	
	Jan. 3	93.87
	4	42.50
	6	61.75
	9	54.26
	10	38.60
	31	49.72
		1 426.10

GST Input Tax Credit

Unit 14 of this chapter introduced the new accounts used by a merchandising company. You learned that the Purchases account is used to record the cost of merchandise bought for resale. To simplify the introduction of these accounts, GST was not included in the discussion. The following example will show the purchase of merchandise including GST. When Campbell Sports purchased the mountain bike from a wholesaler, it received the following purchase invoice (Figure 7-14).

FIGURE 7-14

Cash purchase of
merchandise

Mountain Bike Limited
1035 Quay Street North
Vancouver, BC
V4J 6B7

Date: January 1, 2008
Sold To: Campbell Sports
          3000 Base Line Road
          Niagara Falls, ON   L2J 1H2

Item: 67 Mountain Bike
Quantity: 1
Price: $500.00
GST: 30.00
Total Due: $530.00

Terms of Sale: Cash

What is the amount recorded in the Purchases account? The $500 cost price. Why is the $30 GST not recorded as part of the cost price? As you learned earlier, the retailer deducts the GST paid to suppliers from the GST collected from the consumer before remitting the tax to the federal government. Therefore, Campbell receives an input tax credit for the $30 GST paid to Mountain Bike Limited. How will Campbell record the invoice shown in Figure 7-14? The journal entry will be:

Jan. 1	Purchases	500.00	
	GST Refundable	30.00	
	Cash		530.00
	Cash purchase of mountain bike.		

The amount of GST paid to suppliers is debited to the **GST Refundable** account.

An account used to record the GST paid to suppliers of goods and services.

GST Refundable

Jan.	1	30.00
	4	28.00
	8	42.00
	9	14.00
	11	63.00
	31	49.00
		980.63

The GST Refundable account is a *contra-liability account* since it reduces the amount of a liability. The GST Payable account balance ($1426.10) is reduced by the balance in the GST Refundable account ($980.63) to determine the net amount owed to the federal government ($445.47). This amount is forwarded to the federal government.

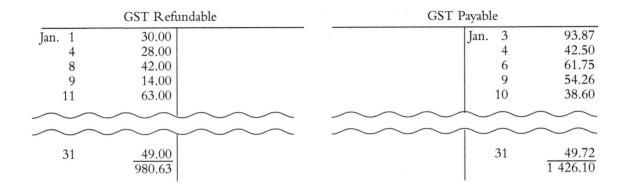

GST Refundable				GST Payable		
Jan. 1	30.00			Jan. 3	93.87	
4	28.00			4	42.50	
8	42.00			6	61.75	
9	14.00			9	54.26	
11	63.00			10	38.60	
31	49.00			31	49.72	
	980.63				1 426.10	

The GST Payable account balance is forwarded to the Receiver General of the federal government monthly, quarterly, or annually, depending on the size of the business.

Jan. 31	GST Payable	1 426.10	
	GST Refundable		980.63
	Cash		445.47
	January GST remitted.		

In the event the GST paid to suppliers exceeds the GST collected from customers, the business is able to apply for a refund from the federal government.

Recording GST for a Service Business

The Goods and Services Tax also applies to services sold and purchased. A service business would follow the same basic accounting procedures you have just learned for a merchandising business. The business collects GST from its customers on the sale of the service, deducts GST paid to suppliers, and remits the difference to the federal government.

Harmonized Sales Tax

A tax that applies at a single rate the combined GST and PST in a province.

The Harmonized Sales Tax (HST) is a tax that applies the GST and PST as a single rate of 14 percent to taxable supplies in the provinces of Newfoundland, Nova Scotia, and New Brunswick. The HST operates in the same way as GST and combines the federal 6 percent GST with an 8 percent PST. Accounting entries for HST are similar to those outlined for GST and PST.

Calculation of HST	
Mountain bike selling price (base price)	$700.00
Harmonized Sales Tax (0.14 × $700)	98.00
Final Price to Customer	$798.00

GST, PST, and Cash Discounts

A sale of $500 worth of merchandise is made on account to J. Woodsworth. The GST at 6 percent is $30, making a total of $530. PST at 8 percent on $500 is $40. The total amount of the sale is $570. The terms of sale are 2/10, n/30.

Suppose that Woodsworth pays for the merchandise within 10 days to take advantage of the 2 percent cash discount. A question arises concerning the amount of the discount. Should it be 2 percent of the merchandise only ($500), or should it be 2 percent of the total owing ($570)? There are arguments for both alternatives. In actual practice, it is generally accepted that the customer is allowed to take a discount of 2 percent of $570, which is $11.40 ($0.02 \times 570 = 11.40$).

UNIT 15

REVIEW QUESTIONS

1. What is the amount of the GST?

2. Is the full amount of GST collected by a business from customers remitted to the federal government? Explain the term "input tax credit."

3. What is the amount of your province's PST? Has it changed since this text was published?

4. What type of account (asset, liability, revenue, or expense) is PST Payable?

5. What does it mean if a product is exempt from sales tax?

6. A sale of merchandise costing $200 is made with terms of net 30. GST is 6 percent and PST is 8 percent calculated on the base price. What accounts are debited and credited in recording this transaction?

7. A customer buys merchandise for $60 on credit. GST is 6 percent and PST is 7 percent calculated on the base price. The merchandise is defective and is returned by the customer. A credit invoice is issued.

   (a) Record this sales return in General Journal form for a seller who uses a Sales Returns and Allowances account.
   (b) Record the same transaction in General Journal form for a seller who does not use a Sales Returns and Allowances account.

8. On November 10, your company received an invoice with terms 2/10, n/30, for $550, plus $33 GST, plus $44 PST.

   (a) By what date must the invoice be paid to take advantage of the discount?
   (b) Will the discount be taken on the $500 or on $627?

9. A service is provided for $200 cash. The GST is 6 percent and the PST is 8 percent calculated on the base price plus GST. What accounts are debited and credited?

10. A taxable item is sold for $478 cash. The GST is 6 percent and the PST is 10 percent on the base price plus GST.

    (a) Calculate the taxes and the total received from the customer.
    (b) What accounts are debited and credited to record the sale?

11. A company collected $510 in PST during March. What is the General Journal entry required to record the cheque issued to the Provincial Treasurer to remit the PST? (Assume there is a 4 percent commission paid by the government.)

1. Complete the chart shown below in your notebook.

   (a) Calculate PST on the base amount of the sale.
   (b) Calculate PST on the base amount of the sale plus GST.

Amount of Sale	GST (6%)	PST (8%)	PST on Total
$ 125.00	?	?	?
7.95	?	?	?
725.00	?	?	?
4 500.00	?	?	?

2. Prepare General Journal entries on June 15, 2008, for the following retail sales:

   (a) Sold goods for $250 to R. Collins, terms net 30, GST $15, PST $20. Total $285.
   (b) Sold goods for $300, GST $18, PST $24, terms 2/10, n/30.
   (c) Received $285 cash from R. Collins.

3. Following is a PST Payable account:

   PST Payable
Apr. 5	90
12	64
19	177
30	105

   (a) How much should be remitted to the provincial government for the month of April?
   (b) In General Journal form, prepare the entry to remit the April tax to the provincial government. Assume that the company is located in a province that does not pay a commission to companies for collecting the tax.

4. Following are GST Payable and GST Refundable accounts:

GST Payable		GST Refundable	
May 5	85	May 4	55
12	90	11	110
19	120	20	85
29	73	30	70

   (a) How much should be remitted to the federal government for the month of May?
   (b) In General Journal form, prepare the entry to remit the May tax to the federal government.

5. (a) Kim Soo Supply made taxable retail sales of $5400 during May. How much is the cheque sent to the provincial government if the PST is 8 percent and Kim Soo Supply is allowed a commission of 3 percent for collecting the PST?
   (b) Prepare the journal entry to record the payment.

6. (a) During June, Kim Soo Supply made sales of $7000, of which $900 was paid for non-taxable items. How much is remitted to the provin-

cial government if the PST is 6 percent and the company's commission is 3 percent?

(b) Prepare the journal entry to record the payment.

7. Record the following source documents on page 307 of a General Journal:

Aug. 1 Cash register tape shows sales of $945, GST $56.70, PST $75.60.

2 Cheque received from C. Ballard for $583 to pay Invoice 803.

2 Cheque received from L. Noble for $317.52 to pay Invoice 799, $324 less $6.48 discount.

4 Cheque received from K. Engel, the owner, for $3700 as an additional investment in the business.

7 Bank credit memo, $10 500 for a bank loan that was deposited in the company bank account.

8 Cheque received from C. Drago for $548.80 to pay Invoice 805, $560 less $11.20 discount.

9 Cash Sales Slips 940 to 955 for $2155 plus $129.30 GST and $172.40 PST.

8. Record the following source documents on page 98 of a General Journal:

Nov. 1 Cheque received for $6300 from the owner, C. White, as a further investment in the business.

2 Cash Sales Slips 340 to 355 for $1275 plus 6 percent PST on base price and 6 percent GST.

3 Cheques received:
From A. Derouin, $372 on account;
From V. Williams, $428.26 to pay Invoice 6061 for $437 less $8.74 discount.

5 Cheque received from A. Derouin for $749.70 to pay Invoice 6059 for $765 less $15.30 discount.

5 Cash Sales Slips 356 to 382 for $3650 plus 6 percent PST on base price and 6 percent GST.

UNIT 16   Bank Credit Cards

Learning Objective

After reading this unit, discussing the applicable review questions, and completing the applications exercises, you will be able to do the following:

1. **EXPLAIN** the accounting procedures and **PREPARE** the journal entries for bank credit cards.

BANK CREDIT CARDS

Many merchandising enterprises accept bank credit cards rather than, or in addition to, extending credit to their customers. Credit card companies such as MasterCard, American Express, and Visa supply an accounts receivable service to businesses. Since both MasterCard and Visa are operated by banking institutions, their cards are called *bank credit cards.*

Why People Use Credit Cards

Two examples are given below to show why consumers and businesses use bank credit cards.

Cindy Hutton has just purchased a sweater from Giselle's Boutique and uses her MasterCard to pay for her purchase. Like many other people, Cindy uses a bank credit card to do much of her shopping. Why do people use credit cards instead of paying with cash or by cheque? Cindy prefers to shop using a credit card for the following reasons:

- She does not have to carry large amounts of cash.
- She can buy things even if she does not have cash at the time she wishes to make a purchase.
- Some businesses do not accept personal cheques and others demand several items of identification before accepting cheques.
- Cindy's card is accepted internationally when Cindy travels. She can obtain cash advances up to a set limit. As well, Cindy simply finds it more convenient to use a credit card. Figure 7-15 below shows the credit card form completed by the store clerk for Cindy's purchase. The form is known as a *sales draft* or *sales slip.*

Producing the Credit Card Sales Slip

Let's follow the steps in producing the credit card slip.

(1) Cindy gives the clerk her credit card. The clerk checks the expiry date on the card to make sure it is still valid. Then, the card is passed through a scanner to authorize use of the card.

FIGURE 7-15

Credit card sales slip

```
            GISELLES BOUTIQUE
            NORTH BAY, ONTARIO

    409009                     01/29/20--
    CLERK 461                                    ——— Customer copy

    1 SWEATER @ $49.95            49.95           ——— Merchant copy
                        GST       3.00
                        PST       4.00
                        TOTAL    56.95


    ACCOUNT 4506 003 200 987
    AUTHORIZATION 004004262


        Cindy Hutton
    CUSTOMER SIGNATURE
```

(2) The clerk enters the information into the point-of-sale terminal and the terminal's printer produces the credit card sales slip. The slip includes all the information found on a regular cash sales slip: the cost of the item, any GST and PST applied to the sale, and the total payable. The credit card slip includes an authorizatin number as well as a signature line.

(3) Cindy is asked to sign the slip. The signature is checked against the sample signature on the back of the card. (If the clerk thinks the signature is not correct, he or she should ask for photo ID.)

(4) Cindy is given a copy of the credit card sales slip, and the store keeps a copy to go in the deposit. Usually, a separate tape printout of the sale is produced that serves as a receipt for customer returns and as the source document for the accounting entry.

Cindy leaves the store with her sweater without having paid any cash for it. She will not have to pay until she receives a statement from the bank credit card company. This is another reason why she uses a bank credit card. If she is able to pay the statement on time, she will not have to pay any interest. Cindy is very careful to pay her balance owing by the due date to avoid the interest charges.

Many of the credit card companies impose a fee for using the credit card. The fee may be a separate charge for each transaction or a monthly or yearly fee for using the card. All credit card companies generally charge interest on balances that have not been paid within 15 to 30 days of the statement. Credit card transactions and balances can be accessed online at any time.

Why Businesses Use Bank Credit Cards

Giselle's Boutique uses the services provided by both Visa and MasterCard. It does so for the following reasons:

- Many people have either Visa or MasterCard credit cards and will shop at stores that accept these cards.
- The store receives its money for credit card sales from the bank as soon as the sales draft forms are deposited in the bank.
- There is no risk of bad debts. The credit card company guarantees payment to the store.
- The store does not have to have an accounts receivable system to record sales to customers and does not have to worry about collecting amounts from customers.

The credit card companies provide a guaranteed, immediate collection service to companies. In return for the service, the companies pay a percentage of each sale to the bank credit card company.

Accounting Example for Bank Credit Card Transactions

In this example, we will use the Visa credit card and the Men's Wear Shop to illustrate accounting procedures for bank credit card transactions.

Sales Recap Form

At the end of the day, the store accountant prepares a merchant sales recap form (Figure 7-16 on the next page). This is a summary of all the sales drafts for the

FIGURE 7-16

Visa sales recap form

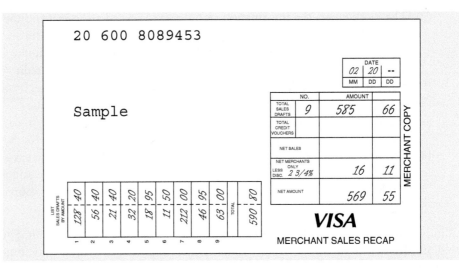

day. Figure 7-16 is the recap form from February 20 and lists nine Visa sales drafts and a total of $585.66 (which includes GST and PST).

The Visa sales drafts are treated as cash and are taken to the bank and deposited at the end of the day. The bank receives the deposit and increases the balance in the account of the business. The store accountant then prepares an accounting entry to record the sales. The entry is:

Feb. 20	Cash	569.55	
	Visa Discount Expense	16.11	
	GST Payable		30.82
	PST Payable		41.10
	Sales		513.74
	To record Visa credit card sales.		

Although no cash has changed hands, the store has received its money — it was placed in the store's bank account by the bank.

Bank Fees

The fee paid by a merchant for using the services of a credit card company.

In return for providing instant cash for sales made, the bank charges the store a fee. The fee is calculated at the time of deposit. On the recap summary sheet (Figure 7-16), the fee is $16.11. The store treats this fee as an expense.

The amount of the fee charged by the bank credit card company is based on the average volume of credit card sales and the average draft size. The fee paid by the Men's Wear Shop is 2 3/4 percent of credit card sales. This is the rate for a business with an average monthly volume of $5000 to $12 499, and an average draft size of $50 to $99.99. Figure 7-17 illustrates the service charges paid to a bank by merchants:

Merchant Statement

In the example described above, the merchant deposited the bank credit card sales drafts each day and deducted the Visa fee from the deposit each day. Some banks use the monthly statement method of charging the fee to the merchant. The business will make a single entry from the statement to record their bank credit card costs.

FIGURE 7-17
Table of Bank credit card charges

SAMPLE BANK CREDIT CARD
MEMBER DISCOUNT SCHEDULE

Average Monthly Volume			AVERAGE DRAFT SIZE			
			Under $30.00	$30.00 to $49.99	$50.00 to $99.99	$100.00 and over
			%	%	%	%
$ 1	–	$ 999	5 1/2	4 1/2	3 1/2	3 1/2
1 000	–	2 499	4 3/4	4	3 1/2	2 3/4
2 500	–	4 999	4 1/2	3 3/4	3	2 3/4
5 000	–	12 499	4 1/2	3 1/2	2 3/4	2 1/2
12 500	–	19 999	4	3 1/2	2 1/2	2 1/2
20 000	–	29 999	3 3/4	3	2 1/2	2 1/2
30 000	–	49 999	3 1/2	2 3/4	2 1/2	2
50 000	–	74 999	3 1/2	2 3/4	2	2
75 000	–	149 999	3	2 1/2	2	2
150 000	–	299 999	2 1/2	2 1/2	2	2
300 000	–	and over	2	2	2	2

The statement illustrated in Figure 7-18 on the next page was received by the Western Motor Inn in Edmonton from its bank. It is called the merchant statement. Once a month, the statement is sent by the Visa bank to the merchant. The statement provides a summary of the Visa deposits made each day, the total deposits, and the fee charged by Visa for the month's transactions. The fee charged for the month covered in Figure 7-18 is $296.10. This accounting entry is made on the books of the Western Motor Inn to record the Visa service fee:

Feb. 28 Visa Discount Expense	296.10	
Cash		296.10
To record the Visa discount fee for February.		

Can you see the advantage of using the monthly statement method as compared to the daily method for recording the fee?

MOVING TOWARD A PAPERLESS ECONOMY

Electronic Commerce

Electronic commerce (**e-commerce**) refers to the conduct of business activities (production, distribution, purchasing, sales, banking, and other transactions) by means of advanced communication and computer technologies. E-commerce is an important vehicle for business to fully participate in the global economy. It allows consumers like you to more easily purchase products and services from around the world. Companies that are networked for e-commerce are able to develop products, receive orders, communicate with suppliers, arrange production, and service customers with no delays. Participation in e-commerce is becoming a competitive necessity for businesses of all size.

Conduct of business activities by means of advanced communication and computer technologies.

FIGURE 7-18

Merchant statement

THE BANK OF NOVA SCOTIA
VISA CENTRE MERCHANT STATEMENT

WESTERN MOTOR INN   MERCHANT NO.   589
11503 FORT RD., N.W.   STATEMENT DATE   Feb. 28, 2008
EDMONTON, AB. T5B 4G1

DATE	DEPOSIT AMOUNT	ADJUSTMENTS	CODE	REFERENCE NO.
01/29	$ 553.76			2 51301045
02/01	822.69			2 57109132
02/03	754.83			2 57109142
02/06	901.64			2 58240108
02/10	711.40			2 62300040
02/10	873.60			2 62300050
02/17	706.38			2 75223840
02/17	489.13			2 70301295
02/17	884.45			2 70301305
02/17	1,066.69			2 70301315
02/20	489.15			2 75223831
02/24	799.06			2 76246395
02/24	731.51			2 76246405
02/25	982.96			2 76246385

TOTALS $10,767.25 + $0.00 = $10,767.25 NET SALES

BRANCH TRANSIT	ACCOUNT NO.	CHAIN NO.	DISCOUNT RATE	CURRENT DISCOUNT
1072	23-00214	0	2.750%	$296.10

NUMBER & AMOUNT OF SALES DRAFTS		NUMBER & AMOUNT OF CREDITS	
125	$10,767.25	0	$0.00

CARRY FORWARD AMOUNT	UNCLEARED ADJUSTMENTS	CURRENT DISCOUNT	STATEMENT TOTAL
0.00 −	0.00 +	$296.10 =	$296.10

Electronic Banking

The Canadian Bankers Association estimates that over 85 percent of banking transactions are done electronically. The most popular forms of electronic banking are automated banking machines (ATMs) and direct payment cards. Over 97 percent of Canadian ATMs belong to the Interac network; Interac Direct Payment is a service that allows customers to use their client cards to pay for purchases at retail outlets, withdraw cash, and pay bills. Electronic banking also features telephone banking and PC/Internet banking services 24 hours per day. All services require account holders to use a personal password and a client card number.

Debit Cards

Financial institutions have introduced debit, or direct payment, cards, which eliminate the need to write cheques to pay for merchandise. The debit card requires account holders to have a Personal Identification Number (PIN) and a client card number to access the service.

Debit cards are part of a system that transfers funds between parties electronically rather than by paper cheques. The exchange of cash using this system is called *electronic funds transfer* (EFT). This method is already used by many employers to deposit employees' pay directly into their bank accounts while withdrawing from the employer's account. The same type of system allows customers to present a debit card to a retailer rather than write a cheque to pay for goods purchased. The debit card is inserted into the retailer's computer terminal, which is connected to the bank. The funds to pay for the purchased goods are automatically transferred out of the customer's account, and into the store's account.

This system eliminates the cost of processing the paper cheque and removes the risk of bad cheques for the retailer. Implementation of this system moves us closer to the "paperless society" where there is little need to carry cash or cheques. It is quickly becoming the norm in Canadian banking.

Stored-value Cards

These cards are usually issued in amounts of $25–$500 and replace cash. Owners swipe the card through phones or computer terminals; when the money has been spent, the owners can then throw them away or reload them with value. Cellular phone paid minute cards are a widely used throwaway stored-value card. Gift cards are another example of stored-value cards and are available from many retailers.

Point-of-Sale Terminals

Electronic banking provides a number of payment options for customers and direct deposit of the funds to the bank account of the business. Retail outlets use point-of-sale (POS) terminals to allow customers to pay by credit card or direct payment card. Of course, many customers still prefer to pay cash for some purchases. The merchant receives a recap form at the end of the day listing the amount deposited automatically to the merchant's account as a result of transactions processed through the POS terminal. For example, the ABC Co. end-of-day recap form shows:

Sales	**January 15, 2008**
Visa	$12 357.10
MasterCard	11 550.30
Direct Payment	11 780.70
Total	$35 688.10

Remember, this deposit represents only the sales processed through the POS terminal. Total sales shown on the cash register summary for the day include both POS terminal sales plus sales paid with actual cash and cheques. These cheques and cash must also be deposited in the bank daily. Total sales for the day for ABC Co. would be:

POS Sales	$35 688.10
Cash/Cheque Sales	9 430.20
Total Sales	$45 118.30

The ABC Co. bank statement would show two deposits for January 15. What would they be? A point-of-sale (direct) deposit of $39 688.10 and a regular deposit of $9430.20. Can you see the advantage for the retailer?

ACCOUNTING TERMS

Cost of Goods Sold	The total of all costs involved in buying the merchandise to be sold. (p. 211)
Credit Invoice	A credit invoice is a source document issued by the seller to indicate the amount of credit allowed to a customer for returned or defective goods. (p. 217)
Delivery Expense	An account used to record the cost of delivering merchandise to customers. (p. 224)
E-commerce	The conduct of business activities by means of advanced communication and computer technologies. (p. 255)
Goods and Services Tax	A tax charged on the sale of most goods and services in Canada. (p. 240)
Goods and Services Tax Payable	An account used to record GST collected. The balance is paid to the federal government. (p. 246)
Goods and Services Tax Refundable	An account used to record the GST paid to suppliers. (p. 247)
Harmonized Sales Tax	A tax that applies, at a single rate, the combined GST and PST in a province. (p. 248)
Input Tax Credit	A credit for GST paid on business purchases. (p. 241)
Manufacturing Company	A company that makes a product. (p. 208)
Merchandise	Goods bought for resale in a merchandising business. (p. 208)
Merchandising Company	A company that sells a product. (p. 208)
Net Purchases	Purchases – Purchases Returns and Allowances – Purchases Discounts. (p. 221)
Net Sales	Sales – Sales Returns and Allowances – Sales Discounts. (p. 220)
Periodic Inventory Method	The actual amount of inventory on hand is determined by physical count when financial statements are prepared. (p. 210)
Perpetual Inventory Method	A record is kept for each item in inventory, and the balance is updated continuously as items are bought or sold. (p. 210)
Provincial Sales Tax	A tax charged on the price of goods sold to consumers. (p. 244)
Provincial Sales Tax Payable	An account used to record the sales tax collected for a period of time that is payable to the provincial government. (p. 245)
Purchases Account	An account used to record the cost of merchandise purchased for resale. (p. 220)
Purchases Discount	A cash discount received off the purchase price in return for early payment of the invoice. (p. 222)
Purchases Returns and Allowances	An account used to record the return of merchandise previously purchased for resale. (p. 221)
Sales Account	An account used to record the cash and credit sales of merchandise by the business. (p. 215)
Sales Discount	A cash discount off the selling price given to a customer for early payment of an invoice. (p. 217)
Sales Returns and Allowances	An account used to record the return of merchandise by a customer. (p. 216)
Sales Tax Commission	An amount of money earned by the retailer for collecting the sales tax on behalf of the province. (p. 246)
Schedule	A supporting statement providing details of an item on a main statement. (p. 211)

Service Company	A company that sells a service. (p. 208)
Terms of Sale	An agreement between the buyer and seller of an item regarding the method of payment. (p. 218)
Transportation-in	An account used to record the transportation charges incurred to bring merchandise purchased for resale to the store. (p. 212)

REVIEW QUESTIONS

1. Why do retailers accept bank credit cards even though there is a fee charged for using this service?

2. (a) Why do consumers use bank credit cards?
   (b) What is the name of the form completed by the merchant when a sale is made to a customer who makes payment with a bank credit card?
   (c) How many copies of the form are prepared and who receives each copy?

3. What is the name of the form completed at the end of each day that summarizes the day's bank credit card sales?

4. (a) What accounts are debited and credited by the retailer when Visa sales drafts are taken to the bank and deposited?
   (b) What accounts are debited and credited to record the fee charged by the bank?

5. What is the bank credit card fee (in percentage terms) for each of the following monthly volumes? Assume the average draft size is under $30 (refer to Figure 7-18, page 256).

   (a) $3000
   (b) $13 000
   (c) $22 000

PROBLEMS: APPLICATIONS

1. Record the following transactions in a General Journal. Use the Visa Discount Expense account to record the fee paid to Visa and the MasterCard Discount Expense account to record the MasterCard fee.

   Jul. 7 Cash sales, $3500 (sales tax exempt), GST $210.

   7 Invoice 6, sale on account to S. Cox, $830, GST 6 percent, PST 6 percent on base price.

   7 Visa credit card sales, $1100 (not taxable), GST 6 percent.

   7 MasterCard credit card sales, $1500 (sales tax exempt), GST 6 percent.

   8 Visa discount fee, $25.50.

   8 MasterCard discount fee, $36.20.

2. Jim Williams Products offers a variety of credit terms to customers. Record the following transactions for January in a General Journal. All sales are subject to 6 percent GST and 8 percent PST.

Jan. 2 Sold merchandise to J. Coon, $2100, terms 2/10, n/30.

4 Sold merchandise to Lee Mazilli, $450, terms EOM.

4 Paid CN the $74.34 ($70.09 plus $4.21 GST) delivery charges for the merchandise shipped to J. Coon.

6 Damaged merchandise was returned by J. Coon. A credit invoice was issued today for $570 (GST $30 and PST $40, $500 merchandise).

7 Received a cheque from B. Lailey for $314 in payment of her account. Since payment was received within the discount period, a $6 discount had been taken.

7 The weekly cash register tape showed cash and Visa sales of $7530, GST $451.80, PST $602.40, total cash $8584.20.

9 Sold merchandise to C. Corbett, $520, terms 2/10, n/30.

9 Refunded $45.60 to a customer who made a cash purchase on Jan. 7 (GST $2.40, PST $3.20, and $40 merchandise).

10 Received a cheque from L. Mako for $360 in full payment of his account.

14 Sales tax for the period was remitted to the provincial government. The tax collected totalled $3900. Jim Williams Products was entitled to a 3 percent commission for collecting the tax.

16 Received a cheque from J. Coon in payment of the January 2 invoice.

21 Cash and Visa sales for the week were $6090, GST $365.40, PST $487.20, total cash $6942.60.

22 A cheque was received today from C. Corbett for $580.94. A discount of $11.86 had been taken; however, the cheque had been received after the discount period. Therefore, the discount was not granted.

30 Received a cheque from L. Mazilli in full payment of January 4 invoice.

30 The Visa merchant statement was received today. The discount fee charged for the month of January was $436.

30 GST remittance to the Receiver General. GST Payable balance $6839; GST Refundable balance $4719.

1. Use the information in the trial balance for Henley Outdoor Supplies.

   (a) Prepare a schedule of cost of goods sold.
   (b) Prepare an income statement.
   (c) Prepare a classified balance sheet.
   (d) Why does the ending inventory amount not appear on the trial balance prepared from Henley Outdoor Supplies ledger on August 31?

CHAPTER 7

PROBLEMS:
CHALLENGES

Henley Outdoor Supplies
Trial Balance
August 31, 2009

ACCOUNT TITLE	ACC. NO.	DEBIT	CREDIT
Cash	101	$ 5 600	
Accounts Receivable	110	2 900	
Merchandise Inventory, August 1	120	30 200	
Supplies	125	600	
Equipment	151	15 000	
Truck	152	28 000	
Furniture	153	45 000	
Accounts Payable	200		$ 2 500
PST Payable	205		400
GST Payable	206		900
GST Refundable	207	600	
Bank Loan (3 years)	210		6 500
W. Creighton, Capital	300		113 600
Sales	400		18 600
Sales Returns and Allowances	401	350	
Sales Discounts	402	50	
Purchases	500	8 300	
Purchases Returns and Allowances	501		325
Purchases Discounts	502		75
Transportation-in	503	600	
Salaries Expense	600	2 100	
Rent Expense	601	2 700	
Delivery Expense	602	300	
Miscellaneous Expense	603	475	
Visa Discount Expense	604	75	
MasterCard Discount Expense	605	50	
		$142 900	$142 900

Note: **The inventory on August 31 is $27 900.**

2. Some of the account balances of Cycle King for the month of May are shown on the following page.

   (a) Prepare a schedule of cost of goods sold.
   (b) Prepare an income statement.
   (c) Prepare the current asset section of the balance sheet.

Purchases Discounts	$ 25
Beginning Inventory	32 100
Purchases	9 100
Purchases Returns and Allowances	300
Transportation-in	450
Ending Inventory	30 200
Sales	18 500
Sales Returns and Allowances	350
Salaries Expense	2 900
Rent Expense	2 900
Delivery Expense	700
Other Expenses	1 400
Cash on Hand	3 500
Accounts Receivable	2 900
Supplies on Hand	500
Sales Discounts	25
Visa Discount Expense	50
MasterCard Discount Expense	75

3. (a) Prepare a schedule of cost of goods sold for Valley Sports for June from the following figures: Beginning Inventory $33 800; June Purchases $7200; Purchases Returns and Allowances $100; Purchases Discounts $25; Transportation-in $400; Ending Inventory $32 100.

   (b) Prepare an income statement for Valley Sports using the cost of goods sold from part (a) and the following figures: Sales for June $14 500; Sales Returns and Allowances $200; Sales Discounts $50; Salaries Expense $2500; Rent Expense $2700; Delivery Expense $600; Other Expenses $800.

CASE 1
Accounts Used by a Merchandising Company

A new accountant began working for Atlas Stores on July 1. During the month of July, the new accountant recorded the following group of purchase invoices:

Merchandise	$2 900
Office Supplies	300
Office Equipment	900
Delivery Expense	250

However, all four items were recorded as debits in the Purchases account.

(a) For each of the invoices, name the account that should have been debited.
(b) What effect will the incorrect recording of these invoices have on the:
   (i)   Balance sheet?
   (ii) Schedule of cost of goods sold?
   (iii) Income statement?

CASE 2
Delivery Costs

Vachon Stores offers a free delivery service to its customers. For years, a local cartage company has provided the delivery service. Business has increased substantially and, on average, 300 deliveries a month are made. The cartage firm has just increased its charges to $15 for every delivery.

   K. Vachon, the owner of Vachon Stores, has asked the store accountant to compare the present delivery charges with the cost of buying and operating the company's own equipment. The accountant has determined several facts:
• A delivery van would cost $27 000.
• The van would last four years and then would be worth $8000 as a trade-in.
• The driver's salary would be about $20 an hour, including all fringe benefits; the driver would work an average of 30 hours a week.
• Insurance, repairs and maintenance, licences, and fuel would average $6590 a year.

(a) What is more economical, buying the delivery equipment or using the services of the cartage firm?
(b) List factors other than costs that could affect the decision.

CASE 3
Cash Discounts

Mavis Porter manages Studio Sound, a stereo components specialty shop. She is in the process of negotiating a $25 000 order from one of her main suppliers. The supplier has offered a 3 percent discount if payment is made within 15 days. Studio Sound does not have cash on hand to take advantage of the discount. However, the bank will lend money to Studio Sound for 30 days at an annual rate of interest of 10 percent. Mavis is sure that within 30 days there will be enough cash on hand to repay the bank.

   Should Mavis take the 3 percent discount using money borrowed from the bank? How much will be gained or lost if the loan is taken?

ETHICS CASE
Personal Decision Making

W. Moscaluk worked for many years as a machinist for a large automobile manufacturer. He lived very frugally and saved money to satisfy a dream — to own his own business.

Three years ago, Moscaluk mortgaged his home, borrowed money, and invested in his own business. Moscaluk now employs six persons and the business has earned a modest net income for two years. He has been able to pay off most of his debts.

This year, there has been a general slump in the economy. Moscaluk's business has suffered, with sales decreasing 30 percent. Moscaluk's accountant has predicted a loss of $80 000 if three full-time workers are not laid off. Moscaluk feels that his employees are like part of his family. They have been loyal and are partly responsible for the business's success of the past two years. If Moscaluk does not lay off the workers, he will not be able to make his mortgage payments, will likely lose his home, and perhaps lose his business as well.

1. If you were Moscaluk, what would you do?
2. Do you see any similarities and differences between this case and the one involving Metalco (Chapter 6)?

Explore these Web sites for information on merchandising and retailing.

CHAPTER 7

**INTERNET
RESOURCES**

1. **Canada Revenue Agency**
    www.cra-arc.gc.ca/tax/business/topics/gst/menu-e.html
    Go to this site for complete information on GST, forms, regulations, and collections.
    www.cra-arc.gc.ca/tax/business/smallbusiness/faq-05-e.html
    This section of the CRA site provides everything you want to know about GST and provincial sales taxes.

2. **Strategis Canada   www.strategis.gc.ca**

    This site provides a complete book on retail marketing strategy and processes called *Winning Retail*. To access the book, go to the Business Information section of the site and do a search for *Winning Retail*. *Winning Retail* is a self-assessment and instructional guide for independent retailers.

3. **Industry Canada   www.ic.gc.ca**

    Information on electronic commerce, and on Internet consumer issues (online shopping, dealing with spam, and finding an Internet Service Provider) can be found here. Go to the site, select Information by Subject, and then Internet.

4. **The Entrepreneurship Institute of Canada   www.entinst.ca**

    This institute provides information and resources for entrepreneurs and companies including books, training programs, and multimedia products.

5. **Canadian Youth Business Foundation   www.cybf.ca**

    Interested in starting a business? The CYBF provides start-up financing, mentoring, and educational resources to young Canadians, ages 18–34, interested in starting a business.

CHAPTER 8

The Subsidiary Ledger System

 **UNIT 17** The Three-Ledger System

Learning Objectives

After reading this unit, discussing the applicable review questions, and completing the applications exercises, you will be able to do the following:

1. **EXPLAIN** the advantages of using a three-ledger system.

2. **DISCUSS** the relationship between the subsidiary ledger and a control account.

3. **VERIFY** each of the three ledgers by preparing a General Ledger trial balance, a schedule of accounts payable, and a schedule of accounts receivable.

4. **EXPLAIN** the division of labour principle and discuss its applicability to the subsidiary ledger system.

GENERAL LEDGER

As a business increases in size, the system used to record accounting data must be adapted to efficiently process an increasing amount of data. The General Ledger is one of the first areas that is affected by the growth of the firm.

Accounts Receivable

A growing firm normally has a rapid increase in the number of customers who purchase goods or services on account. Accounts must be kept for each customer to determine the amount owed and the date payment is due. The number of accounts receivable increases from a small number for a small firm just beginning business to a very large number for a large business. How does this affect the General Ledger? Look at Figure 8-1. The dramatic increase shown for the number of accounts receivable in the General Ledger makes it necessary to devise a more efficient system of ledger accounts.

FIGURE 8-1

Partial General Ledgers for small and large businesses

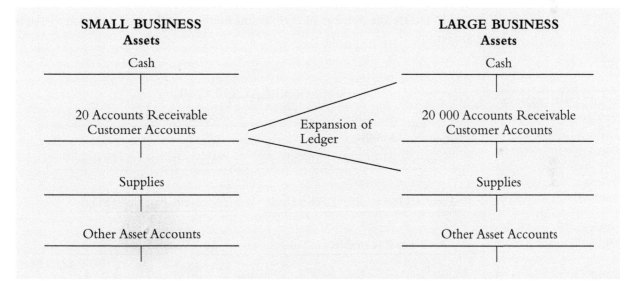

Effect on the Balance Sheet

Consider the effect of this expanded number of accounts receivable on the preparation of the balance sheet. If all the accounts receivable were listed individually on the balance sheet, it would result in a very lengthy financial statement. One of the primary objectives of financial reporting is to provide useful information to financial statement readers. The figure that interests statement readers is the total value of accounts receivable, not the value of each individual account receivable. Therefore, a total for accounts receivable would be more useful when preparing a balance sheet.

Accounts Payable

A similar situation develops in the accounts payable portion of the ledger as the business grows. The number of firms from which goods or services are purchased tends to increase as a business expands. It is necessary to keep individual accounts for each of these creditors to have an accurate record of the amount owed and the payment due date for each. If these data are all recorded in the General

Ledger, the effect is the same as shown previously with the accounts receivable section. There would be a larger number of Accounts Payable accounts in the General Ledger and a very long balance sheet. A summary figure would be more useful on the balance sheet than a large number of individual accounts.

Adapting the General Ledger

An example using T-accounts will demonstrate how the accounting system is changed to handle this increased volume of information more efficiently and also provide the required balance sheet data. A partial ledger and trial balance for Mountain Bike Sales are shown in Figures 8-2 and 8-3. A small number of accounts receivable and payable are shown to demonstrate the concept. In reality, the number of these accounts could be in the thousands, but the change to the accounting system would be similar.

Figure 8-3 is the General Ledger trial balance for Mountain Bike Sales. Each customer account is listed separately. In a large company, there could be many customer accounts. Of course, this would make the trial balance and balance sheet very lengthy.

To reduce the number of accounts in the General Ledger, subsidiary ledgers are set up.

FIGURE 8-2

Partial General Ledger for Mountain Bike Sales

GENERAL LEDGER

Cash		Accounts Payable/S. Dennis	
15 000			3 050

Accounts Receivable/J. Bhinder		Accounts Payable/D. Gill	
3 000			2 500

Accounts Receivable/L. Therriault		Accounts Payable/P. Singh	
550			2 150

Accounts Receivable/G. Wong		Wages Payable	
1 750			3 000

Supplies		GST Payable	
700			370

Land		GST Refundable	
50 000		128	

Building		PST Payable	
85 000			260

Equipment		Bank Loan	
15 300			15 000

		Mortgage Payable	
			80 000

		M. Speza, Capital	
			68 598

		M. Speza, Drawings	
		3 500	

Mountain Bike Sales Trial Balance October 31, 2008		
ACCOUNT TITLE	**DEBIT**	**CREDIT**
Cash	$15 000	
Accounts Receivable/J. Bhinder	3 000	
Accounts Receivable/L. Therriault	550	
Accounts Receivable/G. Wong	1 750	
Supplies	700	
Land	50 000	
Building	85 000	
Equipment	15 300	
Accounts Payable/S. Dennis		$ 3 050
Accounts Payable/D. Gill		2 500
Accounts Payable/P. Singh		2 150
Wages Payable		3 000
GST Payable		370
GST Refundable	128	
PST Payable		260
Bank Loan		15 000
Mortgage Payable		80 000
M. Speza, Capital		68 598
M. Speza, Drawings	3 500	
	$174 928	$174 928

FIGURE 8-3

General Ledger trial balance for Mountain Bike Sales

SUBSIDIARY LEDGERS

A **subsidiary ledger** contains accounts of similar type, usually organized in alphabetical order. The two most commonly used subsidiary ledgers are the Accounts Receivable Ledger and the Accounts Payable Ledger; however, these are not the only subsidiary ledgers used by businesses. Whenever there is a large number of similar accounts in the General Ledger, it is possible to streamline the ledger by utilizing a subsidiary ledger. An example of another common subsidiary ledger used by firms with a large and varied amount of equipment is an Equipment Ledger. An Inventory Subsidiary Ledger could be used by merchandisers who carry varying and extensive stocks of inventory, for example, Zellers.

Let's look at Accounts Receivable and Payable Ledgers in more detail.

A subsidiary ledger is a group of accounts of one type usually organized in alphabetical order.

Accounts Receivable Ledger

The Accounts Receivable accounts are removed from the General Ledger and placed in a special customers' **Accounts Receivable Ledger** (see Figure 8-4 on page 270). Only the customer accounts (J. Bhinder, L. Therriault, and G. Wong) are found in the Accounts Receivable Ledger.

The customers' accounts are replaced in the General Ledger by a single account called the **Accounts Receivable control** account. This account represents the total owing by all the customers ($5300) and is necessary for the General Ledger to remain in balance. The balance in the Accounts Receivable control account should always equal the total of all the individual customer accounts in the Accounts Receivable Ledger — that is why it is called a **control account**. Notice in Figure 8-4 that the balance in the Accounts Receivable control account in the General Ledger ($5300) equals the total of the Accounts Receivable Ledger ($3000 + $550 + $1750).

The Accounts Receivable Ledger is a subsidiary ledger containing only customers' accounts in alphabetical order.

The Accounts Receivable control account replaces the individual customer accounts in the General Ledger.

A control account is an account found in the General Ledger that has a balance equal to a number of accounts found in a subsidiary ledger.

FIGURE 8-4

Three-ledger system: General Ledger Accounts Receivable and Payable control accounts, Accounts Receivable Subsidiary Ledger, and Accounts Payable Subsidiary Ledger

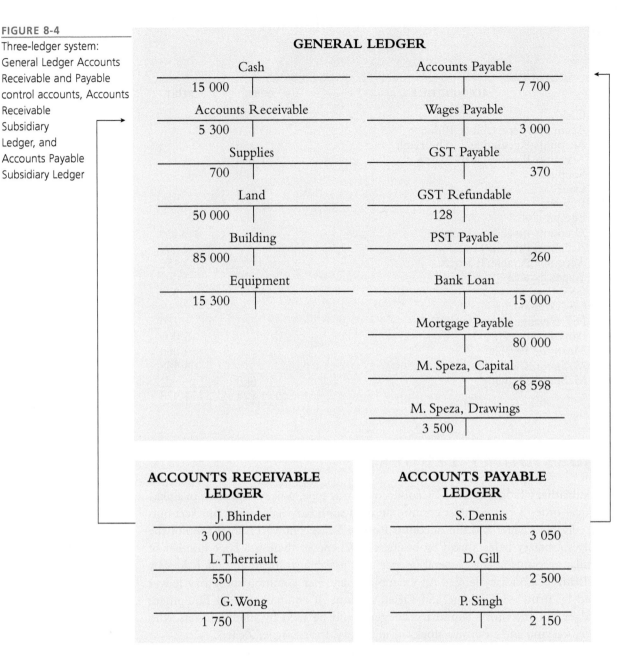

Customer accounts are usually filed alphabetically in the Accounts Receivable Ledger and new accounts are inserted as required.

Accounts Payable Ledger

The Accounts Payable Ledger is a subsidiary ledger containing only creditors' accounts in alphabetical order.

A business with many creditors often removes the creditors' accounts from the General Ledger and places them in alphabetical order in a subsidiary ledger called the **Accounts Payable Ledger**. The creditors' accounts are replaced in the General Ledger by an **Accounts Payable control** account (see Figure 8-4).

The Accounts Payable control account replaces the individual creditors' accounts in the General Ledger.

The total of all of the individual creditors' accounts in the Accounts Payable Ledger ($3050 + $2500 + $2150) should equal the balance of the Accounts Payable control account in the General Ledger ($7700).

Summary

For every subsidiary ledger, there is a control account in the General Ledger. The total of the accounts in the subsidiary ledger must equal the balance of the related control account in the General Ledger.

VERIFYING THE ACCURACY OF THE LEDGERS

General Ledger Trial Balance

A trial balance is prepared to verify the mathematical accuracy of the General Ledger. The procedure to prepare the trial balance is exactly the same in the three-ledger system as in the single-ledger system we used previously. The only difference is that there is now a control account for Accounts Receivable and Accounts Payable rather than the individual Accounts Receivable accounts and Accounts Payable accounts.

A General Ledger trial balance is shown in Figure 8-5. Notice that it contains an Accounts Receivable control account instead of individual customer accounts, and an Accounts Payable control account rather than individual creditor accounts.

FIGURE 8-5
General Ledger trial balance

Mountain Bike Sales
Trial Balance
October 31, 2008

ACCOUNT TITLE	DEBIT	CREDIT
Cash	$ 15 000	
Accounts Receivable	5 300	
Supplies	700	
Land	50 000	
Building	85 000	
Equipment	15 300	
Accounts Payable		$ 7 700
Wages Payable		3 000
GST Payable		370
GST Refundable	128	
PST Payable		260
Bank Loan		15 000
Mortgage Payable		80 000
M. Speza, Capital		68 598
M. Speza, Drawings	3 500	
	$174 928	$174 928

Schedule of Accounts Receivable

The **schedule of accounts receivable** (Figure 8-6) is prepared to verify the accuracy of the Accounts Receivable Ledger. This schedule is a list of the customer accounts showing the balance of each account. The balances are totalled and must equal the value of the Accounts Receivable control account in the General Ledger to be correct.

What is the total of the schedule in Figure 8-6? What is the balance of the Accounts Receivable control account in Figure 8-4?

A schedule of accounts receivable is prepared to prove the mathematical accuracy of the Accounts Receivable Ledger.

FIGURE 8-6

Schedule of accounts
receivable

Mountain Bike Sales
Schedule of Accounts Receivable
October 31, 2008

J. Bhinder	$3 000
L. Therriault	550
G. Wong	1 750
	$5 300

Equals the Accounts
Receivable control account
in the General Ledger

Schedule of Accounts Payable

A schedule of accounts
payable is prepared to
prove the mathematical
accuracy of the Accounts
Payable Ledger.

A similar **schedule of accounts payable** (Figure 8-7) is prepared from the subsidiary Accounts Payable Ledger. This is totalled and must equal the value of the Accounts Payable control account in the General Ledger. This verifies the correctness of the Accounts Payable Ledger.

FIGURE 8-7

Schedule of accounts
payable

Mountain Bike Sales
Schedule of Accounts Payable
October 31, 2008

S. Dennis	$3 050
D. Gill	2 500
P. Singh	2 150
	$7 700

Equals the Accounts
Payable control account
in the General Ledger

What is the total of the schedule in Figure 8-7? What is the balance of the Accounts Payable control account in Figure 8-4?

The Mountain Bike Sales example demonstrates a method of adapting or streamlining the accounting system to meet the needs of the business. Remo Wholesalers will be used throughout the remainder of the chapter to demonstrate how the concept is put into practice in an actual business.

ADVANTAGES OF SUBSIDIARY LEDGERS

There are two main advantages to using subsidiary ledgers in an accounting system:

• Division of labour
• Accounting control

Divide work among several
people who specialize in
completing one component
of the task.

Division of Labour Principle

In a small business, one employee may be able to handle all the accounting tasks from journalizing to the preparation of the financial statements. In a larger firm that must record many business transactions each day, one person cannot handle all the accounting work. Large firms find it necessary and more efficient to divide the work among several people, each of whom specializes in an area of accounting.

Large firms identify the special accounting roles by the job titles accounts receivable clerk, accounts payable clerk, and accounting supervisor. Other companies may use other titles for these same jobs, such as junior clerk, posting clerk, senior accountant, chief accountant, or accounting manager. This division of labour, or segregation of job functions, is one method of internal control used by businesses to prevent errors and detect fraud in the subsidiary ledger accounts.

Accounting Control

In a small business, the owner is involved in most of the transactions that take place. The owner can spot irregularities or errors made by employees or by other businesses with which the owner deals. A large business has a number of people involved in the handling and recording of transactions. A good accounting system controls the recording, the accuracy, and the honesty of the people involved. The control account balances in the General Ledger must equal the totals of the account balances in each of the subsidiary ledgers. When different people are responsible for each of the ledgers, they act as a check on the accuracy of one another's work.

1. In a larger business, why are the customer accounts removed from the General Ledger and placed in an Accounts Receivable Ledger?

2. What is the name of the account in the General Ledger that replaces all the individual customer accounts?

3. What is the name of the account in the General Ledger that replaces all the individual creditor accounts?

4. (a) What is the name of the ledger that contains only customer accounts?
   (b) What is the name of the ledger that contains only creditor accounts?

5. What is a control account? Give two examples.

6. What is a subsidiary ledger? Give two examples.

7. What are the three ledgers in a three-ledger system?

8. Give two advantages of using subsidiary ledgers.

9. From which ledger does one obtain the information required to prepare the financial statements?

10. (a) Which account represents the customers in the General Ledger trial balance?
    (b) Which account represents the creditors in the General Ledger trial balance?

11. (a) What is a schedule of accounts receivable?
    (b) What is a schedule of accounts payable?

12. (a) To what must the total of the schedule of accounts receivable be equal?
    (b) To what must the total of the schedule of accounts payable be equal?

UNIT 17

REVIEW QUESTIONS

 **Accounting Systems**

Learning Objectives

After reading this unit, discussing the applicable review questions, and completing the applications exercises, you will be able to do the following:

1. **PERFORM** the tasks of the accounts payable clerk, the accounts receivable clerk, and the accounting supervisor.

2. **EXPLAIN** the difference between manual and computer accounting systems.

The accounting system for a business consists of all the activities performed to provide the information needed to make business decisions. Managers rely on information provided by the accounting system to answer questions such as the following:

- Did we make a profit?
- Should we expand our business?
- Are sales increasing or decreasing?
- Are expenses increasing or decreasing?
- How efficient are the employees?
- Are we using our resources as efficiently as possible?
- Which products are most profitable?

Questions such as these can be answered when there is an effective accounting system to provide data. A company must record all transactions accurately. It must provide clear financial statements to its managers. If it does not, it will lose money and risk bankruptcy.

INTRODUCING REMO WHOLESALERS

Figure 8-8 illustrates some of the parts of an accounting system. Each part is actually a subsystem. For example, the accounts receivable system consists of a series of tasks completed for all credit sales to customers.

In this unit, part of the accounting system for a company called Remo Wholesalers will be described. The company is a wholesaler of heating and refrigeration equipment. It buys from the manufacturer and sells to companies that, in

FIGURE 8-8

The accounting system provides information to management.

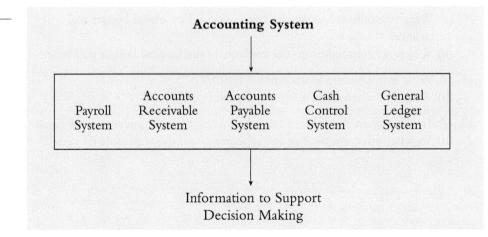

turn, sell or install the equipment. The company's head office is in Mississauga. It has branch offices in Sherbrooke, Québec; Moncton and Fredericton, New Brunswick; Halifax, Nova Scotia; and Pembroke, Sault Ste. Marie, Timmins, and Sudbury, Ontario. Among Remo's customers are fuel oil dealers, engineering firms, and mechanical equipment firms.

℗ROCESSING DATA FOR THE ACCOUNTS PAYABLE SYSTEM

The five tasks listed below make up the accounts payable system for Remo Wholesalers:

Task 1: Processing purchases invoices

Task 2: Recording purchases invoices

Task 3: Paying creditors

Task 4: Updating creditors' accounts

Task 5: Preparing a schedule of accounts payable

At Remo Wholesalers, Yvette Agaton, the accounts payable clerk, performs most of these tasks.

Duties of the Accounts Payable Clerk

Remo Wholesalers purchases goods and services from a number of suppliers or creditors. Yvette Agaton started as a part-time data input clerk at Remo Wholesalers but, after a few months, she took over as accounts payable clerk in the Mississauga office. Now she is kept busy, full time, just handling transactions involving accounts payable.

Figure 8-9 on page 276 is an invoice received from a creditor, Manitoba Supply Co. Yvette calls this a *purchase invoice* because Remo Wholesalers has purchased supplies from Manitoba Supply Ltd. To process the invoice shown in Figure 8-9, Yvette performs the accounting tasks for the accounts payable system.

A purchase invoice is a bill received from a creditor.

Task 1: Processing Purchase Invoices

Yvette's first responsibility is to confirm that her company, Remo Wholesalers, ordered the goods specified in the invoice and that the total amount of the invoice is correct.

In a file of purchase orders that she maintains, Yvette locates Purchase Order 591, sent out about a month before by Remo to Manitoba Supply Co. She checks to see that the order price and the invoice price are the same and that there are no mathematical errors on the invoice.

The details on the purchase invoice and purchase order must match.

Next, she must find out if the goods have actually been received. The person who receives and checks the goods completes a receiving report and sends a copy to Yvette. Yvette checks her file of receiving reports and locates a report showing that the goods have been received. The three documents — the purchase order, the purchase invoice, and the receiving report — are presented to a supervisor for approval before they are recorded.

Task 2: Recording Purchases Invoices

The approved invoice is returned to Yvette, who records the amount owed to Manitoba Supply Co. First, Yvette locates the account in the Accounts Payable

FIGURE 8-9

Purchase invoice received
from Manitoba Supply Co.

MSC
Manitoba Supply Co.
147 McDermot Ave.
Winnipeg, MB   R3B 0R9

SOLD TO: Remo Wholesalers
            77 Thomas Street
            Mississauga, ON L5M 6W3

DATE: Jan. 4, 2009

INVOICE NO: M-31

TERMS: Net 30 days
CUST. ORDER NO: 591

VIA: CN Express

QUANTITY	DESCRIPTION	PRICE	AMOUNT
3	Visual Card Files	$210	$630.00
10 000	Stock Cards	5/1000	50.00
			680.00
		GST	40.80
		Total Due	$720.80

P.O. No. 591
Rec. Rep. No. 609
Price O.K. ✓
Extensions ✓
A.P. Ledger ✓
Journal ✓

Ledger and then raises the balance by entering a credit. (Remember, a liability increases on the credit side.)

The invoice, with the purchase order and receiving report attached, is now placed in a date file until it is due to be paid — which will be within the 30-day period specified on the invoice.

Task 3: Paying Creditors

When the invoice is due to be paid (on February 3), Yvette removes the invoice from the date file. A cheque with a copy is prepared and the original cheque is sent to the creditor.

Task 4: Updating Creditors' Accounts

Using the copy of the cheque as her source of information, Yvette now decreases the balance owed to Manitoba Supply Co. It is Yvette's job to maintain an accurate record of the amount owed to each creditor. She does this by recording purchases as credits and payments as debits.

Task 5: Preparing a Schedule of Accounts Payable

Yvette's job is highly specialized. She works with only one type of account — accounts payable, that is, with creditor accounts. She is responsible for the Accounts Payable Ledger. This is a ledger that contains only creditor accounts. Each month, Yvette prepares a schedule of accounts payable as shown in Figure 8-10. This schedule is a listing of all the accounts payable with their balances.

Figure 8-10, the February schedule, is a shortened version of a schedule of accounts payable. In reality, it would contain many more creditor accounts and would be several pages in length.

Remo Wholesalers
Schedule of Accounts Payable
February 28, 2009

Booth Co.	$ 3 000
Gold Ltd.	9 000
Pitt Ltd.	4 000
Placer, Inc.	6 000
	$22 000

FIGURE 8-10
Schedule of accounts payable

Yvette's job as accounts payable clerk does not include journalizing the purchase invoices. This is done by the accounting supervisor who journalizes the source documents after Yvette is through with them. Yvette posts information directly into the Accounts Payable Ledger from the invoices and cheque copies. Figure 8-11 is a summary of Yvette's duties.

Direct posting is the recording of information from source documents directly into ledger accounts.

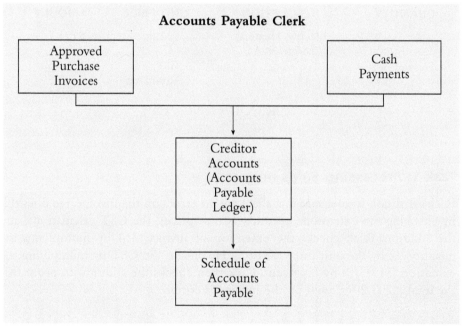

FIGURE 8-11
Duties of an accounts payable clerk

PROCESSING DATA FOR THE ACCOUNTS RECEIVABLE SYSTEM

The four tasks listed below make up the accounts receivable system for Remo Wholesalers:

Task 1: Processing sales invoices
Task 2: Recording sales invoices
Task 3: Processing cash received from customers
Task 4: Preparing a schedule of accounts receivable

Remo Wholesalers has so many customers that Yvette Agaton is unable to service accounts receivable as well as accounts payable. A second accounting clerk,

Rick Nguyen, handles transactions involving the customer accounts. His job title is accounts receivable clerk.

Duties of the Accounts Receivable Clerk

Figure 8-12 is a copy of a sales invoice sent to a customer, L. Henry. When the sale was made to L. Henry, an invoice was prepared in duplicate. The original copy was mailed to Henry. The copy shown in Figure 8-12 was sent to Rick. To process the invoice shown in Figure 8-12, Rick performs the accounting tasks for the accounts receivable system.

FIGURE 8-12

Accounting department copy of the sales invoice sent to L. Henry

Remo Wholesalers

77 Thomas St., Mississauga, ON L5M 6W3

SOLD TO: L. Henry
27 Lakeview Terrace
Ottawa, ON   K1S 3H3

DATE: Feb. 3, 2009
INVOICE NO.: 714
CUSTOMER ORDER NO.: 43015

TERMS: Net 30 days

QUANTITY	DESCRIPTION	UNIT PRICE	AMOUNT
6	Electric Heaters, Model 9-A	$31.95	$191.70
	GST		11.50
	Total Due		$203.20

ACCOUNTING COPY

Task 1: Processing Sales Invoices

Rick's first task is to ensure that there are no errors on the invoice. He does this by checking the extensions (quantity × unit price), the GST calculations, and the addition. Rick checks the extension of Invoice 714 by multiplying the quantity (6) by the unit price ($31.95). He checks the GST by multiplying the extension ($191.70) by 6 percent. Rick then checks the addition to prove that the total ($203.20) shown on the invoice is correct.

Task 2: Recording Sales Invoices

Rick locates Henry's account in the Accounts Receivable Ledger and increases the balance with a debit. (Remember, an account receivable is an asset and assets increase on the debit side.) Rick then initials the invoice and sends it, along with others he has processed, to his accounting supervisor.

Task 3: Processing Cash Received from Customers

When cash (currency, cheques, or money orders) is received from customers, a list is prepared showing the customers' names, the invoices being paid, and the amounts received. The money is deposited in the bank each day. Rick does not actually see the money but is given a list like the one in Figure 8-13.

Rick locates the accounts of the customers shown on the cash receipts list and reduces the balances in these accounts with credits. When Rick is through posting the invoices and daily cash receipts, he passes them on to the accounting supervisor for journalizing.

Remo Wholesalers
Daily Cash Receipts
Feb. 14, 2009

CUSTOMER	AMOUNT
C. Harkies, Invoice 711	$1 200
A. Taulib, Invoice 721	3 000
C. Martino, Invoice 696	2 000
Total Deposited	$6 200

FIGURE 8-13
List of daily cash receipts

Task 4: Preparing a Schedule of Accounts Receivable

At the end of each month, Rick prepares a list showing the balance owed by each customer. A shortened version of this list, called the schedule of accounts receivable, is shown in Figure 8-14:

Remo Wholesalers
Schedule of Accounts Receivable
Feb 28, 2009

CUSTOMER	AMOUNT
C. Harkies	$4 800
C. Martino	5 200
D. Patel	3 500
A. Taulib	$8 000
	$21 500

FIGURE 8-14
Schedule of accounts
receivable

As you will have noticed, Rick's job is also highly specialized. He deals with only one type of account — accounts receivable, that is, with customer accounts. A summary of Rick's duties is presented in Figure 8-15.

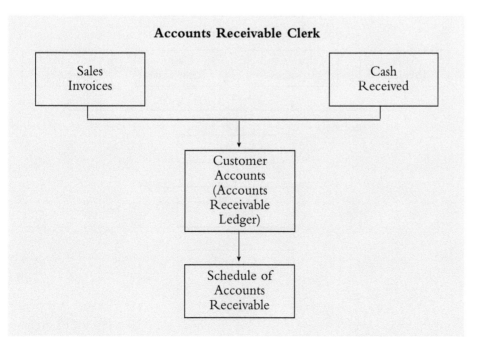

Accounts Receivable Clerk

Sales Invoices → Customer Accounts (Accounts Receivable Ledger) ← Cash Received

Customer Accounts (Accounts Receivable Ledger) → Schedule of Accounts Receivable

FIGURE 8-15
Duties of an accounts
receivable clerk

ⒶCCOUNTING SUPERVISOR

As has been shown in the first two job descriptions, Remo Wholesalers employs two accounting clerks: the accounts payable clerk and the accounts receivable clerk. Both clerks answer to an accounting supervisor who fills a third accounting position in the department. Andrea Wong is the accounting supervisor at Remo Wholesalers. While she was going to school, Andrea worked at Remo Wholesalers as a part-time clerk. When she graduated from college, she was hired as an accounts payable clerk. Several years later, Andrea was promoted to the position of accounting supervisor. Her job involves the supervision of the work of the accounting clerks, the preparation of journal entries, the posting of journal entries to the General Ledger, and the preparation of a General Ledger trial balance.

Andrea is given source documents after they have been posted directly to the Accounts Receivable and Accounts Payable Ledgers by Rick and Yvette. The source documents involved are:

- Sales invoices (copies)
- List of cash receipts
- Purchase invoices
- Cheque copies

Figure 8-16 below illustrates how these documents are processed by the accounting supervisor.

Preparing Journal Entries

The journal entries given under the next four headings are prepared to record the source documents sent to Andrea from Rick and Yvette.

Sales Invoices

The journal entry to record sales invoices is shown below. Notice that in this entry, individual customers are not debited. Instead, the Accounts Receivable

FIGURE 8-16

Documents processed by an accounting supervisor

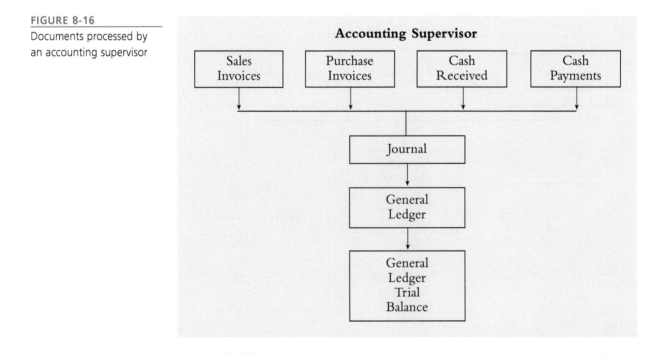

account is debited. Also, several sales documents (Invoices 561–568) are totalled
and recorded in one entry.

Feb. 8	Accounts Receivable	1 272	
	Sales		1 200
	GST Payable		72
	To record Invoices 561–568.		

List of Cash Receipts

The entry to record the cash received from customers is shown below. Notice that
in this entry, the Accounts Receivable account is credited, not the individual customer accounts.

Feb. 8	Cash	1 875	
	Accounts Receivable		1 875
	To record cash receipts for Feb. 8.		

Purchases Invoices

The accounting supervisor's journal entry to record invoices for Supplies ($430),
Miscellaneous Expense ($210), and Equipment ($700) is shown below. Notice
that in this entry, several invoices are recorded. Also, the Accounts Payable account
is credited instead of the individual creditor accounts. Can you explain why there
are four accounts debited but only one account credited?

Feb. 8	Supplies	430	
	Miscellaneous Expense	210	
	Equipment	700	
	GST Refundable	91	
	Accounts Payable		1 431
	To record purchase invoices from		
	Manitoba Supply Co., Nelson Ltd., and		
	Dufferin Equipment.		

Cheque Copies

The entry to record payments to creditors is shown below. This entry records several documents (Cheques 84–87). The Accounts Payable account is debited
instead of the individual creditor accounts.

Feb. 8	Accounts Payable	1 980	
	Cash		1 980
	To record Cheques 84–87.		

Posting the Journal

Andrea is also responsible for posting the journal entries to the General Ledger.
When these entries have been posted to the General Ledger, the Accounts
Receivable account in the General Ledger has the same balance as the total of the
balances of the customer accounts in the Accounts Receivable Ledger.
Remember that the sales invoices were recorded as debits in the customer

The General Ledger is the
main ledger and contains
all asset, liability, equity,
revenue, and expense
accounts.

accounts, and the cash amounts received were recorded as credits in the customer accounts by Rick, the accounts receivable clerk.

The Accounts Payable account in the General Ledger also has the same balance as the total of the balances in the creditor accounts in the Accounts Payable Ledger. Remember that the purchase invoices and cash payments (cheque copies) were recorded by Yvette, the accounts payable clerk.

All the source documents have been recorded twice: once by the accounting supervisor and once by the accounting clerks. This is necessary if the balances of the control accounts in the General Ledger are to equal the total of the accounts in the subsidiary ledgers.

Preparing Other Journal Entries

The accounting supervisor is responsible for journalizing all source documents, not just those involving accounts receivable and accounts payable. Some examples of other journal entries made by Andrea follow:

(1) A $2800 cash sale was made:

Feb. 10 Cash	2 968	
Sales		2 800
GST Payable		168
Cash sale.		

(2) The owner invested $7200:

Feb. 10 Cash	7 200	
C. Remmick, Capital		7 200
Additional investment.		

(3) Cheque 81 for $198.14 was issued to pay the telephone bill:

Feb. 12 Telephone Expense	186.92	
GST Refundable	11.22	
Cash		198.14
Cheque 81.		

(4) The owner withdrew $2000 for personal use:

Feb. 17 C. Remmick, Drawings	2 000	
Cash		2 000
Cheque 85, personal use.		

Summary of Direct Posting Procedure

A summary of the direct posting procedure used by Remo Wholesalers is illustrated below.

DIRECT POSTING PROCEDURE

SOURCE DOCUMENTS

All source documents including accounts payable and accounts receivable are journalized.

Accounts payable and accounts receivable are posted directly to individual or supplier accounts.

GENERAL JOURNAL
Entries
posted to
GENERAL LEDGER

ACCOUNTS PAYABLE AND
ACCOUNTS RECEIVABLE
SUBSIDIARY LEDGERS

SUBSIDIARY LEDGERS SUMMARY

The three previous job descriptions have served as a basic introduction to subsidiary ledgers; a more detailed examination of the theory of subsidiary ledger accounting will now be made.

It is clear from the accounting procedures already covered in this chapter that a company like Remo Wholesalers needs more than one ledger to efficiently process and control the accuracy of its accounting data. Since Remo Wholesalers has numerous creditors and several hundred customers, it would, of course, be inconvenient to list them all on the balance sheet. Instead, the total owing by all the customers ($21 500) is indicated on the balance sheet by the Accounts Receivable control account as shown in Figure 8-17 below. The total owing to all creditors ($22 000) is represented by the Accounts Payable control account, which

Remo Wholesalers Balance Sheet February 28, 2009		
Assets		
Cash	$ 15 500	
Accounts Receivable	21 500	
Supplies	5 000	
Land	100 000	
Building	400 000	
Equipment	35 000	
Total Assets		$577 000
Liabilities and Owner's Equity		
Liabilities		
Accounts Payable	$ 22 000	
Bank Loan	200 000	
Total Liabilities		$222 000
Owner's Equity		
C. Remmick, Capital		355 000
Total Liabilities and Owner's Equity		$577 000

FIGURE 8-17

Balance sheet for Remo Wholesalers

is also shown in Figure 8-17. Both the Accounts Receivable and the Accounts Payable control accounts are found in the main ledger or General Ledger.

In addition, the General Ledger contains all the asset, liability, equity, revenue, and expense accounts. The **General Ledger** is a file of all the accounts that are used to prepare the financial statements — both the income statement and the balance sheet. A simplified example of the General Ledger and the two subsidiary ledgers used by Remo Wholesalers is given in Figure 8–18 below.

The General Ledger is a file of all accounts used to prepare the financial statements.

To effectively process the large number of customer and creditor account transactions, separate or subsidiary ledgers such as the Accounts Receivable Ledger and the Accounts Payable Ledger are used.

Before looking more closely at the two subsidiary ledgers used by Remo Wholesalers, remember that subsidiary ledgers are usually organized in alphabetical order. In the General Ledger, all accounts are numbered. For example, Cash may be number 100 and Capital may be number 300.

Accounts Receivable Ledger

In many firms like Remo Wholesalers, the Accounts Receivable accounts are removed from the General Ledger and placed in a special customers' *Accounts Receivable Ledger*. This subsidiary ledger is required to record the details of the large number of customer accounts of such businesses. Only the customer accounts are found in this Accounts Receivable Ledger.

FIGURE 8-18

Simplified examples of the General Ledger and two subsidiary ledgers used by Remo Wholesalers

GENERAL LEDGER

Cash	Equipment
15 500	35 000
Accounts Receivable	Accounts Payable
21 500	22 000
Supplies	Bank Loan
5 000	200 000
Land	C. Remmick, Capital
100 000	355 000
Building	
400 000	

ACCOUNTS RECEIVABLE LEDGER	ACCOUNTS PAYABLE LEDGER
C. Harkies	Booth Co.
4 800	3 000
C. Martino	Gold Ltd.
5 200	9 000
D. Patel	Pitt Ltd.
3 500	4 000
A. Taulib	Placer Inc.
8 000	6 000

The customers' accounts are replaced in the General Ledger by a single account called the *Accounts Receivable control account*. This account represents the total owing by all the customers and is necessary for the General Ledger to remain in balance. The balance in the Accounts Receivable control account should always equal the total of all the individual customer accounts in the Accounts Receivable Ledger — that is why it is called a control account. Customer accounts are usually filed alphabetically in the Accounts Receivable Ledger and new accounts are inserted as required.

Accounts Payable Ledger

A business with many creditors often removes the creditors' accounts from the General Ledger and places them in a subsidiary ledger called the *Accounts Payable Ledger*. The creditors' accounts are replaced in the General Ledger by an Accounts Payable control account.

The total of all the individual creditors' accounts in the Accounts Payable Ledger should equal the balance of the Accounts Payable control account in the General Ledger. Accounts in the Accounts Payable Ledger are also organized alphabetically. Figure 8-18 shows the relationship of the three ledgers. Notice that the total of the Accounts Receivable Ledger is $21 500 ($4800 + $5200 + $3500 + $8000) and is equal to the balance in Accounts Receivable, the control account in the General Ledger. Similarly, the total of the Accounts Payable Ledger, $22 000 ($3000 + $9000 + $4000 + $6000), is equal to the balance in Accounts Payable, the control account in the General Ledger.

Proof of Accuracy of Ledgers

Each ledger should be proved to be mathematically accurate on a regular basis, for example, monthly. The proof of the accuracy of the General Ledger is a trial balance in which the debit total equals the credit total. The Accounts Receivable Ledger is proved to be correct if the total of the schedule of accounts receivable is equal to the balance of the Accounts Receivable control account in the General Ledger. Similarly, the total of the schedule of accounts payable should be equal to the balance of the Accounts Payable control account in the General Ledger. Figure 8–19 on the next page shows Remo Wholesalers' trial balance and schedules of accounts receivable and accounts payable. Remember this general rule:

> *For every subsidiary ledger, there is a control account in the General Ledger. The total of the accounts in the subsidiary ledger must equal the balance of the related control account in the General Ledger.*

Additional Subsidiary Ledgers

Two common examples of subsidiary ledgers have been described in this chapter. However, these are not the only subsidiary ledgers used by businesses. A subsidiary ledger is a ledger containing accounts of the same type with a control account replacing the individual accounts in the General Ledger. Therefore, whenever there are a large number of similar accounts in the General Ledger, it is possible to streamline the ledger by utilizing a subsidiary ledger. An example of another common subsidiary ledger used by firms with a large and varied amount of equipment is an Equipment Ledger. As well, if a company has many notes receivable, it could set up a subsidiary ledger for **Notes Receivable**.

A written promise to receive cash in the future; usually specifies the interest rate and the maturity date of the note.

FIGURE 8-19

Subsidiary ledger account totals must equal the balance of the related control account in the General Ledger.

Remo Wholesalers
General Ledger Trial Balance
February 28, 2009

Cash	$ 15 500	
Accounts Receivable	21 500	
Supplies	5 000	
Land	100 000	
Building	400 000	
Equipment	35 000	
Accounts Payable		$ 22 000
Bank Loan		200 000
C. Remmick, Capital		355 000
	$577 000	$577 000

Remo Wholesalers
Schedule of Accounts Receivable
February 28, 2009

C. Harkies	$ 4 800
C. Martino	5 200
D. Patel	3 500
A. Taulib	8 000
	$21 500

Remo Wholesalers
Schedule of Accounts Payable
February 28, 2009

Booth Co.	$3 000
Gold Ltd.	9 000
Pitt Ltd.	4 000
Placer Inc.	6 000
	$22 000

JOURNALIZING BATCH TOTALS

Journalizing batch totals is a technique used to efficiently record similar transactions that are frequently repeated. Suppose a business issues 28 invoices to customers over a short period of time. For each invoice, a journal entry such as this is made by the accounting supervisor:

Mar. 7	Accounts Receivable	143.10	
	Sales		135.00
	GST Payable		8.10
	To record Invoice 101.		

However, rather than record this entry 28 separate times for each invoice, a total may be taken of all the invoices and this total recorded as follows:

Mar. 7	Accounts Receivable	5 936	
	Sales		5 600
	GST Payable		336
	To record Invoices 101–128 for sales on account.		

This concept of grouping source documents and recording the total is called **journalizing batch totals**. It can be applied to a variety of documents. This is the entry made when cash receipts are batched:

To journalize batch totals is to record the total of a number of source documents of one type in a single journal entry.

Mar. 7	Cash	3 800	
	Accounts Receivable		3 800
	To record cash received from customers Mar. 1–7.		

Payments made to creditors may also be journalized in batches. For example, a series of cheque copies are journalized as follows:

Mar. 7	Accounts Payable	4 125	
	Cash		4 125
	Cheques 438–453.		

Purchase invoices may be grouped together as well. However, the entry to record purchase invoices may have more than one debit if different items were purchased. The following journal entry illustrates this situation:

Mar. 7	Office Supplies	500	
	Equipment	2 000	
	Heating Expense	300	
	Miscellaneous Expense	100	
	GST Refundable	174	
	Accounts Payable		3 074
	To record purchases Mar. 1–7.		

Summary of Indirect Posting Procedure

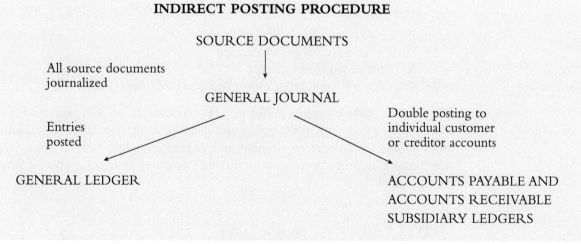

INDIRECT POSTING PROCEDURE

SOURCE DOCUMENTS

All source documents journalized

GENERAL JOURNAL

Double posting to individual customer or creditor accounts

Entries posted

GENERAL LEDGER

ACCOUNTS PAYABLE AND ACCOUNTS RECEIVABLE SUBSIDIARY LEDGERS

DATA COLLECTION

The information for the subsidiary ledgers can be recorded in a variety of ways depending on the size of the business. The concepts demonstrated in the manual system used by Remo Wholesalers are consistent in all systems since only the data collection method changes. These methods fall into two major categories:

- Manual system
- Computerized system

Manual System

A few small firms record all accounting data manually. These firms may use a three-ledger system to have up-to-date accounts receivable and payable information. Different people specialize in recording information in the ledgers assigned to them. This system has been fully explained previously in this chapter.

Computerized System

Most firms use computerized accounts receivable and payable software packages to improve the efficiency of recording into the subsidiary ledgers. Transactions are entered into the computer's data bank of accounting information. The accounts receivable module of the software program processes the data, updates the accounts, and provides a variety of output. The software program generates reports such as the schedule of accounts receivable, as well as a print-out of the accounts showing transaction details.

THE COMPUTERIZED SYSTEM

Up to this point, you have been doing problems and exercises manually, that is, writing by hand the solutions to assignments. As you will see, there are many tasks in accounting that are repeated. For example, sales are made and recorded every day and balance sheets are prepared every month. Such repetitive tasks are ideal for a computer. Consequently, accountants view the computer as a very helpful tool.

Computers can do the following tasks very quickly:

- Perform mathematical calculations
- Store large amounts of information
- Retrieve stored information
- Classify, sort, summarize, move, and compare information

These are all tasks routinely performed by accountants, so it makes sense for accountants to make use of the power and speed of computers. When a computer is combined with other equipment such as printers, additional terminals, and other communication devices, the resulting computer system becomes a very powerful tool.

COMPARING MANUAL
AND COMPUTER ACCOUNTING

Manual Accounting Characteristics

Figure 8-20 on the next page illustrates the steps to complete the accounting cycle. The steps are shown in the order that they are performed when accounting is done by hand, that is, manually. Each step requires that the data be rewritten.

FIGURE 8-20

Steps in a manual
accounting system

SOURCE DOCUMENTS
↓
JOURNAL
↓
LEDGER
↓
TRIAL BALANCE
↓
FINANCIAL STATEMENTS

Computer Accounting Characteristics

Computers have very large storage (memory) capacities. They also have the capability to manipulate and process data in a variety of ways and with great speed. This includes the ability to handle mathematical tasks, such as calculating the balance in accounts, and to print documents.

When accounting data have been input, the computer processes the data and then provides a variety of output (reports). The nature of the processing and the output is determined by the software programs that run the computer system.

Now look at Figure 8-21. The same steps as in Figure 8-20 are illustrated in this figure, but they are listed in the order in which they are completed in a computerized accounting system.

In a computerized accounting system, the accounting cycle is reduced to just three basic steps:

(1) Inputting data
(2) Processing data
(3) Outputting data

Step 1: Inputting Data

Source documents are the source of information for the computer operator. A source document is prepared for every transaction, and the information is entered into the computer system from the source document. Some companies, however, prefer to list the source documents on a data entry sheet prior to computer entry.

FIGURE 8-21

Steps in a computerized
accounting system

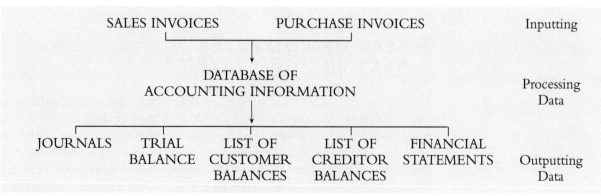

SALES INVOICES   PURCHASE INVOICES   Inputting

DATABASE OF
ACCOUNTING INFORMATION   Processing Data

JOURNALS   TRIAL BALANCE   LIST OF CUSTOMER BALANCES   LIST OF CREDITOR BALANCES   FINANCIAL STATEMENTS   Outputting Data

Step 2: Processing Data

All the information concerning transactions is stored in the computer's *memory*. Here it forms a database (or data bank) of accounting information. This database of information can be manipulated (processed) in a variety of ways. The software program determines what processing will actually occur. The result of the processing can be printed as *output*. It can be recalled from memory and used in a variety of ways depending on the type of output desired. The information does not have to be re-entered each time it is to be used for a report or form. Even though it has been used, it is still stored in memory and can be used again for a different report.

Step 3: Outputting Data

Output refers to the information produced by the computer. Information can be produced in a variety of ways, including printed reports, visual reports on the computer monitor, or electronic reports that can be used by computers.

As illustrated in Figure 8-21, the output can be a journal, a trial balance, ledger account information, or financial statements. The actual type and format of the report is determined by the needs of the company. Of course, a software program that is capable of producing the desired reports must be designed or purchased.

Because of the processing ability of a computer, more detailed schedules can be produced automatically. Once accounting information has been input, it becomes a database of information. Most accounting software programs are capable of producing a schedule that reports how old each customer's debt is.

Summary

The main difference between manual and computer accounting is the ability of the computer to store large amounts of data and to process those data in a variety of ways. The data are only entered into the system once. In a manual system, each accounting step requires that data be written and processed separately.

Information entered into a computerized accounting system forms a database of accounting information. The software program can access and process the information in the database and use it to produce a variety of outputs. Once information is in the database, it can be retrieved in a variety of ways — in the form of a journal, as ledger accounts, or as financial reports. The information does not have to be re-entered each time. In a manual accounting system, each form or report must be written individually. This means that the same information must be obtained and written out each time that a form or report is prepared.

USERS OF COMPUTER ACCOUNTING SYSTEMS

The number of businesses, of all sizes, using computer accounting systems (for example, Simply Accounting®) will continue to increase dramatically as computer hardware and software become more affordable. Processing up-to-date accounting information is a necessity in order to make business decisions. A computer system provides the most efficient method of generating these data. Accounting personnel at all levels in a business are currently expected to exhibit proficiency in accounting procedures as well as basic understanding of computer operation and software application. The theory and practical applications learned in this text will provide you with a solid foundation for a computerized accounting application course.

Ⓐ CCOUNTING TERMS

Accounts Payable Control	Equals the value of all the individual accounts payable found in the Accounts Payable Ledger. (p. 270)
Accounts Payable Ledger	A ledger containing the individual accounts payable of a company. (p. 270)
Accounts Receivable Control	Equals the value of all the individual accounts receivable found in the Accounts Receivable Ledger. (p. 269)
Accounts Receivable Ledger	A ledger containing the individual accounts receivable of a company. (p. 269)
Control Account	An account found in the General Ledger that has a balance equal to a number of accounts found in a subsidiary ledger. (p. 269)
Division of Labour Principle	Divide work among several people who specialize in completing one component of the task. (p. 272)
General Ledger	The General Ledger is a file of all accounts used to prepare the financial statements. (p. 284)
Journalizing Batch Totals	Journalizing batch totals is the recording of the total of a number of source documents of one type in a single journal entry. (p. 287)
Notes Receivable	A written promise to receive cash in the future; usually specifies the interest rate and the maturity date of the note. (p. 285)
Schedule of Accounts Payable	The individual accounts payable found in the subsidiary ledger are listed and totalled to prove they equal the Accounts Payable control account in the General Ledger. (p. 272)
Schedule of Accounts Receivable	The individual accounts receivable found in the subsidiary ledger are listed and totalled to prove they equal the Account Receivable control account in the General Ledger. (p. 271)
Subsidiary Ledger	A ledger containing a group of accounts of similar type, usually organized in alphabetical order. (p. 269)

1. Which source documents does an accounts payable clerk handle?

2. Explain what is meant by direct posting.

3. Who receives the documents after the accounts payable clerk?

4. What is the accounts receivable clerk's first task with the copies of the sales invoices?

5. Specify whether the accounts receivable clerk records:
   (a) Sales invoices as debits or credits
   (b) Cash receipts as debits or credits

UNIT 18

REVIEW QUESTIONS

6. Who gets the sales invoices and the list of cash receipts after the accounts receivable clerk?

7. List the source documents for which the accounting supervisor is responsible.

8. (a) Which two General Ledger accounts are always affected by a list of cash receipts?
    (b) Give an example of a journal entry resulting from a list of cash receipts.

9. (a) Which two General Ledger accounts are always affected by copies of cheques issued on account?
    (b) Give an example of a journal entry resulting from a copy of a cheque on account.

10. What is the name given to the main ledger for a company that has more than one ledger?

11. Accounts in the General Ledger are numbered and organized in numerical sequence. How are the accounts in subsidiary ledgers usually organized?

12. What is the rule concerning the relationship between a subsidiary ledger and the General Ledger?

13. What statement or document is prepared to prove the accuracy of the General Ledger?

14. What statement or document is prepared to prove the accuracy of the Accounts Receivable Ledger?

15. Explain the process of journalizing batch totals.

16. What are the two advantages of using subsidiary ledgers?

17. Explain the three steps in the accounting cycle when a computerized accounting system is used by a firm.

18. What are the two basic components of a computerized accounting system?

UNIT 18

PROBLEMS: APPLICATIONS

1. You are the accounts payable clerk for Brandon Suppliers. Your duties include recording purchase invoices in creditor accounts.

   (a) Head up the following accounts in your Accounts Payable Ledger:

   - Gillan's Service Station
   - Reeves Office Equipment
   - Sethi Supply Ltd.
   - Tomlin Fuels Ltd.

   (b) The following purchase invoices represent purchases on account made by Brandon. Record them in the Accounts Payable Ledger. The price shown is the final cost of the item and includes GST and PST.

   Mar. 1   Tomlin Fuels Ltd., No. 6931 for fuel oil, $285;
            Sethi Supply Ltd., No. K-213 for office supplies, $175;
            Reeves Office Equipment, No. 316 for a printer/fax machine, $339.

        2   Gillan's Service Station, No. 179 for gas and oil for company automobiles, $372.

        4   Reeves Office Equipment, No. 391 for filing equipment, $260;
            Sethi Supply Ltd., No. K-272 for stationery, $50.

8   Gillan's Service Station, No. 225 for gasoline, $48;
Tomlin Fuels Ltd., No. 6983 for furnace servicing, $140.

9   Gillan's Service Station, No. 238 for car repairs, $282;
Sethi Supply Ltd., No. K–317 for miscellaneous supplies, $36.

18   Reeves Office Equipment, No. 421 for cheque protecting machine, $375.

2. Your duties as accounts payable clerk for Brandon Suppliers also include recording payments made to creditors. Record the following copies of cheques issued in the Accounts Payable Ledger used for exercise 1.

Mar. 14   No. 116 to Gillan's Service Station, $372 for Invoice 179;
No. 117 to Tomlin Fuels Ltd., $285 for Invoice 6931.

21   No. 118 to Sethi Supply Ltd., $175 for Invoice K–213;
No. 119 to Gillan's Service Station, $48 for Invoice 225.

28   No. 120 to Reeves Office Equipment, $275 in part payment of Invoice 316;
No. 121 to Sethi Supply Ltd., $50 for Invoice K–272.

3. Prepare a schedule of accounts payable dated March 31, 2008 for the Accounts Payable Ledger of Brandon Suppliers. Your schedule should total $1157.

4. In this exercise, you will act as the accounts receivable clerk for Brandon Suppliers. Your duties include posting sales invoices directly into the customer accounts in the subsidiary Accounts Receivable Ledger.

(a) Head up the following accounts in your Accounts Receivable Ledger:

- J. Hoskins
- V. Lynch

- N. Singh
- R. Williams

(b) The following sales invoices represent sales on account made by your company to your customers. Post them directly into the Accounts Receivable Ledger. The price shown is the final cost of the item and includes GST and PST.

Mar.   1   V. Lynch, No. 76-15, total of $400;
R. Williams, No. 76-16, $572.

3   N. Singh, No. 76-17, $625;
J. Hoskins, No. 76-18, $195.

7   J. Hoskins, No. 76-19, $515;
V. Lynch, No. 76-20, $157.

10   N. Singh, No. 76-21, $247;
R. Williams, No. 76-22, $235.

12   J. Hoskins, No. 76-23, $430;
N. Singh, No. 76-24, $255.

5. The accounts receivable clerk's job at Brandon Suppliers includes recording money received from customers. Record the following cash receipts as credits in the customer accounts used in exercise 4.

Mar. 15 J. Hoskins, $195 for Invoice 76-18;
V. Lynch, $400 for Invoice 76-15;
R. Williams, $270 toward payment of Invoice 76-16.

22 J. Hoskins, $515 for Invoice 76-19;
N. Singh, $625 for Invoice 76-17.

29 R. Williams, $537 for Invoices 76-16 and 76-22;
N. Singh, $247 for Invoice 76-21.

6. Prepare a schedule of accounts receivable dated March 31, 2008 for the Accounts Receivable Ledger of Brandon Suppliers. Your schedule should total $842.

7. (a) How can the total of $1157 for the schedule of accounts payable (exercise 3) be checked for accuracy?
   (b) How can the total of $842 for the schedule of accounts receivable (exercise 6) be checked for accuracy?
   (c) If your totals do not agree with $1157 and $842, what does this indicate?

8. (a) As the accounts receivable clerk for Brandon Suppliers, perform the following duties:

   (i) Set up the following accounts and balances in the Accounts Receivable Ledger:

• J. Hoskins	$430
• V. Lynch	157
• N. Singh	255
• R. Williams	nil

   (ii) Post the following source documents directly to the Accounts Receivable Ledger. Note: All sales are PST exempt.

   Apr. 1 Sales invoices:
   N. Singh, No. 76-25, $355 (sale $334.91, plus $20.09 GST);
   V. Lynch, No. 76-26, $53 (sale $50, plus $3 GST).

   3 Sales invoices:
   V. Lynch, No. 76-27, $670 (sale $632.08, plus $37.92 GST);
   R. Williams, No. 76-28, $212 (sale $200, plus $12 GST).

   5 List of cash receipts:
   V. Lynch, $157 for Invoice 76-20;
   N. Singh, $255 for Invoice 76-24.

   6 Sales invoices:
   J. Hoskins, No. 76-29, $513 (sale $483.96, plus $29.04 GST);
   V. Lynch, No. 76–30, $275 (sale $259.43, plus $15.57 GST);
   R. Williams, No. 76-31, $850 (sale $801.89, plus $48.11 GST).

   8 List of cash receipts:
   J. Hoskins, $430 for Invoice 76-23;
   V. Lynch, $723 for Invoices 76-26 and 76-27;
   R. Williams, $212 for Invoice 76-28.

   (iii) Prepare a schedule of accounts receivable dated April 10, 2008.

(b) As the accounting supervisor for Brandon Suppliers, perform the following duties:

(i) Set up the following accounts and balances in the General Ledger as at April 1:

101	Cash	$2 209
110	Accounts Receivable	842
206	GST Payable	0
400	Sales	0

(ii) In the Student Working Papers, journalize on page 29 the source documents received from the accounts receivable clerk in part (a) of this exercise.

(iii) Post the journal to the General Ledger.

(iv) Compare the Accounts Receivable control account with the schedule of accounts receivable prepared in part (a).

9. Presented below is the Accounts Receivable Ledger for Moe's Service Centre and the Accounts Payable Ledger for Autoparts Supply Store.

Accounts Receivable Ledger

ACCOUNT   Moe's Service Centre

DATE		PARTICULARS	P.R.	DEBIT	CREDIT	DR. CR.	BALANCE
2008							
Oct.	1	Invoice 111–1		315.00		DR.	315.00
	5	For Invoice 109–1			184.00	DR.	131.00
	8	Invoice 112–1		262.00		DR.	393.00
	12	For Invoice 111–1			315.00	DR.	78.00

Accounts Payable Ledger

ACCOUNT   Autoparts Supply Store

DATE		PARTICULARS	P.R.	DEBIT	CREDIT	DR. CR.	BALANCE
2008							
Oct.	1	Forwarded				CR	625.00
	2	Invoice 692			339.00	CR.	964.00
	4	Cheque 63 for Invoice 690		550.00		CR.	414.00
	9	Invoice 693			254.00	CR	668.00

Describe each transaction that has been posted to the subsidiary ledgers. Ignore any taxes.

1. In this problem, you are the accounting clerk for Worldwide Educators, which uses the indirect posting procedure.

(a) Set up the accounts in the General Ledger from the following June 1 information:

CHAPTER 8

PROBLEMS:
CHALLENGES

101	Cash	$ 3 575	
110	Accounts Receivable	8 500	
120	Merchandise Inventory	22 000	
130	Office Supplies	1 275	
151	Furniture and Equipment	27 000	
200	Accounts Payable		$6 250
205	PST Payable		1 975
206	GST Payable		1 560
207	GST Refundable	1 350	
300	P. Grinds, Capital		34 415
400	Sales		47 000
500	Purchases	20 000	
600	Rent Expense	7 500	
607	Office Expense	0	
		$91 200	$91 200

(b) The Accounts Receivable Ledger contains the following accounts and balances on June 1. Open the ledger.

A. Coolman	$4 800
R. Pawa	3 700
	$8 500

(c) The Accounts Payable Ledger contains the following accounts and balances on June 1. Open the accounts.

C. Heath	$2 350
T. Nguyen	2 100
G. Vergara	1 800
	$6 250

(d) Record the entries below on page 51 of a General Journal.

(e) Post the entries to the General Ledger and subsidiary ledgers using the indirect posting method.

(f) Prepare a trial balance, accounts receivable summary, and accounts payable summary on June 9, 2009.

Jun. 1 Purchase invoice:
No. 302 from G. Vergara for merchandise $1050 plus $63 GST.

2 Cheque copy No. 252 to T. Nguyen $2100 full payment of account.

2 Cash purchase of office supplies from Decker's Office Supply $150 plus $9 GST. Cheque copy No. 253.

3 Sales invoices:
R. Pawa No. 1515, $700 plus 6 percent GST and 8 percent PST; A. Coolman No. 1516, $1100 plus GST and PST.

4 Purchase invoices:
No. C475 from C. Heath for merchandise $1450 plus $87 GST; No. 15147 from T. Nguyen for merchandise $2300 plus $138 GST.

5   Cash sales for week $4500, plus $270 GST and $360 PST.

6   Paid rent for the month $2500 plus GST. Cheque copy
No. 254.

9   Cheques received from A. Coolman ($4000) and R. Pawa
($3500) in partial payment of their accounts.

2. Source documents for some of the transactions of Rob's TV Repairs are
shown on pages 297 to 300. Source documents for other transactions are
listed on page 301. The accounts and balances in the three ledgers for Rob's
TV Repairs are as follows:

Rob's TV Repairs
Schedule of Accounts Receivable
April 6, 2008

C. Dunes	$ 287.40
The Wayside Motor Hotel	1 356.70
J. Pothier	642.30
	$2 286.40

Rob's TV Repairs
General Ledger Trial Balance
April 6, 2008

ACCOUNT TITLE	ACC. NO.	DEBIT	CREDIT
Cash	101	$ 7 118.60	
Accounts Receivable	110	2 286.40	
Repair Parts	140	2 470.00	
Equipment	151	25 000.00	
Truck	155	18 000.00	
Accounts Payable	200		$ 2 119.63
GST Payable	206		0
PST Payable	207		0
R. Davies, Capital	300		52 755.37
R. Davies, Drawings	301	0	
Sales	400		0
Truck Expense	602	0	
Rent Expense	604	0	
		$54 875.00	$54 875.00

Rob's TV Repairs
Schedule of Accounts Payable
April 6, 2008

Electronic Suppliers	$1 849.67
Roland's Body Repairs	0
Tinsdale's Service Station	269.96
	$2 119.63

In this problem, you will perform the duties of three different employees of Rob's TV Repairs:

- Accounts receivable clerk
- Accounts payable clerk
- Accounting supervisor

(a) Open the three ledgers and record the balances.

(b) In the Accounts Receivable Ledger, record the appropriate source documents given on April 7 and April 9; then prepare a schedule of accounts receivable.

(c) In the Accounts Payable Ledger, record the appropriate source documents and other transactions given on April 9; then prepare a schedule of accounts payable.

(d) Record all source documents in the journal on page 38; post to the General Ledger; and prepare a trial balance of the General Ledger.

Invoice
Rob's TV Repairs
1750 Elgin Street, Winnipeg, Manitoba   R3E 1C3

Date: April 7, 2008
Inv. No.: 2450
Terms: Net 30 days

Sold to:

The Wayside Motor Hotel
1460 River Road
Winnipeg, Manitoba
R2M 3Z8

RE: TVs in rooms 107 and 214

	Labour	$157.40
	Parts	211.12
		368.52
	GST	22.11
	PST on Parts	16.89
		$407.52

AMOUNT OF THIS INVOICE: $407.52

Daily Cash Receipts
April 7, 2008

CUSTOMER	INVOICE	AMOUNT
J. Pothier	2340	$ 642.30
The Wayside Motor Hotel	2355	1 375.00
Cash Sales: Sales 1 287.74		
GST 77.26		1 365.00
		$3 382.30

Invoice
Rob's TV Repairs
1750 Elgin Street, Winnipeg, Manitoba   R3E 1C3

Date: April 7, 2008
Inv. No.: 2451
Terms: Net 30 days

Sold to:

C. Dunes
141 Dynes Road
Winnipeg, Manitoba
R2J 0Z8

RE: G.E. COLOUR TV

Labour	$ 50.64
Parts	87.30
	137.94
GST	8.28
PST on Parts	6.98
	$153.20

AMOUNT OF THIS INVOICE: $153.20

Invoice
Rob's TV Repairs
1750 Elgin Street, Winnipeg, Manitoba   R3E 1C3

Date: April 7, 2008
Inv. No.: 2452
Terms: Net 30 days

Sold to:

J. Pothier
543 Kilburn Street
Winnipeg, Manitoba
R2B 1B1

RE: Sony Colour TV

Labour	$ 74.71
Parts	175.10
	249.81
GST	14.99
PST on Parts	14.01
	$278.81

AMOUNT OF THIS INVOICE: $278.81

Montreal
Toronto
Winnipeg
Vancouver

Electronic Suppliers
147 Industrial Blvd., Winnipeg, Manitoba   R2W 0J7
Tel.: 475-6643   Terms: Net 15 days

SOLD TO   SHIP TO

Rob's TV Repairs   Same
1750 Elgin Street
Winnipeg, Manitoba   R3E 1C3

PST No.	Date Invoiced	Inv. No.
435 70913	04/09/08	9875

Quantity	Description	Unit Price	Amount
2	X780 Speakers	$257.89	$515.78
		GST	30.95
		Pay this amount	$546.73

Roland's Body Repairs
4765 Borden Road, Winnipeg, Manitoba   R2C 3C6
Telephone: 422-7368

Name:	Rob's TV Repairs	**Inv. No.**	74709
Address:	1750 Elgin Street	**Terms:**	Net 30 days
	Winnipeg, Manitoba		
	R3E 1C3		
Make:	Ford Truck	**Licence:**	A-4597
Date:	April 9, 2008		

Quantity	Description	Unit Price	Amount
1	Fender	$1 380.49	$1 380.49
4	Brackets	13.25	53.00
			1 433.49
	Labour		625.41
			2 058.90
	GST		123.53
	Pay this amount		$2 182.43

ELECTRONIC SUPPLIERS				CHEQUE 576
Date	Item	Amount	Discount	Net Amount
Apr. 7	Inv. 9621	$203.76		
9	Inv. 9632	514.83		$718.59

TINSDALE'S SERVICE STATION				CHEQUE 577
Date	Item	Amount	Discount	Net Amount
Apr. 7	Inv. B-376	$ 24.50		
8	Inv. B-437	209.76		
9	Inv. B-533	35.70		$269.96

COCHRAN REALTIES				CHEQUE 578
Date	Item	Amount	Discount	Net Amount
Apr. 9	Rent for April	$1 500.00		
	GST	90.00		$1 590.00

Source Documents for Other Transactions:

Apr.   9   Sales invoices:
No. 2453 to Wayside Motor Hotel, $278.18, GST $16.69, total $294.87;
No. 2454 to J. Pothier, $87.51, GST $5.25, total $92.76.

Daily cash receipts:
C. Dunes, $235.60 on account;
Cash sales $2100.73, GST $126.04, total $2226.77.

Purchases invoices:
Electronic Suppliers, No. 9778, $273.71 for parts ($258.22 sale, plus $15.49 GST);
Tinsdale's Service Station, No. B-675, $166.84 for a tune-up on the truck ($157.40, plus $9.44 GST).

Cheque copies:
No. 579 to Roland's Body Repairs, $1400 on account;
No. 725 to R. Davies, the owner, $725 for personal use.

3. On December 31, the Accounts Receivable control account in the General Ledger has a balance of $90 000. The company auditor has located the following recording errors.

(1)   A cheque for $800 received from a customer was not recorded in the customer's account receivable account but was recorded in the Accounts Receivable control account in the General Ledger.
(2)   A cheque from a customer for $2000 was deposited but not recorded in the control account.
(3)   A sale to a customer for $2400 was posted to the control account as $4200.
(4)   A sales invoice for $500 was not recorded in either the customer's account or the control account.
(5)   A sale for $1000 was posted to the Sales accounts as $100.
(6)   A sales invoice for $1200 was missed completely and not recorded.
(7)   A purchase invoice for $2000 was not recorded anywhere.
(8)   A $1700 cheque payment for provincial sales tax was not recorded.

Required:

(a)   Outline the corrections to be made for each of the errors.
(b)   Use a T-account to determine the correct balance in the Accounts Receivable control account.

CHAPTER 8

CASE STUDIES

CASE 1
Balancing the Accounts Receivable Ledger

The following transactions were journalized and posted to the General Ledger of Whistler Ltd. during August:

Sales on account	$13 200
Cash received from customers	11 300
Cash sales	8 100

The schedule of accounts receivable prepared on August 31 shows a total of $7800 owed by customers.

(a) Open a T-account for the Accounts Receivable control account. The August 1 balance is $6100.
(b) Record the August transactions involving accounts receivable to the T-account. Determine the August 31 balance in the Accounts Receivable control account.
(c) Have any errors been made involving accounts receivable? Give reasons for your answer.

CASE 2
Locating Errors

As the accounting supervisor, you have prepared a trial balance of the General Ledger at the end of the month and it balances. The accounting clerk prepares a schedule of accounts receivable and accounts payable from the subsidiary ledgers and gives it to you to verify. The accounts receivable schedule balances to the control account in your trial balance but the accounts payable schedule is $72 less than the control account.

(a) Which total is in error — the control account or the schedule of accounts payable? Why?
(b) What type of error could cause the difference?
(c) How would the error be located?

CASE 3
Accounts Receivable Procedures

Reliable Testing Services is located in Alberta. It provides laboratory testing services to companies involved in petroleum and mining in Western Canada. Companies send samples to Reliable, testing is completed, and analysis reports are returned to the customers along with the samples. All work is completed on account; invoices are sent to the customer and payment is due in 30 days.

Alicia Doyle is the office manager and accountant for Reliable Testing Services. She opens and sorts the mail each day and supervises the office employees. Each day cheques received from customers along with remittance slips for the payments are handled by Alicia. She totals the cheques received and prepares a bank deposit. She records the bank deposit. She uses the remittance slip to post the money received to the customer accounts. The total posted to the customer accounts each day agrees with the amount deposited into the company bank account.

One of the annual tasks of the company auditor is to review the accounting systems and to make recommendations. As the company's auditor, what recommendations would you make to Reliable Services?

ETHICS CASE
Personal Values

George Sloan is the accounts payable clerk for Clifford Enterprises. He is considered a reliable employee. Frank Clifford, the firm's owner, lets George "run his own show" and rarely checks the work done by George.

George is responsible for matching purchase orders, receiving reports, and purchase invoices. He audits the invoices and checks them for mathematical accuracy. George then initials the invoices. A cheque is prepared, attached to the invoice, and presented to Mr. Clifford. Mr. Clifford routinely signs the cheques. He assumes the invoice and the cheque amounts are correct because "George never makes mistakes" and "George always catches overcharges made by suppliers."

One night, while having dinner with a friend, George meets Gord Chamberlain who is a major supplier of goods to Clifford Enterprises. Gord insists on paying George's cheque and buys him an expensive bottle of wine, saying, "It's the least we can do for such a good customer."

Soon, George is invited by Chamberlain to play golf at the Hunt Club. After a game of golf and dinner, George receives an offer: In return for accepting phoney invoices from Chamberlain's company and getting them paid by Mr. Clifford, George will be paid half the amount of each cheque. Chamberlain argues that George can earn $500 a month with no risk of being caught, since he has the authority to approve invoices and his work is never questioned. George realizes he could get away with this plan without being caught.

(a) If you were George, what would you do?
(b) List several alternatives open to George.
(c) What are the consequences of each alternative?
(d) What changes do you think should be made to the Clifford Enterprises' accounting system?
(e) How might George get caught if he agrees to participate in this fraud?

CHAPTER 8

INTERNET RESOURCES

Explore these Web sites for a variety of accounting resources.

1. **Canada Customs and Revenue   www.cra-arc.gc.ca/menu-e.html**

   Visit the Canada Customs and Revenue site for key small business and tax information of interest to individuals and business and for an online accounting glossary.

2. **Accounting.Com—Job Seekers   www.accounting.com**

   Go the the Job Seekers section of Accounting.com for valuable background information on currently available jobs. It lists and describes accounting jobs. The site provides a good picture of a variety of accounting positions.

3. **Accounting Education.com**
   ANET www.accountingeducation.com

   This site provides a free weekly newswire, accounting journals and articles, and links to many accounting sites, worldwide.

4. **Bookkeeper List.com**
   http://www.bookkeeperlist.com/tipsandtricks5.shtml

   This site provides tips and tricks, income tax and business information and related material for individuals and businesses.

5. **Accountants World   http://www.accountantsworld.com**

   Visit this site for a business glossary and information on accounting, small business, technology and general business items.

6. **Personal Finance Links**
   http://www.multcolib.org/homework/perfinhc.html

   This site for teachers, parents and students has links and information on banking and budgeting, investments, taxes, money and the stock market.

CHAPTER 9

The Special Journal System

UNIT 19   Purchases Journal

Learning Objectives

After reading this unit, discussing the applicable review questions, and completing the applications exercises, you will be able to do the following:

1. **IDENTIFY** transactions that are recorded in each of the special journals in a five-journal system.

2. **EXPLAIN** the advantages and disadvantages of using a special journal system.

3. **EXPLAIN** the purpose of a purchase requisition, purchase order, purchase invoice, and receiving report.

4. **DISCUSS** the process of matching documents to approve purchase invoices.

5. **EXPLAIN** the importance of filing invoices in a date file according to the date on which terms of sale indicate that payment is due.

6. **RECORD** transactions in a Purchases Journal.

7. **BALANCE** and post a Purchases Journal.

8. **RECORD** purchases returns.

INTRODUCING SPECIAL JOURNALS— THE FIVE-JOURNAL SYSTEM

In Chapter 8, you learned about accounting systems and procedures that made use of the principles of division of labour and specialization.

Chapter 8 described the three-ledger system used by large companies that have many customers and creditors. Now you will learn that *several* special multi-column journals may be used in a manual accounting system or computerized accounting system by companies that have many repetitive transactions.

Examine the General Journal in Figure 9-1. GST and PST have been omitted to simplify the example. Notice that recording of the entries involves writing certain words and account names over and over. How many times is Cash written? Sales? Imagine how many entries involving Cash, Sales, Purchases, and other frequently used accounts a large business would have!

A few small businesses may still use this system, but the more advanced special journal system discussed in this chapter is used most frequently in business.

As the business grows it may have thousands of entries a day. Could one person record and post all of these entries? Of course not! A more efficient method is to use a special journal system where a separate journal is used to record a certain type of transaction. Let's see how that works.

FIGURE 9-1

Two-column General Journal

GENERAL JOURNAL		PAGE 17		
DATE	PARTICULARS	P.R.	DEBIT	CREDIT
2008 May 1	Cash		618.00	
	Sales			618.00
	Cash sales tickets 781–799.			
1	Accounts Receivable/M. Faux		242.80	
	Sales			242.80
	Invoice B-601, n/30.			
1	Cash		603.70	
	Sales			603.70
	Cash sales tickets 800-819.			
1	Purchases		2 100.00	
	Accounts Payable/Frye Ltd.			2 100.00
	Invoice K-206, merchandise, n/30.			
1	Accounts Receivable/S. Chin		323.75	
	Sales			323.75
	Invoice B-602, n/30.			
1	Purchases		1 473.00	
	Cash			1 473.00
	Cheque 16239, merchandise.			
1	Cash		1 250.00	
	Sales			1 250.00
	Cash sales tickets 820-839.			

A large percentage of the transactions that you recorded previously fall into four major categories:

Category	Transaction
1	Purchases of goods or services on account
2	Sales of goods or services on account
3	Receipt of cash
4	Payment of cash

These four types of transactions represent the majority of financial events happening in a business. When there are too many transactions to record in one general journal, several specialized multi-column journals are used.

A **special journal** is used for each type of repetitive transaction. For example, a *Purchases Journal* is used to record all purchases on account (credit purchases). A *Sales Journal* is used to record credit sales. *Cash Receipts* and *Cash Payments Journals* are used to record cash received and cash payments. In addition, a General Journal is used to record transactions that do not fit into these major categories as well as the end-of-period adjusting and closing entries.

Different people are assigned to record transactions in each of the special journals. Thus, as you can see, the five-journal system makes use of the principles of division of labour and specialization.

The chart below is a summary of the major categories of transactions, the source documents for these transactions, and the special journal into which each will be journalized.

In this chapter, we will examine the use of each of the special journals listed in the chart below.

> A special journal system uses separate journals for similar transactions that recur frequently.

Transactions	Common Source Documents	Journals Used
Purchases on account	Purchase invoices	Purchases Journal
Sales of goods on account	Sales invoices	Sales Journal
Cash receipts	Bank credit memos Cash sales slips Cash register slips List of cheques received in the mail	Cash Receipts Journal
Cash payments	Bank debit memos Cheque copies or stubs	Cash Payments Journal
Other transactions	Credit invoices End-of-period entries Memo — correcting entries	General Journal

You will find that operating the five-journal system will not be difficult once you master the concept of channeling routine transactions into the new special journals rather than recording everything in one journal. The chart in Figure 9-2 on the next page will help you make the correct decisions.

FIGURE 9-2
Special journal system

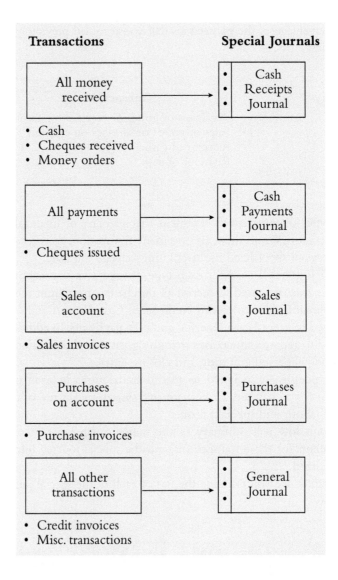

PURCHASING SYSTEMS

The first special journal you will learn to use is the Purchases Journal. Before examining the recording and posting procedures for a Purchases Journal, it is important to understand the purchasing system as a whole. Many documents and company departments are involved in a purchasing system. This is necessary to efficiently divide the work load among a number of people and to control human error and possible dishonesty. Purchasing systems differ from business to business. Henley Sporting Goods is used in the examples that follow to illustrate standard principles used by many businesses.

Ordering Goods

Figure 9–3 illustrates the steps that are usually followed when buying goods:

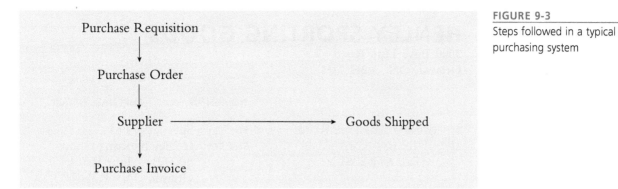

FIGURE 9-3

Steps followed in a typical purchasing system

Purchase Requisition

An employee wishing to purchase goods or services completes a request form called a **purchase requisition**. After it is approved by a supervisor, this form is sent to the purchasing department. Figure 9-4 is an example of a purchase requisition.

A purchase requisition is a form sent to the purchasing department requesting that goods or services be ordered.

FIGURE 9-4

Example of a purchase requisition

HENLEY SPORTING GOODS
3000 Base Line Road
Ottawa, ON K2H 7B3

PURCHASE REQUISITION   **DATE** May 31, 2008

TO PURCHASING DEPARTMENT Please Purchase
                          the Following   No. P-34   **DATE NEEDED** June 25

QUANTITY	STOCK NO.	DESCRIPTION
30		Dolphin clear goggles
30		Olympian clear goggles
12		Assorted earplugs
8		Size 1–4 swim wings

REQUISITIONED BY _Denise Faria_   **APPROVED** _David Carriere_

Purchase Order

It is the responsibility of the purchasing department to acquire the best quality items at the best price. When a supplier has been selected, a **purchase order** is prepared and sent to the supplier. When both the buyer and the seller agree on the terms of the purchase, the purchase order becomes a legal contract. Henley Sporting Goods uses the purchase order shown in Figure 9-5 on the next page.

A purchase order is a form prepared by the buyer and sent to the seller. It describes the items the buyer wants to purchase.

Figure 9-6, also on the next page, shows where each copy of the purchase order is sent. The original is sent to the supplier. The receiving department is sent a copy of the purchase order so that it will know that goods have been ordered and will accept *only* the goods ordered. The accounting department receives a copy of the purchase order so that it will pay only for the goods that have been ordered. The purchasing department retains a copy for its records, and the final copy of the purchase order is sent to the requesting department, so that the requesting department knows that the goods have been ordered and when delivery can be expected.

FIGURE 9-5

Example of a purchase
order

HENLEY SPORTING GOODS
3000 Base Line Road
Ottawa, ON K2H 7B3

NO. 2198   **PURCHASE ORDER**

STORE: 3000 Base Line Road
❏   Tel: 684–1287
          Fax: 684–5381

FACTORY: 5 Melrose Avenue
❏   Tel: 729–7100
          Fax: 729–7288

DATE June 2, 2008

TO: Speedquip Ltd.
SHIP TO: Henley Sporting Goods
               3000 Base Line Road,
               Ottawa, ON   K2H 7B3

Please supply the following by date specified.

REQUIRED BY   June 25
SHIP BY   Parcel Post

QUANTITY	DESCRIPTION
30	Dolphin clear goggles
30	Olympian clear goggles
12	Assorted earplugs
8	Size 1–4 swim wings

PST Licence No. 41902211
GST Registration No. R119282106

PER *David Carriere*

FIGURE 9-6

Distribution of purchase
order and copies

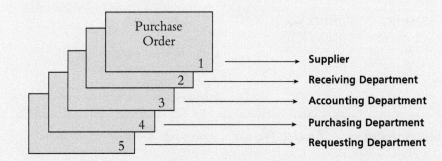

Purchase Invoice

An invoice is a form sent by
the seller to the buyer. It
lists the costs of the items
shipped, along with details
of the shipment.

After the goods have been shipped, the seller sends an *invoice* or bill to the buyer.
Figure 9-7 on the next page is the invoice received by Henley Sporting Goods.
This invoice lists the items shipped to Henley that were ordered on June 2 (Figure
9-5).

The information in the columns headed Quantity Ordered, Quantity Shipped,
Stock Number/Description, Unit Price, and Amount must be carefully checked and
are subject to further detailed controls in Henley's purchasing system.

FIGURE 9-7

Example of a purchase invoice

Speedquip Ltd.   992 St. Mary's Rd., Winnipeg, MB   R2M 3S3   **INVOICE**
Phone: 204-256-3489   Fax: 204-256-7531

SOLD TO	SHIPPED TO	NO. 278
Henley Sporting Goods Ltd.	Same	
3000 Base Line Road		**DATE** June 25, 2008
Ottawa, Ontario K2H 7B3		
		YOUR ORDER NO. 2198

Our Order No.	Salesperson	Terms	F.O.B.	Date Shipped	Shipped Via
52876	Dunn	Net 30 Days	Winnipeg	June 18, 2008	Parcel Post

QUANTITY ORDERED	QUANTITY SHIPPED	STOCK NUMBER/DESCRIPTION	UNIT PRICE	AMOUNT
30	30	Dolphin clear goggles	$4.80	$144.00
30	30	Olympian clear goggles	5.10	153.00
12	12	Assorted earplugs	0.90	10.80
8	8	Size 1–4 swim wings	2.39	19.12
				326.92
		Goods and Services Tax 6%		19.62
		Total Due		$346.54

2% added to overdue accounts

White — Customer's Copy / Pink — Office Copy / Canary — Commission Copy / Green — Salesperson's Copy / Blue — Shipping Copy

Paying for Purchases

To this point, the system for ordering goods from a supplier has been shown. The steps to be followed in receiving the goods and the procedures for paying for them will now be discussed.

Receiving Report

Merchandise received from a supplier must be checked to ensure that:

- Goods received were actually ordered
- Goods are in satisfactory condition
- Correct quantity and quality were shipped

The person receiving and checking the goods completes a **receiving report** (Figure 9-8 on the next page) and sends a copy to the purchasing department. Remember that a copy of the purchase order was initially sent to the receiving department when the goods were ordered. This purchase order copy is used to determine if the goods received were in fact ordered.

A receiving report is a form that lists and describes all goods received.

Some firms do not use a receiving report. Instead, the receiver will check off each item on the purchase order when it is received. The receiver then initials the purchase order copy and sends it to the purchasing department.

FIGURE 9-8
Example of a receiving report

HENLEY SPORTING GOODS
3000 Base Line Road
Ottawa, ON K2H 7B3

RECEIVING REPORT

FROM: Speedquip Ltd.

NO. R-312
DATE June 30, 2008
P.O. NO. 2198

VIA	PREPAID	COLLECT

STOCK NO. QUANTITY	DESCRIPTION	UNIT PRICE
30	Dolphin clear goggles	
30	Olympian clear goggles	
12	Assorted earplugs	
8	Size 1–4 swim wings	

CHECKED BY _M. Khan_   ENTERED IN STORE'S LEDGER BY _A. Lottey_

Matching Process

Before an invoice is approved or recorded, it is checked and compared to the purchase order and the receiving report. This comparison is necessary to ensure that what was ordered was received, and what was charged for was ordered and received. Usually, the **matching process** is the responsibility of the purchasing department. If the three documents match, the invoice is approved and sent to the accounting department.

The matching process is the comparison of the purchase order, purchase invoice, and receiving report.

Approved Invoice

The accounting department receives the invoice and supporting documents from the purchasing department and checks their mathematical accuracy. Each **extension** is checked and the amounts are added to verify the total of the invoice.

An extension is the quantity multiplied by the unit price.

The account to be debited is indicated on the invoice. An accounting clerk then journalizes and posts the transaction. For example, the journal entry for the Speedquip invoice is:

Jun. 30	Purchases	326.92	
	GST Refundable	19.62	
	Accounts Payable/Speedquip Ltd.		346.54
	Invoice 278, net 30 days.		

Payment on the Due Date

The date on which payment is to be made.

After journalizing, the approved invoice is placed in a date file according to the date on which payment is to be made. On that day, the invoice is taken from the file and a cheque is prepared and sent to the supplier. The payment is then journalized and posted. The journal entry to record the payment of the Speedquip invoice is:

Jul. 23	Accounts Payable/Speedquip Ltd.	346.54	
	Cash		346.54
	Invoice 278.		

Figure 9-9 illustrates the steps followed when paying an invoice:

FIGURE 9-9

Typical steps followed when paying an invoice

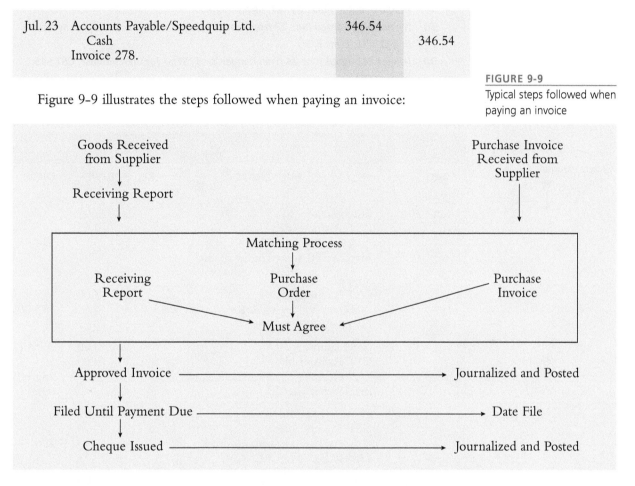

❶NTRODUCING THE PURCHASES JOURNAL

A business that makes many purchases on account uses a **Purchases Journal** instead of a General Journal to record such purchases. When invoices are received, they are approved and then recorded in the Purchases Journal:

A Purchases Journal is a special journal used to record all purchases on account.

Purchase Invoices ⟶ Invoices Approved ⟶ Purchases Journal

Journalizing Purchases on Account

As you know, an invoice received for items purchased on account is called a *purchase invoice*. After the purchase invoice has been approved, it is journalized. On June 30, approved invoices for the following transactions were received by the accounting department of Henley Sporting Goods.

Purchases Transactions

Jun. 30   Invoice 278 dated June 25 from Speedquip Ltd., $326.92 for merchandise, GST $19.62, terms n/30.

30   Invoice W184 dated June 26 from Evans & Kert, $50 for office supplies, GST $3, terms n/30.

30   Invoice 3871 dated June 24 from Tops Service Centre, $150 for repairs to the company automobile, GST $9, terms n/30.

30   Invoice B-519 dated June 27 from Ontario Hydro, $195 for the August hydro bill, GST $11.70, terms n/30.

30   Invoice 281 dated June 26 from Cooper Bros., $750 for merchandise, GST $45, terms n/30.

Figure 9-10, below, shows these transactions recorded in a General Journal.

FIGURE 9-10

Transactions recorded in a General Journal

	GENERAL JOURNAL			PAGE 17
DATE	**PARTICULARS**	**P.R.**	**DEBIT**	**CREDIT**
2008				
Jun. 30	Purchases		326.92	
	GST Refundable		19.62	
	Accts. Pay./Speedquip Ltd.			346.54
	Invoice 278, merchandise, n/30.			
30	Supplies		50.00	
	GST Refundable		3.00	
	Accts. Pay./Evans & Kert			53.00
	Invoice W184, n/30.			
30	Car Expense		150.00	
	GST Refundable		9.00	
	Accts. Pay./Tops Service Centre			159.00
	Invoice 3871, n/30.			
30	Utilities Expense		195.00	
	GST Refundable		11.70	
	Accts. Pay./Ontario Hydro			206.70
	Invoice B-519, n/30.			
30	Purchases		750.00	
	GST Refundable		45.00	
	Accts. Pay./Cooper Bros.			795.00
	Invoice 281, merchandise, n/30.			

Special columns are provided for accounts that are used frequently.

Figure 9-11 on page 316 shows the same invoices recorded in a Purchases Journal. Compare the recording of the five invoices in the General Journal with the recording procedures followed in the Purchases Journal. How many lines does each transaction require in the General Journal and in the Purchases Journal? In the recording of these invoices, which journal requires less writing? Why do you think there are special columns headed Purchases Debit and Utilities Expense Debit? When is the Other Accounts Debit section used?

Note that only purchases on account appear in the Purchases Journal. Cash purchases would be recorded in the Cash Payments Journal.

Special Column Headings

In the Purchases Journal in Figure 9-11, columns are headed Purchases debit, GST Refundable debit, Accounts Payable credit, Utilities Expense debit, and Other Accounts debit. The Accounts Payable credit column is required for every transaction in the Purchases Journal. Merchandise is purchased frequently and that is why there are special columns for Purchases debit and GST Refundable debit in the journal. A special column is headed Utilities Expense debit because, for this particular company, the Utilities Expense account is involved in many transactions. Another company might use this column for Supplies or Delivery Expense or any other account used in repetitive transactions.

The Other Accounts debit section is used to record debits to accounts other than Purchases or Utilities Expense. Notice that the account title must be shown as well as the name of the creditor when the other accounts section is used.

Balancing the Purchases Journal

Since the Purchases Journal in Figure 9-11 has five money columns, it is quite possible to record part of an entry in the wrong column. To locate errors of this type before they are transferred to the ledger in the posting process, each page of the Purchases Journal is balanced. The total of the debit columns must equal the total of the credit columns.

These steps should be followed when balancing a Purchases Journal:

(1) Rule a single line across all money columns below the last line used.
(2) Add the columns; put totals in as pencil footings.
(3) Where there is more than one of each, add all the debit column totals and all the credit column totals.
(4) If the debit totals equal the credit totals, write the column totals in ink at the bottom of each column. Write the debit and credit totals in the creditor column.
(5) Rule double lines across money columns.

Figure 9-12 illustrates the balancing process for page 12 of the Purchases Journal. The Purchases Journal is balanced at the end of each page and at the end of each month. Note that additional transactions have been posted to the journal in addition to the five transactions already covered. This is done to give the Purchases Journal a more realistic appearance.

Locating Errors

If the journal does not balance:

- Start on the first line and check to see if there are equal debit and credit amounts on each line.
- Recheck all addition.
- Follow the locating error steps given in Chapter 4.

Forwarding Totals

When a page of a journal is filled, it should be balanced and the totals carried forward to the next page. Follow the forwarding procedures described earlier in this chapter.

FIGURE 9-11
Transactions recorded in a Purchases Journal

PURCHASES JOURNAL · PAGE 12

DATE	REF. NO.	CREDITOR	TERMS	P.R.	PURCHASES DEBIT	GST REFUND. DEBIT	ACCOUNTS PAYABLE CREDIT	UTILITIES EXPENSE DEBIT	OTHER ACCOUNTS ACCOUNT	P.R.	DEBIT
2008											
Jun. 30	278	Speedquip Ltd.	n/30		326.92	19.62	346.54				
30	W184	Evans & Kert	n/30			3.00	53.00		Supplies		50.00
30	3871	Tops Service Centre	n/30			9.00	159.00		Car Expense		150.00
30	B-519	Ontario Hydro	n/30			11.70	206.70	195.00			
30	281	Cooper Bros.	n/30		750.00	45.00	795.00				

FIGURE 9-12
Balancing the Purchases Journal

PURCHASES JOURNAL · PAGE 12

DATE	REF. NO.	CREDITOR	TERMS	P.R.	PURCHASES DEBIT	GST REFUND. DEBIT	ACCOUNTS PAYABLE CREDIT	UTILITIES EXPENSE DEBIT	OTHER ACCOUNTS ACCOUNT	P.R.	DEBIT
2008											
Jun. 30	278	Speedquip Ltd.	n/30		326.92	19.62	346.54				
30	W184	Evans & Kert	n/30			3.00	53.00		Supplies		50.00
30	3871	Tops Service Centre	n/30			9.00	159.00		Car Expense		150.00
30	B-519	Ontario Hydro	n/30			11.70	206.70	195.00			
30	281	Cooper Bros.	n/30		750.00	45.00	795.00				
Jul. 2	419	Hall Fuel	n/30			12.00	212.00	200.00			
5	801	Coles Ltd.	n/30			.60	10.60		Miscellaneous Expense		10.00
8	291	Speedquip Ltd.	n/30		200.00	12.00	212.00				
11	307	Cooper Bros.	n/30		40.00	2.40	42.40				
12	H-719	CN Express	n/15			6.90	121.90		Trans. on Purchases		115.00
15	3461	City Water Dept.	EOM			21.60	381.60	360.00			
18	319	Cooper Bros.	n/30		900.00	54.00	954.00				
20	W220	Evans & Kert	n/30			5.82	102.82		Supplies		97.00
23	331	Cooper Bros.	n/30		120.00	7.20	127.20				
27	3904	Tops Service Centre	n/30			2.70	47.70		Car Expense		45.00
29	344	Speedquip Ltd.	n/30		400.00	24.00	424.00				
					2736.92	237.54	4196.46	755.00			467.00

Debits = $4196.46
Credits = $4196.46

POSTING TO THE LEDGERS

The main advantage of using the Purchases Journal is that it reduces the recording workload since only one line is needed for most transactions. In contrast, three lines of writing are required when transactions are recorded directly in the General Journal.

Further efficiencies are achieved in the posting process. On the following pages, the steps involved in posting from the Purchases Journal to the Accounts Payable Ledger and the General Ledger will be described. Figure 9-13, on page 318, will illustrate the complete posting process for the Purchases Journal. First, however, we will briefly review the methods of posting to the subsidiary ledgers.

Methods of Posting to the Subsidiary Ledgers

There are two methods commonly used to post to the subsidiary ledgers.

Direct Posting

In this method, source documents are posted *directly* to the subsidiary ledgers. Different people can be assigned the duties of journalizing transactions and updating the subsidiary ledgers. A company with a large number of transactions involving customers and creditors would use this direct posting system.

Companies with a multi-column Purchases Journal usually use the direct posting method for recording source documents in the subsidiary ledgers. Purchase invoices are recorded directly into the Accounts Payable Ledger. Sales invoices are recorded directly into the Accounts Receivable Ledger. Division of responsibility is made possible since different accounting personnel can be used to perform these tasks. In Chapter 8, you learned the accounts payable clerk posted directly to the Accounts Payable Ledger and the accounts receivable clerk to the Accounts Receivable Ledger.

Posting from the Journal

Another posting method is to enter transactions in the journal and *then* to post the entries from the journal to the ledger accounts. This method is used by companies that wish to use special journals but do not have enough transactions to have separate people working on the journals and the ledgers. It will be used here for the Purchases Journal.

PURCHASES JOURNAL

PAGE 12

DATE	REF. NO.	CREDITOR	TERMS	P.R.	PURCHASES DEBIT	GST REFUND. DEBIT	ACCOUNTS PAYABLE CREDIT	UTILITIES EXPENSE DEBIT	ACCOUNT	OTHER ACCOUNTS P.R.	DEBIT
2008											
Jun. 30	278	Speedquip Ltd.	n/30		326.92	19.62	346.54				
30	W184	Evans & Kert	n/30			3.00	53.00		Supplies		50.00
30	3871	Tops Service Centre	n/30			9.00	159.00		Car Expense		150.00
30	B-519	Ontario Hydro	n/30			11.70	206.70	195.00			
30	281	Cooper Bros.	n/30		750.00	45.00	495.00	200.00			
Jul. 2	281	Hall Fuel	n/30			12.00	212.00				
5	801	Coles Ltd.	n/30			.60	10.60		Miscellaneous Expense		10.00
8	291	Speedquip Ltd.	n/30		200.00	12.00	212.00				
11	307	Cooper Bros.	n/30		40.00	2.40	42.40				
12	H-719	CN Express	n/15			6.90	121.90		Trans. on Purchases		115.00
15	3461	City Water Dept.	EOM			21.60	381.60	360.00			
18	319	Cooper Bros.	n/30		900.00	54.00	954.00				
20	W220	Evans & Kert	n/30			5.82	102.82		Supplies		97.00
23	331	Cooper Bros.	n/30		120.00	7.20	127.20				
27	3904	Tops Service Centre	n/30			2.70	47.70		Car Expense		45.00
29	344	Speedquip Ltd.	n/30		400.00	24.00	424.00				
					2 736.92	237.54	4 196.46	755.00			467.00
					(500)	(206)	(200)	(615)			

Debits = $4 196.46
Credits = $4 196.46

FIGURE 9-13
Balancing the
Purchases Journal

Posting the Purchases Journal to the Accounts Payable Ledger

Step 1

Each day, post each entry in the Accounts Payable credit column of the Purchases Journal to the Accounts Payable Ledger. In the following example, Speedquip Ltd.'s account is credited with $346.54 on June 30. P12 is written in the posting reference column of the account to indicate the journal and page number of the posting:

ACCOUNTS PAYABLE LEDGER						
ACCOUNT Speedquip Ltd.						
DATE	PARTICULARS	P.R.	DEBIT	CREDIT	DR. CR.	BALANCE
2008 Jun. 30		P12		346.54	CR.	346.54

Posting from the Purchases Journal to the Accounts Payable Ledger is done daily to keep the balances in the creditors' accounts up-to-date.

Step 2

Place a check mark (✓) in the posting reference column of the Purchases Journal opposite each creditor (e.g., Speedquip Ltd.) to indicate that the amount has been posted to the subsidiary ledger account (see Figure 9-13 on page 318).

Posting the Purchases Journal to the General Ledger

Step 1

At the end of the month, post the individual transactions in the other accounts section to the General Ledger, writing the Purchases Journal page number and abbreviation in the posting reference column of the accounts. Show the ledger account number in the posting reference column of the other accounts section (see Figure 9-13).

Step 2

At the end of the month, post the totals of each column to the appropriate account in the General Ledger, again writing the Purchases Journal page number and abbreviation in the posting reference column of the accounts. The account numbers are shown in brackets under each total (see Figure 9-13). The other accounts total is not posted. The following example shows the Purchases account in the General Ledger after the purchases debit column total from the Purchases Journal has been posted.

GENERAL LEDGER						
ACCOUNT　Purchases						No. 500
DATE	PARTICULARS	P.R.	DEBIT	CREDIT	DR. CR.	BALANCE
2008 Jul.　29		P12	2 736.92		DR.	2 736.92

General Posting Procedure for Special Journals

The posting procedure described for the Purchases Journal is used for all the special journals in this chapter. A summary of this procedure follows.

Step 1

Do the following:

(1) Each day, post all the individual entries in the Accounts Payable or Accounts Receivable columns to the accounts in the subsidiary ledgers.
(2) Place the journal abbreviation and page number in the posting reference column of each account (e.g., P12, S14, CR26, CP31, J8).
(3) Place a check mark (✔) in the first posting reference column in the journal beside each item to indicate that the item has been posted.

Step 2

Do the following:

(1) At the end of the month, post the individual items in the other accounts section to the relevant accounts in the General Ledger.
(2) Place the journal abbreviation and page number in the posting reference column of each account.
(3) Place the account number in the posting reference column of the other accounts section to indicate that posting of the entry is complete.

Step 3

Do the following:

(1) At the end of the month, post all column totals (except the other accounts total) to the relevant accounts in the General Ledger.
(2) Place the journal abbreviation and page number in the posting reference column of each account.
(3) Place the account number in brackets under the total in the journal to indicate that it has been posted.

ADVANTAGES OF MULTI-COLUMN SPECIAL JOURNALS

There are two main advantages to using a multi-column special journal:

- Posting is reduced compared to the posting of a two-column journal.
- The use of special columns saves time and space in recording transactions.

One of the major advantages is the reduction in the amount of posting to the General Ledger. The use of special columns makes it possible to post only the column totals to the accounts. For example, in Figure 9-13 there are 16 transactions in the GST Refundable debit column, yet only one posting is made to the debit side of the GST Refundable account in the General Ledger. Only the total debit is posted.

> *The use of special columns greatly reduces the amount of posting and is an important advantage of the multi-column journal compared to the two-column General Journal.*

DISADVANTAGES OF THE MULTI-COLUMN JOURNAL

There is one major disadvantage to using the multi-column special journal:

- The risk of error is increased by the large number of columns (i.e., the danger of putting the amounts in the wrong columns).

CREDIT INVOICES

Occasionally, a buyer will return goods to the seller. This causes changes on the books of both the buyer and the seller. The source document prepared as a record of the transaction is the credit invoice.

The seller prepares the credit invoice and sends it to the buyer. The seller decreases the amount owed by the buyer. When the buyer receives the credit invoice, the buyer decreases the amount owed to the seller.

Recording Credit Invoices

Credit invoices may be recorded in several ways, depending on the information required by the company and the number of credit invoices to be processed:

(1) Credit invoices may be recorded in the General Journal. This method will be used to complete the exercises in the rest of this chapter.
(2) Credit invoices may be recorded in the Purchases Journal. The circling method can be used, or special columns can be set up in the Purchases Journal for purchases returns.
(3) A special account, the Purchases Returns and Allowances account, may be used to record returns. A Purchases Returns and Allowances account will be used to complete the exercises in this chapter.

The following sample transactions will be used to illustrate the recording of credit invoices in the buyer's books.

Transaction for a Purchase on Account

Apr.   2   *Purchased merchandise from Riley Co., Invoice 322, terms n/30, $650 on account, GST $39.*

This transaction was recorded in the Purchases Journal in the normal way.

Transaction for a Purchase Return

Apr.   9   *Returned unacceptable goods worth $150 plus $9 GST to Riley Co. from merchandise purchased Apr. 2. Riley issued Credit Invoice C-71 for $159.*

The various methods of recording this $159 credit invoice are described below.

Using the General Journal

If the General Journal is used, the credit invoice is recorded as follows:

Apr. 9	Accounts Payable/Riley Co.	✓/200	159	
	Purchases Returns and Allowances	501		150
	GST Refundable	207		9
	To record Credit Invoice C-71.			

When this transaction is posted, the $159 debit is posted to the Accounts Payable control account in the General Ledger and to Riley Co. in the Accounts Payable Ledger. A check mark (✓) is used to show the posting to the subsidiary ledger account, while the account number 200 indicates that the General Ledger has been posted. Both the credit of $150 to the Purchases Returns and Allowances account and the $9 credit to the GST Refundable account are posted in the General Ledger.

Can you explain why the $159 debit is posted twice — once to the control account and once to Riley's account?

Using the Purchases Journal: Circling Method

If special columns are not used, credit invoices can be recorded in the Purchases Journal using the circling method. Any item circled is subtracted when the columns are totalled. Circling is a method of indicating that an item is to be treated as a debit, and not as a credit. This method is illustrated for the Riley transaction in Figure 9-14.

Using the Purchases Journal: Special Columns

The Purchases Journal can have special columns added for Accounts Payable debit and Purchases Returns and Allowances credit. A company would use these two additional columns when it had many credit invoices to be recorded. Credit invoices would then be recorded as illustrated in Figure 9-15. Any item circled is subtracted when the column totals are calculated.

ADVANTAGES OF THE PURCHASES JOURNAL

There are four advantages to using a Purchases Journal. They are:

- Most entries require only one line in a Purchases Journal.
- Posting is reduced.
- Explanations are eliminated.
- Division of labour and responsibilities is possible.

FIGURE 9-14
Purchases Journal showing the circling method. The circled amounts are subtracted when the columns are totalled.

PURCHASES JOURNAL PAGE 12

DATE	REF. NO.	CREDITOR	TERMS	P.R.	PURCHASES DEBIT	GST REFUND. DEBIT	ACCOUNTS PAYABLE CREDIT	UTILITIES EXPENSE DEBIT	OTHER ACCOUNTS ACCOUNT	OTHER ACCOUNTS P.R.	OTHER ACCOUNTS DEBIT
2009											
Apr. 2	322	Riley Co.	n/30		650	39	689				
9	C-71	Riley Co.			(150)	(9)	(159)				
		Totals			500	30	530				

FIGURE 9-15
Purchases Journal with special columns for Purchases Returns and Allowances credit and Accounts Payable debit

PURCHASES JOURNAL PAGE 12

DATE	REF. NO.	CREDITOR	TERMS	P.R.	PURCHASES DEBIT	GST REFUND. DEBIT	ACCOUNTS PAYABLE CREDIT	ACCOUNTS PAYABLE DEBIT	PURCH. RET. & ALL. CREDIT	OTHER ACCOUNTS ACCOUNT	OTHER ACCOUNTS P.R.	OTHER ACCOUNTS DEBIT
2009												
Apr. 2	322	Riley Co.	n/30		650	39	689					
9	C-71	Riley Co.				(9)		159	150			

REVIEW QUESTIONS

1. Answer the following questions about the purchase requisition shown in Figure 9-4:

   (a) Who requested the merchandise?
   (b) Who is the supervisor?
   (c) Why is it necessary to have the supervisor sign the purchase requisition?

2. What factors does the purchasing department consider before issuing the purchase order?

3. Answer the following questions about the purchase order shown in Figure 9-5:

   (a) What company was chosen to supply the goods?
   (b) Why do each of the following receive a copy of the purchase order:

      (i)   Receiving department?
      (ii) Accounting department?
      (iii) Purchasing department?
      (iv) Requesting department?

4. Explain the term "matching process" and indicate what three documents are matched.

5. What department is responsible for matching the documents?

6. What supporting documents are attached to the purchase invoice?

7. What types of transactions are recorded in the Purchases Journal?

8. Explain the steps followed in posting the Purchases Journal. (Assume direct posting is not used.)

9. What is a credit invoice?

10. What is a special journal system?

11. Which accounts are debited and credited when recording a credit invoice for goods returned (purchase return) in the General Journal?

PROBLEMS: APPLICATIONS

1. Carl Wakeland owns Wakeland Supply Ltd.. His firm uses a Cash Receipts Journal (CRJ), Cash Payments Journal (CPJ), Purchases Journal (PJ), Sales Journal (SJ), and General Journal (J). Indicate which journal should be used to record each of the following transactions:

   (a) Sale of merchandise for cash
   (b) Payment of the employees' salaries for the week
   (c) Purchase of equipment on account
   (d) Sale of merchandise on account
   (e) Adjusting entry to record supplies expense for the period
   (f) Purchase of a new printer by paying one-third in cash and the remainder on account
   (g) Purchase of equipment for cash
   (h) Return of merchandise by a customer for a credit to her account
   (i) Return of merchandise by a customer for a cash refund
   (j) Receipt of a cheque from a customer in payment of an outstanding account
   (k) Closing entries for the month
   (l) Payment of creditors on account

2. (a) Record the following approved invoices in a Purchases Journal, page 84.

 (b) Total, balance, and rule the Purchases Journal.

Apr. 2 Purchased merchandise for $2500 from Berko Ltd., GST $150, Invoice 319 dated March 31, terms n/30.

  4 Purchased office supplies for $215 from Ross Office Supplies, GST $12.90, Invoice R29 dated April 1, terms n/30.

  5 Purchased merchandise for $750 from Baskin Bros., GST $45, Invoice 18 dated April 2, terms n/30.

  6 Purchased office equipment for $1200 from Wells, Inc., GST $72, Invoice 4-138 dated April 3, terms n/30.

3. (a) Set up the following accounts and balances for July 1 in the partial General Ledger for Mays Surplus:

101	Cash	$ 3 500	
110	Accounts Receivable	7 100	
125	Office Supplies	1 340	
200	Accounts Payable		$ 4 720
206	GST Payable		750
207	GST Refundable	500	
300	P. Maillette, Capital		14 670
501	Purchases	7 000	
503	Transportation on Purchases	240	
606	Truck Expense	460	
		$20 140	$20 140

 (b) Set up the following accounts and balances on July 1 in the Accounts Payable Ledger for Mays Surplus:

Canadian Tire	$ 335
Sims Wholesalers	3 660
Steck Stationers	635
Wells Trucking	90
	$4 720

 (c) Enter the following approved purchase invoices on page 64 of a Purchases Journal for Mays Surplus; then total, balance, and rule the journal.

Jul. 2 Merchandise from Sims Wholesalers for $576, GST $34.56.

  4 Office supplies from Steck Stationers for $135, GST $8.10.

  6 Gas and oil used in the truck from Canadian Tire for $105, GST $6.30.

  8 Transportation of merchandise from Wells Trucking for $65, GST $3.90.

  9 Merchandise from Sims Wholesalers for $1348, GST $80.88.

 (d) Post the Purchases Journal to the General Ledger.

(e) Prepare a trial balance for the General Ledger.

(f) Post the relevant source documents directly to the Accounts Payable Ledger.

(g) Prepare a schedule of accounts payable. Check your total with the control account, 200, in the General Ledger.

4. (a) In a Purchases Journal for the City Cycle Shop, enter the approved invoices given below. Assign page 158 to the journal. Use the following trial balance to determine the accounts affected:

City Cycle Shop Trial Balance April 30, 2009		
101 Cash	$8 400	
110 Accounts Receivable	6 300	
125 Supplies	1 500	
151 Office Equipment	30 000	
200 Accounts Payable		$ 3 700
206 GST Payable		715
207 GST Refundable	400	
300 G. Watson, Capital		50 885
301 G. Watson, Drawings	0	
500 Purchases	7 000	
503 Transportation on Purchases	500	
600 Delivery Expense	700	
601 Advertising Expense	200	
607 Repairs and Maintenance Expense	300	
	$55 300	$55 300

May 1 Fifteen bicycles from CCM Ltd. for $3800, GST $228.

2 Tires and tubes from Dunlop Tires for $477, GST $28.62.

3 Repairs to the main entrance by Coastal Glass for $635, GST $38.10.

4 Transportation of the bicycles received on May 1, $125 from Hunt Transport, GST $7.50.

6 Gas and oil used in the delivery truck during April, $515 from Gibb's Service Station, GST $30.90.

8 Advertising space, $430 from the *Daily Post,* GST $25.80.

(b) Total, balance, and rule the Purchases Journal.

(c) Assign page 159 to the next journal page and bring the totals forward from page 158; then continue by recording the following approved invoices:

May 9 Repairs to the owner's (G. Watson's) cottage, $2541 plus GST $152.46 from Simcoe Contractors.

9 Bicycle accessories from CCM Ltd. for $862, GST $51.72.

10 A new computer from Gateway Computers for $2685, GST $161.10.

11 Ten bicycles from Mountain Bike Manufacturers for $2960, GST $177.60.

13 Paper bags, wrapping paper, and other store supplies from City
    Pack Supplies for $190, GST $11.40.

(d) Set up a General Ledger and post the Purchases Journal.

(e) Prepare a trial balance.

(f) Describe the procedure you would prefer to use to post the Accounts
    Payable Ledger. Why do you prefer this method to other methods available?

5. The following is a partial chart of accounts for Electronics Unlimited of
   Vancouver.

100	Cash	501	Purchases
121	Office Equipment	502	Transportation on Purchases
201	Accounts Payable	503	Purchases Returns and Allowances
205	PST Payable	604	Delivery Expense
206	GST Payable	610	Building Repairs Expense
207	GST Refundable		

(a) On page 46 of a Purchases Journal, record the approved purchase
    invoices for Electronics Unlimited shown on the following pages.

(b) Record credit invoices in a General Journal.

(c) Total, balance, and rule the Purchases Journal.

BANNEX LTD.

1493 Bridge Road, Toronto, ON   M6A 1Z5

Phone 594-6655   Fax 594-8731

SOLD TO Electronics Unlimited   **INVOICE** 17493
795 Beaver Drive   **DATE**   March 1, 2009
Vancouver, BC   **TERMS**   Net 30 days
V7N 3H6

QUANTITY	DESCRIPTION	UNIT PRICE	TOTAL
5	Spools of #10 copper wire	$23.50	$117.50
		GST	7.05
		Total Due	$124.55

Received March 30

Received by BK
Price O.K.   ✓
Account   501
Payment O.K. CD

Sales Tax Exempt

White and Turner

Received
March 31

Heating Contractors
for all your heating supplies
497 Albion Rd., Vancouver, BC   V7A 3E4

Sold to   Electronics Unlimited
795 Beaver Drive
Vancouver, BC
V7N 3H6

Invoice No. 86B743
Date   March 2, 2009
Terms   2/10, n/30

Stock No.	Description	Quantity	Price	Amount
N-21-2	2 cm x 3 m pipes	7	$4.50	$31.50
R-63-47	Boxes #3 washers	2	0.75	1.50

Cash ☐

Charge ☐

Received by BK
Price O.K.   ✓
Account   510
Payment O.K. CD

	Amount
Subtotal	33.00
GST (6%)	1.98
PST	2.31
Total	$37.29

Received by BK
Price O.K.   ✓
Account   501
Payment O.K. CD

EVC
Limited

Received
March 31

1793 Pennfield Drive, Victoria, BC   V8B 6M2

To   Electronics Unlimited
795 Beaver Drive
Vancouver, BC
V7N 3H6

Invoice No.   E-437073
Terms   Net 30 days F.O.B.
Your Order No. 7434
Ship Via   WCT
Date Shipped   March 28, 2009
Date of Inv.   March 31

Quantity	Description	Unit Price	Amount
20	EVC 40 Speakers	$109	$2 180.00
10	EVC 50 Speakers	129	1 290.00
10	SP-743-H Receivers	133	1 330.00
5	SP-843-H Receivers	152	760.00

Sales Tax
Exempt

	Amount
Sub Total	5 560.00
GST	333.60
Total	$5 893.60

WEST COAST TRANSPORT

Vancouver	Seattle	Los Angeles
73 Commissioner Rd.	1890 Industrial Rd.	734 Green Street
Vancouver, BC	Seattle, WA	Los Angeles, CA
Canada V7R 3T6	U.S.A. 92000-8191	U.S.A. 96300-9852
Phone (604) 937-4370	Phone (206) 347-8650	Phone (213) 474-8503
Fax (604) 937-4819	Fax (206) 347-9190	Fax (213) 474-8888

Shipper:

EVC Limited

1793 Pennfield Drive

Victoria, BC V8B 6M2

Consignee:

Electronics Unlimited

795 Beaver Drive

Vancouver, BC   V7N 3H6

Prepaid   Collect X

Date April 2, 2009   **Terms:** Net 30   **Inv. No.** W.B 74343

No. of Containers		Mass	Rate	Amount
45 boxes		300 kg	$0.40/kg	$120.00
			GST	7.20
			Total	$127.20

Received by	BK
Price O.K.	✓
Account	502
Payment O.K.	CD

Received April 10

Pay this Amount $127.20

Same Day Delivery

LOCAL DELIVERIES

475 Dynes Road   **Invoice No.**   657

Vancouver, BC   V7E 3R1   **Terms**   Net 30

Phone 837-4390   **Date**   April 9, 2009

Charge

Electronics Unlimited

795 Beaver Drive

Vancouver, BC

V7N 3H6

Deliver to

Mr. K. Stafford

473 Elm Street

Vancouver, BC

V6L 2L4

Description		**Amount**
4 boxes		$100.00
	GST	6.00
	Total	$106.00

Received April 10

Received by	BK
Price O.K.	✓
Account	503
Payment O.K.	CD

Jonsson

Office Specialties Ltd.

63 Main Street, Vancouver, BC   V6A 2S2   Phone 343-7512 Fax 343-1817

For All Your Office Needs

Sold to	**Our Invoice No.**	73B4973
Electronics Unlimited	**Your Order No.**	7440
795 Beaver Drive	**Terms**	2/10, n/30
Vancouver, BC	**Date Shipped**	April 9, 2009
V7N 3H6	**Date of Inv.**	April 9, 2009

Quantity	Description	Unit Price	Amount
1	Printer PX585	$465.64	$465.64

Received
April 11

Received by	BK
Price O.K.	✓
Account	121
Payment O.K.	CD

GST	27.94
PST	32.59
Pay this amount	$526.17

EVC
Limited

1793 Pennfield Drive, Victoria, BC   V8B 6M2

TO: Electronics Unlimited   **Credit No.**   1396
795 Beaver Drive   April 9, 2009
Vancouver, BC
V7N 3H6

We credit your account as specified below

Re: Inv. #E-437073, dated March 31, 2009
    1 SP-743-H Receiver $133.00
    1 SP-843-H Receiver   152.00
    Sub Total $285.00
    GST   17.10
                      $302.10

Received
April 11

CREDIT MEMORANDUM

UNIT 20   Sales Journal

Learning Objectives

After reading this unit, discussing the applicable review questions, and completing the applications exercises, you will be able to do the following:

1. **RECORD** sales invoices in a Sales Journal.

2. **RECORD** credit invoices.

3. **TOTAL,** balance, and post a Sales Journal.

4. **EXPLAIN** the purpose of a customer statement.

5. **DISCUSS** the cycle billing method of preparing statements.

In this unit, the system for processing sales of goods on account will be discussed as well as the recording and posting procedures for a Sales Journal.

PROCEDURES FOR SALES INVOICES

For each credit sale, a source document called a *sales invoice* is prepared. This document, commonly called a *bill,* is the seller's evidence that a transaction occurred. The sales invoice in Figure 9-16 was prepared by Henley Sporting Goods:

FIGURE 9-16
Sales invoice

HENLEY SPORTING GOODS

3000 Base Line Road
Ottawa, ON K2H 7B3
Tel: 684–1287   Fax: 684–5381

INVOICE   **Order No.**

Sold To   **Ship To**
Ottawa School of Commerce   Same
300 Rochester Street
Ottawa, ON   K1R 7N4

Date July 15, 2008   **Invoice No.** 97   **Terms** Net 30 days   **Cash**   **Charge**

Quantity	Description	Unit Price	Amount
4	Volleyballs, vinyl specials	$29.95	$119.80
		GST (6%)	7.19
		PST (8%)	9.58
		Total Due	$136.57

GST Registration No. R119282106

See if you can answer the following questions about the invoice in Figure 9-16:

- Who is the seller?
- Who is the buyer?
- What is the total to be paid by the customer and when must it be paid?
- How are the $119.80, $7.19, and $9.58 calculated?

Four copies of the invoice are normally prepared and are distributed as shown in Figure 9-17.

FIGURE 9-17

Distribution of sales invoice copies

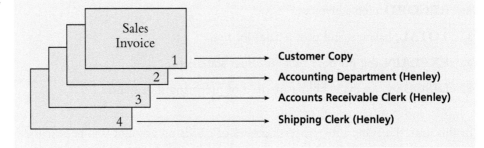

INTRODUCING THE SALES JOURNAL

Earlier in this chapter, you learned that a Purchases Journal is used to record purchases of goods and services on credit. The use of special columns saves time and effort in recording and posting purchases.

Special journal used to record credit sales.

For the same reasons, the **Sales Journal** is used to record sales on account (credit sales) by companies that make many such sales.

In a Sales Journal, each transaction requires only one line. Look at Figure 9-18, the Sales Journal for Henley Sporting Goods. Notice that in some of the transactions the customer is charged PST, while in others there is no PST. This is because some of the sales involve non-taxable items.

FIGURE 9-18

Sales Journal for Henley Sporting Goods showing correct balancing and posting procedures

This Sales Journal in Figure 9-18 has been correctly balanced and posted. The steps involved in both these procedures will now be described.

		SALES JOURNAL					PAGE 14	
DATE	INV. NO.	CUSTOMER	TERMS	P.R.	ACCOUNTS REC. DEBIT	SALES CREDIT	GST PAYABLE CREDIT	PST PAYABLE CREDIT
2008								
Sep. 4	71	J. Grier	n/30	✓	228.00	200.00	12.00	16.00
7	72	C. Setia	n/30	✓	342.00	300.00	18.00	24.00
9	73	M. Wong	n/30	✓	100.70	95.00	5.70	
11	74	L. Will	n/30	✓	477.00	450.00	27.00	
13	75	K. Rice	n/30	✓	798.00	700.00	42.00	56.00
15	76	C. Setia	n/30	✓	456.00	400.00	24.00	32.00
		Debits = $2 401.70			2 401.70	2 145.00	128.70	128.00
		Credits = $2 401.70			(110)	(400)	(206)	(205)

Balancing the Sales Journal

If transactions have been recorded correctly, the total of the debit columns should equal the total of the credit columns.

At the bottom of each page and at the end of the month, these procedures are followed:

(1) Rule a single line across all money columns below the last line used.
(2) Add the columns; put totals in as pencil footings.
(3) Where there is more than one of each, add all the debit column totals and all the credit column totals.
(4) If the debit totals equal the credit totals, write the column totals in ink at the bottom of each column. Write the debit and credit totals in the customer column.
(5) Rule double lines across all money columns.

Look again at Figure 9-18 to see an example of a Sales Journal that has been balanced. If the month has not ended, the totals are carried forward to the next page. At the end of the month, the totals are posted to the General Ledger.

Posting the Sales Journal

The use of a Sales Journal reduces the amount of posting to be done. There are only two steps followed in posting the Sales Journal. The amounts in the Accounts Receivable debit column are posted daily to the customer accounts in the Accounts Receivable Ledger and the four totals are posted to the General Ledger at the end of the month. The posting is similar to the posting of the Purchases Journal and is done as follows:

(1) Each day, post the entries in the Accounts Receivable debit column to the customer accounts in the Accounts Receivable Ledger. Write the Sales Journal page number and abbreviation in the posting reference column of each account. Enter a check mark (✓) in the posting reference column of the journal opposite each customer.
(2) At the end of the month, post the journal totals to the Accounts Receivable account, the Sales account, the GST Payable account, and the PST Payable account in the General Ledger. Enter the Sales Journal page number and abbreviation in the posting reference column of the accounts. Write the account numbers below the totals in the Sales Journal (see Figure 9-18).

ⓇECORDING CREDIT INVOICES

When goods are returned by a customer, a credit invoice is prepared and sent to the customer. Four methods are used to record sales returns on the books of the seller. They are:

(1) In the General Journal, use a Sales Returns and Allowances account and record the credit invoices as debits in that account.
(2) In the General Journal, decrease the Sales account with a debit.
(3) In the Sales Journal, record the return in the Sales Returns and Allowances debit column and decrease the GST Payable, PST Payable, and Accounts Receivable accounts using the circling method.
(4) In the Sales Journal, use the circling method to decrease the Sales, GST Payable, PST Payable, and Accounts Receivable accounts.

The circling method is illustrated in Figure 9-19.

SALES JOURNAL PAGE 17

DATE	INV. NO.	CUSTOMER	TERMS	P.R.	ACCOUNTS REC. DEBIT	SALES CREDIT	GST PAYABLE CREDIT	PST PAYABLE CREDIT
2008								
Sep. 4	71	J. Grier	n/30		228.00	200.00	12.00	16.00
7	72	C. Setia	n/30		342.00	300.00	18.00	24.00
9	73	M. Wong	n/30		100.70	95.00	5.70	
11	74	L. Will	n/30		477.00	450.00	27.00	
13	75	K. Rice	n/30		798.00	700.00	42.00	56.00
15	76	C. Setia	n/30		456.00	400.00	24.00	32.00
22	C-19	C. Setia			(91.20)	(80.00)	(4.80)	(6.40)
		Debits = $2 310.50			2 310.50	2 065.00	123.90	121.60
		Credits = $2 310.50						

FIGURE 9-19

Circled items representing sales returns are subtracted from uncircled items.

If the circling method (see Figure 9-19) is not used and if the Sales Journal does not have special columns to accommodate a sales return transaction, then the transaction is recorded in the General Journal. An example follows:

Sep. 22	Sales Returns and Allowances	401	80.00	
	GST Payable	206	4.80	
	PST Payable	205	6.40	
	Accounts Receivable/C. Setia	110/✓		91.20
	Credit Invoice C-19 for goods returned.			

Note: As you have seen previously, the $91.20 must be posted to both the Accounts Receivable control account in the General Ledger and to the C. Setia account in the Accounts Receivable Ledger to maintain the equality of the control account and the subsidiary ledger.

Each of the exercises in this chapter will state the company's accounting policy for recording credit invoices.

STATEMENT OF ACCOUNT

Suppose a company has a customer by the name of R. Thomson, and another named R. Thompson. A sale of $200 to R. Thomson was incorrectly posted to R. Thompson's account. In the seller's Accounts Receivable Ledger, R. Thomson's account balance would be $200 too low and R. Thompson's account balance would be $200 too high. How would this error be discovered?

A statement of account is a form sent to customers showing charges, amounts credited, and the balance of an account.

To locate errors of this type, many companies send a **statement of account** to their customers (see Figure 9-20). At regular periods, usually every month, a copy of the debits and credits in customer accounts is mailed to every customer. In effect, a copy of the account is sent to the customer. The statement of account serves two purposes:

- It enables a customer to compare his or her records with those of the seller and thus to locate errors.
- It reminds a customer of the balance owing.

The statement of account may be prepared by hand or by computer.

One Stop Printing

COMMERCIAL PRINTING • BOOK PRINTING • PHOTOCOPIES • RUBBER STAMPS

23 Avenue South, Lethbridge, AB   T1J 0P6

Tel 432-6449   Fax 432-1147

TO   Carriere & Associates
       252 Raglan Street S.
       Renfrew, ON   K7V 1R1

MONTH OF   May 2009
AMOUNT OF
REMITTANCE $

PLEASE RETURN THIS PART WITH YOUR REMITTANCE

- -

**IN ACCOUNT
    WITH**

**PLEASE KEEP
THIS PART**

DATE	PARTICULARS	DEBIT	CREDIT	BALANCE
May 1	PREVIOUS BALANCE FORWARD			$178.50
15	5000 #10 Envelopes	$321.82		500.32

**2% PER MONTH (24% PER ANNUM) INTEREST
CHARGED ON OVERDUE ACCOUNTS**

**PLEASE PAY LAST
AMOUNT
IN THIS COLUMN**

FIGURE 9-20

Statement of account sent each month by One Stop Printing to its customers. It shows the balance forwarded from the previous month and the transactions for the current month.

Cycle Billing

A company that has only a few customers usually sends a statement of account to each customer at the end of the month.

A company with a large number of customers may find it impossible to prepare all the statements at the end of the month. A more efficient method of handling the preparation of the statements is to distribute the work evenly over the month. Statements are prepared and mailed to groups of customers at different times of the month. Figure 9-21 illustrates how the work is scheduled.

In **cycle billing**, the records of transactions (source documents such as invoices and cash receipt lists) for someone like R. Thomson would be accumulated from the date of the last statement. These transactions would be entered in the customer's account and the statement of account would be prepared on the 30th day of each month. The statement of account for Remo Ltd. would be prepared on the 21st day of each month.

Cycle billing is a method of spreading over the month the work of preparing and mailing statements to customers.

FIGURE 9-21

Cycle billing

Cycle Billing Schedule

INITIAL OF CUSTOMER'S LAST NAME	INCLUDES TRANSACTIONS UP TO	DAY OF THE MONTH ON WHICH STATEMENT IS PREPARED
A–E	5th	6th
F–L	13th	14th
M–R	20th	21st
S–Z	29th	30th

SUMMARIZING THE SYSTEM FOR RECORDING SALES

Earlier in this text, you learned that a system is a series of steps followed to complete a task. In this unit, you learned the system for recording sales. Figure 9-22 on the next page summarizes that system.

FIGURE 9-22

Complete system for recording sales

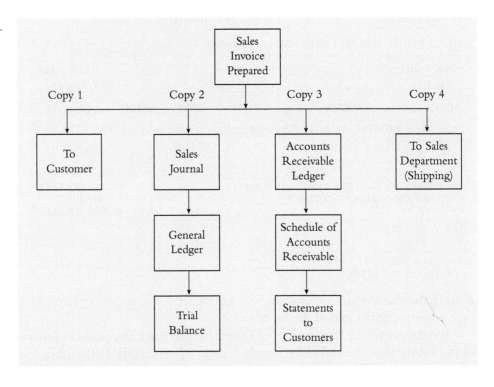

UNIT 20

REVIEW QUESTIONS

1. What source document is prepared for a credit sale?

2. In which special journal is a credit sale recorded?

3. There is a $75 entry circled in a Sales Journal's accounts receivable debit column. Should the $75 be posted as a debit or as a credit to the customer's account?

4. To which ledger are copies of a sales invoice posted when a company uses direct posting?

5. (a) What is a statement of account?
   (b) What two purposes are served by the statement of account?

6. Explain the cycle billing method of preparing customer statements.

UNIT 20

PROBLEMS: APPLICATIONS

1. (a) Answer the following questions about the invoice shown on the next page.

   (i)   Who is the seller?
   (ii) Who is the customer?
   (iii) What is the date of the invoice?
   (iv) What are the terms of sale?
   (v)   What is the last day for payment?

kid bindery

132 Railside Road, Don Mills, ON   M3A 1B8   Phone (416) 449-5565/Fax (416) 449-7516

Quality Printers   **Invoice** 6897   **Date** 4/15/08
1825 Valentine Road   **Docket no.**   3100
Scarborough, ON M1R 3C5   **Terms**   net 30 days
                                Customer's order no.

QUANTITY	DESCRIPTION	PRICE	PER	TOTAL
110 000	Rectangular labels, 45 mm x 330 mm	$0.75	1000	$75.00

Provincial Sales
Tax Exempt

                                GST 6%   4.50
                                Total Due $79.50

GST NO. S22621120
Prov. Lic. 31659012

(vi) How was the $75 calculated?

(vii) Why is PST not added to the invoice?

(b) Assuming you are the seller, record the entry for the invoice above in General Journal form.

2. You are employed by Norton Wholesale Ltd., which sells merchandise to retailers. There is no PST on the sales because the retailer is not the end user of the merchandise, but resells it to the public.

(a) Record the following invoices on page 35 of a Sales Journal:

Mar. 3 No. 171 to Wilkie Co., terms n/15, amount $317.98, GST $19.08.

     6 No. 172 to Lancio Ltd., terms 1/10, n/30, amount $749.95, GST $45.

    12 No. 173 to Frontenac Enterprises, terms 1/10, n/30, amount $247, GST $14.82.

    19 No. 174 to Wilkie Co., terms n/15, amount $260, GST $15.60.

    27 No. 175 to Olsen, Inc., terms n/15, amount $83.25, GST $5.

(b) Total, balance, and rule the journal.

3. You are an accounting clerk for Enza, a high-fashion boutique. Sales invoices are recorded in a Sales Journal and credit invoices in a General Journal. A Sales Returns and Allowances account is used to record credit invoices. Terms of sale for all sales on account are n/30. GST of 6 percent is charged on all sales. PST of 8 percent is calculated on the base price plus GST.

(a) Record the sales invoices listed below on page 51 of the Sales Journal and the credit invoices on page 36 of the General Journal.

Jun.   2   Sales Invoice 201 to I. Ihrig, amount $100.

        4   Credit Invoice C-41 to I. Ihrig, goods returned $65.

        6   Sales Invoice 202 to S. Forge, amount $200.

       10   Sales Invoice 203 to L.T. Ohlhausen, amount $49.50.

       12   Sales Invoice 204 to W. Simone, amount $300.

       13   Credit Invoice C-42 to W. Simone, goods returned $95.

       15   Sales Invoice 205 to I. Ihrig, amount $19.95.

       17   Sales Invoice 206 to S. Forge, amount $28.75.

       20   Sales Invoice 207 to W. Simone, amount $135.

       22   Sales Invoice 208 to L.T. Ohlhausen, amount $89.

       24   Sales Invoice 209 to S. Forge, amount $234.

       26   Credit Invoice C-43 to S. Forge, goods returned $125.

       29   Sales Invoice 210 to L.T. Ohlhausen, amount $165.

(b) Total, balance, and rule the Sales Journal.
(c) Open an Accounts Receivable Ledger and post the source documents to the customer accounts from the journal. You require these customer accounts: S. Forge, I. Ihrig, L.T. Ohlhausen, and W. Simone.
(d) Prepare a schedule of accounts receivable. Compare your total to the General Ledger control account (see (g) below).
(e) Open General Ledger accounts: Accounts Receivable 102, PST Payable 205, GST Payable 206, Sales 410, and Sales Returns and Allowances 411.
(f) Post the transactions in the General Journal to the General Ledger. Post the totals of the Sales Journal to the General Ledger.
(g) Prepare a General Ledger trial balance.

4. Mitchell Wholesalers, Inc. does not use a Sales Returns and Allowances account. It is their accounting policy to record returns and allowances in the Sales Journal using the circling method. All sales are n/30 and are subject to 6 percent GST and 6 percent PST on the base price.

(a) Record the following on page 43 of the Sales Journal.

Oct.   2   Sales Invoice 116, B. Rowan, $800.

        4   Sales Invoice 117, R. Lyttle, $518.

        7   Credit Invoice 5, R. Lyttle, $48.

       10   Sales Invoice 118, G. Gardiner, $687.

       12   Sales Invoice 119, C. Liu, $375.

       16   Sales Invoice 120, L.S. Chin, $800.

       19   Sales Invoice 121, C. Liu, $85.

       21   Sales Invoice 122, M. Hernandez, $613.

       22   Sales Invoice 123, R. Lynch, $950.

       24   Credit Invoice 6, R. Lynch, $50.

25   Sales Invoice 124, S. VanDyke, $330.

29   Sales Invoice 125, P. Lindsay, $250.

(b) Total, balance, and rule the Sales Journal.

UNIT 21   Cash Receipts Journal

Learning Objectives

After reading this unit, discussing the applicable review questions, and completing the applications exercises, you will be able to do the following:

1. **RECORD** cash received in the Cash Receipts Journal.

2. **BALANCE** and post the Cash Receipts Journal.

In the special journal system, all money received is recorded in the **Cash Receipts Journal**. The items considered to be money — that is, cash receipts — include cheques, money orders, bills, and coins.

A special journal used to record cash received.

INTRODUCING THE CASH RECEIPTS JOURNAL

Figure 9-23 on page 341 is a Cash Receipts Journal with seven money columns. There are debit columns for Cash and Sales Discounts and credit columns for Accounts Receivable, Sales, GST Payable, and PST Payable. There is also an Other Accounts credit column that is used to record credits to any account for which a column is not provided.

Most transactions require only one line. However, an occasional compound transaction requires two lines. When the Other Accounts column is used, the name of the account must be shown in the customer or account column. Similarly, the account name must be shown when an entry is made in the Accounts Receivable column. Additional columns may be added to the journal if a particular account is used frequently.

The Cash Receipts Journal is totalled and balanced at the bottom of each journal page and at the end of the month as shown in Figure 9-23. The procedure followed in balancing and posting is the same as the procedure for the Sales or Purchases Journals. The following points regarding posting are illustrated by Figure 9-23:

(1) Accounts receivable are posted to the Accounts Receivable Ledger daily. A check mark in the posting reference column indicates that an entry has been posted to the customer's account.

(2) Other accounts column entries are posted individually at the end of the month to the General Ledger. A number in the posting reference column indicates that an entry has been posted and gives the account number.

(3) Column totals are posted to the General Ledger at the end of the month. A number in brackets under a column indicates that a total has been posted and gives the account number.

RECORDING SOURCE DOCUMENTS FOR CASH RECEIPTS

Cash Receipts from Customers

Source documents for two transactions involving cash received from customers are shown recorded in Figure 9-23. We will examine each of them.

Cheque Received for Payment on Account

A credit sale was made by Henley Sporting Goods to the Ottawa School of Commerce on July 15. The terms of the sale were net 30 days. This meant that a cheque should be received by Henley Sporting Goods by August 14, 30 days from the invoice date.

The cheque received by Henley Sporting Goods is shown in Figure 9-24 on page 342. Notice that this cheque is different from the personal cheques used by most individuals. It is called a *voucher cheque* and contains two parts:

- Cheque
- Attached statement describing the purpose of the payment

When the cheque is received, it is recorded in the Cash Receipts Journal as shown in Figure 9-23. Cash is debited $137.77 and the customer's account is decreased with a credit of $137.77. Notice that the credit is written in the Accounts Receivable credit column and the customer's name is shown in the section next to the date. As with many transactions in special journals, the recording procedure is completed on one line.

Cheque Received for Account Payment Less Sales Discount

Cash discounts are offered to encourage early payment of customer account balances.

You have learned that sellers offer discounts to customers to encourage early payment of account balances. When sales are being made, the buyer and seller agree on payment terms. When the final details of a sale have been completed, both parties should understand clearly when and how payment is to be made. The payment terms should appear on the purchase invoice, the sales invoice, and the monthly statement. Any penalty for late payment should also be clearly outlined on the sale documents.

Figure 9-23 on page 341 shows how the receipt of a cheque for the payment of a sales invoice less a sales discount is recorded in the Cash Receipts Journal. On August 18, a customer, M. Mulvihill, paid $601.40, being $620 less a cash discount of $18.60 ($620 × 0.03 = $18.60) for paying the invoice within 10 days. The customer's account is credited for the full amount of the invoice, $620. The credit of $620 is recorded in the Accounts Receivable credit column. The sales discount of $18.60 is recorded in the Sales Discounts debit column. The cash received, $601.40, is recorded in the Cash debit column.

Other Cash Receipts

As well as money received from customers paying the balances in their accounts, cash is received from the following types of transactions:

- Cash sales to customers

FIGURE 9-23
Cash Receipts Journal after balancing and posting

CASH RECEIPTS JOURNAL

PAGE 26

DATE	REF. NO.	P.R.	CUSTOMER OR ACCOUNT	CASH DEBIT	SALES DISCOUNTS DEBIT	ACCOUNTS REC. CREDIT	SALES CREDIT	GST PAYABLE CREDIT	PST PAYABLE CREDIT	OTHER ACCOUNTS CREDIT
2008										
Aug. 14			Forwarded	3 110.60		1 955.00	1 000.00	75.60	80.00	
14		✓	Ottawa School of Commerce	137.77		137.77				
18			M. Mulvihill	601.40	18.60	620.00				
21	71			26.50			25.00	1.50		
28		300	W. Lyons, Capital	6 000.00						6 000.00
31		420	Bank Interest Earned	75.00						75.00
				9 951.27	18.60	2 712.77	1 025.00	77.10	80.00	6 075.00
				(100)	(410)	(102)	(400)	(206)	(221)	

Debits = $9 969.87
Credits = $9 969.87

FIGURE 9-24
Voucher cheque

OTTAWA SCHOOL OF COMMERCE
300 Rochester St.
Ottawa, Ontario K1R 7N4

CURRENT ACCOUNT
CHEQUE NUMBER 80479
Aug. 2, 2008

**PAY TO THE
ORDER OF** Henley Sporting Goods -------------------------- $137.77

SUM OF One hundred thirty-seven----------------------- 77/100 **DOLLARS**

THE ROYAL BANK OF CANADA
1517 Woodward Ave.
Ottawa, ON K1Z 7W5

Canning and Associates
OTTAWA SCHOOL OF COMMERCE

⑤1428 003 124 5802

(Detach and retain this statement)

THE ATTACHED CHEQUE IS IN PAYMENT OF ITEMS LISTED BELOW

DATE	ITEM	AMOUNT	DISCOUNT	NET AMOUNT
Aug. 2	Invoice 97	$137.77		$137.77

- Owner investments
- Cash refunds received for purchase returns
- Interest earned on bank accounts and other investments
- Miscellaneous sources

Source documents for three transactions of this type are shown recorded in Figure 9-23. Each will be examined.

Cash Sales Slip

A $25 cash sale that is exempt from PST is made by Henley to a customer on August 21. The customer pays for the item and receives Cash Sales Slip 71, which describes the transaction and serves as proof of payment. Cash sales slips are prenumbered and the number of the slip is often recorded in the reference number column of the journal. This transaction is shown in the Cash Receipts Journal in Figure 9-23. Notice that for this cash sale it is not necessary to show anything in the customer or account column.

Cheque Received for New Investment

On August 28, W. Lyons, the owner of Henley Sporting Goods, uses a personal cheque to invest an additional $6000 in the business. Figure 9-23 shows the entry made to record the cheque in the Cash Receipts Journal. Cash is debited $6000. The credit to the Capital account is recorded in the Other Accounts credit column because there is no column entitled Capital credit.

Bank Credit Memorandum

A bank credit memo indicates an increase in a bank account.

A **bank credit memorandum (memo)** is a source document received from a bank when the bank adds money to a customer's account. Henley received a bank credit memo for $75 on August 31. It indicated that $75 interest had been earned and added by the bank to Henley's account. The $75 is recorded on the debit side of the Cash account (an asset increasing), and on the credit side of the Bank Interest Earned account.

Bank Interest Earned is a revenue account. It increases Capital, and that is why interest received is recorded on the credit side of the Bank Interest Earned account. This transaction is shown in T-accounts below:

Bank Interest Earned is a revenue account and has a credit balance.

Cash		Bank Interest Earned	
Aug. 31 75		Aug. 31 75	

This transaction represents money received; therefore, it is recorded in the Cash Receipts Journal (see Figure 9-23). The $75 debit to the Cash account is placed in the cash debit column. The $75 credit to the Bank Interest Earned account is entered in the Other Accounts credit column.

UNIT 21

REVIEW QUESTIONS

1. What source document is prepared for a cash sale?

2. What is a voucher cheque?

3. What is the purpose of the voucher that is attached to the voucher cheque?

4. Does a bank credit memo indicate that a company's bank account has increased or decreased?

UNIT 21

PROBLEMS: APPLICATIONS

1. Record the following source documents in a General Journal:

Nov. 15   Cash sales slip for $30 plus $2.40 PST plus $1.80 GST.

16   Cheque received from the owner, A. Price, for $3800 as an additional investment in the business.

18   Bank credit memo from the Bank of Montreal showing that $127 in interest has been added to the bank account.

19   Cheque received from R. Karasch for $294 to pay Invoice 518 of $300 less 2 percent discount allowed. Invoice date November 10. Invoice terms 2/10, n/30.

20   Cheque received from S. Wooten for $356 to pay Invoice 479, no discount.

21   Cash sales slip for $240 plus $19.20 PST plus $14.40 GST.

2. (a) Record the following source documents on page 274 of a Cash Receipts Journal:

Oct.   1   Cash register tape shows sales of $2465 plus $147.90 GST and $197.20 PST.

2   Cheque received from M. Gillan for $825 to pay Invoice 619, $825 dated September 4. Terms: n/30.

2   Cheque received from V. O'Brien for $317.52 to pay Invoice 621, $324 less 2 percent discount. Invoice dated September 5. Terms: n/30.

3 Bank credit memo, $189 for interest deposited into the bank account.

5 Cheque received from L. Baird, the owner, for $5100 as an additional investment in the business.

7 Bank credit memo, $12 750 for a bank loan that was deposited in the company bank account.

8 Cheque received from B. Sandhu for $548.80 to pay Invoice 623, $560 less 2 percent discount. Invoice dated September 18. Terms: n/30.

10 Cash Sales Slips 940 to 955 for $2875 plus $172.50 GST and $230 PST.

12 Cash register tape for sales of $1890 plus $113.40 GST and $151.20 PST.

13 Money order received from G. Vaz for $875.14 to pay Invoice 628, $893 less 2 percent discount. Invoice dated September 24. Terms: n/30.

(b) Total, balance, and rule the Cash Receipts Journal.
(c) Describe how you would post this journal if this firm did not use a direct posting system for customer accounts.

3. (a) Record the source documents given below on page 210 of a Cash Receipts Journal.
(b) Total, balance, and rule the Cash Receipts Journal.
(c) Set up a General Ledger and an Accounts Receivable Ledger for June 1 with the following accounts and balances; then post the Cash Receipts Journal.
(d) Prove that the total of the customer account balances in the Accounts Receivable Ledger equals the Accounts Receivable general ledger balance as of June 7, 2009.

Cash	101	1 400	
Accounts Receivable	102	3 808	
PST Payable	205		350
GST Payable	206		400
R. Lynch, Capital	301		15 000
Sales	401		0
Sales Discounts	402	0	

**Schedule of
Accounts Receivable
June 1, 2009**

B. Ebel	$2 400
S. Kassam	693
P. Soto	715
	$3 808

Jun. 1 Cheque received for $4500 from the owner,
         R. Lynch, as a further investment in the business.

      2 Cash Sales Slips 340 to 355 for $1115 plus $66.90 GST and $89.20
         PST.

      4 Cheques received:
         $1100 from B. Ebel on account;
         $428.26 from P. Soto to pay Invoice 4372 for $437, Invoice dated
         May 28. Terms: 2/10, n/30.

      5 Bank credit memo for $693 the bank collected from S. Kassam on
         account.

      6 Cheque received from B. Ebel for $749.70 to pay Invoice 4375 for
         $765. Invoice dated May 29. Terms: 2/10, n/30.

      7 Cash Sales Slips 356 to 382 for $3250 plus $195 GST and $260
         PST.

UNIT 22 Cash Payments Journal

Learning Objectives

After reading this unit, discussing the applicable review questions, and
completing the applications exercises, you will be able to do the following:

1. **RECORD** payments, including refunds, in the Cash Payments Journal.

2. **BALANCE** and post the Cash Payments Journal.

So far in this chapter, special columnar journals for purchases, sales, and cash
receipts have been described. Now the recording of cash payments in a special
journal called the *Cash Payments Journal* will be discussed.

MAKING CASH PAYMENTS

Payment By Cheque

A basic accounting principle is that all payments, except very small ones, should
be made by cheque. Each cheque should be authorized. Documents such as
receiving reports and approved invoices should be available to support the issuing
of the cheque.

Cheque Requisition

In many companies, a cheque request form is completed before a cheque is issued.
This form is called a *cheque requisition*. The cheque requisition is accompanied by
all the documents related to the transaction, because the person with the responsibility to authorize the issuing of a cheque may wish to trace the entire history
of the transaction.

Voucher Cheque

Many firms use the voucher form of a cheque as shown in Figure 9-25 below. The cheque is prepared with three copies. Copy 1 is the cheque sent to the creditor. Copy 2 is kept and used by the accounting department as the source document for the journal entry. Copy 3 is filed with the invoice. Notice that the cheque in Figure 9-25 requires two signatures. Many firms require two people to sign all cheques so that there is some control over the cash (see Cash Control).

FIGURE 9-25

Voucher cheque showing distribution of copies

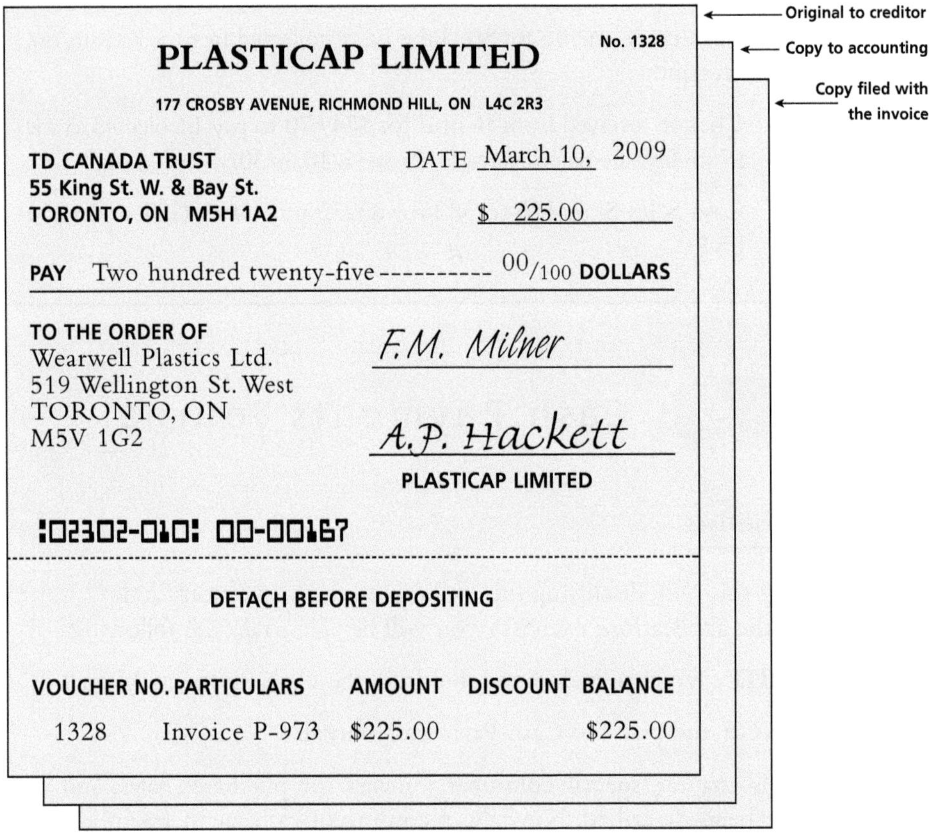

→ Original to creditor
→ Copy to accounting
→ Copy filed with the invoice

INTRODUCING THE CASH PAYMENTS JOURNAL

The Cash Payments Journal is used to record all payments.

Because of the large number of payments made, many companies record their cheques in a **Cash Payments Journal**. Special columns are provided for accounts that are used often. In the Cash Payments Journal in Figure 9-26 on page 347, special columns are headed Cash credit, Accounts Payable debit, GST Refundable debit, Purchases debit, and Purchases Discounts credit. The Other Accounts debit column is provided for those accounts that do not fit into the special columns. Source documents for various transactions involving cash payments are shown recorded in Figure 9-26. In the following section, each will be examined.

FIGURE 9-26
Cash Payments Journal

CASH PAYMENTS JOURNAL

PAGE 31

DATE	CH. NO.	CREDITOR OR ACCOUNT	P.R.	CASH CREDIT	ACCOUNTS PAYABLE DEBIT	GST REFUNDABLE DEBIT	PURCHASES DEBIT	PURCHASES DISCOUNTS CREDIT	OTHER ACCOUNTS DEBIT
2008									
Sep. 24	278	Sporting Goods Ltd.		831.04	848.00			16.96	
27	DM	Bank Interest Expense		230.00					230.00
29	279	Ryan Hoskins		165.30					
		Sales Returns & Allow.							145.00
		PST Payable							11.60
		GST Payable							8.70

Recording Source Documents for Cash Payments

Cheque Issued for Account Payment Less Purchase Discount

On September 10, Henley Sporting Goods received Purchase Invoice 5316 for $800 worth of basketballs, plus $48 GST, from Sporting Goods Ltd. Terms of sale on the invoice were 2/15, n/30. The invoice was checked for accuracy and since the order was received in good condition, the invoice was passed for payment. The invoice was recorded in Henley's books as shown by the following T-accounts:

Purchases	Accounts Payable/ Sporting Goods Ltd.	GST Refundable
Sep. 10 800	Sep. 10 848	Sep. 10 48

The invoice was placed in the date file in a folder dated September 24. On September 24, a cheque for $831.04 was prepared and sent to Sporting Goods Ltd. From the cheque copy, entries were made in Henley's books as shown by the following T-accounts:

Cash	Accounts Payable/ Sporting Goods Ltd.	Purchases Discounts
Sep. 24 831.04	Sep. 24 848 | Sep. 10 848	Sep. 24 16.96

In General Journal form, the entries shown in these two sets of T-accounts would appear as follows:

Sep.10	Purchases	800.00	
	GST Refundable	48.00	
	Accts. Payable/Sporting Goods Ltd.		848.00
	Invoice 5316, terms 2/15, n/30.		
24	Accts. Payable/Sporting Goods Ltd.	848.00	
	Cash		831.04
	Purchases Discounts		16.96
	Invoice 5316, less discount.		

The Purchases Discounts account is a negative cost account.

This payment on account was recorded in a Cash Payments Journal as illustrated in Figure 9-26.

Bank Debit Memo

A bank debit memo indicates a decrease in a customer's bank account.

A **bank debit memo** indicates a decrease in a bank account. On September 27, Henley Sporting Goods received a bank debit memo from TD Canada Trust. The memo indicated that $230 had been deducted from Henley's bank account for the monthly interest on their bank loan.

The $230 is an expense, and must be recorded in the Bank Interest Expense account. In Figure 9-26, the debit to Bank Interest Expense is placed in the Other Accounts debit column and the credit is entered in the Cash credit column.

Cheque Issued for Refund on Cash Sale with GST and PST

On September 22, Ryan Hoskins purchased a pair of tennis shoes for $120 and a racquet for $145. He paid a total of $302.10 cash for his purchases, which included GST of $15.90 (0.06 × 265 = 15.90) and PST of $21.20 (265 × 0.08 = 21.20). The seller, Henley Sporting Goods, recorded the sales as follows:

Sep. 22	Cash	302.10	
	Sales		265.00
	GST Payable		15.90
	PST Payable		21.20
	To record a cash sale.		

Ryan was unhappy with the quality of the racquet and returned it on September 29. He received Cheque 279 for $165.30 as a cash refund. The cheque consisted of $145 plus $8.70 GST (0.06 × 145 = 8.70) and PST of $11.60 (145 × 0.08 = 11.60) for a total of $165.30.

   This refund cheque affected the books of Henley Sporting Goods as shown by the following T-accounts:

Cash		Sales Returns & Allowances	
Sep. 22 302.10	Sep. 29 165.30	Sep. 29 145.00	

PST Payable		GST Payable	
Sep. 29 11.60	Sep. 22 21.20	Sep. 29 8.70	Sep. 22 15.90

The refund cheque of $165.30 is recorded in the cash credit column of the Cash Payments Journal (Figure 9-26, page 347). The sale amount, $145, is debited to Sales Returns and Allowances using the other accounts debit column. Since Henley Sporting Goods refunded the $8.70 GST and the $11.60 PST to Ryan, it no longer owes this amount to the government. Therefore, Henley decreased its liability to the government by debiting GST Payable $8.70 and PST Payable $11.60 in the Other Accounts debit column of the journal. Notice that the entry on September 29 in Figure 9-26 requires four lines because the journal does not have a Sales Returns and Allowances debit column, a PST Payable debit column, or a GST Payable debit column.

Recording Transactions in a Cash Payments Journal

The transactions shown in Figure 9-27 on page 350 provide examples of a number of common cash payment transactions that occur in business. See if you can trace them to the journal from the list of sample transactions.

Sample Transactions

Oct.	1	Issued Cheque 101 for $530 to Abrams Trading for cash purchase of merchandise, $500 plus $30 GST.
	3	Issued Cheque 102 for $183 to Speedquip Ltd. for Invoice B-231 dated Sep. 9.
	8	Issued Cheque 103 for $75 to Len's Service Centre to pay for repairs to the company automobile (repairs $70.75, GST $4.25).
	12	Issued Cheque 104 for $310 to Willson's Ltd. as partial payment of account.
	15	Issued Cheque 105 for $500 to The Daily News for advertising ($471.70 plus $28.30 GST).

FIGURE 9-27
Recording transactions in a
Cash Payments Journal

CASH PAYMENTS JOURNAL
PAGE 31

DATE	CH. NO.	CREDITOR OR ACCOUNT	P.R.	CASH CREDIT	ACCOUNTS PAYABLE DEBIT	GST REFUNDABLE DEBIT	PURCHASES DEBIT	PURCHASES DISCOUNTS CREDIT	OTHER ACCOUNTS DEBIT
2008									
May 1	101	Abrams Trading		530.00		30.00	500.00		
3	102	Speedquip Ltd.		183.00	183.00				
8	103	Car Repairs Expense		75.00		4.25			70.75
12	104	Willson's Ltd.		310.00	310.00				
15	105	Advertising Expense		500.00		28.30			471.70
17	106	B. Poirier, Drawings		420.00					420.00
22	107	Supplies Expense		49.00		2.77			46.23
23	108	PST Payable		142.00					142.00
25	109	Willson's Ltd.		286.20		16.20	270.00		
28	110	Abrams Trading		343.00	350.00			7.00	
31	111	Salaries Payable		4 500.00					4 500.00
31	112	GST Payable		300.00					300.00

17   Issued Cheque 106 for $420 to Angelo's Masonry to pay for a patio at the home of the owner, B. Poirier.

22   Issued Cheque 107 for $49 to The Office Place for the cash purchase of supplies (supplies $46.23, GST $2.77).

23   Issued Cheque 108 for $142 to the Provincial Treasurer for last month's PST collections.

25   Issued Cheque 109 for $286.20 to Willson's Ltd. for cash purchase of merchandise (merchandise $270, GST $16.20).

28   Issued Cheque 110 for $343 to Abrams Trading in payment of Invoice 673 (amount of invoice $350, discount taken $7).

31   Issued Cheque 111 for $4500 for monthly salaries.

31   Issued Cheque 112 for $300 to Receiver General for GST remittance.

Balancing and Posting the Cash Payments Journal

Procedures similar to those used with the other special journals are followed when balancing and posting the Cash Payments Journal:

(1) Each page is totalled and balanced. Page totals are carried forward if the month has not ended.

(2) At the end of each month, the journal is totalled, balanced, and ruled; it is then posted.

(3) Entries in the Accounts Payable debit column are posted daily to the creditor accounts in the Accounts Payable Ledger.

(4) The Other Accounts debit column entries are posted individually at the end of each month.

(5) The column totals are posted to the General Ledger at the end of the month.

(6) The Other Accounts column total is not posted.

SUMMARY OF DIRECT POSTING TO THE SUBSIDIARY LEDGERS

Figures 9-28 and 9-29 summarize the procedures followed when source documents are posted directly to the subsidiary ledgers. Figure 9-28 shows how transactions involving customers are posted directly from the source documents to the customer accounts in the Accounts Receivable Ledger. Transactions involving creditors are posted directly to the accounts in the Accounts Payable Ledger.

FIGURE 9-28

Direct posting to the subsidiary ledgers

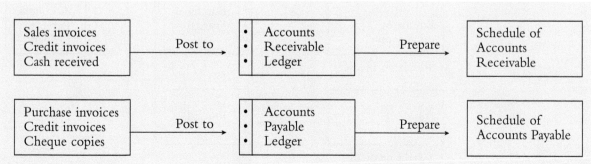

FIGURE 9-29

Posting to the General
Ledger

The same transactions are entered in the journals and then posted to the General Ledger. Figure 9-29 illustrates how this is done:

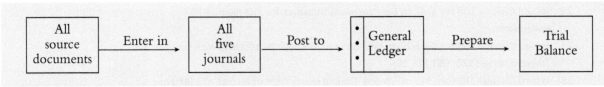

SUMMARY OF THE SPECIAL JOURNAL SYSTEM

Since many business transactions are similar in nature, journals may be specially designed to handle the recording of transactions that occur frequently. The following special journals are used by many firms:

- Purchases Journal: used for recording purchases on account
- Sales Journal: used for recording sales of merchandise on account
- Cash Receipts Journal: used for recording all cash received
- Cash Payments Journal: used for recording all payments of cash

The special journal system is summarized in Figure 9-30.

FIGURE 9-30

Special journal system

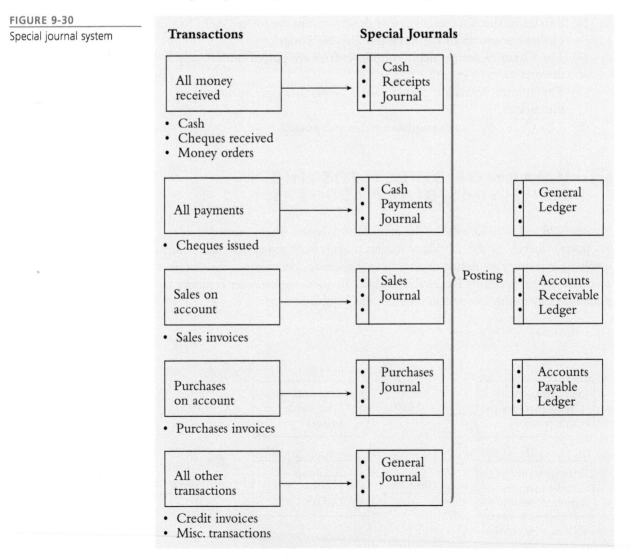

ACCOUNTING TERMS

Bank Credit Memo	A memorandum from the bank indicating an increase in a bank account. (p. 342)
Bank Debit Memo	A memorandum from the bank indicating a decrease in a bank account. (p. 348)
Cash Payments Journal	Special journal used to record cash payments. (p. 346)
Cash Receipts Journal	Special journal used to record cash received. (p. 339)
Cycle Billing	Method of spreading over the month the work of preparing and mailing statements to customers. (p. 335)
Due Date	The date on which payment is to be made. (p. 313)
Extension	An extension is the quantity multiplied by the unit price. (p. 312)
Matching Process for Purchases	Comparing the purchase order, the purchase invoice, and the receiving report before payment is made. (p. 312)
Purchase Order	A form prepared by the buyer and sent to the seller containing the details regarding the goods to be purchased. (p. 309)
Purchase Requisition	A form sent to the purchasing department requesting that goods or services be ordered. (p. 309)
Purchases Journal	Special journal used to record purchases on account. (p. 313)
Receiving Report	Form listing all goods received. (p. 311)
Sales Journal	Special journal used to record credit sales. (p. 332)
Special Journal System	Uses separate journals for similar transactions that recur frequently. (p. 307)
Statement of Account	Form sent to a customer showing charges, amounts credited, and the balance of the customer's account. (p. 334)

UNIT 22 REVIEW QUESTIONS

1. (a) What is a cheque requisition?
   (b) What is a voucher cheque?

2. Are purchases discounts recorded as debits or credits? Why?

3. Does a bank debit memo indicate that the bank account has increased or decreased?

4. Should the PST Payable account be increased or decreased when a customer returns goods on which tax has been charged?

5. Is anything other than a cheque number recorded in the cheque number column of the Cash Payments Journal?

6. Briefly describe the types of transactions recorded in each of the following:

   (a) Sales Journal
   (b) Cash Receipts Journal
   (c) Purchases Journal
   (d) Cash Payments Journal
   (e) General Journal

7. Hancock Supply Ltd. uses a five-journal accounting system. Answer the following questions regarding their system:

   (a) In which journal will you find the closing entries?
   (b) Which journal will contain the fewest entries?

(c) If Accounts Payable and Accounts Receivable Ledgers are used, explain how transactions are posted to these ledgers. (Assume a direct posting system is not used.)

(d) When are transactions usually posted to the General Ledger?

(e) Which journals contain information that must be posted to the Accounts Receivable control account?

UNIT 22

PROBLEMS: APPLICATIONS

1. (a) Using the accounts below, record the following documents on page 53 of a Cash Payments Journal:

Feb.   1   Cheque 1890, $1100 to P. Dean for a week's salary.

     2   Cheque 1891, $2125 to R. LaGrange, the owner, for personal use.

     4   Bank debit memo, $28.50 for service charges.

     6   Cheque 1892, $833 to Rolf Distributors for $850 less $17 discount.

     7   Cheque 1893, $189.10 to Gilles Service Centre on account.

     9   Bank debit memo, $830 for monthly payment on the bank loan.

     10   Cheque 1894, $4410 to Manwani Suppliers, for $4500 invoice less $90 discount.

(b) Total, balance, and rule the Cash Payments Journal.

(c) Set up a General Ledger and an Accounts Payable Ledger for February 1 with the following accounts and balances; then post the Cash Payments Journal.

101	Cash	18 493	
200	Accounts Payable		8 340
210	Bank Loan		25 000
300	R. LaGrange, Drawings	0	
502	Purchases Discounts		0
600	Salaries Expense	0	
615	Bank Charges Expense	0	

**Schedule of
Accounts Payable
February 1, 2008**

Gilles Service Centre	$ 269
Manwani Suppliers	6 500
Rolf Distributors	1 571
	$8 340

2. (a) Record the following source documents on page 87 of a Cash Payments Journal:

Aug.   1   Cheque 705, $2700 plus GST to Tompkins Realty Inc. for the August rent.

2 Cheque 706, to Monet Manufacturers for Invoice 17849 for $14 500 less 1 percent discount. Invoice dated July 24. Terms: 1/10, n/30.

3 Bank debit memo M85192 for $35 for bank charges.

5 Refund Cheque 707, $433.20 to J. Means, a customer, for a $380 coffee table (returned today) plus $30.40 PST and $22.80 GST.

6 Cheque 708 for Invoice 11529 for $7100 to Jiannis Cabinets on account. Invoice dated July 10. Terms: n/30.

8 Cheque 709 to Southern Electric for Invoice B8521 for $7561 less discount. Invoice dated July 25. Terms: 2/10, n/30.

10 Cheque 710, $1800 to M. Pothier for personal use.

(b) Total, balance, and rule the Cash Payments Journal.
(c) Set up a General Ledger and Accounts Payable Ledger with the accounts and balances below; then post the Cash Payments Journal.
(d) Does the Accounts Payable General Ledger balance equal the total of the Accounts Payable Ledger?

101	Cash	41 453.72	
202	Accounts Payable		35 696.67
205	PST Payable		0
206	GST Payable		0
207	GST Refundable	1 126.10	
302	M. Pothier, Drawings	13 490.44	
403	Sales Returns and Allowances	2 376.49	
503	Purchases Discounts		6 273.91
600	Rent Expense	28 600.00	
613	Bank Charges Expense	1 875.95	

**Schedule of
Accounts Payable
August 1, 2009**

Monet Manufacturers	$14 500.00
Jiannis Cabinets	9 400.23
Southern Electric	11 796.44
	$35 696.67

1. The cash receipts and cash payments journals are presented on the next page. Certain transactions in each of the journals have been incorrectly recorded, and there are other errors as well; each journal contains five errors. However, each journal has at least one correct entry.

(a) Identify the errors in each of the journals.
(b) Identify the correct transaction(s) in each of the journals.

CHAPTER 9

**PROBLEMS:
CHALLENGES**

CASH RECEIPTS JOURNAL

DATE	REF. NO.	CUSTOMER OR ACCOUNT	P.R.	CASH CREDIT	SALES DISC. DEBIT	ACCOUNTS REC. CREDIT	SALES CREDIT	PST PAYABLE CREDIT	OTHER ACCOUNTS CREDIT
2008									
Mar. 1	1	Bank Loan	210	10 000		10 000			
2	2	Palmer, Capital	301	3 500					3 500
4	71	A. Butler	✓	597.80	12.20	610			
6	3	Land	160	71 000					71 000
9		Cash Register Tape		3 162.50			2 750	220	
				(100)	(410)	(102)	(400)	(221)	

CASH PAYMENTS JOURNAL

DATE	REF. NO.	CUSTOMER OR ACCOUNT	P.R.	CASH CREDIT	ACCOUNTS PAYABLE CREDIT	GST REFUND DEBIT	PURCHASE DEBIT	PURCHASES DISC. CREDIT	OTHER ACCOUNTS CREDIT
2008									
Mar. 1	74	Salaries Expense	600	1 300	1 300				
3		Bank Charges Expense	615	25					25.00
5	75	Lee Ltd.	✓	1 470	1 500			30	
7	76	Purina	✓	795	795				
9	77	Palmer, Drawings	300	1 250			1 250		
		Debits = $1280 Credits = $8460		4 840	3 595		1 280		25.00
				(100)	(200)	(207)	(500)	(502)	

2. The accounting system of Best Care Kennels includes a General Journal, four special journals, a General Ledger, and two subsidiary ledgers. All credit sales have terms of n/30. GST of 6 percent is charged on all sales of service or merchandise. PST of 8 percent calculated on the base price is charged on pet food sales only. Grooming is performed on a cash basis only. The firm's chart of accounts appears on page 353.

(a) Enter the April 2008 transactions given below in the five journals used by Best Care Kennels.

(b) Total, balance, and rule the journals.

(c) Show how the postings would be made by placing the ledger account numbers and check marks in the appropriate columns of the journals. Best Care Kennels does not use a direct posting system to the subsidiary ledgers.

Apr. 1   The owner, C. Erdman, deposited $2000 in the firm's bank account as a further personal investment in the business.

3   Purchased additional grooming equipment from Jayco Supplies ($2897.20 + $173.83 GST), paying $1000 cash and agreeing to pay the remaining $2071.03 EOM.

4   Signed an agreement with J. Johnson to train and exhibit her dog at a price of $250 per month plus expenses, to be billed at the end of each month.

5   Sold dog food on account for $85 plus taxes to Orion Kennels Invoice 874.

6   Received $175 plus $10.50 GST for boarding T. Bach's dog for the past three weeks.

7   Purchased a load of Quality Dog Food for resale, $2400 plus $144 GST, terms n/30.

7   Sold two bags of dog food for $78 plus taxes.

8   Grooming income for the week was $1200 plus $72 GST, per cash sales slips.

9   Billed K. Bailey $500 plus $30 GST for training her dog for the past month, Invoice 875.

10   Orion Kennels returned one bag of feed for credit, $42 plus taxes. Credit Invoice 73 was issued today.

11   Purchased supplies for $75 plus $4.50 GST, cash.

13   Purchased dog food for use in our kennel for $900 plus $54 GST, from Purina on account.

14   Grooming income for the week was $1500 plus $90 GST, per cash sales slips.

15   Received payment from Orion Kennels for the April 5 purchase less returns.

15   Sold pet food for $250 plus taxes to Halton Kennels on account, Invoice 876.

16   Purchased additional fencing materials for the kennel from Huron Farm Supply, $875 plus $52.50 GST, on 30-day account.

16   Received a credit invoice today from Quality Dog Food for $100 plus $6 GST for damaged goods we had returned previously.

17   Billed Vinelands Kennels $1000 plus $60 GST for the monthly training fee, Invoice 877.

18   Billed B. Iannizzi $125 plus $7.50 GST for boarding his dog for four days, Invoice 878.

19   Received $490 from R. Skolnick in payment of training fee previously billed.

21   Grooming revenue for the week, $1350 plus $81 GST.

22   Purchased dog food for resale from Beatrice Foods, $1450 plus $87 GST, on 30-day account.

22   Paid the freight charges on the Beatrice shipment, $75 plus $4.50 GST, cash.

23   Paid Purina $3100 on account.

24   Sold an old set of grooming clippers to R. Steel for $175 on account. The clippers were recorded in the Grooming Equipment account at a cost of $250.

26   Borrowed $3800 from the bank and signed a note payable.

28   Sold pet food on account to Brookfield Kennels, $375 plus taxes, Invoice 879.

28   Grooming fees for the week, $1400 plus $84 GST, cash.

29   Paid the monthly salaries, $2200 cash.

30   Paid Jayco Supplies in full for the April 3 purchase.

30   Sold pet food on account to R. Skolnick, $83 plus taxes, Invoice 880.

30   Received $530 from K. Bailey in payment of her account.

100	Cash	301	C. Erdman, Drawings
110	Accounts Receivable	302	Income Summary
120	Merchandise Inventory	410	Pet Food Sales
125	Supplies	420	Grooming Revenue
126	Feed Supply	430	Boarding Revenue
135	Prepaid Insurance	440	Training Revenue
150	Building	450	Interest Earned
153	Kennel Fencing	475	Sales Returns & Allow.
155	Furniture and Fixtures	500	Purchases
158	Grooming Equipment	525	Purchases Returns & Allow.
160	Land	550	Transportation-in
200	Accounts Payable	600	Salaries Expense
205	PST Payable	601	Taxes Expense
206	GST Payable	602	Supplies Expense
207	GST Refundable	603	Insurance Expense
210	Bank Loan	604	Interest Expense
250	Mortgage Payable	605	Feed Expense
300	C. Erdman, Capital	606	Loss on Sale of Equip.

3. Hannah's Designs offers terms of 2/10, n/30 to credit customers. All sales are exempt from PST. A chart of accounts (showing only those accounts necessary for this exercise) appears on page 360, and schedules of accounts receivable and payable as of June 30 appear on page 360.

(a) Record the July 2009 transactions given below in the following journals:
   • Sales Journal, page 49
   • Purchases Journal, page 53
   • Cash Receipts Journal, page 59
   • Cash Payments Journal, page 64
   • General Journal, page 71

(b) Total, balance, and rule all special journals.

(c) Indicate how the postings would be made to the General Ledger by placing the ledger account numbers in the appropriate places in the journals.

(d) Post to the subsidiary ledgers.

(e) Prepare schedules of accounts receivable and payable as of July 31. The control accounts in the General Ledger on this date show Accounts Receivable $9084.57 and Accounts Payable $7472.

Jul.   2   Purchased merchandise from R. Williams, Inc. for $15 000

($14 150.94 plus $849.06 GST). Invoice 39187 dated today with terms 2/15, n/30.

3 Issued cheque 232 for $21 000 to R. Williams, Inc. for a June purchase, Invoice 38714. No discount was taken.

4 Sold merchandise to F. Lunney, $5900 plus GST, Invoice 275.

5 Sold merchandise for cash, $9200 plus GST.

6 Received Credit Invoice C1826 from R. Williams, Inc. for returned merchandise valued at $1000 ($943.40 plus $56.60 GST).

8 Issued Cheque 233 for $159 ($150 plus $9 GST) to B. Hogan for merchandise returned today.

10 Purchased merchandise from K. Singh & Associates for $7500 plus $450 GST. Invoice 4499 dated July 9 with terms 2/10, n/30.

12 Sold merchandise to N. Blazina for $7943.93 plus GST, Invoice 276.

13 Received payment from F. Lunney to pay her account in full.

13 Issued Credit Invoice 78 to N. Blazina for $636 ($600 plus $36 GST).

15 Sold old store fixtures for $10 500 plus GST to Watson Industries. A cash down payment of $3000 was received with the remainder due on a promissory note in 60 days. The fixtures originally cost $11 425.

18 Received a cheque from N. Blazina for $15 300 for a June sale.

20 Purchased a one-year liability insurance policy from Hensell Insurance for $1200 plus $72 GST on account.

20 Paid K. Singh & Associates, Cheque 234.

21 Paid R. Williams Inc. for the July 2 purchase less the return, Cheque 235.

22 Received $4000 on account from N. Blazina.

24 Purchased new store fixtures for $35 000 plus $2100 GST. Paid 10 percent down (Cheque 236) and signed a promissory note with Avco Finance for the remainder.

25 Sold merchandise to F. Lunney, $5500 plus GST, on account, Invoice 277.

27 Purchased merchandise from K. Singh & Associates, $5849.06 plus $350.94. Invoice dated today with terms 2/10, n/30.

28 Paid the $3600 monthly mortgage payment, of which $1500 was interest expense, Cheque 237.

29 Paid the monthly office salaries, $8200, Cheque 238.

30 Issued Credit Invoice 79 to F. Lunney, $500 plus $30 GST, for goods returned today.

31 Purchased merchandise from Blackburn Wholesalers, $1800 plus $108 GST, Cheque 239.

100	Cash	475	Sales Returns & Allow.
120	Accounts Receivable	480	Sales Discounts
125	Notes Receivable	500	Purchases
130	Supplies	525	Purchases Returns & Allow.
135	Prepaid Insurance	550	Purchases Discounts
160	Store Fixtures	555	Transportation-in
200	Accounts Payable	601	Salaries Expense
206	GST Payable	602	Supplies Expense
207	GST Refundable	603	Insurance Expense
210	Notes Payable	604	Loss on Sale of Equipment
220	Mortgage Payable	605	Interest Expense
400	Sales		

Schedule of Accounts Receivable June 30, 2009

N. Blazina	$15 300.00
F. Lunney	10 750.00
	$26 050.00

Schedule of Accounts Payable June 30, 2009

K. Singh & Associates	12 000.00
R. Williams, Inc.	21 000.00
	$33 000.00

CHAPTER 9

CASE STUDIES

CASE 1

Information that an Effective Accounting Information System Can Provide

Your friend owns a small pet store. It sells household pets and supplies, and provides dog and cat grooming services. Your friend uses a two-column page to record sales dollars and expenses. He believes that as long as it "keeps track of sales dollars and expenses," he is satisfied.

You have learned that "processing up-to-date accounting information is a necessity to make business decisions." A system, either manual or computerized, that will process accounting information and prepare financial reports quickly and easily is of great importance to any organization, regardless of its size.

(a) With that in mind, what would you tell your friend about what an accounting system can do?

(b) What other information would be available if your friend expanded his "basic" accounting system to one that does more than just record sales dollars and expenses?

CASE 2
Duplicate Information—What To Do?

Chevalier Designs is an upscale fashion boutique for women. Pat, the owner, while reviewing the August purchase invoices for payment, noticed that there were duplicate invoices from Fashion Accessories, Inc. for the same line of fall accessories she had ordered. Chevalier knows that she would not have placed a duplicate fall accessory order and wonders if perhaps Fashion Accessories, Inc. has mistakenly sent two invoices for the same order.

(a) What would you suggest that Chevalier do to determine whether her store had indeed ordered the same line of fall accessories twice or whether Fashion Accessories, Inc. had mistakenly billed her twice for the same purchase order?

(b) If Chevalier Designs had placed a duplicate order in error, how can Chevalier prevent this from occurring again?

CASE 3
Special Journal System

Remo Industries uses a five-journal accounting system. On September 30 upon completion of all posting for the month, the Accounts Receivable control account had a debit balance of $161 000, and the Accounts Payable control account had a credit balance of $67 000. The October transactions recorded in the four special journals are summarized below.

- Purchases Journal: total transactions $84 900
- Sales Journal: total transactions $139 000
- Cash Receipts Journal: Accounts Receivable column total $186 300
- Cash Payments Journal: Accounts Payable column total $106 700

(a) From the above information, indicate the figures that would be posted to the Accounts Receivable and Accounts Payable control accounts.

(b) Based on this information, what would the control account balances be upon completing the October 31 posting?

CASE 4
Terms of Sale

You are the credit manager for a large manufacturer of sporting goods. One of your main jobs is to decide if a new customer is to be allowed to buy on credit. Depending on the customer, your firm allows one of the following terms of payment.

- C.O.D. (cash on delivery)
- 30 days
- 90 days

Athletes Sports Inc., a new customer, has ordered $15 000 worth of merchandise. Which term of payment would you grant to Athletes Sports Inc.? Its balance sheet follows. Give reasons for your answer.

Athletes Sports Inc.
Balance Sheet
April 30, 2008

Assets		Liabilities	
Cash	$ 2 500	Accounts Payable	$ 91 000
Accounts Receivable	21 400	Bank Loan	42 000
Inventory	83 000	Mortgage Payable	140 000
Land	85 000	Total Liabilities	273 000
Building	175 000		
Equipment	30 000		
		Owner's Equity	
		R. Holmes, Capital	123 900
		Total Liabilities and	
Total Assets	$396 900	Owner's Equity	$396 900

ETHICS CASE
Personal Values

Jeanne Southcott has been transferred by her company from Toronto to Winnipeg. Jeanne has $4000 in her Toronto bank account. Rather than taking the $4000 cash with her to Winnipeg, Jeanne instructs her bank to transfer the funds to a branch of the bank in Winnipeg.

When Jeanne arrives in Winnipeg, she receives a statement from her new bank that shows a balance of $14 000 in her new account. Jeanne realizes that someone has made a mistake because there should only be $4000 in the account and she wonders what to do.

(a) Does the extra $10 000 in the account belong to Jeanne?
(b) How could such an error occur?
(c) What alternatives does Jeanne have?
(d) What are the consequences of each alternative?
(e) Which alternative do you recommend?

1. **Financial Consumer Agency of Canada   www.fcac-acfc.gc.ca**

    This Canadian federal government agency works to protect and educate consumers of financial services. On this site is an interactive tool that provides information and quizzes to check understanding about consumers' rights and responsibilities, getting the most from credit cards, managing money, and understanding credit reports and scores.

2. **Bankrate.com   www.bankrate.com/brm/rate/cc_home.asp**

    On this site is information on credit card rates, calculators, in-depth articles, and professional advice. You can analyze your credit rating and figure out your score. Included are 5 Must Do's for credit card shoppers.

3. **Office of Consumer Affairs
    strategis.ic.gc.ca/epic/internet/inoca-bc.nsf/en/ca00458e.html**

    Information is provided through Industry Canada's Office of Consumer Affairs. This interactive tool is designed to help identify the cost of credit cards and provide guidance on their use.

4. **Federal Trade Commission
    www.ftc.gov/bcp/conline/pubs/credit/choose.htm**

    This American site provides detailed descriptions of credit card terms, costs, and features to guide consumers in the choice and use of credit cards.

CHAPTER 10

Cash Control and Banking

 **UNIT 23**   Cash Control

Learning Objectives

After reading this unit, discussing the applicable review questions, and completing the applications exercises, you will be able to do the following:

1. **EXPLAIN** the purpose and importance of the internal control system of a business.

2. **DISCUSS** the importance of cash control, and **EXPLAIN** why the tasks of handling and recording cash are separated for control purposes.

3. **EXPLAIN** why source documents are prenumbered. **PREPARE** a daily cash proof and **RECORD** shortages or overages. **DEPOSIT** cash receipts daily.

4. **DISCUSS** why cash payments should be made by cheque.

5. **ESTABLISH** and **MAINTAIN** a petty cash fund to pay small bills.

The internal control system of a business refers to the method and procedures used to:

(1) Protect the assets from waste, loss, theft, and fraud
(2) Ensure reliable accounting records
(3) Ensure accurate and consistent application of the firm's policies
(4) Evaluate the performance of departments and personnel

These components of an effective internal control system can be divided into administrative controls and accounting controls. **Administrative controls** normally relate to components (3) and (4). They increase the efficiency of the business and ensure company policies are followed. **Accounting controls** relate to components (1) and (2). They protect assets and ensure the reliability of accounting records and statements.

> *Accountants must be familiar with both administrative and accounting controls. Proper internal control ensures that the accounting system is dependable and efficient and provides security for the resources of the business.*

In this chapter, we will discuss one portion of the accounting control system of a business — the need for control of cash. We will examine a number of procedures that are used to protect this important asset, as well as methods of keeping accurate cash records. It should be understood that the term "cash" includes cheques, money orders, bills, and coins.

IMPORTANCE OF CASH CONTROL

Lisa Khan works for Batista Bakery Ltd. One of Lisa's duties is to handle cash sales. When a customer buys merchandise for cash, a cash sales slip is completed in duplicate. One copy is given to the customer and the second is placed in the cash register with the money received from the sale. Lisa is often left alone in the store and has learned that a sale can be made, a cash sales slip given to the customer, the duplicate copy destroyed, and the money placed in Lisa's pocket instead of in the company's cash register.

This story is an example of why all companies, both large and small, require accounting systems that provide control over dishonesty and error.

Because of the ease with which cash may be lost or stolen and errors may be made in counting cash, systems are needed that give effective control over all cash received and all payments made. No two businesses operate in exactly the same way. Some have many cash sales every day while others have only a few. It is the accountant's task to design a system that suits the particular needs of a company. The system should effectively control cash, but it should not be overly complicated or expensive to operate.

In the case of Batista Bakery Ltd., the solution can be as simple as prenumbering all the sales slips and having Lisa's supervisor check them periodically to ensure that none are missing. Cash is involved in a large portion of the transactions of a business and therefore presents opportunities for errors to occur. Cash is also an attractive target for theft and fraud. Therefore, control of cash is very important to the owner or manager of the enterprise.

Presented on the next page are the Comparative Balance Sheets for the Bank of Montreal, years 2004 and 2005. Note the amount of cash holdings. You can easily see why control over cash is so very important to business managers and owners!

Internal accounting control is used to protect assets and to ensure the reliability of records and statements.

Procedures used to ensure application of company policies and evaluate performance.

Procedures used to protect assets and ensure reliable accounting records.

Cash includes cheques, money orders, bills, and coins.

FIGURE 10-1

Comparative balance sheets
for the Bank of Montreal,
years 2004 and 2005

Consolidated Financial Statements

Consolidated Balance Sheet

As at October 31 (Canadian $ in millions)	2005	2004
		Restated (see Note 20)
Assets		
Cash Resources (Notes 2 and 27)	$ 20,721	$ 18,045
Securities (Notes 3 and 27)		
Investment (fair value $12,933 in 2005 and $15,103 in 2004)	12,936	15,017
Trading	44,309	35,444
Loan substitutes	11	11
	57,256	50,472
Loans (Notes 4 and 7)		
Residential mortgages	60,871	56,444
Consumer instalment and other personal	27,929	24,887
Credit cards	4,648	3,702
Businesses and governments	47,803	44,559
Securities borrowed or purchased under resale agreements	28,280	22,609
	169,531	152,201
Customers' liability under acceptances (Note 4)	5,934	5,355
Allowance for credit losses (Note 4)	(1,128)	(1,308)
	174,337	156,248
Other Assets		
Derivative financial instruments (Note 9)	31,517	25,448
Premises and equipment (Note 10)	1,847	2,020
Goodwill (Note 13)	1,091	1,507
Intangible assets (Note 13)	196	480
Other (Note 14)	10,567	10,974
	45,218	40,429
Total Assets	$ 297,532	$ 265,194
Liabilities and Shareholders' Equity		
Deposits (Note 15)		
Banks	$ 25,473	$ 20,654
Businesses and governments	92,437	79,614
Individuals	75,883	74,922
	193,793	175,190
Other Liabilities		
Derivative financial instruments (Note 9)	28,868	23,973
Acceptances (Note 16)	5,934	5,355
Securities sold but not yet purchased (Note 16)	16,142	10,441
Securities lent or sold under repurchase agreements (Note 16)	22,657	21,345
Other (Note 16)	12,203	12,156
	85,804	73,270
Subordinated Debt (Note 17)	2,469	2,395
Preferred Share Liability (Note 20)	450	450
Capital Trust Securities (Note 18)	1,150	1,150
Shareholders' Equity		
Share capital (Note 20)	4,618	4,453
Contributed surplus (Note 21)	20	10
Net unrealized foreign exchange loss	(612)	(497)
Retained earnings	9,840	8,773
	13,866	12,739
Total Liabilities and Shareholders' Equity	$ 297,532	$ 265,194

The accompanying notes to consolidated financial statements are an integral part of these statements.
Certain comparative figures have been reclassified to conform with the current year's presentation.

F. Anthony Comper
President and Chief Executive Officer

Jeremy H. Reitman
Chairman, Audit Committee

92 | BMO Financial Group 188th Annual Report 2005

Source: BMO Financial Group, *188th Annual Report*, 2005, p. 92.

CASH CONTROL PROCEDURES

A business owned and operated by one person or by a small family has little need for control procedures. However, as a company grows and employs an increasing number of people, it is often necessary to pass on to others those tasks that include financial responsibilities. This makes it necessary to control theft, fraud, and errors made by people within the company. As well, control procedures can result in more efficient use of employee time. There are a number of established accounting procedures that have been designed to provide internal control over cash. In this chapter, we will discuss the eight cash control procedures listed here:

- Procedure 1: Separation of Duties
- Procedure 2: Immediate Listing of Cash Receipts
- Procedure 3: Daily Cash Proof
- Procedure 4: Daily Deposit of Cash
- Procedure 5: Payment by Cheque
- Procedure 6: Petty Cash Procedures
- Procedure 7: Periodic Audit
- Procedure 8: Monthly Bank Reconciliation

Procedure 1: Separation of Duties

A key component of all control systems is the **separation of duties** of employees. To discourage fraud and theft as well as to ensure the accuracy of accounting data, the duties of the accounting personnel should be arranged so that one employee verifies the accuracy of another employee's work. In a cash control system, it is important that the employee responsible for preparing and depositing the cash in the bank not be the employee responsible for recording the cash receipts. This provides a verification of the cash recorded and minimizes the chance of theft since both employees would have to work together to remove cash from the company. The recording function should be divided among employees also, where possible, to provide additional verification of accuracy of the records and protection for the asset. You have already seen this type of division of duties where the work of the accounts receivable clerk is verified by the accounting supervisor, who compares the schedule of accounts receivable total to the control account in the General Ledger. The importance of this control procedure for both cash receipts and cash payments will be demonstrated throughout this chapter.

Duties of employees should be arranged so that one employee verifies the work of another employee.

Different people should carry out the task of recording cash received and the task of actually handling the cash.

CONTROL OF CASH RECEIPTS

The accounting controls in Procedures 2, 3, and 4 ensure the accuracy of cash receipts.

Procedure 2: Immediate Listing of Cash Receipts

Cash receipts consist of cash received at the time of the sale, over the counter, cheques received by mail, in payment of accounts receivable, and electronic receipts.

Electronic Receipts

A system to transfer cash using electronic communictions.

Electronic funds transfer (EFT) uses electronic communications to move cash from one bank account to another, without the use of paper. EFT cash receipts are listed with deposits and other credits on the monthly bank statement.

Since no cash or cheques are handled by employees, an EFT system provides very good internal cash control. The accounting department records EFT cash receipts directly from the information on the company's monthly bank statement.

Cash Sales

All cash should be recorded as soon as it is received.

Cash registers or terminals are usually used to record cash sales as they occur. The cash register should be set up to allow the customer to see the amount being recorded. The customer assists with the control system by preventing an error in recording a cash sale and by preventing the employee from ringing in a lower amount than that charged to the customer and then pocketing the difference. The cash register tape provides a total of the cash sales for the day. It is compared to the actual cash receipts by the manager, supervisor, or owner when preparing the daily cash proof. This allows a person other than the cashier to verify the accuracy of the cash.

This procedure follows the concept of separation of duties explained previously. In addition, the immediate recording of the sale by the cash register eliminates the possibility of cash being stolen and the sale remaining unrecorded.

Computerized cash register systems provide additional accounting controls by verifying prices and updating inventory records.

Prenumbered Sales Slips

Multiple-copy sales slips prepared for each cash sale.

In many businesses, a prenumbered, multiple-copy sales slip is prepared for each cash sale. One copy is given to the customer and two are kept on file in the business. At the end of the day, the sales slips are totalled and compared to the cash register tape and the actual cash on hand. One set of sales slips is forwarded with the cash to the person responsible for making a bank deposit. The other set is forwarded to the accounting department to act as a source document to record the cash sales for the day.

Cancelled sales slips are marked void and are kept on file.

If all documents are prenumbered, all of them must be accounted for. It is therefore impossible for the sales clerk to destroy a cash sales slip and pocket the money, since it would mean that one of the numbered slips would be destroyed. If a sales slip is spoiled or cancelled, it must be marked *void* and kept with the rest of the day's source documents. The principle of prenumbering documents is applied to many forms. For example, cheques, sales invoices, and petty cash vouchers are all prenumbered. This ensures that every document is accounted for.

Cash Received by Mail

The employee who opens the mail should prepare a list of the cheques received. One copy of this list, along with the cheques, is forwarded to the person responsible for making the daily deposit. The second copy is sent to the accounting department to act as a source document to record these cash receipts. In some firms, a third copy is kept on file for future reference by the employee opening the mail.

These procedures ensure a separation in duties between the employees handling the cash and the employees recording the cash receipts. This is important to verify the accounting records and to prevent theft.

Procedure 3: Daily Cash Proof

Each day, the owner or supervisor should balance the cash received against the source documents used to record the cash transactions. By preparing this proof daily, any major shortages or overages can be dealt with immediately. In the case of Cooper's Drugstore, a daily **cash proof** form is completed by the owner of the business, F. Cooper. This form is shown in Figure 10-2.

Verifies cash on hand equals cash sales slips for the day.

Introducing the Cash Short and Over Account

As Figure 10-2 illustrates, the cash is counted and a $200 cash float (change fund) is removed from the cash and kept for the next day's business. On October 5, the cash is short $4.80. Since the company has lost funds, an expense must be recorded in an expense account called **Cash Short and Over**.

The Cash Short and Over account is used to record shortages and overages of cash.

FIGURE 10-2
Daily cash proof showing a cash shortage

DAILY CASH PROOF

DATE _oct. 5_ 2008	
TOTAL CASH	$2 178.25
LESS CASH FLOAT	200.00
TOTAL DEPOSITED	$1 978.25
SALES SLIPS	
NO.s _923_ to _961_	$1 983.05
CASH SHORT	4.80
or	
CASH OVER	
AUTHORIZED _F. Cooper_	

The daily cash proof is the source document for a journal entry to record the day's sales. For October 5, the journal entry is:

Oct. 5	Cash	1 978.25	
	Cash Short and Over	4.80	
	Sales		1 983.05
	To record Sales Slips 923 to 961.		

DAILY CASH PROOF

DATE ___Oct. 6___ ____2008____

TOTAL CASH	$1 834.51
LESS CASH FLOAT	200.00
TOTAL DEPOSITED	$1 634.51

SALES SLIPS

NO.s ___962___ to ___994___ $1 632.40

CASH SHORT

or

CASH OVER 2.11

AUTHORIZED ___F. Cooper___

The daily cash proof for the next day, October 6, is shown in Figure 10-3. Notice that the total cash deposited is $2.11 more than it should be according to the cash sales slips. In this entry, the overage is recorded as a credit to Cash Short and Over. The journal entry for October 6 is:

Oct. 6	Cash	1 634.51	
	Sales		1 632.40
	Cash Short and Over		2.11
	To record Sales Slips 962 to 994.		

Cash shortages are recorded as debits in the Cash Short and Over account.

Cash overages are recorded as credits in the Cash Short and Over account.

These two journal entries may be summarized as follows. In the daily cash proof in Figure 10-2, the cash is short by $4.80. This shortage represents a loss to the company and is charged as a debit (a decrease in owner's equity) to the Cash Short and Over account. If the cash is over (see Figure 10-3), the amount is recorded in the same Cash Short and Over account. However, an overage is recorded as a credit (an increase in owner's equity).

When an income statement is prepared, the Cash Short and Over account may appear in either the revenue or the expense section. It appears in the revenue section if the account has a credit balance or the overages have been greater than the shortages. It appears in the expense section if the account has a debit balance or the shortages have been greater than the overages.

Some companies prefer to use a separate section at the bottom of the income statement for miscellaneous items such as cash short and over. This section, called Other Income and Expenses, includes such items as bank interest earned, cash short and over, and gain or loss on sale of assets. The use of this section clearly indicates how much of the net income comes from the regular operations of the business and how much comes from miscellaneous sources.

Cash Short and Over Policy

A company that handles a lot of cash transactions and prepares a daily cash proof is faced with a problem. What should be done about shortages and overages?

There are several possibilities, including these:

- Absorb all shortages and overages.
- Deduct shortages from the cashier's pay.

Many companies prefer to keep all shortage information from the cashier. The daily cash proof is prepared by someone from the accounting office. Shortages and overages are absorbed by the company and are not mentioned to the cashier, unless they are frequent and fairly large. If this occurs, the situation is discussed with the cashier. Retraining may be necessary. If errors still continue on a large scale, the cashier may be transferred or dismissed.

Procedure 4: Daily Deposit of Cash

Each day, the total cash receipts of the business (cash sales and cheques received) should be deposited in the bank. Therefore, no large amounts of money (which could be stolen) are kept on the premises. No bills should be paid out of these funds. Thus, the amount of the deposit each day will be the same as the amount recorded in the Cash Receipts Journal by the accounting department. This allows a further verification of the records by the company's bank when the bank sends the bank statement at the end of the month. After completing the daily cash proof (see Figure 10-2), F. Cooper, the owner of Cooper's Drugstore, completes the deposit slip shown in Figure 10-4. The cash is deposited in the bank. A copy of the deposit slip is kept by the company.

FIGURE 10-4
Bank deposit slip

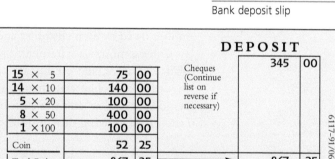

REMO WHOLESALERS' CASH RECEIPTS CONTROL SYSTEM

The example of Remo Wholesalers, a large wholesaler of heating and refrigeration equipment, is used to demonstrate the cash control procedures we have discussed to this point. The principle of separation of duties is used by Remo Wholesalers to control and record cash receipts. Each day, a list of all cash received is prepared by the mail clerk. This list shows the name of the customer, the amount received, and the invoice that is being paid. Two copies of the list are prepared. They are sent to the accounting department where the money received is recorded.

The actual cash is taken to the bank each day by the office manager. Cheques received are endorsed using a restrictive endorsement stamp as shown in Figure 10-5. This endorsement ensures that the cheque is deposited in the company account. It cannot be cashed by anyone. A duplicate deposit slip is prepared, and one copy is kept by the bank. The second copy, signed by the bank teller, is kept by the company.

FIGURE 10-5

Restrictive endorsement stamp on the back of a cheque

DEPOSIT TO THE CREDIT OF
REMO WHOLESALERS
The Bank of Montreal
Meadowvale Branch
Mississauga, Ontario
L5N 1P7

Using the List of Cash Received

When the two copies of the list of cash received are sent to the accounting department, one copy goes to the accounts receivable clerk for posting and the other copy goes to the accountant for journalizing.

Duties of the Accounts Receivable Clerk

From the list of cash received, the accounts receivable clerk posts to the customer accounts. Each account is lowered with a credit. Once every week, the accounts receivable clerk prepares a schedule of accounts receivable. This is a list showing the amount owed by each customer and the total owed by all the customers as a group.

Once a month, a statement is sent to each customer. The statement shows the balance, charges, and credits for cash received, and it acts as a reminder of the amount owing. The statement also is used to check on the accuracy of both Remo Wholesalers' and the customer's records. The customer is sure to complain if the balance owing shown on the statement is too high!

Duties of the Accountant

The second copy of the list of cash receipts is sent to the accountant, who is responsible for recording cash received in the Cash Receipts Journal. The total recorded in the Cash Receipts Journal each day must equal the total of the daily bank deposit. The Cash Receipts Journal is posted to the General Ledger. A trial balance is prepared to prove the accuracy of the General Ledger. One of the accounts on the General Ledger trial balance is the *Accounts Receivable control account*. The balance in this account must equal the total of the schedule of accounts receivable prepared by the accounts receivable clerk.

Control Features

In the system just described, four people are involved in the cash receipts procedures. One person prepares the deposit and another takes the money to the bank. The duty of recording the receipt of cash is handled by two other people. The duties are *separated*. Figure 10-6 illustrates all these tasks that have been described.

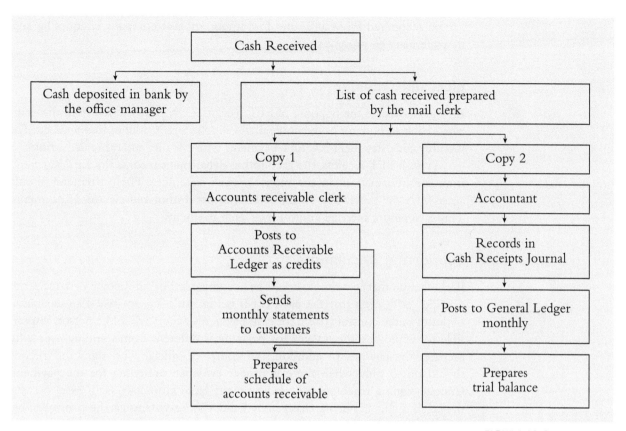

FIGURE 10-6

The duties of depositing and recording cash received are carried out by four people — the mail clerk, the office manager, the accounts receivable clerk, and the accountant.

The separation of duties shown in Figure 10-6 has several built-in control features:

- The entries in the Cash Receipts Journal each day should equal the total of the day's bank deposit.
- The customer should discover any errors in the customer account when the statement is sent out.
- The total of the schedule of accounts receivable should always equal the balance of the Accounts Receivable control account in the General Ledger trial balance.

The separation of duties concept is observed by most large companies. The separation is more difficult to achieve in small businesses because there are fewer employees. To achieve the necessary controls, it is important for the owner of the enterprise to become involved.

CONTROL OF CASH PAYMENTS

Although most people think of protecting cash receipts when discussing control procedures, it is just as important to control cash payments. Procedures 5 and 6 are important parts of a cash payment control system.

Procedure 5: Payment by Cheque

All cash payments should be made by cheque or by EFT payments. The exception is small bills paid out of petty cash, as discussed in Procedure 6. Cheques are prenumbered and spoiled cheques should be marked *void*. Therefore, all cheques can be accounted for at any time. It is important that company cheques be kept in a safe place to prevent theft.

Electronic Payments

EFT payments are the opposite of EFT receipts. Cash is transferred from the company's bank account for payment of salaries, suppliers, rent, utilities, insurance, etc. The monthly bank statement lists EFT payments with cheques and other deductions.

As with EFT receipts, the accounting department records the EFT payments from the information on the monthly bank statement. These payments should agree with the previously established list of pre-authorized electronic payments. This is to ensure internal control over such payments.

Supporting Documents

Each cheque that is written should be accompanied by an invoice or voucher to provide verification that the payment is being made legitimately. The separation of duties in the control system for cash payments occurs when the person responsible for approving the invoice for payment is different from the employee who prepares the cheque. In addition, the company official who signs the cheque should do so only when there is proper evidence presented for the payment. Cheque-signing machines are used by many large businesses as an extra precaution against cheques being changed by hand. Cash payments can be controlled by:

- Using prenumbered cheques for all payments
- Issuing cheques only when there are supporting documents to justify payment
- Separating the duties of employees involved in the cash payment function within the firm

Procedure 6: Petty Cash Procedures

It is often necessary to make a payment by cash because the amount involved is small or because a cheque is not acceptable. For example:

- Parcel post C.O.D. charge: $3.15
- Shortage of postage on incoming mail: 86¢
- Taxi charge for a rush order of supplies: $21.40
- Payment for office supplies: $18.25

The petty cash fund is an amount of cash used to make small payments.

To meet these situations, a small amount of cash is kept on hand. This **petty cash fund** is given to one person, the petty cashier, to maintain. The petty cashier usually has no connection with the accounting system of the company. The petty cash fund operates on an **imprest system**. This means that a specified sum of money has been advanced to the petty cashier to set up the petty cash fund.

A system wherein a designated amount of cash is set aside for a specific purpose, for example, a petty cash fund.

Setting Up the Petty Cash Fund

To establish the petty cash fund, a cheque is issued and given to the petty cashier. The cheque is cashed and the money is usually kept in a petty cash box.

When a petty cash fund is established, this journal entry is made:

Apr. 1	Petty Cash	200	
	Cash		200
	Cheque 217 to set up a petty cash fund.		

The Petty Cash account debited in this entry is found in the General Ledger. It is an asset and appears in the current assets section of the balance sheet. Its balance is combined with that of the Cash account for financial statement purposes.

The Petty Cash account is a current asset.

Making Payments

The petty cashier is the only person who handles petty cash. Payments made must be authorized by a properly supporting **petty cash voucher** (Figure 10-7 below).

Petty cash vouchers are kept in the petty cash box with the remaining cash. Because they have been signed by the party receiving the cash payment, the vouchers prove that legitimate, authorized payments have been made.

The petty cash voucher is a signed authorization for small payments.

Proving the Petty Cash

Suppose a petty cashier starts with $200 cash in the petty cash fund. At any time, the petty cash can be proven by adding the total of the cash in the box to the total of the vouchers in the box. Cash plus vouchers should always equal $200.

Replenishing the Petty Cash Fund

When the petty cash fund runs low, it must be replenished. The petty cashier presents the vouchers and a summary of all payments to the accountant. The vouchers prove that authorized payments have been made. The accountant then issues a cheque equal to the total of the vouchers. The petty cashier cashes the cheque and places the money in the petty cash box. This brings the petty cash fund back to its original amount. This process will now be examined in detail.

Suppose that on April 28, the petty cashier notes that there is only $14.60 cash left in the petty cash fund. Along with this cash are 14 vouchers for payments

Replenishing the petty cash fund means bringing the total currency on hand up to the original amount.

FIGURE 10-7
Petty cash voucher

Petty Cash Voucher

No.   **56**
Date **April 28, 2008**

Amount	$59.87

For   **Office supplies**

Charge to	**Office Supplies Expense**	**$55.95**
	GST Refundable	**3.92**

Approved by   **R. Lincoln**
Received by   **F. Gardiner**

made. Since the original amount of the fund was $200 and there is only $14.60 left, the payment vouchers should total $185.40.

The petty cashier adds the 14 vouchers; they total $185.40. This means that there were no errors in handling the petty cash. The vouchers are then used to prepare the summary below.

Petty Cash Summary
April 1 to April 28

T. Muldoon, Drawings	$ 75.00
Office Supplies Expense	55.95
Delivery Expense	28.00
Miscellaneous Expense	18.42
GST Refundable	8.03
Total Payments	$185.40
Cash on hand	14.60
Total of fund	$200.00

Cheque request: $185.40
Number of vouchers: 14

The 14 vouchers and the summary are then presented to the accountant. The accountant checks to see that all payments are supported by numbered, signed vouchers and that all the vouchers have been accounted for. Then a replenishing cheque for $185.40 is issued by the accountant and given to the petty cashier. This journal entry is made by the accountant:

2008			
Apr. 28	T. Muldoon, Drawings	75.00	
	Office Supplies Expense	55.95	
	Delivery Expense	28.00	
	Miscellaneous Expense	18.42	
	GST Refundable	8.03	
	Cash		185.40
	Cheque 419 to replenish petty cash, vouchers 1–14.		

A journal entry similar to this one is made each time the petty cash fund is replenished. The accounts to be debited are determined by referring to the vouchers and the summary submitted by the petty cashier. Notice that expense accounts are debited each time the fund is replenished. The Petty Cash account is used only when the fund is established or the size of the fund is changed.

The petty cashier cashes the $185.40 cheque, obtaining a variety of denominations of bills, and places the cash in the petty cash box. When this $185.40 is placed in the petty cash box, the total cash is increased to $200. (Remember, there was a $14.60 cash balance before the fund was replenished.)

The petty cash fund is replenished in the way that has been described whenever it runs low. In addition to replenishing petty cash when needed, the fund is also normally replenished at the end of the fiscal period whether the fund is low or not. This is necessary to provide current expense account balances for financial statement preparation.

Petty Cash Guidelines

The petty cashier is usually given a set of guidelines like the following:

- The amount of the fund is $200.
- An approved voucher is required for every payment.
- Replenish the fund when the cash level reaches $15.
- The maximum for any one payment is $18.
- Approved vouchers must be presented to the accountant when requesting a replenishing cheque.

Changing the Size of the Petty Cash Fund

At some point, the office manager may find that the petty cash fund is constantly running out of money during the month and may therefore want to increase the size of the fund. If the fund were to be increased to $250, the journal entry at the time of replenishing (using the previous example) would be as follows:

```
2008
Apr. 28  T. Muldoon, Drawings                    75.00
         Office Supplies Expense                 55.95
         Delivery Expense                        28.00
         Miscellaneous Expense                   18.42
         GST Refundable                           8.03
         Petty Cash                              50.00
            Cash                                           235.40
         Cheque 419 to replenish petty cash,
         vouchers 1–14, and to increase fund.
```

Notice that this entry *does* contain a debit to the Petty Cash account as well as to the expense accounts. This is due to the fact that the amount of the fund has been increased. How would you decrease the original fund to $150 if you found it was too large? Here is an example:

```
2008
Apr. 28  T. Muldoon, Drawings                    75.00
         Office Supplies Expense                 55.95
         Delivery Expense                        28.00
         Miscellaneous Expense                   18.42
         GST Refundable                           8.03
            Cash                                           135.40
            Petty Cash                                      50.00
         Cheque 419 to replenish petty cash,
         vouchers 1–14, and to decrease fund.
```

In this example, the fund is only replenished with enough cash to reach the new value of $150. Petty cash is credited since the amount of the fund is being decreased.

1. What is the purpose of an internal control system?

2. Explain the difference between administrative controls and accounting controls.

3. Why is control of cash necessary?

4. What items are included when cash control is discussed?

5. What type of business must consider cash control systems?

6. What is the first principle of cash control?

7. How can the customer assist in the control of cash when an over-the-counter cash sale is made?

8. What is the purpose of prenumbering source documents?

9. What should be done with cancelled or voided cash sales slips in a prenumbered system?

10. What is a cash float?

11. The day's cash total is $982.40. The sales slips total $984.05. Is the cash short or over and by how much?

12. (a) Is a cash shortage recorded as a debit or a credit in the Cash Short and Over account?
    (b) How is an overage recorded?

13. The Cash Short and Over account has a debit balance of $28.60 at the end of a fiscal period. Is this considered a revenue or an expense? Does it increase or decrease net income?

14. Who receives the two copies of the deposit slip?

15. When all the day's cash receipts are deposited, both the company's records and the bank's record show the cash the company has received on that day. How is this an advantage for the company?

16. Give an advantage of making all payments by cheque.

17. How is a separation of duties achieved when making cash payments by cheque?

18. What is the purpose of a petty cash fund?

19. How does the petty cash voucher prove that a legitimate payment was made?

20. One cash control procedure states that all payments must be made by cheque. Explain how the petty cash fund is designed so that this principle is followed.

21. What type of account is Petty Cash?

22. Some of the following practices contribute to a strong cash control system and some weaken the system. Identify each as a strength or a weakness and explain your reasons.

    (a) Any cash shortage or overage in the daily cash proof is added to or removed from petty cash.
    (b) All cash receipts are deposited daily.
    (c) Cheques are issued for all cash payments other than petty cash disbursements.
    (d) All payments under $150 are made through the petty cash fund.
    (e) Cheques received through the mail are listed and recorded by the accounts receivable clerk.

1. The change fund for Lanark Florist consists of:

BILLS	COINS
2 × $20	6 × $2
3 × $10	13 × $1
6 × $ 5	24 × 25¢
	25 × 10¢
	20 × 5¢
	50 × 1¢

The cash on hand for Lanark Florist consists of:

BILLS	COINS
1 × $50	20 × $2
12 × $20	42 × $1
15 × $10	40 × 25¢
22 × $ 5	33 × 10¢
	50 × 5¢
	57 × 1¢

The calculator tape of the day's cash sales slips for Lanark Florist consists of:

Date: March 8, 2008
Cash Sales Slips: 671–714
Total: $511.92

(a) Remove the $135 change fund from the cash on hand and prepare a deposit slip for account no. 36104-13 at TD Canada Trust.
(b) Prepare the daily cash proof.

2. Prepare the journal entry to record the daily cash proofs prepared for exercise 1.

3. A petty cash fund was established with $150. At present, the petty cash box contains:

Bills	Coins	Vouchers
1 × $20	2 × $1	7 totalling $49.75
4 × $10	3 × $2	
6 × $ 5		

Have any errors been made in the handling of the petty cash?

4. Edmonton Supply Co. decides to establish a petty cash fund. The office supervisor is chosen to be responsible for petty cash. The accountant issues Cheque 213 for $200 on Nov. 1 and gives it to the supervisor to establish the fund. Record the $200 cheque in a General Journal.

5. On November 3, a summary of vouchers in a petty cash box shows:

Office Supplies Expense	$ 63.25
N. Henry, Drawings	80.00
Donations Expense	25.00
Delivery Expense	18.60
Miscellaneous Expense	12.15
Total	$199.00

In a General Journal form, record the $199 cheque issued by the accountant to replenish the petty cash fund.

6. On June 1, Tweed Photo Store decided to begin using a petty cash fund. A cheque for $150 was issued and cashed. The $150 cash was given to the receptionist who was to act as petty cashier. The receptionist/petty cashier was told to obtain authorized vouchers for all payments. The petty cash was to be replenished when the balance in the cash box reached $25. When this happened, a summary of vouchers was to be prepared and given to the accountant.

(a) Record the $150 cheque to establish the fund on June 1.
(b) On June 15, this summary was prepared:
   Prepare the entry to replenish the petty cash.

A. Perretta, Drawings	$ 40.00
Delivery Expense	25.60
Miscellaneous Expense	23.55
Office Supplies Expense	29.35
GST Refundable	7.75
Total	$126.25

(c) It was decided to increase the amount of the petty cash fund from $150 to $175. A cheque for $25 was issued. Record this cheque.

7. If only one cheque were issued in 6(b) and (c) to both replenish and increase the fund, how would the cheque be recorded in a General Journal?

8. June 30 was the end of the fiscal year for Tweed Photo Store. The following summary of vouchers from the petty cash fund was prepared:

Office Supplies Expense	$ 55.34
Miscellaneous Expense	29.75
Delivery Expense	21.25
A. Perretta, Drawings	25.00
GST Refundable	7.16
	$138.50

(a) Record the cheque issued to replenish the petty cash fund on June 30.
(b) Why was the fund replenished even though it still contained a substantial amount of cash?

UNIT 24   Checking Cash Records

Learning Objectives

After reading this unit, discussing the applicable review questions, and completing the applications exercises, you will be able to do the following:

1. **EXPLAIN** audit, bank debit memo, bank credit memo, NSF cheque, electronic funds transfer (EFT), cancelled cheque, outstanding cheque, and reconciliation statement.

2. **PREPARE** a reconciliation statement.

3. **PREPARE** journal entries involving banking transactions.

CONCLUDING CASH CONTROL PROCEDURES

In Unit 23, we examined the first six cash control procedures. Now, in this unit, we will look at the two concluding procedures.

Procedure 7: Periodic Audit

Periodically, a check or an **audit** is made to determine that all cash is properly accounted for. Any system, no matter how complicated or foolproof, can break down. Those involved in the system can devise ways to break the system. People can get together and contrive to defraud a company. The periodic — often unannounced — audit is designed to thwart such attempts.

> An audit is a periodic check on the accuracy of an accounting system.

An auditor, employed either by the company or by an outside accounting firm, is given the task of checking the company records. Transactions are traced from their source documents to their posting in the ledgers. Invoices and deposit slips are checked for accuracy. As you learned when studying Procedure 2, prenumbered documents should be used to record cash. However, if a check is not made to ensure that all documents and cash are accounted for, the system breaks down.

EXAMINING THE BANKING CONNECTION

Procedure 8 will involve making sure that a company's record of its money agrees with the bank's record of the company's money. This requires an understanding of the banking connection or, in other words, an understanding of the relationship between a bank and its depositors. What is the relationship between the bank and a company or person who deposits money? Do banks follow the same accounting rules and the same theory of debits and credits as everyone else? The following example is a good illustration of the banking connection. Note: GST and PST have been excluded from these transactions to simplify the examples.

Halifax Printers Ltd. makes cash sales of $3250 and deposits the $3250 in a savings account at Royal Bank of Canada. In the books of Halifax Printers Ltd., the following occurs, as shown in T-account form:

Halifax Printers' Books

Cash		Sales	
3 250			3 250

Through this transaction, Halifax Printers Ltd. has more money: Its Cash account increases (debit) and its Sales account increases (credit). When Royal Bank of Canada receives the deposit, its books also change, as shown by the following T-accounts:

Royal Bank of Canada's Books

Cash		Halifax Printers Ltd.	
3 250			3 250

Through this transaction, Royal Bank of Canada has more money: Its asset Cash increases (debit). The bank *owes* this $3250 to Halifax Printers Ltd.; in other words, Halifax Printers Ltd. is an account payable on the bank's books. At any time, the depositor can demand the money owing and withdraw cash from the account. The bank records the debt by placing a credit of $3250 in the liability account, Halifax Printers Ltd.

Transactions Involving the Bank's Source Documents

Some of the bank's source documents are the same as those of other companies. For example, banks receive purchase invoices and write cheques. The source document that is evidence that a depositor has withdrawn money from the bank is the *withdrawal slip*. The *deposit slip* is the source document proving that money was deposited by a depositor. Two other source documents commonly used by banks are the *bank credit memo* and the *bank debit memo*. Transactions involving these two documents follow.

A bank debit memo is a source document indicating a decrease in a depositor's account.

Bank Debit Memo

To give notice of a service charge of $25 for cashing cheques on Halifax Printers' account, Royal Bank of Canada issues the debit memo shown in Figure 10-8. As shown in the T-accounts following Figure 10-8, the bank deducts the $25 by debiting Halifax's account. Remember, a liability decreases on the debit side.

FIGURE 10-8

A bank debit memo is the source document prepared when the bank decreases a customer's account.

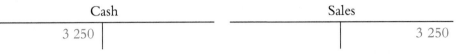

ROYAL BANK OF CANADA

26189-57   November 17, 2009
    Account Number   Date

DEBIT   Service charge for month $25

Authorized by **M.J.**   Checked by *R.W.*   Entry made by **D.P.**

This slip must be initialled by an authorized signing officer.

Royal Bank of Canada's Books

Halifax Printers Ltd.

25.00	3 250.00

A depositor's account is a liability of the bank. Service charges decrease the liability of the bank.

When the depositor, Halifax Printers Ltd., receives the debit memo, the following changes are made in its books:

Halifax Printers' Books

Cash			Bank Charges Expense	
3 250.00	25.00		25.00	

Since this transaction is a payment, it is recorded in the Cash Payments Journal of Halifax Printers Ltd..

Bank Credit Memo

If Halifax Printers Ltd. has a savings account, it will earn interest that is periodically calculated by the bank. Suppose interest amounting to $41.85 has been earned by Halifax Printers Ltd. This means that the bank owes Halifax Printers more money and the bank will increase the amount in its liability account, Halifax Printers Ltd.

Royal Bank of Canada's Books

Halifax Printers Ltd.

25.00	3 250.00
	41.85

A **bank credit memo** (Figure 10-9) is completed and serves to instruct the bank's clerk to increase the Halifax Printers account. A copy of the memo is sent to Halifax Printers to inform the company that its bank account has been increased.

ROYAL BANK OF CANADA

November 17, 2009
Date

CREDIT Halifax Printers Ltd.
        $41.85   Interest earned on term deposit.
        Deposit to Halifax Printers Ltd.'s account   26189-57.

R. Cummings

FIGURE 10-9
A bank credit memo is the source document prepared when the bank increases a customer's account.

When the depositor, Halifax Printers Ltd., receives the credit memo, it will change its accounts as follows:

Halifax Printers' Books

Cash			Interest Earned	
3 250.00	25.00			41.85
41.85				

This transaction represents cash received and is recorded in the Cash Receipts Journal. After the debit and credit transactions, what is the balance in the bank's liability account, Halifax Printers Ltd.? What is the balance in Halifax Printers' Cash account?

A company's Cash account should, theoretically, always have the same balance as the bank's record of the company's bank account. However, in actual practice this is rarely the situation. We will now look at Procedure 8 to see what is done to determine if the bank's records agree with the depositor's records.

Procedure 8: Monthly Bank Reconciliation

Personal Chequing Account Reconciliation

Joy and Dennis Richards are a young couple striving to make ends meet. Because they are making payments on their new home and on furniture, they have little money left over for savings. Several months ago, they received telephone calls from their insurance company and the company holding their house mortgage. Both companies said that the cheques given to them by Joy and Dennis were **NSF** — that is, the cheques had been returned by the bank with the explanation that there were **not sufficient funds** in the Richards' account to cash the cheques.

> An NSF cheque is one that cannot be paid because there are not sufficient funds in the account of the person who wrote the cheque.

The Richards were quite upset because, according to their records, there was enough money in their bank account to cover the cheques. They called the bank and suggested that the bank had made an error. They were right. Somehow, the combined deposit for both their paycheques had ended up in someone else's account! Do banks make errors? Of course they do! People who work in banks are human and can make mistakes just like anyone else. Can you remember instances of banks making errors in your own or your family's bank account? The Richards felt good about discovering this error in their account because it demonstrated that they kept a good record of their bank account balance. Let's look at their account records for the month of December. This will illustrate how the Richards always check the accuracy of the bank's records by observing Procedure 8.

The Richards have a joint personal chequing account at Canada Bank. They use this account to make payments for their personal expenses such as mortgage payments, utilities, and charge accounts. Every month, the bank sends them a bank statement and returns their cancelled cheques. At the end of December, the Richards received from the bank the bank statement shown in Figure 10-10 on page 385. According to the bank statement, the Richards' balance was $1521.45. Enclosed with the bank statement were four **cancelled cheques**, numbered 94, 95, 96, and 97. (Figure 10-11 on page 385).

> Cancelled cheques are cheques that have been cashed by the bank.

The cheque book provided to the Richards by the bank included cheque record pages as shown in Figure 10-12. These provided the Richards with a record of cheques written, deposits made, and the balance. According to their cheque record, the Richards had a December balance of $1672.72. Which was correct — the bank statement balance of $1521.45, the Richards' balance of $1672.72, or neither?

FIGURE 10-10
Bank statement received by
the Richards

CANADA BANK

Joy and Dennis Richards
792 Cannon Street
Hamilton, ON
L7P 2E4

ACCOUNT NUMBER
4258-91

STATEMENT OF	FROM	TO	PAGE
Personal Chequing Account	Dec. 1, 2008	Dec. 31, 2008	1

			DATE		
DESCRIPTION	DEBITS	CREDITS	M	D	BALANCE
Balance forward			07	01	486.79
Deposit		2800.00	07	02	3 286.79
Cheque 94	22.84		07	05	3 263.95
Cheque 95	980.00		07	07	2 283.95
Cheque 96	499.00		07	11	1 784.95
Cheque 97	250.00		07	22	1 534.95
SC	13.50		07	29	1 521.45

NO. OF DEBITS	TOTAL AMOUNT OF DEBITS	NO. OF CREDITS	TOTAL AMOUNT OF CREDITS	NO. OF ENCLOSURES
5	1 765.34	1	2 800.00	4

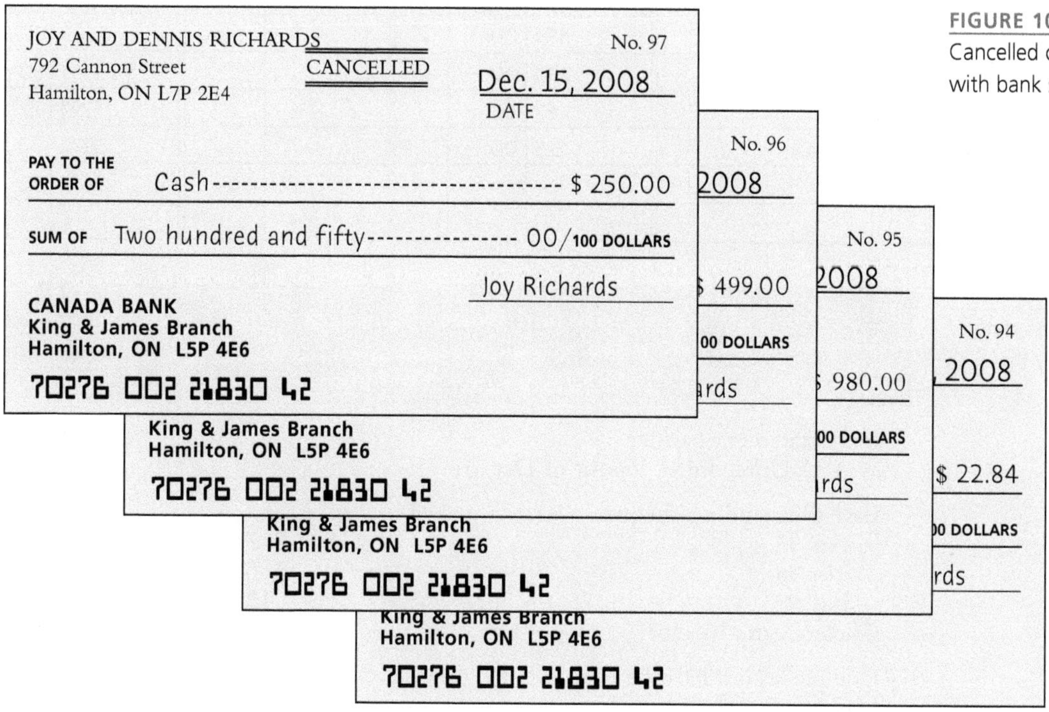

FIGURE 10-11
Cancelled cheques enclosed
with bank statement ·

JOY AND DENNIS RICHARDS   No. 97
792 Cannon Street   CANCELLED
Hamilton, ON L7P 2E4   Dec. 15, 2008
                                           DATE

PAY TO THE
ORDER OF   Cash------------------------------ $ 250.00

SUM OF   Two hundred and fifty---------------- 00/100 DOLLARS

                                  Joy Richards

CANADA BANK
King & James Branch
Hamilton, ON L5P 4E6

7027�6 00� 2⑱830 42

No. 96
2008
$ 499.00
00 DOLLARS
rds

King & James Branch
Hamilton, ON L5P 4E6

7027⑥ 00�", 2⑱830 42

No. 95
2008
$ 980.00
00 DOLLARS
rds

King & James Branch
Hamilton, ON L5P 4E6

7027⑥ 00⑰ 2⑱830 42

No. 94
2008
$ 22.84
00 DOLLARS
rds

King & James Branch
Hamilton, ON L5P 4E6

7027⑥ 00⑰ 2⑱830 42

Preparing the Personal Bank Reconciliation Statement

To determine the correct balance, the Richards did the following:

(1) In their cheque record (Figure 10-12), they ticked off (✔) each of the cancelled cheques returned by the bank. The three unticked ones were **outstanding cheques**; that is, they were cheques that had been issued but had not yet been cashed by the bank. Cheques 93, 98, and 99 were outstanding.

Outstanding cheques are cheques issued but not yet cashed by the bank.

(2) They matched and ticked off the deposits on the bank statement with deposits in their cheque book record. The last deposit of $500 was not shown in the bank statement — probably because the statement was being prepared and mailed before the Richards made the deposit.

(3) They looked for items that appeared on the bank statement but not on their records. The Richards then prepared a **reconciliation statement** (Figure 10-13), which brought their records into agreement with the bank's records. This statement indicated that their correct balance was $1659.22.

A reconciliation statement brings into agreement the bank's records with the depositor's records.

(4) After preparing the reconciliation statement, the Richards record the service charges on their cheque record. They did this by recording the $13.50 SC (service charge) in the Amount of Cheque column on their cheque record. Their new balance in the cheque record was then $1659.22.

FIGURE 10-12

Page from the Richards' cheque book showing their record of banking transactions

CHEQUE NO.	DATE	DESCRIPTION OF TRANSACTION	AMOUNT OF CHEQUE		✔	AMOUNT OF DEPOSIT		BALANCE	
	Dec. 1	Balance forward						486	79
	2	Deposit			✔	2800	00	3286	79
93	2	MasterCard	175	15				3111	64
94	3	Bell Canada	22	84	✔			3088	80
95	3	Central Mortgage Corp.	980	00	✔			2108	80
96	4	CIAG Insurance	499	00	✔			1609	80
97	15	Cash	250	00	✔			1359	80
98	24	The Bay	62	08				1297	72
99	29	Shell Canada	125	00				1172	72
	31	Deposit				500	00	1672	72

FIGURE 10-13

Bank reconciliation statement prepared by the Richards

Joy and Dennis Richards
Bank Reconciliation Statement
December 31, 2008

Bank statement balance		$1 521.45
Add: Unrecorded deposit of Dec. 31		500.00
		2 021.45
Less: Outstanding cheques		
No. 93	$175.15	
No. 98	62.08	
No. 99	125.00	362.23
Correct bank balance		$1 659.22
Cheque record balance		$1 672.72
Less: Service charges		13.50
Correct cheque book balance		$1 659.22

People like the Richards wisely prepare monthly bank reconciliation statements. This ensures that their records and the bank's records agree. Reconciliation statements will bring to light errors made by the bank or by the depositor. Companies follow similar procedures.

Business Current Account Reconciliation

Remo Wholesalers has a current account with Bank of Montreal. Each month, the bank sends a statement to Remo Wholesalers and encloses cancelled cheques that were paid out of Remo's account. The company accountant compares the bank statement balance with the balance in Remo's books. A reconciliation statement is then prepared to bring the two into agreement. Figure 10-14 is the bank statement received by Remo Wholesalers. It shows a balance of $2592.59 on June 16. Figure 10-15 on pages 389 and 390 is the company's cash records. The Cash account shows a balance of $3219.25 on June 16. Which of the two balances is correct — the bank's or Remo's? Or is neither correct?

FIGURE 10-14

Bank statement received by Remo Wholesalers

BANK OF MONTREAL

Remo Wholesalers
77 Thomas St.
Mississauga, ON
L5M 6W3

ACCOUNT NUMBER
3848-691

STATEMENT OF	FROM	TO	PAGE
Current Account	May 16, 2009	June 15, 2009	1

DESCRIPTION	DEBITS	CREDITS	M	D	BALANCE
Balance forward			05	16	1371.89
EFT—Rent		875.00 ✓	05	17	2246.89
Cheque 134	75.00 ✓		05	17	
Deposit		1500.00 ✓	05	19	3671.89
Cheque 135	284.30 ✓		05	23	3387.59
RI	85.00		05	25	
SC	20.00		05	25	
Deposit		250.00 ✓	05	31	3532.59
Cheque 137	675.00 ✓		06	02	
Cheque 138	2100.00 ✓		06	06	
Deposit		2115.00 ✓	06	09	2872.59
Cheque 139	29.60 ✓		06	12	2842.99
EFT—Insurance	269.00		06	15	
SC	25.00		06	16	2548.99
CM		43.60	06	16	2592.59

NO. OF DEBITS	TOTAL AMOUNT OF DEBITS	NO. OF CREDITS	TOTAL AMOUNT OF CREDITS	NO. OF ENCLOSURES
9	3562.90	5	4783.60	6

Preparing the Business Bank Reconciliation Statement

To determine the correct balance, a bank reconciliation statement is prepared. This statement will bring the bank's balance into agreement with the company's balance to determine the true, or correct, cash balance. These procedures are followed in preparing the bank reconciliation statement:

Subtract outstanding cheques.

(1) Prepare a list of the outstanding cheques. This is done by ticking off in the Cash Payments Journal all the cancelled cheques returned by the bank (see Figure 10-15). Unticked cheques are outstanding; they have not been cashed by the bank. The cancelled cheques are also ticked off on the bank statement debits column (see Figure 10-14). The outstanding cheques (in the case of Remo Wholesalers, Nos. 136, 140, and 141) are subtracted from the bank statement balance on the reconciliation statement to bring the bank's balance into agreement with the company's balance (see Figure 10-16 on page 391).

Add outstanding deposits.

(2) Compare the deposits shown in the cash debit column of the Cash Receipts Journal (see Figure 10-15) with those shown in the credits column of the bank statement (see Figure 10-14). Tick off the deposits on both records. Deposits not recorded on the bank statement are added to the bank statement balance on the reconciliation statement (refer to the $1845 unrecorded June 16 deposit in Figure 10-16).

Add credit memos. Subtract debit memo.

(3) Locate all unticked items on the bank statement. Add unticked items in the credits column to the company's record of the cash balance (on the cheque book stub). In this case, CM, or credit memo, indicates that $43.60 in interest must be added. Subtract the unticked items in the debits column of the bank statement from the company's record of the cash balance (on the cheque book stub). Two items must be subtracted in this example: SC (service charges) of $45 and RI of $85. RI stands for returned item and in this case is a not-sufficient-funds cheque. Note: The $20 service charge under the RI is the bank charge for the NSF cheque. For more information on NSF cheques, see page 392.

(4) Journal entries to adjust the company's Cash account to reflect the unticked items on the bank statement are prepared after the bank reconciliation statement. Adjust both the bank's and the company's balance for any obvious errors. For example, cheque amounts could have been recorded incorrectly or arithmetic errors might have been made. If you have problems in understanding whether the bank's or the company's balance should be adjusted on a bank reconciliation statement, here are a couple of rules to follow:

- Adjust the balance of whoever makes a mistake (the company or the bank).
- Adjust the balance of whoever is last to know about an adjustment (e.g., NSF cheque).

FIGURE 10-15

Remo Wholesalers' cash records

CASH RECEIPTS JOURNAL

PAGE 18

DATE	REF. NO.	CUSTOMER OR ACCOUNT	P.R.	CASH DEBIT	SALES DISCOUNTS DEBIT	ACCOUNTS REC. CREDIT	SALES CREDIT	GST PAYABLE CREDIT	PST PAYABLE CREDIT	OTHER ACCOUNTS CREDIT
2009										
May 19		Deposit		1500.00 ✓						
31				250.00						
		May total		1750.00						
Jun. 9		Deposit		2115.00 ✓						
16				1845.00						
				5710.00						
				(101)						

Deposits made from May 16 to June 16

CASH PAYMENTS JOURNAL

PAGE 23

DATE	CH. NO.	CREDITOR OR ACCOUNT	P.R.	CASH CREDIT	ACCOUNTS PAYABLE DEBIT	GST REFUNDABLE DEBIT	PURCHASES DEBIT	PURCHASES DISCOUNTS CREDIT	OTHER ACCOUNTS DEBIT
2009									
May 17	134			75.00 ✓					
23	135			284.30 ✓					
25	136			85.00					
Jun. 2	137			675.00 ✓					
6	138			2100.00 ✓					
12	139			29.60 ✓					
16	140			81.74					
16	141			532.00					
				3862.64					
				(101)					

Cheques written from May 16 to June 16

ACCOUNT Cash   NO. 101

DATE	PARTICULARS	P.R.	DEBIT	CREDIT	DR. CR.	BALANCE
May 16	Forwarded	✓			DR.	1371.89
Jun. 16	Cash Receipts	CR18	5710.00		DR.	7081.89
16	Cash Payments	CP23		3862.64	DR.	3219.25

Cash account in the General Ledger

FIGURE 10-16

Bank reconciliation statement prepared by Remo Wholesalers

Remo Wholesalers		
Bank Reconciliation Statement		
June 16, 2009		
Bank statement balance		$2 592.59
Add: Unrecorded June 16 deposit		1 845.00
		4 437.59
Less: Outstanding cheques		
No. 136	$ 85.00	
No. 140	81.74	
No. 141	532.00	698.74
Correct bank balance		$3 738.85
Cash balance per ledger		3 219.25
Add: EFT—Rent collection	875.00	
Interest earned (CM)	43.60	918.60
		4 137.85
Less: EFT—Insurance payment	269.00	
Service charges	45.00	
RI (NSF cheque)	85.00	399.00
Correct cash balance		$3 738.85

Figure 10-15 is the bank reconciliation statement prepared after completing the preceding four steps. It shows that the correct Cash account balance is $3738.85.

Journal Entries After Bank Reconciliation

After the reconciliation statement has been prepared, the company's Cash account balance must be brought up-to-date. Remember, Figure 10-15 showed that, according to the company's Cash account, the cash balance was $3219.25. However, the correct balance is $3738.85, as shown on the reconciliation statement. The company's Cash account is brought up-to-date by preparing journal entries for any unrecorded items brought to light by the reconciliation statement. A journal entry decreasing cash is made for items such as service charges, NSF cheques, and interest charged. A journal entry increasing cash is made for an item such as interest earned that was added by the bank.

Service Charges

The bank has deducted $25 for service charges and $269 for the EFT payment of the monthly insurance premium; therefore, in both cases the company should record an expense and decrease its cash. The following entries are made:

Jun. 16	Bank Service Charges Expense	45	
	Cash		45
	To record bank service charges.		
16	Insurance Expense	269	
	Cash		269
	To record insurance premium for the month.		

The following section outlines the procedures for recording NSF cheque service charges.

NSF Cheques

An NSF cheque is usually a customer's cheque that has been deposited by the company but cannot be cashed by the bank because there are not sufficient funds in the customer's bank account. Since the bank cannot collect from the writer of the cheque, it will deduct the amount of the cheque from Remo Wholesalers' account. The company will charge the amount plus the bank service charge back to its customer's account as an account receivable and will try to collect the amount. This entry is made:

Jun. 16	Accounts Receivable/R. Amodeo	105	
	Cash		105
	NSF cheque ($85) and bank charges ($20) charged back to R. Amodeo.		

Interest Earned

Remo Wholesalers has earned $43.60 interest on a term deposit. Since the bank has added the $43.60 to Remo Wholesalers' bank account, the company must now prepare a journal entry to record the $ 43.60. The following entry is made to record the revenue earned and to increase the Cash account:

Jun. 16	Cash	43.60	
	Interest Earned		43.60
	To record interest earned on a term deposit.		

Also, there was an EFT cash receipt ($875) relating to rent income that Remo Wholesalers had earned. The bank added this amount to Remo Wholesalers' bank account; the company must prepare a journal entry to record the $875.

Jun. 16	Cash	875	
	Rent Revenue		875
	To record rental income for the month.		

Interest Expense

In addition to the entries described above, it is sometimes necessary to record interest expense deducted from a company's bank account. Suppose a company has a bank loan and $175 interest is paid each month. When the bank deducts interest for the loan from the company's bank account, this entry is made on the company's books:

Jun. 16	Interest Expense	175	
	Cash		175
	To record interest on the bank loan deducted by the bank.		

SUMMARY

In this chapter, you have learned eight procedures that are used to ensure that a firm has a proper accounting system in place to control cash:

- Procedure 1: Separation of Duties
- Procedure 2: Immediate Listing of Cash Receipts
- Procedure 3: Daily Cash Proof
- Procedure 4: Daily Deposit of Cash
- Procedure 5: Payment by Cheque
- Procedure 6: Petty Cash Procedures
- Procedure 7: Periodic Audit
- Procedure 8: Monthly Bank Reconciliation

ACCOUNTING TERMS

Accounting Controls	Procedures used to protect assets and ensure reliable accounting records. (p. 365)
Administrative Controls	Procedures used to ensure application of company policies and evaluate performance. (p. 365)
Audit	Verification of the accuracy of company records. (p. 381)
Bank Credit Memo	Source document indicating an increase in a depositor's account. (p. 383)
Bank Debit Memo	Source document indicating a decrease in a depositor's account. (p. 382)
Cancelled Cheque	A cheque that has been cashed by the bank. (p. 384)
Cash Proof	Verifies cash on hand equals cash sales slips for the day. (p. 369)
Cash Short and Over	An account used to record the amount of cash over or under the cash proof total each day. (p. 369)
Electronic Funds Transfer	A system to transfer cash using electronic communications. (p. 368)
Imprest System	A system wherein a designated amont of cash is set aside for a specific purpose. For example, the Petty Cash Fund. (p. 374)
NSF (Not Sufficient Funds) Cheque	A cheque that cannot be cashed because there are not sufficient funds in the account of the person who wrote the cheque. (p. 384)
Outstanding Cheque	A cheque that has not been cashed by the bank. (p. 386)
Petty Cash Fund	A small amount of cash kept on hand to make small payments. (p. 374)
Petty Cash Voucher	A signed authorization for petty cash payments. (p. 375)
Prenumbered Sales Slip	Multiple-copy sales slip prepared for each cash sale. (p. 368)
Reconciliation Statement	A statement that brings into agreement the bank's records with the depositor's records. (p. 386)
Replenishing Petty Cash	Bringing the total currency on hand up to the original amount. (p. 375)
Separation of Duties	Duties of employees should be arranged so that one employee verifies the work of another employee. (p. 367)

REVIEW QUESTIONS

1. Explain the role of the auditor.

2. Paul Coté has a savings account with ScotiaBank. In which section of its ledger will the bank locate Coté's account — the asset, liability, owner's equity, revenue, or expense section?

3. Will a debit memo increase or decrease the balance of a depositor's account?

4. Will a credit memo increase or decrease the balance of a depositor's account?

5. In which journal is a bank credit memo recorded? A bank debit memo?

6. What is an NSF cheque?

7. What is a bank statement?

8. What is a cancelled cheque?

9. What is an outstanding cheque?

10. What is an EFT transfer?

11. Some cheques that have been issued will not appear on the bank statement. Explain how such a situation can happen.

12. Some deposits that have been recorded in the depositor's records may not appear on the bank statement. Explain how such a situation can happen.

13. Give examples of certain items that appear on a bank statement but not on the depositor's records.

14. A bank reconciliation statement brings into agreement two sets of records. What are they?

15. Who prepares the bank reconciliation statement, the bank or the depositor?

16. When a company prepares a bank reconciliation statement, to what is the balance on the bank statement compared?

17. What is the General Journal entry to record a customer's cheque returned NSF?

18. Does cash control mean anything more than procedures used to prevent losses from fraud or theft? Explain.

UNIT 24

PROBLEMS: APPLICATIONS

1. Below are the types of reconciling items found on the bank reconciliation:

(a) added to the book balance
(b) deducted from the book balance
(c) added to the bank balance
(d) deducted from the bank balance
(e) omitted from the reconciliation

_____ 1. Cheques 318 and 321 were not among the cancelled cheques returned by the bank.

_____ 2. The bank statement indicated an EFT collection of a note receivable of $1500 with interest of $105.

_____ 3. The bank statement included $32 in monthly service charges.

_____ 4. The bookkeeper discovered an error. A $535 cheque disbursement was recorded as $53.50.

_____ 5. A $500 deposit made by Langdon, Ltd. on April 30 did not appear on the bank statement.

_____ 6. A $400 deposit was recorded by the bookkeeper as $4000.

_____ 7. The bank statement included an NSF cheque from Poirier Pottery, in the amount of $335.

_____ 8. A March 31 deposit, which was included as a deposit in transit on the March 31 bank reconciliation, was recorded by the bank on April 2.

_____ 9. Included in the cancelled cheques returned by the bank were cheques 294 and 297, which had been outstanding on March 31.

_____10. The bank had charged Langdon's account for a cheque written by Langley Ltd., and included it among the cancelled cheques.

Tasks Required:

(a) For each of the above items taken from the records of Langdon Ltd., put a letter in the space provided that identifies the treatment it would receive on the April 30 bank reconciliation.

(b) Circle the letters that would require an adjustment on the books of Langdon Ltd.

2. Record the following transactions in a General Journal for Wellington County Sports Equipment Ltd.:

Nov. 15   Cash sales slips totalled $4130 + $247.80 GST. Cash was deposited.

16   Issued Sales Invoice 317-B to R. Vlasic, terms 2/10, n/30, amount $1700, non-taxable, GST $102.

19   Received bank credit memo for $84 interest earned by the company.

21   Received bank debit memo for $35, plus $2.10 GST, for the annual charge for a safety deposit box.

27   Received cheque from R. Vlasic, for amount owed on Invoice 317-B less $36.04 discount. Cheque was deposited.

30   Received bank debit memo for $25 for service charges on current account.

3. Record the following transactions in a General Journal for Wellington County Sports Equipment Ltd.:

Dec. 1   Received bank credit memo for a $12 000 loan granted and deposited in the company account, term two months, annual interest at 7.5 percent payable monthly.

31   Received bank debit memo for $75 deducted from the company account for interest on the loan.

Jan. 31 Received bank debit memo for $12 075 deducted from the company account ($12 000 repayment of the bank loan, $75 interest on the loan).

4. At April 30, Mary and Greg Faux have a balance of $635.54 in their cheque record. The bank statement shows a balance of $1242.71. The bank statement contains a service charge deduction of $12 and an EFT receipt for interest earned on an investment certificate on April 15 for $235.72. This deposit is not recorded in the Faux'a cheque record. Cheque 51 for $48.60, Cheque 53 for $117.35, and Cheque 54 for $217.50 are outstanding. Prepare the April reconciliation statement.

5. (a) Prepare the July reconciliation statement for V. Best Furniture Co. using the following information:

   Company Records:

   - Cash account balance is $1990.11.
   - These cheques are recorded in the Cash Payments Journal but not on the bank statement:
     No. 161 $49.50   No. 170 $150   No. 176 $75
   - A deposit for $400 was recorded in the Cash Receipts Journal on July 31 but did not appear on the bank statement.

   Bank Statement:

   - Bank statement balance is $1839.86.
   - Bank service charges of $24.75 are shown on the bank statement.

   (b) In a General Journal, record any entries required to bring the company records up-to-date.

6. (a) Prepare the August reconciliation statement for V. Best Furniture Co. using the following information:

   - Cash account balance is $2090.51.
   - Bank statement balance is $1684.51.
   - These cheques were recorded in the Cash Payments Journal but did not appear on the bank statement:
     No. 186 $87   No. 193 $297.30   No. 199   972.30
   - A deposit for $1910 dated July 31 was recorded in the Cash Receipts Journal but did not appear on the bank statement.
   - Service charges of $27.25 are shown on the bank statement.
   - A cheque for $37.50 has been cashed (correctly) by the bank but was incorrectly recorded in the company's Cash Payments Journal as $375.50. The cheque was issued for the purchase of office supplies.
   - An NSF cheque for $143.35 appeared on the bank statement as a returned item. It was deducted by the bank. It had been received from R. Lynch and was recorded in the company's Cash Receipts Journal. A bank charge of $20 was levied.

   (b) In a General Journal, record any entries required to bring the company records up-to-date.

1. Record the following selected transactions on page 61 in a General Journal for Marv's Graphic Designs:

Aug.   1   Established a petty cash fund by issuing Cheque 186 for $200.

     7   Cash sales slips for the week totalled $1800. PST on sales is 8 percent, GST is 6 percent.

     7   The cash proof indicated a shortage of $1.80.

     9   Issued Cheque 187 for $628 plus 6 percent GST for a cash purchase of merchandise from Pentagon Supplies.

   12   Issued sales invoices (all sales tax exempt, terms 2/10, n/30):
No. 951, $500 + $30 to Red Deer Ltd.;
No. 952, $79.80 + $4.79 to Hannah and Zoey Co.;
No. 953, $465 + $27.90 to Lamarr & Family;
No. 954, $720 + $43.20 to S. Wong.

   14   Cash sales slips for the week totalled $2300. PST was $184, GST $138.

   15   Replenished the petty cash and increased it to $250. Issued Cheque 188.
Summary of petty cash vouchers:

Janitorial Services	$85.00
Advertising Expense	51.25
Postage Expense	28.75
Office Supplies Expense	22.50
GST Refundable	8.00

   16   Received a cheque for $82.90 from Hannah and Zoey Co. in payment of Invoice 952 less $1.69 discount.

   17   The cash proof indicated that cash was over by $1.83.

   19   Received a bank debit memo for $82.90 plus $15 service charge. Hannah and Zoey's cheque was returned NSF.

   20   Purchased merchandise on account from Fordham Ltd., $765 + $45.90 GST, terms 30 days.

   22   Received a cheque for $483.04 from J. Lamarr & Family in payment of Invoice 953 less the applicable discount.

   28   Received a cheque for $530 from Red Deer Ltd. in payment of Invoice 951.

   30   The monthly bank reconciliation was prepared. The bank statement included a debit of $27 for bank service charges.

   31   Replenished the petty cash fund. Issued Cheque 189. On this date the fund had $6.22 in cash and the following vouchers: Entertainment Expense $75.88, Delivery Expense $53, Marv Williams, Drawings $50, Postage Expense $31.45, Computer Repairs Expense $21.65 and GST Refundable $10.40.

2. The following data have been gathered for Brandon Marketing, Inc.:

(a) The November 30 bank balance was $3900.

(b) The bank statement included $45 in service charges.

(c) There was an EFT deposit of $1415 on the bank statement for the monthly rent from a tenant.

(d) Cheques 939, 941and 943 for $89, $146, and $235, respectively, were not among the cancelled cheques returned with the statement.

(e) The November 30 deposit of $425 did not appear on the bank statement.

(f) The bookkeeper had erroneously recorded a $4500 cheque as $4050. The cheque was written to an office supply store as a payment on account.

(g) Included with the cancelled cheques was a cheque written by Brandon Consulting Ltd., for $175, which was deducted from Brandon Marketing's account.

(h) The bank statement also included an NSF cheque written by Lucenti Enterprises, for a $285 payment on account.

(i) There was an EFT debit on the bank statement for the monthly insurance premium, $375.

(j) The cash account showed a balance of $2852 on November 30.

Tasks Required:

(a) Prepare the November 30, 2008, bank reconciliation for Brandon Marketing, Inc.

(b) Prepare the necessary journal entries.

3. The information listed below pertains to Chandler Construction, Inc., for August 2009:

(1) Balance per bank on August 31, $8725.

(2) Bank collected Note Receivable, $520, plus accrued interest of $25; a collection fee of $15 was charged to Chandler Construction's bank account.

(3) An August 31 deposit of $750 did not appear on the bank statement.

(4) Cheques 1375, 1379 and 1383 for $87, $185 and $401, respectively, were not included with the bank statement.

(5) Bank error: an EFT debit of $315 on August 25 was in error; Chandler Lumber Company's account should have been debited, not Chandler Construction's account.

(6) EFT credit of $1475 for rent, August 1.

(7) NSF cheque returned by bank, $179.

(8) EFT debit of $275 for monthly insurance premium, August 15.

(9) Interest earned on bank balance during August, $42.

(10) Book error: a cheque for $548 for August's utility bill was recorded as $845 in the Cash Payments Journal.

(11) Bank service charges for the month, $25.

Tasks Required:

Determine the August 31 cash ledger balance for Chandler Construction, Inc.

4. Listed on the next page are items from the bank reconciliation for Windmill Garage for the month ending June 30, 2010:

(1) A $635 deposit dated June 29 did not appear on the bank statement.

(2) Bank service charges for the month were $28.

(3) The bank returned a customer's NSF cheque for $287. The cheque was from A. Jones for payment in full of her Accounts Receivable balance. The bank charged an NSF cheque fee of $20.

(4) Interest earned on Windmill's bank balance for the month was $38.

(5) The bank balance on June 30 was $3625.

(6) The bank collected a Note Receivable for $1700. The bank charged a $20 collection fee. Interest earned on the note was $135.

(7) Bank error: the bank debited Windmill Garage's bank account for $1819. The account of Windmere Motors should have been debited.

(8) Cheques totalling $783 were not among the cancelled cheques returned by the bank.

(9) Book error: a $425 cheque written to Auto Supply Store for three new batteries was recorded at $45 in the Cash Payments Journal.

Tasks Required:

Record in the General Journal any entries that are required to bring Windmill Garage's records up to date as of June 30, 2010.

5. You have just been hired by a small company to work in the accounting department. As an accounting graduate, one of your tasks is to prepare the monthly bank reconciliation. The person you are replacing, Jas Rohini, did not have an accounting background and had many problems preparing the bank reconciliation every month. Presented below is the bank reconciliation for September 30, 2010. It does balance, but there are a few mistakes in it!

Fay's Wholesale Flowers **Bank Reconciliation** **September 30, 2010**		
Book balance		$31 039
Add: Error cheque 1119		171
		31 210
Less: Service charges	$ 25	
Interest	38	
EFT receipt	175	
EFT payment	1 795	2 033
Correct cash balance		29 177
Bank balance		32 997
Add: EFT receipt		175
		33 172
Less: NSF cheque	299	
NSF cheque charge	21	
Outstanding cheques:		
1124	480	
814	1 400	
EFT payment	1 795	$ 3 995
Correct bank balance		$29 177

Additional information:

(1) Cheque 814 was incorrectly debited to Fay's Wholesale Flowers' account by the bank. The account of Fern's Wholesale Bakery should have been charged.

(2) The interest of $38 was interest revenue as indicated on the bank statement, not interest expense as Jas thought.

(3) The error in cheque 1119 was a book error. The cheque was written for the monthly utilities expense, $365, but was recorded in the Cash Payments Journal as $536.

(4) The EFT receipt was an Accounts Receivable collection from customer, Louise Chang, as payment in full on her outstanding balance.

(5) The EFT payment was for the monthly rent.

(6) Cheque 1110 for $2,374 is still outstanding from the August 31 bank statement. Cheques 1118 and 1120 for $8000 and $4000 respectively, were issued September 29 and were not returned with the bank statement.

(7) The NSF cheque for $299 was received from Sam Cabral as a partial payment on his Accounts Receivable balance. The bank charged Fay's Wholesale Flowers an NSF service fee of $21.

(8) The monthly bank service charges are $25.

(9) The Cash ledger account is as follows:

CASH

Aug. 30	Bal.	31 039	52 667	CPJ	Sep. 30
Sep. 30	CRJ	41 000			
Sep. 30	Bal.	19 372			

Tasks required:

(a) Prepare the correct bank reconciliation for Fay's Wholesale Flowers for September 30, 2010.

(b) In the General Journal, page 73, record any entries that are necessary to bring the company's records up to date.

6. Means Art Gallery Ltd. has a current account with Scotiabank. The May bank statement that follows was sent to Means Art Gallery Ltd. by the bank.

   The bank also sent the following four cancelled cheques — Nos. 301, 303, 304, and 305 — and an NSF cheque for $75 which had been deposited by Means Art Gallery Ltd. The NSF cheque was from Bloom & Co. Inc., a customer of Means Art Gallery Ltd. A bank debit memo for $20 (NSF charge) was also sent.

Cheques:

MEANS ART GALLERY LTD. 575 Goulding St. Winnipeg, MB R3G 2S3	CANCELLED
	301 May 1, 2008
	No. Date

PAY TO THE
ORDER OF   Malcolm Enterprises --------------------------------- $ 200.00

SUM OF   Two hundred ----------------------------- 00/**100 DOLLARS**

J. Means

SCOTIABANK   MEANS ART GALLEY, LTD.
319 Graham Ave.
Winnipeg, MB   R3C 2Y5

CANCELLED

MEANS ART GALLERY LTD.
575 Goulding St.
Winnipeg, MB   R3G 2S3

303   May 15, 2008
No.   Date

PAY TO THE
ORDER OF   Salaries -- $ 1,200.00

SUM OF   One thousand two hundred----------------- 00/100 DOLLARS

SCOTIABA
Winnipeg,

CANCELLED

MEANS ART GALLERY LTD.
575 Goulding St.
Winnipeg, MB   R3G 2S3

304   May 16, 2008
No.   Date

PAY TO THE
ORDER OF   T. Clements--- $ 50.00

SUM OF   Fifty--- 00/100 DOLLARS

CANCELLED

MEANS ART GALLERY LTD.
575 Goulding St.
Winnipeg, MB   R3G 2S3

305   May 23, 2008
No.   Date

PAY TO THE
ORDER OF   Clayton Ltd. ------------------------------------ $ 17.00

SUM OF   Seventeen ----------------------------------- 00/100 DOLLARS

J. Means
MEANS ART GALLEY, LTD.

SCOTIABANK
319 Graham Ave.
Winnipeg, MB   R3C 2Y5

BLOOM & CO. INC.
99 Jefferson Ave.
Winnipeg, MB   R2V 0M2

PURSUANT TO CLEARING RULES THIS ITEM
MAY NOT BE CLEARED AGAIN UNLESS CERTIFIED

576   May 8, 2008
No.   Date

PAY TO THE
ORDER OF   Means Art Gallery Ltd.----------------------------- $ 75.00

SUM OF   Seventy-five -------------------------------- 00/100 DOLLARS

A. Bloom
BLOOM & CO. INC.

SCOTIABANK
9 Keewatin St.,
Winnipeg, MB   R3E 3B6

Bank Statement:

SCOTIABANK

Means Art Gallery Ltd.
575 Goulding St.
Winnipeg, MB
R3G 2S3

ACCOUNT NUMBER
81720-00

STATEMENT OF	FROM	TO	PAGE
Current Account	Apr. 30, 2008	May 31, 2008	1

			DATE		
DESCRIPTION	**DEBITS**	**CREDITS**	**M**	**D**	**BALANCE**
Balance forward			04	30	2,690.50
Deposit		700.00	05	01	3,390.50
Deposit		200.00	05	05	3,590.50
Cheque 301	200.00		05	08	3,390.50
Deposit		75.00	05	10	3,465.50
Cheque 303	1,200.00		05	15	2,265.50
Deposit		225.00	05	19	2,490.50
Deposit		600.00	05	22	3,090.50
Cheque 304	50.00		05	23	3,040.50
Cheque 305	17.00		05	28	3,023.50
SC	22.25		05	29	3,001.25
RI	75.00		05	31	2,926.25
DM	20.00		05	31	2,906.25

NO. OF DEBITS	TOTAL AMOUNT OF DEBITS	NO. OF CREDITS	TOTAL AMOUNT OF CREDITS	NO. OF ENCLOSURES
6	1,584.25	5	1,800.00	5

Company Records:

The cash records kept by Means Art Gallery Ltd. are illustrated below:

| | CASH RECEIPTS JOURNAL | | | | PAGE | 14 |

DATE	REF. NO.	CUSTOMER OR ACCOUNT	P.R.	CASH DEBIT	SALES DISCOUNTS DEBIT	ACCOUNTS REC. CREDIT	SALES CREDIT	GST PAYABLE CREDIT	PST PAYABLE CREDIT	OTHER ACCOUNTS CREDIT
2008										
May 1		Cash Sales		700.00						
5		J. Bentley		200.00						
10		Bloom & Co. Inc.		75.00						
19		T. Gabriel		225.00						
22		Cash Sales		600.00						
31		Cash Sales		450.00						
				2 250.00						
				(101)						

CASH PAYMENTS JOURNAL									PAGE 17
DATE	CH. NO.	CREDITOR OR ACCOUNT	P.R.	CASH CREDIT	ACCOUNTS PAYABLE DEBIT	GST REFUND-ABLE DEBIT	PURCHASES DEBIT	PURCHASES DISC. CREDIT	OTHER ACCOUNTS CREDIT
2008									
May 1	301	Purchases		200.00					
8	302	A. Baker		100.00					
15	303	Salaries		1 200.00					
16	304	T. Clements		50.00					
23	305	Supplies		17.00					
24	306	Aster Ltd.		250.00					
30	307	Purchases		170.00					
				1 987.00					
				(101)					

ACCOUNT Cash						NO. 101
DATE	PARTICULARS	P.R.	DEBIT	CREDIT	DR. CR.	BALANCE
2008						
May 1	Forwarded	✓			DR.	2 690.50
31	Cash Receipts	CR14	2 250.00		DR.	4 940.50
31	Cash Payments	CP17		1 987.00	DR.	2 953.50

Tasks Required:

(a) Prepare the bank reconciliation statement dated May 31, 2008.
(b) Prepare the necessary journal entries.

CASE 1
Cash Shortages

CHAPTER 10

CASE STUDIES

You are an accountant for The Jones Store, a department store. Sales for the year are $5 million and 25 cashiers work in the store. At the end of the year, you determine that there are 150 debits that account for $148 in the Cash Short and Over account. There are 124 credits to that account for $59.

(a) Should you be concerned about the resulting $89 net debit in Cash Short and Over?
(b) What action, if any, would you recommend to the company's senior accountant?

CASE 2
Embezzlement!

Mary McBride has worked for many years at Burnaby Bank. During that time, she has performed many functions—was a teller, counted cash at other teller windows, recorded many transactions in the accounting records, worked late many evenings to finish any postings from the day's deposits and filled in at the last minute if another teller became ill. Mary does not like to take any vacation time or even a sick day! She is very well liked by the other employees and is a valuable, trusted employee. The bank manager is a personal friend.

Recently, it was decided to have a formal audit done—the bank has been operating for five years and this would be the first formal one to be done. Smith and Jones, both CAs, were hired for this audit. Mary was upset—she thought that the accounting records were correct and felt that the money spent on this audit should be put to other use.

As Smith and Jones were examining the bank's records they discovered that $100 000 cash was missing! There were many unauthorized cash payments for office supplies and other small expenses, as well as adjustments made to customer accounts using credit memos. Also, there were numerous "cash shorts" from the tellers' drawers. Since Mary was involved in everything at the bank, it appeared that she was the culprit! Her friend, the bank manager was astounded. How did all of these things happen and no one noticed?

CASE 3
Petty Cash System

You are the assistant to the office manager of a very large company. She asks you to develop a system and procedures for a petty cash fund. At present, there is no such fund. Prepare a report with a recommended system. Include in your report an analysis of which cash principles are used in your system.

CASE 4
Cash Control

Barbara Jones performed all the accounting tasks for Hannah Sales, a small home accessories store. Finding herself in financial difficulty, she devised the following plan to steal money from the business.

She believed she could, at any time, remove an amount of cash from the daily deposit and replace the cash with a cheque received in the mail from a customer. She would not include the cheque in her list of cheques received for the day. To prevent the customer from complaining about an incorrect amount owing, the following General Journal entry would be made by Barbara for the amount of the cheque and posted to the ledger accounts affected:

Sales Returns and Allowances	75	
Accounts Receivable/Customer Account		75
To record goods returned today.		

(a) Would Hannah Sales' General Ledger be out of balance?
(b) Would the control account balance to the schedule of accounts receivable?
(c) Would this action be discovered or prevented by current cash control procedures? Explain.
(d) What are the weaknesses in Hannah Sales' cash control system?
(e) What procedures would you implement in a small business such as Hannah Sales to have effective cash control?

ETHICS CASE
Periodic Audits

Faye Borowski worked for five years as a receptionist-secretary for Dr. P. Chau, a dentist. Her duties included billing patients, receiving cash from customers, issuing receipts, depositing money, and handling the patients' accounts. One day, Faye reduced a patient's account to zero by mistake. A month later, the patient paid the $50 that was actually still owing. Faye *pocketed* the $50.

Yielding to temptation, Faye began to embezzle money regularly from Dr. Chau. When money was received from patients, she would lower the patients' accounts and prepare a bank deposit but keep some of the cash for herself. The deposit was always lower than the cash received. For example, one week she received $1900 from customers, kept $200, and deposited $1700. She lowered the customers' accounts by $1900. Over a period of 30 weeks she stole $3500. She is now awaiting trial on criminal charges! *How was she caught?*

Explore these Web sites for information banking and cash control.

CHAPTER 10

INTERNET RESOURCES

1. **Canadian Bankers Association   www.cba.ca**

   This site provides consumers and businesses with information and free brochures on topics such as: Debit Card Security; Identity Theft; Financial Information for Youth; Small Business Services. Also available online is a glossary of financial, banking, and investment terms.

2. **Canada Business Service Centre   www.cbsc.org**

   This site leads you to a dedicated site for each province. There you can obtain business information such as: Preventing Theft; Dealing with your Banker; Bad Cheque Control; Starting and Operating a Business.

3. **Association of Certified Fraud Examiners   www.acfe.com**

   Go to this site and do a search for "cash control." You will discover a number of real cases that illustrate the principles of cash control taught in this chapter.

4. **University of Chicago**
   www.adminet.uchicago.edu/admincompt/pettycashmanual
   This site provides the petty cash guidelines followed by a university.

5. **University of California   www.audit.ucsb.edu/ccontrol.html**
   This site provides the cash control guidelines followed by a university.

Completing the Accounting Cycle for a Merchandising Company

 UNIT 25   Adjusting the Books

Learning Objectives

After reading this unit, discussing the applicable review questions, and completing the applications exercises, you will be able to do the following:

1. **EXPLAIN** why adjustments are necessary.

2. **PREPARE** the adjustment for bad debts using the income statement method and the balance sheet method.

3. **PREPARE** entries for uncollectible accounts.

4. **PREPARE** adjustments for accrued expenses.

5. **PREPARE** adjustments for accrued revenue.

In Chapter 6, you were introduced to the accounting procedures performed at the end of the fiscal period for a service business. These included adjustments, financial statements, adjusting and closing entries, and the post-closing trial balance. A service business, Management Consultant Services, was used to explain the adjusting and closing procedures. Adjustments were prepared for prepaid expenses such as supplies and prepaid rent and to record amortization expense on capital assets.

You will remember that a service company sells a service to its customers. For example, a movie theatre sells entertainment; a dentist sells a dental health service; Sylvan Learning® sells tutoring services.

A merchandising company sells merchandise to its customers. For example, a clothing store sells clothes; a sporting goods store sells sports equipment; La-Z-Boy® stores sell chairs and other furniture.

A merchandising firm must prepare adjustments for the same reason that a service company must — so that the financial statements will be accurate. Adjustments to prepaid expense accounts and amortization on capital assets are similar to those prepared for a service business. However, additional adjustments are necessary for merchandising companies. These include adjusting the Merchandise Inventory account and recording purchases of merchandise at the end of the fiscal period.

Some new adjustments that apply to both service and merchandising companies will be outlined in this chapter. These are the adjustment for **bad debts** and the adjustments for recording, at the end of the accounting periods, amounts that have not yet been recorded.

> Bad debts are uncollectible amounts owed by customers.

INTRODUCING THE BAD DEBTS ADJUSTMENT

Almost all companies and many consumers buy on credit at some time. They buy when they need or desire goods, and they pay when they have cash or according to the terms of sale. Our economy relies heavily on credit — there are more credit sales made than cash sales. In many product areas, a business cannot survive if it does not offer customers the opportunity to *buy now and pay later*. Unfortunately, however, sometimes customers do not pay — leading to uncollectible accounts. This can mean problems for a company making credit sales. However, the increase in sales revenues generally is considered to be an advantage that outweighs the disadvantage of non-paying customers.

> Selling on credit is necessary for most companies.

Accounting Problems Caused by Bad Debts

Accounting problems arise when customers do not pay their debts and the resulting loss of revenue becomes a **bad debts expense** for the company. Let us take, as an example, two consecutive years in the business affairs of Robeson's Department Store.

Suppose that, in 2009, Robeson's Department Store makes sales worth $4 980 000. The net income for the year is $1 140 000. If in the next year, 2010, customers default on 2009 sales worth $70 000, the net income of $1 140 000 will be incorrect. It includes sales of $70 000 for which money will never be received. A more accurate net income figure is $1 070 000.

In Figure 11-1, an expense of $70 000, from the Bad Debts Expense account, has been included in the expense section of Robeson's Department Store's

> Bad debts expense is the loss due to uncollectible accounts.

FIGURE 11-1

Income statement for 2009

Robeson's Department Store
Income Statement
For the Year Ended December 31, 2009

Revenue		
Sales		$4 980 000
Cost of Goods Sold		
Cost of Goods Sold (per schedule)		3 015 000
Gross Profit		1 965 000
Operating Expenses		
Bad Debts Expense	$ 70 000	
Other Expenses	825 000	
Total Expenses		895 000
Net Income		$1 070 000

income statement for 2009. This results in an adjusted net income for the year of $1 070 000, which is more accurate than the $1 140 000 figure.

The inclusion of the $70 000 expense for bad debts is based on an important Generally Accepted Accounting Principle — the matching principle. The matching principle states that expenses for an accounting period should be matched against the revenue produced during the accounting period. If the $70 000 bad debts expense were not included, the proper total for the expenses would not be matched against revenue for the 2009 accounting period.

Figure 11-2 shows part of the balance sheet for 2009. The Accounts Receivable figure of $3 460 000 includes the $70 000 in credit sales that will never be paid by customers.

When the balance sheet was prepared at the end of 2009, the business hoped to collect all $3 460 000 of the accounts receivable. However, during 2009, $70 000 worth of the accounts receivable proved to be uncollectible. The $3 460 000 amount for the Accounts Receivable account in Figure 11-2 is therefore not accurate. A figure of $3 390 000 more correctly describes the value of the Accounts Receivable.

FIGURE 11-2

Partial balance sheet for 2009

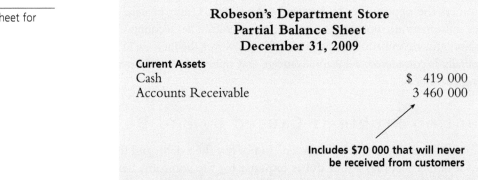

Robeson's Department Store
Partial Balance Sheet
December 31, 2009

Current Assets	
Cash	$ 419 000
Accounts Receivable	3 460 000

Includes $70 000 that will never
be received from customers

It is the accountant's task to prepare financial statements that are as accurate as possible. For this reason, an adjustment of $70 000 is required at the end of 2009 to establish the correct value for the Accounts Receivable account on the balance sheet and for the expenses on the income statement.

From past experience, the accountant knows that despite anything a business does, there will be bad debts. Some customers will not, or cannot, pay their debts. However, the accountant does not know which customers will not pay, nor does the accountant know the exact amount that will not be paid. Past experience only indicates that there will be a loss due to bad debts.

In our example, the accountant for Robeson's Department Store knows, based on past experience, that about $70 000 worth of credit sales will become uncollectible. However, the accountant does not know which customers will not pay their bills until quite some time into the next accounting period, or even later. Therefore, using past experience as a guide, the accountant prepares an adjustment for bad debts to improve the accuracy of the financial statements.

Preparing the Adjustment for Bad Debts

Based on the estimated bad debts for 2009, the accountant prepares this adjustment before preparing the 2009 financial statements:

Dec. 31 Bad Debts Expense	70 000	
Allowance for Bad Debts		70 000
To record the estimated bad debts		
for the year 2009.		

The effect of this entry is shown here in T-account form:

Accounts Receivable	Allowance for Bad Debts	Bad Debts Expense
Dec. 31	Dec. 31 70 000	Dec. 31 70 000
3 460 000		
Appears on the balance sheet	**Appears on the balance sheet**	**Appears on the income statement**

Examining the Bad Debts Expense Account

Bad Debts Expense appears as an expense account on the income statement as shown in Figure 11-1. At the end of the fiscal period, Bad Debts Expense is closed into the Income Summary account. During the fiscal period, there is no balance in the Bad Debts Expense account. It is opened with the adjustment made at the end of the fiscal period. It is then reduced to a zero balance when the closing entries are prepared.

Examining the Allowance for Bad Debts Account

The partial balance sheet in Figure 11-2 contains the Account Receivable control account with a balance of $3 460 000. Robeson's Department Store estimates that $70 000 worth of the Accounts Receivable balance will become bad debts. Why is the asset Accounts Receivable not credited $70 000 when the adjustment is made?

This is not done because it is not known which customer balances will become uncollectible. Therefore, it is not possible to credit any customer in the Accounts Receivable Ledger. Furthermore, it is not possible to credit the Accounts Receivable control account in the General Ledger because the control account must always be equal to the total of the individual customer balances in the Accounts Receivable Ledger. This is why the **Allowance for Bad Debts** (or Allowance for Uncollectible Accounts) account is credited instead with the estimated uncollectible amount.

A contra-asset account used to determine a realistic value for Accounts Receivable on the balance sheet.

The Allowance for Bad Debts account appears in the asset section of the balance sheet, as shown in Figure 11-3, but it is considered to be a contra account or a valuation account. As explained earlier in the text, a contra account reduces the value of the account that it describes. The Allowance for Bad Debts account is used to determine a realistic valuation for the Accounts Receivable account. The accounts used to record the accumulated amortization on various assets are also considered to be valuation or contra accounts. Examples of such accounts are shown later in this chapter in Figure 11-12 on page 437.

FIGURE 11-3

Partial balance sheet with Allowance for Bad Debts included

Robeson's Department Store Partial Balance Sheet December 31, 2009		
Current Assets		
Cash		$ 419 000
Accounts Receivable	$3 460 000	
Less: Allowance for Bad Debts	70 000	3 390 000

ESTIMATING BAD DEBTS EXPENSE

A company may use any one of several methods for estimating bad debts expense. Whichever method is used must be consistently followed. The two methods commonly used — the income statement (percent-of-sales) method and the balance sheet method (aging of accounts receivable) — are described below.

Using the Income Statement Method

The income statement method of estimating bad debts uses a percentage of net sales.

The **income statement method** is based on the question: "How much of this year's sales will become bad debts?" This is how it works. The accountant examines the bad debt losses in previous years. If, for instance, the losses have consistently been about 1 percent of net sales, then 1 percent is used for the adjustment. If sales are $2 160 000 and sales returns are $48 000, then net sales are $2 112 000. Since 1 percent of $2 112 000 is $21 120, this is the amount used for the adjustment. This entry is made:

Dec. 31 Bad Debts Expense	21 120	
Allowance for Bad Debts		21 120
To record bad debts at 1 percent of net sales.		

Using the Balance Sheet Method

The balance sheet method uses a percentage of accounts receivable as a basis for estimating bad debts expense.

A listing of all customers' balances and how long each balance has been owed.

Many companies examine their customer accounts to estimate the value of the uncollectible balances. This method is known as the **balance sheet method** because it uses the asset Accounts Receivable as a basis for estimating the bad debts expense. To determine the value of the uncollectible accounts, it is necessary to prepare an **accounts receivable age analysis** as shown in Figure 11-4 for Moncton Building Supplies Ltd. This is a listing of all customers, showing the balance owed by each one. It also shows how long the balance has been owed.

FIGURE 11-4
Age analysis prepared for accounts receivable

Moncton Building Supplies Ltd.
Accounts Receivable Age Analysis
December 31, 2009

CUSTOMER	BALANCE OF ACCOUNTS RECEIVABLE	CURRENT ACCOUNTS RECEIVABLE	1–30 DAYS OVERDUE	31–60 DAYS OVERDUE	61–90 DAYS OVERDUE	90+ DAYS OVERDUE
J. Butler	$ 510	$ 510				
R. Henry	375	180	$ 95	$ 100		
P. O'Brien	890	625	265			
S. Tariq	1 620	1 620				
B. Vaz	715				715	
All Others	194 600	105 600	44 700	26 200	12 500	$5 600
Total	$198 710	$108 535	$45 060	$26 300	$13 215	$5 600

The age analysis tells a company manager which customer balances have not been paid for various time periods. With this information, a manager can decide when to stop giving credit to a customer or when to start collection proceedings against a customer.

At the end of a fiscal period, the age analysis is used to determine the amount required for the bad debts expense adjustment. Here is how it is done. For each age group, the accountant estimates a percentage loss. For example, past experience might indicate that 50 percent of all debts over 90 days past due will be uncollectible. Figure 11-4 shows that an amount of $5600 is over 90 days old. Therefore, $2800 (0.50 $\times$ 5600 = 2800) will probably be uncollectible. In a similar way, estimates are made for each of the age groups. Figure 11-5 shows the percentage considered uncollectible for each group and the total amount of estimated bad debts. The total of $12 072.10 shown in Figure 11-5 is the amount required in the Allowance for Bad Debts account and is used to prepare the adjustment.

FIGURE 11-5
Estimated amount of accounts receivable that will become bad debts

Estimated Bad Debts
For the Year 2009

AGE OF ACCOUNTS	AMOUNT	PERCENTAGE ESTIMATED TO BE UNCOLLECTIBLE	BAD DEBTS ESTIMATE
Current	$108 535	1%	$ 1 085.35
1–30 days	45 060	5%	2 253.00
31–60 days	26 300	10%	2 630.00
61–90 days	13 215	25%	3 303.75
90+ days	5 600	50%	2 800.00
Total	$198 710		$12 072.10

Accounts Receivable less estimated bad debts is often referred to as **net realizable accounts receivable.**

Net realizable accounts receivable is Accounts Receivable less estimated bad debts.

Balance Sheet Method Steps

The following three steps are completed when using the balance sheet method of estimating the amount of bad debts:

- **Step 1:** Prepare an accounts receivable age analysis. A list of all customers is prepared (see Figure 11-4) showing the balance owed by each customer.

The amounts owed by each customer are classified according to how long they have been owed. The normal terms of payment are net 30 days. This means the customer must pay the invoice amount within 30 days from the invoice date. Let's look at one customer as an example.

In Figure 11-4, Henry owes $375. This represents several different sales to Henry. Of the $375 owing, $180 is current. That means $180 worth of merchandise was bought on credit and 30 days from the invoice date have not elapsed. However, Henry does have another $195 in the overdue columns. Of this $195 owing, $95 is for an invoice that is 1 to 30 days overdue. This means Henry has not paid the amount within the normal terms of payment. Henry also has $100 that is 31 to 60 days overdue. In summary, Henry owes $375 represented by more than one sale or invoice. One invoice is overdue 1 to 30 days; another invoice is overdue 31 to 60 days; another invoice is current and is not overdue.

- **Step 2:** Estimate a percentage loss.
- **Step 3:** Prepare the adjusting entry.

Previous Balance in the Allowance for Bad Debts Account

When using the balance sheet method of estimating bad debts expenses, any existing balance in the Allowance for Bad Debts account must be considered.

When using the balance sheet method of estimating bad debts, any existing balance in the contra account (Allowance for Bad Debts) *must* be considered. For example, the age analysis indicates an estimate for bad debts of $12 072 (rounded), but there is already a credit balance of $380 in the Allowance for Bad Debts account. The $380 credit balance of actual bad debts occurring during the period is less than the estimate (Allowance for Bad Debts $11 600 − $11 220 Accounts Receivable written off = $380 balance). A credit of only $11 692 is required to attain the balance of $12 072 for this period in the Allowance for Bad Debts account. This would be the adjusting entry:

Dec. 31 Bad Debts Expense	11 692	
Allowance for Bad Debts		11 692
To increase the Allowance account to $12 072.		
Previous *credit* balance	380	
Adjustment	11 692	
New balance	12 072	

The result of the adjusting entry in T-account form would appear as follows:

Bad Debts Expense		Allowance for Bad Debts	
Dec. 31 11 692		Balance	380
		Dec. 31	11 692
		New balance	12 072
Appears on the income statement		**Appears on the balance sheet**	

Where does the $380 beginning balance in the Allowance for Bad Debts account originate? It could be caused by a collection of an account previously written off or by an overestimate of bad debts from the last accounting period. Remember, the adjustment for bad debts is an estimate only. It is usually impossible to estimate the exact amount of the bad debts. There will generally be a debit or a credit balance in the Allowance account. When using the balance sheet method of adjusting bad debts, the previous balance must be considered. With the income statement method, it is ignored. The reason for this is that the income statement method identifies "new" bad debts based on "new" credit sales, whereas the balance sheet method estimates "cumulative" bad debts based on all accounts receivable.

When using the income statement method of estimating bad debts, the previous balance in the Allowance for Bad Debts account is ignored.

It is possible to have a debit balance in the Allowance for Bad Debts account. This occurs when the actual amount of bad debts for the period exceeds the estimated allowance. The age analysis indicates an estimate of $12 072 for bad debts. There is an existing debit balance of $453 in the Allowance for Bad Debts account. An adjustment of $12 525 is necessary. This is the entry:

2009			
Dec. 31 Bad Debts Expense		12 525	
Allowance for Bad Debts			12 525
To increase the Allowance			
account to $12 072.			
Previous *debit* balance	453		
Adjustment, credit	12 525		
New balance, credit	12 072		

Ⓦ RITING OFF UNCOLLECTIBLE ACCOUNTS

Accounts receivable that cannot be collected.

Three accounts are involved in the adjustment for bad debts: Accounts Receivable, Allowance for Bad Debts, and Bad Debts Expense. The first two accounts appear in the asset section on the balance sheet. The third, Bad Debts Expense, is an expense on the income statement. It is closed at the end of the fiscal period. At the beginning of the new fiscal period, these three accounts will appear in T-account form as follows:

Accounts Receivable		Allowance for Bad Debts	
Dec. 31 198 710		Balance	380
		Dec. 31	11 692
		2009	
		New balance	12 072

Appears on the balance sheet

Appears on the balance sheet as a contra-asset account

Bad Debts Expense	
Dec. 31 11 692	Dec. 31 11 692

Appears on the income statement

What does a company do when it determines that it will never be able to collect a debt owed by a customer? Examine the following system used by Moncton Building Supplies. Suppose that after several months, a customer of Moncton Building Supplies, M. Parr, declares bankruptcy. By July 14, it is clearly determined that the $1075 owed by M. Parr will never be collected. The following entry is made:

2010			
Jul. 14	Allowance for Bad Debts	1075	
	Accounts Receivable/M. Parr		1075
	To write off M. Parr's account as uncollectible.		

Notice that in this entry, the Bad Debts Expense account is not used. The loss is written off against the Allowance for Bad Debts account which was set up in expectation of, or to allow for, such losses. Remember that a total of $10 000 was recorded in the Bad Debts Expense account when the adjustment was made. To record the $1075 loss in the Bad Debts Expense account would be wrong because this would mean the expense would be recorded twice: once in the adjustment and once in the write-off. After M. Parr's account is written off, the T-accounts would appear as follows:

Accounts Receivable	
Dec. 31 198 710	

Allowance for Bad Debts	
2010	2009
Jul. 14 1 075	Dec. 31 12 072

Accounts Receivable/M. Parr	
	2010
Balance 1 075	Jul. 14 1 075

Bad Debts Expense	
2009	2009
Dec. 31 11 692	Dec. 31 11 692

This account now closed   **No change in this account**

During the year, write-off entries are made whenever it is certain that a debt is uncollectible. At the end of the year, there will probably be a balance in the Allowance for Bad Debts account. It is almost impossible to be exactly correct in estimating a year's uncollectible accounts. When the next fiscal period ends, the balance in the Allowance for Bad Debts account must be considered if the balance sheet method of adjusting for bad debts is used. The income statement method ignores any such balance.

The Comparative Balance Sheets from the 2005 annual reports for Canadian Tire Corporation are presented in Figure 11-6 on the next page. Note the dollar amounts for Accounts Receivable for that time period. What has happened?

An excerpt from the Notes to the Consolidated Financial Statements for Canadian Tire is shown below:

Note 1, Significant Accounting Policies:
Loans Receivable   Loans receivable include credit card and personal loans receivable. Loans receivable are recorded at cost net of unearned interest income and of allowances for credit losses. Interest income is recorded on an accrual basis. An allowance for credit losses is calculated using the historical loss experience of account balances based on aging and arrears status, with certain adjustments for other relevant circumstances influencing the recoverability of the loans. Personal

FIGURE 11-6

Comparative balance sheets
from the 2005 annual
report for Canadian Tire
Corporation

Consolidated Balance Sheets

As at (Dollars in millions)	December 31, 2005	January 1, 2005
ASSETS		
Current assets		
Cash and cash equivalents (Note 12)	$ 838.0	$ 802.2
Accounts receivable (Note 12)	652.8	370.7
Loans receivable (Note 2)	728.7	592.4
Merchandise inventories	675.5	620.6
Prepaid expenses and deposits	42.4	24.1
Future income taxes (Note 11)	43.6	24.6
Total current assets	2,981.0	2,434.6
Long-term receivables and other assets (Note 3)	132.1	129.7
Goodwill (Note 4)	46.2	41.7
Intangible assets (Note 4)	52.4	52.0
Property and equipment (Note 5)	2,743.9	2,585.2
Total assets	$ 5,955.6	$ 5,243.2
LIABILITIES		
Current liabilities		
Accounts payable and other	$ 1,545.5	$ 1,437.6
Income taxes payable	71.2	44.2
Current portion of long-term debt (Note 6)	204.3	5.6
Total current liabilities	1,821.0	1,487.4
Long-term debt (Note 6)	1,171.3	1,081.8
Future income taxes (Note 11)	89.0	67.2
Other long-term liabilities (Note 7)	63.2	55.6
Total liabilities	3,144.5	2,692.0
Minority interest (Note 17)	300.0	300.0
SHAREHOLDERS' EQUITY		
Share capital (Note 9)	702.7	709.0
Contributed surplus	1.5	1.3
Accumulated foreign currency translation adjustment	(5.7)	(6.0)
Retained earnings	1,812.6	1,546.9
Total shareholders' equity	2,511.1	2,251.2
Total liabilities, minority interest and shareholders' equity	$ 5,955.6	$ 5,243.2

(SIGNED)   (SIGNED)

Gilbert S. Bennett   **Maureen J. Sabia**
Director   Director

Source: Canadian Tire Corporation, *Canadian Tire 2005 Audited Annual Report*, March 2006, p. 84.

loans are considered impaired when principal or interest payments are over 90 days past due and are written off when they are over one year past due. Credit card loans are written off when they are in arrears for over 180 days. Payments received on loans that have been written off are recorded first against any previous write-offs or allowances and then as revenue.

What is Canadian Tire's policy/policies with respect to credit losses (bad debts)? How does the company record interest income? Why do you think that Canadian Tire's policy for personal loans differs from that of credit cards?

Payment of an Account Receivable Previously Written Off

Sometimes, an account that was assumed uncollectible and was written off is unexpectedly collected. Such payments are termed *recovery of bad debts.* When this occurs, it is necessary to make two entries.

In the previous example, M. Parr's account was written off on July 14. On September 19, Parr unexpectedly pays Moncton Building Supplies Ltd. the full amount ($1075). Two entries are made. The first one records the debt in the customer's account again and re-establishes the amount in the Allowance for Bad Debts account:

2010			
Sep. 19	Accounts Receivable/M. Parr	1 075	
	Allowance for Bad Debts		1 075
	To set up previously written-off account.		

The second entry records the money received and decreases the customer's account:

2010			
Sep. 19	Cash	1 075	
	Accounts Receivable/M. Parr		1 075
	Received payment in full.		

After the entries have been posted, M. Parr's account appears as below:

Accounts Receivable/M. Parr

	2009		2010		
Original sale ⟶	Feb. 8	1 075	Jul. 14	1 075	⟵ **Account written off**
	2010		2010		
Sale rerecorded ⟶	Sep. 19	1 075	Sep. 19	1 075	⟵ **Payment received**

Direct Write-Off Method

Another method to account for bad debts. It is not based on a bad debts estimate calculation and is not used by many companies.

Another method for recording bad debts is the **direct write-off** method. It is used mainly by companies that have very few uncollectible Accounts Receivable or that have very few receivables.

An example of a journal entry using the direct write-off method follows:

Apr. 19	Bad Debts Expense	485	
	Accounts Receivable A. Ganesh		485
	Wrote off an uncollectible account using the direct write-off method.		

This method does not comply with the matching principle because the expense from the uncollectible account is usually not recorded in the same period as the revenue was earned. Therefore, net income is overstated in the period when the sale occurred and is understated when the expense is recorded. Also, Accounts Receivable are reported at their full value, not at their net realizable value, thus assets are overstated.

Many companies use the income statement and the balance sheet methods together. For the *interim statements* (monthly or quarterly), the income statement method is used because it is quick and easy. This method focuses on the amount of bad debts expense. At year-end, however, the balance sheet method is preferred because it focuses on assets. Any receivables are reported at their net realizable value.

Now that we have looked at the adjustment for bad debts, we will examine two other adjustments, called accrued expenses and accrued revenue.

INTRODUCING ACCRUED EXPENSES

Adjusting entries are required for any expenses that are owed but not yet recorded. These are called **accrued expenses** because as time goes on the liability "accrues." They have been incurred but not journalized and posted to the General Ledger. Interest owed but not recorded is an example.

Accrued expenses are expenses that have been incurred but not yet recorded in the books.

Accrued Interest

Suppose $150 000 was borrowed by Moncton Building Supplies Ltd. from a bank on August 1, 2009, and is to be repaid in six months, on January 31. Interest at 6.25 percent is charged by the bank. The following entry is made when the money is borrowed:

Aug. 1	Cash	150 000	
	Bank Loan		150 000
	Borrowed $150 000 for six months at 6.25 percent interest.		

On December 31, at the end of the fiscal period, the bank is owed five months' interest. This amount owing is an expense and should be on the income statement. The interest figure for five months is $3906.25. This amount must be shown in an account called Interest Expense. The adjustment necessary is:

2009			
Dec. 31	Interest Expense	3 906.25	
	Interest Payable		3 906.25
	To record interest for five months from August 1 (150 000 × 0.0625 × 5/12 = $3906.25).		

After this entry has been posted, the Interest Expense, Bank Loan, and Interest Payable accounts appear as follows:

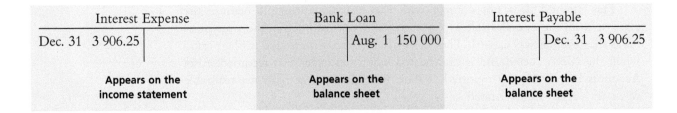

Interest Expense	Bank Loan	Interest Payable
Dec. 31 3 906.25	Aug. 1 150 000	Dec. 31 3 906.25
Appears on the income statement	**Appears on the balance sheet**	**Appears on the balance sheet**

What would be wrong with the financial statements if this adjustment were not made? Which accounting principle would be violated if these expenses were not recorded at the end of the accounting period? First of all, the expenses would be too low and this would cause the net income to be $3906.25 too high. Because net income would be overstated, the final owner's equity total would also be too high. A mismatch would have occurred between the expenses and revenue for the period.

Such an error would be a result of not matching all the expenses of a period with the revenue for that period. If the interest was not recorded until it was paid in the next accounting period, the net income in this fiscal period would be too low. By how much would the net income be incorrect during the second fiscal period? The expenses in the next fiscal period would be too high and this would cause the net income to be $3906.25 too low. Can you explain why the owner's equity would be correct at the end of the second fiscal period even though the income statement was incorrect? Failure to record the expense in the first instance would result in an overstatement of net income of $3906.25 while recording too high an expense in the second instance would result in an understatement of net income of $3906.25. The total net income added to the owner's equity over the two fiscal periods would be correct even though both income statements were incorrect.

Accrued Salaries

A second example of accrued expenses is salaries and commissions earned but not yet paid. The most common reason for this is that the pay period does not coincide with the end of the financial period.

The employees of Moncton Building Supplies Ltd. are paid every second Friday. Presented below are the calendars for September and October with the pay periods circled.

	SEPTEMBER							OCTOBER					
S	M	T	W	T	F	S	S	M	T	W	T	F	S
					1	2	1	2	3	4	5	(6)	7
3	4	5	6	7	(8)	9	8	9	10	11	12	13	14
10	11	12	13	14	15	16	15	16	17	18	19	(20)	21
17	18	19	20	21	(22)	23	22	23	24	25	26	27	28
24	25	26	27	28	29	30	29	30	31				

The payroll for each two-week period is $3800. The employees were last paid on September 22. The journal entry on that date was:

Sep. 22	Salary Expense	3 800	
	Cash		3 800
	To record two weeks' salaries.		

The next payday is Friday, October 6. An adjusting entry is required on September 29, the end of the finance reporting period, to record the accrued salaries for one week.

Sep. 29	Salary Expense	1 900	
	Salary Payable		1 900
	To record one week's salaries.		
	($3 800/2 weeks = $1 900)		

When this entry is posted, the accounts appear as follows:

Salary Expense				Salary Payable			
Sep. 22	3 800					Sep. 29	1 900
Sep. 29	1 900						
Balance	5 700						

If this entry had not been recorded, by how much would the expenses be understated, the net income be overstated, and the liability be understated?

On October 6, when the next payday occurs, the following entry is recorded:

Oct. 6	Salary Payable	1 900	
	Salary Expense	1 900	
	Cash		3 800
	To record two weeks' salaries		
	including one week's accrued in September.		

When this entry is posted, the accounts for Salary Expense and Salary Payable appear as follows:

Salary Expense				Salary Payable			
Sep. 22	3 800			Oct. 6	1 900	Sep. 29	1 900
Sep. 29	1 900						
Oct. 6	1 900						
Balance	7 600						

Many companies use computerized accounting systems. These systems will include a payroll component. At the end of the financial period, any adjusting entries for accrued expenses are automatically journalized and posted.

INTRODUCING ACCRUED REVENUE

Accrued revenue is revenue that has been earned but not recorded or collected. Here is an example.

Moncton Building Supplies Ltd. purchased a three-year guaranteed investment certificate worth $20 000 from its bank. The certificate earns interest at the rate of 4 percent, or $800, a year. The interest (a total of $2400) will be received at the end of three years. However, $800 in interest is actually earned each year, as illustrated:

Accrued revenue is revenue earned during the fiscal period but not yet recorded in the books.

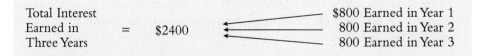

Total Interest Earned in Three Years	=	$2400		$800 Earned in Year 1
				800 Earned in Year 2
				800 Earned in Year 3

Since $800 interest is earned at the end of Year 1, that interest should be recorded as revenue and should be included in the income statement for Year 1. If it is not recorded, there would be a mismatch between revenue and expenses. Some of the revenue for the year ($800) would not be matched against the expenses for the year. To avoid that error, this adjustment is made:

Dec. 31 Interest Receivable	800	
Interest Revenue		800
To record one year's interest on the guaranteed investment certificate.		

Here is another example of accrued revenue. If Moncton Building Supplies Ltd. performed a service on account ($1500) for a customer in December, revenue was earned. If by December 31, this transaction had not been recorded in Moncton's accounting records and the customer had not paid the amount owed, Moncton Building Supplies Ltd. would record an adjusting entry to reflect the receivable and the revenue. The year-end adjusting entry is as follows:

Dec. 31	Accounts Receivable	1 500	
	Service Revenue		1 500
	To record the accrued service revenue.		

SUMMARY OF ACCRUED ADJUSTMENTS

Adjusting entries are necessary for accrued revenue and for accrued expenses so that the financial statements will be accurate. This is in agreement with the matching principle and the revenue principle. If accrued expenses are not recorded, there will be a mismatch between expenses and revenue and the following will occur:

- Expenses will be too low.
- Net income will be overstated.
- Liabilities will be too low.
- Owner's equity will be too high.

If accrued revenue is not recorded, the following will occur:

- Revenue will be too low.
- Net income will be understated.
- Assets will be too low.
- Owner's equity will be understated.

1. Explain the difference between a service company and a merchandising company.

2. On which financial statements do the following two accounts appear:

    (a) Bad Debts Expense
    (b) Allowance for Bad Debts

3. (a) What is the General Journal entry to record estimated bad debts?
    (b) Name the financial statement on which each account in the entry from (a) would appear.
    (c) Which of the two accounts in (a) are closed at the end of the fiscal period?

4. (a) Name the two methods of estimating bad debts.
    (b) Which method takes into consideration the previous balance in the Allowance for Bad Debts account?

5. What is the General Journal entry to write off an uncollectible account?

6. When is an account written off as uncollectible?

7. What is the adjusting entry to record interest owed but not recorded?

8. What is the adjusting entry to record salaries owed to employees?

9. Define accrued expenses and give two examples.

10. Define accrued revenue and give two examples.

UNIT 25

REVIEW QUESTIONS

---

1. At the end of the fiscal period, December 31, 2009, Whistler Ski Shoppe has a balance of $12 750 in the Accounts Receivable account. The Allowance for Bad Debts account has a zero balance. It is estimated that the bad debts will be $876.

    (a) Prepare the adjusting entry to record the estimated bad debts of $876.
    (b) Copy the T-accounts that follow. Post the adjusting entry to your own T-accounts.

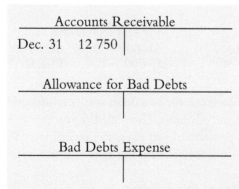

    (c) How much will appear on the income statement for Bad Debts Expense?
    (d) Show how Accounts Receivable and Allowance for Bad Debts will appear on the balance sheet.

2. The Georgian Bay Marine Store has a balance of $20 800 in the Accounts Receivable account. The Allowance for Bad Debts account has a zero balance. The estimated amount for bad debts is $1075.

UNIT 25

PROBLEMS: APPLICATIONS

(a) Prepare the adjusting entry to record the estimated bad debts for December 31, 2008.
(b) How much will appear in the income statement for Bad Debts Expense?
(c) Show how Accounts Receivable and Allowance for Bad Debts will appear on the balance sheet.

3. The three companies in the following description all use the income statement method of estimating bad debts. For each, prepare the adjusting entry.

(a) Company A: Net sales were $163 000. Bad debts are estimated to be 1 percent of net sales.
(b) Company B: Net sales were $249 000. Bad debts are estimated to be 0.5 percent of net sales.
(c) Company C: Net sales were $310 000. Bad debts are estimated to be 1.25 percent of net sales.

4. For each of the following cases, give the adjusting entry for bad debts if the balance sheet method of estimating bad debts is being used.

(a) Estimated bad debts: $9370; balance in the Allowance for Bad Debts account: $625 credit.
(b) Estimated bad debts: $24 680; balance in the Allowance for Bad Debts account: $1715 debit.

5. (a) Copy the T-accounts that follow:

Accounts Receivable		Allowance for Bad Debts		Bad Debts Expense	
Dec. 31 179 800			Dec. 31 965		

(b) An age analysis shows that $2780 worth of the Accounts Receivable account is estimated to be uncollectible. Journalize and post the necessary adjusting entry for December 31, 2010.

6. The accounts receivable age analysis for the James Bay Trading Company on December 31, 2009 shows the following totals:

			Days Overdue		
Balance	**Current**	**1–30**	**31–60**	**61–90**	**90+**
$126 800	$86 800	$24 300	$7 700	$4 200	$3 800

(a) Calculate the allowance for bad debts if it is estimated that the following percentages are uncollectible: Current, 1.5 percent; 1–30 days, 6 percent; 31–60 days, 12 percent; 61–90 days, 25 percent; over 90 days, 50 percent.
(b) Calculate the estimated value of the net realizable accounts receivable.

7. (a) Copy the T-accounts that follow:

Accounts Receivable		Allowance for Bad Debts		Bad Debts Expense	
Apr. 30 33 100			Apr. 30 1 125		

(b) Record these transactions in a General Journal on page 54 and post the entries to the T-accounts:

May   19   Write off S. Mateen's account of $360 as uncollectible. Mateen has gone out of business.

      24   Write off B. Schultz 's account of $475 as uncollectible. Schultz has left town and cannot be located.

      31   An age analysis shows that $825 worth of the Accounts Receivable account is estimated to be uncollectible. Prepare the necessary adjusting entry. Use the balance sheet method, remembering that the balance in the Allowance for Bad Debts account must be considered.

Jun. 30   B. Schultz 's cheque for $475 was received in payment of his account previously written off.

8. Journalize these transactions in a General Journal on page 73:

Jul.   1   The balance in the Allowance for Bad Debts account is $265 credit.

      10   Write off K. Babbar's account of $138 as uncollectible.

      21   Write off R. Awad's account of $182 as uncollectible.

      30   The age analysis indicates that $380 is required in the Allowance for Bad Debts account. The balance sheet method is being used. Prepare the adjusting entry.

9. (a) Copy the T-accounts that follow:

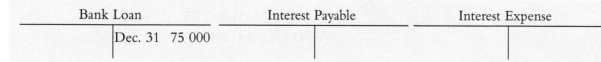

Bank Loan	Interest Payable	Interest Expense
Dec. 31 75 000		

   (b) At the end of the fiscal period, $930 interest has accrued. Prepare the adjusting entry to record the $930 interest.
   (c) Post the adjusting entry to the T-accounts.

10. For each of the following cases, give the adjusting entry for interest owing:

   (a) Loan of $15 000 for one year at an annual interest rate of 5.5 percent to be repaid on April 30. Date of adjustment: October 31.
   (b) Loan of $7500 for nine months at an annual interest rate of 6 percent, to be repaid on November 30. Date of adjustment: May 31.

11. (a) Copy the T-accounts that follow:

Salaries Expense	Salaries Payable
Dec. 31 87 000	

   (b) At the end of the fiscal period, $6900 is owed to the employees. Prepare the adjusting entry to record the salaries owing.
   (c) Post the adjusting entry to the T-accounts.

12. For each of the following cases, give the adjusting entry for salaries owing:

   (a) Sales staff receive a 6 percent commission on their monthly sales. In November, they sold $72 000 worth of goods for which they are to be paid on December 31. The date of the adjustment is November 30.

   (b) The total earnings of all hourly employees is $4900 per day, excluding Saturdays and Sundays. They are paid every Friday. What will the adjusting entry be if the financial statements are prepared at the end of the working day on Thursday?

13. At the end of the fiscal period, S. Bowman, an accountant, had completed $16 750 worth of work for clients, but had not yet prepared the invoices.

   (a) Prepare the journal entry to record the information.
   (b) Post the entry to T-accounts for July 31.

14. On June 1, 2008, Walden Trucking Co. purchased a new truck for $95 000. A down payment of $30 000 was made and Walden signed a two-year 6 percent note payable for the balance.

   Journalize the following on page 43 of the General Journal:

   (a) The purchase of the truck.
   (b) The December 31, 2008, adjusting entry for the accrued interest.
   (c) The entry to repay the note for the full amount owed.

Adjustments and the Work Sheet

Learning Objectives

After reading this unit, discussing the applicable review questions, and completing the applications exercises, you will be able to do the following:

1. **RECORD** the beginning and ending inventory on a work sheet.

2. **RECORD** adjustments on a work sheet.

3. **COMPLETE** a work sheet for a merchandising company.

In the first unit of this chapter, you learned how to prepare adjustments for bad debts, accrued expenses, and accrued revenue. These adjustments were described in General Journal form. In this unit, the work sheet will be used to plan the adjustments for a merchandising company.

RECORDING ADJUSTMENTS ON THE WORK SHEET

The accountant for Henley Sporting Goods has prepared the trial balance for the fiscal period ended December 31, 2010. It is shown on the work sheet in Figure 11-7 on page 426. The following information is used to prepare the adjustments on the work sheet:

- The age analysis indicates that a balance of $2400 is required in the Allowance for Bad Debts account.
- Supplies worth $1800 are left at the end of the year.
- Amortization is recorded using the straight line method.
- Interest of $300 is owed on the bank loan.
- Salaries of $1900 are owed to the employees.

Analysis of the Work Sheet Adjustments

Adjustment for Bad Debts

Henley Sporting Goods uses the balance sheet method for estimating bad debts. The age analysis indicates that $2400 is required in the Allowance for Bad Debts account. Since there is already a credit balance, an adjustment of $2250 is made. Bad Debts Expense is added to the work sheet and is debited $2250. A credit of $2250 is written on line 3 opposite Allowance for Bad Debts. The debit and credit amounts in the adjusting columns are coded (a). The adjustments are coded to provide easy identification of the debit and credit portions of the entry.

Adjustment for Prepaid Expenses

As you may recall, prepaid expenses such as prepaid rent, prepaid insurance, and supplies must be adjusted on the work sheet.

An inventory of supplies shows an $1800 total for supplies on hand at the end of the year. The Supplies account on the work sheet has a $4500 balance. An adjustment of $2700 is required. Supplies Expense is added to the work sheet and is debited $2700, the amount of the supplies used. Supplies (line 5) is credited $2700. This adjustment is coded (b).

Adjustment for Amortization

The straight-line method of amortizing capital assets is used by Henley Sporting Goods.

The building has a residual value of $30 000 and its useful life is 25 years. Amortization Expense—Building is added to the work sheet and debited $5200 [(160 000 – 30 000)/25 = 5200]. Accumulated Amortization Building is credited $5200 (line 7). The adjustment is coded (c).

The same method is used for equipment, which has an estimated life of seven years and a $2000 residual value. Amortization Expense—Equipment is added to the work sheet and debited $3000 [(23 000 – 2000)/7 = 3000]. Accumulated Amortization—Equipment is credited $3000 (line 9). This adjustment is coded (d).

If Henley Sporting Goods had instead used the declining-balance method, amortization for the building would be at the rate of 5 percent per year on the declining balance which is now $113 200 (160 000 – 46 800 accumulated amortization = 113 200). Amortization Expense—Building would be added to the work sheet and debited $5660 (113 200 × 0.05 = 5660). Accumulated Amortization—Building would be credited $5660 (line 7).

The declining balance of the Equipment account is $11 000 (23 000 – 12 000 accumulated amortization = 11 000). The rate of amortization is 20 percent per year. Amortization Expense—Equipment is added to the work sheet and debited

FIGURE 11-7
Completed work sheet for a merchandising business

Henley Sporting Goods, Work Sheet
For the Year Ended December 31, 2010

	ACC. NO.	ACCOUNT TITLE	TRIAL BALANCE DEBIT	TRIAL BALANCE CREDIT	ADJUSTMENTS DEBIT	ADJUSTMENTS CREDIT	INCOME STATEMENT DEBIT	INCOME STATEMENT CREDIT	BALANCE SHEET DEBIT	BALANCE SHEET CREDIT	
1	101	Cash	112 400						112 400		1
2	110	Accounts Receivable	43 000						43 000		2
3	111	Allowance for Bad Debts		150		(a) 2 250				2 400	3
4	120	Merchandise Inventory, January 1	90 000				90 000	81 800	81 800		4
5	125	Supplies	4 500			(b) 2 700			1 800		5
6	150	Building	160 000						160 000		6
7	151	Accum. Amort. — Building		46 800		(c) 5 200				52 000	7
8	160	Equipment	23 000						23 000		8
9	161	Accum. Amort. — Equipment		12 000		(d) 3 000				15 000	9
10	200	Accounts Payable		23 450						23 450	10
11	205	PST Payable		2 130						2 130	11
12	206	GST Payable		1 870						1 870	12
13	207	GST Refundable	640						640		13
14	210	Bank Loan		20 000						20 000	14
15	250	Mortgage Payable		88 000						88 000	15
16	300	R. Henley, Capital		200 640						200 640	16
17	301	R. Henley, Drawings	28 000						28 000		17
18	400	Sales Revenue		330 000				330 000			18
19	500	Purchases	120 000				120 000				19
20	600	Advertising Expense	5 000				5 000				20
21	601	General Expense	4 000				4 000				21
22	602	Salaries Expense	120 000		(f) 1 900		121 900				22
23	603	Utilities Expense	7 500				7 500				23
24	604	Insurance Expense	7 000				7 000				24
25			725 040	725 040							25
26	605	Bad Debts Expense			(a) 2 250		2 250				26
27	606	Supplies Expense			(b) 2 700		2 700				27
28	607	Amort. Expense — Building			(c) 5 200		5 200				28
29	608	Amort. Expense — Equipment			(d) 3 000		3 000				29
30	609	Interest Expense			(e) 300		300				30
31	215	Interest Payable				(e) 300				300	31
32	220	Salaries Payable				(f) 1 900				1 900	32
33					15 350	15 350	368 850	411 800	450 640	407 690	33
34		Net Income					42 950			42 950	34
35							411 800	411 800	450 640	450 640	35
36											36

Note: **(1)** Adjustments coded with letters for easy identification. **(2)** Opening inventory extended to income statement debit column. **(3)** Ending inventory extended to income statement credit and balance sheet debit columns.

$2200 (0.20 × 11 000 = 2200). Accumulated Amortization—Equipment would be credited $2200 (line 9).

Adjustment for Accrued Interest

Three months' interest is owed on the bank loan and amounts to $300 (20 000 × 0.06 × 3/12 = 300). Both Interest Expense and Interest Payable are added to the work sheet. The $300 adjustment is coded (e).

Adjustment for Accrued Salaries

The salaries adjustment is made to record the $1900 owed to the employees. Salaries is debited $1900. Salaries Payable is added to the work sheet and is credited $1900. The adjustment is coded (f).

Adjustment for Merchandise Inventory — Perpetual Inventory System

Under the perpetual inventory system discussed in Chapter 7, the Merchandise Inventory account is continually adjusted as merchandise is bought and sold during the accounting period. However, an entry may be necessary to ensure the accuracy of the inventory account at the end of the accounting period. The entry to record the difference between the physical inventory (counting and pricing the inventory) taken at the end of the fiscal period and the Merchandising Inventory ledger account is as follows:

Calculation:

Dec. 31 Merchandise Inventory (Ledger Balance)	$76 000	
Physical Inventory	75 450	
Inventory Shortage	$ 550	

Journal Entry:

Dec. 31 Inventory Shortage (or Cost of Goods Sold)	550	
Merchandise Inventory		550
To adjust the balance of Merchandise Inventory		
to equal physical inventory.		

Inventory Shortage (or Cost of Goods Sold) is an expense account and is shown on the income statement.

  The entries required to adjust inventory for a firm, like Henley Sporting Goods, that uses a periodic inventory system are somewhat different.

Adjustment for Merchandise Inventory — Periodic Inventory System

The work sheet in Figure 11-7 contains the Merchandise Inventory account with a January balance of $90 000. This means that at the beginning of the fiscal period, there were goods on hand that cost $90 000. During the year, merchandise was sold and the sales transactions were recorded in the Sales account. Merchandise was purchased when it was required and recorded in the Purchases account.

  At the end of the year, the Merchandise Inventory account must be adjusted since it contains the cost of the merchandise on hand at the beginning of the year, January 1. This figure is incorrect. It has changed because of sales and purchases of merchandise during the year. The Merchandise Inventory must be adjusted so that it contains the value of the inventory on hand at the end of the year (December 31). This value is obtained by taking a physical inventory at the end of the fiscal year. This adjustment will now be examined in greater detail.

EXAMINING THE MERCHANDISE INVENTORY ADJUSTMENT

In line with the periodic inventory method used to date in the examples given in this book, entries were not made in the Henley Sporting Goods Merchandise Inventory account during the accounting period. At the end of the accounting period, an adjustment is needed to update the balance of the Merchandise Inventory account. We will look first at the steps involved in making this adjustment and at the journal entries required.

Steps in Inventory Adjustment

Three steps are completed in adjusting the Merchandise Inventory account.

Step 1: Determine the Value of the Inventory

At the end of the fiscal period, a physical count called taking an inventory is made of merchandise on hand. This results in a new dollar amount of $81 800 for the Merchandise Inventory account. This is the actual value of the merchandise on hand.

Step 2: Prepare the Closing Entry for Merchandise Inventory

An entry is made to remove the beginning inventory figure. This is necessary because the beginning merchandise value has been replaced by the end-of-the-year inventory figure of $81 800. This entry is made to close out the beginning inventory to the Income Summary account:

Dec. 31 Income Summary	90 000	
Merchandise Inventory		90 000
To close the beginning inventory into the		
Income Summary account.		

Step 3: Prepare the Entry to Record the Value of the Inventory

This entry is made to record the new inventory figure:

Dec. 31 Merchandise Inventory	81 800	
Income Summary		81 800
To record the ending inventory.		

This entry is necessary because the inventory on hand at the end of the year is an asset and must be recorded.

The Merchandise Inventory account now appears as follows:

The balance of the Merchandise Inventory account is now $81 800, the value of the ending inventory. When the financial statements are prepared, Merchandise Inventory of $81 800 will appear in the current assets section of the balance sheet.

The Income Summary T-account follows. Note that it has a debit and a credit in it as a result of the inventory adjustments:

The beginning inventory of $90 000 is on the left, or expenses and cost side, of the Income Summary account. The new inventory figure of $81 800 (the cost of goods not yet sold) is on the revenue side. The debit of $90 000 and the credit of $81 800 were recorded on the work sheet shown earlier in Figure 11-7.

Two entries involving inventory have been described. One entry reduces the Merchandise Inventory account to zero by transferring the beginning inventory to the Income Summary account. The other entry records the ending inventory in the Merchandise Inventory account.

Recording the Inventory Adjustment on the Work Sheet

The two entries that have just been described explain how the Merchandise Inventory account is adjusted at the end of the accounting period. This adjustment can be organized on a work sheet before the journal entries are made. Figures 11-8, 11-9, and 11-10 on page 430 illustrate, in three steps, the recording of the adjustment on a work sheet:

- **Step 1:** Transfer the beginning inventory ($90 000) to the debit column of the income statement section. This $90 000 figure is the cost of merchandise sold, which is an asset. This is why it is recorded as a debit and why it decreases the net income (see Figure 11-8 on page 430).
- **Step 2:** Record the new inventory ($81 800) in the credit column of the income statement section (see Figure 11-9 on page 430). This is the cost of inventory not sold yet.
- **Step 3:** Record the new inventory ($81 800) in the debit column of the balance sheet section. This records the ending inventory as an asset at cost (see Figure 11-10 on page 430).

Trace the three steps described above through Figures 11-8, 11-9, and 11-10. Rather than preparing separate entries to adjust Merchandise Inventory, the account is adjusted as part of the closing entry procedure discussed in the next unit.

Using Danier Leather's 2004 and 2005 comparative balance sheets shown in Figure 11-11 on page 431, find the two Inventory dollar amounts. What was the beginning Inventory figure for 2005? What has occurred with Accounts Receivable and with Capital Assets?

FIGURE 11-8

Transfer the beginning inventory balance of $90 000 from the trial balance section to the debit column of the income statement section of the work sheet.

Henley Sporting Goods, Work Sheet
For the Year Ended December 31, 2010

	ACCOUNT TITLE	ACC. NO.	TRIAL BALANCE DEBIT	TRIAL BALANCE CREDIT	ADJUSTMENTS DEBIT	ADJUSTMENTS CREDIT	INCOME STATEMENT DEBIT	INCOME STATEMENT CREDIT	BALANCE SHEET DEBIT	BALANCE SHEET CREDIT	
1	Cash	101	112 400						112 400		1
2	Accounts Receivable	110	43 000						43 000		2
3	Allowance for Bad Debts	111		150		(a) 2 250				2 400	3
4	Merchandise Inventory, January 1	120	90 000				90 000				4
5	Supplies	125	4 500			(b) 2 700			1 800		5

FIGURE 11-9

Record the new inventory of $81 800 in the credit column of the income statement section of the work sheet.

Henley Sporting Goods, Work Sheet
For the Year Ended December 31, 2010

	ACCOUNT TITLE	ACC. NO.	TRIAL BALANCE DEBIT	TRIAL BALANCE CREDIT	ADJUSTMENTS DEBIT	ADJUSTMENTS CREDIT	INCOME STATEMENT DEBIT	INCOME STATEMENT CREDIT	BALANCE SHEET DEBIT	BALANCE SHEET CREDIT	
1	Cash	101	112 400						112 400		1
2	Accounts Receivable	110	43 000						43 000		2
3	Allowance for Bad Debts	111		150		(a) 2 250				2 400	3
4	Merchandise Inventory, January 1	120	90 000				90 000	81 800			4
5	Supplies	125	4 500			(b) 2 700			1 800		5

FIGURE 11-10

Record the new inventory of $81 800 in the debit column of the balance sheet section of the work sheet.

Henley Sporting Goods, Work Sheet
For the Year Ended December 31, 2010

	ACCOUNT TITLE	ACC. NO.	TRIAL BALANCE DEBIT	TRIAL BALANCE CREDIT	ADJUSTMENTS DEBIT	ADJUSTMENTS CREDIT	INCOME STATEMENT DEBIT	INCOME STATEMENT CREDIT	BALANCE SHEET DEBIT	BALANCE SHEET CREDIT	
1	Cash	101	112 400						112 400		1
2	Accounts Receivable	110	43 000						43 000		2
3	Allowance for Bad Debts	111		150		(a) 2 250				2 400	3
4	Merchandise Inventory, January 1	120	90 000				90 000	81 800	81 800		4
5	Supplies	125	4 500			(b) 2 700			1 800		5

Beginning Inventory and Ending Inventory value required to calculate Cost of Goods Sold on the income statement

Ending Inventory value required for the balance sheet

FIGURE 11-11
Danier Leather's 2004 and
2005 comparative balance
sheet

consolidated financial statements

For the years ended June 25, 2005 and June 26, 2004

CONSOLIDATED BALANCE SHEETS (THOUSANDS OF DOLLARS)

	June 25, 2005	June 26, 2004
ASSETS		
Current Assets		
Cash	$ 21,193	$ 22,576
Accounts receivable	594	626
Income taxes recoverable	939	-
Inventories (Note 3)	29,031	29,483
Prepaid expenses	516	903
Assets of discontinued operations (Note 2)	23	884
Future income tax asset (Note 8)	159	107
	52,455	54,579
Other Assets		
Capital assets (Note 4)	25,314	28,891
Goodwill (Note 5)	342	342
Assets of discontinued operations (Note 2)	-	1,321
Future income taxes asset (Note 9)	5,254	4,736
	$ 83,365	$ 89,869
LIABILITIES		
Current Liabilities		
Accounts payable and accrued liabilities	$ 8,170	$ 9,355
Income taxes payable	-	952
Liabilities of discontinued operations (Note 2)	-	70
	8,170	10,377
Accrued litigation provision and related expenses (Note 10)	18,000	15,450
Deferred lease inducements	1,838	2,283
Future income tax liability (Note 9)	420	472
	28,428	28,582
SHAREHOLDERS' EQUITY		
Share capital (Note 7)	22,493	24,166
Contributed surplus	230	219
Retained earnings	32,214	36,902
	54,937	61,287
	$ 83,365	$ 89,869

Approved by the Board

Edwin F. Hawken, Director   *Jeffrey Wortsman*, Director

Source: Danier Leather, *2005 Audited Annual Report*, September 2005, p. 2.

COMPLETING THE WORK SHEET

The individual amounts on the trial balance are then transferred to either the income statement section or the balance sheet section of the work sheet. The columns are totalled and the net income is determined. Then, the work sheet columns are balanced and double ruled.

Look again at Figure 11-7 to see the completed work sheet for Henley Sporting Goods. The major difference between this work sheet and that of a service company is the addition of the Purchases and Merchandise Inventory accounts. The Purchases account is transferred to the income statement section. As regards the Merchandise Inventory account, the new inventory value is shown in the debit column of the balance sheet section and in the credit column of the income statement section. The old, or beginning, inventory value is shown in the debit column of the income statement section.

UNIT 26

REVIEW QUESTIONS

1. Where is the beginning inventory figure found on the work sheet?

2. Why is the inventory figure in the trial balance section of the work sheet different from the inventory figure in the balance sheet section of the work sheet?

3. How is the ending inventory determined?

4. What is the General Journal entry to set up the new inventory value at the end of the fiscal period?

5. What is the General Journal entry to close the beginning inventory?

6. How is the inventory adjustment shown on the work sheet?

7. What are the major differences between a work sheet for a service business and a work sheet for a merchandising business?

8. Does the perpetual inventory system require an end-of-period adjusting entry? Why or why not?

1. (a) A business uses the perpetual inventory system. At the end of its fiscal period, February 28, the Merchandise Inventory ledger account has a balance of $118 600. On February 28, the physical inventory taken (counting and pricing) amounts to $116 800. Record the journal entry necessary to ensure the accuracy of the balance in the Merchandise Inventory ledger account.

   (b) Another business uses the periodic inventory system. At the end of its fiscal period, January 31, the Merchandise Inventory ledger account has a balance of $101 750. After taking an inventory, the physical count is $89 250. Record the journal entries necessary to adjust the balance in the Merchandise Inventory ledger account.

2. The first four columns of Wade's Book Store's work sheet for 2009 appear below. Complete the work sheet in your workbook. The December 31 inventory was determined to be $6300.

   Note: The straight-line method for the amortization of capital assets is used in all of the exercises.

UNIT 26

PROBLEMS: APPLICATIONS

ACCOUNT TITLE	ACC. NO.	TRIAL BALANCE DEBIT	TRIAL BALANCE CREDIT	ADJUSTMENTS DEBIT	ADJUSTMENTS CREDIT
Cash	101	750			
Accounts Receivable	110	1 920			
Merchandise Inventory, December 1	120	7 100			
Unexpired Insurance	130	580			(b)360
Store Fixtures	160	3 500			
Accum. Amortization — Store Fixt.	161		900		(a)280
Accounts Payable	200		3 350		
PST Payable	205		352		
GST Payable	206		308		
GST Refundable	207	210			
S. Wade, Capital	300		7 400		
S. Wade, Drawings	301	1 800			
Sales Revenue	400		59 540		
Sales Returns & Allowances	401	1 600			
Sales Discounts	402	1 200			
Purchases	500	43 000			
Purchases Returns & Allowances	501		1 900		
Purchases Discounts	502		800		
Transportation-in	508	1 200			
Advertising Expense	600	5 390			
Rent Expense	601	2 800			
Salaries Expense	602	3 500			
		74 550	74 550		
Amortization Expense — Store Fixt.	603			(a) 280	
Insurance Expense	604			(b) 360	
				640	640

3. From the year-end trial balance shown below and the following additional information, prepare a work sheet. Set up your own account names and numbers.

Additional Information:

- Merchandise Inventory, December 31, valued at $72 000.
- Supplies on hand, December 31, valued at $1800.
- The Allowance for Bad Debts account must be increased to $950 using the balance sheet method.
- Store Fixtures: eight-year estimated life and no residual value.
- Interest owing but unrecorded, $810.
- Salaries owing to employees, $1680.

Heritage Antiques Ltd.
Trial Balance
December 31, 2009

ACCOUNT TITLE	ACC. NO.	DEBIT	CREDIT
Cash	100	$ 13 730	
Accounts Receivable	102	19 500	
Allowance for Bad Debts	103		$ 250
Merchandise Inventory, January 1	120	80 000	
Supplies	131	5 000	
Store Fixtures	141	20 000	
Accum. Amortization — Store Fixtures	142		7 500
Accounts Payable	200		7 500
PST Payable	205		1 730
GST Payable	206		1 520
GST Refundable	207	470	
Bank Loan	221		11 000
F. Will, Capital	300		65 750
F. Will, Drawings	301	39 000	
Sales Revenue	400		305 000
Purchases	500	115 000	
Advertising Expense	610	9 150	
Office Expense	611	4 000	
Store Expense	612	7 200	
Rent Expense	613	24 000	
Salaries Expense	614	62 000	
Interest Expense	615	1 200	
		$400 250	$400 250

4. Prepare a work sheet for Cooper's Hardware Store using the trial balance shown below and the following additional information.

Additional Information:

- Merchandise Inventory, December 31, valued at $8500.
- Supplies on hand valued at $450.
- Insurance expired, $1200.
- Building: $30 000 residual value and an estimated life of 25 years.
- Store Fixtures: six year useful life and a residual value of $5000.
- Bad debts are recorded at 1 percent of net credit sales.

Cooper's Hardware Store
Trial Balance
December 31, 2009

ACCOUNT TITLE	ACC. NO.	DEBIT	CREDIT
Cash	100	$ 5 200	
Accounts Receivable	102	8 000	
Merchandise Inventory, January 1	120	21 000	
Supplies	121	1 700	
Prepaid Insurance	122	2 000	
Land	140	40 000	
Building	141	120 000	
Store Fixtures	143	35 000	
Accounts Payable	200		$ 8 700
PST Payable	205		1 800
GST Payable	206		1 640
GST Refundable	207	560	
Mortgage Payable	210		55 000
M. Cooper, Capital	300		172 620
M. Cooper, Drawings	301	35 500	
Sales Revenue	400		195 000
Sales Returns & Allowances	401	1 000	
Sales Discounts	402	300	
Purchases	500	95 000	
Transportation on Purchases	501	7 000	
Purchases Returns & Allowances	502		3 300
Purchases Discounts	503		3 000
Salaries Expense — Selling	610	30 000	
Salaries Expense — Administrative	611	20 000	
Delivery Expense	612	7 000	
Utilities Expense	613	6 300	
Property Tax Expense	614	5 500	
		$441 060	$441 060

5. Ian Baird formed Baird's Furniture Store on January 1, 2010. At year-end, the trial balance shown below was prepared. Prepare an eight-column work sheet for Baird's Furniture Store using the trial balance and the additional information given. Set up any additional accounts you require. Choose appropriate account names and numbers.

Additional Information:

- Merchandise Inventory, December 31, valued at $165 000.
- Cost of insurance that expired during the year, $780.
- Supplies on hand, $640.
- Building: $45 000 residual value and a useful life of 30 years; Store Fixtures: five-year estimated life and a $3000 residual value.
- Interest to date on the Mortgage Payable, $1100.
- Salaries and wages owing at the end of the year, $3960.
- Property taxes accrued but unpaid, $2400.
- An Allowance for Bad Debts account must be set up with bad debts recorded at 1 percent of gross sales.

Baird's Furniture Store
Trial Balance
December 31, 2010

ACCOUNT TITLE	ACC. NO.	DEBIT	CREDIT
Cash	101	$ 12 800	
Accounts Receivable	110	38 000	
Merchandise Inventory, January 1	120	205 000	
Supplies	126	2 840	
Unexpired Insurance	127	1 080	
Land	140	140 000	
Building	150	225 000	
Store Fixtures	155	24 000	
Accounts Payable	200		$ 72 100
PST Payable	205		2 540
GST Payable	206		2 225
GST Refundable	207	1 320	
Mortgage Payable	210		83 000
I. Baird, Capital	300		376 415
I. Baird, Drawings	301	45 000	
Sales Revenue	400		568 700
Sales Returns & Allowances	401	9 000	
Sales Discounts	402	3 500	
Purchases	500	287 500	
Purchases Returns & Allowances	501		6 500
Purchases Discounts	502		2 100
Transportation-in	503	19 640	
Advertising Expense	601	14 000	
Delivery Expense	602	3 500	
Salaries and Wages Expense	603	72 900	
Property Tax Expense	604	8 500	
		$1 113 580	$1 113 580

UNIT 27 Financial Statements

Learning Objectives

After reading this unit, discussing the applicable review questions, and completing the applications exercises, you will be able to do the following:

PREPARE the following for a merchandising company:

- Schedule of cost of goods sold

- Classified income statement

- Classified balance sheet

- Adjusting, closing, and reversing entries

MERCHANDISING BUSINESS USING A PERIODIC INVENTORY SYSTEM

Once the work sheet has been completed, financial statements are prepared. These include the schedule of cost of goods sold, the income statement, and the balance sheet. The financial statements may also include a separate statement of owner's equity. If such a statement is used, the complete equity calculation is not included in the owner's equity section of the balance sheet. Examples of this situation were shown in Chapter 5 in Figures 5-9 and 5-10.

PREPARING THE SCHEDULE OF COST OF GOODS SOLD

The first statement prepared is the **schedule of cost of goods sold**. The cost information used to prepare this schedule is found in the income statement section of the work sheet. The cost information used by Henley Sporting Goods includes Merchandise Inventory — beginning and ending inventories — and Purchases. Other cost accounts that appear in the schedule of cost of goods sold of some merchandising companies are:

> A schedule used to indicate how the cost of goods sold on the balance sheet was determined.

- Transportation on Purchases
- Purchases Returns and Allowances
- Purchases Discounts

Henley Sporting Goods uses a periodic inventory system. The schedule of cost of goods sold for the year 2010 is shown in Figure 11-12:

Henley Sporting Goods Schedule of Cost of Goods Sold For the year ended December 31, 2010		
Merchandise Inventory, January 1	$ 90 000	
Add: Purchases	120 000	
Total Cost of Merchandise	210 000	
Less: Merchandise Inventory, December 31	81 800	
Cost of Goods Sold		$128 200

FIGURE 11-12

Schedule of cost of goods sold for Henley Sporting Goods

ⓟREPARING THE INCOME STATEMENT (OR STATEMENT OF EARNINGS)

Statement of earnings is another name for an income statement.

Now that the cost of goods sold figure has been determined from the schedule of cost of goods sold, the income statement can be prepared. Figure 11-12 reveals that the goods sold during the year cost $128 200. This figure is now used on the income statement (Figure 11-13) to determine the gross profit. The items in the revenue and expenses sections of the income statement are obtained from the work sheet.

Classified Income Statement

The grouping of accounts using a standardized format is an aid to those who examine and interpret financial statements. Owners, managers, creditors, and government officials examine the financial statements of a variety of companies. Their task is made easier by the use of standard or classified financial statements.

A classified financial statement is one that groups accounts in a standard format as an aid to those who examine and interpret the statement.

The income statement shown in Figure 11-13 is a classified statement. There are three main sections in a **classified income statement**: revenue, cost of goods sold, and operating expenses. Two separate categories may be found in the expenses sections of merchandising companies: administrative expenses and selling expenses, illustrated in Figure 11-13.

FIGURE 11-13

Income statement for Henley Sporting Goods

Henley Sporting Goods Income Statement For the Year Ended December 31, 2010			
Revenue			
Sales			$330 000
Cost of Goods Sold			
Cost of Goods Sold (per schedule)			128 200
Gross Profit			201 800
Operating Expenses			
Administrative Expenses			
Amortization Expense — Building	$ 5 200		
Amortization Expense — Equipment	3 000		
Interest Expense	300		
General Expense	4 000		
Office Salaries Expense	73 140		
Office Supplies Expense	1 620		
Office Insurance Expense	4 200		
Utilities Expense	7 500		
Total Administrative Expenses		$98 960	
Selling Expenses			
Advertising Expense	$ 5 000		
Bad Debts Expense	2 250		
Salespersons' Salaries Expense	48 760		
Sales Supplies Expense	1 080		
Sales Insurance Expense	2 800		
Total Selling Expenses		59 890	
Total Operating Expenses			158 850
Net Income			$ 42 950

Administrative Expenses

Money spent in the general operation of a business is usually classified as an **administrative expense**. This would include expenses involved in the operation of the business office and all departments other than sales. Office salaries, office supplies, and building maintenance are a few examples.

Money spent in the general operation of a business.

Selling Expenses

Money spent for the direct purpose of selling goods is classified as a **selling expense**. Some examples include salespersons' salaries, advertising, deliveries, and sales supplies.

Money spent for the direct purpose of selling goods.

Allocating Responsibility for Expenses

Classifying expenses as administrative or selling expenses provides a detailed breakdown of where the money is being spent. It also allows the top management of a company to allocate responsibility for the spending of money. For example, if the sales manager is held responsible for all selling expenses, it is the responsibility of the sales manager to justify the spending of money for all the selling expenses. The responsibility for administrative expenses may be allocated to someone in the same manner. A person such as an office manager may be held responsible for controlling the administrative expenses.

Some expenses may be allocated as both selling and administrative expenses. For example, Insurance Expense may be incurred on behalf of both the office and the sales departments. Amortization may have to be divided between the administrative and the sales sections. It is the accountant's task to determine a fair basis for allocating the expense. For example, if the office occupies 30 percent of the building, then 30 percent of the amortization on the building would be charged as an administrative expense. If the remaining 70 percent is occupied by the sales sections, then 70 percent of the amortization on the building would be charged as a selling expense.

ⓟ PREPARING THE BALANCE SHEET OR STATEMENT OF FINANCIAL POSITION

Another name for a balance sheet is a **statement of financial position**. The data required for the balance sheet are found in the balance sheet section of the work sheet. The balance sheet for Henley Sporting Goods is shown in Figure 11-14 on page 440. Notice how Capital is updated in the equity section. The additional investments and the difference between the Net Income and Drawings are added to the Capital account.

Statement of financial position is another name for a balance sheet.

An alternative to this presentation would be to prepare the Statement of Owner's Equity as shown below:

Henley's Sporting Goods Statement of Owner's Equity For the Year Ended December 31, 2010		
R. Henley, Capital, January 1, 2010		$125 640
Add: Additional investment	$75 000	
Net Income for the year	42 950	
Less: R. Henley, Drawings	(28 000)	89 950
R. Henley, Capital, December 31, 2010		$215 590

FIGURE 11-14

Balance sheet for Henley
Sporting Goods

Henley Sporting Goods
Balance Sheet
December 31, 2010

ASSETS

Current Assets

Cash		$112 400	
Accounts Receivable	$ 43 000		
Less: Allowance for Bad Debts	2 400	40 600	
Merchandise Inventory		81 800	
Supplies		1 800	
Total Current Assets			$236 600

Capital Assets

Building	160 000		
Less: Accumulated Amortization	52 000	108 000	
Equipment	23 000		
Less: Accumulated Amortization	15 000	8 000	
Total Capital Assets			116 000
Total Assets			$352 600

LIABILITIES AND OWNER'S EQUITY

Current Liabilities

Accounts Payable		$ 23 450	
Salaries Payable		1 900	
PST Payable		2 130	
GST Payable		1 870	
GST Refundable		(640)	
Interest Payable		300	
Bank Loan		20 000	
Total Current Liabilities			$ 49 010

Long-Term Liabilities

Mortgage Payable			88 000
Total Liabilities			137 010

Owner's Equity

R. Henley, Capital, January 1		125 640	
Add: Investment for Year	$ 75 000		
Add: Net Income for Year	42 950		
Less: R. Henley, Drawings	(28 000)		
Increase in Capital		89 950	
R. Henley, Capital, December 31			215 590
Total Liabilities and Owner's Equity			$352 600

Classified Balance Sheet or Statement of Financial Position

The balance sheet shown in Figure 11-14 is also a classified statement. As was said previously in regard to the income statement, it is much easier for users to examine and interpret such standard or classified financial statements.

As you learned in Chapter 5, Unit 10, assets are divided into two sections on a classified balance sheet — *current* and *capital* (sometimes called Plant and Equipment or Property, Plant, and Equipment) — as shown in Figure 11-14. The current assets are listed in order of liquidity, that is, in the order in which they will be converted into cash. The capital assets that have the longest life are listed first in the capital assets section.

Current assets are listed in order of liquidity.

Order of liquidity is the order in which current assets can be converted into cash.

Capital assets are listed in order of longest life first.

Current Assets	Capital Assets
Cash	Land
Accounts Receivable	Building
Merchandise Inventory	Equipment
Prepaid Expenses	Store Fixtures
	Vehicles

Liabilities are also divided into two sections — current and long-term. Current liabilities are those that will be paid within one year. They are listed according to maturity, that is, in the order in which they will be paid. Long-term liabilities are those that have a due date longer than one year. They are also listed according to maturity.

Current Liabilities	Long-Term Liabilities
Accounts Payable	Bank Loan (3 years)
Salaries Payable	Mortgage Payable (25 years)
Interest Payable	
Bank Loan (6 months)	

PREPARING JOURNAL ENTRIES

The adjustments on the work sheet are recorded in the General Journal and then posted to the General Ledger.

Adjusting Entries

You have learned that adjusting journal entries are required so that the adjustments made on the work sheet will become part of the permanent records. When the adjustments on the work sheet are coded with letters such as (a), (b), (c), etc., the preparation of the adjusting entries is made quite simple. The adjusting entries for Henley Sporting Goods are shown in the General Journal in Figure 11-15 (page 442.) See if you can trace these entries back to the work sheet (see Figure 11-7).

Closing Entries

Closing entries are required to prepare the ledger for the next fiscal period and to update the owner's Capital account. The revenue, expense, and cost of goods sold accounts are closed into the Income Summary account. The Income Summary and Drawings accounts are closed into the Capital account. Four basic closing entries are prepared as follows:

(1) Close the credits from the income section of the work sheet.
(2) Close the debits from the income section of the work sheet.
(3) Close the Income Summary account into the Capital account.
(4) Close the Drawings account into the Capital account.

Included in are two entries involving the adjustment for the Merchandise Inventory account. One entry closes the beginning inventory amount and the other records the ending inventory amount in the Merchandise Inventory account.

FIGURE 11-15

Adjusting entries in the
General Journal

GENERAL JOURNAL				PAGE 78
DATE	**PARTICULARS**	**P.R.**	**DEBIT**	**CREDIT**
2010				
Dec. 31	Bad Debts Expense		2 250	
	Allowance for Bad Debts			2 250
	To record estimated bad debts			
	according to age analysis.			
31	Supplies Expense		2 700	
	Supplies			2 700
	To record supplies used.			
31	Amortization Expense — Building		5 200	
	Accum. Amortization — Building			5 200
	To record amortization at 5 percent			
	using declining-balance method.			
31	Amortization Expense — Equipment		3 000	
	Accum. Amortization — Equipment			3 000
	To record amortization at 20 percent			
	using declining-balance method.			
31	Interest Expense		300	
	Interest Payable			300
	To record three months' interest			
	owed on bank loan.			
31	Salaries Expense		1 900	
	Salaries Payable			1 900
	To record salaries owed to employees.			

The General Journal in Figure 11-16 contains the closing entries prepared from the work sheet (see Figure 11-7). Can you trace each entry back to the work sheet? What effect does the credit of $90 000 have on the Merchandise Inventory account? What effect does the debit of $81 800 have on the Merchandise Inventory account?

In Chapter 7 you learned about the perpetual inventory system. Recall that Purchases and the Purchases contra accounts are not used. Therefore, these accounts are not listed on the worksheet or included in the closing entries. If Henley Sporting Goods had used the perpetual inventory system instead of the periodic system, the first two closing entries would be as follows:

2010			
Dec. 31	Sales	330 000	
	Income Summary		330 000
	To close the Sales account.		
Dec. 31	Income Summary	287 050	
	Cost of Goods Sold		128 200
	Advertising Expense		5 000
	•		•
	•		•
	•		•
	•		•
	Interest Expense		300
	To close the Cost of Goods Sold account		
	and the other expense accounts.		

FIGURE 11-16

Closing entries in the General Journal

DATE	PARTICULARS	P.R.	DEBIT	CREDIT
2010				
Dec. 31	Merchandise Inventory		81 800	
	Sales		330 000	
	Income Summary			411 800
	To record the new inventory			
	and to close the Sales account.			
31	Income Summary		368 850	
	Merchandise Inventory			90 000
	Purchases			120 000
	Advertising Expense			5 000
	General Expense			4 000
	Salaries Expense			121 900
	Utilities Expense			7 500
	Insurance Expense			7 000
	Bad Debts Expense			2 250
	Supplies Expense			2 700
	Amortization Expense — Building			5 200
	Amortization Expense — Equipment			3 000
	Interest Expense			300
	To close the inventory account,			
	the cost of goods sold accounts,			
	and the expense accounts.			
31	Income Summary		42 950	
	R. Henley, Capital			42 950
	To transfer the year's net income to			
	the Capital account.			
31	R. Henley, Capital		28 000	
	R. Henley, Drawings			28 000
	To close the Drawings account.			

GENERAL JOURNAL   **PAGE 79**

Notice that Cost of Goods Sold is the first account to be credited. This is because the work sheet would list it as the first expense account. Remember: Cost of Goods Sold is the single largest expense for most merchandising companies! Also notice that Merchandise Inventory is not part of either the first or second closing entry. Being an asset, its ending balance, after any adjustment for shortages, would be listed on the work sheet, balance sheet debit column.

POSTING TO THE LEDGER

The adjusting and closing entries in the General Journal are posted to the General Ledger. After this is done, the revenue, expense, and cost of goods sold accounts, as well as the Drawings account, will have zero balances. They will be ready to receive the revenue, expense, and cost of goods sold transactions for the new fiscal period. The Merchandise Inventory account will contain the new inventory figure. The Capital account will be updated. It will contain the new balance, which takes into consideration the operating results for the fiscal period.

FIGURE 11-17

Partial General Ledger showing some of the ledger accounts after posting of adjusting and closing entries

ACCOUNT   Merchandise Inventory   NO. 120

DATE	PARTICULARS	P.R.	DEBIT	CREDIT	DR. CR.	BALANCE
2010						
Jan. 1	Beginning balance	✓	90 000		DR.	90 000
Dec. 31	To close	J79		90 000		0
31	To record new inventory	J79	81 800		DR.	81 800

ACCOUNT   S. Campbell, Capital   NO. 300

DATE	PARTICULARS	P.R.	DEBIT	CREDIT	DR. CR.	BALANCE
2010						
Jan. 1	Balance	✓			CR.	125 640
Oct. 31	Add'l Investment	J51		75 000	CR.	200 640
Dec. 31	Net Income	J79		42 950	CR.	243 640
31	Drawings	J79	28 000		CR.	215 590

ACCOUNT   S. Campbell, Drawings   NO. 301

DATE	PARTICULARS	P.R.	DEBIT	CREDIT	DR. CR.	BALANCE
2010						
Dec. 31	Balance	✓			DR.	28 000
31	To close	J79	28 000			0

ACCOUNT   Income Summary   NO. 302

DATE	PARTICULARS	P.R.	DEBIT	CREDIT	DR. CR.	BALANCE
2010						
Dec. 31	Merch. Inventory and Sales	J79		411 800	CR.	411 800
31	Merch. Inv., Costs and Exp.	J79	368 850		CR.	42 950
31	Net Income to Capital	J79	42 950			0

ACCOUNT   Sales   NO. 400

DATE	PARTICULARS	P.R.	DEBIT	CREDIT	DR. CR.	BALANCE
2010						
Dec. 31	Balance	✓			CR.	330 000
31	To close	J79	330 000			0

In Figure 11-17, several of the General Ledger accounts are shown after the adjusting and closing entries have been posted. Notice that the Sales account is prepared for the next fiscal period. It has a zero balance and has been ruled closed. The Merchandise Inventory account has been closed and re-opened. It contains the new inventory of $81 800. The Capital account has a balance of $215 590, the same as the new Capital amount on the balance sheet in Figure 11-14.

ⓅREPARING THE POST-CLOSING TRIAL BALANCE

A final proof is required to ensure that the General Ledger is in balance to start the new fiscal period. Figure 11-18 shows the trial balance prepared after the closing entries have been posted. It contains only asset, liability, and equity accounts. All the revenue, expense, and cost of goods sold accounts have been closed and do not have to be shown on the last trial balance.

FIGURE 11-18

Post-closing trial balance proving the accuracy of the recording process in preparation for the new fiscal period

ACCOUNT TITLE	ACC. NO.	DEBIT	CREDIT
\multicolumn{4}{c}{**Henley Sporting Goods**}			

ACCOUNT TITLE	ACC. NO.	DEBIT	CREDIT
Cash	100	$112 400	
Accounts Receivable	102	43 000	
Allowance for Bad Debts	103		$ 2 400
Merchandise Inventory	120	81 800	
Supplies	131	1 800	
Building	140	160 000	
Accumulated Amortization — Building	141		52 000
Equipment	142	23 000	
Accumulated Amortization — Equipment	143		15 000
Accounts Payable	200		23 450
Interest Payable	201		300
Salaries Payable	202		1 900
PST Payable	205		2 130
GST Payable	206		1 870
GST Refundable	207	640	
Bank Loan	221		20 000
Mortgage Payable	231		88 000
R. Henley, Capital	300		215 590
		$422 640	$422 640

Henley Sporting Goods
Post-Closing Trial Balance
December 31, 2010

EXAMINING REVERSING ENTRIES

Earlier in this chapter, you learned how to adjust accrued expenses. The example used was $300 interest, which was owed on a bank loan. The loan was for six months. At the end of the fiscal period, three months' interest of $300 was owed but had not been recorded because it was not due to be paid until March 31. The following T-accounts illustrate the adjusting and closing entries made on December 31:

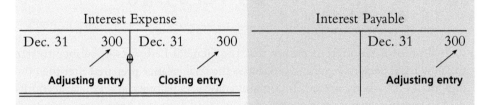

On March 31, payment was made to the bank for six months' interest of $600. This covered the full period of the loan, October 1 to March 31. When this entry was made, Interest Expense was debited $600 and Cash was credited $600 as shown here:

Interest Expense				Cash			
Dec. 31	300	Dec. 31	300			Mar. 31	600
Mar. 31	600						

But there is a dilemma here. Can you see it? How much interest on this loan had already been recorded in December?

Because of the adjusting entry, the interest for October 1 to December 31 ($300) was recorded twice — once when the adjustment was made and again when the interest was actually paid to the bank in March. A total of $900 ($300 + $600) has been recorded in the Interest Expense account. The actual amount of the interest is $600. This double recording of interest is avoided by the use of a **reversing entry**.

On January 3, the first working day after the end of the fiscal period, this reversing entry is made:

Reversing entries are entries necessary to make accurate adjustments to accrued revenue.

Jan. 3	Interest Payable	300	
	Interest Expense		300
	To reverse the adjusting entry of Dec. 31.		

The effect of this entry is shown in the following T-accounts:

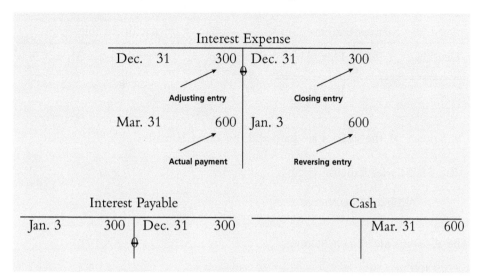

Notice that the reversing entry of January 3 has the effect of allocating half the actual interest paid to the new fiscal period and half to the previous fiscal period. This is correct and results in the correct matching of expenses and revenue for each fiscal period.

Other Reversing Entries

Reversing entries are required for all accrued expense and accrued revenue adjustments. Earlier in this chapter, an adjusting entry for salaries owed ($1900) was explained. The adjusting entry is shown in these T-accounts:

Salaries Expense		Salaries Payable	
Dec. 31 1 900			Dec. 31 1 900

This entry was necessary because salaries are paid the month after they have been earned. The closing entries resulted in the following:

Salaries Expense	
Dec. 31 1 900	Dec. 31 1 900

The following reversing entry was made on January 3. This entry was necessary to avoid a double recording of the salaries:

Jan. 3	Salaries Payable	1 900	
	Salaries Expense		1 900
	To reverse the adjusting entry of Dec. 31.		

The accounts now appear as follows:

Salaries Expense						Salaries Payable			
Dec. 31	1 900	Dec. 31	1 900		Jan. 31	1 900	Dec. 31	1 900
		Jan. 3	1 900					

On January 31 the salaries are paid and this entry is made:

Jan. 31	Salaries Expense	1 900	
	Cash		1 900
	To pay December salaries.		

The accounts are shown below:

Salaries Expense						Cash		
Dec. 31	1 900	Dec. 31	1 900				Jan. 31	1 900
Jan. 31	1 900	Jan. 3	1 900					

The reversing entry avoids double recording of the $1900. Similar reversing entries are prepared on the first working day of the new fiscal period for all accrued expense and revenue adjustments.

Reversing entries could be avoided by debiting the payable account when payment is made in the new fiscal period. However, this is *not* done; with a number of accruals and payments spread out over months, it would be easy to forget to handle the transactions correctly. To avoid errors and reliance on one person's memory, it is standard accounting practice to use the reversing entry procedure.

COMPLETING THE ACCOUNTING CYCLE

You have now learned the final steps in the accounting cycle for a merchandising company. Figure 11-19 on page 449 summarizes the complete accounting cycle and illustrates all the tasks completed during the accounting period.

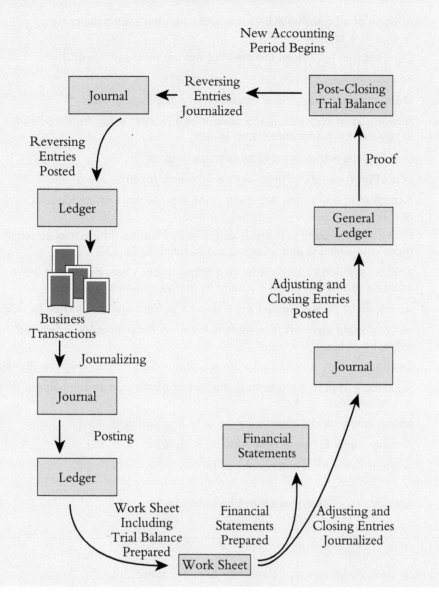

ACCOUNTING CYCLE

FIGURE 11-19
The accounting cycle is a continuous process.

ⒶCCOUNTING TERMS

Accounts Receivable Age Analysis	A listing of all customers' balances and how long each balance has been owed. (p. 410)
Accrued Expenses	Expenses that have been incurred but not yet recorded. (p. 417)
Accrued Revenue	Revenue earned but not yet recorded. (p. 419)
Administrative Expenses	Money spent in the general operation of a business. (p. 439)
Allowance for Bad Debts	A contra-asset account used to determine a realistic value for Accounts Receivable on the balance sheet. (p. 409)
Bad Debts	Uncollectible amounts owed by customers. (p. 407)
Bad Debts Expense	Loss of revenue due to uncollectible accounts. (p. 407)
Balance Sheet Method	A method of estimating bad debts using a percentage of accounts receivable. (p. 410)
Classified Statements	Financial statements that group accounts in a standard format as an aid to those who examine and interpret the statements. (p. 438)
Direct Write-Off Method	Another method to account for bad debts. It is not based on a bad debts estimate calculation and is not used by many companies. (p. 416)
Income Statement Method	A method of estimating bad debts using a percentage of net sales. (p. 410)
Net Realizable Accounts Receivable	Net realizable accounts receivable is Accounts Receivable less estimated bad debts. (p. 411)
Reversing Entries	Entries necessary to make accurate adjustments to accrued revenue. (p. 446)
Schedule of Cost of Goods Sold	A schedule used to indicate how the cost of goods sold on the balance sheet was determined. (p. 437)
Selling Expenses	Money spent for the direct purpose of selling goods. (p. 439)
Statement of Earnings	Another name for an income statement. (p. 438)
Statement of Financial Position	Another name for a balance sheet. (p. 439)
Uncollectible Accounts	Accounts receivable that cannot be collected. (p. 413)

REVIEW QUESTIONS

1. What is the purpose of classifying financial statements?

2. What are the two classes into which operating expenses may be divided?

3. What are the five separate sections on a classified balance sheet?

4. Explain why reversing entries are necessary.

5. Which adjusting entries require reversing entries?

6. Explain how the closing entries result in the Merchandise Inventory account being both closed and opened.

7. What is the purpose of the post-closing trial balance?

1. (a) Prepare schedules of cost of goods sold for each of the following
       companies. The fiscal period is the month of July 2009.

Company X

Beginning Merchandise Inventory	$34 000
Purchases	62 000
Transportation on Purchases	1 650
Purchases Returns and Allowances	3 500
Ending Merchandise Inventory	26 650

Company Y

Beginning Merchandise Inventory	$50 000
Purchases	91 800
Transportation on Purchases	6 400
Duty	7 900
Purchases Returns and Allowances	4 100
Purchases Discounts	1 800
Ending Merchandise Inventory	42 800

Company Z

Beginning Merchandise Inventory	$ 36 900
Purchases	101 300
Transportation on Purchases	5 000
Sales Discounts	5 600
Sales Returns and Allowances	7 800
Purchases Returns and Allowances	7 500
Ending Merchandise Inventory	53 200

   (b) Which inventory system do Companies X, Y, and Z use?

2. (a) Shown below is a list of expenses. Divide the list into two sections —
       administrative expenses and selling expenses. Insurance, Utilities,
       Telephone, and Amortization — Building are all divided 70 percent to
       selling expenses and 30 percent to administrative expenses.
   (b) What is the total of the selling expenses and the total of the administra-
       tive expenses?
   (c) What is the net income if the gross profit is $59 820?
   (d) What are net sales if the cost of goods sold is $49 330?

Expenses

Advertising	$ 3 500
Utilities	2 800
Salaries — Office	10 300
Delivery	6 000
Office Supplies (used)	630
Insurance	690
Amortization — Building	4 150
Amortization — Truck	2 650
Store Supplies (used)	970
Telephone	470

3. (a) Prepare a classified income statement for exercise 3 on page 434. Heritage Antiques Ltd. classifies Bad Debts Expense as a selling expense and allocates Supplies Expense, Rent Expense, Amortization Expense, and Salaries Expense 75 percent to selling expenses and 25 percent to administrative expenses.
   (b) Prepare a classified balance sheet.
   (c) Journalize the adjusting and closing entries. Use journal page 96.
   (d) Post the adjusting and closing entries.
   (e) Prepare a post-closing trial balance.

4. The following adjustments were prepared on December 31. In a General Journal, prepare the reversing entries that would be made on January 3.

2008			
Dec. 31	Interest Expense	1 175	
	Interest Payable		1 175
	To record interest owed but not yet paid.		
31	Salaries Expense	3 650	
	Salaries Payable		3 650
	To record salaries owed to workers but not yet paid.		

5. A company pays its workers every two weeks. The next payday is January 4. Employees are owed (but have not been paid) $2970 for work in December.

   (a) Prepare the adjusting entry to record salaries owing on December 31, 2010.
   (b) Prepare the reversing entry on January 2, 2011.

6. At the end of fiscal period 2007, a company has earned, but not received, interest of $4250 on a long-term deposit. Prepare the adjusting and reversing entries.

7. At the beginning of 2009, Davis Manufacturing Company purchased a new colour copier for its office. The copier cost $40 000. It is expected to have a five-year useful life and a $4000 residual value.
   (a) Calculate the amortization for each of the five years, assuming that the company uses
      (1) Straight-line amortization.
      (2) Declining-balance amortization at twice the straight-line rate.
   (b) Record the December 31 amortization expense for the second year under both methods.

8. The Giant Bookstore uses the perpetual inventory system. A partial list of the store's accounting records follows:

Cash	15 870
Interest Expense	8 450
J. Tinsdale, Drawings	80 000
Interest Revenue	10 250
Salaries Payable	4 780
Cost of Goods Sold	348 600
Accounts Receivable	22 400
Office Supplies	6 340
General Expenses	127 900
Merchandise Inventory, December 31	273 400
Selling Expenses	196 800
Sales	759 125

Required: Prepare the December 31, 2009, closing entries for The Giant Bookstore.

CHAPTER 11

**PROBLEMS:
CHALLENGES**

1. The completed adjusted work sheet for Sandals Unlimited is shown on page 454.
   (a) In a general journal, prepare the adjusting entries.
   (b) Prepare the closing entries.
   (c) Open T-accounts for Income Summary and M. Pitre, Capital.
   (d) Post relevant entries to the Income Summary and Capital accounts.
   (e) What is Pitre's capital beginning the new year?

2. Using the work sheet completed for Cooper's Hardware Store in exercise 4 on page 435:

   (a) Prepare an income statement.
   (b) Prepare a statement of owner's equity.
   (c) Prepare a classified balance sheet.
   (d) Journalize on page 87 the adjusting and closing entries.

3. The accounts and balances shown on page 455 appear on The Uptowne Store's partial work sheet as of June 30, 2008, the end of its fiscal year.

   (a) Without completing the work sheet, prepare an income statement.
   (b) Prepare a classified balance sheet.

   Note: Inventory on hand June 30 is $27 400. All operating expenses are summarized in the General Expense account.

Sandals Unlimited
Worksheet
December 31, 20--

ACCOUNT TITLE	ACC. NO.	TRIAL BALANCE DEBIT	TRIAL BALANCE CREDIT	ADJUSTMENTS DEBIT	ADJUSTMENTS CREDIT	INCOME STATEMENT DEBIT	INCOME STATEMENT CREDIT	BALANCE SHEET DEBIT	BALANCE SHEET CREDIT
Cash		3 000						3 000	
Accounts Receivable		9 000						9 000	
Inventory		145 000						145 000	
Prepaid Rent		10 000			(a) 5 000			5 000	
Equipment		50 000						50 000	
Accumulated Amortization			20 000		(b) 6 000				26 000
Accounts Payable			12 000						12 000
Salaries Payable					(c) 2 000				2 000
Interest Payable					(d) 1 000				1 000
Note Payable (long-term)			30 000						30 000
M. Pitre, Capital			115 000						115 000
M. Pitre, Withdrawals		80 000						80 000	
Sales			339 000				339 000		
Cost of Goods Sold		130 000				130 000			
Salaries Expense		50 000		(c) 2 000		52 000			
Rent Expense		15 000		(a) 5 000		20 000			
Advertising Expense		9 000				9 000			
Utilities Expense		7 000				7 000			
Amortization Expense				(b) 6 000		6 000			
Insurance Expense		5 000				5 000			
Interest Expense		3 000		(d) 1 000		4 000			
Totals		516 000	516 000	14 000	14 000	233 000	339 000	292 000	186 000
Net Income						106 000			106 000
						339 000	339 000	292 000	292 000

The Uptowne Store
Partial Worksheet
June 30, 2008

ACCOUNT TITLE	TRIAL BALANCE DEBIT	TRIAL BALANCE CREDIT	ADJUSTMENTS DEBIT	ADJUSTMENTS CREDIT
Cash	$ 10 200			
Accounts Receivable	8 900			
Inventory, July 1	38 300			
Store Supplies	2 800			$ 1 900
Land	55 000			
Building	165 000			
Accumulated Amortization — Building		$ 18 000		6 000
Store Equipment	43 000			
Accumulated Amortization — Store Equipment		7 000		3 500
Accounts Payable		7 850		
Interest Payable				1 500
Salaries Payable				2 850
PST Payable		1 427		
GST Payable		1 877		
GST Refundable	1 150			
Property Tax Payable				1 750
Mortgage Payable		108 000		
K. Barclay, Capital		119 346		
K. Barclay, Drawings	42 000			
Sales		289 550		
Sales Returns and Allowances	4 500			
Sales Discounts	3 100			
Purchases	110 500			
Purchases Returns and Allowances		2 800		
Purchases Discounts		4 100		
Transportation on Purchases	6 400			
Selling Expenses	37 500		$ 2 850	
General Expenses	25 800		1 900	
Amortization Expense — Building			6 000	
Amortization Expense — Store Equipment			3 500	
Property Tax Expense			1 750	
Interest Expense	5 800		1 500	
Totals	$559 950	$559 950	$17 500	$17 500

CASE 1
Advice for a Friend

Your friend, Sandeep, has recently received a small inheritance. He wishes to purchase a small business and has located two that are of interest to him. They both are successful enterprises, are in the same industry, and their present owners are willing to sell. Sandeep has graduated from a college business management program and is certain that whichever one he purchases, the business will prosper further under his guidance.

He presents you with only one piece of information about each of them. Company A uses the income statement method for estimating uncollectible accounts and Company B, the balance sheet method.

Do you have enough information to advise Sandeep as to which is the better purchase? Explain your answer.

CASE 2
Interpreting Accounting Data

The following table presents the new sales and the actual bad debts for four years. For each of these years, calculate the percentage of bad debts in relation to sales. Then project (or estimate) the percentage of sales that will become bad debts for Year 5.

Year	Net Sales	Actual Bad Debts	Bad Debts Percentage
1	$ 47 000	$1 200	?
2	135 800	2 100	?
3	268 000	3 750	?
4	335 000	5 100	?

CASE 3
Taking Inventory

At the end of the fiscal period, employees for Sheridan Wholesalers, Inc. made a count of all merchandise on hand. However, a complete section of the warehouse was missed when the inventory was taken. The cost of the merchandise that was missed and not included in the ending inventory figure was $10 400.

(a) What effect does this error have on the income statement and on the balance sheet this year?
(b) If the error went undiscovered, would the net income in the second year be too high or too low?
(c) Over the two-year period, what is the total error in the net income?
(d) Is the owner's equity total correct or incorrect in the second-year balance sheet? Explain your answer.

CASE 4
Accounting Analysis

You are considering buying The Quick Print Store. The income statements for the last four years include the following key figures:

	Year 4	Year 3	Year 2	Year 1
Net Sales	$565 000	$500 000	$445 000	$400 000
Cost of Goods Sold	310 750	280 000	262 550	248 000
Gross Profit	$254 250	$220 000	$182 450	$152 000
Gross Profit Percentage	45%	44%	41%	38%

Note: Operating expenses are 25 percent of net sales each year.

The current owner informs you that the statements indicate that the business is becoming more profitable each year and that it would be an ideal time for you to purchase The Quick Print Store. He explains that not only is the total gross profit increasing, but also the gross profit percentage (gross profit expressed as a percentage of sales) is increasing.

You hire an accountant to examine the books of The Quick Print Store before you make a final decision. She finds the following previously undetected errors:
- The inventory was too high by $18 000 at the end of Year 1.
- The inventory was too low by $5500 at the end of Year 4. All the remaining records of the firm were found to be accurate.
- No change in inventory figures for Year 3.
- Operating expenses were actually 30 percent of net sales for the last two years.

(a) Prepare a revised four-year schedule of gross profit.
(b) Recalculate the gross profit percentage for each year.
(c) Compare the statement trends before and after the correction.
(d) Would you be willing to pay as much for this firm now as you would have before the audit? Explain.
(e) Would you still consider purchasing the business? Why?

ETHICS CASE
Revenue Recognition

Macorreta Fashions is a fairly small but successful men's fashion clothier located in a high-traffic shopping mall. It is owned and managed by Larry Macorreta who, for years, has had a good reputation in the community. It is organized as a sole proprietorship.

Susan is the part-time bookkeeper for the business. She is also an accounting student working toward her professional designation. Susan enjoys her work and feels the experience is very worthwhile for her studies and her future career in accounting. She is also very grateful for the part-time job as it allows her to continue her education in accounting.

At the end of each day, sales totals are entered on a weekly summary sheet that has columns for cash sales, cheques, Visa, and MasterCard. A deposit slip is completed and Larry takes the deposit to the bank. Susan is responsible for recording the sales and deposits in the company's accounting system. Often, when Larry returns the sales summary sheet to Susan for recording her accounting entries, the totals have been changed (i.e. decreased) by hand.

Susan notices that each week the cash totals and deposits have been altered by about $500 and monthly gross sales revenue is about $2000 less than it should be.

The owner/manager is the only person to handle the cash and the bank deposits. He also prepares and files the provincial and federal sales tax reports with the two levels of government. When Susan discusses the differences in cash deposited, sales revenue reported, and taxes paid, the owner insists that all sales revenue is reported for tax purposes. Larry also states that, since Susan did not sign the tax forms, she shouldn't worry about anything.

(a) What are the accounting implications of decreasing the bank deposits and sales revenues recorded in the accounting system?
(b) What are the provincial and federal tax implications?
(c) What are the personal income tax implications?
(d) What alternatives are available to Susan?
(e) What would you recommend that Susan do?
(f) What are the personal ethical and legal risks being taken by the owner?

CHAPTER 11

INTERNET RESOURCES

Explore these Web sites for information on the accounting cycle for merchandising companies.

1. **Principles of Accounting**
   www.pearsoned.ca/principlesofaccounting/

   Visit this site for a listing of accounting Web sites, an accounting quiz and reviews of basic accounting concepts and principles.

2. **Business Owner's Toolkit** **www.toolkit.cch.com/text/P06_2900.asp**

   This site explains the various methods of handling and recording bad debts including the cash method, accrual method, estimating allowances, writing off accounts and recovery of bad debts.

3. **It's Simple Biz** **www.itssimple.biz**

   This site provides information on various accounting topics including bad debts and accruals. It has a glossary of business terms. Also included is information on planning, starting and financing a business.

4. **NetMBA** **www.netmba.com/accounting/fin/process/adjusting/**

   This section of the NetMBA site provides explanations and samples of adjusting and reversing entries as well as other accounting information.

THE ACCOUNTING CYCLE

Bronte Office Supplies Ltd.

❶NTRODUCTION

Integrative Activity 2 takes you through the accounting cycle for a merchandising company.

On September 1, M. Burke started a business called Bronte Office Supplies Ltd. Burke went to a public accounting firm, P. London and Associates, and obtained recommendations for an accounting system for the new business. London recommended a five-journal system (Purchases, Sales, Cash Payments, Cash Receipts, and General) and a three-ledger system (General Ledger, Accounts Payable Ledger, and Accounts Receivable Ledger). It was also recommended that Bronte Office Supplies Ltd. use a periodic inventory system and that the accounts shown below be set up in the General Ledger. (Notice that the chart of accounts contains six sections and the accounts commonly used by merchandising companies.) Burke has further engaged London and Associates to make recommendations concerning a computerized accounting system and to set up a system of internal accounting control for Bronte Office Supplies Ltd.

General Ledger Accounts

100	Cash	400	Sales
101	Petty Cash	401	Sales Returns and Allowances
110	Accounts Receivable	402	Sales Discounts
120	Merchandise Inventory	500	Purchases
125	Supplies	501	Purchases Returns and Allow.
126	Prepaid Insurance	502	Purchases Discounts
150	Store Fixtures	503	Transportation on Purchases
151	Accum. Amort. — Store Fixts.	600	Advertising Expense
200	Accounts Payable	601	Delivery Expense
205	PST Payable	602	Accounting Fees Expense
206	GST Payable	603	Miscellaneous Expense
207	GST Refundable	604	Rent Expense
210	Salaries Payable	605	Salaries Expense
300	M. Burke, Capital	606	Telephone Expense
301	M. Burke, Drawings	607	Utilities Expense
302	Income Summary		

Part A

1. Record the September, 2009 transactions (see below, following Part C) in the special journals in your work book. Use Sales Journal, page 10; Cash Receipts Journal, page 20; Purchases Journal, page 11; Cash Payments Journal, page 21; and General Journal, pages 1 and 2. You will note that Bronte Office Supplies Ltd. records GST collected as well as the input tax credits. Therefore, GST Refundable DR. and GST Payable CR. columns are included in the journal.
2. Total, balance, and rule the journals.
3. Post the journals to the General Ledger at the end of the month and to the subsidiary ledgers daily.
4. Prepare a General Ledger trial balance on work sheet paper on September 30.
5. On September 30 prepare schedules for each of the subsidiary ledgers.

Part B

Complete the work sheet and prepare financial statements using the following information:

* Store Fixtures: $2000 residual value, five-year estimated life.
* One month of the 12-month insurance policy has expired.
* At the end of the month, there was $85 worth of supplies on hand.
* The ending inventory is $1625.
* GST is 6 percent; PST is 8 percent.

Part C

1. Journalize the adjusting and closing entries in a General Journal and post.
2. Prepare a post-closing trial balance.

September Transactions

Sep. 1 M. Burke invested $50 730 to start Bronte Office Supplies Ltd.

2 Cheque copies:
No. 1 to P. London and Associates, $1500 plus GST for organizing an accounting system;
No. 2 to Dot Personnel, $1000 plus GST for hiring services (Miscellaneous Expense);
No. 3 to Wexford Realty Ltd., $2800 plus GST for September rent;

3 No. 4 to Preston Wholesalers Co., $3500 plus GST for a cash purchase of merchandise;
No. 5 to *Daily Times*, $450 plus GST for advertising.

3 Purchase invoices:
Butler Supply, T-5986, $2400 plus GST for merchandise, terms net 60 days;
Willson's Ltd., 9324, $250 plus GST for letterhead, business forms, and miscellaneous office supplies, terms net 30 days; Hornby Designs Ltd., 4438, $12 000 plus GST for store fixtures and furnishings, terms: three equal payments, September 15, September 30, and October 31; Lawrence Discount Suppliers, Inc., LD7955, $2000 plus GST for merchandise, terms 2/10, n/30.

4　Cash sales:
　　Sales Invoices 1 to 4, $3250 plus GST and PST.

5　Sales invoices (terms 2/10, n/30 for all sales on account):
　　No. 5, $200 to R. Babbar, plus GST and PST;
　　No. 6, $300 plus GST and PST, to M. Charters;
　　No. 7, $1200 plus GST and PST, to E. Erdman;
　　No. 8, $140 plus GST and PST, to M. Perez.

7　Purchase invoices:
　　Bell Canada, 4987321, $125 plus GST for installation services; CP, H4836, $120
　　plus GST for transportation on merchandise purchases; Jenkins Enterprises,
　　3952, $2900 plus GST for merchandise, terms 3/10, n/60.

9　Credit invoices received:
　　Butler Supply, C-8924, $120 for defective merchandise plus GST, total credit
　　$127.20; Hornby Designs, C-5558, $250 allowance off the price of scratched fix-
　　tures plus GST, total credit $265.

10　Cash sales:
　　Sales Invoices 9 to 12, $4400, plus GST and PST.

11　Credit invoice issued:
　　No. C-1 to M. Charters, $114 for $100 worth of merchandise returned,
　　$8 PST, $6 GST.

12　Sales invoices:
　　No. 13 to L. Becker, $1200, plus GST and PST;
　　No. 14 to A. Gupta, $5000, plus GST and PST;
　　No. 15 to M. Charters, $2200, plus GST and PST.

14　Cheque copies:
　　No. 6 to Bell Canada, $132.50 on account;
　　No. 7 to CP, $127.20 on account;
　　No. 8 to Hornby Designs, $4240 on account;
　　No. 9 to Lawrence Discount Suppliers, Inc., $2077.60 for invoice of September
　　3 less 2 percent discount.

15　Purchase invoice:
　　Lawrence Discount Suppliers, Inc., LD8347, $275 for merchandise plus GST,
　　terms 2/10, n/30.
　　Cheque copies:
　　No. 10, $3000 for a 12-month comprehensive business insurance policy to
　　Metropolitan Life;
　　No. 11, $200 to establish a petty cash fund.
　　Cash received from customers:
　　R. Babbar $223.44 for September 5 invoice less 2 percent cash discount;
　　M. Perez, $156.41 for September 5 invoice less 2 percent cash discount.

16　Sales invoices:
　　No. 16 to L. Becker, $4000, plus GST and PST;
　　No. 17 to A. Gupta, $650, plus GST and PST;
　　No. 18 to M. Braganolo, $940, plus GST and PST;
　　No. 19 to P. LeDuc, $895, plus GST and PST.

18 Cheque copies:
No. 12 for $126 plus GST to pay for an invoice received today from Quick Delivery Service, terms C.O.D.;
No. 13 for $1500 to M. Burke for personal use;
No. 14 for $2981.78 to Jenkins Enterprises for September 7 invoice, less 3 percent cash discount.

19 Cash sales:
Sales Invoices 20 to 26, $5200, plus GST and PST.

22 Purchase invoices:
CP, H5981, $79 for transportation on purchases of merchandise plus GST;
Willson's Ltd., 9947, $58 for office supplies plus GST.

24 Credit invoice issued:
No. C-2 to P. LeDuc, $45 plus GST and PST, for defective merchandise.

25 Cheque copy:
No. 15 for $155 to replenish petty cash.
Summary of petty cash vouchers:
Office Supplies $35; Miscellaneous Expenses $65;
M. Burke, Drawings $50; GST Refundable $5.

25 Sales invoices:
No. 27 to R. Babbar, $798 plus GST and PST;
No. 28 to A. Gupta, $240 plus GST and PST.

27 Cheque copies:
No. 16 for $3210 to Hornby Designs Ltd. on account;
No. 17 for $2500 to M. Burke for personal use.

29 Purchase invoices:
Bell Canada, 4988412, $55.50, plus GST;
City Light and Power, D4941, $225, plus GST for hydro bill;
Daily Times, 8348, $870 plus GST for newspaper advertising.

30 Cheque No. 18 for $261.50 to the Receiver General for Canada for the GST payment.

CHAPTER **1 2**

Payroll Accounting

 **Paying Employees**

Learning Objectives

After reading this unit, discussing the applicable review questions, and completing the applications exercises, you will be able to do the following:

1. SPECIFY three compulsory deductions.

2. LIST five voluntary deductions.

3. DETERMINE a net claim code for income tax deduction purposes.

4. EXPLAIN the purpose of the social insurance number.

5. OUTLINE the benefits and services provided by Canada Pension Plan, Employment Insurance, health insurance, registered pension plans, credit unions, group insurance, and extended health service.

6. CALCULATE net earnings.

7. SPECIFY five pay periods and six payment plans used by businesses.

8. DEFINE payroll, compulsory deductions, voluntary deductions, TD1 form, gross earnings, statement of earnings and deductions, and net earnings.

All companies pay their employees a wage or a salary and have a payroll accounting procedure as part of the accounting system. The word **payroll** means a list (*roll*) of employees and the money (*pay*) to be given to them. Thus you can see the origin of the phrase "being on the payroll."

The type of accounting procedures used by a company to prepare the payroll depends on the number of employees, the type of equipment available, the complexity of the payroll, and the number of people available in the accounting department.

Payroll procedures may be performed manually or using a computer system. Some companies prefer to buy a payroll service from an accounting firm or from a bank. Such businesses do the payroll work for other companies and charge a fee for providing the service.

A payroll is a list of employees and the amount of money to be paid to them.

EMPLOYMENT LAWS

Companies are required by law to keep certain payroll records, to prepare payroll reports, and to provide each employee with a statement of earnings and deductions. There are both federal and provincial laws governing the payment of employees. One of these is the **Employment Standards Act**.

Provincial laws governing the payment of employees.

Provincial Laws

All provinces have an *Employment Standards Act*. These provincial laws govern:

- Minimum wages
- Hours of work
- Statutory holidays
- Vacation pay
- Overtime
- Many other employment practices

Provincial ministries of labour or departments of labour administer these acts. One of their tasks is to investigate employee complaints of unfair treatment.

These laws ensure that all employees receive fair treatment. For example, all employees must receive the statutory holidays, which are: New Year's Day, Good Friday, Victoria Day, Canada Day, Labour Day, Thanksgiving, and Christmas. The acts also set out the payroll records that must be kept and give provincial government auditors the authority to inspect company records.

Federal Laws

A number of federal laws impose payroll requirements on employers and affect the pay received by all employees. The federal laws include the *Income Tax Act,* the *Canada Pension Act,* the *Employment Insurance Act,* and the *Workers' Compensation Act.* The example of M. Lostracco used in this chapter will illustrate how all workers are affected by the federal laws.

EARNINGS

A statement of earnings and deductions is provided to all employees and shows how net earnings are determined.

M. Lostracco is an employee of Eastern Systems, a computer consulting firm located in Niagara-on-the-Lake. Lostracco earns a salary of $800 a week as a supervisor. However, the paycheque received by Lostracco for one week's pay is for $597.11. The cheque is shown in Figure 12-1. Notice that it also includes a pay statement showing employee earnings and payroll deductions.

If Lostracco earns $800 and receives only $ 597.11, what happens to the difference of $202.89? Does the company keep it? Of course not! The $202.89 deducted from Lostracco's cheque by the employer is passed on to other agencies for Lostracco. For example, $151.25 is sent to the federal government to pay Lostracco's personal income tax; $15.60 is paid out for employment insurance; and $36.04 is paid out for the Canada Pension Plan.

FIGURE 12-1

Paycheque with statement of employee earnings and deductions

Pay statement

STATEMENT OF EMPLOYEE EARNINGS AND PAYROLL DEDUCTIONS

1620	800.00		800.00	36.04	15.60	151.25	0			202.89	597.11	648.72	3821	May 7, 20--
EMP. NO.	REGULAR	OVERTIME	TOTAL GROSS EARN.	CPP	EI	INC. TAX	HLTH.	GR. INS.	OTHER	TOTAL DEDUC-TIONS	NET EARNINGS	TOTAL CPP TO DATE	CH. NO.	PAY PERIOD ENDING
	GROSS EARNINGS					DEDUCTIONS								

MISCELLANEOUS DEDUCTIONS

1 PENSION _____

2 BONDS _____

3 UNION _____

4 _____

5 _____

EASTERN SYSTEMS
19 Queen St.
Niagara-on-the-Lake, ON L0S 1N0

PAYROLL ACCOUNT

CHEQUE NO. __3821__

DATE __May 7, 20--__

PAY TO THE ORDER OF   M. Lostracco ---------------------- $ 597.11

SUM OF   Five hundred ninety-seven ------------- 11/100 DOLLARS

Harry Lock

EASTERN SYSTEMS

THE BANK OF NOVA SCOTIA
3549 Hudson St.
Niagara-on-the-Lake, ON L0S 1N0

Cathy M. Drummond

EASTERN SYSTEMS

Cheque

DEDUCTIONS

The amounts deducted from an employee's pay are called payroll **deductions**. Some deductions are *compulsory* — they apply to all workers. Others are voluntary on the part of the employee.

Deductions are amounts subtracted from an employee's gross earnings.

Compulsory Deductions

Employers are required by law to make three payroll deductions for their employees:

- Personal income tax
- Employment Insurance contributions
- Canada Pension Plan contributions

In some provinces, health insurance is also a compulsory deduction. In Ontario, however, employers must pay an Employer Health Tax rather than deduct premiums from employees.

Employers may also have collective agreements (contracts) with unions that require union dues to be deducted from the employees' earnings. The union dues are then forwarded to the union by the company.

Compulsory payroll deductions include income tax, Canada Pension Plan, and Employment Insurance.

Voluntary Deductions

There are a large number of deductions that an employee may ask the employer to make. These include:

- Charitable donations
- Payments to a credit union
- Group life insurance payments
- Purchase of government bonds
- Extended health insurance premiums
- Private pension plan contributions

These deductions are made by the company if *an employee requests that they be made.* They are then forwarded to the appropriate agency by the company. In effect, the company is handling the payment of some of the employee's personal bills.

ⒺXAMINING COMPULSORY DEDUCTIONS

Canada Pension Plan

All employees over 18 and under 70 contribute a percentage of their earnings during their working years and receive a pension at age 65.

Every employee who is over 18 and under 70 years of age and working in Canada (with minor exceptions) must contribute to the **Canada Pension Plan** (CPP). The amount of the contribution is 4.95 percent of the employee's salary calculated on pensionable earnings of $41 000 equal to a maximum yearly contribution of $1861.20. Upon retirement, anyone who has contributed will receive a pension at the age of 65. A reduced pension is available to those who retire at an earlier age. In the event of death, the contributor's dependants receive a pension.

Federal legislation requires that the employer also make contributions to the Canada Pension Plan on behalf of each employee. The employer contributes an amount equal to the employee's contribution (4.95 percent). Thus, both the employee and the employer are paying for the employee's future pension. Once a month, the company sends all the employees' deductions along with the employer's share to the federal government. In effect, the business is acting as a collection agent for the government and also helping to finance the Canada Pension Plan benefits for the employee.

In Quebec, the province has organized the Quebec Pension Plan. It is operated in much the same way as the Canada Pension Plan.

Employment Insurance

Employees contribute a percentage of their earnings while employed to a fund that is designed to provide income to those workers who later become unemployed.

Employment insurance is designed to provide income to those workers who become unemployed through no fault of their own. Most workers in Canada must contribute to the employment insurance fund. Benefits are received only when a person becomes unemployed. This means that those workers who are fortunate enough never to be unemployed will contribute to the fund but will not receive payments from it.

With minor exceptions, all full-time employees are required to make employment insurance payments. The employer makes payroll deductions from the employees' earnings and forwards the money to the federal government. The amount of contributions is 1.95 percent of earnings, to maximum insurable earnings of $39 000. The maximum employee contribution is $760.50.

The employer must also contribute to the employment insurance fund for its employees. The employer contributes 1.4 times the amount deduction for each employee. Thus for an employee who contributes $760.50 per year, the employer contributes $1064.70 (1.4 × $760.50).

Employment Insurance and the Record of Employment

A form called the Record of Employment must be completed and given to an employee who leaves employment. This form is used to decide if a person is eligible for employment insurance benefits, the amount of the benefits, and how long the person can collect benefits. In effect, it is the employee's proof that contributions have been made and that the employee is entitled to receive benefits from the employment insurance fund. The Record of Employment form must be issued by the employer within five days of the stoppage in employment.

Personal Income Tax

Each year before April 30, Canadians must complete a **personal income tax** return. The *Income Tax Act* requires that employers deduct an amount for income tax from each employee's earnings each payday. Once a month, the employer must send the amounts deducted to the federal government. Through these deductions, workers pay their income tax to the government on a regular basis.

> A percentage of personal income remitted to the federal and provincial governments.

The form, called the T1, is used to determine the amount of income tax deducted from each person's paycheque. The total amount payable is compared to the amount the employee has already paid through payroll deductions each payday. The result may be a refund (money back) for the employee if the payroll deductions were too large or an extra amount owing if the payroll deductions were too low.

The amount of tax payable is determined in two steps.

Step 1: Calculation of Taxable Income

The amount of **taxable income** is determined by the amount of income earned minus deductions. Allowable deductions include payments made for items such as registered pension plan contributions, child care expenses, and union dues.

> Income earned minus allowable deductions such as pension contributions.

Income − (Registered Pension Plan Contributions +
Child Care Expenses + Union Dues) = Taxable Income

Step 2: Calculation of Income Tax

The amount of tax payable is determined by subtracting non-refundable tax credits from the amount of tax owing on taxable income. Non-refundable **tax credits** for items such as dependants, CPP or EI contributions, and tuition reduce the amount of federal income tax payable. They are called non-refundable because, if these credits are more than your federal income tax, the difference is not refunded to you.

> Credits for items such as dependent children, CPP and EI contributions, and tuition reduce the amount of federal income tax payable.

To determine an employee's credits, the employer is required to have each employee complete a *Personal Tax Credits Return* (**TD1** form) when hired, or when there is a new change of credits. This form is used to determine a person's tax credits, which affect the amount of income tax paid. Tax credits are amounts of income on which income tax is not paid. Therefore, a person with a number of credits (e.g., for spouse or infirm dependants) pays less income tax than a person with few credits. Since many provinces have their own tax rates, as well as their own non-refundable tax credits, you have to complete both a federal and a

> A TD1 form shows an employee's claim for non-refundable tax credits. It must be completed by all employees when credits change.

provincial personal tax credit return. Figures 12-2 through 12-4 show the Federal Personal Tax Credit Return (TD1) and Worksheet while Figures 12-5 through 12-7 show the Ontario Personal Tax Credit Return (**TD1ON**) and Worksheet completed for M. Lostracco. All provinces with the exception of Quebec have a Provincial Personal Tax Credit form. The example in this text uses the Ontario forms for tax calculation. Tax forms and tables for all provinces are available at www.cra-arc.gc.ca/lists. You will notice that the employee lists all personal credits to arrive at a net claim code. For Lostracco, the net claim code is 1 for both federal and provincial tax calculations. This code is used by the employer to determine the tax deduction to be made each payday.

EXAMINING VOLUNTARY DEDUCTIONS

Group Life Insurance

Many companies provide a group life insurance plan for their employees. Because of the large number of people joining the plan, the insurance companies provide a group discount rate. The amount paid by each employee is determined by the amount of insurance requested and the age of the employee. For example, an employee who decides to purchase $50 000 worth of life insurance for a premium of 25 cents per $1000 per month, would pay $12.50. The $12.50 is deducted from earnings by the employer and sent to the insurance company for the employee.

Credit Union

A *credit union* is a non-profit banking organization operated by the employees of a company or organization. A credit union is similar to a banking institution. It receives deposits from members and gives interest on the deposits. Funds contributed by the employees are lent to other members who pay interest on money borrowed. The expenses of a credit union are low because it is operated by its own members, facilities are often provided by the employer, and bad debts on loans are rare since loans are made only to the members who are all employed workers. Credit unions provide many banking services, including:

- Loans
- Chequing accounts
- Savings accounts
- Mortgages
- Registered retirement savings plans

Deposits to the credit union, or payments on loans granted by the credit union, may be made through payroll deductions. The employer deducts the appropriate amounts from the employees' earnings and transfers them to the credit union for the employees.

Health Insurance

In Canada, there is *universal health coverage*. This means that everyone is able to obtain health insurance. Each province operates its own health plan. The benefits provided by provincial health insurance plans include:

- Payment of doctors' fees for required services
- Hospital expenses

FIGURE 12-2
Federal Personal Tax Credits
(TD1) form

**Canada Customs
and Revenue Agency**   Agence des douanes
et du revenu du Canada   **2005 PERSONAL TAX CREDITS RETURN**   TD1

Complete this TD1 form if you have a new employer or payer and you will receive salary, wages, commissions, pensions, Employment Insurance benefits, or any other remuneration, or if you wish to increase the amount of tax deducted at source. Be sure to sign and date it on the back page and give it to your employer or payer, who will use it to determine the amount of your tax deductions.

If you do not complete a TD1 form, your new employer or payer will deduct taxes after allowing the basic personal amount **only**.

You **do not** have to complete a new TD1 form every year unless there is a change in your entitlement to personal tax credits. Complete a new TD1 form no later than seven days after the change.

You can get the forms and publications mentioned on this form from our Web site at **www.cra.gc.ca/forms** or by calling **1-800-959-2221**.

Last name Lostracco	First name and initial(s) Mary W.	Date of birth (YYYY/MM/DD) 1979/08/14	Employee number 620

Address including postal code 219 Queen St. Niagara-on-the-Lake LOS 1N0	For non-residents only – Country of permanent residence	Social insurance number 4 5 2 6 3 8 5 2 9

1. Basic personal amount – Every resident of Canada can claim this amount. If you have more than one employer or payer at the same time, see the section called "Income from other employers or payers" on the back page. If you are a non-resident, see the section called "Non-residents" on the back page. — **8,148**

2. Age amount – If you will be 65 or older on December 31, 2005, and your net income for the year will be $29,619 or less, enter $3,979. If your net income will be between $29,619 and $56,146 and you want to calculate a partial claim, get the *Worksheet for the 2005 Personal Tax Credits Return* (TD1-WS) and complete the appropriate section. — 0

3. Pension income amount – If you will receive regular pension payments from a pension plan or fund (excluding Canada or Quebec Pension Plans (CPP/QPP), Old Age Security, and guaranteed income supplements), enter $1,000 or your estimated annual pension income, whichever is less. — 0

4. Tuition and education amounts (full time and part time) – If you are a student enrolled at a university, college, or educational institution certified by Human Resources and Skills Development Canada, and you will pay more than $100 per institution in tuition fees, complete this section. If you are enrolled full time, or if you have a mental or physical disability and are enrolled part time, enter the total of the tuition fees you will pay, plus $400 for each month that you will be enrolled. If you are enrolled part time and do not have a mental or physical disability, enter the total of the tuition fees you will pay, plus $120 for each month that you will be enrolled part time. — 0

5. Disability amount – If you will claim the disability amount on your income tax return by using Form T2201, *Disability Tax Credit Certificate*, enter $6,596. — 0

6. Spouse or common-law partner amount – If you are supporting your spouse or common-law partner who lives with you, and whose net income for the year will be $692 or less, enter $6,919. If his or her net income for the year will be between $692 and $7,611 and you want to calculate a partial claim, get the *Worksheet for the 2005 Personal Tax Credits Return* (TD1-WS) and complete the appropriate section. — 0

7. Amount for an eligible dependant – If you do not have a spouse or common-law partner and you support a dependent relative who lives with you, and whose net income for the year will be $692 or less, enter $6,919. If his or her net income for the year will be between $692 and $7,611 and you want to calculate a partial claim, get the *Worksheet for the 2005 Personal Tax Credits Return* (TD1-WS) and complete the appropriate section. — 0

8. Caregiver amount – If you are taking care of a dependant who lives with you, whose net income for the year will be $13,141 or less, and who is either your or your spouse's or common-law partner's:
• parent or grandparent (aged 65 or older), **or**
• relative (aged 18 or older) who is dependent on you because of an infirmity,
enter $3,848. If the dependant's net income for the year will be between $13,141 and $16,989 and you want to calculate a partial claim, get the *Worksheet for the 2005 Personal Tax Credits Return* (TD1-WS) and complete the appropriate section. — 0

9. Amount for infirm dependants age 18 or older – If you are supporting an infirm dependant aged 18 or older who is your or your spouse's or common-law partner's relative, who lives in Canada, and whose net income for the year will be $5,460 or less, enter $3,848. You cannot claim an amount for a dependant you claimed on line 8. If the dependant's net income for the year will be between $5,460 and $9,308 and you want to calculate a partial claim, get the *Worksheet for the 2005 Personal Tax Credits Return* (TD1-WS) and complete the appropriate section. — 0

10. Amounts transferred from your spouse or common-law partner – If your spouse or common-law partner will not use all of his or her age amount, pension income amount, tuition and education amounts, or disability amount on his or her income tax return, enter the unused amount. — 0

11. Amounts transferred from a dependant – If your dependant will not use all of his or her **disability amount** on his or her income tax return, enter the unused amount. If your or your spouse's or common-law partner's dependent child or grandchild will not use all of his or her **tuition and education amounts** on his or her income tax return, enter the unused amount. — 0

12. TOTAL CLAIM AMOUNT – Add lines 1 through line 11. Your employer or payer will use this amount to determine the amount of your tax deductions. — **8148.00**

Form continues on the back ➡

TD1 E (05)   (Vous pouvez obtenir ce formulaire en français à www.arc.gc.ca/formulaires ou au 1 800 959-3376.)   Canada

FIGURE 12-3

Back of Federal Personal Tax
Credits (TD1) form

┌─ Deduction for living in a prescribed zone ──────────────────────────────────

If you live in the Northwest Territories, Nunavut, Yukon, or another prescribed **northern** zone for more than six months in a row beginning or ending in 2005, you can claim:

- $7.50 for each day that you live in the prescribed northern zone, or
- $15 for each day that you live in the prescribed northern zone if, during that time, you live in a dwelling that you maintain, and you are the only person living in that dwelling who is claiming this deduction.

Employees living in a prescribed **intermediate** zone can claim 50% of the total of the above amounts.

$ _____

For more information, get Form T2222, *Northern Residents Deductions*, and the publication called *Northern Residents Deductions – Places in Prescribed Zones* (T4039).

┌─ Total income less than total claim amount ──────────────────────────────────

Will your total income for the year from all employers and payers be less than your total claim amount on line 12? Yes ☐ No ☐

If *yes*, your employer or payer will not deduct tax from your earnings.

┌─ Additional tax to be deducted ──────────────────────────────────

You may want to have more tax deducted from each payment, especially if you receive other income, including non-employment income such as CPP or QPP benefits, or Old Age Security pension. By doing this, you may not have to pay as much tax when you file your income tax return.

To choose this option, state the amount of additional tax you want to have deducted. To change this deduction later, you will have to complete a new TD1 form, *Personal Tax Credits Return.*

$ _____

┌─ Reduction in tax deductions ──────────────────────────────────

You can ask to have less tax deducted if on your income tax return you are eligible for deductions or non-refundable tax credits that are not listed on this form (for example, periodic contributions to an RRSP, child care or employment expenses, and charitable donations). To make this request, complete Form T1213, *Request to Reduce Tax Deductions at Source,* to get a letter of authority from your tax services office.

Give the letter of authority to your employer or payer. You do not need a letter of authority if your employer deducts RRSP contributions from your salary.

┌─ Non-residents ──────────────────────────────────

If you are a non-resident of Canada, tick this box and answer the question below. If you are unsure of your residency status, call the International Tax Services Office at **1-800-267-5177**. Non-resident ☐

Will you include 90% or more of your world income when determining your taxable income earned in Canada in 2005? If *yes*, complete the front page. If *no*, enter "0" on line 12 on the front page and do not complete lines 2 to 11 as you are not entitled to the personal tax credits. Yes ☐ No ☐

┌─ Income from other employers or payers ──────────────────────────────────

If you have more than one employer or payer at the same time and you have already claimed personal tax credit amounts on another TD1 form for 2005, you can choose not to claim them again. By doing this, you may not have to pay as much tax when you file your income tax return. To choose this option, enter "0" on line 12 on the front page and do not complete lines 2 to 11.

┌─ Certification ──────────────────────────────────

I certify that the information given in this return is, to the best of my knowledge, correct and complete.

Signature _*Mary Lostracco*_   Date *Jan 4/05*

It is a serious offence to make a false return.

┌─ Provincial or territorial personal tax credits return ──────────────────────────────────

In addition to this federal personal tax credits return, you may have to complete a provincial or territorial personal tax credits return.

If your claim amount on line 12 on the front page is more than $8,148, complete a provincial or territorial TD1 form in addition to this form. If you are an employee, use the TD1 form for your province or territory of employment. If you are a pensioner, use the TD1 form for your province or territory of residence. Your employer or payer will use both this form and your most recent provincial or territorial TD1 form to determine your tax deductions.

If you are claiming the basic personal amount **only** (your claim amount on line 12 on the front page is $8,148), do not complete a provincial or territorial TD1 form. Your employer or payer will deduct provincial or territorial taxes after allowing the provincial or territorial basic personal amount.

Note: If you are a Saskatchewan resident supporting children under 18 at any time during 2005, you may be entitled to claim the child amount on the *2005 Saskatchewan Personal Tax Credits Return* (TD1SK). Therefore, you may want to complete the TD1SK form even if you are claiming the basic personal amount **only** on the front page of this form (your claim amount on line 12 is $8,148).

If you entered "0" on line 12 on the front page because you are a non-resident and you will not include 90% or more of your world income when determining your taxable income earned in Canada in 2005, do not complete a provincial or territorial TD1 form. You are not entitled to the provincial or territorial personal tax credits.

Printed in Canada

FIGURE 12-4

Worksheet for the 2005
Personal Tax Credits Return
(TD1-WS) (Canada Customs
and Revenue Agency)

Canada Customs and Revenue Agency   **Agence des douanes et du revenu du Canada**

**WORKSHEET FOR THE
2005 PERSONAL TAX CREDITS RETURN**

TD1-WS

Complete this worksheet if you want to calculate partial claims for your Form TD1, *2005 Personal Tax Credits Return*, for the following:

- Age amount
- Spouse or common-law partner amount
- Amount for an eligible dependant
- Caregiver amount
- Amount for infirm dependants age 18 or older

Do not give your completed worksheet to your employer or payer. Keep it for your records.

Line 2 of your TD1 form – Age amount

If you will be 65 or older on December 31, 2005, and your estimated net income from all sources for the year will be between $29,619 and $56,146, calculate your partial claim as follows:

Maximum age amount	3,979	1
Your estimated net income for the year		2
Base amount	− 29,619	3
Line 2 minus line 3	=	4
Multiply the amount on line 4 by 15% × 15% =	−	5
Line 1 minus line 5. Enter this amount on line 2 of your TD1 form.	=	

Line 6 of your TD1 form – Spouse or common-law partner amount

If your spouse's or common-law partner's estimated net income for the year (including the income earned before and during the marriage or common-law relationship) will be between $692 and $7,611, calculate your partial claim as follows:

Base amount	7,611	1
Your spouse's or common-law partner's estimated net income for the year	−	2
Line 1 minus line 2. Enter this amount on line 6 of your TD1 form.	=	

Line 7 of your TD1 form – Amount for an eligible dependant

If your dependant's estimated net income for the year will be between $692 and $7,611, calculate your partial claim as follows:

Base amount	7,611	1
Your dependant's estimated net income for the year	−	2
Line 1 minus line 2. Enter this amount on line 7 of your TD1 form.	=	

Line 8 of your TD1 form – Caregiver amount

If your dependant's estimated net income for the year will be between $13,141 and $16,989, calculate your partial claim as follows:

Base amount	16,989	1
Your dependant's estimated net income for the year	−	2
Line 1 minus line 2 (maximum $3,848)	=	3
Minus: the amount claimed on line 7 of your TD1 form for this dependant	−	4
Line 3 minus line 4. Enter this amount on line 8 of your TD1 form.	=	

Line 9 of your TD1 form – Amount for infirm dependants age 18 or older

You cannot claim this amount for a dependant for whom you claimed the caregiver amount on line 8 of your TD1 form.

If your infirm dependant's estimated net income for the year will be between $5,460 and $9,308, calculate your partial claim as follows:

Base amount	9,308	1
Your infirm dependant's estimated net income for the year	−	2
Line 1 minus line 2 (maximum $3,848)	=	3
Minus: the amount claimed on line 7 of your TD1 form for this dependant	−	4
Line 3 minus line 4. Enter this amount on line 9 of your TD1 form.	=	

TD1-WS E (05)
Printed in Canada

(Vous pouvez obtenir ce formulaire en français à **www.arc.gc.ca/formulaires** ou au **1 800 959-3376**.)

Canada

FIGURE 12-5

Ontario Personal Tax Credits
(TD1ON) form

Ontario   **2005 ONTARIO PERSONAL TAX CREDITS RETURN**   TD1ON

Do you have to complete this form?

Complete this form if you have not previously given an Ontario TD1 form to your employer or payer, or if there has been a change in your entitlement to personal tax credits, and you are:

- an employee working in Ontario; or
- a pensioner residing in Ontario.

If you complete this form, be sure to sign and date it on the back page and give it to your employer or payer. Your employer or payer will use both this form and your most recent federal TD1 form to determine the amount of your tax deductions.

Last name	First name and initial(s)	Date of birth (YYYY/MM/DD)	Employee number
Lostracco	Mary W.	1979/08/14	620

Address including postal code	For non-residents only – Country of permanent residence	Social insurance number
219 Queen St. Niagara-on-the-Lake LOS 1N0		4 5 2 6 3 8 5 2 9

1. Basic personal amount – Every person employed in Ontario and every pensioner residing in Ontario can claim this amount. If you will have more than one employer or payer at the same time in 2005, see the section called "Income from other employers or payers" on the back page. — **8,196**

2. Age amount – If you will be 65 or older on December 31, 2005, and your net income from all sources will be $29,793 or less, enter $4,002. If your net income will be between $29,793 and $56,473 and you want to calculate a partial claim, get the *Worksheet for the 2005 Ontario Personal Tax Credits Return* (TD1ON-WS) and complete the appropriate section. — ∅

3. Pension income amount – If you will receive regular pension payments from a pension plan or fund (excluding Canada or Quebec Pension Plans (CPP/QPP), Old Age Security, and guaranteed income supplements), enter $1,133 or your estimated annual pension income, whichever is less. — ∅

4. Tuition and education amounts (full time and part time) – If you are a student enrolled at a university, college, or educational institution certified by Human Resources and Skills Development Canada, and you will pay more than $100 per institution in tuition fees, complete this section. If you are enrolled full time, or if you have a mental or physical disability and are enrolled part time, enter the total of the tuition fees you will pay, plus $441 for each month that you will be enrolled. If you are enrolled part time and do not have a mental or physical disability, enter the total of the tuition fees you will pay, plus $132 for each month that you will be enrolled part time. — ∅

5. Disability amount – If you will claim the disability amount on your income tax return by using Form T2201, *Disability Tax Credit Certificate*, enter $6,622. — ∅

6. Spouse or common-law partner amount – If you are supporting your spouse or common-law partner who lives with you, and whose net income for the year will be $696 or less, enter $6,960. If his or her net income for the year will be between $696 and $7,656 and you want to calculate a partial claim, get the *Worksheet for the 2005 Ontario Personal Tax Credits Return* (TD1ON-WS) and complete the appropriate section. — ∅

7. Amount for an eligible dependant – If you do not have a spouse or common-law partner and you support a dependent relative who lives with you, and whose net income for the year will be $696 or less, enter $6,960. If his or her net income for the year will be between $696 and $7,656 and you want to calculate a partial claim, get the *Worksheet for the 2005 Ontario Personal Tax Credits Return* (TD1ON-WS) and complete the appropriate section. — ∅

8. Caregiver amount – If you are taking care of a dependant who lives with you, whose net income for the year will be $13,218 or less, and who is either your or your spouse's or common-law partner's:
- parent or grandparent (aged 65 or older), or
- relative (aged 18 or older) who is dependent on you because of an infirmity,

enter $3,863. If the dependant's net income for the year will be between $13,218 and $17,081 and you want to calculate a partial claim, get the *Worksheet for the 2005 Ontario Personal Tax Credits Return* (TD1ON-WS) and complete the appropriate section. — ∅

9. Amount for infirm dependants age 18 or older – If you are supporting an infirm dependant aged 18 or older who is your or your spouse's or common-law partner's relative, who lives in Canada, and whose net income for the year will be $5,492 or less, enter $3,863. You cannot claim an amount for a dependant you claimed on line 8. If the dependant's net income for the year will be between $5,492 and $9,355 and you want to calculate a partial claim, get the *Worksheet for the 2005 Ontario Personal Tax Credits Return* (TD1ON-WS) and complete the appropriate section. — ∅

10. Amounts transferred from your spouse or common-law partner – If your spouse or common-law partner will not use all of his or her age amount, pension income amount, tuition and education amounts, or disability amount on his or her income tax return, enter the unused amount. — ∅

11. Amounts transferred from a dependant – If your dependant will not use all of his or her **disability amount** on his or her income tax return, enter the unused amount. If your or your spouse or common-law partner's dependent child or grandchild will not use all of his or her **tuition and education amounts** on his or her income tax return, enter the unused amount. — ∅

12. TOTAL CLAIM AMOUNT – Add lines 1 through line 11. Your employer or payer will use your claim amount to determine the amount of your provincial tax deductions. — **8196.00**

Form continues on the back ⟶

TD1ON E (05)   (Vous pouvez obtenir ce formulaire en français à www.arc.gc.ca/formulaires ou au 1 800 959-3376.)   **Canada**

FIGURE 12-6

Back of Ontario Personal Tax
Credit (TD1ON) form

Forms and publications

You can get forms and publications on our Web site at **www.cra.gc.ca/forms** or by calling **1-800-959-2221**.

Why is there an Ontario TD1 form?

Your employer or payer uses the personal tax credit amounts you claim on your Ontario TD1 form to calculate how much provincial tax to deduct from each payment.

Total income less than total claim amount

Will your total income for the year from all employers and payers be less than your total claim amount on line 12?   Yes ☐   No ☒
If *yes*, your employer or payer will not deduct tax from your earnings.

Addition or reduction to tax deductions

If you wish to have **more tax deducted**, complete the section called "Additional tax to be deducted" on the federal TD1 form.

You can ask to have **less tax deducted** if on your income tax return you are eligible for deductions or non-refundable tax credits that are not listed on this form. To make this request, complete Form T1213, *Request To Reduce Tax Deductions At Source,* to get a letter of authority from your tax services office. Give the letter of authority to your employer or payer. You do not need a letter of authority if your employer deducts RRSP contributions from your salary.

Income from other employers or payers

If you have more than one employer or payer at the same time and you have already claimed personal tax credit amounts on another Form TD1ON for 2005, you can choose not to claim them again. By doing this, you may not have to pay as much tax when you file your income tax return. To choose this option, enter "0" on line 12 on the front page and do not complete lines 2 to 11.

Certification

I certify that the information given in this return is, to the best of my knowledge, correct and complete.

Signature _____*Mary Lostracco*_____   Date __Jan 4/05__
It is a serious offence to make a false return.

Printed in Canada

The cost to the public for this insurance varies from province to province. Many companies pay part or all of the health insurance premium as a fringe benefit for their employees. Often this is part of a contract negotiated with the union. The portion of the monthly premium paid by the company is an expense of operating the business and is recorded in an account called Health Insurance Expense or in an account called Payroll Expense. In Ontario, the public does not pay directly for health insurance. Employers pay an Employer Health Tax, which will be explained later in this chapter.

In provinces where employees pay part or all of the premium, the premium is deducted from earnings by the employer and is sent to the provincial health plan organization.

FIGURE 12-7
Worksheet for the 2005
Ontario Personal Tax Credits
Return (TD1ON-WS)

WORKSHEET FOR THE 2005 ONTARIO PERSONAL TAX CREDITS RETURN

Ontario   TD1ON-WS

Complete this worksheet if you want to calculate partial claims for your Form TD1ON, *2005 Ontario Personal Tax Credits Return*, for the following:
- Age amount
- Spouse or common-law partner amount
- Amount for an eligible dependant
- Caregiver amount
- Amount for infirm dependants age 18 or older

Do not give your completed worksheet to your employer or payer. Keep it for your records.

Line 2 of your TD1ON form – Age amount

If you will be 65 or older on December 31, 2005, and your estimated net income from all sources for the year will be between $29,793 and $56,473, calculate your partial claim as follows:

Maximum age amount	4,002	1
Your estimated net income for the year		2
Base amount	− 29,793	3
Line 2 minus line 3	=	4
Multiply the amount on line 4 by 15% × 15% =	→ −	5
Line 1 minus line 5. Enter this amount on line 2 of your TD1ON form.	=	

Line 6 of your TD1ON form – Spouse or common-law partner amount

If your spouse's or common-law partner's estimated net income for the year (including the income earned before and during the marriage or common-law relationship) will be between $696 and $7,656, calculate your partial claim as follows:

Base amount	7,656	1
Your spouse's or common-law partner's estimated net income for the year	−	2
Line 1 minus line 2. Enter this amount on line 6 of your TD1ON form.	=	

Line 7 of your TD1ON form – Amount for an eligible dependant

If your dependant's estimated net income for the year will be between $696 and $7,656, calculate your partial claim as follows:

Base amount	7,656	1
Your dependant's estimated net income for the year	−	2
Line 1 minus line 2. Enter this amount on line 7 of your TD1ON form.	=	

Line 8 of your TD1ON form – Caregiver amount

If your dependant's estimated net income for the year will be between $13,218 and $17,081, calculate your partial claim as follows:

Base amount	17,081	1
Your dependant's estimated net income for the year	−	2
Line 1 minus line 2 (maximum $3,863)	=	3
Minus: the amount claimed on line 7 of your TD1ON form for this dependant	−	4
Line 3 minus line 4. Enter this amount on line 8 of your TD1ON form.	=	

Line 9 of your TD1ON form – Amount for infirm dependants age 18 or older

You cannot claim this amount for a dependant for whom you claimed the caregiver amount on line 8 of your TD1ON form.

If your infirm dependant's estimated net income for the year will be between $5,492 and $9,355, calculate your partial claim as follows:

Base amount	9,355	1
Your infirm dependant's estimated net income for the year	−	2
Line 1 minus line 2 (maximum $3,863)	=	3
Minus: the amount claimed on line 7 of your TD1ON form for this dependant	−	4
Line 3 minus line 4. Enter this amount on line 9 of your TD1ON form.	=	

TD1ON-WS E (05)
Printed in Canada

(Vous pouvez obtenir ce formulaire en français à www.arc.gc.ca/formulaires ou au 1 800 959-3376.)

Canada

FIGURE 12-8
Federal Claim Codes

Chart 1 – Tableau 1
2006 federal claim codes – Codes de demande fédéraux pour 2006

Total claim amount ($) Montant total de la demande ($)		Claim code Code de demande	Total claim amount ($) Montant total de la demande ($)			Claim code Code de demande
No claim amount – Nul		0	18,274.01	–	20,121.00	7
Minimum	–	9,039.00	1	20,121.01	–	21,968.00	8
9,039.01	–	10,886.00	2	21,968.01	–	23,815.00	9
10,886.01	–	12,733.00	3	23,815.01	–	25,662.00	10
12,733.01	–	14,580.00	4	25,662.01	and over – et plus	X
14,580.01	–	16,427.00	5	The employer must do a manual calculation of tax. L'employeur doit faire le calcul manuel de l'impôt.	
16,427.01	–	18,274.00	6	No withholding – Aucune retenue	E

FIGURE 12-9
Ontario Claim Codes

Chart 2 – Tableau 2
2006 Ontario claim codes – Codes de demande de l'Ontario pour 2006

Total claim amount ($) Montant total de la demande ($)		Claim code Code de demande	Total claim amount ($) Montant total de la demande ($)			Claim code Code de demande
No claim amount – Nul		0	17,402.01	–	19,207.00	7
Minimum	–	8,377.00	1	19,207.01	–	21,012.00	8
8,377.01	–	10,182.00	2	21,012.01	–	22,817.00	9
10,182.01	–	11,987.00	3	22,817.01	–	24,622.00	10
11,987.01	–	13,792.00	4	24,622.01	and over – et plus	X
13,792.01	–	15,597.00	5	The employer must do a manual calculation of tax. L'employeur doit faire le calcul manuel de l'impôt.	
15,597.01	–	17,402.00	6	No withholding – Aucune retenue	E

Source: Figures 12-2 through 12-9 copyright © Canada Revenue Agency. Reproduced with permission of the Minister of Public Works and Government Services Canada, 2006.

Extended Health Insurance Plans

Provincial health plans do not pay for all health services. Many employees like to have additional health insurance provided by insurance companies. The premiums for additional health insurance are deducted from the employees' earnings by the employer and sent to the appropriate insurance organization.

Extended health plans provide benefits not covered by provincial plans such as:

- Cost of prescription drugs
- Special medical services and supplies
- Semi-private or private hospital accommodation
- Home-care nursing

Registered Pension Plans

Employees of some companies can voluntarily join a private pension plan. This plan provides pension benefits to the employee upon retirement. The pension is in addition to the benefits the employee would receive from the Canada Pension Plan.

While working, the employee contributes to the private pension plan through payroll deductions. The employer sends the money deducted to the insurance company. Usually, the employer makes a matching contribution on behalf of the employee.

Private pension plans are usually registered with the federal government. Contributions made to a registered pension plan (RPP) are an eligible income tax deduction. Each year when completing their personal income tax returns (T1), employees are allowed to deduct, for income tax purposes, the payments made to an RPP. This lowers the amount of income tax to be paid by the worker.

GOVERNMENT REQUIREMENTS

To receive benefits from employment insurance and the Canada Pension Plan, a person must have contributed to the plans. The contributions are recorded using each person's social insurance number (SIN).

Social Insurance Number

The recording of contributions is much more efficiently done by SIN than by name. Can you imagine how many *Jack Chins, Mary Smiths,* or *Maurice Leblancs* there are in Canada? By assigning numbers to each person, the possibilities of error due to similarities in names is eliminated. The Canada Revenue Agency also uses the SIN to handle the tax records of Canadians.

Books and Records

Every person carrying on a business in Canada is required by law to keep records and accounts for income tax, Canada Pension Plan, and employment insurance purposes. The records must contain enough information to determine the correct payroll deductions. On request, the records must be made available to officers of the Canada Revenue Agency. Normally, the records must be kept for a minimum of six years. Written permission of the Minister of National Revenue is required before records are destroyed.

CALCULATING NET EARNINGS

Net earnings is the balance remaining after deductions have been subtracted from gross earnings.

Gross earnings are the total earnings of an employee before deductions.

The **net earnings** for an employee are determined as follows:

$$\text{Gross Earnings} - \text{Deductions} = \text{Net Earnings}$$

In M. Lostracco's case:

$$\$800 - \$202.89 = \$597.11$$

The deductions of \$202.89 are as follows:

Canada Pension Plan	\$ 36.04
Employment Insurance	15.60
Income Tax	151.25
Total Deductions	\$202.89

Let's examine the calculation of each of these deductions.

Canada Pension Plan Deduction

Lostracco's employer consults the Canada Revenue Agency booklet, Payroll Deductions Tables, to get the CPP deduction. Figure 12-10 on pages 479–481 shows pages from this booklet. It indicates that the CPP contribution required on weekly earnings of $800 is $36.04. Note: Taking 4.95 percent of an employee's earnings will not give the same figures as on the CPP chart. The reason for this is that there is a basic yearly exemption (currently $3500).

Employment Insurance Deduction

The same booklet contains a section on employment insurance. Figure 12-11 on pages 482–484 shows that the maximum EI premium deduction required on gross weekly earnings of $800 is $15.60. Notice, however, that maximum premium deduction for the year is $760.50. According to the table, Lostracco's EI contribution on a weekly salary of $800 is $15.60. Once the year-to-date deduction reaches $760.50, no more is deducted.

Income Tax Deduction

Lostracco's income tax deduction for the week is determined by referring again to the Payroll Deductions Tables and using the taxable earnings amount and the net claim code from the TD1 and TD1ON forms. Figure 12-12 on page 485 and Figure 12-13 on page 486 show that for taxable earnings of $800 and with a net claim code of 1, the income tax deduction is:

Federal Tax	+	Provincial Tax	=	Total Income Tax
$102.00	+	$49.25	=	$151.25

When an employee contributes to an RPP or pays union dues, the contribution reduces taxable earnings. To find the taxable earnings for employees who have these deductions, the calculation is:

Taxable Earnings = Gross Earnings − (Registered Pension Plan Contributions + Union Dues + Other Authorized Deductions [Alimony Payments, Living Away from Home Deductions, Child Care, etc.])

Taxable earnings are the earnings that remain after non-taxable deductions. Taxable earnings are used to determine the amount of income tax that will be deducted.

Would Lostracco's income tax deduction change if she had paid union dues or made an RPP contribution during the pay period? Yes, it would, since the income tax deduction is based on taxable earnings.

Example:

Gross Earnings	−	RPP	−	Union Dues	=	Taxable Earnings
$800	−	$50.00	−	$14.50	=	$735.50

Figures 12-12 and 12-13 show the income tax deduction for taxable earnings of $735.50 at net claim code 1 is $88.40 + $43.50 = $131.90. Therefore Lostracco's tax deduction is reduced as a result of having approved income tax deductions.

Net Earnings

Lostracco's cheque, Figure 12-1, was for net earnings of $597.11. This figure was arrived at as follows:

Gross Earnings	–	Deductions	=	Net Earnings
$800	–	$202.89	=	$597.11

Ⓟ AYROLL ACCOUNTING PROCEDURES

Lostracco is paid a salary of $800 for a work period of one week. A variety of other pay periods can also be used for payroll.

Pay Periods

Payrolls are prepared for different time periods, such as:

- Weekly: every week, or 52 times a year
- Bi-weekly: every two weeks, or 26 times a year
- Monthly: every month, or 12 times a year
- Semi-monthly: twice a month, or 24 times a year

Payment Plans

A variety of payment plans are used by companies. Lostracco is paid on a salary basis.

Salary

The employee's earnings are a set amount for a stated period of time. The salary is an amount for a week, a month, or a year, for example, $1000 a week, $4250 a month, or $52 000 a year. A common practice is to hire on a yearly basis and then to pay the worker according to one of the pay periods described above.

Hourly Rate

In this plan, workers are paid an hourly rate for each hour worked. An employee working at the rate of $12 an hour who works 40 hours a week would earn $480 (before deductions).

Commission

Sales personnel are often paid on a commission basis. Their earnings are determined by the amount of sales they make. The gross earnings for a person who gets a 4 percent commission and has sales of $15 000 are $600 ($15 000 × 0.04 = $600).

Combination of Salary and Commission

It is more common to see a combination of a set minimum salary plus a commission on sales. An employee might receive a base salary of $300 a week plus a 2 percent commission on sales. If the week's sales are $10 000, the employee receives a total of $600 ($300 + 0.02 × $15 000 = $600).

Piece Rate

Manufacturing companies often use the piece-rate method. To provide an incentive to workers, payment is based on the number of units the worker produces. If an employee is paid $1.75 per unit and completes 350 units, the earnings are $612.50.

FIGURE 12-10
CPP Contribution Tables

Canada Pension Plan Contributions
Weekly (52 pay periods a year)

Cotisations au Régime de pensions du Canada
Hebdomadaire (52 périodes de paie par année)

Pay Rémunération From - De	To - À	CPP RPC	Pay Rémunération From - De	To - À	CPP RPC	Pay Rémunération From - De	To - À	CPP RPC	Pay Rémunération From - De	To - À	CPP RPC
649.02	649.21	28.80	663.57	663.76	29.52	678.11	678.31	30.24	692.66	692.85	30.96
649.22	649.42	28.81	663.77	663.96	29.53	678.32	678.51	30.25	692.86	693.05	30.97
649.43	649.62	28.82	663.97	664.16	29.54	678.52	678.71	30.26	693.06	693.25	30.98
649.63	649.82	28.83	664.17	664.37	29.55	678.72	678.91	30.27	693.26	693.46	30.99
649.83	650.02	28.84	664.38	664.57	29.56	678.92	679.11	30.28	693.47	693.66	31.00
650.03	650.22	28.85	664.58	664.77	29.57	679.12	679.32	30.29	693.67	693.86	31.01
650.23	650.43	28.86	664.78	664.97	29.58	679.33	679.52	30.30	693.87	694.06	31.02
650.44	650.63	28.87	664.98	665.17	29.59	679.53	679.72	30.31	694.07	694.26	31.03
650.64	650.83	28.88	665.18	665.38	29.60	679.73	679.92	30.32	694.27	694.47	31.04
650.84	651.03	28.89	665.39	665.58	29.61	679.93	680.12	30.33	694.48	694.67	31.05
651.04	651.23	28.90	665.59	665.78	29.62	680.13	680.33	30.34	694.68	694.87	31.06
651.24	651.44	28.91	665.79	665.98	29.63	680.34	680.53	30.35	694.88	695.07	31.07
651.45	651.64	28.92	665.99	666.18	29.64	680.54	680.73	30.36	695.08	695.27	31.08
651.65	651.84	28.93	666.19	666.39	29.65	680.74	680.93	30.37	695.28	695.48	31.09
651.85	652.04	28.94	666.40	666.59	29.66	680.94	681.13	30.38	695.49	695.68	31.10
652.05	652.24	28.95	666.60	666.79	29.67	681.14	681.34	30.39	695.69	695.88	31.11
652.25	652.45	28.96	666.80	666.99	29.68	681.35	681.54	30.40	695.89	696.08	31.12
652.46	652.65	28.97	667.00	667.19	29.69	681.55	681.74	30.41	696.09	696.28	31.13
652.66	652.85	28.98	667.20	667.40	29.70	681.75	681.94	30.42	696.29	696.49	31.14
652.86	653.05	28.99	667.41	667.60	29.71	681.95	682.14	30.43	696.50	696.69	31.15
653.06	653.25	29.00	667.61	667.80	29.72	682.15	682.35	30.44	696.70	696.89	31.16
653.26	653.46	29.01	667.81	668.00	29.73	682.36	682.55	30.45	696.90	697.09	31.17
653.47	653.66	29.02	668.01	668.20	29.74	682.56	682.75	30.46	697.10	697.29	31.18
653.67	653.86	29.03	668.21	668.41	29.75	682.76	682.95	30.47	697.30	697.50	31.19
653.87	654.06	29.04	668.42	668.61	29.76	682.96	683.15	30.48	697.51	697.70	31.20
654.07	654.26	29.05	668.62	668.81	29.77	683.16	683.36	30.49	697.71	697.90	31.21
654.27	654.47	29.06	668.82	669.01	29.78	683.37	683.56	30.50	697.91	698.10	31.22
654.48	654.67	29.07	669.02	669.21	29.79	683.57	683.76	30.51	698.11	698.31	31.23
654.68	654.87	29.08	669.22	669.42	29.80	683.77	683.96	30.52	698.32	698.51	31.24
654.88	655.07	29.09	669.43	669.62	29.81	683.97	684.16	30.53	698.52	698.71	31.25
655.08	655.27	29.10	669.63	669.82	29.82	684.17	684.37	30.54	698.72	698.91	31.26
655.28	655.48	29.11	669.83	670.02	29.83	684.38	684.57	30.55	698.92	699.11	31.27
655.49	655.68	29.12	670.03	670.22	29.84	684.58	684.77	30.56	699.12	699.32	31.28
655.69	655.88	29.13	670.23	670.43	29.85	684.78	684.97	30.57	699.33	699.52	31.29
655.89	656.08	29.14	670.44	670.63	29.86	684.98	685.17	30.58	699.53	699.72	31.30
656.09	656.28	29.15	670.64	670.83	29.87	685.18	685.38	30.59	699.73	699.92	31.31
656.29	656.49	29.16	670.84	671.03	29.88	685.39	685.58	30.60	699.93	700.12	31.32
656.50	656.69	29.17	671.04	671.23	29.89	685.59	685.78	30.61	700.13	700.33	31.33
656.70	656.89	29.18	671.24	671.44	29.90	685.79	685.98	30.62	700.34	700.53	31.34
656.90	657.09	29.19	671.45	671.64	29.91	685.99	686.18	30.63	700.54	700.73	31.35
657.10	657.29	29.20	671.65	671.84	29.92	686.19	686.39	30.64	700.74	700.93	31.36
657.30	657.50	29.21	671.85	672.04	29.93	686.40	686.59	30.65	700.94	701.13	31.37
657.51	657.70	29.22	672.05	672.24	29.94	686.60	686.79	30.66	701.14	701.34	31.38
657.71	657.90	29.23	672.25	672.45	29.95	686.80	686.99	30.67	701.35	701.54	31.39
657.91	658.10	29.24	672.46	672.65	29.96	687.00	687.19	30.68	701.55	701.74	31.40
658.11	658.31	29.25	672.66	672.85	29.97	687.20	687.40	30.69	701.75	701.94	31.41
658.32	658.51	29.26	672.86	673.05	29.98	687.41	687.60	30.70	701.95	702.14	31.42
658.52	658.71	29.27	673.06	673.25	29.99	687.61	687.80	30.71	702.15	702.35	31.43
658.72	658.91	29.28	673.26	673.46	30.00	687.81	688.00	30.72	702.36	702.55	31.44
658.92	659.11	29.29	673.47	673.66	30.01	688.01	688.20	30.73	702.56	702.75	31.45
659.12	659.32	29.30	673.67	673.86	30.02	688.21	688.41	30.74	702.76	702.95	31.46
659.33	659.52	29.31	673.87	674.06	30.03	688.42	688.61	30.75	702.96	703.15	31.47
659.53	659.72	29.32	674.07	674.26	30.04	688.62	688.81	30.76	703.16	703.36	31.48
659.73	659.92	29.33	674.27	674.47	30.05	688.82	689.01	30.77	703.37	703.56	31.49
659.93	660.12	29.34	674.48	674.67	30.06	689.02	689.21	30.78	703.57	703.76	31.50
660.13	660.33	29.35	674.68	674.87	30.07	689.22	689.42	30.79	703.77	703.96	31.51
660.34	660.53	29.36	674.88	675.07	30.08	689.43	689.62	30.80	703.97	704.16	31.52
660.54	660.73	29.37	675.08	675.27	30.09	689.63	689.82	30.81	704.17	704.37	31.53
660.74	660.93	29.38	675.28	675.48	30.10	689.83	690.02	30.82	704.38	704.57	31.54
660.94	661.13	29.39	675.49	675.68	30.11	690.03	690.22	30.83	704.58	704.77	31.55
661.14	661.34	29.40	675.69	675.88	30.12	690.23	690.43	30.84	704.78	704.97	31.56
661.35	661.54	29.41	675.89	676.08	30.13	690.44	690.63	30.85	704.98	705.17	31.57
661.55	661.74	29.42	676.09	676.28	30.14	690.64	690.83	30.86	705.18	705.38	31.58
661.75	661.94	29.43	676.29	676.49	30.15	690.84	691.03	30.87	705.39	705.58	31.59
661.95	662.14	29.44	676.50	676.69	30.16	691.04	691.23	30.88	705.59	705.78	31.60
662.15	662.35	29.45	676.70	676.89	30.17	691.24	691.44	30.89	705.79	705.98	31.61
662.36	662.55	29.46	676.90	677.09	30.18	691.45	691.64	30.90	705.99	706.18	31.62
662.56	662.75	29.47	677.10	677.29	30.19	691.65	691.84	30.91	706.19	706.39	31.63
662.76	662.95	29.48	677.30	677.50	30.20	691.85	692.04	30.92	706.40	706.59	31.64
662.96	663.15	29.49	677.51	677.70	30.21	692.05	692.24	30.93	706.60	706.79	31.65
663.16	663.36	29.50	677.71	677.90	30.22	692.25	692.45	30.94	706.80	706.99	31.66
663.37	663.56	29.51	677.91	678.10	30.23	692.46	692.65	30.95	707.00	707.19	31.67

Employee's maximum CPP contribution for the year 2005 is $1,861.20   B-11   La cotisation maximale de l'employé au RPC pour l'année 2005 est de 1 861,20 $

FIGURE 12-10
continued

Canada Pension Plan Contributions
Weekly (52 pay periods a year)

Cotisations au Régime de pensions du Canada
Hebdomadaire (52 périodes de paie par année)

Pay Rémunération From - De	To - À	CPP RPC	Pay Rémunération From - De	To - À	CPP RPC	Pay Rémunération From - De	To - À	CPP RPC	Pay Rémunération From - De	To - À	CPP RPC
707.20 -	707.40	31.68	721.75 -	721.94	32.40	736.29 -	736.49	33.12	750.84 -	751.03	33.84
707.41 -	707.60	31.69	721.95 -	722.14	32.41	736.50 -	736.69	33.13	751.04 -	751.23	33.85
707.61 -	707.80	31.70	722.15 -	722.35	32.42	736.70 -	736.89	33.14	751.24 -	751.44	33.86
707.81 -	708.00	31.71	722.36 -	722.55	32.43	736.90 -	737.09	33.15	751.45 -	751.64	33.87
708.01 -	708.20	31.72	722.56 -	722.75	32.44	737.10 -	737.29	33.16	751.65 -	751.84	33.88
708.21 -	708.41	31.73	722.76 -	722.95	32.45	737.30 -	737.50	33.17	751.85 -	752.04	33.89
708.42 -	708.61	31.74	722.96 -	723.15	32.46	737.51 -	737.70	33.18	752.05 -	752.24	33.90
708.62 -	708.81	31.75	723.16 -	723.36	32.47	737.71 -	737.90	33.19	752.25 -	752.45	33.91
708.82 -	709.01	31.76	723.37 -	723.56	32.48	737.91 -	738.10	33.20	752.46 -	752.65	33.92
709.02 -	709.21	31.77	723.57 -	723.76	32.49	738.11 -	738.31	33.21	752.66 -	752.85	33.93
709.22 -	709.42	31.78	723.77 -	723.96	32.50	738.32 -	738.51	33.22	752.86 -	753.05	33.94
709.43 -	709.62	31.79	723.97 -	724.16	32.51	738.52 -	738.71	33.23	753.06 -	753.25	33.95
709.63 -	709.82	31.80	724.17 -	724.37	32.52	738.72 -	738.91	33.24	753.26 -	753.46	33.96
709.83 -	710.02	31.81	724.38 -	724.57	32.53	738.92 -	739.11	33.25	753.47 -	753.66	33.97
710.03 -	710.22	31.82	724.58 -	724.77	32.54	739.12 -	739.32	33.26	753.67 -	753.86	33.98
710.23 -	710.43	31.83	724.78 -	724.97	32.55	739.33 -	739.52	33.27	753.87 -	754.06	33.99
710.44 -	710.63	31.84	724.98 -	725.17	32.56	739.53 -	739.72	33.28	754.07 -	754.26	34.00
710.64 -	710.83	31.85	725.18 -	725.38	32.57	739.73 -	739.92	33.29	754.27 -	754.47	34.01
710.84 -	711.03	31.86	725.39 -	725.58	32.58	739.93 -	740.12	33.30	754.48 -	754.67	34.02
711.04 -	711.23	31.87	725.59 -	725.78	32.59	740.13 -	740.33	33.31	754.68 -	754.87	34.03
711.24 -	711.44	31.88	725.79 -	725.98	32.60	740.34 -	740.53	33.32	754.88 -	755.07	34.04
711.45 -	711.64	31.89	725.99 -	726.18	32.61	740.54 -	740.73	33.33	755.08 -	755.27	34.05
711.65 -	711.84	31.90	726.19 -	726.39	32.62	740.74 -	740.93	33.34	755.28 -	755.48	34.06
711.85 -	712.04	31.91	726.40 -	726.59	32.63	740.94 -	741.13	33.35	755.49 -	755.68	34.07
712.05 -	712.24	31.92	726.60 -	726.79	32.64	741.14 -	741.34	33.36	755.69 -	755.88	34.08
712.25 -	712.45	31.93	726.80 -	726.99	32.65	741.35 -	741.54	33.37	755.89 -	756.08	34.09
712.46 -	712.65	31.94	727.00 -	727.19	32.66	741.55 -	741.74	33.38	756.09 -	756.28	34.10
712.66 -	712.85	31.95	727.20 -	727.40	32.67	741.75 -	741.94	33.39	756.29 -	756.49	34.11
712.86 -	713.05	31.96	727.41 -	727.60	32.68	741.95 -	742.14	33.40	756.50 -	756.69	34.12
713.06 -	713.25	31.97	727.61 -	727.80	32.69	742.15 -	742.35	33.41	756.70 -	756.89	34.13
713.26 -	713.46	31.98	727.81 -	728.00	32.70	742.36 -	742.55	33.42	756.90 -	757.09	34.14
713.47 -	713.66	31.99	728.01 -	728.20	32.71	742.56 -	742.75	33.43	757.10 -	757.29	34.15
713.67 -	713.86	32.00	728.21 -	728.41	32.72	742.76 -	742.95	33.44	757.30 -	757.50	34.16
713.87 -	714.06	32.01	728.42 -	728.61	32.73	742.96 -	743.15	33.45	757.51 -	757.70	34.17
714.07 -	714.26	32.02	728.62 -	728.81	32.74	743.16 -	743.36	33.46	757.71 -	757.90	34.18
714.27 -	714.47	32.03	728.82 -	729.01	32.75	743.37 -	743.56	33.47	757.91 -	758.10	34.19
714.48 -	714.67	32.04	729.02 -	729.21	32.76	743.57 -	743.76	33.48	758.11 -	758.31	34.20
714.68 -	714.87	32.05	729.22 -	729.42	32.77	743.77 -	743.96	33.49	758.32 -	758.51	34.21
714.88 -	715.07	32.06	729.43 -	729.62	32.78	743.97 -	744.16	33.50	758.52 -	758.71	34.22
715.08 -	715.27	32.07	729.63 -	729.82	32.79	744.17 -	744.37	33.51	758.72 -	758.91	34.23
715.28 -	715.48	32.08	729.83 -	730.02	32.80	744.38 -	744.57	33.52	758.92 -	759.11	34.24
715.49 -	715.68	32.09	730.03 -	730.22	32.81	744.58 -	744.77	33.53	759.12 -	759.32	34.25
715.69 -	715.88	32.10	730.23 -	730.43	32.82	744.78 -	744.97	33.54	759.33 -	759.52	34.26
715.89 -	716.08	32.11	730.44 -	730.63	32.83	744.98 -	745.17	33.55	759.53 -	759.72	34.27
716.09 -	716.28	32.12	730.64 -	730.83	32.84	745.18 -	745.38	33.56	759.73 -	759.92	34.28
716.29 -	716.49	32.13	730.84 -	731.03	32.85	745.39 -	745.58	33.57	759.93 -	760.12	34.29
716.50 -	716.69	32.14	731.04 -	731.23	32.86	745.59 -	745.78	33.58	760.13 -	760.33	34.30
716.70 -	716.89	32.15	731.24 -	731.44	32.87	745.79 -	745.98	33.59	760.34 -	760.53	34.31
716.90 -	717.09	32.16	731.45 -	731.64	32.88	745.99 -	746.18	33.60	760.54 -	760.73	34.32
717.10 -	717.29	32.17	731.65 -	731.84	32.89	746.19 -	746.39	33.61	760.74 -	760.93	34.33
717.30 -	717.50	32.18	731.85 -	732.04	32.90	746.40 -	746.59	33.62	760.94 -	761.13	34.34
717.51 -	717.70	32.19	732.05 -	732.24	32.91	746.60 -	746.79	33.63	761.14 -	761.34	34.35
717.71 -	717.90	32.20	732.25 -	732.45	32.92	746.80 -	746.99	33.64	761.35 -	761.54	34.36
717.91 -	718.10	32.21	732.46 -	732.65	32.93	747.00 -	747.19	33.65	761.55 -	761.74	34.37
718.11 -	718.31	32.22	732.66 -	732.85	32.94	747.20 -	747.40	33.66	761.75 -	761.94	34.38
718.32 -	718.51	32.23	732.86 -	733.05	32.95	747.41 -	747.60	33.67	761.95 -	762.14	34.39
718.52 -	718.71	32.24	733.06 -	733.25	32.96	747.61 -	747.80	33.68	762.15 -	762.35	34.40
718.72 -	718.91	32.25	733.26 -	733.46	32.97	747.81 -	748.00	33.69	762.36 -	762.55	34.41
718.92 -	719.11	32.26	733.47 -	733.66	32.98	748.01 -	748.20	33.70	762.56 -	762.75	34.42
719.12 -	719.32	32.27	733.67 -	733.86	32.99	748.21 -	748.41	33.71	762.76 -	762.95	34.43
719.33 -	719.52	32.28	733.87 -	734.06	33.00	748.42 -	748.61	33.72	762.96 -	763.15	34.44
719.53 -	719.72	32.29	734.07 -	734.26	33.01	748.62 -	748.81	33.73	763.16 -	763.36	34.45
719.73 -	719.92	32.30	734.27 -	734.47	33.02	748.82 -	749.01	33.74	763.37 -	763.56	34.46
719.93 -	720.12	32.31	734.48 -	734.67	33.03	749.02 -	749.21	33.75	763.57 -	763.76	34.47
720.13 -	720.33	32.32	734.68 -	734.87	33.04	749.22 -	749.42	33.76	763.77 -	763.96	34.48
720.34 -	720.53	32.33	734.88 -	735.07	33.05	749.43 -	749.62	33.77	763.97 -	764.16	34.49
720.54 -	720.73	32.34	735.08 -	735.27	33.06	749.63 -	749.82	33.78	764.17 -	764.37	34.50
720.74 -	720.93	32.35	735.28 -	735.48	33.07	749.83 -	750.02	33.79	764.38 -	764.57	34.51
720.94 -	721.13	32.36	735.49 -	735.68	33.08	750.03 -	750.22	33.80	764.58 -	764.77	34.52
721.14 -	721.34	32.37	735.69 -	735.88	33.09	750.23 -	750.43	33.81	764.78 -	764.97	34.53
721.35 -	721.54	32.38	735.89 -	736.08	33.10	750.44 -	750.63	33.82	764.98 -	765.17	34.54
721.55 -	721.74	32.39	736.09 -	736.28	33.11	750.64 -	750.83	33.83	765.18 -	765.38	34.55

Employee's maximum CPP contribution for the year 2005 is $1,861.20   B-12   La cotisation maximale de l'employé au RPC pour l'année 2005 est de 1 861,20 $

FIGURE 12-10
continued

Canada Pension Plan Contributions
Weekly (52 pay periods a year)

Cotisations au Régime de pensions du Canada
Hebdomadaire (52 périodes de paie par année)

Pay Rémunération		CPP RPC	Pay Rémunération		CPP RPC	Pay Rémunération		CPP RPC	Pay Rémunération		CPP RPC
From - De	To - À		From - De	To - À		From - De	To - À		From - De	To - À	
765.39	765.58	34.56	779.93	780.12	35.28	990.44	1000.43	45.94	1710.44	1720.43	81.58
765.59	765.78	34.57	780.13	780.33	35.29	1000.44	1010.43	46.44	1720.44	1730.43	82.08
765.79	765.98	34.58	780.34	780.53	35.30	1010.44	1020.43	46.93	1730.44	1740.43	82.57
765.99	766.18	34.59	780.54	780.73	35.31	1020.44	1030.43	47.43	1740.44	1750.43	83.07
766.19	766.39	34.60	780.74	780.93	35.32	1030.44	1040.43	47.92	1750.44	1760.43	83.56
766.40	766.59	34.61	780.94	781.13	35.33	1040.44	1050.43	48.42	1760.44	1770.43	84.06
766.60	766.79	34.62	781.14	781.34	35.34	1050.44	1060.43	48.91	1770.44	1780.43	84.55
766.80	766.99	34.63	781.35	781.54	35.35	1060.44	1070.43	49.41	1780.44	1790.43	85.05
767.00	767.19	34.64	781.55	781.74	35.36	1070.44	1080.43	49.90	1790.44	1800.43	85.54
767.20	767.40	34.65	781.75	781.94	35.37	1080.44	1090.43	50.40	1800.44	1810.43	86.04
767.41	767.60	34.66	781.95	782.14	35.38	1090.44	1100.43	50.89	1810.44	1820.43	86.53
767.61	767.80	34.67	782.15	782.35	35.39	1100.44	1110.43	51.39	1820.44	1830.43	87.03
767.81	768.00	34.68	782.36	782.55	35.40	1110.44	1120.43	51.88	1830.44	1840.43	87.52
768.01	768.20	34.69	782.56	782.75	35.41	1120.44	1130.43	52.38	1840.44	1850.43	88.02
768.21	768.41	34.70	782.76	782.95	35.42	1130.44	1140.43	52.87	1850.44	1860.43	88.51
768.42	768.61	34.71	782.96	783.15	35.43	1140.44	1150.43	53.37	1860.44	1870.43	89.01
768.62	768.81	34.72	783.16	783.36	35.44	1150.44	1160.43	53.86	1870.44	1880.43	89.50
768.82	769.01	34.73	783.37	783.56	35.45	1160.44	1170.43	54.36	1880.44	1890.43	90.00
769.02	769.21	34.74	783.57	783.76	35.46	1170.44	1180.43	54.85	1890.44	1900.43	90.49
769.22	769.42	34.75	783.77	783.96	35.47	1180.44	1190.43	55.35	1900.44	1910.43	90.99
769.43	769.62	34.76	783.97	784.16	35.48	1190.44	1200.43	55.84	1910.44	1920.43	91.48
769.63	769.82	34.77	784.17	784.37	35.49	1200.44	1210.43	56.34	1920.44	1930.43	91.98
769.83	770.02	34.78	784.38	784.57	35.50	1210.44	1220.43	56.83	1930.44	1940.43	92.47
770.03	770.22	34.79	784.58	784.77	35.51	1220.44	1230.43	57.33	1940.44	1950.43	92.97
770.23	770.43	34.80	784.78	784.97	35.52	1230.44	1240.43	57.82	1950.44	1960.43	93.46
770.44	770.63	34.81	784.98	785.17	35.53	1240.44	1250.43	58.32	1960.44	1970.43	93.96
770.64	770.83	34.82	785.18	785.38	35.54	1250.44	1260.43	58.81	1970.44	1980.43	94.45
770.84	771.03	34.83	785.39	785.58	35.55	1260.44	1270.43	59.31	1980.44	1990.43	94.95
771.04	771.23	34.84	785.59	785.78	35.56	1270.44	1280.43	59.80	1990.44	2000.43	95.44
771.24	771.44	34.85	785.79	785.98	35.57	1280.44	1290.43	60.30	2000.44	2010.43	95.94
771.45	771.64	34.86	785.99	786.18	35.58	1290.44	1300.43	60.79	2010.44	2020.43	96.43
771.65	771.84	34.87	786.19	786.39	35.59	1300.44	1310.43	61.29	2020.44	2030.43	96.93
771.85	772.04	34.88	786.40	786.59	35.60	1310.44	1320.43	61.78	2030.44	2040.43	97.42
772.05	772.24	34.89	786.60	786.79	35.61	1320.44	1330.43	62.28	2040.44	2050.43	97.92
772.25	772.45	34.90	786.80	786.99	35.62	1330.44	1340.43	62.77	2050.44	2060.43	98.41
772.46	772.65	34.91	787.00	787.19	35.63	1340.44	1350.43	63.27	2060.44	2070.43	98.91
772.66	772.85	34.92	787.20	787.40	35.64	1350.44	1360.43	63.76	2070.44	2080.43	99.40
772.86	773.05	34.93	787.41	787.60	35.65	1360.44	1370.43	64.26	2080.44	2090.43	99.90
773.06	773.25	34.94	787.61	787.80	35.66	1370.44	1380.43	64.75	2090.44	2100.43	100.39
773.26	773.46	34.95	787.81	788.00	35.67	1380.44	1390.43	65.25	2100.44	2110.43	100.89
773.47	773.66	34.96	788.01	788.20	35.68	1390.44	1400.43	65.74	2110.44	2120.43	101.38
773.67	773.86	34.97	788.21	788.41	35.69	1400.44	1410.43	66.24	2120.44	2130.43	101.88
773.87	774.06	34.98	788.42	788.61	35.70	1410.44	1420.43	66.73	2130.44	2140.43	102.37
774.07	774.26	34.99	788.62	788.81	35.71	1420.44	1430.43	67.23	2140.44	2150.43	102.87
774.27	774.47	35.00	788.82	789.01	35.72	1430.44	1440.43	67.72	2150.44	2160.43	103.36
774.48	774.67	35.01	789.02	789.21	35.73	1440.44	1450.43	68.22	2160.44	2170.43	103.86
774.68	774.87	35.02	789.22	789.42	35.74	1450.44	1460.43	68.71	2170.44	2180.43	104.35
774.88	775.07	35.03	789.43	789.62	35.75	1460.44	1470.43	69.21	2180.44	2190.43	104.85
775.08	775.27	35.04	789.63	789.82	35.76	1470.44	1480.43	69.70	2190.44	2200.43	105.34
775.28	775.48	35.05	789.83	790.02	35.77	1480.44	1490.43	70.20	2200.44	2210.43	105.84
775.49	775.68	35.06	790.03	790.22	35.78	1490.44	1500.43	70.69	2210.44	2220.43	106.33
775.69	775.88	35.07	790.23	790.43	35.79	1500.44	1510.43	71.19	2220.44	2230.43	106.83
775.89	776.08	35.08	790.44	800.43	36.04	1510.44	1520.43	71.68	2230.44	2240.43	107.32
776.09	776.28	35.09	800.44	810.43	36.54	1520.44	1530.43	72.18	2240.44	2250.43	107.82
776.29	776.49	35.10	810.44	820.43	37.03	1530.44	1540.43	72.67	2250.44	2260.43	108.31
776.50	776.69	35.11	820.44	830.43	37.53	1540.44	1550.43	73.17	2260.44	2270.43	108.81
776.70	776.89	35.12	830.44	840.43	38.02	1550.44	1560.43	73.66	2270.44	2280.43	109.30
776.90	777.09	35.13	840.44	850.43	38.52	1560.44	1570.43	74.16	2280.44	2290.43	109.80
777.10	777.29	35.14	850.44	860.43	39.01	1570.44	1580.43	74.65	2290.44	2300.43	110.29
777.30	777.50	35.15	860.44	870.43	39.51	1580.44	1590.43	75.15	2300.44	2310.43	110.79
777.51	777.70	35.16	870.44	880.43	40.00	1590.44	1600.43	75.64	2310.44	2320.43	111.28
777.71	777.90	35.17	880.44	890.43	40.50	1600.44	1610.43	76.14	2320.44	2330.43	111.78
777.91	778.10	35.18	890.44	900.43	40.99	1610.44	1620.43	76.63	2330.44	2340.43	112.27
778.11	778.31	35.19	900.44	910.43	41.49	1620.44	1630.43	77.13	2340.44	2350.43	112.77
778.32	778.51	35.20	910.44	920.43	41.98	1630.44	1640.43	77.62	2350.44	2360.43	113.26
778.52	778.71	35.21	920.44	930.43	42.48	1640.44	1650.43	78.12	2360.44	2370.43	113.76
778.72	778.91	35.22	930.44	940.43	42.97	1650.44	1660.43	78.61	2370.44	2380.43	114.25
778.92	779.11	35.23	940.44	950.43	43.47	1660.44	1670.43	79.11	2380.44	2390.43	114.75
779.12	779.32	35.24	950.44	960.43	43.96	1670.44	1680.43	79.60	2390.44	2400.43	115.24
779.33	779.52	35.25	960.44	970.43	44.46	1680.44	1690.43	80.10	2400.44	2410.43	115.74
779.53	779.72	35.26	970.44	980.43	44.95	1690.44	1700.43	80.59	2410.44	2420.43	116.23
779.73	779.92	35.27	980.44	990.43	45.45	1700.44	1710.43	81.09	2420.44	2430.43	116.73

Employee's maximum CPP contribution for the year 2005 is $1,861.20   B-13   La cotisation maximale de l'employé au RPC pour l'année 2005 est de 1 861,20 $

FIGURE 12-11
EI Premiums Table

Employment Insurance Premiums   **Cotisations à l'assurance-emploi**

Insurable Earnings Rémunération assurable		EI premium Cotisation d'AE	Insurable Earnings Rémunération assurable		EI premium Cotisation d'AE	Insurable Earnings Rémunération assurable		EI premium Cotisation d'AE	Insurable Earnings Rémunération assurable		EI premium Cotisation d'AE
From - De	To - À		From - De	To - À		From - De	To - À		From - De	To - À	
591.03	591.53	11.53	627.95	628.46	12.25	664.88	665.38	12.97	701.80	702.30	13.69
591.54	592.05	11.54	628.47	628.97	12.26	665.39	665.89	12.98	702.31	702.82	13.70
592.06	592.56	11.55	628.98	629.48	12.27	665.90	666.41	12.99	702.83	703.33	13.71
592.57	593.07	11.56	629.49	629.99	12.28	666.42	666.92	13.00	703.34	703.84	13.72
593.08	593.58	11.57	630.00	630.51	12.29	666.93	667.43	13.01	703.85	704.35	13.73
593.59	594.10	11.58	630.52	631.02	12.30	667.44	667.94	13.02	704.36	704.87	13.74
594.11	594.61	11.59	631.03	631.53	12.31	667.95	668.46	13.03	704.88	705.38	13.75
594.62	595.12	11.60	631.54	632.05	12.32	668.47	668.97	13.04	705.39	705.89	13.76
595.13	595.64	11.61	632.06	632.56	12.33	668.98	669.48	13.05	705.90	706.41	13.77
595.65	596.15	11.62	632.57	633.07	12.34	669.49	669.99	13.06	706.42	706.92	13.78
596.16	596.66	11.63	633.08	633.58	12.35	670.00	670.51	13.07	706.93	707.43	13.79
596.67	597.17	11.64	633.59	634.10	12.36	670.52	671.02	13.08	707.44	707.94	13.80
597.18	597.69	11.65	634.11	634.61	12.37	671.03	671.53	13.09	707.95	708.46	13.81
597.70	598.20	11.66	634.62	635.12	12.38	671.54	672.05	13.10	708.47	708.97	13.82
598.21	598.71	11.67	635.13	635.64	12.39	672.06	672.56	13.11	708.98	709.48	13.83
598.72	599.23	11.68	635.65	636.15	12.40	672.57	673.07	13.12	709.49	709.99	13.84
599.24	599.74	11.69	636.16	636.66	12.41	673.08	673.58	13.13	710.00	710.51	13.85
599.75	600.25	11.70	636.67	637.17	12.42	673.59	674.10	13.14	710.52	711.02	13.86
600.26	600.76	11.71	637.18	637.69	12.43	674.11	674.61	13.15	711.03	711.53	13.87
600.77	601.28	11.72	637.70	638.20	12.44	674.62	675.12	13.16	711.54	712.05	13.88
601.29	601.79	11.73	638.21	638.71	12.45	675.13	675.64	13.17	712.06	712.56	13.89
601.80	602.30	11.74	638.72	639.23	12.46	675.65	676.15	13.18	712.57	713.07	13.90
602.31	602.82	11.75	639.24	639.74	12.47	676.16	676.66	13.19	713.08	713.58	13.91
602.83	603.33	11.76	639.75	640.25	12.48	676.67	677.17	13.20	713.59	714.10	13.92
603.34	603.84	11.77	640.26	640.76	12.49	677.18	677.69	13.21	714.11	714.61	13.93
603.85	604.35	11.78	640.77	641.28	12.50	677.70	678.20	13.22	714.62	715.12	13.94
604.36	604.87	11.79	641.29	641.79	12.51	678.21	678.71	13.23	715.13	715.64	13.95
604.88	605.38	11.80	641.80	642.30	12.52	678.72	679.23	13.24	715.65	716.15	13.96
605.39	605.89	11.81	642.31	642.82	12.53	679.24	679.74	13.25	716.16	716.66	13.97
605.90	606.41	11.82	642.83	643.33	12.54	679.75	680.25	13.26	716.67	717.17	13.98
606.42	606.92	11.83	643.34	643.84	12.55	680.26	680.76	13.27	717.18	717.69	13.99
606.93	607.43	11.84	643.85	644.35	12.56	680.77	681.28	13.28	717.70	718.20	14.00
607.44	607.94	11.85	644.36	644.87	12.57	681.29	681.79	13.29	718.21	718.71	14.01
607.95	608.46	11.86	644.88	645.38	12.58	681.80	682.30	13.30	718.72	719.23	14.02
608.47	608.97	11.87	645.39	645.89	12.59	682.31	682.82	13.31	719.24	719.74	14.03
608.98	609.48	11.88	645.90	646.41	12.60	682.83	683.33	13.32	719.75	720.25	14.04
609.49	609.99	11.89	646.42	646.92	12.61	683.34	683.84	13.33	720.26	720.76	14.05
610.00	610.51	11.90	646.93	647.43	12.62	683.85	684.35	13.34	720.77	721.28	14.06
610.52	611.02	11.91	647.44	647.94	12.63	684.36	684.87	13.35	721.29	721.79	14.07
611.03	611.53	11.92	647.95	648.46	12.64	684.88	685.38	13.36	721.80	722.30	14.08
611.54	612.05	11.93	648.47	648.97	12.65	685.39	685.89	13.37	722.31	722.82	14.09
612.06	612.56	11.94	648.98	649.48	12.66	685.90	686.41	13.38	722.83	723.33	14.10
612.57	613.07	11.95	649.49	649.99	12.67	686.42	686.92	13.39	723.34	723.84	14.11
613.08	613.58	11.96	650.00	650.51	12.68	686.93	687.43	13.40	723.85	724.35	14.12
613.59	614.10	11.97	650.52	651.02	12.69	687.44	687.94	13.41	724.36	724.87	14.13
614.11	614.61	11.98	651.03	651.53	12.70	687.95	688.46	13.42	724.88	725.38	14.14
614.62	615.12	11.99	651.54	652.05	12.71	688.47	688.97	13.43	725.39	725.89	14.15
615.13	615.64	12.00	652.06	652.56	12.72	688.98	689.48	13.44	725.90	726.41	14.16
615.65	616.15	12.01	652.57	653.07	12.73	689.49	689.99	13.45	726.42	726.92	14.17
616.16	616.66	12.02	653.08	653.58	12.74	690.00	690.51	13.46	726.93	727.43	14.18
616.67	617.17	12.03	653.59	654.10	12.75	690.52	691.02	13.47	727.44	727.94	14.19
617.18	617.69	12.04	654.11	654.61	12.76	691.03	691.53	13.48	727.95	728.46	14.20
617.70	618.20	12.05	654.62	655.12	12.77	691.54	692.05	13.49	728.47	728.97	14.21
618.21	618.71	12.06	655.13	655.64	12.78	692.06	692.56	13.50	728.98	729.48	14.22
618.72	619.23	12.07	655.65	656.15	12.79	692.57	693.07	13.51	729.49	729.99	14.23
619.24	619.74	12.08	656.16	656.66	12.80	693.08	693.58	13.52	730.00	730.51	14.24
619.75	620.25	12.09	656.67	657.17	12.81	693.59	694.10	13.53	730.52	731.02	14.25
620.26	620.76	12.10	657.18	657.69	12.82	694.11	694.61	13.54	731.03	731.53	14.26
620.77	621.28	12.11	657.70	658.20	12.83	694.62	695.12	13.55	731.54	732.05	14.27
621.29	621.79	12.12	658.21	658.71	12.84	695.13	695.64	13.56	732.06	732.56	14.28
621.80	622.30	12.13	658.72	659.23	12.85	695.65	696.15	13.57	732.57	733.07	14.29
622.31	622.82	12.14	659.24	659.74	12.86	696.16	696.66	13.58	733.08	733.58	14.30
622.83	623.33	12.15	659.75	660.25	12.87	696.67	697.17	13.59	733.59	734.10	14.31
623.34	623.84	12.16	660.26	660.76	12.88	697.18	697.69	13.60	734.11	734.61	14.32
623.85	624.35	12.17	660.77	661.28	12.89	697.70	698.20	13.61	734.62	735.12	14.33
624.36	624.87	12.18	661.29	661.79	12.90	698.21	698.71	13.62	735.13	735.64	14.34
624.88	625.38	12.19	661.80	662.30	12.91	698.72	699.23	13.63	735.65	736.15	14.35
625.39	625.89	12.20	662.31	662.82	12.92	699.24	699.74	13.64	736.16	736.66	14.36
625.90	626.41	12.21	662.83	663.33	12.93	699.75	700.25	13.65	736.67	737.17	14.37
626.42	626.92	12.22	663.34	663.84	12.94	700.26	700.76	13.66	737.18	737.69	14.38
626.93	627.43	12.23	663.85	664.35	12.95	700.77	701.28	13.67	737.70	738.20	14.39
627.44	627.94	12.24	664.36	664.87	12.96	701.29	701.79	13.68	738.21	738.71	14.40

Yearly maximum insurable earnings are $39,000   Le maximum annuel de la rémunération assurable est de 39 000 $
Yearly maximum employee premiums are $760.50   La cotisation maximale annuelle de l'employé est de 760,50 $
The premium rate for 2005 is 1.95 %   C-5   Le taux de cotisation pour 2005 est de 1,95 %

FIGURE 12-11
continued

Employment Insurance Premiums   Cotisations à l'assurance-emploi

Insurable Earnings Rémunération assurable		EI premium Cotisation d'AE	Insurable Earnings Rémunération assurable		EI premium Cotisation d'AE	Insurable Earnings Rémunération assurable		EI premium Cotisation d'AE	Insurable Earnings Rémunération assurable		EI premium Cotisation d'AE
From - De	To - À		From - De	To - À		From - De	To - À		From - De	To - À	
738.72	739.23	14.41	775.65	776.15	15.13	812.57	813.07	15.85	849.49	849.99	16.57
739.24	739.74	14.42	776.16	776.66	15.14	813.08	813.58	15.86	850.00	850.51	16.58
739.75	740.25	14.43	776.67	777.17	15.15	813.59	814.10	15.87	850.52	851.02	16.59
740.26	740.76	14.44	777.18	777.69	15.16	814.11	814.61	15.88	851.03	851.53	16.60
740.77	741.28	14.45	777.70	778.20	15.17	814.62	815.12	15.89	851.54	852.05	16.61
741.29	741.79	14.46	778.21	778.71	15.18	815.13	815.64	15.90	852.06	852.56	16.62
741.80	742.30	14.47	778.72	779.23	15.19	815.65	816.15	15.91	852.57	853.07	16.63
742.31	742.82	14.48	779.24	779.74	15.20	816.16	816.66	15.92	853.08	853.58	16.64
742.83	743.33	14.49	779.75	780.25	15.21	816.67	817.17	15.93	853.59	854.10	16.65
743.34	743.84	14.50	780.26	780.76	15.22	817.18	817.69	15.94	854.11	854.61	16.66
743.85	744.35	14.51	780.77	781.28	15.23	817.70	818.20	15.95	854.62	855.12	16.67
744.36	744.87	14.52	781.29	781.79	15.24	818.21	818.71	15.96	855.13	855.64	16.68
744.88	745.38	14.53	781.80	782.30	15.25	818.72	819.23	15.97	855.65	856.15	16.69
745.39	745.89	14.54	782.31	782.82	15.26	819.24	819.74	15.98	856.16	856.66	16.70
745.90	746.41	14.55	782.83	783.33	15.27	819.75	820.25	15.99	856.67	857.17	16.71
746.42	746.92	14.56	783.34	783.84	15.28	820.26	820.76	16.00	857.18	857.69	16.72
746.93	747.43	14.57	783.85	784.35	15.29	820.77	821.28	16.01	857.70	858.20	16.73
747.44	747.94	14.58	784.36	784.87	15.30	821.29	821.79	16.02	858.21	858.71	16.74
747.95	748.46	14.59	784.88	785.38	15.31	821.80	822.30	16.03	858.72	859.23	16.75
748.47	748.97	14.60	785.39	785.89	15.32	822.31	822.82	16.04	859.24	859.74	16.76
748.98	749.48	14.61	785.90	786.41	15.33	822.83	823.33	16.05	859.75	860.25	16.77
749.49	749.99	14.62	786.42	786.92	15.34	823.34	823.84	16.06	860.26	860.76	16.78
750.00	750.51	14.63	786.93	787.43	15.35	823.85	824.35	16.07	860.77	861.28	16.79
750.52	751.02	14.64	787.44	787.94	15.36	824.36	824.87	16.08	861.29	861.79	16.80
751.03	751.53	14.65	787.95	788.46	15.37	824.88	825.38	16.09	861.80	862.30	16.81
751.54	752.05	14.66	788.47	788.97	15.38	825.39	825.89	16.10	862.31	862.82	16.82
752.06	752.56	14.67	788.98	789.48	15.39	825.90	826.41	16.11	862.83	863.33	16.83
752.57	753.07	14.68	789.49	789.99	15.40	826.42	826.92	16.12	863.34	863.84	16.84
753.08	753.58	14.69	790.00	790.51	15.41	826.93	827.43	16.13	863.85	864.35	16.85
753.59	754.10	14.70	790.52	791.02	15.42	827.44	827.94	16.14	864.36	864.87	16.86
754.11	754.61	14.71	791.03	791.53	15.43	827.95	828.46	16.15	864.88	865.38	16.87
754.62	755.12	14.72	791.54	792.05	15.44	828.47	828.97	16.16	865.39	865.89	16.88
755.13	755.64	14.73	792.06	792.56	15.45	828.98	829.48	16.17	865.90	866.41	16.89
755.65	756.15	14.74	792.57	793.07	15.46	829.49	829.99	16.18	866.42	866.92	16.90
756.16	756.66	14.75	793.08	793.58	15.47	830.00	830.51	16.19	866.93	867.43	16.91
756.67	757.17	14.76	793.59	794.10	15.48	830.52	831.02	16.20	867.44	867.94	16.92
757.18	757.69	14.77	794.11	794.61	15.49	831.03	831.53	16.21	867.95	868.46	16.93
757.70	758.20	14.78	794.62	795.12	15.50	831.54	832.05	16.22	868.47	868.97	16.94
758.21	758.71	14.79	795.13	795.64	15.51	832.06	832.56	16.23	868.98	869.48	16.95
758.72	759.23	14.80	795.65	796.15	15.52	832.57	833.07	16.24	869.49	869.99	16.96
759.24	759.74	14.81	796.16	796.66	15.53	833.08	833.58	16.25	870.00	870.51	16.97
759.75	760.25	14.82	796.67	797.17	15.54	833.59	834.10	16.26	870.52	871.02	16.98
760.26	760.76	14.83	797.18	797.69	15.55	834.11	834.61	16.27	871.03	871.53	16.99
760.77	761.28	14.84	797.70	798.20	15.56	834.62	835.12	16.28	871.54	872.05	17.00
761.29	761.79	14.85	798.21	798.71	15.57	835.13	835.64	16.29	872.06	872.56	17.01
761.80	762.30	14.86	798.72	799.23	15.58	835.65	836.15	16.30	872.57	873.07	17.02
762.31	762.82	14.87	799.24	799.74	15.59	836.16	836.66	16.31	873.08	873.58	17.03
762.83	763.33	14.88	799.75	800.25	15.60	836.67	837.17	16.32	873.59	874.10	17.04
763.34	763.84	14.89	800.26	800.76	15.61	837.18	837.69	16.33	874.11	874.61	17.05
763.85	764.35	14.90	800.77	801.28	15.62	837.70	838.20	16.34	874.62	875.12	17.06
764.36	764.87	14.91	801.29	801.79	15.63	838.21	838.71	16.35	875.13	875.64	17.07
764.88	765.38	14.92	801.80	802.30	15.64	838.72	839.23	16.36	875.65	876.15	17.08
765.39	765.89	14.93	802.31	802.82	15.65	839.24	839.74	16.37	876.16	876.66	17.09
765.90	766.41	14.94	802.83	803.33	15.66	839.75	840.25	16.38	876.67	877.17	17.10
766.42	766.92	14.95	803.34	803.84	15.67	840.26	840.76	16.39	877.18	877.69	17.11
766.93	767.43	14.96	803.85	804.35	15.68	840.77	841.28	16.40	877.70	878.20	17.12
767.44	767.94	14.97	804.36	804.87	15.69	841.29	841.79	16.41	878.21	878.71	17.13
767.95	768.46	14.98	804.88	805.38	15.70	841.80	842.30	16.42	878.72	879.23	17.14
768.47	768.97	14.99	805.39	805.89	15.71	842.31	842.82	16.43	879.24	879.74	17.15
768.98	769.48	15.00	805.90	806.41	15.72	842.83	843.33	16.44	879.75	880.25	17.16
769.49	769.99	15.01	806.42	806.92	15.73	843.34	843.84	16.45	880.26	880.76	17.17
770.00	770.51	15.02	806.93	807.43	15.74	843.85	844.35	16.46	880.77	881.28	17.18
770.52	771.02	15.03	807.44	807.94	15.75	844.36	844.87	16.47	881.29	881.79	17.19
771.03	771.53	15.04	807.95	808.46	15.76	844.88	845.38	16.48	881.80	882.30	17.20
771.54	772.05	15.05	808.47	808.97	15.77	845.39	845.89	16.49	882.31	882.82	17.21
772.06	772.56	15.06	808.98	809.48	15.78	845.90	846.41	16.50	882.83	883.33	17.22
772.57	773.07	15.07	809.49	809.99	15.79	846.42	846.92	16.51	883.34	883.84	17.23
773.08	773.58	15.08	810.00	810.51	15.80	846.93	847.43	16.52	883.85	884.35	17.24
773.59	774.10	15.09	810.52	811.02	15.81	847.44	847.94	16.53	884.36	884.87	17.25
774.11	774.61	15.10	811.03	811.53	15.82	847.95	848.46	16.54	884.88	885.38	17.26
774.62	775.12	15.11	811.54	812.05	15.83	848.47	848.97	16.55	885.39	885.89	17.27
775.13	775.64	15.12	812.06	812.56	15.84	848.98	849.48	16.56	885.90	886.41	17.28

Yearly maximum insurable earnings are $39,000
Yearly maximum employee premiums are $760.50
The premium rate for 2005 is 1.95 %

C-6

Le maximum annuel de la rémunération assurable est de 39 000 $
La cotisation maximale annuelle de l'employé est de 760,50 $
Le taux de cotisation pour 2005 est de 1,95 %

FIGURE 12-11

continued

Employment Insurance Premiums / Cotisations à l'assurance-emploi

Insurable Earnings Rémunération assurable From - De	To - À	EI premium Cotisation d'AE	Insurable Earnings Rémunération assurable From - De	To - À	EI premium Cotisation d'AE	Insurable Earnings Rémunération assurable From - De	To - À	EI premium Cotisation d'AE	Insurable Earnings Rémunération assurable From - De	To - À	EI premium Cotisation d'AE
886.42	886.92	17.29	923.34	923.84	18.01	960.26	960.76	18.73	997.18	997.69	19.45
886.93	887.43	17.30	923.85	924.35	18.02	960.77	961.28	18.74	997.70	998.20	19.46
887.44	887.94	17.31	924.36	924.87	18.03	961.29	961.79	18.75	998.21	998.71	19.47
887.95	888.46	17.32	924.88	925.38	18.04	961.80	962.30	18.76	998.72	999.23	19.48
888.47	888.97	17.33	925.39	925.89	18.05	962.31	962.82	18.77	999.24	999.74	19.49
888.98	889.48	17.34	925.90	926.41	18.06	962.83	963.33	18.78	999.75	1000.25	19.50
889.49	889.99	17.35	926.42	926.92	18.07	963.34	963.84	18.79	1000.26	1000.76	19.51
890.00	890.51	17.36	926.93	927.43	18.08	963.85	964.35	18.80	1000.77	1001.28	19.52
890.52	891.02	17.37	927.44	927.94	18.09	964.36	964.87	18.81	1001.29	1001.79	19.53
891.03	891.53	17.38	927.95	928.46	18.10	964.88	965.38	18.82	1001.80	1002.30	19.54
891.54	892.05	17.39	928.47	928.97	18.11	965.39	965.89	18.83	1002.31	1002.82	19.55
892.06	892.56	17.40	928.98	929.48	18.12	965.90	966.41	18.84	1002.83	1003.33	19.56
892.57	893.07	17.41	929.49	929.99	18.13	966.42	966.92	18.85	1003.34	1003.84	19.57
893.08	893.58	17.42	930.00	930.51	18.14	966.93	967.43	18.86	1003.85	1004.35	19.58
893.59	894.10	17.43	930.52	931.02	18.15	967.44	967.94	18.87	1004.36	1004.87	19.59
894.11	894.61	17.44	931.03	931.53	18.16	967.95	968.46	18.88	1004.88	1005.38	19.60
894.62	895.12	17.45	931.54	932.05	18.17	968.47	968.97	18.89	1005.39	1005.89	19.61
895.13	895.64	17.46	932.06	932.56	18.18	968.98	969.48	18.90	1005.90	1006.41	19.62
895.65	896.15	17.47	932.57	933.07	18.19	969.49	969.99	18.91	1006.42	1006.92	19.63
896.16	896.66	17.48	933.08	933.58	18.20	970.00	970.51	18.92	1006.93	1007.43	19.64
896.67	897.17	17.49	933.59	934.10	18.21	970.52	971.02	18.93	1007.44	1007.94	19.65
897.18	897.69	17.50	934.11	934.61	18.22	971.03	971.53	18.94	1007.95	1008.46	19.66
897.70	898.20	17.51	934.62	935.12	18.23	971.54	972.05	18.95	1008.47	1008.97	19.67
898.21	898.71	17.52	935.13	935.64	18.24	972.06	972.56	18.96	1008.98	1009.48	19.68
898.72	899.23	17.53	935.65	936.15	18.25	972.57	973.07	18.97	1009.49	1009.99	19.69
899.24	899.74	17.54	936.16	936.66	18.26	973.08	973.58	18.98	1010.00	1010.51	19.70
899.75	900.25	17.55	936.67	937.17	18.27	973.59	974.10	18.99	1010.52	1011.02	19.71
900.26	900.76	17.56	937.18	937.69	18.28	974.11	974.61	19.00	1011.03	1011.53	19.72
900.77	901.28	17.57	937.70	938.20	18.29	974.62	975.12	19.01	1011.54	1012.05	19.73
901.29	901.79	17.58	938.21	938.71	18.30	975.13	975.64	19.02	1012.06	1012.56	19.74
901.80	902.30	17.59	938.72	939.23	18.31	975.65	976.15	19.03	1012.57	1013.07	19.75
902.31	902.82	17.60	939.24	939.74	18.32	976.16	976.66	19.04	1013.08	1013.58	19.76
902.83	903.33	17.61	939.75	940.25	18.33	976.67	977.17	19.05	1013.59	1014.10	19.77
903.34	903.84	17.62	940.26	940.76	18.34	977.18	977.69	19.06	1014.11	1014.61	19.78
903.85	904.35	17.63	940.77	941.28	18.35	977.70	978.20	19.07	1014.62	1015.12	19.79
904.36	904.87	17.64	941.29	941.79	18.36	978.21	978.71	19.08	1015.13	1015.64	19.80
904.88	905.38	17.65	941.80	942.30	18.37	978.72	979.23	19.09	1015.65	1016.15	19.81
905.39	905.89	17.66	942.31	942.82	18.38	979.24	979.74	19.10	1016.16	1016.66	19.82
905.90	906.41	17.67	942.83	943.33	18.39	979.75	980.25	19.11	1016.67	1017.17	19.83
906.42	906.92	17.68	943.34	943.84	18.40	980.26	980.76	19.12	1017.18	1017.69	19.84
906.93	907.43	17.69	943.85	944.35	18.41	980.77	981.28	19.13	1017.70	1018.20	19.85
907.44	907.94	17.70	944.36	944.87	18.42	981.29	981.79	19.14	1018.21	1018.71	19.86
907.95	908.46	17.71	944.88	945.38	18.43	981.80	982.30	19.15	1018.72	1019.23	19.87
908.47	908.97	17.72	945.39	945.89	18.44	982.31	982.82	19.16	1019.24	1019.74	19.88
908.98	909.48	17.73	945.90	946.41	18.45	982.83	983.33	19.17	1019.75	1020.25	19.89
909.49	909.99	17.74	946.42	946.92	18.46	983.34	983.84	19.18	1020.26	1020.76	19.90
910.00	910.51	17.75	946.93	947.43	18.47	983.85	984.35	19.19	1020.77	1021.28	19.91
910.52	911.02	17.76	947.44	947.94	18.48	984.36	984.87	19.20	1021.29	1021.79	19.92
911.03	911.53	17.77	947.95	948.46	18.49	984.88	985.38	19.21	1021.80	1022.30	19.93
911.54	912.05	17.78	948.47	948.97	18.50	985.39	985.89	19.22	1022.31	1022.82	19.94
912.06	912.56	17.79	948.98	949.48	18.51	985.90	986.41	19.23	1022.83	1023.33	19.95
912.57	913.07	17.80	949.49	949.99	18.52	986.42	986.92	19.24	1023.34	1023.84	19.96
913.08	913.58	17.81	950.00	950.51	18.53	986.93	987.43	19.25	1023.85	1024.35	19.97
913.59	914.10	17.82	950.52	951.02	18.54	987.44	987.94	19.26	1024.36	1024.87	19.98
914.11	914.61	17.83	951.03	951.53	18.55	987.95	988.46	19.27	1024.88	1025.38	19.99
914.62	915.12	17.84	951.54	952.05	18.56	988.47	988.97	19.28	1025.39	1025.89	20.00
915.13	915.64	17.85	952.06	952.56	18.57	988.98	989.48	19.29	1025.90	1026.41	20.01
915.65	916.15	17.86	952.57	953.07	18.58	989.49	989.99	19.30	1026.42	1026.92	20.02
916.16	916.66	17.87	953.08	953.58	18.59	990.00	990.51	19.31	1026.93	1027.43	20.03
916.67	917.17	17.88	953.59	954.10	18.60	990.52	991.02	19.32	1027.44	1027.94	20.04
917.18	917.69	17.89	954.11	954.61	18.61	991.03	991.53	19.33	1027.95	1028.46	20.05
917.70	918.20	17.90	954.62	955.12	18.62	991.54	992.05	19.34	1028.47	1028.97	20.06
918.21	918.71	17.91	955.13	955.64	18.63	992.06	992.56	19.35	1028.98	1029.48	20.07
918.72	919.23	17.92	955.65	956.15	18.64	992.57	993.07	19.36	1029.49	1029.99	20.08
919.24	919.74	17.93	956.16	956.66	18.65	993.08	993.58	19.37	1030.00	1030.51	20.09
919.75	920.25	17.94	956.67	957.17	18.66	993.59	994.10	19.38	1030.52	1031.02	20.10
920.26	920.76	17.95	957.18	957.69	18.67	994.11	994.61	19.39	1031.03	1031.53	20.11
920.77	921.28	17.96	957.70	958.20	18.68	994.62	995.12	19.40	1031.54	1032.05	20.12
921.29	921.79	17.97	958.21	958.71	18.69	995.13	995.64	19.41	1032.06	1032.56	20.13
921.80	922.30	17.98	958.72	959.23	18.70	995.65	996.15	19.42	1032.57	1033.07	20.14
922.31	922.82	17.99	959.24	959.74	18.71	996.16	996.66	19.43	1033.08	1033.58	20.15
922.83	923.33	18.00	959.75	960.25	18.72	996.67	997.17	19.44	1033.59	1034.10	20.16

Yearly maximum insurable earnings are $39,000
Yearly maximum employee premiums are $760.50
The premium rate for 2005 is 1.95 %

C-7

Le maximum annuel de la rémunération assurable est de 39 000 $
La cotisation maximale annuelle de l'employé est de 760,50 $
Le taux de cotisation pour 2005 est de 1,95 %

FIGURE 12-12
Federal Tax Deduction Table

Federal tax deductions
Effective January 1, 2005
Weekly (52 pay periods a year)
Also look up the tax deductions
in the provincial table

Retenues d'impôt fédéral
En vigueur le 1er janvier 2005
Hebdomadaire (52 périodes de paie par année)
Cherchez aussi les retenues d'impôt
dans la table provinciale

Pay Rémunération		Federal claim codes/Codes de demande fédéraux										
From De	Less than Moins de	0	1	2	3	4	5	6	7	8	9	10
		Deduct from each pay — Retenez sur chaque paie										
493	501	74.55	49.50	46.70	41.15	35.60	30.05	24.50	18.90	13.35	7.80	2.25
501	509	75.75	50.70	47.90	42.35	36.80	31.25	25.65	20.10	14.55	9.00	3.45
509	517	76.95	51.90	49.10	43.55	38.00	32.40	26.85	21.30	15.75	10.20	4.60
517	525	78.15	53.05	50.30	44.75	39.15	33.60	28.05	22.50	16.95	11.35	5.80
525	533	79.35	54.25	51.50	45.90	40.35	34.80	29.25	23.70	18.10	12.55	7.00
533	541	80.50	55.45	52.65	47.10	41.55	36.00	30.45	24.85	19.30	13.75	8.20
541	549	81.70	56.65	53.85	48.30	42.75	37.20	31.65	26.05	20.50	14.95	9.40
549	557	82.90	57.85	55.05	49.50	43.95	38.40	32.80	27.25	21.70	16.15	10.60
557	565	84.10	59.05	56.25	50.70	45.15	39.55	34.00	28.45	22.90	17.35	11.75
565	573	85.30	60.20	57.45	51.90	46.30	40.75	35.20	29.65	24.10	18.50	12.95
573	581	86.50	61.40	58.65	53.05	47.50	41.95	36.40	30.85	25.25	19.70	14.15
581	589	87.65	62.60	59.80	54.25	48.70	43.15	37.60	32.00	26.45	20.90	15.35
589	597	88.85	63.80	61.00	55.45	49.90	44.35	38.80	33.20	27.65	22.10	16.55
597	605	90.05	65.00	62.20	56.65	51.10	45.55	39.95	34.40	28.85	23.30	17.75
605	613	91.25	66.20	63.40	57.85	52.30	46.70	41.15	35.60	30.05	24.50	18.90
613	621	92.45	67.35	64.60	59.05	53.45	47.90	42.35	36.80	31.25	25.65	20.10
621	629	93.65	68.55	65.80	60.20	54.65	49.10	43.55	38.00	32.40	26.85	21.30
629	637	94.80	69.75	66.95	61.40	55.85	50.30	44.75	39.15	33.60	28.05	22.50
637	645	96.00	70.95	68.15	62.60	57.05	51.50	45.95	40.35	34.80	29.25	23.70
645	653	97.20	72.15	69.35	63.80	58.25	52.70	47.10	41.55	36.00	30.45	24.90
653	661	98.40	73.35	70.55	65.00	59.45	53.85	48.30	42.75	37.20	31.65	26.05
661	669	99.60	74.50	71.75	66.20	60.60	55.05	49.50	43.95	38.40	32.80	27.25
669	677	100.80	75.70	72.95	67.35	61.80	56.25	50.70	45.15	39.55	34.00	28.45
677	685	101.95	76.90	74.10	68.55	63.00	57.45	51.90	46.30	40.75	35.20	29.65
685	693	103.45	78.35	75.60	70.00	64.45	58.90	53.35	47.80	42.20	36.65	31.10
693	701	105.10	80.05	77.25	71.70	66.15	60.55	55.00	49.45	43.90	38.35	32.75
701	709	106.75	81.70	78.90	73.35	67.80	62.25	56.70	51.10	45.55	40.00	34.45
709	717	108.45	83.35	80.60	75.05	69.45	63.90	58.35	52.80	47.25	41.65	36.10
717	725	110.10	85.05	82.25	76.70	71.15	65.60	60.05	54.45	48.90	43.35	37.80
725	733	111.80	86.70	83.95	78.40	72.80	67.25	61.70	56.15	50.60	45.00	39.45
733	741	113.45	88.40	85.60	80.05	74.50	68.95	63.35	57.80	52.25	46.70	41.15
741	749	115.15	90.05	87.30	81.70	76.15	70.60	65.05	59.50	53.90	48.35	42.80
749	757	116.80	91.75	88.95	83.40	77.85	72.30	66.70	61.15	55.60	50.05	44.50
757	765	118.50	93.45	90.65	85.10	79.55	74.00	68.40	62.85	57.30	51.75	46.20
765	773	120.20	95.15	92.35	86.80	81.25	75.65	70.10	64.55	59.00	53.45	47.85
773	781	121.90	96.85	94.05	88.50	82.95	77.35	71.80	66.25	60.70	55.15	49.55
781	789	123.60	98.55	95.75	90.20	84.65	79.05	73.50	67.95	62.40	56.85	51.25
789	797	125.30	100.26	97.46	91.90	86.35	80.80	75.25	69.66	64.10	58.55	53.00
797	805	127.10	102.00	99.25	93.65	88.10	82.55	77.00	71.45	65.85	60.30	54.75
805	813	128.85	103.75	101.00	95.45	89.85	84.30	78.75	73.20	67.65	62.05	56.50
813	821	130.60	105.55	102.75	97.20	91.65	86.05	80.50	74.95	69.40	63.85	58.25
821	829	132.35	107.30	104.50	98.95	93.40	87.85	82.25	76.70	71.15	65.60	60.05
829	837	134.10	109.05	106.25	100.70	95.15	89.60	84.05	78.45	72.90	67.35	61.80
837	845	135.90	110.80	108.05	102.45	96.90	91.35	85.80	80.25	74.65	69.10	63.55
845	853	137.65	112.55	109.80	104.25	98.65	93.10	87.55	82.00	76.45	70.85	65.30
853	861	139.40	114.35	111.55	106.00	100.45	94.85	89.30	83.75	78.20	72.65	67.05
861	869	141.15	116.10	113.30	107.75	102.20	96.65	91.05	85.50	79.95	74.40	68.85
869	877	142.90	117.85	115.05	109.50	103.95	98.40	92.85	87.25	81.70	76.15	70.60
877	885	144.70	119.60	116.85	111.25	105.70	100.15	94.60	89.05	83.45	77.90	72.35
885	893	146.45	121.35	118.60	113.05	107.45	101.90	96.35	90.80	85.25	79.65	74.10
893	901	148.20	123.15	120.35	114.80	109.25	103.65	98.10	92.55	87.00	81.45	75.85
901	909	149.95	124.90	122.10	116.55	111.00	105.45	99.85	94.30	88.75	83.20	77.65
909	917	151.70	126.65	123.85	118.30	112.75	107.20	101.65	96.05	90.50	84.95	79.40
917	925	153.50	128.40	125.65	120.05	114.50	108.95	103.40	97.85	92.25	86.70	81.15
925	933	155.25	130.15	127.40	121.85	116.25	110.70	105.15	99.60	94.05	88.45	82.90

This table is available on TOD   D-3   Vous pouvez obtenir cette table sur TSD

FIGURE 12-13
Provincial Tax Deduction Table

Ontario provincial tax deductions
Effective January 1, 2005
Weekly (52 pay periods a year)
Also look up the tax deductions in the federal table

Retenues d'impôt provincial de l'Ontario
En vigueur le 1er janvier 2005
Hebdomadaire (52 périodes de paie par année)
Cherchez aussi les retenues d'impôt dans la table fédérale

Pay Rémunération From De / Less than Moins de	0	1	2	3	4	5	6	7	8	9	10
559 - 567	37.70	28.15	27.10	25.05	23.00	20.95	18.90	16.85	14.80	12.40	8.30
567 - 575	38.15	28.60	27.55	25.50	23.45	21.40	19.35	17.30	15.25	13.20	9.20
575 - 583	38.60	29.05	28.00	25.95	23.90	21.85	19.80	17.75	15.70	13.65	10.10
583 - 591	39.05	29.50	28.45	26.40	24.35	22.30	20.25	18.20	16.15	14.10	11.00
591 - 599	39.50	29.95	28.90	26.85	24.80	22.75	20.70	18.65	16.60	14.55	11.90
599 - 607	39.95	30.40	29.35	27.30	25.25	23.20	21.15	19.10	17.05	15.00	12.80
607 - 615	40.40	30.85	29.80	27.75	25.70	23.65	21.60	19.55	17.50	15.45	13.40
615 - 623	40.85	31.30	30.25	28.20	26.15	24.10	22.05	20.00	17.95	15.90	13.85
623 - 631	41.30	31.75	30.70	28.65	26.60	24.55	22.50	20.45	18.40	16.35	14.30
631 - 639	41.75	32.20	31.15	29.10	27.05	25.00	22.95	20.90	18.85	16.80	14.75
639 - 647	42.20	32.65	31.65	29.55	27.50	25.45	23.40	21.35	19.30	17.25	15.20
647 - 655	42.65	33.10	32.10	30.00	27.95	25.90	23.85	21.80	19.75	17.70	15.65
655 - 663	43.25	33.70	32.70	30.65	28.60	26.50	24.45	22.40	20.35	18.30	16.25
663 - 671	43.95	34.40	33.40	31.35	29.30	27.20	25.15	23.10	21.05	19.00	16.95
671 - 679	44.65	35.10	34.10	32.05	29.95	27.90	25.85	23.80	21.75	19.70	17.65
679 - 687	45.35	35.80	34.80	32.75	30.65	28.60	26.55	24.50	22.45	20.40	18.35
687 - 695	46.05	36.50	35.50	33.45	31.35	29.30	27.25	25.20	23.15	21.10	19.05
695 - 703	47.15	37.60	36.60	34.55	32.45	30.40	28.35	26.30	24.25	22.20	20.15
703 - 711	48.30	38.80	37.75	35.70	33.65	31.60	29.55	27.50	25.45	23.40	21.30
711 - 719	49.50	39.95	38.95	36.90	34.85	32.75	30.70	28.65	26.60	24.55	22.50
719 - 727	50.70	41.15	40.10	38.05	36.00	33.95	31.90	29.85	27.80	25.75	23.70
727 - 735	51.85	42.30	41.30	39.25	37.20	35.15	33.10	31.00	28.95	26.90	24.85
735 - 743	53.05	43.50	42.45	40.40	38.35	36.30	34.25	32.20	30.15	28.10	26.05
743 - 751	53.80	44.30	43.25	41.20	39.15	37.10	35.05	33.00	30.95	28.85	26.80
751 - 759	54.50	45.00	43.95	41.90	39.85	37.80	35.75	33.70	31.65	29.60	27.50
759 - 767	55.25	45.70	44.65	42.60	40.55	38.50	36.45	34.40	32.35	30.30	28.25
767 - 775	55.95	46.40	45.40	43.30	41.25	39.20	37.15	35.10	33.05	31.00	28.95
775 - 783	56.65	47.10	46.10	44.05	41.95	39.90	37.85	35.80	33.75	31.70	29.65
783 - 791	57.35	47.80	46.80	44.75	42.70	40.65	38.55	36.50	34.45	32.40	30.35
791 - 799	58.10	48.55	47.50	45.45	43.40	41.35	39.30	37.25	35.20	33.15	31.10
799 - 807	58.80	49.25	48.25	46.20	44.15	42.10	40.05	37.95	35.90	33.85	31.80
807 - 815	59.55	50.00	49.00	46.90	44.85	42.80	40.75	38.70	36.65	34.60	32.55
815 - 823	60.25	50.75	49.70	47.65	45.60	43.55	41.50	39.45	37.40	35.35	33.25
823 - 831	61.00	51.45	50.45	48.40	46.35	44.30	42.20	40.15	38.10	36.05	34.00
831 - 839	61.75	52.20	51.15	49.10	47.05	45.00	42.95	40.90	38.85	36.80	34.75
839 - 847	62.45	52.95	51.90	49.85	47.80	45.75	43.70	41.65	39.60	37.50	35.45
847 - 855	63.20	53.65	52.65	50.60	48.55	46.45	44.40	42.35	40.30	38.25	36.20
855 - 863	63.95	54.40	53.35	51.30	49.25	47.20	45.15	43.10	41.05	39.00	36.95
863 - 871	64.65	55.15	54.10	52.05	50.00	47.95	45.90	43.85	41.75	39.70	37.65
871 - 879	65.40	55.85	54.85	52.80	50.70	48.65	46.60	44.55	42.50	40.45	38.40
879 - 887	66.15	56.60	55.55	53.50	51.45	49.40	47.35	45.30	43.25	41.20	39.15
887 - 895	66.85	57.35	56.30	54.25	52.20	50.15	48.10	46.00	43.95	41.90	39.85
895 - 903	67.60	58.05	57.05	55.00	52.90	50.85	48.80	46.75	44.70	42.65	40.60
903 - 911	68.35	58.80	57.75	55.70	53.65	51.60	49.55	47.50	45.45	43.40	41.30
911 - 919	69.05	59.50	58.50	56.45	54.40	52.35	50.30	48.20	46.15	44.10	42.05
919 - 927	69.80	60.25	59.25	57.15	55.10	53.05	51.00	48.95	46.90	44.85	42.80
927 - 935	72.50	62.95	61.95	59.90	57.85	55.75	53.70	51.65	49.60	47.55	45.50
935 - 943	74.15	64.60	63.55	61.50	59.45	57.40	55.35	53.30	51.25	49.20	47.15
943 - 951	74.85	65.35	64.30	62.25	60.20	58.15	56.10	54.05	52.00	49.90	47.85
951 - 959	75.60	66.05	65.05	63.00	60.95	58.85	56.80	54.75	52.70	50.65	48.60
959 - 967	76.35	66.80	65.75	63.70	61.65	59.60	57.55	55.50	53.45	51.40	49.35
967 - 975	77.05	67.55	66.50	64.45	62.40	60.35	58.30	56.25	54.15	52.10	50.05
975 - 983	77.80	68.25	67.25	65.20	63.15	61.05	59.00	56.95	54.90	52.85	50.80
983 - 991	78.55	69.00	67.95	65.90	63.85	61.80	59.75	57.70	55.65	53.60	51.55
991 - 999	79.25	69.75	68.70	66.65	64.60	62.55	60.50	58.45	56.35	54.30	52.25

Provincial claim codes/Codes de demande provinciaux
Deduct from each pay / Retenez sur chaque paie

This table is available on TOD — E-3 — Vous pouvez obtenir cette table sur TSD

Source: Figures 12-10 through 12-13 copyright © Canada Revenue Agency. Reproduced with permission of the Minister of Public Works and Government Services Canada, 2006.

Overtime

Provincial laws require that extra pay be given after a certain number of hours have been worked in a week. For example, if 40 hours were the maximum number of hours at regular pay, an employee who worked more than that would receive extra pay for the time worked over 40 hours.

Suppose a person earns $15/h for the first 40 hours worked each week, plus time and a half for overtime. The overtime hours are paid at the rate of $15/h: the regular rate of $15 plus one-half, $7.50. If the person works 48 hours in the week, a total of $780 would be earned. The earnings are calculated as follows:

$$
\begin{array}{rclr}
\$15.00 & \times & 40 & = & \$600.00 \\
22.50 & \times & 8 & = & \underline{180.00} \\
& & & & \$780.00
\end{array}
$$

Overtime regulations are set by the provincial governments and by agreements between the employer and the employees.

UNIT 28

REVIEW
QUESTIONS

1. What does the word "payroll" mean?

2. List three federal laws that affect payroll accounting procedures.

3. (a) What are the two parts of Lostracco's cheque in Figure 12-1?
   (b) What is the purpose of the pay statement?

4. What are the compulsory deductions in your province?

5. List five voluntary deductions.

6. (a) Who must contribute to the Canada Pension Plan?
   (b) What percentage of gross earnings must be contributed by employees?
   (c) If all the employees of a company together made CPP contributions of $575.50 in the week, what must the company also contribute?

7. (a) Who must pay employment insurance premiums?
   (b) If all the employees of a company together paid EI premiums of $414.60, what is the amount of the premium paid by the company?

8. (a) What is a TD1 form?
   (b) What is a TD1ON form?
   (c) Explain why Lostracco's net claim code is 1.
   (d) What is a non-refundable tax credit?

9. (a) What are the gross earnings?
   (b) What are the net earnings?
   (c) What are the deductions?
   (d) What is Lostracco's take-home pay?
   (e) For which deductions must the employers also make a contribution? How much is the contribution of the employer?

10. What purpose is served by the SIN?

11. Describe five commonly used pay periods.

12. Describe four of the six payment methods.

13. What benefits or services are provided by the following:
    (a) Provincial health insurance
    (b) Extended health insurance
    (c) Canada Pension Plan
    (d) Employment insurance
    (e) Group life insurance
    (f) Credit unions
    (g) Registered pension plans

Note: Where necessary, use either current payroll deduction booklets or the tables given on pages 479–486 to complete the exercises in this chapter.

UNIT 28

PROBLEMS: APPLICATIONS

1. (a) Calculate each week's gross earnings for Agnes Davis, a salesperson who earns a 6 percent commission on weekly sales.

WEEK	SALES
1	$10 152.60
2	13 420.33
3	12 366.29
4	14 986.50

   (b) Calculate the total sales and commission for the four weeks.

2. What are Nancy Koosman's gross earnings if she receives a 5 percent commission and had sales of $24 230 during the week?

3. Motoko Haslam is paid a basic salary of $280 plus 3.5 percent commission on sales. The sales made for four weeks are shown below:

WEEK	SALES
1	$23 570
2	25 450
3	29 610
4	19 375

   (a) Calculate gross earnings for each week.
   (b) Calculate total earnings for the month.
   (c) If Motoko had received a straight commission of 5 percent of sales, what would the month's commission be?
   (d) Which method would you prefer — salary and commission or commission only? Why?

4. Ulla Eckhardt works for a firm producing electronic components. She is paid according to the number of components she assembles. Calculate Eckhardt's gross earnings for each day of the week if she is paid $2.25 for each assembly.

Day	No. of Components
Monday	70
Tuesday	74
Wednesday	81
Thursday	87
Friday	75

5. Determine the gross earnings for each of the following employees:

Name	Hourly Rate	Hours
C. Giamberardino	$13.20	40
C. Murphy	9.60	39
D. Kimura	15.25	40
R. Trites	14.75	38

6. If each employee in exercise 5 works four hours of overtime in addition to the regular hours, and is paid time and a half for each hour of overtime, what are the gross earnings for each?

7. Charmaine Hooper, a welder, is paid on a piece-rate basis. She receives $3.75 for each sheet metal part produced. What are her earnings for each day and for the week?

Day	Number Produced
Monday	42
Tuesday	57
Wednesday	65
Thursday	51
Friday	47

8. Lois Belincki is paid at the rate of $8.50/h and time and a half for overtime. Any work over eight hours in one day is considered overtime. Calculate her week's gross earnings if she worked the following hours:

Day	Hours
Monday	8.00
Tuesday	7.50
Wednesday	10.00
Thursday	7.75
Friday	8.00

9. During the month of July, Veronica Drepko's gross earnings were as follows:

Week	Gross Earnings
1	$887.50
2	773.27
3	871.45
4	884.92

Calculate the CPP and EI premium for the month of July.

10. (a) Charles Mazer contributes $42 per week to the company pension plan and $10 per week to union dues. Calculate his taxable earnings in July if his gross earnings for the four weeks were as follows:

Week	Gross Earnings
1	$790.25
2	815.80
3	839.45
4	810.75

    (b) Mazer's net claim code for both federal and provincial income tax deduction purposes is 6. Calculate the income tax deduction for each week in July.

    (c) Calculate the CPP and EI premiums that Mazer pays each week.

    (d) As well as the deductions that you have calculated in parts (a), (b), and (c), Mazer also has the following weekly deductions: group life insurance for $30 000 at a premium of 15¢ per $1000. In the fourth week, he chose to buy a Canada Savings Bond at $50 per week. Calculate his total deductions and his net earnings for the four weeks.

11. Grace Trumball contributes $11.25 per week to her company's pension plan. She also has the following weekly deductions: group life insurance for $25 000 at a cost of 17¢ per $1000; union dues $6.75. Her net claim code for tax purposes is 1. Her gross earnings in March were as follows:

Week	Gross Earnings
1	$830.40
2	892.80
3	861.50
4	828.62

    (a) Calculate the taxable earnings and income tax payable.

    (b) Calculate the CPP contributions and the EI premium.

    (c) Calculate net earnings.

12. Use the TD1 and TD1ON forms shown in Figures 12-2, 12-3, 12-4, 12-5, 12-6, and 12-7 to determine both the federal and provincial net claim codes for each of the following:

    (a) Richard Rancourt has one dependent, 21 years old. The dependent attends college for eight months of the year, earns $7000 per year, and pays tuition fees of $3400.

    (b) Gerald Ouellette has a dependent spouse who earns no income.

    (c) Pat Brophy is a university student for eight months of the year and pays tuition of $4050. This year Pat receives a scholarship for $1250.

    (d) B. Falconer is 66 years old, has a dependent spouse, and receives a $24 000 pension.

UNIT 29   Payroll Records and Journal Entries

Learning Objectives

After reading this unit, discussing the applicable review questions and completing the applications exercises, you will be able to do the following:

1. **COMPLETE** and **PROVE** the accuracy of a Payroll Journal.

2. **EXPLAIN** the purpose of the employee's earnings record.

3. **PREPARE** the four basic types of payroll entries in the General Journal.

4. **DESCRIBE** the process of remitting payroll deductions to the federal government.

5. **DEFINE** Payroll Journal, T4, employee's earnings record, Employer Health Tax, and workers' compensation.

IMPLEMENTING PAYROLL PROCEDURES

Various forms and procedures are used for payroll. We will begin this unit by examining them.

Using the Payroll Journal

To determine the amount to be paid to employees (net earnings), a number of calculations are necessary. The deductions for each employee must be listed, totalled, and subtracted from gross earnings. These calculations are performed on an accounting form called a **Payroll Journal**, which is sometimes called a Payroll Register.

> A Payroll Journal is the form used to record gross earnings, deductions, and net earnings for all of a firm's workers.

    A Payroll Journal records the payroll details for employees for each pay period. It shows the gross earnings, deductions, and net earnings. It is a form that helps the payroll accountant to organize the calculation of the payroll. An example is shown in Figure 12-14 on page 492. Notice in Figure 12-14 how the totals of the Payroll Journal are balanced as a form of mathematical proof of accuracy. Two separate proofs are prepared to avoid errors:

(1) Gross Earnings – Total Deductions = Net Earnings

(2) Gross Earnings – Individual Deduction Totals = Net Earnings

Using the Employee's Earnings Record

On or before April 30 each year, Canadians must file their income tax returns with the federal government. To complete an income tax return, an employee must know how much he or she earned and the amounts of payroll deductions withheld by the employer throughout the year. The federal government requires all employers to give their employees a Statement of Remuneration Paid form, commonly called a **T4 slip**, that provides this information. The employer must provide the T4 slip to all employees by February 28. An example is shown in Figure 12-15 on page 493.

> A T4 slip provides an employee with the total earnings and deductions for the year.

FIGURE 12-14
Completed Payroll Journal

COMPANY NAME EASTERN SYSTEMS

PAY PERIOD ENDING MAY 7, 20--

PAYROLL JOURNAL

PAGE

EMPL. NO.	NAME OF EMPLOYEE	NET CLAIM CODE	GROSS EARNINGS	NON-TAXABLES		TAXABLE EARNINGS	OTHER DEDUCTIONS							TOTAL DEDUC-TIONS	NET EARNINGS
				RPP*	UNION DUES		FED. INC. TAX	PROV. INC. TAX	TOTAL INC. TAX	CPP	EI	HEALTH INS.	GROUP INS.		
617	Barlow, J.	7	900.00			900.00	99.35	8.75	108.10	41.34	18.90			168.34	731.66
618	Campbell, K.	2	900.00			900.00	125.85	30.90	156.75	41.34	18.90			216.99	683.01
619	Campbell, R.	1	600.00			600.00	66.20	15.90	82.10	26.37	12.60			121.07	478.93
620	Lostracco, M.	1	800.00			800.00	107.40	27.05	134.45	36.39	16.80			187.64	612.36
621	Palmer, R.	2	550.00			550.00	55.20	8.55	63.75	23.89	11.55			99.19	450.81
622	Weeks, D.	8	800.00			800.00	83.55	4.90	88.45	36.39	16.80			141.64	658.36
			4 550.00			4 550.00	537.55	96.05	633.60	205.72	95.55			934.87	3 615.13

*The term *Registered Pension Plan (RPP)* identifies deductions payable to a pension plan provided by the employer.

Proof 1

Gross Earnings	$	$4 550.00
Less: Total Deductions		934.87
Net Earnings	$	$3 615.13

Proof 2

Gross Earnings		$4 550.00
Less: Income Tax	633.60	
CPP	205.72	
EI	95.55	934.87
Net Earnings		$3 615.13

The T4 slip in Figure 12-15 shows the employee's gross earnings and all deductions that will affect the personal income tax calculations. To prepare the T4 slip, an employer must keep cumulative totals of the employee's earnings and deductions. The totals are kept on a form called an **employee's earnings record.**

An employee's earnings record is a record of all the payroll information for an employee for one year.

The employee's earnings record provides all the information required for the preparation of the T4 slip. Figure 12-16 on page 494 shows the earnings record for M. Lostracco. Notice which figures are transferred from this form to the T4 slip in Figure 12-15.

At the present time, every worker in Canada is required to pay 4.95 percent of contributory earnings, to a maximum of $1861.20 yearly, to the Canada Pension Plan. Many employees will have paid their total year's premium of $1861.20 before the end of the year. For this reason, a special column is used on the earnings record to accumulate the CPP premiums. When the total reaches $1861.20 for the year, the employee will no longer have the CPP deduction made. At the year's end, the earnings record is totalled and balanced. Similarly, EI contributions have a maximum of $760.50. When the EI maximum is reached, there are no further deductions.

FIGURE 12-15

Statement of remuneration paid (T4)

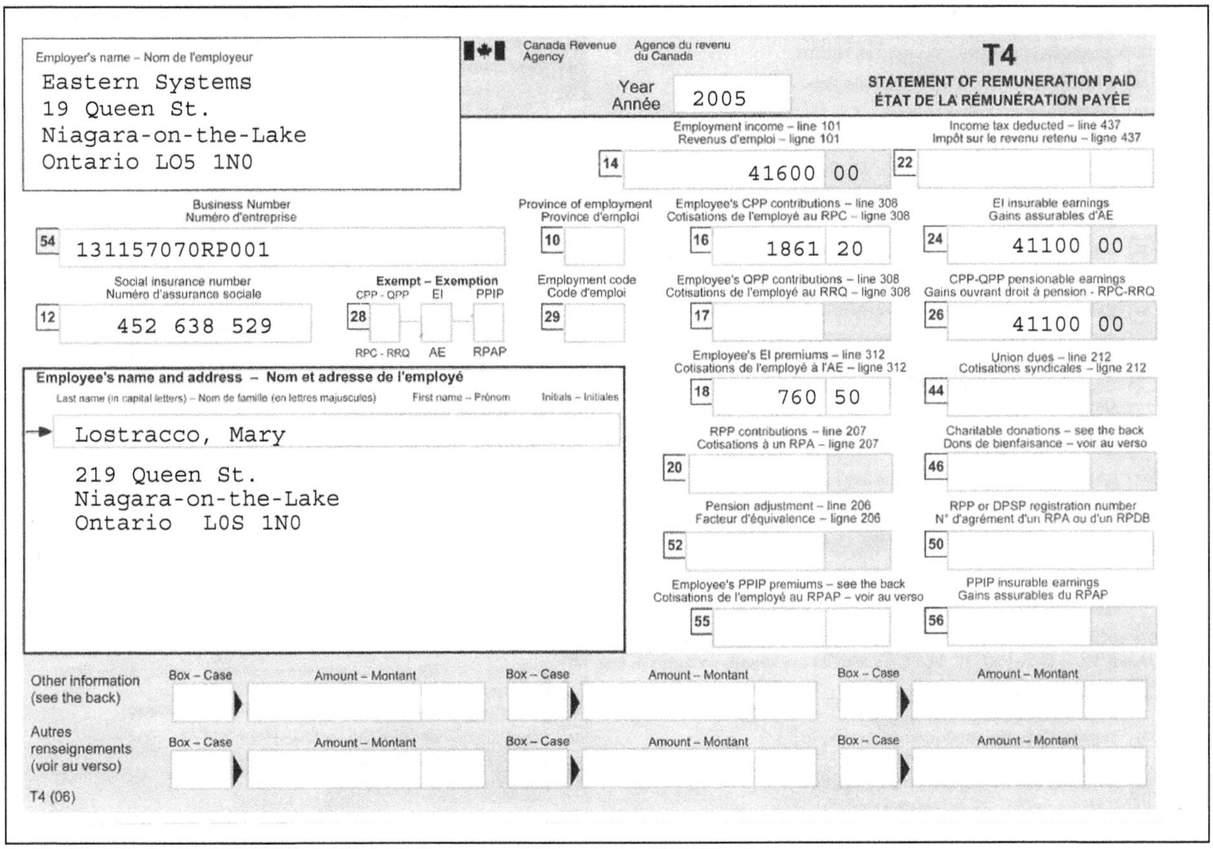
Employer's name – Nom de l'employeur
Eastern Systems
19 Queen St.
Niagara-on-the-Lake
Ontario L05 1N0

Canada Revenue Agency / Agence du revenu du Canada

T4

Year / Année 2005

STATEMENT OF REMUNERATION PAID / ÉTAT DE LA RÉMUNÉRATION PAYÉE

14 Employment income – line 101 / Revenus d'emploi – ligne 101: 41600 00

22 Income tax deducted – line 437 / Impôt sur le revenu retenu – ligne 437:

54 Business Number / Numéro d'entreprise: 131157070RP001

10 Province of employment / Province d'emploi:

16 Employee's CPP contributions – line 308 / Cotisations de l'employé au RPC – ligne 308: 1861 20

24 EI insurable earnings / Gains assurables d'AE: 41100 00

12 Social insurance number / Numéro d'assurance sociale: 452 638 529

28 Exempt – Exemption: CPP-QPP / RPC-RRQ, EI / AE, PPIP / RPAP

29 Employment code / Code d'emploi:

17 Employee's QPP contributions – line 308 / Cotisations de l'employé au RRQ – ligne 308:

26 CPP-QPP pensionable earnings / Gains ouvrant droit à pension - RPC-RRQ: 41100 00

Employee's name and address – Nom et adresse de l'employé

Last name (in capital letters) – Nom de famille (en lettres majuscules) / First name – Prénom / Initials – Initiales

Lostracco, Mary
219 Queen St.
Niagara-on-the-Lake
Ontario L0S 1N0

18 Employee's EI premiums – line 312 / Cotisations de l'employé à l'AE – ligne 312: 760 50

44 Union dues – line 212 / Cotisations syndicales – ligne 212:

20 RPP contributions – line 207 / Cotisations à un RPA – ligne 207:

46 Charitable donations – see the back / Dons de bienfaisance – voir au verso:

52 Pension adjustment – line 206 / Facteur d'équivalence – ligne 206:

50 RPP or DPSP registration number / N° d'agrément d'un RPA ou d'un RPDB:

55 Employee's PPIP premiums – see the back / Cotisations de l'employé au RPAP – voir au verso:

56 PPIP insurable earnings / Gains assurables du RPAP:

Other information (see the back) / Autres renseignements (voir au verso)

Box – Case | Amount – Montant | Box – Case | Amount – Montant | Box – Case | Amount – Montant

T4 (06)

Source: Copyright © Canada Revenue Agency. Reproduced with permission of the Minister of Public Works and Government Services, Canada, 2006.

FIGURE 12-16
Employee's earnings record

EMPLOYEE EARNINGS RECORD FOR THE YEAR 2005

NAME Lostracco, M.
ADDRESS 19 Queen St.
Niagara-on-the-Lake, ON L0S 1N0
TELEPHONE 825-6621

DEPARTMENT Info. Tech.
POSITION Supervisor
SOCIAL INS. NO. 452-638-529
SALARY $800/week

DATE EMPLOYED 06/01/96
DATE TERMINATED
NO. OF DEPENDANTS 0
NET CLAIM CODE 1

| EMP. NO. | REGULAR OVERTIME | GROSS EARNINGS | DEDUCTIONS | | | | | TOTAL DEDUCTIONS | NET EARNINGS | TOTAL EI TO DATE | CH. NO. | PAY PERIOD ENDING |
			CPP	EI	INC. TAX	GR. INS.	OTHER					
1620	19 200.00	19 200.00	946.14	436.80	3 495.70			4 878.64	14 321.36	405.60		Jan.–Jun.
	800.00	800.00	36.04	15.60	151.25			202.89	597.11	421.20		Jul. 5
	800.00	800.00	36.04	15.60	151.25			202.89	597.11	436.80		12
	800.00	800.00	36.04	15.60	151.25			202.89	597.11	452.40		19
	800.00	800.00	36.04	15.60	151.25			202.89	597.11	468.00		26
	800.00	800.00	36.04	15.60	151.25			202.89	597.11	483.60		Aug. 2

Paying Employees

Generally, employers use one of three methods to pay employees:

(1) Cash
(2) Cheque
(3) Bank, credit union, or trust company deposit

Paying by Cash

Although this method is not preferred by employers, it is sometimes necessary to pay by cash because of agreements with employees or in remote areas where banks are not readily available.

Paying by Cheque

Many companies prefer to pay by cheque. To simplify the end-of-month bank reconciliations, a separate payroll bank account is opened. Each month, a cheque is written on the regular account. The amount of this cheque is exactly the total required to pay all of the employees. This cheque is deposited in the special payroll bank account. The entry to record this cheque is:

May 28 Salaries Payable	30 000	
Cash		30 000
To transfer funds to the payroll bank account for the May 28 payroll.		

Next, cheques are issued to each employee. These cheques have the pay statements attached and are usually identified as payroll cheques by the words "payroll account" printed on the cheque face. When workers cash their cheques, the bank will cash them from the company's special payroll account. If all the workers cash their cheques, the special payroll account balance will be reduced to zero.

Paying by Deposit

Many companies and employees prefer the deposit method. In this case, a bank provides a payroll service to companies. The employer gives the bank a list of employees, showing the amount earned by each. In return for a fee, the bank pays the employees by depositing the money in their accounts in various banks, credit unions, or trust companies.

 The deposit method frees the employer from having to prepare paycheques or having to handle cash when paying employees. Employees like this system because money is placed directly in their accounts. No matter which method is used, provincial labour laws require that each employee receive a statement (like the one shown at the beginning of the chapter in Figure 12-1) outlining gross earnings, deductions, and net pay. Why do you think this law was passed?

Remitting Deductions

Once a month, the employer must remit the deductions taken from the employee's wages and salaries to the proper agencies. Income tax, CPP, and EI deductions must be sent to the Receiver General for Canada by the 15th of the following month.

Canada Revenue Agency supplies companies with the official remittance form, PD7AR, which is used to send deductions to Canada Revenue Agency. Other deductions, such as union dues and life insurance premiums must also be remitted to the appropriate agencies.

RECORDING THE PAYROLL

Up to this point, we have described the procedures for determining and keeping track of the earnings and deductions for employees. Now, we will examine the recording of the payroll information in the accounting system.

Payroll involves expenses, liabilities, and payment of funds. Therefore, journal entries must be made to record these items so that the accounts and financial statements will be accurate. There are four basic types of payroll entries in the General Journal:

- **Step 1:** Make an entry to record the Salaries Expense and the payroll liabilities for each pay period. The figures for this entry are taken from the Payroll Journal.
- **Step 2:** Make an entry to record the payment to workers for each pay period.
- **Step 3:** Make entries to record the employer's share of CPP and EI premiums for each pay period.
- **Step 4:** Make entries to remit the payroll deductions to the government and other agencies. These entries are made once a month.

All these entries will now be examined.

Step 1: Record the Salaries Expense and Payroll Liabilities

The first entry involves recording the total Salaries Expense and the amounts owed to the employees, government, and other agencies, such as insurance companies.

The figures for the entry come from the Payroll Journal, Figure 12-14 on page 492:

May 7	Salaries Expense	4 550.00	
	CPP Payable		205.72
	EI Payable		95.55
	Income Tax Payable		633.60
	Salaries Payable		3 615.13
	To record the May 7 payroll.		

This first entry records the deductions held back from the employees and recorded as liabilities on the books of the employer. As you will see, these amounts must be paid out once a month, and until they are paid are debts owed by the employer. The first entry also records the figures for a liability account called *Salaries Payable*. This is the amount owed to the workers and is a liability until the workers are paid.

Step 2: Record the Payment to Employees

The second entry is made when the employees are paid. In the previous entry, a credit was entered in the Salaries Payable account to record the liability to the employees. When the employees are paid, this liability is cancelled:

May 7	Salaries Payable	3 615.13	
	Cash		3 615.13
	Payment of May 7 payroll.		

Step 3: Record the Employer's Payroll Expenses

As you learned earlier, the employer is required to contribute to the Canada Pension Plan and to the employment insurance fund on behalf of employees. *For CPP, the employer must contribute an amount equal to that contributed by employees. For EI, the employer's contribution is 1.4 times the employee premiums.*

In the case of Eastern Systems (Figure 12-14), the employees' CPP contribution is $205.72; therefore, the employer's contribution is $205.72. The employees' EI contribution is $95.55; therefore, the employer's EI contribution is $133.77 (1.4 × $95.55).

The company records its contribution to CPP in an expense account called CPP Expense. This account is debited for the employer's contribution to CPP. The company's contribution to EI is debited to an expense account called EI Expense. The entries for Eastern Systems are as follows:

May 7	CPP Expense	205.72	
	CPP Payable		205.72
	To record the employer's contribution to CPP.		
7	EI Expense	133.77	
	EI Payable		133.77
	To record the employer's contribution to EI.		

Employer Health Tax

In Ontario, all employers must pay an **Employer Health Tax** (EHT) calculated at a graduated tax rate on total gross payroll. This tax replaces employee contributions to provincial health care plans.

A graduated health tax, payable by Ontario employers, which is based on total gross payroll.

Employer Health Tax Rates

The rate of EHT is determined by the total annual gross earnings of employees during the year. The chart in Figure 12-17 shows the earnings categories and applicable rates:

Quebec calculates EHT on the basis of a flat rate of 3.45 percent of the gross payroll amount, while the Manitoba EHT is based on the following schedule:

Gross Payroll	Rate
Less than $600 000	0%
$600 000 – $1 200 000	4.5%
Over $1 200 000	2.25%

Employer Health Tax Calculation

Employer Health Tax is calculated by multiplying the appropriate rate by the total gross earnings for the period. Eastern Systems' gross earnings can be found on the Payroll Journal (Figure 12-14). The gross earnings are $4400 per week. Eastern

FIGURE 12-17

Employer Health Tax rates

Tax Rates

APPLICATION   The amount of tax payable is a percentage of the total annual remuneration paid by employers during a calendar year. The tax is calculated by multiplying the total amount of remuneration paid in a year by the tax rate applicable to that amount of remuneration.

The tax rate on total remuneration is graduated, ranging from 0.98% to 1.95%, with the highest rate applying in those cases where total annual remuneration paid by the employer exceeds $400 000.

RATES   Ranges of remuneration and applicable tax rates are outlined below:

TOTAL ONTARIO ANNUAL REMUNERATION	RATE
up to $200 000	0.98%
over $200 001 to $230 000	1.101%
over $230 000 to $260 000	1.223%
over $260 000 to $290 000	1.344%
over $290 000 to $320 000	1.465%
over $320 000 to $350 000	1.586%
over $350 000 to $380 000	1.708%
over $380 000 to $400 000	1.829%
over $400 000	1.95%

Systems has an annual payroll between $200 001 and $230 000 ($4400 × 52 weeks = $228 800). Can you find the appropriate EHT rate in the chart in Figure 12-17? Eastern Systems' rate is 1.101 percent. Therefore, the Employer Health Tax owing is $4550 × 0.01101 = $50.10 for this pay period. The following entry is made to record the EHT for the pay period.

May 7	Employer Health Tax Expense	50.10	
	Employer Health Tax Payable		50.10
	To record EHT for May 7 payroll.		

The entries just described to record and pay the payroll and to record the employer's payroll expenses are made each pay period and posted to the General Ledger. The partial ledger in Figure 12-18 on page 500 shows the entries in the accounts relating to payroll after four pay periods have been posted in May. Notice that CPP Payable and EI Payable include entries for both the employees' and employer's contributions.

Step 4: Record the Payment of Payroll Deductions

Once a month, the employer's contributions and deductions withheld from employees are forwarded to the appropriate agencies. The payment is recorded with the entries illustrated below. The entries are made on the 15th of the following month and record the remittance of the deductions for all the pay periods of the previous month. The amounts are obtained from the ledger accounts shown in Figure 12-18.

The first entry shown records the payment of money to the federal government. The amounts include both the employee and employer contributions to CPP and EI and the employees' income tax deductions:

Jun. 15	CPP Payable	1 645.76	
	EI Payable	917.28	
	Income Tax Payable	2 534.40	
	Cash		5 097.44
	To record the payment of the May		
	payroll deductions to the Receiver General.		

The next entry shown records the payment to the Provincial Treasurer for the Employer Health Tax when remittance is made monthly.

Jun. 15	Employer Health Tax Payable	200.40	
	Cash		200.40
	To record the payment of Employer Health		
	Tax to the Provincial Treasurer.		

Other payroll liabilities are also paid once a month. Similar entries are made for union dues, life insurance, health care plans in provinces that require employee contributions, and other payroll liabilities, if applicable.

Figure 12-19 on page 501 illustrates the ledger accounts after the June 15 entries have been posted. The debts owed to the federal and provincial governments have been paid, and these liability accounts are reduced to zero.

ⓈOME CONCLUDING POINTS ABOUT PAYROLL

Workers' Compensation

All provinces provide an insurance plan for the protection of workers who suffer personal injuries or occupational diseases related to their jobs. Compensation is paid to injured workers from a fund administered by a provincial Workers' Compensation Board. Employers supply the money for the fund. The amount paid by an employer varies according to the type of business and its accident record.

In return for providing money to the fund, the employer is relieved of liability for injuries suffered by workers. The amount of compensation received by an injured worker is based on the average salary earned while working. The employer's payment to the fund is an expense of operating the business. When premiums are paid, this entry is made:

> An insurance plan provided by provinces for the protection of workers injured on the job.

Jun. 30	Workers' Compensation Expense	250	
	Cash		250
	To pay semi-annual premium to Workers'		
	Compensation Board.		

Payroll Ledger Accounts

Payroll accounting involves a number of expense accounts. For example, Wages Expense is the account used for earnings of hourly rated workers. Salaries Expense is used for the earnings of salaried employees.

FIGURE 12-18
Partial General Ledger
showing the May payroll
entries recorded in the
payroll accounts

PARTIAL GENERAL LEDGER

Cash			101
May 1	30 000.00	May 7	3 615.13
		14	3 615.13
		21	3 615.13
		28	3 615.13

Employee Health Tax Payable			223
		May 7	50.10
		14	50.10
		21	50.10
		28	50.10
			200.40

CPP Payable			220
		May 7	205.72
		7	205.72
		14	205.72
		14	205.72
		21	205.72
		21	205.72
		28	205.72
		28	205.72
			1 645.76

Salaries Payable			224
May 7	3 615.13	May 7	3 615.13
14	3 615.13	14	3 615.13
21	3 615.13	21	3 615.13
28	3 615.13	28	3 615.13
	14 460.52		14 460.52

Salaries Expense			620
May 7	4 550.00		
14	4 550.00		
21	4 550.00		
28	4 550.00		
	18 200.00		

EI Payable			221
		May 7	95.55
		7	133.77
		14	95.55
		14	133.77
		21	95.55
		21	133.77
		28	95.55
		28	133.77
		28	917.28

CPP Expense			621
May 7	205.70		
14	205.70		
21	205.70		
28	205.70		
	822.80		

EI Expense			622
May 7	133.77		
14	133.77		
21	133.77		
28	133.77		
	535.08		

Income Tax Payable			222
		May 7	633.60
		14	633.60
		21	633.60
		28	633.60
			2 534.40

Employer's Health Tax Expense			623
May 7	50.10		
14	50.10		
21	50.10		
28	50.10		
	200.40		

FIGURE 12-19
Partial General Ledger after the June 15 entries have been posted

PARTIAL GENERAL LEDGER

Cash				101
May	1	30 000.00	May 7	3 615.13
			14	3 615.13
			21	3 615.13
			28	3 615.13
			Jun. 15	5 097.44
			15	200.40

CPP Payable				220
Jun. 15	1 645.76	May	7	205.72
			7	205.72
			14	205.72
			14	205.72
			21	205.72
			21	205.72
			28	205.72
			28	205.72
	1 645.76			1 645.76

EI Payable				221
Jun. 15	917.28	May	7	95.55
			7	133.77
			14	95.55
			14	133.77
			21	95.55
			21	133.77
			28	95.55
			28	133.77
	917.28		28	917.28

Income Tax Payable				222
Jun. 15	2 534.40	May	7	633.60
			14	633.60
			21	633.60
			28	633.60
	2 534.40			2 534.40

Employer's Health Tax Payable				223
Jun. 15	200.40	May	7	50.10
			14	50.10
			21	50.10
			28	50.10
	200.40			200.40

Salaries Payable				224
May	7	3 615.13	May 7	3 615.13
	14	3 615.13	14	3 615.13
	21	3 615.13	21	3 615.13
	28	3 615.13	28	3 615.13
		14 460.52		14 460.52

Salaries Expense			620
May	7	4 500.00	
	14	4 500.00	
	21	4 500.00	
	28	4 500.00	
		18 200.00	

CPP Expense			621
May	7	205.70	
	14	205.70	
	21	205.70	
	28	205.70	
		822.80	

EI Expense			622
May	7	113.77	
	14	113.77	
	21	113.77	
	28	113.77	
		535.08	

Employer's Health Tax Expense			623
May	7	50.10	
	14	50.10	
	21	50.10	
	28	50.10	
		200.40	

Several expense accounts are used to record employers' contributions required by various laws. These include CPP Expense, EI Expense, and Workers' Compensation Expense. Rather than use these individual accounts, some companies prefer to use one account called Payroll Expense. This account is used for all employer payments such as the employer's share of CPP, EI, EHT, and other insurances. A sample entry using the Payroll Expense account follows:

Jun. 30	Payroll Expense	369	
	CPP Payable		85
	EI Payable		99
	Workers' Compensation Payable		50
	Group Insurance Payable		45
	Employer Health Tax Payable		90
	To record the employer's payroll expenses.		

SUMMARY OF PROCEDURES

Figure 12-20 illustrates the payroll accounting procedures covered in this chapter.

FIGURE 12-20

Summary of payroll procedures

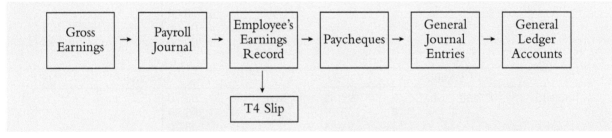

ACCOUNTING TERMS

Canada Pension Plan   All employees over 18 and under 70 contribute a percentage of their earnings during their working years and receive a pension at age 65. (p. 466)

Compulsory Deductions   Personal income tax, Employment Insurance, and Canada Pension Plan contributions are deductions required by law. (p. 465)

Deductions   Amounts deducted from an employee's pay. (p. 465)

Employee's Earnings Record   An employee's earnings record is a record of all of the payroll information for an employee for one year. (p. 493)

Employer Health Tax   A graduated health tax, payable by Ontario employers, which is based on total gross payroll. (p. 497)

Employment Insurance   Employees contribute a percentage of their earnings while employed to a fund that is designed to provide income to those workers who later become unemployed. (p. 466)

Employment Standards Act   Provincial laws governing the payment of employees. (p. 464)

Health Insurance   Each province has its own version of health insurance plans and all citizens are covered for basic health services that they require. (p. 468)

Net Earnings	Gross earnings minus deductions. (p. 476)
Payroll	A list of employees and the amount of pay earned. (p. 464)
Payroll Journal	Records gross earnings, deductions, and net earnings for each employee for all pay periods. (p. 491)
Personal Income Tax	A percentage of personal income remitted to the federal and provincial governments. (p. 467)
TD1	A form completed annually by employees to determine personal tax credits for federal tax. (p. 467)
TD1ON	A form completed annually by employees to determine personal tax credits for provincial tax. (p. 468)
T4 Slip	A statement of remuneration provided yearly to employees showing gross earnings and deductions that offset personal income tax calculations. (p. 491)
Tax Credits	Credits for items such as dependent children, CPP and EI contributions, and tuition reduce the amount of federal income tax payable. (p. 467)
Taxable Income	Income earned minus allowable deductions such as pension contributions. (p. 467)
Workers' Compensation	An insurance plan provided by provinces for the protection of workers injured on the job. (p. 499)

1. Explain how a Payroll Journal is proved to be mathematically correct.

2. Pat has just completed a Payroll Journal and the totals balance, yet there is an error in the journal. How can this happen?

3. When must the employer remit payroll deductions to the federal government?

4. Which payroll deductions are remitted to the federal government?

5. To whom is the cheque made payable when deductions are remitted to the government?

6. What form is completed when remitting to the federal government?

7. What is the purpose of the employee's earnings record?

8. Describe the four basic types of payroll entries in the General Journal.

9. (a) Which insurance compensates workers injured on the job?
   (b) Who pays the premiums for this insurance?

10. What single expense account may be used instead of CPP Expense, EI Expense, and Workers' Compensation Expense?

11. How is Ontario's Employer Health Tax calculated?

UNIT 29

REVIEW QUESTIONS

Note: Where necessary, use either current payroll deduction booklets or the tables given previously on pages 479–486 to complete the exercises in this chapter.

1. D. Houston Ltd. has six employees on the salary payroll.

   (a) Record the following information in a Payroll Journal.
   (b) Determine the taxable earnings and the income tax deduction for each employee.
   (c) Determine the CPP and EI deductions for each employee.
   (d) Calculate the net earnings for each employee.
   (e) Balance the Payroll Journal.

UNIT 29

PROBLEMS: APPLICATIONS

EMP. NO.	NAME	NET CLAIM CODE	GROSS EARNINGS	CO. PENSION
103	Jaswinder Singh	8	$780.00	$19.50
104	Bill Strahan	1	740.00	19.50
105	Linda Lo	10	660.00	19.50
106	Lesley Durvan	4	710.00	19.50
107	Stan Trudeau	9	660.00	19.50
108	Tracey St. James	1	660.00	19.50

2. The payroll information for Maingot Manufacturers for the week ended March 24 follows. Every employee also pays union dues of $7.25 weekly and has $30 000 worth of group life insurance for which 12¢ per $1000 is contributed weekly.

EMP. NO.	NAME	NET CLAIM CODE	GROSS EARNINGS
101	P. Dagenais	4	$660.00
102	L. Rasmussen	8	680.00
103	C. Hayashi	1	780.00
104	T. Chan	6	660.00
105	F. Brammel	9	710.00
106	C. Lazzari	3	740.00

(a) Record the payroll in a Payroll Journal, determining the CPP contributions, EI premiums, and income tax deductions.
(b) Total and prove the Payroll Journal.

3. The payroll information for Eastern Distributors for the week ended August 18 follows:

EMP. NO.	NAME	NET CLAIM CODE	GROSS EARNINGS	CO. PENSION
201	T. Fong	1	$765.75	$2.13
202	A. Hjelt	9	781.91	2.34
203	A. Covington	6	807.34	2.59
204	C. Amato	1	823.70	2.64
205	P. Surat	4	792.41	2.41
206	S. Betterworth	7	773.56	2.27

Every employee also pays union dues of $9 weekly and has $35 000 worth of group life insurance for which 15¢ per $1000 is contributed weekly.

(a) Record the payroll in a Payroll Journal; determine CPP, EI, and income tax.
(b) Total and prove the Payroll Journal.

4. The Payroll Journal for the pay period ended September 22 showed the following totals: gross earnings $5783.20; CPP contributions, $104.09; EI premiums, $62.70; income tax, $983.14; health insurance, $132; union dues, $142.50; net earnings, $4358.77. Prepare journal entries to record:

(a) The payroll
(b) The paying of the employees
(c) The employer's share of the CPP contributions and EI premiums

5. The Payroll Journal for the pay period ended July 21 showed the following totals: gross earnings, $46 793.55; CPP contributions, $842.28; EI premiums, $495; registered pension plan, $1544.19; income tax, $7954.90; union dues,

$1325.25; group insurance, $797.53; net earnings, $33 834.40. The Employer Health Tax is $912.47. Prepare journal entries on page 10 to record:

(a) The payroll
(b) The paying of the employees
(c) The employer's share of the CPP contributions and EI premiums and Employer Health Tax

6. Refer to the completed Payroll Journal for exercise 1, D. Houston Ltd.

(a) Prepare the journal entry on page 8 to record the payroll on May 24.
(b) Prepare the entry to pay the employees.
(c) Prepare the entry to record the company's share of CPP and EI.
(d) Prepare the entry to record the EHT of $46.35.

7. Presented below are selected data from the August 15 payroll register for Darwin and Goodall Manufacturers. Some amounts have been intentionally omitted.

Gross earnings	$22 412
Deductions	
CPP	578
EI	637
Income Tax	(?)
Group Insurance	265
Registered Pension Plan	706
Total Deductions	(?)
Net Pay	15 483
Accounts debited	
Office Salaries	11 875
Shop Wages	(?)

(a) Calculate the missing amounts.
(b) Calculate the company's share of CPP and EI.
(c) Prepare the journal entry to record the payroll.
(d) Prepare the journal entry to record the company's share of CPP and EI.
(e) Prepare the journal entry to pay the employees on August 22.

1. Delmonte Manufacturing pays its salaried employees once a month. The Payroll Journal at the end of June for these employees is shown on the following page. Prepare journal entries to record:

(a) the payroll journal at the end of June
(b) the employer's share of the CPP and the EI
(c) the cheques to pay the employees
(d) the remittance to Clarica for group insurance
(e) the remittance to Clarica for the pension
(f) the remittance to the Provincial Treasurer for the Employer Health Tax if the rate is 1.344 percent
(g) the remittance to the Receiver General for the payroll liabilities

CHAPTER 12

PROBLEMS:
CHALLENGES

2. Refer to the completed Payroll Journal for exercise 3, page 504, Eastern Distributors. Prepare journal entries to record:

(a) the payroll
(b) the cheques to pay the employees
(c) the employer's share of the CPP and the EI
(d) the remittance to Great West Life for group insurance
(e) the remittance to the union for the union dues
(f) the remittance to the Provincial Treasurer for the Employer Health Tax if the rate is 1.344 percent
(g) the remittance to the Receiver General for the payroll liabilities

COMPANY NAME DELMONTE MANUFACTURING   **PAYROLL JOURNAL**   **PAGE 307**

PAY PERIOD ENDING JUNE 30, 20--

EMPL. NO.	NAME OF EMPLOYEE	NET CLAIM CODE	GROSS EARNINGS	NON-TAXABLES RPP*	UNION DUES	TAXABLE EARNINGS	INCOME TAX	CPP	EI	HEALTH INS.	GROUP INS.	TOTAL DEDUC- TIONS	NET EARNINGS
65	O'Connell, P.	9	4 025.00	125.69		3 899.31	678.10	145.74	96.60		33.61	1 079.74	2 945.26
66	Dooner, C.	1	2 875.00	77.20		2 797.80	524.55	100.75	69.00		22.93	794.43	2 080.57
67	Greenspoon, L.	3	3 115.00	110.58		3 004.42	548.45	110.11	74.76		31.50	875.40	2 239.60
68	Ritcher, F.	10	3 897.00	118.72		3 778.28	610.35	140.67	93.53		35.90	999.17	2 897.83
69	Lapchinski, C.	6	4 250.00	136.70		4 113.30	842.85	154.32	102.00		29.88	1 265.75	2 984.25
70	Karklins, A.	4	4 250.00	136.70		4 113.30	904.95	154.32	102.00		29.88	1 327.85	2 922.15
			22 412.00	705.59		21 706.41	4 109.25	805.91	537.89		183.70	6 342.34	16 069.66

*The term *Registered Pension Plan (RPP)* identifies deductions payable to a pension plan provided by the employer.

Proof 1

Gross Earnings	$22 412.00
Less: Total Deductions	6 342.34
Net Earnings	$16 069.66

Proof 2

Gross Earnings		$ 22 412.00
Less: RPP	$ 705.59	
Income Tax	4 109.25	
CPP	805.91	
EI	537.89	
Group Insurance	183.70	6 342.34
Net Earnings		$16 069.66

CASE 1
Personal Values

Canada's employment insurance (EI) plan provides temporary financial assistance for unemployed Canadians while they look for work or upgrade their skills. The goal is to encourage people to return to the job market, as well as to provide funds while unemployed through no fault of their own.

The money in the fund comes from the federal government, employees, and employers. Employees pay insurance premiums of 1.95 percent of their earnings to a maximum of $760.50 per year. Employers contribute 1.4 times the employee contribution. For example, if 10 employees contributed total premiums of $100, then the employer would contribute $140 for the same pay period. The employee payroll deduction is based on the first dollar earned to a yearly maximum of $39 000 per employee. The maximum contribution by an employer for each employee is $1064.70 (1.4 $\times$ $760.50).

Earnings subject to employment insurance premiums include wages, salary, paid leave, and payment in kind to employees.

The employment insurance system can be a costly operation each year. Costs increase as a result of:

(a) Improved benefits paid to the unemployed
(b) Rising unemployment
(c) Claimants cheating the system

Read each of the following mini-cases.

1. Maria is an employee working for her friend Trudy's small firm. They have an agreement that Trudy will not deduct employment insurance from Maria's earnings. This saves Maria about $760.50 per year and it saves Trudy about $1064.70 per year. *Besides being illegal, what risk is Maria taking?*
2. Parveen has worked for several years and has never been unemployed. She decides to take a six-month trip. After deliberately getting herself laid off from her job, Parveen completes the required forms and begins the process to receive employment insurance. She has her friend Romi complete forms for her indicating that she is actively seeking employment. Parveen is actually away on her trip while her friend completes the paperwork. Romi forges Parveen's name on the government cheques and deposits them in Parveen's bank account.
3. Brian and Anne Marie are both working and earning good salaries. Each year one of them deliberately becomes unemployed and receives employment insurance and then goes back to work. Although they are able to find employment, they feel that they deserve the money because they have contributed the premiums for so many years. An employer, Sandra, figures out what they are doing but does not report them because she does not want to get involved in a court case that might hurt the reputation of the business.
4. Toni has worked for 25 years at a number of low-level jobs and has never had to claim employment insurance. As Toni approaches retirement he feels it is not fair that after contributing so much, he has never benefited from the system. He works out a scheme to be laid off prior to retirement so that he can claim employment insurance, and then when the funds run out he can retire.

Discuss each of the mini-cases with two members of your class. Answer the following questions:

(a) Rank each of the people according to their honesty. Give each a number from 1 to 8, with 1 being the most dishonest (Marie, Trudy, Parveen, Romi, Brian, Anne Maria, Sandra, Toni).

(b) Do you think each person is guilty of wrongdoing? If not, which person has not done nothing wrong?

(c) For each mini-case, suggest procedures the government could use to prevent wrongdoing by the person involved.

(d) For each mini-case, suggest a fair penalty for those you feel have committed an illegal action.

CASE 2
Canada Pension Plan and Employment Insurance

Canada Revenue Agency (CRA) administers the *Income Tax Act*, and Human Resources and Skills Development Canada (HRSDC) is responsible for the *Canada Pension Act* and the *Employment Insurance Act*.

The Canada Pension Plan (CPP) came into effect in 1966 to provide financial assistance to Canadians when they retired from the workforce. Every individual in Canada who worked and contributed to CPP is entitled to benefits when they retire. The employer is responsible for deducting CPP contributions from the employee and for matching the contribution.

The Employment Insurance Program provides temporary financial assistance for unemployed Canadians while they look for work or upgrade their skills. Information, rules, regulations, and news on the Employment Insurance program are available on the HRSDC Web site: www.hrsdc.gc.ca

Canada Revenue Agency provides information brochures, rules and regulations, and payroll deduction tables for income tax, CPP, and EI on its Internet Web site: www.cra-arc.gc.ca/payroll. Booklets and deduction tables are available online, can be printed, or can be ordered in print form. Deduction tables are also available electronically on CDs.

Obtain or print a current copy of the deduction booklet *Canada Pension Plan Contribution and Employment Insurance Premium Tables*, or work from information on the Canada Revenue Agency Web site to prepare a research report that includes the following information:

Canada Pension Plan

(a) The current year's maximum pensionable earnings
(b) The year's basic exemption
(c) Maximum weekly earnings on which premiums are based
(d) Maximum employee contributions for a year
(e) The percentage of earnings contributed by an employee
(f) The employer contribution for each employee
(g) The responsibilities of employers
(h) Three examples of "excepted employment"

Employment Insurance

(a) The minimum hours below which premiums are not payable
(b) The percentage of earnings contributed by an employee
(c) The employer's premium rate

(d) For a person paid weekly, the maximum deduction for one week

(e) For a person paid monthly, the maximum deduction for one month

CASE 3
Payroll Costs

Technology Wizards is a computer service business. It provides installation, networking and support services to computer users. Its main customers are small businesses that do not have their own technical support staff. There is a lot of competition in this area and being profitable is increasingly difficult.

Technology Wizards has ten technical support staff who are permanent employees and who each earn an average gross salary of $60 000. Average fringe benefits include vacation pay, 4 percent; extended medical insurance, 1 percent; CPP and EI, 5 percent; pension 2 percent.

Because of declining profit and stiff competition, the company is considering converting to a contract basis instead of having permanent employees. This would mean that the ten support staff would no longer be employees of the company. They would become independent contractors and would receive no benefits from the company. They would have to pay for their own benefits such as CPP and medical insurance. Their contracts would be for 49 weeks and would be renewed at that time if their work was satisfactory. The average salary would increase to $62 000 and they would be guaranteed this amount if they worked 49 weeks.

(a) Describe the financial implications if this proposal is implemented. Use specific figures to illustrate the implications.

(b) What other factors enter into this decision?

(c) What decision would you make? Why?

ETHICS CASE
Wellington's Department Store

Wellington's is a large department store, that employs many students part time. Minimum wage laws specify the number of hours of work per week above which a student must be paid the general worker's rate. There is about a 10 percent difference between the general rate and the student rate. Wellington's offers several fringe benefits to its full-time employees. These include a free life insurance policy, 50 percent of the cost of a medical plan, and 20 days annual sick leave. Part-time employees do not receive fringe benefits. Management of the store behaves as follows:

- The owner of the store encourages the use of many part-time students because the minimum rate for students is lower and because they do not receive fringe benefits.

- The personnel manager occasionally, but deliberately, contravenes the minimum wage law by not paying overtime as required. The owner is not aware of this.

- The manager of the sporting goods department has hired his son-in-law as a salesperson and often offers him overtime work. No one else in the department works overtime.

(a) Who do you think is the most ethical person in the store? Who is the least ethical? Rank the following on an ethical scale, from 1 to 4, with 4 being the least ethical:
  (i)   The owner
  (ii) The personnel manager
  (iii) The sporting goods manager
  (iv) The son-in-law
(b) Provide reasons for your ranking.
(c) What is your definition of the word "ethical?"
(d) Suppose you worked for Wellington's and felt that you were not being treated fairly according to several of your province's employment standard laws. What would you do?
  (i) List your alternatives.
  (ii) What are the possible consequences of each alternative?

CHAPTER 12

INTERNET RESOURCES

These Web sites provide payroll accounting information and resources.

1. **Canadian Payroll Association   www.payroll.ca**

   This association represents the payroll community with government and provides payroll groups with news and information on legislation and policy, educational opportunities, job opportunities, and payroll resources.

2. **Canada Revenue Agency**

   http://www.cra-arc.gc.ca/tax/business/topics/payroll/menu-e.html
   The Canada Revenue Agency site provides employers with up-to-date government requirements for payroll deductions and taxation. Electronic payroll forms may be downloaded from this site, including payroll deduction tables, and information pamphlets such as "How Payroll Works" and "Calculating and Remitting Deductions."

3. **ABOUT.com   http://sbinfocanada.about.com/od/payrolltaxes/**

   Everything you need to know about payroll taxes, from how to fill out the ROE to payroll deductions, is provided at this site. Many topics and resources are offered for anyone interested in business.

4. **Payroll Services Companies**

   Visit any of these sites to review companies that provide payroll services to other companies.
   • TDCanada Trust
     http://www.tdcanadatrust.com/smallbusiness/resources.jsp
   • OnPayroll.ca www.onpayroll.ca/
   • Outsourcing Canadian Payroll Inc. http://www.cdnpay.com/

3

Claymore Industries

❶NTRODUCTION

In this activity, you will perform the duties of a payroll accountant employed by Claymore Industries and responsible for hourly rated workers. You will complete the payroll for four weeks in February, 20-- and then journalize and post the entries to record the payroll. Payroll information and time cards for employees follow.

Payroll Information

Every employee pays weekly group insurance premiums of 20¢ per $1000. Other information is given in the following table:

Emp. No.	Name	Net Claim Code	Co. Pension	Union Dues	Group Ins.
101	T.A. Means	2	$3.70	$5.50	$35 000.00
102	S.M. Tompkins	9	2.78	5.50	45 000.00
103	R.P. Lynch	6	2.80	5.50	60 000.00
104	E.A. Erdman	1	2.78	5.50	30 000.00

Time Cards for the Week of February 7, 20--
for Three Employees

NO. 101
NAME T. A. Means
Regular Hours
Overtime Hours

Pay Period Ending Feb. 7, 20--

Regular Rate	$16.80
Overtime Rate	25.20
Total Earnings	

	MORN	NOON	NOON	NIGHT	EXTRA		
	IN	OUT	IN	OUT	IN	OUT	HOURS
M	07:58	12:01	13:00	17:00			
T	08:00	12:01	13:00	17:00	18:00	21:00	
W	07:56	12:04	13:00	17:01			
T	07:59	12:03	12:55	17:01			
F	07:58	12:02	12:56	17:02			
S							
S							

NO. 102
NAME S. M. Tompkins
Regular Hours
Overtime Hours

Pay Period Ending Feb. 7, 20--

Regular Rate	$18.50
Overtime Rate	27.75
Total Earnings	

	MORN	NOON	NOON	NIGHT	EXTRA		
	IN	OUT	IN	OUT	IN	OUT	HOURS
M	07:59	12:01	12:59	17:01			
T	07:58	12:02	12:58	17:00	18:00	21:00	
W	08:02	12:01	13:02	17:02			
T	08:03	12:03	13:05	17:03			
F	07:59	12:01	13:00	17:05			
S							
S							

NO. 103
NAME R. P. Lynch
Regular Hours
Overtime Hours

Pay Period Ending Feb. 7, 20--

Regular Rate	$18.20
Overtime Rate	27.30
Total Earnings	

	MORN	NOON	NOON	NIGHT	EXTRA		
	IN	OUT	IN	OUT	IN	OUT	HOURS
M			12:50	17:01			
T	07:59	12:00	12:51	17:02			
W	07:58	12:01	12:57	17:00	17:59	21:02	
T	07:57	12:04	12:55	17:05			
F	07:56	12:05	12:50	17:04			
S							
S							

Payroll Rules

In calculating the hours worked, the following rules apply:

- Any time worked on Saturday or Sunday is paid at time and a half.
- Any time worked after 5:00 p.m. is overtime and is paid at time and a half. Overtime is recorded in the extra (in, out) columns of the time cards.
- Regular hours of work are 8:00 a.m. to 12:00 noon and 1:00 p.m. to 5:00 p.m. Employees lose 15 minutes' pay if they are between 2 and 15 minutes late, and 30 minutes' pay if they are between 16 and 30 minutes late.

NO. 104
NAME E. A. Erdman
Regular Hours 35.75
Overtime Hours 3.0

Pay Period Ending Feb. 7, 20--

Regular Rate	$18.20
Overtime Rate	27.30
Total Earnings	

	MORN	NOON	NOON	NIGHT	EXTRA		
	IN	OUT	IN	OUT	IN	OUT	HOURS
M			12:52	17:02			4.0
T	08:00	12:00	13:04	17:02			7.75
W	07:55	12:02	13:00	17:01			8.0
T	07:58	12:01	12:59	17:00	18:00	21:01	8.0/3.0
F	07:58	12:02	12:59	17:01			8.0
S					Regular		35.75
S					O.T.		3.0

Part A

1. (a) Complete the time cards and calculate the gross earnings. The time card for E.A. Erdman is done as an example.
   (b) Complete the February 6 payroll in the Payroll Journal.
   (c) Total and prove the Payroll Journal.

2. Prepare General Journal entries to record:

   (a) The payroll
   (b) The employer's share of CPP contributions, EI premiums, and EHT at the rate of 1.223 percent
   (c) The transfer of funds to the employees' bank accounts

3. Post the General Journal entries to the General Ledger. (You may use T-accounts.) The accounts required are:

101	Cash (Balance $15 000)	216	Group Insurance Payable
210	Wages Payable	217	Union Dues Payable
211	CPP Payable	610	Wages Expense
212	EI Payable	611	CPP Expense
213	EHT Payable	612	EI Expense
214	Income Tax Payable	613	EHT Expense
215	RPP Payable		

4. For the week ended February 14, the gross earnings for the four employees are:

101	T.A. Means	$672.00
102	S.M. Tompkins	740.00
103	R.P. Lynch	728.00
104	E.A. Erdman	755.30

   (a) Complete the Payroll Journal for the week.
   (b) Total and prove the Payroll Journal.
   (c) Prepare General Journal entries to:

      (i) Record the payroll.
      (ii) Record the employer's share of CPP contributions, EI premiums, and EHT.
      (iii) Post the General Journal entries.

5. For the week ended February 21, the gross earnings for the four employees are:

101	T.A. Means	$722.40
102	S.M. Tompkins	740.00
103	R.P. Lynch	728.00
104	E.A. Erdman	728.00

   (a) Complete the Payroll Journal for the week.
   (b) Total and prove the Payroll Journal.
   (c) Prepare General Journal entries to record:

      (i) The payroll
      (ii) The employer's share of CPP contributions, EI premiums, and EHT
      (iii) The transfer of funds to the employees' bank accounts

   (d) Post the General Journal entries.

6. For the week ended February 28, the gross earnings for the four employees are:

101	T.A. Means	$747.60
102	S.M. Tompkins	767.75
103	R.P. Lynch	691.60
104	E.A. Erdman	728.00

   (a) Complete the Payroll Journal for the week.
   (b) Total and prove the Payroll Journal.
   (c) Prepare General Journal entries to record:

   (i)   The payroll
   (ii) The employer's share of CPP contributions, EI premiums, and EHT
   (iii) The transfer of funds to the employees' bank accounts

   (d) Post the General Journal entries.

7. (a) Prepare the journal entries that would be made on March 15 to remit
        the February payroll deductions.
   (b) Post these entries to the General Ledger and total the accounts.

Part B — Optional — Computer Accounting

Complete Payroll Journals for the weeks ended February 6 and February 13 using
a computer.

Part C — Optional — Report

Prepare a written comparison of the two systems used in this project (manual and
computer). Include the advantages and disadvantages of each system.

Accounting for Partnerships and Corporations

 **UNIT 30** Accounting for Partnerships

Learning Objectives

After reading this unit, discussing the applicable review questions, and completing the applications exercises, you will be able to do the following:

1. **EXPLAIN** the difference between a sole proprietorship, a partnership, and a corporation.

2. **DISCUSS** the major advantages and disadvantages of each form of business organization.

3. **PREPARE** the accounting entries required to form and operate a partnership.

4. **CALCULATE** each partner's share of net income or net loss based on a variety of acceptable apportionment methods.

5. **PREPARE** closing entries for a partnership.

6. **PREPARE** financial statements for a partnership.

TYPES OF BUSINESS OWNERSHIP

In the first part of this book, most of the accounting theory involved businesses owned by one person. For example, Chapter 4 described the journal and ledger system used by M. Jacobs, the owner of Jacobs Painting Contractors. A business owned by one person is known as a **sole proprietorship**. Two other types of ownership are the partnership and the corporation.

A sole proprietorship is a business owned by one person.

SOLE PROPRIETORSHIP

The owner of a sole proprietorship is legally responsible for all its debts and legal obligations. Many small businesses are sole proprietorships. These include small stores, restaurants, and many service businesses such as barbershops, TV repair firms, and hairstylists.

Advantages of Proprietorships

- pride of ownership
- ease of formation and dissolution
- freedom of action
- privacy
- simplified decision making
- owner receives all the net income
- personal satisfaction
- possible tax savings

Disadvantages of Proprietorships

- unlimited personal liability
- limited capital
- heavy personal responsibilities
- lack of continuity
- limited talent

In a sole proprietorship, the proprietor has unlimited personal liability for the debts and legal obligations of the business.

Taxation and the Proprietorship

A proprietorship does not pay income tax on its net income. The owner must add the net income of the business to his or her own income and then pay personal income tax on the total. There can be a tax advantage with this form of ownership when the combined net income is quite low. However, when net income becomes fairly high, there may be a tax advantage in switching to a corporate form of ownership. This is explained in detail in Unit 31.

PARTNERSHIPS

Two or more persons may find it worthwhile to combine their talents and money to form a **partnership**. Doctors, lawyers, dentists, and small retail and service businesses are frequently owned by partners. Some of the characteristics of the partnership are exactly like those of the proprietorship except when related to transactions that directly affect the partners' equities. Because ownership rights in a partnership are divided between two or more partners, there must be a capital and withdrawals account for each partner and a division of earnings. The net income or net loss belongs to the owners, and they have *unlimited personal liability* for the debts of the business. This means there is no ceiling on the liability of a partner; thus, his or her personal property can legally be taken, if necessary, to pay these debts. The net income becomes the personal income of the individual partners for income tax purposes.

A partnership is a business owned by two or more persons.

A *limited partnership* could be formed for those individuals who want to invest but are unwilling to accept the risk of unlimited liability. One class of partners must assume unlimited liability.

In a partnership, the partners have unlimited personal liability for the debts and legal obligations of the business.

Advantages of Partnerships

- Two or more persons are available to share the work load.
- Varied skills will be brought to a partnership.
- The partnership has access to more capital (i.e., personal savings or increased borrowing capacity).
- There are low start-up costs.

Disadvantages of Partnerships

When doing business related to the partnership, each partner acts for all other partners.

- **Mutual agency** means that in doing business, each partner acts for all other partners.
- The partners have unlimited personal liability.
- There is a risk of personality conflicts.
- The partnership has a limited life — death or the withdrawal of a partner immediately dissolves the partnership.

CORPORATIONS

A corporation is a business owned by one or more persons and has a legal existence of its own.

Term that is sometimes used to describe the corporate form of ownership.

Unlike a sole proprietorship or a partnership, a **corporation** has a legal existence of its own and may have many owners. However, the owners are not personally responsible for the debts and obligations of the corporation. In the partnership and proprietorship, the owners have unlimited personal liability for the business and risk the loss of their own personal assets. The owners of a corporation do not risk their personal assets but only their direct investment in the corporation. For this reason, the term **limited company** is sometimes used to describe the corporate form of ownership.

Advantages of the Corporate Form of Ownership

In a corporation, the owners' liability is limited to their investment in the corporation.

- The owners have limited liability.
- The company has access to more capital (i.e., by selling shares).
- The company has a greater chance to borrow funds.
- A corporation has a continuous life — it does not cease to exist if a shareholder dies.
- There is no mutual agency concerns.
- A shareholder can sell his or her shares and the business will continue to operate.
- A corporation can be used to split income among family members — a privately held corporation — for example, McCain Foods.

Disadvantages of the Corporate Form of Ownership

- There are complicated legal requirements to form corporations (i.e., the owners must hire a lawyer).
- There are high start-up costs.
- There is a complex decision-making process (i.e., a hierarchy of management).

- A corporation is less likely to have strong employee dedication.
- Corporate earnings are subject to double taxation.

ACCOUNTING PROCEDURES FOR PARTNERSHIPS

Two or more persons may agree orally or in writing to establish a partnership. Each of the provinces has a *Partnership Act*, which establishes rules and regulations for partnerships. It is a general practice to prepare a written contract of partnership or "declaration of partnership." This contract outlines the rights and responsibilities of each of the parties concerned. The contract could also contain the provision for settlement in case a partner dies or a partner withdraws from the partnership. In the absence of an oral or written agreement, all profits and losses are shared among the partners on an equal basis.

The partnership agreement outlines the rights and responsibilities of the partners.

Formation of a Partnership

There are several ways in which a partnership may be formed. Five basic examples and the journal entries involved follow.

Example 1

Omar Malik and Le Cheung agree to contribute $45 000 each to form a partnership. A Capital account is required for each partner. The entry to open the books of Malik and Cheung Services is:

Jan. 2	Cash	90 000	
	O. Malik, Capital		45 000
	L. Cheung, Capital		45 000
	To record the investments of O. Malik and		
	L. Cheung.		

Example 2

W. Mills and L. Poirier have been operating businesses of their own. Their balance sheets are shown in Figure 13-1.

FIGURE 13-1

Balance sheets for W. Mills and L. Poirier

W. Mills
Balance Sheet
January 1, 2008

ASSETS		LIABILITIES AND EQUITY	
Cash	9 200	Accounts Payable	4 000
Accounts Receivable	3 500	Bank Loan	13 700
Inventory	19 000	Mortgage Payable	61 000
Land	40 000		
Building	95 000	W. Mills, Capital	88 000
	166 700		166 700

L. Poirier			
Balance Sheet			
January 1, 2008			
ASSETS		**LIABILITIES AND EQUITY**	
Cash	25 000	Accounts Payable	8 000
Accounts Receivable	5 600	L. Poirier, Capital	123 800
Inventory	21 200		
Equipment	80 000		
	131 800		131 800

They decide to merge their companies and to form a partnership. A separate journal entry is made for each of the partners' contributions to the new business.

Jan. 1	Cash	25 000	
	Accounts Receivable	5 600	
	Inventory	21 200	
	Equipment	80 000	
	Accounts Payable		8 000
	L. Poirier, Capital		123 800
	To record L. Poirier's assets, liabilities, and capital.		

Jan. 1	Cash	9 200	
	Accounts Receivable	3 500	
	Inventory	19 000	
	Land	40 000	
	Building	95 000	
	Accounts Payable		4 000
	Bank Loan		13 700
	Mortgage Payable		61 000
	W. Mills, Capital		88 000
	To record W. Mills' assets, liabilities, and capital.		

Example 3

S. O'Malley and A. MacTavish operate competing businesses. O'Malley's firm is thriving, profitable, and uses modern equipment. MacTavish's business is not as successful. The equipment is older and the building is in need of major repairs. Simplified versions of the accounts of the two businesses follow:

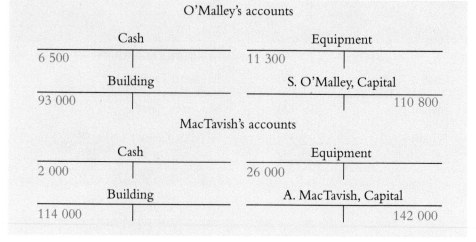

The two proprietors agree to merge their business assets with the following provision: MacTavish's assets are to be devalued by $39 000 (Equipment to be decreased by $10 000 and Building by $29 000).

The entry to decrease the assets of the MacTavish business is:

Jan. 15	A. MacTavish, Capital	39 000	
	Equipment		10 000
	Building		29 000
	To devalue equipment and building according to partnership agreement.		

After the entry above has been posted, the two businesses close their books and a new set of books is opened for the partnership, O'Malley & MacTavish Associates. The following two entries are made to open the partnership's books:

Jan. 15	Cash	6 500	
	Equipment	11 300	
	Building	93 000	
	S. O'Malley, Capital		110 800
	To record the assets and capital of S. O'Malley.		

Jan. 15	Cash	2 000	
	Equipment	16 000	
	Building	85 000	
	A. MacTavish, Capital		103 000
	To record the assets and capital of A. MacTavish.		

After posting this entry, the accounts of the partnership appear as follows:

Cash		Equipment		Building	
6 500		11 300		93 000	
2 000		16 000		85 000	
Balance 8 500		Balance 27 300		Balance 178 000	

A. MacTavish, Capital		S. O'Malley, Capital	
	103 000		110 800

Example 4

T. Mohammed, the sole owner of Mohammed Security Services, decides that to expand his business he will take in a partner. C. Bhatti invests $65 000 and becomes a partner in Mohammed & Bhatti Security Services. The entry to record Bhatti as a partner in the firm is:

May 1	Cash	65 000	
	C. Bhatti, Capital		65 000
	To record Bhatti's investment.		

Two proprietorships merge to form a partnership. Assets are revalued and capital accounts are adjusted to reflect the change.

A proprietor sells an interest in a business to a partner. Cash is paid to the owner personally.

The same ledger used by Mohammed Security Services will continue to be used by the new partnership. The $65 000 contributed by Bhatti was deposited into the bank account of the business. The Cash account increased and a new Capital account was opened.

Example 5

Jean French, the sole proprietor of French Antiques, has agreed to sell part of her business. French's Capital account has a balance of $155 000. E. Lynch has offered $90 000 to become an equal partner in the firm. French accepts the offer. French will personally receive the $90 000. In return she will give up half of her capital in the business. The Cash account of the business does not change since the transaction is between French and Lynch and not Lynch and the business. The only change in the books of the business is a decrease in French's capital and the addition of a second Capital account, E. Lynch, Capital. The entry to record the new account is:

Jul. 31	J. French, Capital	77 500	
	E. Lynch, Capital		77 500
	Admission of a partner to the business.		

It should be noted that this is a private exchange of money outside of the business. The assets and the total capital remain the same, but there are now two Capital accounts.

PARTNERSHIPS AND INCOME TAXES

The partners in a business pay personal income tax on their share of the partnership's net income.

As a business, a partnership does not pay income taxes on its net income. Each partner is taxed on his or her share of the partnership's net income, in addition to any income received from other sources.

Suppose the partnership of O. Malik and L. Cheung (Example 1, page 519) earned a net income of $140 000, and the partnership agreement stipulated that the partners were to share the net income equally. The business, Malik and Cheung Services, is not taxed. The net income is treated as personal income of the owners. Malik must include his share of the partnership's net income ($70 000) on his personal income tax return. Cheung must include her share ($70 000) on her personal income tax return.

LEDGER ACCOUNTS OF A PARTNERSHIP

The accounts in the General Ledger of a partnership are the same as those of a proprietorship except that there is one Drawings account and one Capital account for *each* partner.

Drawings Account

There is a Drawings account and a Capital account for each partner in the General Ledger of a partnership.

The Drawings account of each partner is used in the same way in a partnership as the Drawings account in a sole proprietorship. The relevant Drawings account is debited whenever assets are withdrawn by a partner from the business. Typical transactions involving Drawings accounts are:

- payment of salaries to partners
- withdrawal of cash or other business assets by a partner
- payments of a personal nature for a partner using partnership funds

It should be emphasized that salaries paid to partners during the year *must* be recorded in the Drawings accounts. Since partners are not employed by the partnership, their salaries cannot be treated as a company expense and debited to Salaries Expense. One of the difficulties encountered by accountants is to decide if a transaction involves a legitimate business expense or should be treated as a personal withdrawal and recorded in the owner's Drawings account. Personal expenses charged to the business have the effect of lowering the net income of the business and, in the long run, the income taxes paid by the owners. By charging personal expenses to the business, owners can obtain free fringe benefits illegally.

Salaries paid to partners must be recorded in the Drawings account.

CLOSING THE PARTNERSHIP BOOKS

In a proprietorship, revenue and expense accounts are closed into an Income Summary account. The balance of the summary account would be the net income or the net loss. This balance is then transferred to the owner's Capital account. The owner's Drawings account is then closed into the Capital account.

The books of a partnership are closed in a similar way but with one difference. The balance of the Income Summary account is closed into each of the partner's Capital accounts according to the partnership agreement for dividing net income and net loss. Figure 13-2 illustrates the closing of the books when there is a net income of $180 000 to be divided equally between the two partners. In General Journal form this entry is:

Dec. 31	Income Summary	180 000	
	Partner W, Capital		90 000
	Partner X, Capital		90 000
	To divide the net income equally as per partnership agreement.		

After the net income has been transferred to the partners' Capital accounts, the partners' Drawings accounts are closed into the Capital accounts. The partners' Drawings accounts contain the salaries paid to the owners during the year as well as any other personal withdrawals. The debit balance of the Drawings accounts represents a decrease in equity and this decrease is reflected by closing the Drawings account into the Capital account with this entry:

Dec. 31	Partner W, Capital	65 000	
	Partner X, Capital	65 000	
	Partner W, Drawings		65 000
	Partner X, Drawings		65 000
	To close the Drawings accounts.		

The steps in closing the books of a partnership include:

(1) Close revenue accounts into the Income Summary account.
(2) Close expense accounts into the Income Summary account.
(3) Close the Income Summary account into the partners' Capital accounts (based on the terms of the partnership agreement).

(4) Close the partners' Drawings accounts into the partners' Capital accounts.

These steps are illustrated in Figure 13-2.

FIGURE 13-2

The partnership agreement in this example states that the net income is to be divided equally between partners W and X.

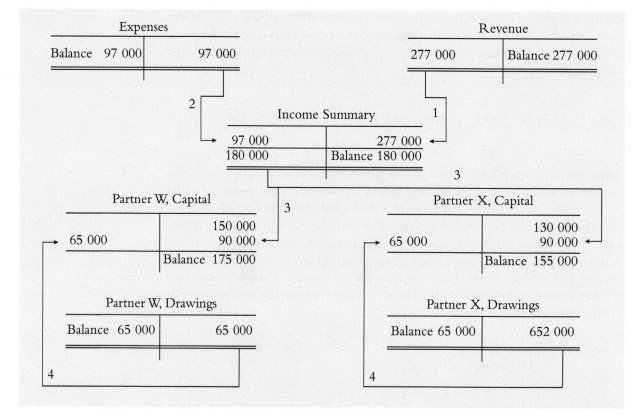

DIVIDING NET INCOME

The partnership contract states how net income or net losses are to be shared.

Partners may make any agreement they wish for the division of the partnership's net income or net loss. One of the most important clauses of the partnership contract is the one stating how these will be shared. Four factors considered by partners in coming to an agreement on the sharing of net income and net loss are:

- payment for amount of work performed
- return on capital
- amount of capital invested
- skills, talent, reputation

Payment for Amount of Work Performed

Suppose one partner is very actively engaged in running a business while another contributes money but does not work in the business. It seems fair that the working partner should be paid for the work performed. In some partnerships, both partners work in the business but one has a more responsible position or puts in more hours of work than the other. In preparing the partnership agreement, the partners may consider the amount of work performed in deciding how to share the net income or net loss.

Return on Capital

If a partner invested money in government bonds, term deposits, or mortgages, interest would be earned on that money. Likewise, if a partner invests in a partnership, it seems reasonable for the partner to receive interest on the money invested. This is especially so when one partner invests more funds in the partnership than the others. If interest is paid on all funds contributed to a partnership proportionately to all partners, the partner who invested more money would appropriately receive more interest.

Amount of Capital Invested

If partners contribute an equal amount of money, work, time, and skills to a partnership, it seems fair to distribute net income equally to the partners. However, if one of the partners contributes more money, that partner could expect to receive a greater share. Suppose one partner contributes $60 000 and another partner contributes $75 000. The second partner could demand a greater share of net income because of the larger investment.

Skills, Talent, and Reputation

Sometimes partners use factors such as skills, talents, and reputation of the owners in deciding how to share net income or net losses. It can be argued that if a net income is earned, it is because of the personal contributions of the partners. The differing levels of skills, talent, and reputation of partners may be reflected in how the partners agree to share net income or net loss.

METHODS OF DIVIDING NET INCOME OR NET LOSS

Among the many methods used to divide net income and net loss are:

- fixed ratio
- capital ratio
- salaries and remaining net income (or net loss) to partners on a fixed ratio
- interest on capital, salaries, and remaining net income (or net loss) to partners on a fixed ratio

Fixed Ratio

On forming their partnership, Malik and Cheung (Example 1, page 519) agreed to divide net income and net loss equally. Thus 50 percent of net income will belong to Malik and 50 percent to Cheung. They felt that a 50:50 ratio was fair since both contributed the same amount of capital, both would work full time in the business, and both had special skills to offer to the new business. At the end of a year, net income is $160 000. According to the partnership agreement, this amount is divided 50:50. When the books are closed, the division is made by the following entry:

Dec. 31	Income Summary	160 000	
	O. Malik, Capital		80 000
	L. Cheung, Capital		80 000
	To divide the net income equally between		
	the partners, per partnership agreement.		

Figure 13-3 shows how the division of net income is included on the bottom of the income statement.

FIGURE 13-3

Distribution of net income as shown on the income statement

Malik and Cheung
Income Statement
For the Year Ended December 31, 2009

REVENUE		
Sales Revenue		$285 000
EXPENSES		
Selling Expenses	$90 000	
Administrative Expenses	35 000	125 000
Net Income		$160 000
Distribution of net income		
O. Malik (50%)	$80 000	
L. Cheung (50%)	80 000	$160 000

Capital Ratio

The capital ratio method is used when the success of the business depends to some extent on the contribution of capital. In some businesses, such as auto dealerships, substantial investments in equipment, buildings, and merchandise are required. The capital ratio method recognizes the importance of capital to the business and divides the net income or net loss accordingly.

W. Mills and L. Poirier (Example 2, page 519) have invested $88 000 and $123 800, respectively, in their partnership. They agree to share net income and net loss in the ratio of their beginning capital. The ratio is determined as follows:

	Beginning Capital	Percentage of Total
W. Mills	$ 88 000	42%
L. Poirier	123 800	58%
Total	$211 800	100.0%

Mills receives 42 percent of any net income and Poirier 58 percent. They share net losses in the same way, that is, in the ratio of 42:58. Suppose there is net income of $130 000. The division of the net income would be calculated as follows:

		Share of Net Income
W. Mills	$0.42 \times 130\ 000$	$ 54 600
L. Poirier	$0.58 \times 130\ 000$	75 400
	Total	$130 000

The entry to record the division of net income is:

Dec. 31 Income Summary	130 000	
W. Mills, Capital		54 600
M. Stedman, Capital		75 400
To divide net income in the ratio of		
42:58, per partnership agreement.		

The division of the net income would be shown on the bottom of the income statement as was the case in Figure 13-3.

Salaries and Remaining Profits in a Fixed Ratio

In their partnership agreement (Example 4, page 521), T. Mohammed and C. Bhatti agreed to the following:

- a salary of $60 000 to Mohammed and $55 000 to Bhatti per year
- any remaining net income after salaries to be shared 50:50

At the end of the year, there is a net income of $180 000. A special report called a *statement of distribution of net income* is prepared as shown in Figure 13-4.

Mohammed & Bhatti Security Services Statement of Distribution of Net Income December 31, 2008			
Net Income to be divided			$180 000
	T. Mohammed	C. Bhatti	Total
Salaries	$60 000	$55 000	$ 115 000
Remaining net income shared equally (50:50)	32 500	32 500	65 000
Totals	$92 500	$87 500	$180 000

FIGURE 13-4

Statement of distribution of net income for two partners, Mohammed & Bhatti Security Services

The statement of distribution of net income outlines clearly to the partners how the net income is shared between them. Two entries are required in the General Ledger.

Dec. 31 Income Summary	115 000	
T. Mohammed, Capital		60 000
C. Bhatti, Capital		55 000
To credit partners with their net salaries,		
per partnership agreement.		
Dec. 31 Income Summary	65 000	
T. Mohammed, Capital		32 500
C. Bhatti, Capital		32 500
To divide remainder of net income on a 50:50 ratio,		
per partnership agreement.		

Interest, Salaries, and Fixed Ratio

In forming their partnership, A. Major and B. Minor agreed to the following division of net income and net loss:

- each partner to receive a $45 000 salary per year
- 10 percent interest on the beginning capital to be credited annually to each partner from net income (Major, Capital $90 000, Minor, Capital $120 000)
- any remaining net income or net loss after interest and salaries to be divided equally

In the last fiscal year, the partnership earned net income of $131 000. The statement of distribution of net income was prepared to divide the net income as shown in Figure 13-5.

FIGURE 13-5

Statement of distribution of net income for Major & Minor Enterprises

Major and Minor Enterprises
Statement of Distribution of Net Income
December 31, 2007

	A. Major	B. Minor	Total
Net income to be divided			$131 000
Salaries	$45 000	$45 000	$ 90 000
Interest on beginning capital 10%	9 000	12 000	21 000
Remaining net income shared equally	10 000	10 000	20 000
Total	$64 000	$67 000	$131 000

Three entries are required to record this division of net income in the General Ledger accounts.

Dec. 31 Income Summary		90 000	
A. Major, Capital			45 000
B. Minor, Capital			45 000
To credit partners with salaries, per partnership agreement.			
Dec. 31 Income Summary		21 000	
A. Major, Capital			9 000
B. Minor, Capital			12 000
To credit each partner with interest based on beginning capital, per partnership agreement.			
Dec. 31 Income Summary		20 000	
A. Major, Capital			10 000
B. Minor, Capital			10 000
To divide remainder ($20 000) of net income equally, per partnership agreement.			

DIVIDING NET LOSS AND INSUFFICIENT NET INCOME

In each of the situations discussed to this point, there was a net income large enough to give each partner what was owing according to the partnership agreement. However, businesses often suffer losses or do not earn enough net income to pay the partners according to the agreement. Two examples of such situations follow.

First, W. Mills and L. Poirier agreed to share net income and net loss in the ratio of their beginning capital balances. This ratio was 42:58. This means that if there is a net loss, Mills absorbs 42 percent of the net loss and Poirier 58 percent. Suppose the partnership suffers a net loss of $18 000. The division of the net loss would be calculated as follows:

		Share of Net Loss
W. Mills	0.42 × 18 000 =	$ 7 560
L. Poirier	0.58 × 18 000 =	10 440
	Total	$18 000

The entry to record this division of the net loss is:

Dec. 31	W. Mills, Capital	7 560	
	L. Poirier, Capital	10 440	
	Income Summary		18 000
	To close the Income Summary account and to divide the net loss per partnership agreement.		

Second, when there is an agreement on how to allocate salary, interest, and earnings, it is normal to follow the same procedure whether allocating a loss or a profit. For example, Brick and Brack agree to the following provisions: Brick would receive a salary of $25 000 plus $5000 interest on capital while Brack would receive $20 000 salary and $6000 interest. They also agree to divide profits or losses equally. The distribution of a net income for the year of $25 000 is shown on the following page.

Brick and Brack Group Statement of Distribution of Net Income December 31, 2009			
Net income to be divided			$25 000
	Brick	Brack	Total
Salaries	$25 000	$20 000	$45 000
Interest on capital	5 000	6 000	11 000
Total salaries plus interest	30 000	26 000	56 000
Remainder of net income shared equally	(15 500)	(15 500)	(31 000)
Partner's share	$14 500	$10 500	$25 000

The entry to record this division of a net income that was insufficient to meet salary and interest obligations of the partners is:

Dec. 31 Income Summary	25 000	
Brick, Capital		14 500
Brack, Capital		10 500

℗ARTNERS' SALARIES

Journal entries involving partners' salaries are handled as follows. A debit entry is made to the partners' Drawings accounts during the year each time salaries are paid to the partners and when personal withdrawals are made. Another entry is made at the end of the year when the net income or net loss is divided between the partners. For example, suppose Dunn and Dugal invest $18 000 each and become partners in a masonry business. Their partnership agreement states that they are to receive salaries and to share equally any remaining net income or net loss after salaries. Each receives a salary of $42 000 a year. Once a month, each partner receives a cheque for $3500. At the end of the year, each partner will have received cash payments of $42 000. The following T-accounts show the entries for salaries on the debit side of the Drawings accounts.

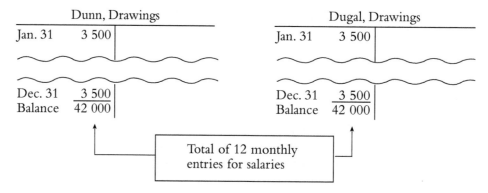

Suppose the partnership has earned a net income of $126 000 for the year. According to the partnership agreement, the partners share this $126 000 by:

- receiving salaries of $42 000 each (total $84 000)
- sharing the remainder ($42 000) equally

These entries are made to distribute the net income:

Dec. 31 Income Summary	84 000	
Dunn, Capital		42 000
Dugal, Capital		42 000
To credit each partner with $42 000 salary, per the partnership agreement.		
Dec. 31 Income Summary	42 000	
Dunn, Capital		21 000
Dugal, Capital		21 000
To distribute the remaining net income equally, per the partnership agreement.		

Finally, the Drawings accounts are closed into the Capital accounts with this entry:

Dec. 31	Dunn, Capital	42 000	
	Dugal, Capital	42 000	
	Dunn, Drawings		42 000
	Dugal, Drawings		42 000
	To close the Drawings accounts.		

See if you can understand these principles:

(1) The debits in the Drawings accounts represent actual withdrawals of cash made during the year.

(2) Each partner's share of the net income ($63 000 in this example, which is made up of $42 000 salary and $21 000 remainder) appears as a credit in each Capital account.

(3) Each partner's share of the net income is $63 000. The partners' Capital accounts increase by only $21 000 each because they withdrew $42 000 during the year as salaries.

FINANCIAL STATEMENTS

In a partnership, the following four financial statements may be prepared:

- income statement
- statement of distribution of net income
- balance sheet
- statement of partners' equity

Income Statement

The income statement of a partnership is very similar to that of a proprietorship. However, a section may be added to the bottom to show the division of the net income or net loss (see Figure 13-3).

Statement of Distribution of Net Income

If the division of the net income or net loss is not shown on the income statement, a *statement of distribution of net income* is prepared (Figure 13-5). This is a more formal report that is prepared when there are salaries, interest, and a remainder of net income or loss to be divided.

The Balance Sheet

There are at least two people in every partnership. For every partner there is a Capital account. Each partner's capital appears in the equity section of the balance sheet, as shown in Figure 13-6.

FIGURE 13-6

Balance sheet for Vaz &
Vieira Computer Services

Vaz & Vieira Computer Services Balance Sheet December 31, 2008			
ASSETS			
Current Assets			
Cash		$ 9 000	
Accounts Receivable		4 100	
Office Supplies		1 100	
Prepaid Rent		12 000	
Prepaid Advertising		300	
Total Current Assets			$ 26 500
Capital Assets			
Land		50 000	
Building	$149 000		
Less: Accumulated Amortization	9 000	140 000	
Equipment	35 000		
Less: Accumulated Amortization	3 000	32 000	
Total Capital Assets			222 000
Total Assets			$248 500
LIABILITIES AND PARTNERS' EQUITY			
Current Liabilities			
Accounts Payable			$ 3 500
Partners' Equity			
S. Vaz, Capital		$134 500	
J. Vieira, Capital		110 500	245 000
Total Liabilities and Partners' Equity			$248 500

Statement of Partners' Equity

Partners are usually interested in seeing the changes in their Capital accounts from year to year. A *statement of partners' equity* is prepared to provide this information (see Figure 13-7). The information in this statement could be placed in the equity section of the balance sheet if it did not make the balance sheet unduly long.

The statement of partners' equity is a picture of all the activity involving the partners' investments; it shows additions to the business contributed during the year; it shows all withdrawals made; it shows the share of the net income or net loss credited to each partner.

Partners' equity is the claim of the partners against the assets of a partnership.

FIGURE 13-7

Statement of partners' equity for Vaz & Vieira Computer Services

Vaz & Vieira Computer Services Statement of Partners' Equity For the Year Ended December 31, 2008			
	Vaz	**Vieira**	**Total**
Capital, Jan. 1	$110 000	$ 85 000	$195 000
Add: Additional Investment	9 500	8 000	17 500
Share of Net Income	70 000	60 500	130 500
Total	$189 500	$153 500	$343 000
Less: Withdrawals	55 000	43 000	98 000
Total Capital, Dec. 31	$134 500	$110 500	$245 000

1. Explain what is meant by the following:

    (a) sole proprietorship   (b) partnership   (c) corporation

2. Explain the term "mutual agency."

3. If a proprietorship does not pay income tax on its net income, how does the net income get taxed?

4. How many persons may form:

    (a) a partnership?   (b) a corporation?

5. Give three advantages and three disadvantages for each of the three forms of business ownership.

6. What do you think are the three main items that should be included in a partnership agreement?

7. Why might some assets be revalued when two persons combine their businesses to form a partnership?

8. Explain how income tax is paid on the income of a partnership.

9. Which account is used to record the payment of salaries to partners?

10. What accounts are debited and credited when a partner withdraws merchandise from the business for personal use?

11. In closing partnership books at the end of a fiscal period, into which account (or accounts) are the following closed?

    (a) the balance of the Income Summary account
    (b) revenue and expenses
    (c) the Drawings account

12. List the four steps followed in closing the books of a partnership.

13. List four methods of dividing the net income of a partnership.

14. Lord and Locke use the ratio of beginning capital balances as their method of dividing net income. Lord's capital balance is $22 000 and Locke's is $33 000. In what ratio is the net income divided?

15. Name the four financial statements that may be prepared for a partnership.

1. For each of the following, prepare General Journal entries to record the formation of the partnership.

    (a) D. Agaton, M. Cabral, and B. Khan each contribute $50 000 cash to a new partnership.
    (b) M. Dolson and A. Mateen form a partnership with Dolson contributing $5000 cash, land valued at $90 000, and a building worth $135 000. Mateen invests $35 000 cash and equipment worth $55 000.

2. A. Sethi and L. Singh agree to join their two businesses to form a partnership. Sethi's assets and liabilities are: Cash $2800; Accounts Receivable $4300; Equipment $15 000; Accounts Payable $2700. Singh's assets and liabilities are: Cash $5000; Accounts Receivable $3000; Land, $40 000; Building $95 000; Mortgage Payable $35 000; Bank Loan $8500. Prepare General Journal entries to set up the partnership.

3. S. Lundy wishes to expand her business and agrees to take L. Hoskins in as an equal partner. S. Lundy has a capital balance of $55 000. L. Hoskins contributes $55 000 cash to the business. Prepare the General Journal entry to record Hoskins' investment in the business.

4. S. Patel has an investment of $68 000 in a sole proprietorship. To share the work of running the company, he sells an equal share of the company to S. Pawa. In return, he personally receives $75 000 cash from Pawa. The assets of the business do not change. Prepare the General Journal entry to admit Pawa as a partner.

5. Gill and Hall agree to join their businesses and to form a partnership.

Gill's Accounts		Hall's Accounts	
Cash	$ 7 500	Cash	$ 3 500
Accounts Receivable	10 000	Accounts Receivable	7 000
Equipment	40 000	Land	60 000
Accounts Payable	5 000	Building	55 000
		Equipment	19 000
		Mortgage Payable	31 000

Their agreement includes the following:

- Gill's equipment is to be reduced in value to $25 000 from the balance of $40 000.
- Hall's building is to be increased in value to $95 000 from $55 000.
- Hall's equipment is to be reduced in value to $9000 from $19 000.

(a) Prepare General Journal entries to revalue assets for Gill and for Hall.
(b) Prepare General Journal entries to set up the partnership.

6. (a) Prepare General Journal entries to record these transactions for Brian Wong and Cecilia Au:

Sep.	10	Au withdrew cash for personal use, $600.
	20	Wong took home merchandise worth $150.
	31	Paid salaries, $2500 each to partners.
Oct.	15	Paid $145 for piano lessons for Wong's daughter.
	30	Paid partners' salaries $2500 each.
Nov.	25	Wong invested an additional $10 000 in the business.

(b) After closing the expense and revenue accounts, there is a credit balance of $86 000 in the Income Summary account. This net income is to be divided equally between Wong and Au. Prepare the General Journal entry to close the Income Summary account and to divide the net income between the partners.

(c) Wong's Drawings account has a debit balance of $26 000 and Au's a debit balance of $28 000. Prepare the General Journal entry to close the Drawings accounts.

(d) The next year, the firm of Wong and Au Services incurs a net loss of $18 000. This is represented by a debit balance in the Income Summary account. Prepare the General Journal entry to close the Income Summary account and to divide the net loss equally.

7. (a) Red and Green divide net income and net loss according to the ratio of their beginning capital balances. Red has a capital balance of $40 000 and Green $60 000. What is the ratio used?

   (b) Using the ratio from part (a), how much is received by each partner if the net income is $110 000?

   (c) If Red and Green incurred a net loss of $12 000, how much of the net loss would be shared by each partner?

8. Henry and Lyons divide net income from their partnership in the ratio of their capital. The ratio is 30:70.

   (a) The net income or net loss for each of three years follows. For each year determine how much of the net income or net loss is allocated to Henry and how much is allocated to Lyons.

Year 1	Net Income	$160 000
Year 2	Net Loss	90 000
Year 3	Net Income	250 000

   (b) Prepare General Journal entries to close the Income Summary account and to divide the net income or net loss each year.

9. Casey and Lynch divide net income and net loss on the following basis:

   • Casey's salary is $46 000 and Lynch's salary is $38 000.
   • Any remaining net income or net loss after salaries is shared equally.

   (a) Prepare a statement of distribution of net income for each of these years:

Year 1	Net Income	$126 000
Year 2	Net Income	72 000

   (b) Prepare General Journal entries to distribute the net income each year.

10. Dionne and LaPorte share the net income of their partnership in the following manner:

    • Salaries are $50 000 each.
    • Interest on beginning capital is 10 percent. Dionne's capital is $70 000, LaPorte's $82 000.
    • Remaining net income or loss after salaries and interest is shared equally.

    (a) Prepare a December 31 statement of distribution of net income for each of these years:

Year 1	Net Income	$140 000
Year 2	Net Income	78 000
Year 3	Net Loss	30 000

    (b) Prepare the General Journal entries to distribute the net income or net loss each year.

11. Prepare a December 31, 2008, statement of partners' equity for Bach and Beethoven:

    • January 1 capital balances: Bach $35 000; Beethoven $22 000.
    • Additional investment: $12 000 each.
    • Withdrawals: Bach $24 000; Beethoven $20 000.
    • Share of net income: Bach $27 000; Beethoven $19 500.

12. Jana and Jones decide to form a partnership. Jana invests $70 000 cash and Jones $50 000 cash. They are each to receive a salary of $32 000 and interest of 10 percent on their beginning capital. The balance of the net income or net loss is to be divided in the ratio of the Capital accounts at the time of formation.

(a) Prepare the General Journal entry to record the formation.
(b) Prepare a December 31, 2009, statement of distribution of net income if the year's net income is $95 000.

UNIT 31 Accounting for Corporations

Learning Objectives

After reading this unit, discussing the applicable review questions, and completing the applications exercises, you will be able to do the following.

1. **EXPLAIN** the difference between the two types of business corporations.

2. **IDENTIFY** and discuss the types of shares and their basic rights.

3. **PREPARE** the accounting entries required to form a corporation, issue shares, and pay dividends.

4. **PREPARE** the closing entries for a corporation.

5. **PREPARE** the financial statements for a corporation.

UNLIMITED LIABILITY

The proprietorship and partnership forms of ownership, discussed in previous chapters, have several disadvantages. One of these is illustrated by the following example.

Jason Scott operated a very successful business as a sole proprietorship for 15 years. Through hard work and good management, Jason's company earned substantial net income for him. Over the years, Jason invested the money earned by his business by purchasing a cottage, two expensive cars, and several apartment buildings, which he rented out.

However, his business suddenly became unprofitable as new products and competitors caused several large losses in consecutive years. Jason's business was unable to pay a number of debts on time and, as a result, the business was forced into bankruptcy. To pay off his creditors, Jason was ordered by the court to sell his cottage and the apartment buildings. Jason had to do so despite the fact that the properties belonged to him, personally, and not to his business.

Jason was personally liable for all the business debts. He lost his business investment and some of his personal assets.

The case of Jason Scott illustrates a major disadvantage of partnerships and proprietorships: unlimited liability. It also points out one of the advantages of forming a corporation. In the corporate form of ownership, an investor risks the investment

> The proprietor of a business is personally responsible for its debts.

in the business, but not personal assets. Limited liability is an important advantage of the corporate form of ownership. Because of this characteristic, the term *limited company* is often used instead of *corporation*. Other advantages of the corporate form of ownership were given in Unit 30.

WHAT IS A CORPORATION?

A corporation is a business that has a legal existence of its own. It is separate from its owners. Each owner is liable only for the amount of his or her investment in the business. In a partnership or proprietorship, the owners are not separate from the business. A corporation has the right to sue and can be sued by others.

Forming a Corporation

A corporation is formed by applying to a provincial government or to the federal government for its articles of incorporation. The application, signed by one or more persons, must include the following information:

- name and address of the corporation
- types and number of shares to be authorized for issue
- names and addresses of the incorporators
- nature of the business to be conducted

Generally, a corporation that will do business in only one province will apply to that province for incorporation. A business that will operate in more than one province usually applies to the federal government for incorporation. A business that is federally incorporated is required to comply with the Canadian *Business Corporations Act*.

Shareholders (owners) of corporations have limited legal liability. This means each owner is only liable up to the amount of his or her investment in the company for the debts or obligations of the business.

Corporation Name

Have you ever wondered why so many businesses use Limited or Ltd. in their names? The reason for this is that the corporation laws require the words "Limited," "Limitée," "Incorporated," or "Incorporée" to be part of the name. The short forms "Ltd.," "Ltée.," or "Inc." may also be used. Other requirements for the corporation name are:

- The proposed name must differ from that of any other Canadian business.
- The name must be acceptable to the public.
- The name must be clearly displayed on the outside of the business in all its locations and in notices and advertisements.

After the application has been accepted by the government and the incorporation fee paid, the limited company or corporation comes into existence. The persons who applied for incorporation receive a document from the government. It is called a *charter* or *articles of incorporation* if issued by the federal government, or *letters patent* or *memorandum of association* depending on the province involved.

Once a business is incorporated, a meeting is held to elect directors of the corporation. The **board of directors** then hire people (**officers**) to manage the business. Shares are sold or exchanged for assets and the company is in business.

An important difference between a corporation and partnership or proprietorship is that the corporation has a continuous life or perpetual existence.

A group of persons, elected by the shareholders, who are responsible for the operation of the corporation.

Hired employees of a corporation who manage the day-to-day operations of the corporation.

Owners may change for a variety of reasons but the corporation continues under the management of employees hired by the board of directors, who represent all shareholders.

TYPES OF BUSINESS CORPORATION

There are two types of business corporation:

- private corporation
- public corporation

Private Corporation

A private business corporation is limited in the number of shareholders it may have and in the way it raises its capital. It may not have more than 50 shareholders, and it must obtain its funds privately. It cannot sell shares or bonds to the public. Many small proprietorships and partnerships change their form of ownership to that of a private corporation to take advantage of the limited liability feature of the corporation. The owners still control and own the business and yet have protection for their personal assets — for example, Irving Oil.

Public Corporation

A public business corporation can have any number of shareholders. It can sell shares and bonds to the public, but it is subject to the requirements of the provincial Securities Commission — for example, Bell Canada..

ACCOUNTING PROCEDURES FOR CORPORATIONS

Share Certificates

A share certificate is a form issued by a corporation indicating the number of shares owned.

Ownership of a corporation is represented by shares in the company. A person who invests in a corporation buys a portion or a share of the corporation. A share certificate is a form issued by a corporation showing the number of shares owned. The person purchasing the shares receives the share certificate and is called a **shareholder**.

Shareholders are owners of shares in a corporation.

Shareholders' Equity Accounts

The books and accounts of a corporation are similar to those of proprietorships and partnerships except for differences in the equity section.

Figure 13-8 illustrates the different types of Owner's Equity accounts. In the corporate form of ownership, there are no Drawings accounts. The shareholders, or owners, of a corporation may not withdraw assets. They may, however, receive a portion of the corporate net income in the form of *dividends*. Dividends are the amount of earnings that may be declared by the board of directors for distribution to the shareholders in proportion to the number of shares owned if the year-end profits are favourable.

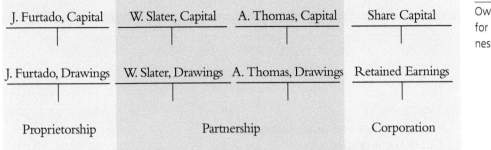

FIGURE 13-8

Owner's Equity accounts for the three types of business ownership

The equity section of the corporate balance sheet for WestJet Airlines Ltd. is shown in Figure 13-9. In the simplified balance sheet on page 540, Figure 13-10, note the two new accounts in the equity section. The **Share Capital** account is a record of shares sold. The **Retained Earnings** account contains the balance of net income earned by the corporation after dividends have been paid.

Retained Earnings, like the owner's Capital account, has a normal credit balance. If a company experiences a few years of net losses, Retained Earnings could have a debit balance. This is called a **deficit**. A company whose Retained Earnings account is in a deficit (negative) position cannot pay dividends to its shareholders. In Figure 13-11 on page 540, Barrick Gold Corporation's Retained Earnings account shows a deficit.

A Share Capital account is a record of shares sold.

The Retained Earnings account is an equity account containing the balance of undistributed net income.

A deficit is a debit (negative) balance in the Retained Earnings account.

FIGURE 13-9

The consolidated balance sheets for WestJet Airlines Ltd. Has the company's financial position improved from December 31, 2004 to December 31, 2005? If so, in what areas do you see improvement?

CONSOLIDATED BALANCE SHEETS

WestJet Airlines Ltd.

December 31, 2005 and 2004
(Stated in Thousands of Dollars)

	2005	2004
Assets		
Current assets:		
Cash and cash equivalents	$ 259,640	$ 148,532
Accounts receivable	8,022	12,814
Income taxes recoverable	13,909	2,854
Prepaid expenses and deposits	31,746	25,493
Inventory	6,259	5,382
	319,576	195,075
Property and equipment (note 2)	1,803,497	1,601,546
Other assets (note 3)	90,019	80,733
	$ 2,213,092	$ 1,877,354
Liabilities and Shareholders' Equity		
Current liabilities:		
Accounts payable and accrued liabilities	$ 100,052	$ 91,885
Advance ticket sales	127,450	81,991
Non-refundable guest credits	32,814	26,704
Current portion of long-term debt (note 4)	114,115	97,305
Current portion of obligations under capital lease (note 6)	2,466	6,564
	376,897	304,449
Long-term debt (note 4)	1,044,719	905,631
Obligations under capital lease (note 6)	1,690	–
Other liabilities (note 5)	16,982	10,000
Future income tax (note 8)	102,651	67,382
	1,542,939	1,287,462
Shareholders' equity:		
Share capital (note 7(b))	429,613	390,469
Contributed surplus (note 7(g))	39,093	21,977
Retained earnings	201,447	177,446
	670,153	589,892
Subsequent events (note 6)		
Commitments and contingencies (notes 6 and 9)		
	$ 2,213,092	$ 1,877,354

See accompanying notes to consolidated financial statements.

On behalf of the Board:

Clive Beddoe, Director   Wilmot Matthews, Director

Source: WestJet Airlines, *Annual Report for 2005*, p. 40.

FIGURE 13-10

Equity section on the Beatty Incorporated balance sheet

Beatty Incorporated Balance Sheet December 31, 2008		
ASSETS		
Cash		$ 5 000
Other Assets		125 000
Total Assets		$130 000
LIABILITIES AND SHAREHOLDERS' EQUITY		
Current Liabilities		
Accounts Payable		$ 15 000
Shareholders' Equity		
Share Capital	$70 000	
Retained Earnings	$45 000	115 000
Total Liabilities and Shareholders' Equity		$130 000

FIGURE 13-11

Consolidated balance sheets for 2004 and 2005 for Barrick Gold Corporation

Consolidated Balance Sheets

Barrick Gold Corporation
At December 31 (in millions of United States dollars)

	2005	2004
Assets		
Current assets		
Cash and equivalents (note 16a)	$ 1,037	$ 1,398
Accounts receivable (note 12)	54	58
Inventories (note 12)	402	215
Other current assets (note 12)	255	288
	1,748	1,959
Available-for-sale securities (note 11)	62	61
Equity method investments (note 11)	138	86
Property, plant and equipment (note 13)	4,146	3,391
Capitalized mining costs (note 2e)	–	226
Non-current ore in stockpiles (note 12)	251	65
Other assets (note 14)	517	499
Total assets	$ 6,862	$ 6,287
Liabilities and Shareholders' Equity		
Current liabilities		
Accounts payable	$ 386	$ 335
Current part of long-term debt (note 16b)	80	31
Other current liabilities (note 15)	94	54
	560	420
Long-term debt (note 16b)	1,721	1,655
Asset retirement obligations (note 17)	409	334
Other long-term obligations (note 18)	208	165
Deferred income tax liabilities (note 19)	114	139
Total liabilities	3,012	2,713
Shareholders' equity		
Capital stock (note 20)	4,222	4,129
Deficit	(341)	(624)
Accumulated other comprehensive income (loss) (note 21)	(31)	69
Total shareholders' equity	3,850	3,574
Contingencies and commitments (notes 8 and 13d)		
Total liabilities and shareholders' equity	$ 6,862	$ 6,287

The accompanying notes are an integral part of these consolidated financial statements.

Signed on behalf of the Board,

Gregory C. Wilkins, Director   Steven J. Shapiro, Director

Source: Barrick Gold Corporation, *Barrick Annual Report 2005*, p. 80.

Par Value and No Par Value Shares

When a company applies to the government for the articles of incorporation, it indicates the number of shares that will be sold (authorized) and the type of share. The two types of common shares are par value and no par value shares. The *Canada Business Corporations Act* requires the use of no par value shares, while some provinces allow the use of both types of share issue. Par value shares have a specific value, but it is important to note that this does not indicate the actual selling price of the share.

For example, a company may issue common shares with a $20 par value. This does not mean that each share is worth $20. A share is worth whatever buyers will pay for it.

No par value shares have no specific value. These shares are recorded on the corporate books at the price for which they are sold. The par value of a share (if any) is the amount entered in the Share Capital account. It represents legal capital per share. It does not mean market value. By law, dividends may *not* be declared if the payment of the dividend causes the shareholders' equity to fall below the par value of the outstanding shares. If the board of directors assigns a value to the no par value shares when they are issued, this is referred to as a *stated value*. It is worth noting that more than 90 percent of Canadian public companies issue no par value shares.

Journal Entries

W. Slater and A. Thomas operate a business as a partnership. To have the benefits of limited liability, they have applied to their provincial government for permission to incorporate their company. They have received permission to incorporate as a private corporation with 10 000 authorized shares, no par value.

Five hundred shares at $50 per share are sold in the new corporation to Slater, Thomas, and several of their friends. The entry to record the issuing of the shares for cash in General Journal form is:

May 1	Cash	25 000	
	Share Capital		25 000
	Sold 500 shares at $50:		
	W, Slater　150 shares		
	A. Thomas　150 shares		
	P. Nelson　　75 shares		
	S. Patel　　25 shares		
	J. Au　　　100 shares		
	500 shares		

Shares for Assets

W. Slater and A. Thomas turned over to the corporation the assets of their previous business in return for shares in the corporation. Equipment worth $20 000 and a building valued at $160 000 are exchanged for company shares.

Jul. 2	Equipment	20 000	
	Building	160 000	
	Share Capital		180 000
	Issued 3 600 shares for property at $50:		
	W. Slater　1 600 shares		
	P. Bush　　2 000 shares		
	3 600 shares		

Authorized shares are the
number of shares that a
company may issue
according to the terms of
its articles of incorporation.

The corporation, S and T Ltd., is now formally established. Its balance sheet is shown in Figure 13-12. In the equity section of the balance sheet, it is necessary to show both the authorized shares and the value of the shares actually issued or sold.

FIGURE 13-12

Balance sheet for the new corporation — S and T Ltd.

Issued, or outstanding, shares are the number of authorized shares that have been sold and issued to shareholders.

S and T Ltd. Balance Sheet May 2, 2007		
ASSETS		
Current Assets		
Cash		$ 25 000
Capital Assets		
Equipment	$ 20 000	
Building	160 000	180 000
Total Assets		$205 000
SHAREHOLDERS' EQUITY		
Share Capital		
Authorized 10 000 shares, no par value		
Issued 4 100 shares		$205 000

Organization Costs

Organization Costs is an account used to record costs of organizing a business.

A number of costs are incurred in organizing a corporation. These include legal fees, a fee to the government, and miscellaneous items such as share certificates and a company seal. These costs are charged to an account called **Organization Costs**. Generally, this account is treated in one of two ways:

- as an expense charged to the first year's operations
- as an asset that is *written off* as an expense over a short time period. Each year, the balance in the account, Organization Costs, is shown after the capital assets on the balance sheet.

The first of these two methods is used when the amount involved is small. Whichever method is followed, the entry to record organizational costs is:

Jun. 1	Organization Costs	5 200	
	Cash		5 200
	Paid organizing costs.		

Corporate Net Income

The net income of a corporation increases the shareholders' equity. The decision concerning what happens to the net income is made by the board of directors. The board has several alternatives:
- distribute all of the net income to the shareholders
- leave all the net income in the corporation
- a combination of the above — leave part of the net income in the business and distribute part to the shareholders

The shareholders do not participate directly in deciding what is done with corporate net income. However, if they are not satisfied with the decision of the board of directors, they can make their displeasure known at the annual share-holders' meeting. Every business corporation must hold a meeting of sharehold-ers each year. At this meeting, the board of directors is elected by the shareholders. If enough shareholders are displeased with the operation of the corporation, some or all of the directors may be replaced. Elections are based on a majority vote of shareholders, with one vote allowed for each share owned. Shareholders must also approve the annual report, which contains the latest set of financial statements.

IVIDENDS

Generally speaking, the owners of a proprietorship or partnership may withdraw money from their business as they wish. The Drawings account is a record of withdrawals.

There is no opportunity for shareholders in a corporation to withdraw cash in the way that proprietors or partners do. Because of the limited liability feature of corporations, the creditors must be protected from the possibility of corporate owners withdrawing the assets and leaving no funds for the payment of corporate debts. In that event, the creditors would lose their investment since shareholders are not personally liable for the corporation's debts.

The portion of a corporation's net income that is distributed to the share-holder is called a **dividend**. Payment of a dividend must be approved by the board of directors of the corporation. Corporate laws allow dividends to be paid to owners or shareholders only out of accumulated net income. The accumulated net income is recorded in the Retained Earnings account. This account appears in the shareholders' equity section of the balance sheet (see Figure 13-10). If there is a balance in this account, dividends may be declared.

Dividends are the portion of a corporation's net income paid to the shareholders.

Dividends are paid out of retained earnings.

Closing the Books of a Corporation

The closing phase of the accounting cycle for a corporation is very similar to those of partnerships and proprietorships. The steps in closing the books include:

(1) Close Revenue and Expense accounts into the Income Summary account.

(2) Close the Income Summary account balance (which is the net income or the net loss) into the Retained Earnings account.

These steps are illustrated in Figure 13-13.

There is no change in the Share Capital account. The Retained Earnings account balance represents the accumulated net income (credit balance) or net loss (debit balance) of the corporation. It presents a historical picture of the com-pany's profitability.

If dividends are to be paid, the Retained Earnings account must have a cred-it balance. Dividends may be paid in a year when the corporation has sustained a loss, as long as the net income from previous years leaves a credit balance in the Retained Earnings account.

Distributing Dividends

After the first year, the board of directors has decided to pay a dividend of $2 on each of the outstanding shares of S and T Ltd. November 15 was the date that the

FIGURE 13-13

Closing the books

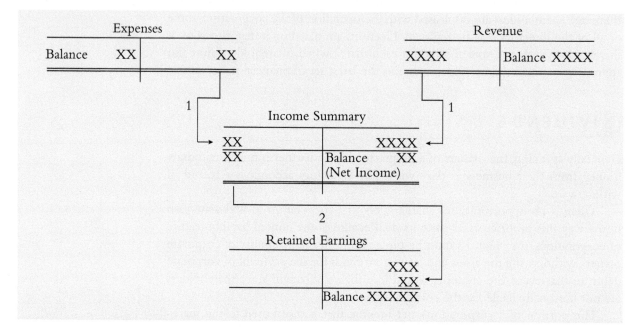

decision was made (Date of Declaration). It was also decided that the $2 dividend would be paid to all owners of shares on record as of November 25 (Date of Record). The dividend cheques would be issued on December 10 (Date of Payment). This entry is made on November 15 to establish a liability on the corporate books:

Nov. 15 Retained Earnings	8 200	
Dividends Payable		8 200
Declared a $2 dividend on the		
4100 outstanding shares.		

This entry results in a decrease in the shareholders' equity because some of the accumulated net income will be taken out of the business. The debit to Retained Earnings reduced the equity. This entry also establishes a current liability called *Dividends Payable*.

On December 10, cheques are issued to the shareholders of record on November 25. The entry to record the payment is:

Dec. 10 Dividends Payable	8 200	
Cash		8 200
Issued dividend cheques to shareholders.		

The payment cancels the liability created by the previous declaration of the dividend. After two years of profitable operation, the shareholders' equity section of S and T Ltd. appears as in Figure 13-14.

The balance of $33 000 in retained earnings indicates that a net income has been earned and that not all the net income was distributed in the form of dividends.

FIGURE 13-14

SHAREHOLDERS' EQUITY

Share Capital
    Authorized   10 000 shares, no par value
    Issued   4100 shares $205 000
Retained Earnings   33 000
                                 $238 000

Shareholders' equity portion of the balance sheet

Statement of Retained Earnings

The shareholders' equity section of the balance sheet shown in Figure 13-14 indicates retained earnings of $33 000 when the balance sheet was prepared at the end of the fiscal period. However, it does not show the beginning balance or changes during the year.

    A **retained earnings statement** as shown in Figure 13-15, after S and T Ltd. had been operating for four years, provides a complete description of changes in retained earnings. It shows the beginning balance, net income added, dividends paid, and ending balance in retained earnings. A retained earnings statement is prepared in addition to the income statement and the balance sheet.

Provides a complete description of changes to retained earnings.

CORPORATE INCOME TAX

A corporation has a legal existence of its own and is a taxpayer. Corporations pay income tax on net income in excess of $300 000, to the federal government (22 percent of taxable income) and to the provinces in which they earn income (2.5 percent to 17 percent, depending on the province). A special income tax rate is available to small Canadian-owned corporations. This deduction, if applicable, results in a small Canadian business paying income tax at a rate of less than 22 percent, an average rate. Special accounting procedures must be followed if the reduced rate is to be obtained.

    The income tax paid by a corporation is an expense of operating the business and appears as a deduction on the income statement, as shown in Figure 13-16.

    S and T Ltd. had a net income of $72 500 *before* income taxes. This income is the difference between total revenue and total expenses. From the information on the income statement, there was a net income of $58 000 *after* taxes. This amount is the increase in the shareholders' equity as a result of the year's activity and appears on the retained earnings statement as shown in Figure 13-15. This is the net income that a corporation reports to its shareholders. Figure 13-15 also shows that $8200 in dividends was distributed to the shareholders during the year.

FIGURE 13-15

S and T Ltd.
Retained Earnings Statement
For the Year Ended December 31, 2010

Retained Earnings, January 1, 2010	$ 48 300
Add: Net Income for the Year	58 000
Total	106 300
Less: Dividends	8 200
Retained Earnings, December 31, 2010	$ 98 100

The retained earnings statement provides a complete description of changes to retained earnings.

FIGURE 13-16
Income statement for
S and T Ltd.

S and T Ltd. Income Statement For the Year Ended December 31, 2010		
Revenue		
Sales Revenue		$172 000
Expenses		
Selling	$62 000	
Administrative	37 000	
Amortization	6 800	105 800
Operating Income		66 200
Other Income		
Investments		6 300
Net Income Before Income Taxes		72 500
Income Taxes		14 500
Net Income After Income Taxes		$ 58 000

Double Taxation

A shareholder receiving a dividend from a corporation like S and T Ltd. must add the dividend to personal income. As a result, the shareholder ends up paying income tax on this dividend. Shareholders, unlike the owners of sole proprietorships and partnerships, are not taxed directly for any profits earned by their companies. The corporation, however, pays income tax on the same income from which the shareholder received a dividend. This can be considered to be a case of double taxation: The corporation was taxed and so was the shareholder on the same net income.

To alleviate the burden of double taxation, the federal government generally taxes dividends from a taxable Canadian corporation at a reduced rate.

TYPES OF SHARES

The capital of a corporation takes the form of shares. Shares are sold for cash or exchanged for assets or for services performed for the corporation. Shares may be issued with a *par value* (a *stated value*) or *without par value* (see page 541). The shares may be common shares alone or a mixture of common shares and preferred shares.

Common Shares

Common shares have one vote per share but no guaranteed dividend.

The basic shares issued by a corporation are **common shares**. Each common share entitles the owner to one vote at shareholders' meetings. There is no guarantee that owners of common shares will receive a dividend since only the board of directors may decide if dividends are to be paid on common shares. The board also decides the amount of any dividend. The person or group owning a majority of common shares controls the voting at shareholders' meetings — and thus the makeup of the board of directors and how the business will be managed.

When a corporation offers additional shares for sale, it usually provides common shareholders the first opportunity to purchase the shares, often at less than the current market price. The term *rights* is used to describe the privilege of buying new shares at special prices.

Preferred Shares

Sometimes a corporation, to attract investors and cash, offers shares with special features. These shares, called **preferred shares**, have the following advantages:

- fixed dividend
- preferred position for dividends and assets

For instance, a $2 preferred share entitles the shareholder to a $2 dividend if the corporation earns a profit. A 5 percent preferred share entitles the holder to a dividend of 5 percent of the par value of the share. Thus a 5 percent preferred share, par value $50, would pay a dividend of $2.50 on each preferred share. These dividends must be paid before any dividends are allocated to the common shares. In the event that a corporation dissolves or goes into bankruptcy, the holders of preferred shares have a right to the assets *before* the holders of common shares. Normally, preferred shares do *not* carry voting rights.

Other special features that may be attached to preferred shares are:

- cumulative dividends
- convertibility
- participating
- callable

Cumulative Preferred Share

A *cumulative* preferred share is a share for which the dividends build up or accumulate if they are not paid. For example, a $3 cumulative preferred shareholder might not be given the $3 dividend in a year when a loss is suffered by the corporation. However, the next year, a $6 dividend is paid before any portion of the net income is given to common shareholders.

Convertible Preferred Share

A convertible preferred share is a share that the owner may exchange for common shares at a set price. For example, the owner might be given the right to exchange each convertible preferred share for two common shares.

Callable Preferred Share

A callable preferred share gives the corporation the right to repurchase the share at a set price.

Participating Preferred Share

The shareholder of a participating preferred share has the right to share in any remaining net income along with the common shareholders. This means that the preferred shareholder receives the fixed dividend and may also share in any remaining net income after dividends have been paid to the common shareholders.

Journal Entries

Separate equity accounts are used for each class of share. The following entries record the issue of both common and preferred shares.

Jan. 2	Cash	20 000	
	Share Capital — Common		20 000
	Issued 1000 common shares, stated value $20.		
2	Cash	50 000	
	Share Capital — Preferred		50 000
	Issued 1000, 5% preferred shares, par value $50.		

The accounts for the different classes of shares are shown below:

Share Capital — Preferred		Share Capital — Common	
	Jan. 2 50 000		Jan. 2 20 000

The shareholders' equity section of the balance sheet is shown in Figure 13-17. For each class of share, the total number of shares authorized and issued is shown.

FIGURE 13-17

Number of shares authorized and issued is shown on the balance sheet.

SHAREHOLDERS' EQUITY

Share Capital
Authorized
10 000 5% preferred shares, $50 par value
70 000 common shares, $20 stated value
Issued

2 000 preferred shares	$ 100 000
30 000 common shares	600 000
	700 000
Retained Earnings	350 000
	$1 050 000

Dividends — Common and Preferred

The board of directors of a corporation decides if dividends are to be paid and their amount. Suppose net income is $90 000. The board of directors declares a dividend of 5 percent of the par value for preferred shares and of $1 for common shares. Since there is a total of 2000 preferred shares outstanding at $50 each, the preferred share dividend is $2.50 per share ($50 × 5%) or a total of $5000 ($2.50 × 2 000 shares). The dividend for the common shares amounts to $30 000 or $1 for each of the 30 000 common shares that have been issued.

The Declaration Reduces Retained Earnings

The entry to record the declaration of dividends is as follows:

Jun. 1	Retained Earnings	35 000	
	Dividends Payable — Preferred		5 000
	Dividends Payable — Common		30 000
	Dividends declared, $1 per common share		
	and $2.50 per 5% preferred share.		

The Payment Reduces the Asset

When the dividends are paid, this entry is made:

Jul. 15	1	Dividends Payable — Preferred	5 000	
		Dividends Payable — Common	30 000	
		Cash		35 000
		Issued dividend cheques.		

Suppose that in the next fiscal period, the net income went down to $30 000. The board of directors decided to pay the 5 percent dividend on the preferred shares, but to pay nothing to the common shareholders. They felt that a common share dividend would put a strain on the corporation's finances by removing too much cash. They hoped that by keeping the cash in the corporation, the operations and net income would improve in the next fiscal period. An entry for $5000 was made to record only the preferred dividend.

In the next fiscal period, the net income of the corporation increased dramatically to $150 000. The board of directors was right! The board decided to again declare a 5 percent dividend on each preferred share, but to raise the dividend on the common shares to $3. The following entry was made:

Jun.	1	Retained Earnings	95 000	
		Dividends Payable — Preferred		5 000
		Dividends Payable — Common		90 000
		Dividends declared, $3 per common share		
		and $2.50 per 5% preferred share.		

The three examples just covered illustrate some of the differences in types of shares and dividend payments. The preferred shares have first claim on net income. Common shares may receive no dividend at all when net income is low. However, common shares may receive high dividends when net income increases significantly. It should be noted that the preferred shareholders could also miss their dividends if the directors decide that sufficient funds are not available.

Market Value of Shares

W. Slater and A. Thomas own the majority of shares in the private corporation, S and T Ltd. The corporation has no need of additional funds and does not plan to issue more shares. Both Slater and Thomas paid $50 a share when the corporation was formed.

M. Pothier is aware of the success of the corporation and feels that S and T Ltd. will continue to be successful in the future. She would like to invest in the company, but it is not issuing any new shares. She offers W. Slater $85 a share for 75 of his shares. Slater agrees and receives $6375. He has made a gain of $35 per share, a total of $2625 on the 75 shares sold, since he originally paid only $50 per share. This example illustrates the **market value** of a share. Market value is the price at which a buyer and seller agree to exchange shares.

Market value is the price at which buyers and sellers agree to exchange shares.

THE STOCK MARKET

The **stock market** is a place where shares in a corporation are bought and sold after they have been issued. It is a place where a shareholder who wishes to sell shares may find a buyer willing to purchase the shares. Large public corporations

The stock market is a place where shares in a corporation are bought and sold after they have been issued.

such as the CN Corporation, Laidlaw Inc., and Bombardier Inc., know it is important to make it easy for the public to buy and sell their shares. One reason for this is that these corporations may wish to expand their operations. Expansion requires financing, which can be obtained by issuing more shares.

To facilitate this process, large public corporations list their companies on a *stock exchange*, where shares are bought and sold. To be listed on a stock exchange, a corporation must follow detailed regulations and must provide the public with much information concerning the operation of the company. In Canada, there are stock exchanges in Calgary, Toronto, and Montreal. *Stockbrokers* act as agents for those who wish to buy and sell shares. The brokers arrange the sale in return for a commission on the sale. As well as handling the sale of shares between shareholders and people who wish to buy shares, stockbrokers sell large blocks of new shares for corporations in need of funds.

(A)CCOUNTING TERMS

Board of Directors	A group of persons, elected by the shareholders, who are responsible for the operation of the corporation. (p. 537)
Common Shares	Shares that have one vote per share but no guaranteed dividend. (p. 546)
Corporation	A business owned by one or more persons whose liability is limited to their investment in the corporation. A corporation has a legal existence of its own. (p. 518)
Deficit	A debit (negative) balance in the Retained Earnings account. (p. 539)
Dividends	The portion of the corporation's net income paid out of retained earnings to the shareholders. (p. 543)
Limited Company	Term sometimes used to describe the corporate form of ownership. (p. 518)
Market Value	The price at which buyers and sellers agree to exchange shares. (p. 549)
Mutual Agency	When doing business related to the partnership, each partner acts for all other partners. Any action that one partner takes is binding on every partner. That is, each partner is acting as an "agent" for the partnership. (p. 518)
Officers	Hired employees of a corporation who manage the day-to-day operations of the corporation. (p. 537)
Organization Costs	An account used to record the costs incurred in organizing a corporation. (p. 542)
Partnership	A business owned by two or more persons, each of whom has unlimited personal liability for the debts and legal obligations of the business. (p. 517)
Preferred Shares	Shares that do not have voting rights but have prior claim on assets and net income over common shares. (p. 547)
Retained Earnings	An equity account containing the balance of undistributed net income. (p. 539)
Retained Earnings Statement	A statement that provides a complete description of changes in the Retained Earnings account. (p. 545)
Share Capital	An account that is a record of shares sold. (p. 539)
Shareholders	Owners of shares in a corporation. (p. 538)
Sole Proprietorship	A business owned by one person who has unlimited personal liability for the debts and legal obligations of the business. (p. 517)
Stock Market	A place where shares in a corporation are bought and sold after they have been issued. (p. 549)

1. Explain why limited liability is an advantage of the corporate form of ownership.

2. Explain what is meant by the phrase "a corporation has a legal existence of its own."

3. (a) Why do creditors need to know whether the company applying for credit is a corporation?
   (b) Why must the name of the corporation be clearly displayed in all its notices and advertisements?

4. The firm of S and T Ltd. is a corporation, not a partnership. How does the public know this?

5. What is the board of directors?

6. What is the difference between a private and a public business corporation?

7. What is the name of the form that indicates that a person owns shares in a corporation?

8. Name the two main equity accounts in a corporation's Shareholders' Equity section of the balance sheet.

9. What information does the Retained Earnings account provide?

10. What is the difference between shares authorized and shares issued?

11. Which account is debited to record the costs of forming a corporation?

12. What are the three options for distributing the net income of a corporation?

13. Who decides what will be done with the net income of a corporation?

14. What is the name given to the portion of a corporation's net income that is paid to the shareholders?

15. What is the name of the account that is used to record the accumulated net income of a business?

16. Into which account are the Revenue and Expense accounts of a corporation closed?

17. Into which account is the balance of the Income Summary account closed?

18. What does the balance of the Retained Earnings account represent?

19. (a) What effect do declared dividends have on the Retained Earnings account?
    (b) What effect does net income have on the Retained Earnings account?
    (c) What effect does net loss have on the Retained Earnings account?

20. What is the term that is used when the Retained Earnings account has an abnormal (debit) balance?

21. What is a common share?

22. Explain three main features of common shares.

23. What are rights?

24. What is a preferred share?

25. Explain why preferred shares are generally considered to be a safer investment than common shares.

26. Explain the following terms:

    (a) cumulative preferred shares
    (b) convertible preferred shares
    (c) callable preferred shares
    (d) participating preferred shares

27. What does the "par value" of a share mean?

28. What does "stated value" mean?

29. What is the market value of a share?

30. After a corporation has sold its shares to the public, how can a person purchase shares in that corporation?

UNIT 31

PROBLEMS: APPLICATIONS

1. A group of business people have received the articles of incorporation to operate a Canadian corporation called Meds Corporation. They were authorized to issue 50 000 shares at $30 stated value per share. Record the following in a General Journal using these accounts: Cash; Land; Building; Equipment; Share Capital.

  Jun. 1 Sold 2000 shares for $60 000 cash ($30 per share).

         4 Issued 600 shares to R. Clark, a founding shareholder, in return for equipment ($30 per share).

         5 Issued 6000 shares to G. Jones in return for a building (2000 shares) and land (4000 shares) ($30 per share).

         8 M. Tompkins was issued 200 shares in return for legal services for incorporating the business.

2. A. Hackett, a sole proprietor, has received letters patent that allow her to organize her business as a private corporation to be called First Class Travel Ltd. The accounts of the proprietorship are exchanged for common shares in the new company. First Class Travel Ltd. has authorized 100 000 no par value common shares. The accounts of the proprietorship had these balances:

ACCOUNT TITLE	ACC. NO.	DEBIT	CREDIT
Cash		15 000	
Supplies		4 500	
Furniture		42 000	
Land & Building		300 000	
A. Hackett, Capital			361 500

  (a) Record the journal entry to take over the accounts of the proprietorship in return for common shares:

  Apr. 1 Issued shares in return for assets of the proprietorship.

  (b) Record the following transactions:

  Apr. 6 Issued 50 shares to S. Meier in return for legal services valued at $4500 to set up the corporation.

10 Sold common shares for $50 each to:
 M. Sims 70 shares,
 P. Toms 100 shares,
 S. Ways 150 shares.

12 Paid $10 500 cash for computers.

15 Paid $3000 cash for advertising.

3. (a) Prepare closing General Journal entries using the balances in the T-accounts below:

Expense Account		Revenue Account	
210 000			185 000

Income Summary		Retained Earnings	
			150 000

(b) Close the Expense account into the Income Summary account.
(c) Close the Revenue account.
(d) Close the Income Summary account into the Retained Earnings account.
(e) Post the journal to the T-accounts.

4. An Income Summary account has a credit balance (net income) of $85 000. Prepare the Journal entries from the following information:

- Close the Income Summary account and transfer net income into the Retained Earnings account; dividends of $38 000 are declared.
- Dividends are paid by cheque.

5. An Income Summary account has a credit balance of $91 000 on June 30, 2008. Prepare the General Journal entries from the following information:

- Close the Income Summary account. On July 15, the board of directors of the company declared a $2 per share dividend to the shareholders of record, July 31. There are 40 000 common shares issued and outstanding.
- Dividends are paid by cheque on August 31.

6. Prepare a statement of retained earnings dated December 31, 2008 for S and T Ltd. using the following information:

- net income for the year, $90 000
- dividends paid, $40 000
- retained earnings, beginning balance January 1, $72 000

7. Prepare the next year's (from exercise 6) statement of retained earnings dated December 31, 2009 for S and T Ltd. using the following information:

- net income for the year, $65 000
- dividends paid, $45 000
- retained earnings, January 1, $122 000

8. Carriere Dental Services Ltd. pays income tax at the rate of 22 percent. This year, the company's net income before taxes is $145 000.

   (a) What is the income tax expense for this year?
   (b) What is the net income after taxes?

9. Windsor Mfg. Ltd. was organized on July 2 with the following capital authorized:

   • 5000, 5 percent cumulative preferred shares, par value $50
   • 100 000 common shares, stated value $5

   Record the following transactions in a General Journal.

   Jul. 2 Issued 400 preferred shares for cash.

         6 Received cash for 10 000 common shares sold at stated value.

        10 Paid legal fees for incorporation of $2500 by issuing common shares at stated value.

        12 Received title to land in exchange for 2000 preferred shares and 10 000 common shares at stated value.

        15 Sold 500 preferred shares and 10 000 common shares at stated value for cash.

10. Prepare the shareholders' equity section of a balance sheet from the following information:

    • 150 000 common shares authorized, no par value
    • 50 000 common shares issued with a total value of $300 000
    • 10 000, 5 percent preferred shares authorized, $100 par value
    • 500 preferred shares issued with a total value of $50 000
    • retained earnings, $128 000

11. Prepare the shareholders' equity section of a balance sheet from the following:

    • 300 000 common shares authorized, no par value
    • issued 80 000 common shares for $800 000
    • 30 000 preferred shares authorized, $20 par value
    • issued 10 000 preferred shares at par
    • retained earnings, $317 000

12. Prepare a statement of retained earnings and the shareholders' equity section of the balance sheet dated December 31, 2008, for First Class Travel Ltd.

    • authorized share capital, 100 000 common shares
    • shares issued, 2825 common shares valued at $282 500
    • retained earnings, beginning balance January 1, $155 000
    • net income for the year, $88 000

13. Windsor Mfg. Ltd. has issued 3500, 5 percent cumulative preferred shares, par value $50.

    (a) How much is the total annual dividend on the preferred shares?
    (b) Assume no dividends were paid the first year. How much is the total of dividends owing to preferred shareholders at the end of the second year?

14. During 2009, its third year of operations, a corporation earned a net income of $118 000. Dividends of $1.25 per share were paid on the 50 000 common shares outstanding. The next year, a net loss of $28 000 was reported. No dividends were paid that year. On January 1, 2009, the balance in the Retained Earnings account was $54 000.

   (a) Calculate the balance in the Retained Earnings account at December 31, 2010.
   (b) Prepare the journal entry to close the Income Summary account at December 31, 2010.

---

1. Following is the trial balance of J. Chang and S. Wong, who are partners. They share net income and net loss in the ratio of 2:1. Each receives a salary of $35 000. The ending inventory, December 31, is $31 000. Prepare:

   (a) an income statement
   (b) a statement of distribution of net income
   (c) a statement of partners' equity
   (d) a balance sheet
   (e) the closing entries

CHAPTER 13

**PROBLEMS:
CHALLENGES**

Chang and Wong
Trial Balance
December 31, 2008

ACCOUNT TITLE	ACC. NO.	DEBIT	CREDIT
Cash		$ 16 000	
Accounts Receivable		8 500	
Inventory, January 1		46 000	
Equipment		72 000	
Accumulated Amortization: Equipment			$ 8 000
Accounts Payable			10 000
J. Chang, Capital			39 000
S. Wong, Capital			35 000
J. Chang, Drawings		30 000	
S. Wong, Drawings		29 000	
Sales Revenue			307 000
Purchases		90 000	
Transportation on Purchases		2 500	
Selling Expense		75 000	
Administrative Expense		30 000	
		$399 000	$399 000

2. The Nichols Corporation was formed with the following capitalization:

   • authorized Share Capital:

      20 000, 5 percent preferred shares, par value $30
      100 000 common shares, no par value

   (a) Record the following transactions in a General Journal:

   Jan.   3   Sold 10 000 common shares for $8 each.
              Received cash, $80 000.

4   Issued for cash, 600 preferred shares at par value.

8   Purchased equipment for $10 500 cash.
    Issued a cheque.

10 Paid legal fees of incorporation by issuing 100 preferred shares to the company lawyers.

12 Sold 10 000 common shares for $8 each.

16 Purchased land and a building valued at $360 000 in return for $155 000 cash, an $85 000 mortgage, and 15 000 common shares at $8 per share. Note: Land value is $100 000.

(b) Prepare T-accounts and post the General Journal entries.

3. Prepare the year's income statement for The Nichols Corporation from the adjusted trial balance that follows. Use an income tax rate of 22 percent.

ACCOUNT TITLE	ACC. NO.	DEBIT	CREDIT
The Nichols Corporation			
Adjusted Trial Balance			
December 31, 2008			
Cash		$ 47 000	
Supplies		21 000	
Accounts Receivable		42 000	
Inventory		115 000	
Land		100 000	
Building		260 000	
Accumulated Amortization — Building			$ 15 000
Equipment		10 500	
Accumulated Amortization — Equipment			1 900
Accounts Payable			7 000
Mortgage Payable			85 000
Preferred Shares			21 000
Common Shares			280 000
Retained Earnings			100 000
Sales Revenue			375 600
Selling Expense		245 000	
Administrative Expense		45 000	
		$885 500	$885 500

4. (a) Record these General Journal entries for The Nichols Corporation. Refer to problems 2 and 3:

Oct.   1   Declared a 5 percent dividend on preferred shares, par value $30 and a $2.50 per share dividend on common shares.

       28 Issued dividend cheques.

(b) Prepare closing entries for revenue and expenses including Income Tax Expense.

(c) Post the closing entries to a T-account for Income Summary.

(d) Journalize and post the entry to close the Income Summary account into the Retained Earnings account.

5. Prepare a retained earnings statement and the shareholders' section of The
   Nichols Corporation balance sheet using information from exercises 2 to 4
   and the following:

   - dividends paid, $98 000
   - net income after taxes, $66 768

6. Menards Ltd., has 1000 outstanding shares of 6 percent preferred shares, $30
   par value, and 30 000 no par value common shares outstanding. Assume that
   the preferred shares carry the cumulative feature. During a five-year-period,
   the company paid out the following amounts in dividends:

2007	$ 0
2008	21 000
2009	18 000
2010	0
2011	24 000

   No dividends were owed to the preferred shareholders prior to 2007.

   (a) Set up a table using the following format to show the distribution of
       dividends to each class of shareholder:

Year	**Preferred**	**Common**	**Total**

   (b) For the year 2011, what is the dividend per share that was paid to each
       common shareholder?

7. A group of investors decided to set up and incorporate a business called
   Imperial Enterprises Ltd. The company has this authorized share capital:

   - 200 000 common shares, par value $20
   - 30 000, 4.5 percent cumulative preferred shares, par value $40

   (a) Record the following transactions in a General Journal.

   Oct. 1. Sold 10 000 common shares for $20 each. Received $200 000
            cash.

   3   Issued 2000 preferred shares for $80 000 cash.

   6   Paid $3000 to have a computerized accounting system set up for
       the business.

   10 Paid $10 000 cash for office equipment.

   14 Received cash for 20 000 common shares sold at par value.

   15 Issued 125 preferred shares to a legal firm for incorporating costs.

   19 Purchased office supplies for $2000 cash.

   20 Purchased a building and land valued at $500 000 in return
       for $200 000 cash, 2000 preferred shares, and a mortgage of
       $220 000. The land is valued at $100 000.

   31. Paid salaries, $40 000.

   (b) Post the transactions to a T-account ledger.
   (c) Prepare a trial balance dated October 31.

CASE 1
Forms of Business

Maria Alverez and Cindy Hines are thinking about opening a new hair and esthetics salon to be called THE NEW YOU. Maria will mainly attend to the "hair" side of the business. Cindy is both a hair stylist and esthetician but her expertise is in esthetics. Both will work in this new business but Alverez will provide most of the start-up capital. Alverez and Hines cannot decide whether to operate their business as a partnership or corporation.

(a) Describe the advantages and disadvantages of each form of business.
(b) What type of business structure would you suggest?
(c) Give reasons for your recommendation.

CASE 2
Allocation of Partnership Income or Loss

A friend asks you to enter into a partnership this summer running a small business. Your friend is a very talented artist and you have a great deal of computer skill. Your friend's idea is to create a CD-ROM of local graphical images that could be sold to local businesses. Your friend only has $2000 of the estimated $10 000 required to purchase the equipment needed to produce and market the CD-ROMs. You both will work full time in the business.

If you provide the remaining $8000 and the computer expertise, what method would you recommend for dividing any net income or net loss that may result at the end of the summer? Give reasons for your decision.

CASE 3
Corporation—"Unlimited Life"

Rai Bhalla's small import/export company became so successful that he decided to apply for a certificate of incorporation. He paid all the necessary fees, a board of directors was elected, and shares were sold. Unfortunately, as the company flourished Rai became quite ill and later died of natural causes. At the time of his death, Rai owned 10 percent of all outstanding shares in the company. Rai 's wife was overcome with grief and blamed the business for contributing to her husband's early death. She demanded that the board of directors sell all the company assets and shut the company down.

Will Rai 's wife be able to shut down the company? Explain why or why not.

ETHICS CASE
Insider Trading

Insider trading refers to the buying or selling of publicly traded shares by corporate insiders, such as officers, directors, and employees, who have access to non-public information about the shares of a particular company.

There are two types of insider trading: legal or illegal. Legal insider trading refers to transactions of trades that are made once material information on a company is made public. When this occurs, the insider has no direct advantage over other investors. Illegal insider trading occurs when an insider buys or sells shares in a company while in possession of confidential, or non-public, information about the company. This special knowledge gives the insider an unfair advantage over other investors who do not have access to the same information.

In Canada, each province is responsible for controlling or regulating stock trading by insiders. For example, the Ontario Securities Commission requires that insiders report all trades to the Commission.

The following is an example of illegal insider trading:

J. Rathbone is the vice-president of a large, successful telecommunications company. Annual sales are over a billion dollars a year and the company is profitable. Company share prices are at an all time high on the stock market. Near the end of the current fiscal year, Rathbone is aware of the following: several large contracts have fallen through, two major products will not be developed on time, and the company may be sued by one of its customers. Before this information becomes public knowledge, Rathbone sells a large number of shares at the current high price and earns a significant gain on the sale of the shares. Several weeks later, the company announces it will have a substantial net loss for the year and its shares decrease significantly in value. Many investors, unaware of the bad news, stand to lose a great deal of their investment.

The provincial Securities Commission is investigating Rathbone. If found guilty, he is subject to a fine or a jail term and he could be barred from serving as a director or senior officer of a corporation.

(a) Why is this considered to be illegal insider trading?
(b) Who is taken advantage of because of the insider trading?
(c) What responsibilities to the general public do persons in positions of corporate authority have?
(d) In your province, what agency regulates insider trading?
(e) In your province, what type of penalty can be imposed on those guilty of insider trading?
(f) Celebrity Martha Stewart was investigated on charges of insider trading related to 4000 shares she owned and sold. She was convicted of lesser charges of conspiracy, obstruction of justice, and making false statements. She was sentenced to five months in prison and five months of monitored house arrest and was fined $30 000. Some people felt that this sentence was not harsh enough. How do you feel about the sentence?

Explore these Web sites for information on various types of business organizations.

CHAPTER 13

INTERNET RESOURCES

1. **GlobeInvestor.Com**
   http://globeinvestor.ar.wilink.com/asp/A169_search_ENG.asp
   This link provides access to over 1000 company financial reports as well as financial information, advice, and analysis. The Annual Reports Service provides you with quick access to annual reports and other information on select companies.

2. **Canada Business   www.cbsc.org**
   This federal government business service site provides information on a variety of business topics. Links to provincial business service centres supply information on individual provincial requirements for businesses. Select

"Business Start Up" and then "Choosing a Business Structure" to see a description and summary of the advantages and disadvantages of the carious forms of business organization.

3. **BusinessEthics.ca   www.businessethics.ca**

This site is a clearing house for business ethics resources, both Canadian and International. It provides case studies, Canadian regulations and guidelines, articles, consultants, and news about business ethics.

4. **TSX Group   www.tsx.com**

This is the site for the Toronto Stock Exchange and the TSX Venture Exchange. It includes stock trading services and information, real-time stock quotations, financial links, and information. The Education section has an on-line investment quiz at three levels of difficulty, a business glossary, and links to related sites. One link is to all provincial securities commissions.

Index